Stockholm Arbitration Yearbook 2025

Stockholm Arbitration Yearbook

VOLUME 7

Editors

Patrik Schöldström is a Judge of Appeal of the Svea Court of Appeal. He is also an Associate Professor of the Faculty of Law of Stockholm University. He has a doctorate in arbitration law and is a former member of the Swedish Bar. He regularly writes articles and case notes. He has extensive experience as an arbitrator – chairman, sole arbitrator, co-arbitrator and emergency arbitrator – in international and domestic disputes, ad hoc and institutional.

James Hope is a dual-qualified Swedish Advokat and English Solicitor-Advocate, with over thirty years of experience working as a dispute resolution lawyer. He has acted as counsel or arbitrator in more than 100 international arbitration cases, including, *inter alia*, under ICC, SCC, LCIA, UNCITRAL, ICDR, Danish Institute of Arbitration, and Finnish Chamber of Commerce arbitration rules, as well as under ICSID. In addition to private practice, he is a guest lecturer in arbitration at Stockholm and Uppsala universities. He was previously a member of the Board of the SCC Arbitration Institute and a member of the LCIA Court.

Introduction

The Yearbook is published under the auspices of the Stockholm Centre for Commercial Law, a part of the Stockholm University Faculty of Law. It is designed to meet the information needs of arbitration practitioners and parties from all over the world. The first volume was published in 2019.

Objective

The Yearbook is designed to meet the information needs of arbitration practitioners and parties from all over the world. It provides authoritative articles, some of them with a Swedish angle, that address current matters of global concern in arbitration. Each volume includes one or more chapters accounting for developments in Swedish case law and legislation since the previous volume.

Frequency

The publication is annual.

The titles published in this series are listed at the end of this volume.

Stockholm Arbitration Yearbook 2025

Edited by

Patrik Schöldström
James Hope

Assistant Editor

Philip Mellberg

Editorial Committee

Stockholm Centre for Commercial Law
Faculty of Law

Stockholm University

Wolters Kluwer

Published by:
Kluwer Law International B.V.
PO Box 316
2400 AH Alphen aan den Rijn
The Netherlands
E-mail: lrs-sales@wolterskluwer.com
Website: www.wolterskluwer.com/en/solutions/kluwerlawinternational

Sold and distributed by:
Wolters Kluwer Legal & Regulatory U.S.
920 Links Avenue
Landisville, PA 17538
United States of America
E-mail: customer.service@wolterskluwer.com

ISBN 978-94-035-4979-8

e-Book: ISBN 978-94-035-4989-7
web-PDF: ISBN 978-94-035-4999-6

Editors

Patrik Schöldström is a Judge of Appeal of the Svea Court of Appeal and an Associate Professor of the Faculty of Law of Stockholm University. He has a doctorate degree in arbitration law and is a former member of the Swedish Bar. He regularly writes articles and case notes. He also sits as an arbitrator, and has participated in a number of domestic and international arbitrations (ad hoc and institutional) as chair of arbitral tribunal, sole arbitrator, emergency arbitrator, wing arbitrator, and counsel.

James Hope is a dual-qualified Swedish Advokat and English Solicitor-Advocate, with over thirty years of experience working as a dispute resolution lawyer. He has acted as counsel or arbitrator in more than 100 international arbitration cases, including, *inter alia*, under ICC, SCC, LCIA, UNCITRAL, ICDR, Danish Institute of Arbitration, and Finnish Chamber of Commerce arbitration rules, as well as under ICSID. In addition to private practice, he is a guest lecturer in arbitration at Stockholm and Uppsala universities. He was previously a member of the Board of the SCC Arbitration Institute and a member of the LCIA Court.

Contributors

Narmin Abdulova, Legal Counsel at ROXCEL Holding. She holds an LLM degree in International Business Law from the Central European University (CEU) in Vienna with arbitration experience from her previous roles at the Vienna International Arbitral Centre (VIAC) and Baker Mckenzie, Austria.

Artem N. Barsukov, FCIArb, Partner at Bennett Jones LLP in Edmonton, Alberta, Canada, where he carries on a global arbitration practice. Artem is one of Canada's few true arbitration specialists, having dedicated the entirety of his legal career to arbitration, both international and domestic. Over the years, Artem has acted on more than USD 3.5 billion worth of complex disputes across three continents, appearing before the world's leading arbitrators under the world's leading arbitration systems. Artem is a Fellow of the Chartered Institute of Arbitrators, holds the SCC/SAA Diploma for Foreign Arbitrators, and is an active member of the Swedish arbitration community.

Artem is a Director of the Swedish-Canadian Chamber of Commerce and a Secretary-General of the EU-Canada Chamber of Commerce

Miljana Bigović, Managing Associate in the Dispute Resolution group at DLA Piper Sweden. She holds an LLM in International Commercial Arbitration Law from Stockholm University, an LLM in International Investment Protection and Banking Law (summa cum laude) from the University of Novi Sad, and has undertaken an LLM at Harvard Law School with a focus on business strategy and organisational impact in 2025. She is a qualified attorney in the Republic of Serbia and has extensive experience representing clients in international arbitration proceedings seated both in Sweden and abroad. In addition to her work at DLA Piper in Stockholm, Miljana brings international arbitration experience from Wilmer Cutler Pickering Hale and Dorr in London, DLA Piper's arbitration team in Paris, and academic research at Stockholm University. She is actively engaged in the international arbitration community and regularly contributes to academic and professional initiatives in the field.

Joel Dahlquist, International Arbitration Advisor at Arnold & Porter, London. He is a Swedish-trained lawyer who holds a doctorate in public international law. He practices international commercial and investment arbitration, with a particular focus on representing sovereign states, and also teaches international commercial arbitration at the London School of Economics and Political Science.

Michael F. Decker, Partner at Advokatfirmaet Schjødt in Oslo, Norway. He is qualified as an attorney in New York state, as a solicitor in England & Wales, and as a lawyer (advokat) in Norway.

Alain Farhad, International arbitrator at Farhad Arbitration.

Alexander Foerster works as an independent arbitrator in Stockholm. He is dual-qualified as a Swedish Advokat and a German Rechtsanwalt and was previously a partner at one of Scandinavia's leading law firms, where he was a member of its renowned dispute resolution group. He has experience in numerous international arbitrations under the ICC, SCC, DIS, VIAC, DAI and Swiss arbitration rules, and teaches international arbitration at the University of Applied Sciences in Frankfurt am Main. He is also a member of the advisory board of the Africa Moot Initiative.

Erik Forsin, Partner and head of Baker Mckenzie's Dispute Resolution Practice Group in Stockholm. He joined Baker Mckenzie in 2020. Prior to joining the firm, he worked at the Stockholm office of another global law firm. He graduated from Stockholm University (LLM, jur.kand.) in 2008. He also has experience working in Swedish courts and the Swedish Enforcement Agency. In addition to acting in commercial disputes, Erik serves as an arbitrator and has completed the SCC Institute and Swedish Arbitration Association Arbitrator Training Program (class of 2021/2022).

Nico Gielen, Rechtsanwalt at HANEFELD. He acts as counsel in a variety of litigation and arbitration matters and as a tribunal secretary.

Erlend Haaskjold, Partner at Advokatfirmaet Schjødt in Oslo, Norway. He is qualified as a lawyer (advokat) in Norway and as a barrister in England & Wales. He is also the author of multiple leading treatises on topics related to Norwegian contract law.

Jimmy Skjold Hansen, Head of Arbitration at Plesner and the main contributor to the 2025 DAA Rules. He also participated in the preparation of the IBA Rules on the Taking of Evidence in International Arbitration of 17 December 2020. Together with other partners and colleagues at Plesner, Peter Schradieck and Jimmy Skjold Hansen have an extensive international arbitration practice covering some of the most significant cases relating to Denmark or Greenland

Anna Bladh Redzic, Partner at Sandart & Partners in Stockholm. She specialises in intellectual property, commercial disputes, and arbitration. A former associate judge, she has experience from both general and specialised courts. She holds LLM degrees from Lund University and Columbia Law School.

Olof Heggemann, Lawyer with experience from the Swedish judiciary. He is the founder of a legal tech company focusing on risk assessments in a dispute resolution context. He is specialised in litigation risk analysis and strategy, and regularly gives talks on the topic.

David Johansson, Partner at DLA Piper Sweden, with an LLM from the University of Örebro and an MSc from Linnaeus University. He represents clients in both ad hoc and institutional arbitration proceedings, with a focus on arbitrations under the auspices of the SCC. David has extensive experience in dealing with disputes in the wake of the Russo-Ukrainian war.

Clara Grønborg Juul, Assistant Attorney in Gorrissen Federspiel's dispute resolution practice in Copenhagen, where she focuses on international arbitration. She also regularly serves as Tribunal Secretary in international arbitrations.

Elena Koch, Deputy Counsel at the International Court of Arbitration of the International Chamber of Commerce (ICC). She is an advocate qualified in Ukraine with ten years of professional experience in France, Germany and Ukraine in the field of private international law and international arbitration. She also holds a PhD.

Marie-Anne Lindhardt, Partner at MAQS Advokatbyrå and head of the firm's Sports & Event practice. She has extensive experience assisting federations, clubs, athletes and agents in commercial, regulatory and dispute-related matters. She is internationally recognised by Lexology as a Thought Leader within Sports.

Jan Heiner Nedden, Rechtsanwalt and Managing Partner at HANEFELD, a leading dispute resolution boutique with offices in Hamburg and Paris. He acts as counsel and arbitrator in complex disputes and has been involved in numerous arbitrations in the Nordic region.

Anne-Karin Nesdam, Specialist Counsel and member of the International Arbitration Team of Wikborg Rein Advokatfirma AS in Oslo, Norway. She specialises in and has extensive experience with international arbitration.

Marie Nesvik, Partner, PhD and member of the International Arbitration Team of Wikborg Rein Advokatfirma AS in Oslo, Norway. She specialises in and has extensive experience with international arbitration.

Julie Alexandra Bech Nosch, Military Legal Advisor to the Danish Defence Command. She holds an LLM from both Cambridge University, with a public international law designation, and the University of Copenhagen.

Tetiana Osypenko, Associate at AGA Partners, where she specialises in international arbitration proceedings under various institutional rules, as well as in the enforcement of arbitral awards and interim relief proceedings in Ukraine. Prior to joining AGA Partners, Tetiana interned with the dispute resolution group of an international law firm in Stockholm. She holds an LLM in International Commercial Arbitration Law (ICAL) from Stockholm University.

Peter Schradieck, Partner at Plesner. Together with other partners and colleagues at Plesner, Peter Schradieck and Jimmy Skjold Hansen have an extensive international arbitration practice covering some of the most significant cases relating to Denmark or Greenland.

Raoul J. Sievers is a Research Assistant at ArbBoutique and a PhD candidate at Humboldt University specialising in international arbitration. He holds an LLM in international commercial arbitration law from Stockholm University and spent six months as a visiting professional at the SCC Arbitration Institute.

Bohdana Sokoliuk, LLM graduate in International Commercial Arbitration Law from Stockholm University and LLB graduate in International Law from Taras Shevchenko National University of Kyiv. She previously interned in the dispute resolution practice at DLA Piper Sweden, assisting with international commercial arbitration proceedings conducted under the auspices of the SCC Arbitration Institute.

Malin Stenberg, Lawyer at MAQS Advokatbyrå, and specialises in commercial dispute resolution, including both Swedish civil proceedings and arbitration. She has a particular focus towards the sports and events industry, representing companies, federations, clubs, athletes and agents in disputes mostly related to contract law, association law, and the rules and regulations of sports.

Christian Johannes Wahnschaffe, Rechtsanwalt at HANEFELD. He acts as counsel in a variety of litigation and arbitration cases and as a tribunal secretary.

Dustin Zojaji, Associate in Baker Mckenzie's Dispute Resolution Practice Group in Stockholm since 2023. In addition to holding a Swedish law degree from Stockholm University (LLM, juristexamen), he also holds an LLM from the New York University School of Law. He focuses his practice mainly on litigation and arbitration, representing clients in various types of disputes within the field of commercial law. Dustin is also admitted to practice law in New York.

Roman Zykov, Secretary General of the Russian Arbitration Association and founding partner of Mansors Law Firm (Russia). He is also a lecturer at the Institute of Energy and Mining Law, Gubkin Russian State University of Oil and Gas, Correspondent at UNIDROIT, Rapporteur at ICCA, and Observer at UNCITRAL. In addition to his LLM degree, he holds a PhD.

Summary of Contents

Table of Contents

Preface

Welcome to the seventh edition of the Stockholm Arbitration Yearbook!

You will find articles on arbitration law in general and Swedish arbitration law in particular. Some contributions are by senior and well-known authors, others by more junior ones.

We are happy to receive – at any time of the year – proposals for future contributions in the form of a short abstract.

Patrik Schöldström
James Hope

CHAPTER 1
Swedish Arbitration-Related Case Law 2024-2025

Patrik Schöldström

§1.01 INTRODUCTION

This chapter accounts for arbitration cases from the Swedish Supreme Court and Swedish courts of appeal from 1 May 2024 to 30 April 2025. It is not exhaustive; the aim is to highlight cases that may interest a non-Swedish reader.

§1.02 BACKGROUND

The Swedish Arbitration Act of 1999[1] (the 'Act') applies to all arbitration proceedings seated in Sweden, whether the parties have any connection to Sweden or not.[2] The Act also sets out, incorporating the 1958 New York Convention, the requirements for foreign arbitral awards to be recognised and enforced in Sweden.[3]

Sweden has a three-tier court system: district courts, six regional courts of appeal and the Supreme Court. However, district courts are only rarely involved in arbitration cases since the courts of appeal are courts of first instance for invalidity and set-aside cases. Recognition and enforcement cases are exclusively handled by the Svea Court of Appeal, seated in Stockholm.

A Swedish arbitral award can be declared *invalid* if it determines an issue which under Swedish law cannot be decided by arbitrators or if the award, or the way in which it came about, is clearly incompatible with the basic principles of the Swedish

1. Lagen (1999:116) om skiljeförfarande, as amended 1 March 2019.
2. The Act, section 46.
3. The Act, sections 52 et seq.

legal system, i.e., public policy (*ordre public*).[4] An arbitral award can be *set aside* (wholly or partially) at the request of a party, *inter alia*, when the arbitrators have exceeded their mandate and when, without fault of the party, an irregularity has occurred in the course of the proceedings which probably influenced the outcome of the case.[5]

Invalidity and set-aside cases are handled by the Court of Appeal within whose district the arbitral proceedings were seated.[6] The Court of Appeal's permission is required to appeal its judgment.[7] Such leave to appeal is denied in most cases. And even if leave to appeal is granted by the Court of Appeal, the Supreme Court can decline to take the case.[8]

Invalidity and set-aside actions are rarely successful. A statistical survey covering ten years (1 January 2004 to 31 May 2014) showed that only 6% of all invalidity and set-aside actions were successful; one award was declared invalid pursuant to section 33 of the Act, and seven awards were set aside pursuant to section 34 of the Act.[9]

The following account is chronological, starting with the first judgment in the period covered (1 May 2024 to 30 April 2025).

§1.03 *ROLFS FLYG- & BUSSRESOR AKTIEBOLAG V. RK TRAVEL GROUP AB*

This set-aside case was not successful.[10] The Court of Appeal found that the arbitral tribunal had made a mistake in basing its award in part on a fact not asserted by the respondent in the arbitration. However, said the Court, the award was also based on facts that the respondent had asserted, and it was therefore not probable that the outcome in the arbitration had been any different if the tribunal had not based its award on the fact in question.

§1.04 *LINK NORGE A/S V. OXE MARINE AB*

This set-aside case was successful.[11] The Court of Appeal set aside those parts of the arbitral award that the set-aside claimant, Link Norge, had requested. The Court found that the arbitral tribunal had exceeded its mandate by ordering Link Norge to pay more

4. The Act, section 33, which also provides that an award is invalid if it is not in writing and signed.
5. The Act, section 34(1), items 3 and 7. Section 34 provides for five other grounds for setting aside an arbitral award, but the two mentioned are those most frequently invoked in set-aside proceedings.
6. The Act, section 43(1). Most invalidity and set-aside proceedings are handled by the Svea Court of Appeal because most Swedish arbitrations are seated in Stockholm.
7. The Act, section 43(2), which provides that leave to appeal shall be granted 'where it is of importance, as a matter of precedent, that the appeal be considered by the Supreme Court'.
8. The Act, section 43(2). That requirement was introduced in an amendment to the Act which came into force 1 March 2019.
9. Översyn av lagen om skiljeförfarande ('Review of the arbitration act'), SOU 2015:37, p. 79.
10. The Court of Appeal for West Sweden, judgment of 8 May 2024 in case T 2710-22.
11. The Court of Appeal for West Sweden, judgment of 20 May 2024 in case T 1747-23.

than Oxe Marine had claimed and that this, of course, had affected the outcome of the arbitration.[12]

This is a clear-cut example of excess of mandate in the form of an award *ultra petita*. Regarding the rules governing the determination of the mandate, the Court said the following in view of one of the parties being non-Swedish: 'The Court of Appeal [...] is obliged to take into account that those involved have been familiar with and adjusted themselves to the rules of Swedish procedural law when it comes to how prayers for relief and their bases are determined [...].' In other words, domestic procedural principles were not applied 'automatically', but because that was in line with the party's expectation.

Also set aside was the costs part of the award related to the part set aside for excess of mandate. The Court set aside the costs part – as opposed to making a new costs decision – saying that the Court was unable to reallocate the costs of the arbitration because that would be going into the substance of how the costs should be allocated to various parts of the arbitrated dispute.

§1.05 FOUR CASES IN THE WAKE OF *ACHMEA, KOMSTROY* AND *PL HOLDINGS*: (A) *REPUBLIC OF ITALY V. CEF ENERGIA B.V.*, (B) *REPUBLIC OF ITALY V. ATHENA INVESTMENTS A/S ET AL.*, (C) *REPUBLIC OF POLAND V. MERCURIA ENERGY GROUP LIMITED*, AND (D) *KINGDOM OF SPAIN V. FORESIGHT LUXEMBOURG SOLAR 1 S.À.R.L. ET AL.*

In all four cases, the Svea Court of Appeal declared the arbitral awards, resulting from arbitrations under Article 26 of the Energy Charter Treaty, invalid.[13] The Court's reasons in the cases are in effect identical, referring to the Court of Justice of the European Union cases *Achmea*,[14] *Komstroy*[15] and *PL Holdings*.[16] The Svea Court's conclusion in each case is modelled on the Swedish Supreme Court's conclusion in the Swedish *PL Holdings* case.[17] This is the Court of Appeal's conclusion in the second case:

> This present award has been rendered in an investment dispute between a member state and an investor from another member state in accordance with

12. The explanation seems to be that the tribunal had added up the sums of a number of invoices submitted by Oxe Marine, but did not observe that Oxe Marine had not asked for the total amount of all invoices.
13. Svea Court of Appeal, judgments of 27 May 2024 in case T 4236-19 (*Italy v. CEF Energia*), of 17 June 2024 in case T 3229-19 (*Italy v. Athena*), of 28 June 2024 in case T 1626-23 (*Spain v. Foresight*), and of 23 December 2024 in case T2613-23 (*Poland v. Mercuria*).
14. C-284/16, EU:C:2018:158.
15. C-741/19, EU:C:2021:655.
16. C-109/20, EU:C:2021:875.
17. Judgment of 14 December 2022 in case T 1569-19. NJA 2022, p. 965.

> Article 26 of the Energy Charter Treaty. It would therefore be obviously incompatible with Swedish public policy if the arbitral award were upheld. This means that the award is invalid under section 33(1) item 2 of the Arbitration Act.[18]

The Court gave permission to appeal only in *Italy v. Athena*, but there was no appeal.

§1.06 *OAO TYUMENNEFTEGAZ V. FIRST NATIONAL PETROLEUM CORPORATION*

This case, for setting aside or invalidating the arbitral award, was not successful.[19] The lead role in this case was played by the EU sanctions regime against Russia.[20] In summary, the set-aside claimant argued that the sanctions regime had made it impossible to find replacement counsel for the arbitration, the consequence being that the claimant had not had a sufficient possibility to present its case there, and that the regime also had made the dispute non-arbitrable.

The claimant asked the Court to start with its set-aside claim and then, if that was not successful, its invalidity claim; the order is usually reversed. The Court followed the order requested by the claimant. The first part, the set-aside claim, concerned allegations of procedural inadequacies, one being that the claimant had not been given an equal and reasonable opportunity to present its case. Another allegation was that the arbitral tribunal had not decided on the claimant's assertion that the dispute was not arbitrable because of the EU sanctions against Russia, prohibiting transactions, including the ongoing arbitration. The claimant's other grounds for setting aside or invalidating the award, the Court said, had mainly to do with whether the arbitrated dispute was arbitrable and how the EU sanction regime affects the parties' relationship.

As for the allegation of lack of opportunity to present its case, the Court first stated that the burden of proof is on the party alleging and then found that the arbitral tribunal had given each party an equal and reasonable opportunity to argue its case, as provided in the applicable SCC Rules (Article 23(2)).

Regarding the assertion that the tribunal had failed to decide on the arbitrability of the dispute, the Court noted that no such express decision was taken, but that the lack of such a decision was not a sufficient reason to set aside the award because it in any event had probably not affected the outcome. In the author's opinion, such a decision would have been superfluous because it could not have affected the arbitrability of the dispute. A dispute is or is not arbitrable, no matter what an arbitral tribunal 'decides'. An arbitral tribunal cannot make a non-arbitrable dispute arbitrable.

The Court then went into the issue of arbitrability in substance, concluding that the arbitrated dispute was arbitrable. Among other things, the Court stated that it was obvious that the EU sanctions regime does not in itself forbid parties to settle disputes

---

18. Author's translation.
19. Judgment of 28 June 2024 in case T 2082-23.
20. Council Regulation (EU) 833/2014 of 31 July 2014 concerning restrictive measures in view of Russia's actions destabilising the situation in Ukraine, as amended by Council Regulations (EU) 2022/428 and 2022/1269.

through arbitration, and the Court noted that the regime does not provide for civil law consequences, such as contract invalidity, for sanctions breach.

The Court gave permission to appeal. An appeal was filed but the Supreme Court declined the case.[21]

§1.07 *GOVERNMENT OF GEORGIA V. INTER RAO UES PJSC ET AL.*

This is another unsuccessful invalidity and set-aside case.[22] The Svea Court found that the three arbitral awards in question were not obviously incompatible with Swedish public policy (*ordre public*) for any of the reasons advanced by the claimant and that there had not been any excess of mandate or procedural irregularity as alleged by the claimant.

The arbitrated dispute was rather complex in both substance and form. In addition to the three challenged awards in the same arbitration, rendered by three arbitrators, the same three persons thereafter, as an ICSID tribunal, also rendered an award between the set-aside claimant and two of the parties in the first arbitration. The parties had agreed to coordinate the two arbitrations.

The first of the claimant's main arguments for invalidity of the awards was that the counterparty in the ICSID arbitration had been doubly compensated for the same damage, which is incompatible with fundamental principles of Swedish law regarding compensation for damage. Among other things, the Svea Court concluded from the three challenged awards and the ICSID award that double compensation had not been intended by the tribunal. And anyway, the Court said, double compensation could be prevented at the enforcement stage.

The claimant's second argument was that the awards in part violated fundamental principles of Swedish competition law, either directly or indirectly, by way of fundamental principles of international competition law. The Court did not agree.

The claimant's allegation in support of its set-aside claim was that the tribunal in one of the awards had failed to give sufficient reasons. The Court found otherwise.

The Court did not give permission to appeal.

§1.08 *UKRAINE V. STATE DEVELOPMENT CORPORATION, VEB.RF (RUSSIAN FEDERATION)*

This case was about the jurisdiction of an arbitral tribunal.[23] It was rooted in a bilateral investment treaty between Ukraine and Russia, and particularly the treaty's arbitration clause. VEB requested arbitration of a dispute, invoking the arbitration clause. Ukraine countered that the arbitral tribunal did not have jurisdiction because VEB was not entitled to arbitration under the treaty. But the tribunal decided that it did have jurisdiction. Ukraine challenged the decision, asking the Svea Court of Appeal to

21. Decision 5 December 2024 in case T 5961-24.
22. Svea Court of Appeal, Judgment of 15 July 2024 in cases T 7600-21, T 15496-21 and T 13071-22.
23. Svea Court of Appeal, judgment of 11 October 2024 in case T 2406-21.

declare that the tribunal did not have jurisdiction. Such an action may be brought under section 2(2) of the Arbitration Act.

Ukraine's argument against jurisdiction was that VEB in effect was a part of the Russian state – or at least a representative of the Russian state or an entity exercising Russian state functions – and as such was not entitled to arbitration under the treaty; the Russian state was not an 'Investor' as defined in the treaty.

The Svea Court however found that VEB was an Investor within the treaty's terms and that Ukraine had not shown that VEB had been a representative of the Russian state or exercised state functions. Ukraine's jurisdictional challenge was therefore dismissed.

The Court gave permission to appeal. An appeal was filed but the Supreme Court declined the case.[24]

§1.09 *GEORGIA V. ZAZA OKUASHVILI*

This case too was an action under section 2(2) of the Arbitration Act; Georgia asked the Svea Court to reverse the SCC arbitral tribunal's decision (by majority) that it did have jurisdiction.[25] The Court did so.

The Court said: The case concerns mainly three issues where the parties differ; *whether* Zaza Okuashvili belongs to the category of persons embraced by the relevant investment treaty (between Georgia and the United Kingdom), *whether* he may request arbitration under the SCC Rules by invoking the treaty's Most Favoured Nation Clause (MFN-Clause) together with the dispute resolution clause in the investment treaty between Georgia and the Belgian-Luxemburg Economic Union, *and whether* the dispute resolution clause in the investment treaty between Georgia and the United Kingdom violates EU law.

The Court chose to start with whether the jurisdiction of the arbitral tribunal may be based on the investment treaty's MFN-Clause.

Having first stressed some legal points, the Court moved on to the case at hand, saying, among other things, that Georgia's agreement in the treaty to dispute resolution through arbitration can be understood only as an agreement to ICSID arbitration exclusively. The question is then, the Court continued, if the agreement by virtue of the MFN-Clause could be extended to embrace also SCC arbitration. The Court arrived at a negative answer, in so doing citing a previous judgment of the Court to the effect that an arbitral tribunal's jurisdiction cannot be founded on a dispute resolution clause in another investment treaty.[26]

The Court thus concluded that the arbitral tribunal did not have jurisdiction. It was therefore not necessary for the Court to consider whether Zaza Okuashvili belongs to the category of people entitled to rely on the relevant investment treaty or whether its dispute resolution clause is incompatible with EU law.

24. Decision of 6 May 2025 in case T 8464-24.
25. Svea Court of Appeal, judgment of 12 November 2024 in case T 11278-22.
26. Svea Court of Appeal, judgment of 18 January 2016 in case T 9128-14.

The Court gave permission to appeal. An appeal has been filed but the Supreme Court has not yet decided whether it will take the case.

§1.10 *COREMAN TRADING FZ-LLC V. CARBONES HOLDING GMBH*

This was an unsuccessful set-aside case where the issue was whether the arbitral tribunal had based its judgment on a material fact, i.e., a clause in the parties' contract not alleged by the claimant in the arbitration (Carbones Holding).[27] This amounted to, said the claimant in the set-aside action (Coreman Trading), an excess of mandate by the tribunal. The Svea Court of Appeal agreed. The Court however also found that the excess of mandate had not affected the outcome in the arbitration, and therefore upheld the award.

The Court did not give permission to appeal.

§1.11 *GASUM OY V. GAZPROM EXPORT LLC*

In this case, the Svea Court of Appeal set aside parts of an arbitral award as requested by Gasum, notably the obligation of Gasum to pay EUR 158 million with interest.

It was common ground in the set-aside case that the arbitral tribunal had not considered whether a certain contractual obligation – of Gasum to buy annually a certain minimum of gas – violated the prohibition on anticompetitive contracts in Article 101 Treaty on the Functioning of the European Union (TFEU). It was however disputed whether Gasum had alleged in the arbitration that that obligation was invalid under Article 101 TEUF. It was also disputed whether Gasum in the arbitration had invoked relevant material facts in support of its claim in relation to Article 101 TEUF.

The Court answered both questions in the affirmative. The Court further found that there was no indication that Gasum had abandoned its position in this part of the case or given the tribunal or Gazprom that impression. The conclusion of the Court was that the tribunal had exceeded its mandate. Next, the Court also found that the excess of mandate probably had affected the outcome. Finally, the Court said that there were no further circumstances in the case that could lead to the award not being set aside.

The Court did not give permission to appeal.

§1.12 *BORDO MANAGEMENT LIMITED ET AL V. UKRAINE*

This was a case where the main claim – for setting aside the arbitral award – failed, but the counterclaim – for changing the costs part of the award – succeeded.[28]

Three companies, jointly called LBB, requested arbitration against Ukraine, alleging that Ukraine in violation of the ECT had taken measures lowering the value of their shares in the Ukrainian company Ukrnafta. LBB claimed USD 6 billion.

27. Svea Court of Appeal, judgment of 28 November 2024 in case T 8492-23.
28. Svea Court of Appeal, judgment of 31 January 2025 in cases T 5378-21 and T 5288-21.

The arbitral tribunal however declined jurisdiction on three grounds, out of eight invoked by Ukraine. The first ground was that two of the claimant companies 'did not have an investment as required under Article 1(6) ECT at the time this Arbitration was commenced'. The second was that the 'Claimants' alleged investment in Ukraine, including their conduct in obtaining and maintaining management control of Ukrnafta, is tainted by bribery and corruption and violates international public policy'. And the third was that 'Respondent validly invoked Article 17(1) ECT to deny Claimants the benefits of Part III ECT.'

The tribunal also ordered each side to bear its own costs.

In the set-aside case, LBB requested the arbitral award to be set aside in its entirety, while Ukraine requested the award be changed so that LBB was ordered to pay Ukraine's arbitration costs in the amount of almost USD 23 million.

The Svea Court of Appeal did not set aside the award. The following is the Court's summing up of the set-aside part of the case:

> The Court of Appeal has found that the arbitral tribunal was unable to decline LLB's request either with reference to Article 17(1) ECT or the existence of corruption. A treaty party's invocation of Article 17(1) is to be assessed as a part of the substance of the case, not as a question of jurisdiction. Nor is there sufficient support in the ECT, international public policy *(ordre public)* or international law for declining an action where there has been corruption in the manner alleged by Ukraine in this set-aside action.
>
> However, the arbitral tribunal could have declined LBB's case on the ground that LBB had not made an investment in the ECT's sense since the ECT requires that some form of compensation must have been given and LBB has not shown that they had given any compensation for their shares in Ukrnafta. The arbitral tribunal could have declined all three companies' actions on the ground that no investment had been made. It does not matter for the Court's assessment of whether the arbitral award shall be set aside or not that the arbitral tribunal has declined the companies' cases, especially [one of the companies], on a different ground.

The Court then moved on to Ukraine's counterclaim for arbitration costs. The starting point for assessing that issue, the Court reasoned, should be the Court's findings in the set-aside part of the case. Namely: 'that the arbitral tribunal lacked jurisdiction on one of the grounds invoked by Ukraine, that two of the grounds could not result in the tribunal declining jurisdiction, and that five grounds were not considered'. The Court also said that the main rule in both Swedish arbitration law and the applicable SCC Rules is that costs follow the event, but that exceptions may be made, for example, if the winning party has made unfounded allegations.

The Court found that neither the five grounds not considered by the tribunal, nor the two grounds where the tribunal in the Court's opinion got it wrong, were unfounded or had otherwise overburdened the arbitration. That Ukraine in the arbitration had lost several partial issues along the way, such as requests for document production, should not, said the Court, affect the distribution of costs.

The Court summed up the costs part of the case thus:

> The Court of Appeal has found that the main rule in the SCC Rules is that the winning party is entitled to compensation for its costs in the arbitration and that Ukraine is to be considered completely victorious in the arbitration. In assessing Ukraine's claim for costs, the Court of Appeal has concluded that Ukraine is entitled to a reasonable amount of USD 16,5 million for counsel and the whole amount claimed for expert opinions and expenses.
>
> When it comes to other circumstances relevant to the distribution of costs, the Court of Appeal has found reason to make an adjustment equivalent to a reduction of USD 100.000 in view of Ukraine's actions concerning the two requests for document production.

The Court also ordered LBB to pay interest on the awarded amounts from the date of the award, as requested by Ukraine.

The Court gave permission to appeal. An appeal has been filed but the Supreme Court has not yet decided whether it will take the case.

§1.13 *KOMAKSAVIA AIRPORT INVEST LTD V. THE REPUBLIC OF MOLDOVA*

This was a case where the court was asked to reverse the arbitral tribunal's decision that it did not have jurisdiction.[29] The Svea Court of Appeal did not do so.

The Court summed up its conclusions thus:

> The Court has arrived at the conclusion that – failing an arbitration agreement between the parties – it was not sufficient with the assertion that Komaksavia had made an investment according to the Investment treaty to give the arbitral tribunal jurisdiction under the doctrine of assertion.[30] The Court has also found that none of the dispositions invoked by Komaksavia constitute an investment within the meaning of the investment treaty. The arbitral tribunal did therefore not err when it said that it did not have jurisdiction to try the dispute between the parties.

The Court gave permission to appeal. An appeal has been filed but the Supreme Court has not yet decided whether it will take the case.

§1.14 *KSP STEEL LLP V. DANIELI & C. OFFICINE MECCANICHE S.P.A.*

This was a set-aside case where the claimant, KSP Steel, alleged that the arbitral tribunal had exceeded its mandate and that the arbitration also was flawed by reason

29. Svea Court of Appeal, judgment of 14 February 2025 in case T 13314-22.
30. This doctrine, which since long applies in civil procedure in court, is believed to have been extended to (or confirmed for) arbitration in the Supreme Court case NJA 2008, p. 406. However, the Supreme Court's statements in that case as regards arbitrations based on arbitration agreements are all *obiter dicta*; the case concerned setting aside an arbitral award based not on an arbitration agreement but on legislative provisions.

of other procedural irregularities, all this having to do with the set-off of a sum of money specified in one of the parties' contracts.[31]

This is, in short, the Svea Court of Appeal's conclusion concerning KSP Steel's main argument in the set-aside case:

> It is clear to the Court that the parties have introduced into the arbitration both the relevant contract and the question of setting off the relevant sum of money in such a way that it was within the arbitral tribunal's mandate to decide the issue. Therefore, the arbitral tribunal has not exceeded its mandate or committed a procedural irregularity as alleged by KSP Steel. The Court also finds that the arbitral tribunal has not conducted the arbitration in such a manner that KSP Steel has not been given sufficient opportunity to present its case.

KSP Steel had two further arguments in the set-aside case, but the Court also dismissed those arguments, essentially referring to its findings concerning KSP Steel's excess of mandate argument.

The Court did not give permission to appeal.

31. Svea Court of Appeal, judgment of 5 March 2025 in case T 11225-23.

CHAPTER 2

I Won But Where Is My Money? The Fate of Cost Decisions When Arbitral Awards Are Invalid or Set Aside

Joel Dahlquist[*]

§2.01 INTRODUCTION

The gap between the extent of doctrinal attention to any given arbitration topic and the real-life relevance for the users of arbitration is arguably never bigger than when it comes to the costs of arbitration. One of the first questions any potential litigant asks its lawyer is 'how much will this cost me', but the answer to that question is often fluid. This is partly because tribunals typically enjoy a considerable degree of discretion in allocating the costs, and partly because tribunals, courts and scholars alike have historically been rather terse on the topic.

Very briefly, the costs that a party to an arbitration incurs may be divided into two categories: (i) the fees and expenses incurred by the arbitrators and the administering institution; and (ii) the expenses incurred by a party in bringing its case, including for legal representation, experts, and witnesses.

The first category of costs is often handled by both parties paying an advance into a deposit, from which these running costs are paid throughout the case. The second category, of course, is typically entirely in the discretion of each party to structure as it sees fit. At the end of the proceedings, the two categories of costs are tallied up and the tribunal assesses the reasonableness of the parties' claimed expenses, and ultimately allocates the liability for both categories as between the parties.

* The author wishes to thank Ellen Johnsson, international arbitration clerk at Arnold & Porter, for research assistance. The usual caveats apply.

Precisely how this allocation is done depends on factors such as the parties' agreement, the applicable arbitration rules, and the *lex loci arbitri*, the law of the seat. To paint with the broadest possible brush, however, in modern arbitration practice, the amount of the first category of costs is generally determined by the administering institution (if there is one), and then the tribunal exercises its discretion in deciding on the distribution of both categories.

While in some domestic jurisdictions, it is customary for each litigating party to cover its own costs, the prevailing starting point in international arbitration is often to recognise, at least to some degree, that the unsuccessful party should compensate some or all of the costs incurred by the prevailing party.

It is this common approach that sets the stage for the scenario discussed in this chapter. It is a scenario that, while relatively unusual, should be familiar to seasoned arbitration practitioners. Imagine that a party is at least partly successful on the merits of an arbitration, and the award's cost decision recognises this by ordering the unsuccessful counterparty to pay a certain amount to the successful party for its costs. The losing party then successfully challenges the award at the seat of arbitration.

In this scenario, what happens with the tribunal's cost decision? Unfortunately, it depends. It depends, again, on the applicable rules. In practice, it probably also depends on whether the parties have already acted on the cost decision. However, it seems that the general starting point in most jurisdictions is that if a domestic court, for whatever reason, finds that the 'main' arbitral award is invalid, the tribunal's associated cost decision will be collateral damage, as it were, and also declared invalid. This chapter will elaborate on this situation and highlight some ways in which it is not always entirely satisfactory.

This seemingly esoteric procedural issue has recently been brought to the fore by its interaction with a much more publicised hot topic in international arbitration, namely intra-EU investment arbitration. Please bear with your author; this will make sense in due course. For now, it is sufficient to note that, following a series of judgments from the Court of Justice of the European Union (CJEU), it is settled law, at least as far as domestic courts in the European Union are concerned, that there can be no consent to arbitration in cases based on treaties between EU Member States. Most arbitration lawyers are by now at least somewhat familiar with this general development, which has been the subject of many arbitrations and arbitration-related court proceedings, not to mention conferences and academic work. As we shall see, the intra-EU issue has now also begun to impact tribunal decisions on costs.

This chapter discusses three different court cases, from three different jurisdictions, addressing three very different scenarios that together shine some light on the issue of the relationship between cost decisions and invalid arbitral awards.

The first is a June 2021 judgment from the Singapore Court of Appeal, in which the court set aside two substantive arbitral awards as well as a separate cost award. In doing so, the Singapore court identified, but failed to resolve, some of the very issues that this chapter seeks to discuss.

We then turn our attention to two more recent court judgments. First, a December 2023 judgment, in which the Svea Court of Appeal in Stockholm declared an arbitral award based on the Energy Charter Treaty (ECT) invalid on public policy grounds, including the cost decision incorporated therein. Second, a September 2024 judgment by the Supreme State Court of Bavaria, upheld by the German Federal Supreme Court in March 2025, in which the German courts rejected the recognition and enforcement of a cost decision with reference to the underlying award having been based on an invalid arbitration agreement.

These two latter cases have in common that they featured jurisdictional discussions based on the intra-EU nature of the underlying arbitration. As we shall see, in an ironic twist, this resulted in unintended consequences for the two EU Member States which, despite prevailing on the merits in the arbitrations and having been granted cost orders recognising this fact, have so far been unable to collect on those costs orders (and in fact have incurred further costs associated with the domestic proceedings).

Finally, the chapter discusses these different cases together, in an attempt to answer the question of what should happen with cost decisions associated with awards that are subsequently declared invalid or set aside.

§2.02 *CBX V. CBZ*

[A] The Arbitration

In *CBX v. CBZ*, a Singapore-seated tribunal heard two parallel ICC arbitrations between the seller and the buyer under a share purchase agreement. The proceedings resulted, among other things, in two partial awards and a separate, final award on costs.

In the partial awards, the tribunal ordered the buyer to pay to the seller certain identified amounts, which the seller had claimed were due because their due dates had been accelerated by contractual language that moved up the due date with reference to the buyer's conduct. The tribunal rejected that 'accelerated' basis for the claim, and instead found that the amounts would become due in any event, i.e., without the acceleration. None of those dates had yet occurred at the time of the parties' pleadings in the arbitration, but some did occur before the partial awards were issued. The tribunal also ordered the buyer to pay 15% interest, compounded annually, on the amounts due. This was done despite an agreement between the parties that compound interest was unlawful under the applicable Thai law.[1]

The buyer applied to set aside the partial awards, as well as the final cost award, in Singapore. The Court of First Instance dismissed the application in full.[2] The buyer appealed to the Court of Appeal, which allowed the appeal.

[B] The Challenge Proceedings

CBX v. CBZ is a rare example of an arbitral award having been set aside by the Singapore Court of Appeal.

1. *CBX and anor v. CBZ and ors* [2021] SGCA(I) 3 ('*CBX*'), para. 7.
2. *CBX*, para. 9.

In the Court of Appeal's view, the tribunal's decision to order payment on a basis that was not claimed by the seller – and which the buyer had objected in its post-hearing brief that the tribunal did not have jurisdiction to do – fell outside of the scope of the parties' submission to arbitration.[3] The court also noted that it would have separately set aside the award on the basis of the compound interest that had been ordered contrary to the parties' agreement and the applicable law, but that it was not necessary to do so under the circumstances.[4]

However, the discerning reader will have understood that it is the cost award that is of interest here. In the cost award, which covered both parallel arbitrations, the tribunal had found that the (losing) buyer should pay 66% of the (winning) seller's costs.[5]

The question now before the Singapore Court of Appeal was what to do with this separate cost award, given that the court had concluded that the two substantive awards must be set aside. The court engaged in an extensive analysis of this issue.

The court noted that the parties had not made any submissions on whether, despite the awards having been set aside and the tribunal therefore rendered *functus officio*, the parties could nevertheless rely on the still-valid arbitration agreement to have the cost issue heard before 'a freshly constituted tribunal'.[6] There was some case law to suggest that this would be possible, although none that specifically related to the issue of cost orders.

Instead, the court said, '[t]he parties will have to advise themselves and to agree or decide how to proceed'. Short of agreeing that the same tribunal issue a new cost order – which the court seemed to recognise was not particularly likely – the court could 'do no more than identify some of the considerations that are in play'.[7]

The court made four such observations. *First*, it noted that it would be 'a matter of regret' if no 'sensible method' of addressing the unfortunate situation raised by the setting aside of the main awards could be found. *Second*, the court suggested that since any cost award is intrinsically linked to the substance of the award, it would seem more appropriate for the same tribunal, as opposed to a new tribunal in a separate arbitration, to resolve the outstanding cost issue. But the court was careful not to express any view 'as to whether that is in the present context possible'.[8]

Here, the court noted that section 10 of the Singapore International Arbitration Act specifically allows a court or tribunal to make an award or order of costs if it finds that there is no jurisdiction during a pending arbitration. But – crucially – the Act does not contain an equivalent provision applicable to set-aside proceedings, nor does the UNCITRAL Model Law upon which the Singapore Act is based.[9] The court also noted that the applicable ICC Rules similarly granted the arbitral tribunal that determined the substantive issue the power to decide on costs.

3. *CBX*, para. 64.
4. *CBX*, para. 95.
5. *CBX*, para. 67.
6. *CBX*, paras 79-80.
7. *CBX*, para. 80.
8. *CBX*, para. 81.
9. *CBX*, para. 82.

Third, on the footing that 'arbitration is essentially consensual', the court concluded that there may be scope to argue both ways as to whether a tribunal in the present case was *functus officio* in relation to the cost award. But given that there was no express guidance in either the parties' direct agreement, the applicable law or the arbitration rules, the court was reluctant to take a position and instead 'leave it to the parties to agree or decide individually how to proceed'.[10]

Finally, the court also signalled to the Singapore legislature that it might 'wish to consider' the *lacunae* that is the inability of a party (such as the seller in *CBX*, or for that matter, an EU Member State in the type of scenarios that will soon be discussed) to seek a new, valid cost order from 'some tribunal' or 'even the court' when the cost order has been set aside because the main award was set aside.[11] In other words, the court was noting an unsatisfactory decision for which its hands were tied by the existing legal framework.

The Singapore Court of Appeal's conclusion – and call for further legislative consideration – brings us neatly to the next part of this chapter, which will address two cases that highlight the challenging situation identified by the court.

§2.03 *FESTORINO V. POLAND*

[A] The Arbitration

In the *Festorino Investment Limited et al v. Republic of Poland* arbitration,[12] two Cyprus-incorporated entities and three individuals (two of whom were EU citizens, one of whom was Swiss) brought claims against Poland under the ECT. The claims were based on administrative delays related to gas mining licences held by the investors, which allegedly resulted in the ultimate bankruptcy of a Polish company jointly owned by the investors. The case was brought pursuant to the SCC Rules, and the SCC Board designated Stockholm as the seat of arbitration.[13]

Poland raised a jurisdictional objection, which was also supported by way of an *amicus curiae* submission from the European Commission, to the effect that the tribunal lacked jurisdiction because of the intra-EU nature of the dispute (the 'Intra-EU Objection'), to which the investors objected.[14] Poland's objection was based primarily on the CJEU's *Achmea* judgment, even though that judgment only explicitly concerned *bilateral* investment treaties between EU Member States, and the treaty invoked by the *Festorino* investors was the *multilateral* ECT. Notably, the parties' exchanges on this

10. *CBX*, para. 84.
11. *CBX*, para. 85.
12. *Festorino Investment Limited, Fosontal Limited, Petra Salesny, Peter Derendinger and Petr Rojicek v. Republic of Poland*, SCC Case No. V2018/098, Award, 30 June 2021 ('*Festorino Award*').
13. *Festorino Award*, ¶ 18.
14. *Festorino Award*, ¶¶ 446-461.

point, as well as the tribunal's award, pre-dated the CJEU judgment in *Komstroy*, which explicitly extended the *Achmea* ruling to the ECT.[15]

In any event, the tribunal dismissed the Intra-EU Objection. In an otherwise factually and legally complex dispute, the award's treatment of the Intra-EU Objection is relatively sparse.[16]

The tribunal also rejected numerous other jurisdictional objections and accordingly proceeded to examine the merits of the investors' case. Ultimately, the tribunal rejected all of the investors' claims under the ECT.

The tribunal's cost decision is of particular relevance for the present purposes. The SCC Rules grant arbitral tribunals discretion to apportion costs, taking into consideration 'the outcome of the case, each party's contribution to the efficiency and expeditiousness of the arbitration and any relevant circumstances'.[17] In exercising this discretion, the *Festorino* tribunal noted that '[i]t is fairly common practice to allocate costs and fees based on the "costs follow the event" principle. In these proceedings, however, neither party was fully successful in its claims. That is, the Claimants prevailed on numerous jurisdictional objections, while the Respondent prevailed on the merits'.[18] This mixed outcome, to the tribunal, justified a 'more balanced approach', but upon weighing the relative significance of Poland's failed jurisdictional objections and the investors' case, which 'failed in its entirety', the tribunal concluded that the investors should bear a 'more significant share of the costs and fees' than Poland.[19]

The tribunal accordingly ordered the investors jointly and severally liable for the entire costs of the arbitration (i.e., the arbitrator fees and the SCC administrative fee), as well as part of Poland's legal fees. The cost of the arbitration amounted to EUR 571,075 plus VAT, although the tribunal did not specify how much of this should be paid in a context where both parties had already made advance payments to the SCC. The share of the legal fees that the tribunal found reasonable amounted to PLN 1,296,584.50.[20] The tribunal also ordered that a 5% per annum interest rate should apply to the legal fees owed by the investors.[21]

Shortly after it had rendered the award, the tribunal indicated to the parties that it would be issuing certain non-substantive corrections to the award.[22] Following submissions and requests from both parties, the tribunal issued a correction and interpretation of its award, as well as an additional award, on 30 July 2021 (the 'Festorino Additional Award'). This correction and additional award primarily concerned the tribunal's cost order in the first award.

15. Case C-741/19, *Republic of Moldova v. Komstroy*.
16. *Festorino Award*, paras 462-473.
17. SCC Arbitration Rules 2023, Art. 49(6).
18. *Festorino Award*, para. 766.
19. *Festorino Award*, paras 767-770.
20. *Festorino Award*, paras 772-776.
21. *Festorino Award*, para. 777.
22. *Festorino Investment Limited, Fosontal Limited, Petra Salesny, Peter Derendinger and Petr Rojicek v. Republic of Poland*, SCC Case No. V2018/098, Correction and Interpretation of Award and Additional Award, 30 July 2021 ('*Festorino Additional Award*'), para. 2.

The tribunal clarified its award by, among other things, specifying the specific amounts that the investors were to pay Poland for the costs of the arbitration: EUR 340,973.75.[23] The tribunal also granted Poland's request for an additional award to the effect that the 5% interest rate should apply not only to the legal fees but also to the cost of the arbitration.[24]

[B] The Challenge Proceedings

The investors challenged the Festorino Award in the Svea Court of Appeal, the court with jurisdiction pursuant to the Swedish Arbitration Act (the 'SAA'), applicable by virtue of the *Festorino* tribunal having been seated in Stockholm.

Before venturing into the court proceedings, and if the reader will look past the fact that the author is a Swedish-trained lawyer writing in the Stockholm Arbitration Yearbook, it is helpful to first add a few words about the relevant aspects of the SAA to situate the *Festorino* proceedings in their proper context.

The SAA provides for two main ways to challenge the validity of an arbitral award.[25] This is because the SAA makes a distinction between circumstances of such serious nature that they result in the award becoming invalid *ipso facto* and *ab initio* (section 33) and circumstances where the award may otherwise be set aside as the result of a challenge (section 34).[26]

Section 33 provides that an award is invalid if it meets either of three listed grounds. First, if it 'includes determination of an issue which, in accordance with Swedish law, may not be decided by arbitrators' (i.e., the award decides a matter that is non-arbitrable). Second, if it, or the manner in which it arose, 'is clearly incompatible with the basic principles of the Swedish legal system' (i.e., violates public policy). Third, if it 'does not fulfil the requirements with regard to the written form and signature'.

One further provision of potential relevance in the present context is section 37 SAA, which provides that:

> The parties shall be jointly and severally liable to pay reasonable compensation to the arbitrators for work and expenses. However, *if the arbitrators have stated in the award that they lack jurisdiction to determine the dispute, the party that did not request arbitration shall be liable to make payment only insofar as required due to special circumstances.*

---

23. *Festorino Additional Award*, ¶ 67.
24. *Festorino Additional Award*, ¶ 67.
25. It should be noted that the SAA differs from many other arbitration laws by also providing for a specific avenue for challenging negative jurisdictional awards – section 36, *see* Joel Dahlquist, 'Arbitral Tribunal Jurisdiction', in Annette Magnusson, Jakob Ragnwaldh and Martin Wallin, *International Arbitration in Sweden: A Practitioner's Guide* (2nd ed., Wolters Kluwer, 2021), p. 144; Kaj Hobér, *International Commercial Arbitration* (2nd ed., OUP, 2020), pp. 326-329.
26. Kaj Hobér, *International Commercial Arbitration* (2nd ed., OUP, 2020), pp. 270-271; Finn Madsen, *Commercial Arbitration in Sweden* (5th ed., Jure, 2020), p. 359.

This provision authorises the tribunal to order the parties to pay the arbitrators' fees. The second sentence establishes a main rule to the effect that if the tribunal has declined jurisdiction, the claimant shall bear the arbitrators' fees. There is some commentary suggesting that this provision could be applicable by analogy also in a situation where the tribunal finds that it has jurisdiction, but a reviewing court subsequently comes to a different conclusion.[27] As we shall see, the Svea Court of Appeal rejected that argument.

In their 29 October 2021 application,[28] the investors requested that the Svea Court of Appeal annul *or* set aside the award. The claims under section 33 SAA were that the award was contrary to Swedish public policy or, alternatively, that the award had determined a matter that was non-arbitrable under Swedish law.[29] The investors' alternative claim under section 34 SAA was that the award should be set aside because there was no valid arbitration agreement.[30]

The investors also asked that regardless of the outcome on the main claims, the award's cost decision should be either declared invalid or set aside in any event because there were procedural errors, not attributable to the investors, that affected the tribunal's cost decision.[31]

Poland disputed the investors' application that the entire award be declared invalid, but agreed with the investors' request so far as the award dealt with the relationship between Poland and those investors who were EU nationals.[32]

With respect to the cost decision, however, Poland requested that regardless of the outcome of the application, the cost decision should stand.[33] In developing this request, Poland suggested that it ought to be 'uncontroversial that a request for the invalidity or set-aside does not encompass an award in the parts that concern compensation to the arbitrators'.[34]

As mentioned, these costs - which in the average international arbitration typically amount to much less than the fees associated with legal representation - are governed by section 37 SAA. Pursuant to section 37, the parties shall be jointly and severally liable to pay reasonable compensation to the arbitrators. Despite this, the *Festorino* tribunal had ordered the investors to carry these costs. Poland pointed out that the investors had not made use of the special avenue available under section 41 SAA for a party to appeal a tribunal's decision on these costs to the district court at the seat of arbitration. Furthermore, Poland drew the Svea Court's attention to the second sentence of section 37, which states that if the tribunal has found that there is no

27. Stefan Lindskog, *Skiljeförfarande*, En kommentar (3rd ed., 2020), p. 1045.
28. *Festorino Investment Limited, Fosontal Limited, Petra Salesny, Peter Derendinger and Petr Rojicek v. Republic of Poland*, Svea Court of Appeal, Case No. T 12646-21, Claimants' Application, 29 October 2021 (Case File Entry No. 1) ('Festorino Application').
29. Festorino Application, paras 5-6.
30. Festorino Application, para. 7.
31. Festorino Application, para. 8.
32. *Festorino Investment Limited, Fosontal Limited, Petra Salesny, Peter Derendinger and Petr Rojicek v. Republic of Poland*, Svea Court of Appeal, Case No. T 12646-21, Poland's Response, 19 May 2022, (Case File Entry No. 41) ('Poland Response'), para. 4.
33. Poland Response, para. 6.
34. Poland Response, para. 67.

jurisdiction, the respondent party shall only be liable for these costs in special circumstances.

Although the wording of section 37 is only directly applicable to negative jurisdictional decisions by a *tribunal*, Poland argued that it should apply by analogy to negative jurisdictional decisions also by the *reviewing court*. Therefore, Poland argued, the court should reject the investors' request that the tribunal's cost decision also be declared invalid or set aside.[35]

Moreover, Poland argued that the cost award should be maintained in any event, because of the intra-EU nature of the arbitration agreement. According to Poland, the investors had initiated the arbitration almost six months after the *Achmea* judgment, and thereby forced Poland to defend itself (to the tune of much more than what the tribunal's cost decision reflected, it said) against a claim that was inevitably destined to fail on jurisdictional grounds. In this respect, Poland maintained that the court should invalidate the award as contrary to public policy, but that it should not apply the same reasoning to the cost decision. Anything else, the state argued, would punish Poland for having been the respondent to a claim brought in bad faith in violation of public policy.[36] Doing so would also be contrary to section 37, applied analogously, because the intention behind that provision is to insulate respondents from costs in situations where arbitrations are initiated in the absence of jurisdiction.[37]

Importantly, Poland argued that the same line of reasoning should also apply to Poland's own costs in the arbitration (i.e., separate from the arbitrators' fees that are explicitly regulated by section 37 SAA). Had the tribunal reached the correct decision – i.e., had it rejected jurisdiction on the intra-EU basis, something that Poland noted the parties now seemed to agree was correct – the case would have been dismissed at that stage, and Poland most likely awarded costs. Poland argued that it should not be put in a worse position solely because the tribunal erred on jurisdiction, only for the Svea Court to then rectify this by declaring the award invalid.

Finally, Poland made what could best be characterised as a policy argument: given the development of CJEU case law on this area, it would be unsatisfactory, Poland suggested, if investors could initiate arbitration based on arbitration agreements that are plainly invalid under EU law, only to then avoid having to compensate the respondent state for its costs when the case duly fails for lack of jurisdiction. Such a situation seemed to Poland 'neither reasonable nor intended'.[38]

By the time the case reached the Svea Court of Appeal, the CJEU's *Komstroy* judgment had been issued. The investors – who, it must be repeated, had disputed Poland's Intra-EU Objection during the arbitration – relied on the *Komstroy* judgment to support their argument before the Svea Court of Appeal that the award was manifestly incompatible with fundamental norms and principles of EU law, and

35. Poland Response, paras 68-72.
36. Poland Response, para. 76.
37. Poland Response, para. 77.
38. Poland Response, paras 79-82.

thereby of Swedish law, and should be deemed invalid pursuant to section 33(2) SAA.[39]

Svea Court of Appeal agreed, declaring the award invalid pursuant to section 33(2). This was not particularly surprising, given: (i) that the parties at this stage agreed that the award was based on an arbitration agreement that was contrary to mandatory EU law; and (ii) that the Swedish Supreme Court only a year earlier had held that such arbitration agreements are contrary to EU public policy, and thereby Swedish public policy.[40]

While this conclusion was unsurprising, the court's judgment in *Festorino* is more interesting as it relates to two other, subsidiary issues on which the parties were *not* in agreement: how to handle the fact that one of the investors was not an EU national, and how to handle the tribunal's cost decision.

On the first point, the Svea Court noted that Swedish courts had never before been faced with a situation in which EU nationals and non-EU nationals jointly had brought an arbitration against an EU Member State, and it was clear that the award was invalid in relation to the EU nationals. However, it follows expressly from section 33 that awards may be declared partially invalid, and the court cited a leading commentator on the SAA, who had suggested that the test for partial invalidity on public policy grounds is whether a 'distinguishable and independent' part of the award violates public policy.[41] Applying this test, the court found that the invalidity was not of the kind that could be distinguished in this manner. The court therefore declared the award invalid in its entirety, i.e., also vis-à-vis the third-country investor.[42]

On the cost point, the court's reasoning was relatively short. Having found that the award was invalid in its entirety, the court did not see a reason to make any different assessment with respect to the cost decision contained in the award. The court also briefly noted that this conclusion was unaffected by Poland's arguments: the court said that 'the fact that the investors at the time of the request for arbitration, unlike Poland' considered that the tribunal had jurisdiction did not change its conclusion. Nor was it possible, the court said, to apply section 37 SAA analogously, as Poland had argued.[43]

One judge issued a partial dissenting opinion, with respect to the majority's reasoning as to whether it should be possible to partially uphold the arbitral award with respect to the one claimant who was not an EU citizen. The dissenting judge agreed with the outcome – i.e., that the arbitral award was invalid also vis-à-vis the third-country investor – but noted that in his view, it should be possible to 'partially' uphold an award to the extent it is only partly an intra-EU dispute, because '[t]he various parts of a proceeding may be more or less distinguishable, and the intra-EU element may be greater or lesser'. Partially upholding an award that is otherwise

39. Svea Court of Appeal Judgment, pp. 9-10.
40. NJA 2022, p. 965, *Poland v. PL Holdings*, 14 December 2022, paras 59-60.
41. Svea Court of Appeal Judgment, p. 28, referencing Stefan Lindskog, *Skiljeförfarande*, En kommentar (3rd ed., 2020), pp. 918 et seq.
42. Svea Court of Appeal Judgment, p. 28.
43. Svea Court of Appeal Judgment, pp. 28-29.

invalid, however, should only be possible if the part of the award concerning third-country investors could be sufficiently separated from the other issues before the tribunal 'in such a way that the invalidity does not arise in relation to the third country investor'. In the present case, the dissenting judge found that it was not possible to separate the issue in this manner, and he therefore agreed with the ultimate outcome that the award was invalid in its entirety.[44]

The application having been successful, the court also ordered Poland to bear the investors' costs associated with the challenge proceedings. In doing so, the court notably rejected Poland's argument that the investor had initiated the arbitration in bad faith; in the court's view, there was at least some ambiguity as to the status of intra-EU arbitration by the time that the arbitration had been initiated.[45]

On appeal from Poland, the Swedish Supreme Court decided to consider only a part of the case.[46] While the Supreme Court rejected Poland's request for a preliminary reference from the CJEU (finding that the EU law aspects of the case were not in doubt), it did decide to try the question of whether 'the award is invalid pursuant to Section 33 [...] in the part that concerns the relationship between the Republic of Poland and [the non-EU citizen]'.[47]

In a judgment of 26 May 2025, the Supreme Court came to a different conclusion than the Svea Court of Appeal with respect to the issue of partial invalidity. In doing so, the Supreme Court's starting points were that awards rendered in intra-EU contexts were invalid, but that it is possible for awards to be partially invalid.[48]

With respect to partial invalidity, the Supreme Court stated that courts should avoid invalidating arbitral awards unnecessarily, because of the important principle that awards should generally be final and binding (as expressed not only in the ECT itself but also in the New York Convention and Swedish law).[49] A reviewing court must therefore consider whether it is possible to distinguish different parts of the awards for the purposes of invalidity, for example, if – as in the *Festorino* case – several different parties are involved.[50]

With respect to the obligations to pay costs that are part of the award, the Supreme Court said that if an award is declared partially invalid 'the court, as a rule, needs to consider the extent to which the decision on cost apportionment between the parties are covered by the invalidity'.[51]

44. Svea Court of Appeal Judgment, pp. 35-36.
45. Svea Court of Appeal Judgment, pp. 29-32.
46. *The Republic of Poland v. Festorino Investment Limited, Fosontal Limited, Petra Salesny, Peter Derendinger and Petr Rojicek,* Swedish Supreme Court, Case No T 555-24, 28 October 2024.
47. *The Republic of Poland v. Festorino Investment Limited, Fosontal Limited, Petra Salesny, Peter Derendinger and Petr Rojicek,* Swedish Supreme Court, Case No. T 555-24, 28 October 2024, p. 4.
48. *The Republic of Poland v. Festorino Investment Limited, Fosontal Limited, Petra Salesny, Peter Derendinger and Petr Rojicek,* Swedish Supreme Court, Case No T 555-24, Judgment 26 May 2025 ('Supreme Court Judgment'), paras 8-16.
49. Supreme Court Judgment, para. 12.
50. Supreme Court Judgment, paras 13-16.
51. Supreme Court Judgment, para. 21.

Applying these considerations to the case at hand, the Supreme Court noted that by virtue of the Svea Court of Appeal's judgment (which was not subject to the appeal), the *Festorino* award was invalid vis-à-vis the EU investors. However, the Supreme Court made a different assessment of the award's validity with respect to the non-EU investor, finding that his third-country nationality meant that the basis for the invalidity did not extend to him.[52] The fact that the ground for invalidity was public policy did not change this assessment.[53] The court noted that it was clear from the award itself that the investors brought separate claims based on their clearly identified respective shares in the investment.[54]

In sum, the Supreme Court found that the part of the award that concerned the non-EU investor should be distinguished from the rest of the award. The court also pointed out that this conclusion, letting the award stand in part, did not prevent the other investors from bringing another claim against Poland should they so wish.[55]

According to the award, the non-EU investor was jointly and severally liable for Poland's costs and Poland's share of the arbitrators' fees. Following the Supreme Court's judgment, this part of the award still stands. Presumably, this means that Poland could now seek to enforce the cost decision against this single investor, even if the award remains invalid vis-à-vis the others.

Given this outcome, the Supreme Court also ordered that the non-EU investor should compensate Poland for its costs in both the Svea Court of Appeal and in the Supreme Court.[56]

§2.04 *ANTARIS V. CZECHIA*

[A] The Arbitration

In yet another intra-EU investment arbitration, German company Antaris and its German CEO Mr Michael Gode relied on both the Germany-Czechia bilateral investment treaty and the ECT. The arbitration relates to Czechia's reduction of incentives for renewable energy, which the investors argued had affected their solar energy plants in Czechia.

In the arbitration, the European Commission had intervened as an amicus curiae, arguing that the tribunal lacked jurisdiction due to the intra-EU nature of the dispute.[57] However, the award was rendered in May 2018, i.e., two months after the CJEU's *Achmea* judgment, meaning that the parties exchanged pleadings without the benefit

52. Supreme Court Judgment, paras 23, 8.
53. Supreme Court Judgment, paras 23, 13.
54. Supreme Court Judgment, para. 24.
55. Supreme Court Judgment, paras 25, 15.
56. Supreme Court Judgment, para. 28.
57. *Antaris Solar GmbH and Dr. Michael Göde v. Czech Republic*, PCA Case No. 2014-01, Award, 2 May 2018 ('*Antaris Award*').

of this judgment. Czechia did attempt to introduce the *Achmea* judgment, once rendered, onto the record, but the tribunal rejected the request as too late.[58]

The tribunal upheld jurisdiction and therefore ruled on the merits of the claim, ultimately finding, by majority, in favour of Czechia. The tribunal's costs decision reflected the state's win on the merits, ordering the claimants to pay Czechia USD 1.75 million and GBP 178,125.50 for its legal costs.[59]

[B] The Recognition and Enforcement Proceedings

This last court case to be discussed is not a set-aside case, but instead reached domestic courts by way of an application for recognition and enforcement. It must therefore be noted at the outset that the *Antaris* award, as far as publicly known, as a legal matter appears to stand: the tribunal was seated in Geneva,[60] and no set-aside judgment by Swiss courts has been reported.

Even though the German courts were not the courts at the place of arbitration, they had reason to tackle the intra-EU issues, albeit from a slightly different vantage point. Having prevailed in the arbitration and received a favourable cost decision, Czechia sought recognition and enforcement of the cost part of the award in Germany, the home state of both investors.

Interestingly, in a pattern reminiscent of *Festorino*, at the enforcement stage, the investors, who during the arbitration had argued that the intra-EU nature of the dispute did *not* deprive the tribunal of jurisdiction, now argued that the award was unenforceable precisely because of the intra-EU nature.[61]

Czechia's application was made pursuant to the New York Convention on the Recognition and Enforcement of Foreign Arbitral Awards, which has been incorporated into the German *Zivilprozessordnung* (the 'ZPO').

In examining the enforceability of the cost award under the New York Convention, the *Bayerisches Oberstes Landesgericht* (the 'Bavarian Supreme Court') noted that Article V(1) of the Convention, reflected in Article 1061(1)(1) ZPO, provides that recognition and enforcement 'may be refused' based on the grounds enumerated in that provision. Contrary to the position in many other jurisdictions,[62] the Bavarian Supreme Court found that this language limits the enforcing court's discretion in situations where an Article V ground is present.[63]

The Bavarian Supreme Court then proceeded to examine whether there was any Article V ground that would prevent the Court from enforcing the *Antaris* cost award.

58. *Antaris Award*, para. 73.
59. *Antaris Award*, paras 463-466.
60. *Antaris Award*, para. 38.
61. *Czech Republic v. Antaris GmbH and Michael Göde*, Judgment of the Supreme State Court of Bavaria 101 Sch 146/23, 13 September 2024 ('Bavarian Supreme Court Decision'), paras 17-18.
62. Gary Born, *International Commercial Arbitration* (3rd ed., Kluwer Law International, 2021), 'Chapter 22: Legal Framework for International Arbitral Awards' (Updated March 2024), p. 8.
63. Bavarian Supreme Court Decision, paras 42-44.

In particular, the court discussed Article V(1)(a), i.e., whether the underlying arbitration agreement was 'not valid under the law to which the parties have subjected it or, failing any direction thereon, under the law of the country where the award was made'.

In language that should be familiar to anyone with a surface-level interest in the intersection between EU law and international arbitration, the Bavarian Supreme Court reasoned that, in line with the established case law of the CJEU, intra-EU treaties that provide for arbitration violate Articles 267 and 344 of the Treaty of the Functioning of the European Union, because such treaties authorise tribunals to apply EU law without granting them the opportunity to refer preliminary requests to the CJEU.[64] The arbitration clauses in the two treaties on which the *Antaris* tribunal had based its jurisdiction – the Germany-Czechia BIT (which the High Court noted was materially identical to the very BIT at issue in the *Achmea* case) and the ECT (which the Bavarian Supreme Court noted that the CJEU had explicitly ruled on in *Komstroy*) respectively – were therefore in violation of EU law. Accordingly, the Bavarian Supreme Court concluded that there was no valid arbitration agreement between the disputing parties, which prevented the Court from enforcing any resulting award.[65]

The Bavarian Supreme Court also discussed another German court case, *Vocklinghaus*, relied upon by Czechia in its submissions before the Court, which had reached the opposite conclusion and enforced a cost award incorporated in an arbitral award in a scenario where the arbitration respondent (co-incidentally also Czechia, in another investment treaty arbitration) had prevailed.[66] For the Bavarian Supreme Court, the distinguishing factor between this earlier *Vocklinghaus* case and the *Antaris* award was the fact that in the earlier case, the tribunal had declined jurisdiction, whereas in the *Antaris* case, the tribunal had found that it had jurisdiction and dismissed the case on the merits.[67] It was this upholding of jurisdiction that violated EU law and prevented the enforceability of the award, a situation that was different from the earlier case.[68]

For the present purposes, it should be noted that Czechia had urged the Bavarian Supreme Court to draw a distinction between the award on the merits and the part of the award that decided on the costs.[69] The court rejected this argument, finding that the award *as a whole* was based on an invalid arbitration agreement.[70]

Czechia appealed the High Court decision to the *Bundesgerichthof* (the 'German Federal Court of Justice' or the 'Federal Court'), which issued its decision on 27 March 2025. The Federal Court upheld the Bavarian Supreme Court's decision that the cost award could not be enforced because the underlying arbitration agreement was invalid under EU law.[71]

64. Bavarian Supreme Court Decision, paras 56, 69.
65. Bavarian Supreme Court Decision, para. 56.
66. Bavarian Supreme Court Decision, paras 74-77.
67. Bavarian Supreme Court Decision, paras 65, 75-77.
68. Bavarian Supreme Court Decision, para. 70.
69. 'Chapter 22: Legal Framework for International Arbitral Awards (Updated March 2024)', paras 27-28.
70. Bavarian Supreme Court Decision, paras 59, 62.
71. *Czech Republic v. Antaris GmbH and Michael Göde*, German Federal Court of Justice Case I ZB 64/24, 27 March 2025 (the 'Federal Court Decision'), paras 49-50.

The Federal Court's analysis, similar to the lower court's, was based on Article V(1)(a) of the New York Convention, as incorporated in German law. In reasoning that is likely to cause some debate – but which is not immediately relevant here – the court found that the law applicable to the arbitration agreement was international law (including EU law), and not the law of the Swiss seat.[72] In applying EU law to the arbitration agreement, the court did not have any difficulty in concluding that there was no arbitration agreement because Czechia had not given a valid offer to arbitrate at the time of the initiation of the arbitration.

With respect to the relationship between the cost award and merits awards resulting from this invalid arbitration agreement, the court stated that its reasoning must apply equally to the cost issue; anything else, the court said, 'would amount to an [arbitrary] division of the arbitral award into the decision on the merits and a decision on costs'.[73]

Similar to Poland in the *Festorino* challenge proceeding, Czechia also argued before the Federal Court that the effectiveness of mandatory EU law required that intra-EU investors not gain an improper advantage by being allowed to bring arbitration against Member States without being sanctioned by way of costs. The Federal Court did not accept this argument, noting that EU courts' obligations to deny the legal effects of awards relying on arbitration agreements that were contrary to EU law extended to *any* award, irrespective of the kind of enforcement sought. In a 'fruit of the poisonous tree' kind of reasoning, the court said that anything else would legitimise proceedings that took place contrary to EU law.[74]

However, seemingly picking up on the lower court's discussion about the *Vocklinghaus* enforcement, the Federal Court also noted that it was not necessary to resolve the question whether a cost decision associated with a tribunal's negative jurisdictional finding in an intra-EU case would be enforced in Germany.[75]

Having dismissed Czechia's enforcement application, the court also ordered the state to pay the investors' costs. Notably, the court exercised an ability under German law to fix the amount owed at the value of the dispute. Converted to EUR, the amount that Czechia had sought – i.e., the amount the *Antaris* tribunal had ordered the investors to pay – was roughly EUR 1.8 million.[76]

§2.05 DISCUSSION: THE FATE OF COST DECISIONS

As could be expected from courts in three different jurisdictions seized with three different kinds of questions, the cases discussed in this chapter address separate but overlapping issues relating to the fate of cost decisions.

To recall, in *CBX*, the Singapore Court seemed to find it relatively uncontroversial that the fate of the 'main' award dictates the fate of the cost decision. The court instead

72. Federal Court Decision, paras 35-37.
73. Federal Court Decision, para. 45.
74. Federal Court Decision, para. 49.
75. Federal Court Decision, para. 50.
76. Federal Court Decision, paras 13-14.

focused its attention on what should happen after the awards were set aside, i.e., where the 'cost-creditor' party could turn for a new cost order to replace the one that was set aside. In this respect, the court explicitly recognised that the party that was the beneficiary of the tribunal's cost order is left in an unsatisfactory position, but that the court's hands were tied. Noting that there was some uncertainty as to whether the original tribunal was *functus officio* with respect to the cost decision, the court considered that the matter was largely in the hands of the disputing parties to resolve. In practice, this seems like an unlikely scenario, as it would require the party that has been 'relieved' of its cost obligations to nevertheless agree to re-submit the cost issue to whatever adjudicatory body may be available.

The Swedish and German courts were less occupied with the practical consequences of their respective findings.

In the Svea Court, perhaps unsurprisingly, the *functus officio* discussion and the broader issue of the avenues available to the parties to resolve the cost issue did not come up. Given that the court had found, and the parties agreed, that the award violated Swedish public policy, there was presumably little reason to consider the hypothetical avenues still available to Poland to collect on the cost decision emanating from that award. Declaring the award invalid under section 33 SAA meant that the award was invalid *ab initio* – legally speaking, it had never existed – and the question of the cost decision contained therein was therefore arguably moot. That would not necessarily have been true had the award instead been set aside under section 34, but that question never arose before the Swedish court.

The German Federal Court, meanwhile, stated that the only way to give full effect to EU law was to refuse recognition of a cost decision emanating from an intra-EU arbitration. Given that context, it should not be surprising that the court did not engage in any hypothetical discussion about the unfortunate situation in which this left Czechia.

While understandably short on the question of remedies available to the parties whose favourable cost decisions had been neutralised, both the Svea Court and the two German courts discussed extensively the predicate question of the relationship between costs and the main award, ultimately finding that the cost decisions in both cases could not be separated from the fate of the main awards. Both states had made various arguments as to why the cost decision should still be respected, but in both cases, the courts rejected them relatively swiftly.

The *Festorino* case contains a twist in this respect, because the arbitration was brought by – and the tribunal's cost decision accordingly jointly directed at – both EU investors and a third-country investor. That inevitably raises the question of whether the main award should be allowed to stand in part, vis-à-vis only the third-country investor. The Svea Court recognised that this was possible in theory, but only if the award could be meaningfully distinguished with respect to the different claimants, a question that the court answered in the negative. The Supreme Court, however, came to the opposite conclusion, with consequences for the cost award as well: if the award remains valid with respect to one party, the cost decision contained in the award is also valid with respect to that party, at least when the tribunal's cost decision orders joint and several liability of all losing parties collectively. This ultimate outcome in the Supreme Court not only makes sense as a legal proposition but it also has the added benefit of potentially providing Poland with a solution to the unfortunate situation in which it was left by the Svea Court of Appeal's judgment. At least in theory, an avenue is now available for Poland to collect on the (still partially valid) cost order.

It must be noted that the more common situation is that an award cannot be distinguished between different cost-owing parties. Indeed, the situation facing the seller in *CBX* – i.e., having prevailed in an arbitration only to see the associated cost decision go away when the award is set aside for reasons not attributable to the party itself – is not unusual in international commercial arbitration. As a general proposition, it is not controversial that if a court has found that the award in its entirety was rendered without a valid arbitration agreement, or indeed if any decisions emanating from the arbitration agreement itself violate public policy, the tribunal also lacked the authority to order costs.

Some further spice is added to the mix in the specific situations that arose in *Festorino* and *Antaris*. The basic fact patterns in these cases are somewhat similar: (i) a party raises a jurisdictional objection before the tribunal (over the other party's objection); (ii) that jurisdictional objection is unsuccessful; (iii) nevertheless, the party that objected to jurisdiction prevails on the merits and receives a favourable cost decision; (iv) at the post-award stage, be it in challenge proceeding or in the enforcement context, the losing party now argues that there was in fact no jurisdiction, making essentially the same argument that the objecting party made before the tribunal; and (v) the domestic court agrees, leading either to the award being declared invalid (in *Festorino*, albeit with the Swedish Supreme Court's partial modification) or to recognition and enforcement being refused (in *Antaris*).

In essence, in both cases, a party – let us call it what it is, an EU Member State – objected to the tribunal's jurisdiction because the arbitration agreement was supposedly manifestly invalid under mandatory EU law. Neither tribunal accepted this argument, but the domestic courts subsequently did. In other words, the two states ended up 'prevailing' twice: first on the merits in the arbitration, and then at the post-award stage where the states' jurisdictional argument was vindicated. Nevertheless, the states will have to carry their costs (not only in the arbitration but also potentially in the domestic court proceedings; that was the case in Germany, and also initially in Sweden, until the Supreme Court's revision of the Svea Court of Appeal's cost decision).

Plainly, the states' position is unsatisfactory. In the investment arbitration context, this situation risks adding to the often-voiced criticism against the system as such that a respondent state can never really win, but in the best-case scenario, merely does not lose. Here, neither state lost but both states nevertheless risk being left with the bill for mounting their defence, despite both tribunals recognising that the unsuccessful claimants ought to cover some of the costs and fees, and despite domestic courts subsequently vindicating the states' jurisdictional concerns.

So, what is the way out of this unsatisfactory situation? In the set-aside context, the Singapore Court of Appeal's suggestion that the parties agree to resolve the outstanding cost issue in another forum is unlikely to be helpful in practice, for the reasons discussed above.

A more legal-doctrinal approach, which would render the scenario envisioned by the Singapore court moot, would be to say that a cost award should be able to survive the invalidity of the main award. But if the reviewing court has found that the award was not based on a valid arbitration agreement, the traditional position is that the award's cost disposition was similarly made without support in the parties' agreement.

Unless it is possible to distinguish between the main award and the cost decision in this respect, that is. But this task is far from easy, as evidenced by the Svea Court of Appeal and both German courts which did not see a basis for making such a distinction. The Swedish Supreme Court found that such a distinction could be made where multiple parties had made clearly distinguishable separate claims in the arbitration, a situation that – while not uncommon – was specific to the multiparty situation in the *Festorino* case.

It is conceivable, of course, that a reviewing court is empowered with discretion to maintain the cost decision even if the substantive award is set aside. For example, the English Arbitration Act – famously deviating from UNCITRAL Model Law principles when it comes to the tools available to reviewing judges – provides that a party challenging the substantive jurisdiction of a tribunal under section 67 may request that the reviewing court 'vary the award' or 'set aside the award in whole or in part'. It would seem that this power allows the reviewing court to 'vary' an award's cost order even if the court finds that the tribunal lacked jurisdiction.[77]

In the intra-EU context, many arbitration practitioners have expressed frustration over what they view as the CJEU jurisprudence's 'retroactive' imposition of jurisdictional obstacles, in the sense that the prevailing EU law position is now that the hundreds of arbitration clauses included in intra-EU treaties were never valid in the first place. If the consequence of this jurisprudence is that arbitral awards resulting from such clauses are invalid, perhaps it's just poetic justice that the respondent states' cost entitlements follow the same fate? After all, these cost decisions concern amounts that are generally dwarfed by the amounts ordered in merits awards that are now regularly set aside by EU Member State courts. According to this sentiment, what is a little bad faith from investors – disputing intra-EU objections in arbitrations only to turn 180 degrees and themselves make that very objection when faced with unfavourable cost orders – compared to the bad faith displayed by the CJEU and EU Member States that have pulled the arbitration clauses out from under the feet of hundreds of investment treaties?

The purpose of this chapter is not to venture into this well-known 'clash' between international arbitration and EU law. Here, the two intra-EU cases discussed are merely employed as examples of a potentially problematic situation that extends beyond the intra-EU context; it is not particularly far-fetched to imagine similar scenarios in the

77. *Republic of Kazakhstan v. Istil Group Inc* [2006] 2 Lloyd's Rep 270, discussed at Robert Merkin and Louis Flannery, *Arbitration Act 1996* (6th ed., Informa Law, 2014), p. 413.

commercial arbitration context, where a party prevails 'twice' yet is left with an invalid cost order in its favour.

The embryo of one potential solution might be found in Poland's arguments in the *Festorino* set-aside. The state unsuccessfully requested the court to apply section 37 SAA analogously. As argued by Poland, section 37 embodies a principle of wider application, potentially helpful in this context, that the respondent party should not be punished by way of cost liability when a claimant initiates an arbitration without there being a valid arbitration agreement. But according to its wording, section 37 only applies to tribunals, and not to reviewing courts, and only to the arbitrators' fees, not to the parties' own costs. Svea Court of Appeal declined, without much explanation, to expand the provision's scope to its own authority to order costs. Perhaps it is time to consider introducing legislative provisions that expressly authorise the court at the seat to grant costs to respondents even if the court invalidates or sets aside the main award.

Another potential solution to the problem – not envisaged by any of the court decisions discussed in this chapter – would be to bring a separate claim for compensation. In many jurisdictions, it might be possible for the cost creditor to bring such a separate claim, assuming a domestic court has jurisdiction to entertain it (pursuant to the jurisdictional rules of the relevant jurisdiction). One could imagine a claim based on the alleged bad faith by the counterparty that disputed the jurisdictional objection in the arbitration, only to then rely on it to avoid cost liability at the post-award stage. That bad faith, if established, could potentially be a self-standing basis for damages. A set aside or invalid cost decision would not be res judicata, such that it could prevent a separate damage claim for the incurred costs, but even if parts of the cost decision remained in force, that would presumably not prevent that kind of tort-type claim.[78]

In the enforcement context, the answer seems more straightforward than in the set-aside context. To recall, both German courts found that the only way to give full effect to the EU law obligation to neutralise the legal effects of intra-EU arbitrations was to refuse the recognition of a cost award resulting from such an arbitration. In reaching this conclusion, the courts assumed that the New York Convention required the courts to refuse recognition in a scenario where the court finds that there was no valid arbitration agreement. This proposition is doubtful at best. Absent any language providing otherwise in the domestic law that incorporates the New York Convention, the Convention itself clearly provides that courts 'may' refuse recognition and enforcement in this scenario. That crucial word 'may', different from a mandatory 'shall', has famously been understood in many jurisdictions to allow courts to take a more 'pro enforcement' approach. In fact, there are plenty of well-known examples of awards being recognised and enforced, in many different Convention jurisdictions, despite having been set aside at the place of arbitration,[79] which was not the case in *Antaris*.

---

78. In the court litigation context, the Svea Court of Appeal has recently stated that the res judicata effect of a court's cost decision does not prevent a party from requesting damages for the costs incurred – on a separate, private law basis – from its counterparty, *see* Svea Court of Appeal, *Bostadsaktiebolaget Esplanaden v. Douglas Bigosinski*, Case Ö 6217-23, 26 February 2024.
79. Gary Born, *International Commercial Arbitration* (3rd ed., Kluwer Law International, 2021), 'Chapter 22: Legal Framework for International Arbitral Awards' (Updated March 2024), p. 8 and references therein.

In other words, at least as far as the New York Convention is concerned, domestic courts faced with enforcement application of a cost decision should be free to recognise it, regardless of the fate or status of the 'main' award. The fact that EU Member State courts are presumably unlikely to exercise this discretion, and risk undermining the effectiveness of EU law as identified by the German Federal Court, is another matter, but the discretion certainly exists. In future proceedings where the cost debtor has argued 'both sides' of a fundamental jurisdictional issue – such as, but not limited to, an intra-EU objection – there is an arguable case for why enforcing courts should make use of the discretion afforded by Article V of the New York Convention to recognise cost awards even in situations where the court finds that that there was no arbitration agreement, or where the underlying award has been declared invalid.

CHAPTER 3

Injunctions and Specific Performance in Arbitrations: Issues at the Crossroads of Substance and Procedure*

Erik Forsin & Dustin Zojaji

§3.01 INTRODUCTION

Ubi jus ibi remedium: where there is a right, there is a remedy. Guided by this maxim, this chapter will examine issues not of rights, but of remedies. More specifically, this chapter will explore issues relating to injunctions and specific performance in international arbitration. As disputes become increasingly global and complex, so do the remedial issues that parties, counsel, tribunals and enforcing courts have to tackle.

One such issue is the choice of law. When a claim for specific performance or an injunction is made before a court in a domestic case, the question of applicable law is of course not an issue. However, when such a claim is made before an arbitral tribunal in an international arbitration, complications may arise. While the trend in civil law jurisdictions generally is to view the availability of different reliefs and remedies as a substantive matter, the traditional common law approach has been to recognize and consider the more procedural elements of such claims. Hence, one pressing issue in such arbitrations is what law the tribunal is to apply in deciding the availability of specific performance. Is it the substantive law applicable to the contract? Is it the law applicable to the arbitration agreement? Or maybe *lex arbitri*?

Another complication that may arise when an injunction or specific performance is sought in an international arbitration is the enforcement of the award and the supervision of the losing party's compliance with it. While certain kinds of specific

* This chapter is partially based on the thesis of Dustin Zojaji: A Comparative Study of Injunctive Relief and Specific Performance in the Arbitral Forum (Stockholm University, 2023).

performance are enforceable through physical acts (such as attaching a ship that a tribunal has ordered be turned over to the claimant), many are not. Examples may include an injunction enjoining the respondent from competing with the claimant or a grant of specific performance consisting of a respondent being required to provide a certain quantity of gas through a pipeline to the claimant. Both these examples would require that there be a body that can determine whether the award is being complied with (which may involve quite substantive determinations), as well as being capable of compelling compliance with the award. This allows for the complex and intricate question of how to allocate responsibilities and powers between arbitral tribunals and the courts enforcing their awards.

The chapter will examine these topics from a functional perspective, focusing on the remedial considerations to be made with respect to the arbitral proceedings themselves, as well as analysing the topic from the viewpoint of enforcement. The purpose of this chapter is not to give, or purport to give, a one-size-fits-all solution to all problems that may arise when seeking specific performance or injunctive relief in arbitration. Instead, we, the authors, aim to put the spotlight on certain issues we believe warrant further discussion.

While this chapter is centred around Swedish arbitration law, some comparative elements are included so as to illuminate the differences in how different jurisdictions tackle these issues.

§3.02 THE FRAMEWORK OF SPECIFIC PERFORMANCE AS A REMEDY IN SWEDEN: A DOMESTIC OVERVIEW

[A] Specific Performance as a Substantive Remedy

'An offer to enter a contract, and an answer to such offer, are, in accordance with Sections 2-9 below, binding for whomever made the offer or answer.' These words constitute the first sentence of the Swedish Contracts Act (Sw. *lagen (1915:218) om avtal och andra rättshandlingar på förmögenhetsrättens område*) and represent the very essence of Swedish (and indeed also non-Swedish) contract law: *pacta sunt servanda* (agreements are made to be kept). In reality, however, things are not always as easy. Parties may disagree, for example, on what they have promised (meaning that there is a dispute as to the construction of the contract), on whether a party has actually performed as promised (e.g., whether a seller's goods actually are conforming or not), or on whether non-performance is excusable (e.g., cases of force majeure). But for an aggrieved party, simply convincing a court or tribunal that the opponent is in breach of the contract is often not enough; the party will typically also seek a remedy. Most breach of contract disputes concern the right to damages. However, some parties may not be interested in damages, but rather in receiving what was promised. While damages are often relatively straightforward (there is usually a right to damages for breach of contract, irrespective of jurisdiction and kind of contract, subject to applicable limitations and caps), the availability of specific performance may be – or appear to be – more unclear.

Unlike many other European legal systems, Swedish statutory law does not provide any provisions on remedies in cases of breach of contract. Indeed, there is not even a statutory definition of breach of contract in Swedish law. Where there is legislation governing certain categories of contracts, that legislation will of course be controlling for those categories of contracts. In the absence of such legislation, parties must rely on the statutes governing other categories of contracts, *ex analogia*, as well as general principles of contract law, as provided in the holdings of the Swedish Supreme Court from time to time.

Returning to the issue of specific performance, the Swedish Sale of Goods Act (Sw. *köplagen (1990:931)*) provides explicit support for a buyer's right to specific performance in the two most common kinds of breach: non-conforming goods and delays. In cases where the seller's time for delivery has expired, the buyer may 'maintain the purchase and demand performance',[1] unless the seller's performance is impossible or unduly burdensome.[2] Similarly, in cases where the goods delivered by the seller are non-conforming to the contract, the buyer may demand that the seller rectify the non-conformity, or that the seller provide delivery of substitute goods which conform to the contract.[3] The Sale of Goods Act is not unique. Similar provisions are contained, *inter alia*, in the Swedish Sale of Consumer Goods Act (Sw. *konsumentköplagen (2022:260)*)[4] and the Swedish Consumer Services Act (Sw. *konsumenttjänstlagen (1985:716)*).[5] There are also examples of cases where specific performance is not available as a remedy for breach, with an example being section 32 of the Commissions Agency Act (Sw. *kommissionslagen (2009:865)*) (providing that if either the principal or agent terminates the commission agreement, the termination is effective irrespective of whether it was warranted or not).[6] Looking at legal commentary, some authors contend that it is 'probable' that the right to specific performance is a general principle of Swedish contract law,[7] while others employ a more reserved stance.[8]

Irrespective of whether there is a general right to specific performance under Swedish law (with certain exceptions), or whether the right to specific performance is limited to certain kinds of contracts, it may in any case be concluded that Swedish law recognizes specific performance as a substantive remedy.

[B] Specific Performance as a Relief Sought Before Courts

Somewhat simplified, Swedish courts may entertain two kinds of civil actions and thus grant two kinds of relief. Between the two, the more uncommon one is the declaratory

1. Section 23 of the Swedish Sale of Goods Act.
2. *Ibid.*
3. *Ibid.*, section 34.
4. Chapter 5 section 4.
5. Section 20.
6. Sw. govt. bill. 2008/09:88, p. 145: 'The Section expresses the general principle of [Swedish] law that in cases of agency, parties cannot be forced to non-monetary performance.'
7. Jan Ramberg and Christina Ramberg, *Allmän avtalsrätt*, p. 270 (12th ed., Norstedts Juridik 2022).
8. Jan Hellner et al., *Speciell avtalsrätt II. Kontraktsrätt. 2 Häftet: Allmänna ämnen*, p. 169 (8th ed., Norstedts Juridik 2024).

action (Sw. *fastställelsetalan*). A declaratory action, like the name suggests, is where the plaintiff seeks that the court declare the existence or non-existence of a certain alleged legal relationship between the parties, for example, that the plaintiff has a better right of ownership to a car than the defendant or that the defendant is liable for damages. The declaratory action is, unlike its more common counterpart (the performance action, described below), not available to plaintiffs as a matter of right. Instead, such an action may be brought only if the uncertainty which has caused the plaintiff to bring the suit causes the plaintiff harm, Chapter 13 section 2 of the Code of Judicial Procedure (Sw. *rättegångsbalken*) and if the action is 'appropriate' (Sw. *lämplig*).[9] In determining whether the action is appropriate, courts may consider the interest of the plaintiff in bringing the suit on the one hand, and the inconvenience for the defendant in being forced to litigate the matter, on the other hand.[10]

The more common kind of action is the performance action (Sw. *fullgörelsetalan*), where the plaintiff seeks an order for the defendant to perform an obligation which the plaintiff believes is owed. While the most common kind of performance sought in courts is monetary performance (e.g., performance of the obligation to pay damages), other kinds of performance reliefs are covered by this kind of action as well, such as specific performance or injunctive relief (i.e., the performance of an obligation not to do something). In principle, a plaintiff may bring a performance action *as a matter of right* provided the obligation to perform is due.[11]

For the purposes of specific performance and injunctions, this means that there are no procedural bars for plaintiffs to bring such actions. As long as they are substantively in the right – that they are entitled to the performance or non-performance as a matter of substantive law – the court must grant the relief. As the renowned professor Olivecrona once expressed it: 'The judgment [which a court may order] may consist of any kind of activity, which someone under the rules of private law may be obliged [to do].'[12] It should be noted, though, that even though an action for performance which is due (whether monetary or specific performance) is available to plaintiffs as a matter of right, courts will still scrutinize complaints to ensure compliance with applicable filing rules under the Code of Civil Procedure before issuing summons. In the specific performance context, plaintiffs should be aware of the requirement that a complaint must contain a specified request for relief. This typically does not pose a problem when the relief sought is monetary. But formulating the exact performance requested in cases of physical acts or omissions may prove to be more challenging.[13]

9. NJA 2013 p. 209 ¶ 7 (Swedish Supreme Court).
10. *Ibid.*, ¶ 8.
11. Chapter 13 section 1 of the Swedish Code of Civil Procedure (Sw. *rättegångsbalken*). The provision also provides certain exceptions where a performance action may be brought even though the obligation is not yet due.
12. Karl Olivecrona, *Domen i tvistemål*, p. 30 (1943).
13. By means of example, while seeking a judgment 'enjoining the defendant from divulging to third parties the monthly fee payable to the plaintiff under their services contract of May 5, 2023' would probably be a specified enough, seeking a judgment 'enjoining the defendant from divulging to third parties confidential information' may be too vague.

[C] Enforcing Court-Awarded Specific Performance

Once a court has awarded a plaintiff specific performance, the next issue for the plaintiff is to enforce that judgment of specific performance. While some kinds of performance, such as payment of a sum or surrendering possession of property, can be physically enforced by the Swedish Enforcement Agency (Sw. *Kronofogdemyndigheten*), other kinds, such as a continuing obligation to perform a service or to refrain from divulging certain information, cannot. In such cases, plaintiffs often request courts to include language in their judgments so that the award of specific performance is made *under penalty of fines* (Sw. *vid äventyr av vite*). While the power of courts to make their judgments under penalty of fines is explicitly set out in some statutes,[14] courts are considered to have the authority to include such language in civil cases generally, also outside the scope of the statutorily provided-for cases.[15] Courts may even include such language in their judgments *sue sponte.*[16] Where the defendant is a legal entity, the plaintiff may seek that the award be made against the legal representatives (Sw. *ställföreträdare*) of the defendant-entity, in their capacity as such, as well.[17]

Unlike what may apply in other jurisdictions, Swedish courts do not hold any general contempt powers. If the defendant does not comply with the judgment, it falls upon the plaintiff to commence a new action against the defendant, before the same court, seeking a judgment for the fines, which the judgment was made under the penalty of.[18] Such fines are a matter of public law. Accordingly, the fines are payable to the government, not to the plaintiff. Additionally, given that it is a matter of public law, courts must generally apply procedural rules applicable to (minor) criminal proceedings.[19]

[D] Seeking Specific Performance Before Arbitral Tribunals

Compared to the Swedish Code of Civil Procedure, the 1999 Swedish Arbitration Act (Sw. *lagen (1999:116) om skiljeförfarande*) contains relatively few provisions governing the proceedings. In spite of the statutory ambiguity,[20] the law is that arbitral tribunals have, at least, the same powers as courts to entertain civil disputes which are amenable to settlement.[21] This is a generally accepted proposition.[22]

14. *See, e.g.*, section 52b para. 1 of the Swedish Act on Copyright in Literary and Artistic Works (Sw. *lagen [1960:729] om upphovsrätt till litterära och konstnärliga verk*).
15. NJA 1981 p. 1129 (Swedish Supreme Court).
16. *Ibid.*
17. NJA 1990 p. 338 (Swedish Supreme Court).
18. Section 7 item 2 of the Swedish Administrative Fines Act (Sw. *viteslagen [1985:206]*).
19. *Ibid.*, section 8.
20. Somewhat anecdotally, it may be noted that many jurisdictions leave the issue of reliefs available in arbitrations open in statutory law. However, there are exceptions. For example, section 48 of the 1996 English Arbitration Act provides clear language which explains what remedies that are available to parties appearing before arbitrators.
21. Sw. govt. bill 1998/99:35, p. 59 ('It is a general conception that the powers of arbitrators to try various issues of a civil nature spans wider than the power of courts'). *See generally* section 1 of

In the context of the kind of non-monetary relief discussed in this chapter, this means that arbitral tribunals have, at least, the same freedom as courts to enforce substantive law by awarding specific performance and injunctive relief.[23] This approach seems to be consistent with what applies in other European civil law jurisdictions.[24]

[E] Enforcing Specific Performance Awarded by Arbitral Tribunals

Unlike courts, arbitral tribunals may not make their awards under the penalty of fines for the respondent. This is because fines - which are payable to the government - are not amenable to settlement,[25] which is a requirement for objective arbitrability under Swedish law.[26]

That arbitral awards cannot be made under the penalty of fines does not however mean that they are not enforceable in Sweden. The plaintiff may still submit the award for enforcement to the Swedish Enforcement Agency. Under Chapter 16 section 2 of the Code of Enforcement (Sw. *utsökningsbalken*), the Enforcement Agency may order the enforcement defendant (i.e., the arbitration respondent) to perform what it is obliged to or to follow an injunction. Further, the order of the Enforcement Agency may be made under the penalty of fines, which is provided in Chapter 2 section 15 of the Code of Enforcement. If the defendant ignores the order, the Enforcement Agency may request a competent court to award the fines which the order was made under the penalty of. While the claimant itself is not entitled to make such a request to a court of competent jurisdiction, it may appeal the Enforcement Agency's decision not to make a request to the competent court.[27]

§3.03 CONSIDERATIONS WHERE SPECIFIC PERFORMANCE IS SOUGHT IN SWEDISH-SEATED INTERNATIONAL ARBITRATIONS

[A] The Problem(s)

It has been said that 'arbitration in Sweden is very Swedish'.[28] While we do not seek to examine the accuracy of that statement, it cannot be denied that it has some truth to it.

---

the Swedish Arbitration Act ('Disputes over issues which the parties may settle may through agreement be left to the determination of one or more arbitrators'). Additionally, arbitrators may also try the existence or non-existence of a factual issue (as opposed to being constrained to 'legal relationships' only) and they may also, where authorized by the parties, supplement contracts beyond mere gap-filling. *Ibid.*

22. For example, Stefan Lindskog, *Skiljeförfarande: En kommentar* § III-0.3.1.1 (3rd online ed., available at juno.nj.se, Norstedts Juridik 2020).
23. *Ibid.*, §§ III-0.3.4.1 and III-0.3.4.3; Lars Heuman, *Skiljemannarätt*, p. 334 (1st ed., Norstedts Juridik 1999).
24. *See generally,* Peter Schlosser, *Right and Remedy in Common Law Arbitration and in German Arbitration Law*, 4 Journal of International Arbitration p. 27, passim (1987).
25. NJA 2000 p. 435 I and II (Swedish Supreme Court).
26. Section 1 of the Swedish Arbitration Act.
27. Chapter 18 section 2 of the Code of Enforcement.
28. Carita Wallgren-Lindholm, 'Chapter 6: Stating the Obvious and Connectivity to Self', in Patrik Schöldström and Christer Danielsson (eds), *Stockholm Arbitration Yearbook 2023, Stockholm*

It is not uncommon for (Swedish) counsel, arbitrators and courts sitting in review of vacatur actions to, almost as a reflex, turn to the Swedish Code of Judicial Procedure, when neither the Arbitration Act nor the applicable arbitrable rules provide an explicit solution to a certain issue. In international arbitrations, complications may arise when seeking to apply domestic procedural analogies to a wholly non-domestic dispute. Below, we discuss a few of these problems that may arise.

[B] The Applicable Standard for Specific Performance

As set out above, under Swedish law, the availability of different remedies is a substantive question. Therefore, courts must look to substance, not procedure, in trying a claim for, e.g., specific performance. The same applies with respect to arbitrators. The fact that an arbitration is international ought not to affect that conclusion.[29] But still, complications may arise.

As hinted in the introduction to this chapter, this conclusion is not as apparent elsewhere on the globe. In common law jurisdictions, there has been a traditional divide between law and equity, with the former conservatively only recognizing a right to damages for an aggrieved party, while the latter body of rules and decisions in some cases allowing parties to seek injunctive relief and specific performance. Making a very long story short, the divide dates back to medieval English law, where courts could only try actions for damages, which caused the citizenry to turn to the chancellor who could use discretionary powers to grant other kinds of relief, such as ordering a trespasser not to trespass as opposed to merely awarding damages after the fact. In time, such pleas were directed to a new court: a court of chancery instead of a court of law.[30] The reliefs that were pleaded before the court of chancery, along with the defences to them, became known as equitable reliefs and defences.

This divide between law and equity is not merely a historical anecdote, but has relevance to this day in common law jurisdictions, such as the United States and its several states. Today, equitable remedies remain discretionary and available only where there is no adequate remedy at law (i.e., damages).[31] Accordingly, courts have held that parties cannot by means of contract bind a court to grant equitable relief, such as specific performance.[32]

This has of course had an influence on the American view on the capacity of arbitrators to grant equitable reliefs such as specific performance. For instance, arbitral

Arbitration Yearbook Series, vol. 5 (© Kluwer Law International; Kluwer Law International 2023), pp. 89–94, n. 3.

29. For example, Stefan *Lindskog, Skiljeförfarande: En kommentar* §§ 46-5.1.2 (3rd online ed., available at juno.nj.se, Norstedts Juridik 2020). *See also* NJA 2017 p. 168, ¶ 10 (Swedish Supreme Court) (holding that the classification of foreign legal concepts must be made *lex fori*).
30. *See generally*, Dan Dobbs, *Law of Remedies: Damages, Equity, Restitution*, § 2.2 (2nd ed., 1993); William Blackstone, *The Oxford Edition of Blackstone's: Commentaries on the Laws of England: Book III: of Private Wrongs*, at 46 et seq. (Thomas P. Gallanis ed., 2016).
31. *See generally*, *Guaranty Trust Co. v. York*, 326 U.S. 99, 105 (1945).
32. For example, *Baker's Aid v. Hussmann Foodservice Co.*, 830 F.2d 13, 16 (2d Cir. 1987).

institutes have included specific provisions on remedies in their arbitration rules. The American Arbitration Association provide the following Rule 49(a):

> The arbitrator may grant any remedy or relief that the arbitrator deems just and equitable and within the scope of the agreement of the parties, including, but not limited to, specific performance of a contract.[33]

Even in the absence of such clear language in the arbitration agreement of the parties, courts have held that arbitrators hold great freedom to formulate remedies,[34] and that this remedial freedom stems from the arbitration agreement (as opposed to the underlying contract, presumably).[35]

Returning to Swedish arbitration law, this may create challenges when there are parties, counsel or arbitrators involved from, for example, the United States. If, for example, New York law is applicable to a contract but any disputes arising under it are to be adjudicated by a Stockholm-seated tribunal under the SCC Arbitration Rules,[36] it may be unclear what standard to apply in determining a request for specific performance or a permanent injunction. As explained, Swedish law, which would govern both the arbitral proceedings and the arbitration agreement,[37] would direct the tribunal to determine the issue under the applicable substantive law, while the applicable substantive law would suggest that the tribunal look to the arbitration agreement.

As previously stated, we do not seek to offer a one-size-fits-all solution to the issues that may arise when seeking specific performance in international arbitrations, and this issue of choice of law provides no exception. Likely, there is no one-size-fits-all solution to determine the exact applicable standard for granting specific performance in Stockholm-seated international arbitrations. In many cases, returning to the example with the New York-law-governed contract, it ought to be prudent to apply New York law to the specific performance issue, irrespective of whether the tribunal thinks the issue is substantive or procedural under New York law.[38] That being said, doing so may not always be appropriate in every case.

In any event, an arbitral tribunal faced with issues of this kind must take the matter under serious consideration. This is because an application by a tribunal of a different law than the one agreed to by the parties may constitute an excess of mandate and thus subject the award to the risk of vacatur proceedings under section 34 of the Swedish Arbitration Act.[39]

33. Commercial Arbitration Rules of the American Arbitration Association, R-49(a).
34. *United Steelworkers of Am. v. Enter. Wheel & Car Corp.*, 363 U.S. 593, 597 (1960).
35. *ReliaStar Life Ins. Co. of N.Y. v. EMC Nat. Life Co.*, 564 F.3d 81, 86 (2d Cir. 2009); *Banco de Seguros del Estado v. Mut. Marine Off., Inc.*, 344 F.3d 255, 262 (2d Cir. 2003).
36. The Arbitration Rules of the SCC Arbitration Institute. Said rules do not provide any guidance on the availability of remedies.
37. Section 48 of the Swedish Arbitration Act.
38. Stefan Lindskog, *Skiljeförfarande: En kommentar* §§ 46-5.1.2 n. 4571 (3rd online ed., available at juno.nj.se, Norstedts Juridik 2020).
39. Sw. govt. bill 1998/99:35, p. 123.

[C] Issues of Objective Arbitrability

The issue of whether a dispute is arbitrable or not (objective arbitrability) is not raised particularly often in Swedish arbitrations or, vacatur or annulment proceedings (at least compared to other issues which are more prevalent in such proceedings). In a commercial arbitration where the claimant is seeking payment of monies, issues relating to objective arbitrability seldom (but still sometimes) arise. But in cases where the claimant is seeking another kind of relief, such as specific performance, there may be a higher risk that issues of objective arbitrability come into play.

Under Swedish law, most disputes are arbitrable. Section 1 of the Swedish Arbitration Act provides that parties may submit to arbitration any dispute which the parties may dispose of by means of settlement. To be clear, though, this does not mean that disputes which touch upon topics governed by mandatory law are precluded from being heard by arbitrators. Instead, the relevant inquiry is whether the parties, once a dispute has arisen, may settle that dispute.[40] For example, Swedish law prevents employees from waiving their right not to be terminated save for where cause exists, and any agreement providing differently is, in that regard, void and unenforceable. Nevertheless, if an employee commences an action against an employer, claiming to have been terminated without cause, the parties are free to enter a settlement regarding their issue. Issues of custody and care of children, however, may not be agreed on by separating parents, even if the agreement takes place after their separation. Hence, a custody dispute may not be heard by arbitrators because the parties (parents) cannot settle the dispute themselves, even if they wanted to.

In certain jurisdictions, there may be limitations on what acts a party may undertake to do, even after a dispute has arisen. For example, there may be provisions entailing that any contract obligation to provide certain products is considered null and void absent pre-approval from competent authorities. Hence, when a contract submitted to arbitration in Sweden is governed by non-Swedish law, we must first determine what jurisdiction(s) the laws of which shall be used to determine whether the relief sought may be agreed upon by the parties if they wish to settle.

The text of the Swedish Arbitration Act does not answer this question. The act's preparatory works state that the issue of the extent to which foreign law should be considered in determining objective arbitrability should be decided on a case-by-case basis.[41] The Swedish Supreme Court has provided some clarity in this regard. In the case NJA 2012 p. 790, a claimant had been awarded a certain sum from a respondent. The respondent commenced an action to have the award declared void based on the fact that the dispute lacked objective arbitrability, as the parties could not even have agreed on the respondent making such payment to the claimant, since that would violate applicable currency restrictions. The Court held that where a dispute is governed by foreign substantive law, mandatory elements of that legal system which may prevent a settlement in that jurisdiction only entail that the dispute is considered

40. *Ibid.*, pp. 48-49.
41. *Ibid.*, p. 49.

non-arbitrable in Sweden when the interest which is protected by the mandatory rules in question is also recognized in Sweden. If there is no Swedish interest in upholding the rule in question, the parties may settle the dispute in Sweden and thus also arbitrate it.[42]

In conclusion, issues of objective arbitrability pertaining to non-amenability to settlement under foreign law may be successfully raised only when the interests underlying such foreign law are also present in Sweden. Consequently, it is important that parties and counsel engage in a careful and thorough analysis of any potential obstacles to settlements both under Swedish law and under the law applicable to the substantive dispute. This is especially important since annulment actions to declare arbitral awards void due to the dispute being non-arbitrable are not time-barred in the same manner as actions to vacate (set aside) arbitral awards are.[43]

[D] Foreseeing Enforcement Issues at the Place of Enforcement

In certain cases, an order to do or cause a certain action may be perfectly allowed under Swedish law as well as under the substantive law governing the dispute. Nevertheless, a prevailing claimant may find itself unable to enforce the specific performance in the jurisdiction or jurisdiction where it had originally contemplated.

Enforcing a judgment or award for specific performance or a permanent injunction is often more complicated than attaching property to satisfy a money judgment or award. Different jurisdictions may have different ways of enforcing specific performance and other kinds of non-monetary relief. In some jurisdictions, compelling a party (under threat of fines or jail) may raise constitutional due process issues. Moreover, the specific performance requested by a claimant may not always be clear-cut and easy to define. This may also cause due process issues (e.g., a respondent could argue that the activity it has been ordered to perform or enjoined from performing is not clearly defined and hard to understand)[44] as well as cause disputes as to whether the relief ordered in the award is being complied with or not (e.g., a respondent ordered by an arbitral tribunal to employ reasonable efforts to reach a certain goal may argue that it is in fact using reasonable efforts, without reaching the intended result).

These considerations are not reserved for the enforcement stage of a dispute. Instead, parties must contemplate these issues already at the arbitration stage. This is because arbitrators have a general duty to render an enforceable award. This obligation follows from, *inter alia*, the SCC Rules[45] and the ICC Rules.[46] Additionally, some

42. NJA 2012 p. 790.
43. Section 33 of the Swedish Arbitration Act. Cf. section 33 of the same.
44. Cf. NJA 2018, p. 189, ¶ 23 (Swedish Supreme Court) (providing that under Swedish law, interim and preliminary injunctions issued by courts must be clear as to what act or omission the defendant is to undertake); Fed. R. Civ. P. 60(d)(1)(C) (providing that any injunction issued by a federal court must 'describe in reasonable detail – and not by referring to the complaint or other document – the act or acts restrained or required').
45. Article 2(2) of the SCC Rules.

authors contend that under Swedish law, arbitrators must dismiss (without adjudication on the merits) such claims that will not lead to enforceable awards.[47] Should an arbitral tribunal share that view, a claimant may need to show that the claim, if awarded, will be enforceable in a relevant jurisdiction.[48]

Even though the law in this regard is undecided, parties and counsel should still keep such issues in mind. Unlike when money is at play, the enforcement of certain acts or omissions may prove harder than merely finding a jurisdiction where the respondent has assets.

[E] Supervising Compliance with the Award: Expanding the Assignment of the Arbitral Tribunal

As already mentioned in [D] above, specific performance may cause issues even after being awarded by the tribunal. Many kinds of injunctions (and orders for specific performance), by their very nature, require continuous supervision as disputes may arise as to whether the awarded order is being complied with or not, and if not, require powers to compel compliance.

As an illustrative example, one may imagine a party entering a non-compete agreement which the party later breaks. Where the parties' disputes are to be arbitrated, the aggrieved party is directed to initiate arbitration, seeking an award containing a permanent injunction against engaging in competitive activities. Typically, enforcement of such an award would require seeking relief from national courts (or judicial authorities) and seeking some sort of judicial sanctions against the respondent, if it elects to violate the awarded injunction. However, when the issue is brought before such a court, the respondent may well deny having ever violated the injunction. It could, for example, be claiming that the activity in which it is or was engaging is outside the scope of the injunction or it could deny having engaged in it at all. Litigating that matter before national courts may necessitate quite substantive determinations and may be the very thing the aggrieved party sought to avoid all along by entering an arbitration agreement. Moreover, there may be confidentiality interests at play, which often cannot be maintained if enforcement is sought before courts. Additionally, in some jurisdictions, the sanctions which courts or judicial authorities may impose could be limited to public-law sanctions such as fines or jail time. While providing motive to comply with the award, such sanctions give little relief to the already aggrieved party. However, initiating an entirely new arbitration to recover additional damages may be unnecessarily complicated and cost-ineffective.

Consequently, many parties may wish to return to the tribunal that rendered the award in the first place. Doing so may even appear as the natural course of action in some jurisdictions. In the United States, for example, it is common for arbitrators,

46. Article 42 of the Rules of Arbitration of the International Court of Arbitration of the International Chamber of Commerce.
47. Stefan Lindskog, *Skiljeförfarande: En kommentar* §§ III-0.3.4.3 (3rd online ed., available at juno.nj.se, Norstedts Juridik 2020).
48. *Ibid.*, n. 2329.

when awarding certain kinds of non-monetary reliefs, to retain jurisdiction with respect to the remedial portion of the awards so as to be able to grant further relief if needed. Federal courts have even held that retaining jurisdiction is 'implicit in any order that grants equitable relief',[49] and that suggesting, in a vacatur proceeding, that the retention of such jurisdiction by an arbitrator is erroneous is such a frivolous argument as to warrant sanctions for counsel.[50]

It may therefore come as a surprise for counsel from jurisdictions like the United States that such an approach, as a general rule, is not possible in Sweden. That is a consequence of the *functus officio* doctrine. Unlike a court, an arbitral tribunal does not exist in the absence of a dispute. When agreeing to arbitration, the parties submit to arbitration and generally not to the jurisdiction of a specific arbitral tribunal. Instead, arbitral tribunals are constituted only when disputes arise and generally cease to perform their functions upon the rendering of a final award. The *functus officio* doctrine provides that once a final award has been rendered, the tribunal loses its jurisdiction.

In Sweden, the doctrine finds statutory support in section 27 of the Arbitration Act which provides that the 'assignment of the arbitrators is deemed finished when they have rendered a final award, if nothing else follows from Sections 32 or 35'. The latter two sections provide the two statutory exceptions to the doctrine. First, under section 32, a tribunal may correct or interpret an award. Second, under section 35, a court may, in a vacatur or annulment action against an award, remand the case to the tribunal. Apart from these two exceptions, Swedish law provides for a third, non-statutory, exception, namely when there is support in the arbitration agreement. Hence, when the parties have authorized the tribunal, it may retain jurisdiction over a dispute even after the rendering of a final award.[51] However, absent such authorization, the tribunal would lack jurisdiction,[52] and any award rendered by it would lack legal significance and effect.[53] Consequently, absent support in the arbitration agreement, a party who has been awarded some kind of specific performance or injunctive relief in a final award is prevented from returning to the arbitral tribunal for further relief.

In conclusion, in contracts where the kind of specific performance or injunctions which would benefit from continuous supervision may become relevant, parties should consider putting extra effort into drafting their arbitration clauses. For example, parties could agree that when an injunction or specific performance is awarded, the tribunal may retain jurisdiction over the dispute. Additionally, while Swedish-seated tribunals may not issue fines, the parties may authorize them to issue (and even determine the value of) liquidated damages as a means of compelling compliance with

49. *Dreis & Krump Mfg. Co. v. Int'l Ass'n of Machinists & Aerospace Workers, Dist. No. 8*, 802 F.2d 247, 250 (7th Cir. 1986).
50. *Cuna Mut. Ins. Soc. v. Off. & Pro. Emps. Int'l Union, Loc. 39*, 443 F.3d 556 (7th Cir. 2006) ('there is an abundance of case law in both this circuit and other circuits that recognizes the propriety of an arbitrator retaining jurisdiction over the remedy portion of an award').
51. Sw. govt. bill 1998/99:34, p. 98.
52. Finn Madsen, *Commercial Arbitration in Sweden*, p. 310 (5th ed. 2020).
53. Lars Heuman, *Skiljemannarätt*, pp. 550-551 (1st ed. 1999).

their awards. The possibilities to construct self-contained one-stop-shop arbitration mechanisms are endless (albeit somewhat unorthodox in Sweden), and are held back (almost) only by the imagination of whoever is drafting the arbitration agreement.

§3.04 CONCLUDING REMARKS

Most of those who are active in both arbitration and litigation have at least one time complained that a dispute had to be resolved through the courts instead of arbitration. Similarly, most have also complained that a dispute which was covered by an arbitration clause could not be brought before the courts. That is not strange. Just as not all disputes are suited for litigation, not all disputes are suited for arbitration either.[54] In short, both ways of resolving disputes have their strong and weak sides.

What then applies in respect of specific performance and injunctive relief? Is arbitration preferable? Or maybe litigation? We do not believe that there is one right answer to that question. Quite to the contrary, it depends. Especially in a cross-border context, parties should consider a multitude of factors when drafting their dispute resolution clauses. As has been discussed above, issues of specific performance and injunctive relief may touch on both procedural and substantive issues, requiring a coordinated approach when drafting the main contract and its dispute resolution clause. For example, in a case where two parties enter a joint venture agreement, foreseeing long-term cooperation, it may be advisable to put some effort into drafting a one-stop-shop arbitration clause of the kind discussed in [E] above. It could also be a good idea – as always, depending on the circumstances – to agree on liquidated damages as a mechanism to ensure compliance with awards made under the arbitration clause. If not, then it may be a good idea to make inquiries about how courts in the jurisdiction(s) of the other party enforce arbitral awards for injunctive relief. If the process appears dauntingly complicated, or if due process or public policy considerations require some level of substantive litigation before the court, then maybe an arbitration clause is not the best idea. When push comes to shove, these considerations may be as crucial as the substantive rights and obligations which the parties and counsel spend significantly more time negotiating and drafting.

Returning to where we started, while there is a remedy where there is a right, it may not be the right remedy. And without the right remedy, is the right even worth having?

54. And some disputes are not suitable for anything.

CHAPTER 4

The Arbitral Tribunal's Investigative Powers: Proactive Fact-Finding in International Arbitration

Jan Heiner Nedden, Nico Gielen & Christian Johannes Wahnschaffe

§4.01 INTRODUCTION

The principle of party autonomy implies that whichever party bears the burden of proof must present the necessary facts.[1] Intuitively, this principle suggests arbitrators should adopt a passive approach, leaving control over the fact-finding process to the parties.

Yet, the role of arbitrators in investigating facts remains more nuanced and indeed differs quite significantly across legal systems. Some arbitrators will instinctively pursue an active approach and investigate wherever they deem necessary. The specific approach arbitrators choose ultimately stems from their understanding of the arbitrator's role, which is typically influenced by their legal training, their professional background, and the judicial practices within their jurisdictions.

When faced with the choice between remaining passive or taking action, arbitrators should always bear in mind the aim of any investigative measure and its implications. Arguably, arbitration proceedings do not seek to find the objective truth, unlike criminal proceedings. Instead, arbitrators are tasked with the efficient resolution of disputes, rendering enforceable awards that deliver legal precision while honouring economic realities. This responsibility may nevertheless demand active engagement on the part of the decision-makers. When parties overlook crucial matters or focus on

1. Phillip Landolt, Arbitrators' Initiatives to Obtain Factual and Legal Evidence, 28 Arb. Int'l 173, 198 (2012); Judith Levine, *Can Arbitrators Choose Who to Call as Witnesses? (And What Can Be Done If They Don't Show Up?)*, p. 315 (Albert Jan van den Berg (ed.), ICCA & Kluwer Law International 2015).

irrelevant issues, timely intervention may help them allocate their resources more efficiently – guidance most parties would welcome.

Consider, for example, a scenario where a party seeks compensation but cannot yet fully quantify its claim. It therefore submits a payment claim along with a request for declaratory relief. During the hearing, the arbitral tribunal learns that new invoices were issued that could extend the payment claim, yet the claimant overlooks the possibility of introducing them. Should the arbitral tribunal proactively seek the production of these invoices or confine itself to awarding the payment claim as originally requested, while leaving the rest to be covered by the declaratory relief?

With such situations in mind, this chapter provides practical guidance for arbitrators deciding whether and how to exercise investigative powers. First, we establish that most arbitration frameworks provide broad fact-finding powers, while procedural safeguards ensure their lawful application [*§4.02*]. Second, we present different investigative tools that arbitral tribunals may employ in exercising their fact-finding authority [*§4.03*].

§4.02 LEGAL FRAMEWORK FOR TRIBUNAL INVESTIGATIONS

In general, express rules equipping arbitral tribunals with fact-finding powers are rare.[2] Nevertheless, some arbitration laws do set out these powers expressly [*A*], as do certain arbitration rules [*B*]. Where arbitral tribunals face ambiguous provisions on fact-finding authority, soft law often provides valuable guidance [*C*]. If arbitral tribunals possess and choose to exercise these powers, they remain subject to fundamental limitations they must observe [*D*].

[A] National Arbitration Laws Empower Tribunals to Take the Initiative

Various arbitration laws are heavily influenced by the UNCITRAL Model Law on International Commercial Arbitration. For example, all Nordic countries follow the Model Law – some to the letter, others less strictly.[3] Denmark, for instance, has tied its arbitration regime closely to the Model Law.[4] Sweden, by contrast, chose not to adopt the Model Law directly, but instead considered each provision separately when developing its own framework.[5] Under Swedish law, arbitral tribunals reportedly only 'very rarely embark on any fact-finding on their own initiative'.[6]

Yet, all Nordic arbitration regimes, including Sweden's, share one common feature. Like the Model Law, they provide arbitral tribunals with sufficient leeway to

2. Landolt, *supra* n. 1, at pp. 174, 180.
3. Prop. 1998/99:35 (Sweden); Regeringens proposition 202/1991 (Finland); Ot.prp. nr. 27, 2003-2004 (Norway); L 127 Forslag til lov om voldgift, 2004-2005 (Denmark); Lög um samningsbundna gerðardóma 53/1989, Athugasemdir við lagafrumvarp þetta (Iceland).
4. L 127 Forslag til lov om voldgift, 2004-2005, p. 10.
5. Prop. 1998/99:35, p. 46.
6. Robin Oldenstam et al., *Concise Guide to Arbitration in Sweden*, p. 68 (2nd ed., Mannheimer Swartling Advokatbyrå 2019).

appoint their own experts.[7] Under Finnish law, arbitral tribunals may additionally request parties to submit 'documents which may be relevant in the case'.[8] They may also require any individual 'in possession of a document or other object which may have relevance as evidence to produce the document or object', and summon any individual 'to be heard in the matter'.[9] The Icelandic arbitration law even expects arbitrators to 'actively participate in the arbitral process'.[10]

Another country following the Model Law is Germany – at least since 1998.[11] Regarding investigative powers, however, Germany has stuck with its previous arbitration law, which required arbitrators to 'investigate the facts underlying the dispute to the extent they consider such investigation necessary'.[12] Legal scholars derived from this wording the 'limited inquisitorial principle', allowing arbitral tribunals to investigate relevant facts independently of the parties' motions for taking evidence.[13] After adopting the Model Law, German literature continued to champion this inquisitorial doctrine – now, as an 'unwritten principle'.[14] The Model Law allowed sufficient room for this continuation; it neither embraces an inquisitorial nor an adversarial approach.[15] It simply empowers an arbitral tribunal to 'conduct the arbitration in such manner as it considers appropriate'.[16]

Looking further, Switzerland and France are known for arbitration laws that have developed independently of the Model Law.[17] Nonetheless, these popular seats provide arbitral tribunals with comparable powers to investigate facts. Swiss arbitration law tasks an arbitral tribunal to 'conduct the taking of evidence itself',[18] which commentators see as a permission – not a duty – for arbitral tribunals to 'take evidence on its own which has not been offered by the parties'.[19] For example, an arbitral tribunal may 'request the production of documents from a party on its own initiative'.[20] Similarly, an arbitral tribunal acting under French law 'shall take all necessary steps concerning

7. Article 26 Model Law; section 25 Swedish Arbitration Act; section 28 Finnish Arbitration Act; section 29 Norwegian Arbitration Act; section 26 Danish Arbitration Act; the laws are accessible in English at www.newyorkconvention.org.
8. Section 25(1) Finnish Arbitration Act.
9. Section 27(1) Finnish Arbitration Act.
10. Article 7(3) Icelandic Arbitration Act (53/1989).
11. Bundestags-Drucksache (BT-Drs.) 13/5274, p. 1.
12. Section 1034(1) German Civil Procedure Code (ZPO) applicable until 1998.
13. Klaus Sachs and Torsten Lörcher, *s. 1042 ZPO*, para. 33 (Patricia Nacimiento, Stefan Kröll and Karl-Heinz Böckstiegel (eds), 2nd ed., Kluwer Law International 2015).
14. Rolf Trittmann and Ramona Schardt, *Art. 28 DIS Rules*, para. 23 (Gustav Flecke-Giammarco et al. (eds), Kluwer Law International 2000).
15. Analytical Commentary on Draft Text of a Model Law on International Commercial Arbitration (A/CN.9/264), p. 46, para. 6; the German legislator copied the Model Law in that regard, *see* BT-Drs. 13/5274, p. 46.
16. Article 19(2) Model Law.
17. Simone Hofbauer, *History of Arbitration*, p. 4 (Manuel Arroyo (ed.), 2nd ed., Kluwer Law International 2018); Jean Rouche, Gerald Pointon and Jean-Louis Delvolvé, *French Arbitration Law and Practice*, para. 21 (2nd ed., Kluwer Law International 2009).
18. Article 184(1) Swiss Private International Law Act.
19. Marc Veit, *Chapter 2, Part II: Commentary on Chapter 12 PILS, Art. 184*, para. 9 (Manuel Arroyo (ed.), 2nd ed., Kluwer Law International 2018).
20. Veit, *supra* n. 19, at para. 35.

evidentiary and procedural matters',[21] including ordering a party 'in possession of an item of evidence ... to produce it'.[22]

Unlike the above civil law jurisdictions, both the United Kingdom and the United States are strongly influenced by the adversarial system which allocates a rather passive role to judges. However, their arbitration frameworks contain significant departures from this tradition. The US Federal Arbitration Act empowers arbitrators to summon 'any person to attend before them' and to bring 'any book, record, document, or paper which may be deemed material as evidence in the case'.[23] Even more expansively, the UK Arbitration Act expressly authorizes arbitral tribunals to decide 'whether and to what extent the tribunal should itself take the initiative in ascertaining the facts'.[24]

Overall, most national arbitration laws grant arbitral tribunals substantial investigative powers and discretion in exercising them, with many jurisdictions allowing arbitrators to take a more active role than might be expected.

[B] Most Institutional Rules Reinforce the Investigative Approach

While the surveyed national laws generally permit arbitral tribunals to exercise an active role, some institutional rules display more variation. Specifically, the Rules of the Stockholm Chamber of Commerce (SCC) reveal a restrictive handling of tribunal investigative powers: an arbitral tribunal may order evidence production only 'exceptionally on its own motion'.[25] Some authors conclude that this wording renders the procedure under the SCC Rules adversarial in nature.[26] The Rules of the Danish Institute of Arbitration (DIA) are equally strict. Arbitral tribunals may only order evidence production upon a party's request – preventing arbitral tribunals from issuing such orders independently.[27]

Interestingly, these arbitration rules significantly constrict tribunal powers that – as we have seen[28] – national arbitration laws would otherwise grant. In contrast, the Rules of the Finland Arbitration Institute (FAI) bear more resemblance to the inquisitorial approach, allowing arbitral tribunals to order any party to produce evidence it 'may consider relevant to the outcome of the case'.[29]

The Rules of the International Chamber of Commerce (ICC) require arbitral tribunals to 'establish the facts of the case by all appropriate means'.[30] Most commentators view this wording as a reflection of the civil law approach, encouraging arbitral

21. Article 1467(1) French Arbitration Law.
22. Article 1467(3) French Arbitration Law.
23. Section 7 US Federal Arbitration Act.
24. Section 34(2)(g) UK Arbitration Act.
25. Article 31(3) SCC Rules 2023.
26. Oldenstam et al., *supra* n. 6, at p. 68.
27. Article 33 DIA Rules 2021; *see also* the Danish Association for Arbitration Rules for the Taking of Evidence in Arbitration Cases, mirroring the approach of the DIA Rules.
28. *See* section §4.02[A], *supra*.
29. Section 34.2(b) FAI Rules 2024.
30. Article 25(1) ICC Rules 2021.

tribunals to actively direct the proceedings.[31] However, the ICC Rules do not oblige arbitral tribunals to investigate the facts ex officio.[32] While most arbitral tribunals seem reluctant to participate in the evidence gathering on their own motion,[33] the ICC Rules, nevertheless, empower them 'to summon any party to provide additional evidence'.[34] This right is most often exercised when a party references a relevant but unproduced document,[35] but it extends to any kind of evidence, including witness testimony. Thus, arbitrators may call witnesses not offered by the parties.[36]

The ICC Rules also stress the arbitrators' duty to 'to conduct the arbitration in an expeditious and cost-effective manner', including facilitating settlements.[37] To that end, the ICC Report on 'Controlling Time and Costs in Arbitration' urges arbitral tribunals to be 'proactive' and provide 'tailormade suggestions on the issues to be addressed'.[38] As the ICC Rules exert considerable persuasive influence and serve as a benchmark for institutional rules worldwide, their endorsement of active arbitral tribunals reflects a broader trend in international arbitration.

In the same vein, the German Arbitration Institute (DIS) reinforces the dedication of the German arbitration law to the 'limited inquisitorial approach' by requiring arbitral tribunals to 'establish the facts of the case that are relevant and material for deciding the dispute'.[39] The DIS Rules underscore this approach by stating that 'tribunals shall not be limited to admit only evidence offered by the parties'.[40] For example, they may 'examine fact witnesses other than those called by the parties'.[41] An arbitrator acting under the DIS Rules is, thus, expected to be an 'active case manager',[42] including fostering amicable settlements,[43] but without having to give directions – some may say: hints – as is required of German judges.[44] In fact, the limitation to the inquisitorial approach lies in its optional character: an arbitral tribunal has the power

31. Heiko Haller and Friederike Strack, *Art. 25 ICC Rules*, para. 8 (Jan Heiner Nedden, Axel Benjamin Herzberg and Ulrich Kopetzki (eds), 2nd ed., Otto Schmidt 2022); Thomas H. Webster and Michael Bühler, *Handbook of ICC Arbitration*, para. 25-7 (5th ed., Sweet & Maxwell 2021).
32. Haller and Strack, *supra* n. 31, at para. 1; Herman Verbist, Erik Schäfer and Christophe Imhoos, *ICC Arbitration in Practice*, p. 140 (2nd ed., Kluwer Law International 2015).
33. Haller and Strack, *supra* n. 31, at paras 9, 44; Webster and Bühler, *supra* n. 31, at paras 25-12, 25-44, 25-45, 25-74.
34. Article 25(4) ICC Rules 2021.
35. Webster and Bühler, *supra* n. 31, at para. 25-74.
36. Cf. Webster and Bühler, *supra* n. 31, at para. 25-24.
37. Article 22(2) ICC Rules 2021 referring to Appendix IV.
38. ICC Commission Report, *Controlling Time and Costs in Arbitration*, para. 28 (2nd. ed., ICC publication 2018).
39. Article 28.1 DIS Rules 2018.
40. Article 28.2 DIS Rules 2018.
41. *Ibid.*
42. Jörg Risse, *s. 27 DIS Rules*, para. 2 (Patricia Nacimiento, Stefan Kröll and Karl-Heinz Böckstiegel (eds), 2nd ed., Kluwer Law International 2015).
43. Cf. Art. 26 DIS Rules 2018 providing that tribunals 'shall, at every stage of the arbitration, seek to encourage an amicable settlement'.
44. Risse, *supra* n. 42, at para. 3; for a contrary view, *see* Paul Hauser, 5. *Freshfields Arbitration Lecture (German Edition): 'Die Ermittlung des Sachverhalts durch das Schiedsgericht, Fluch oder Segen?'*, 3 SchiedsVZ, 141, 142 (2017).

but is not 'obliged to investigate on its own initiative',[45] a distinction the DIS Rules specifically chose to clarify.[46] While the decision to investigate is optional, an arbitrator's toolbox reportedly extends 'beyond the powers that are available to judges', particularly for investigating facts not presented by parties.[47]

Several other prominent arbitration rules also embrace fact-finding powers. The Swiss Rules state that arbitral tribunals 'may require the parties to produce documents, exhibits, or other evidence'.[48] Likewise, the ICDR Rules grant arbitral tribunals the power to 'order the parties to produce documents, exhibits, or other evidence it deems necessary or appropriate',[49] which may be exercised without prior party request.[50] The LCIA Rules also empower arbitral tribunals to 'take the initiative in identifying relevant issues and ascertaining relevant facts, and to order any party to produce evidence'.[51] These powers may be exercised sua sponte, which is why some commentators encourage parties 'to consider this carefully before agreeing to the LCIA Rules'.[52]

In sum, the rules of most arbitral institutions allow for active tribunals, with only limited exceptions, maintaining a strictly party-driven approach.

[C] Soft Law Affirms Tribunal Fact-Finding Authority

Soft law instruments often guide arbitrators through specific questions of international arbitration that national laws or arbitral rules leave unanswered. These instruments are not binding in and of themselves, and parties rarely agree to applying them directly. However, arbitral tribunals are free to consider such frameworks, and procedural orders frequently stipulate that the arbitrators may seek guidance from them without being bound by their provisions.

Soft law also serves an important purpose regarding fact-finding. When the applicable procedural rules are silent on this matter, arbitrators may cite these soft law provisions to justify exercising their implied powers. Various evidentiary guidelines can be consulted for this purpose; some are fairly specific,[53] while three frameworks stand out due to their comprehensive approach.[54]

---

45. Trittmann and Schardt, *supra* n. 14, at para. 5; *see also* Risse, *supra* n. 42, at para. 1; Heiko Haller and Friederike Strack, *Art. 28 DIS Rules*, para. 1 (Jan Heiner Nedden, Axel Benjamin Herzberg and Ulrich Kopetzki (eds), 2nd ed., Otto Schmidt 2022); *see* for the discontent with the previous provision, Paul Hauser, *4. Freshfields Arbitration Lecture (German Edition)*, 5 SchiedsVZ 262, 263 (2016); Hauser, *supra* n. 44, at p. 142.
46. Trittmann and Schardt, *supra* n. 14, at para. 8.
47. *Ibid.*, at para. 66.
48. Article 26(2) Swiss Rules 2021.
49. Article 22(5) ICDR Rules 2021.
50. Martin Gusy and James Hosking, *A Guide to the ICDR International Arbitration Rules*, para. 20.28 (2nd ed., Oxford University Press 2019).
51. Article 22.1(iii) LCIA Rules 2020.
52. Lisa Richman, *Arbitrating under the 2020 LCIA Rules: A User's Guide*, Chapter 17, para. 21 (Maxi Scherer, Lisa Richman and Rémy Gerbay (eds), Kluwer Law International 2021).
53. *See* for the CIArb Protocol for the Use of Party-Appointed Expert Witnesses §4.03[B][3], *infra*.
54. Cf. also ALI/UNIDROIT Principles of Transnational Civil Procedure, which are however focussed on transnational litigation and therefore only carry little persuasive weight for international arbitration.

Most prominently, the IBA Rules on the Taking of Evidence in International Arbitration are recognized as a compromise between legal traditions, bridging the gap from adversarial common law to inquisitorial civil law countries. Under these rules, an arbitral tribunal may request any party to produce documents or to provide for any person's appearance.[55] Further, arbitral tribunals may appoint experts, call witnesses, and conduct site inspections on their own motion.[56] Accordingly, the IBA Rules equip arbitral tribunals with a wide range of fact-finding instruments to establish a robust evidentiary record.

Created as a counterbalance to the IBA Rules, the Prague Rules on the Efficient Conduct of Proceedings in International Arbitration expressly favour an inquisitorial approach. For example, they encourage arbitral tribunals 'to take a proactive role in establishing the facts of the case'.[57] Any form of document production is discouraged,[58] clearly distancing the Prague Rules from the common law tradition. Arbitrators may not only request or gather evidence on their own motion but are also expected to assist parties in reaching amicable settlements.[59]

Based on the background of the parties involved, arbitrators should carefully consider which soft law to consult. The Prague Rules' strong inquisitorial approach may disadvantage parties from common law jurisdictions, although they may offer benefits in purely civil law arbitrations.[60] By contrast, the IBA Rules offer a more balanced compromise, accommodating both legal traditions and thus making them more suitable for arbitral proceedings with parties from diverse legal backgrounds.[61]

A third and equally significant soft law instrument is the UNCITRAL Notes on Organizing Arbitral Proceedings. These Notes recognize that an arbitrator 'may itself take appropriate steps to obtain evidence from a third party',[62] 'may have to take appropriate steps to invite a witness to testify',[63] and may appoint their own experts when party-appointed experts' opinions are insufficient.[64] While always emphasizing consultation with the parties, the Notes affirm arbitral tribunals' discretion to act on their own accord.

55. Article 3.10 IBA Rules 2020.
56. Articles 6, 8.6, 4.10 IBA Rules 2020.
57. Article 3.1 Prague Rules 2018.
58. Article 4.2 Prague Rules 2018.
59. Articles 4.6, 5.5, 6.1, 9 Prague Rules 2018.
60. Peter J. Pettibone, The Prague Rules on the Efficient Conduct of Proceedings in International Arbitration: Are They an Alternative to the IBA Rules on the Taking of Evidence in International Arbitration?, 21 Asian Dispute Rev. 13, 17 (2019); Kabir A.N. Duggal and Rekha Rangachari, A Challenger Approaches: An Assessment of the Prague Rules on the Efficient Conduct of Proceedings in International Arbitration, 37 J. Int'l Arb. 27, 48 (2020) https://doi.org/10.54648/joia2020002 (accessed 1 October 2025).
61. *See also* Gary Born, *International Commercial Arbitration*, p. 2378 (3rd ed., Kluwer Law International 2021), who considers that the Prague Rules' reception in international arbitration is uncertain.
62. UNCITRAL, *Notes on Organizing Arbitral Proceedings*, para. 79 (2nd ed., UNCITRAL 2016).
63. *Ibid.*, at para. 125.
64. *Ibid.*, at para. 101.

Collectively, these soft law instruments complete the picture of a broad international consensus that arbitral tribunals possess inherent authority to conduct fact-finding initiatives.

[D] Fundamental Principles Guide Tribunal Investigations

Whenever arbitrators consider exercising their power to investigate facts, they must recognize the boundaries within which they operate. Three core principles guide their authority: ensuring each party's right to be heard, equal treatment of all parties, and their own independence and impartiality.[65]

The right to be heard does not necessarily present a significant obstacle to arbitrator initiatives. Certainly, arbitral tribunals must avoid surprise decisions by disclosing the factual basis of their considerations and allowing parties to comment.[66] This is particularly important when dealing with facts only personally known to an arbitrator or gathered outside the proceedings.[67] The right to be heard also serves as the relevant yardstick when arbitrators guide parties away from issues they consider irrelevant.

Despite these complexities, safeguarding the right to be heard remains consistently straightforward: arbitrators should allow parties to submit comments at the earliest possible stage. This principle extends to all arbitrator initiatives throughout the proceedings. Whenever arbitrators act *sua sponte*, they should invite comments from the parties before deciding.[68] It can also be meaningful to transparently establish criteria in the initial procedural order to dampen the surprise effect that tribunal initiatives may have on parties.[69]

Beyond the right to be heard, balancing parties' equal treatment and the arbitrator's impartiality requires careful consideration. When an arbitrator raises factual circumstances not identified by the parties, this might appear to favour one party over the other.[70] A distinction must therefore be drawn between legitimate clarification of relevant facts and improper assistance to a party in arguing or improving its case. While arbitral tribunals may properly engage in necessary fact-finding, they should naturally avoid enhancing one party's case and compensating for poor counsel selection or presentation of argument.[71]

65. Harold Frey, *The Arbitrators' Initiative: Fact-finding*, p. 51 (Domitille Baizeau and Frank Spoorenberg (eds), Juris Publishing 2016).
66. Frey, *supra* n. 65, at p. 54; Landolt, *supra* n. 1, at p. 219.
67. Jason Fry, Simon Greenberg and Francesca Mazza, *The Secretariat's Guide to ICC Arbitration*, para. 3-944 (ICC Publishing, 2012).
68. Landolt, *supra* n. 1, at p. 219.
69. *Ibid.*, at p. 192.
70. Paul Friedland, *Fact-Finding by International Arbitrators: Sua Sponte Calls for Evidence*, p. 42 (Domitille Baizeau and Frank Spoorenberg (eds), Juris Publishing 2016).
71. Frey, *supra* n. 65, at p. 59; Kristoffer Löf, Aron Skogman, Sara Johnsson, *International Arbitration in Sweden*, Chapter 9, para. 149 (Annette Magnusson, Jakob Ragnwaldh, Martin Wallin (eds), 2nd ed., Kluwer Law International 2021).

Arbitrators should also consider that tribunal investigations may infringe on the parties' control over the dispute,[72] which is, among other things, defined by the principle of *ne ultra petita*.[73] Accordingly, arbitrators generally should not suggest new claims, modify the requested relief, or substitute whole sets of facts. It should remain solely up to the parties to define the scope and nature of their dispute.[74]

Mindful of these limitations, arbitral tribunals should not, however, simply defer to the burden of proof and abandon initiatives altogether.[75] When they exercise their powers in accordance with the applicable laws, rules, and best practices [*§4.03*], they not only strengthen the reliability and completeness of the factual record. They also diminish the prospect of any challenge, be it to an arbitrator or to the award, especially when their investigative measures serve to establish a more complete and accurate evidentiary foundation for the arbitral tribunal to take an informed decision for resolving the dispute.[76]

[E] Summary: Arbitral Tribunals Generally Possess Fact-Finding Authority

The few divergent approaches underscore the importance of diligently checking the applicable provisions for deviations from the general rule. With this caveat in mind, one can conclude that most rules empower arbitral tribunals to be active, allowing them to call for additional evidence – without obligating them to do so.[77] As institutional rules are trending towards allowing more proactive tribunals, this approach gains more and more momentum.[78] Arbitral tribunals should therefore not turn a blind eye to apparent gaps or inconsistencies in submissions. They should rather indicate to the parties which topics deserve focus.[79] At the same time, arbitral tribunals should beware of the confines of their powers and always safeguard the parties' fundamental procedural rights. Navigating between these aims presents a challenge, but arbitral tribunals should not shy away from intervening proactively when necessary.

§4.03 ARBITRAL TRIBUNALS' INVESTIGATIVE TOOLS TO FACILITATE FACT-FINDING

Having established the legal framework, the following section outlines different investigative tools the arbitral tribunal may employ in exercising its fact-finding

72. Landolt, *supra* n. 1, at pp. 203, 222.
73. Pierre-Yves Tschanz, *Selected Questions regarding Arbitrator's Initiatives*, p. 79 (Domitille Baizeau and Frank Spoorenberg (eds), Juris Publishing 2016).
74. Pierre Mayer, *The Arbitrators' Initiative: Its Foundation and Its Limits*, pp. 5-6 (Domitille Baizeau and Frank Spoorenberg (eds), Juris Publishing 2016).
75. *But see* Friedland, *supra* n. 70, at p. 44, who, however, favours an active approach regarding the quantum of damages, *see* pp. 45-46.
76. Mayer, *supra* n. 74, at p. 5; Landolt, *supra* n. 1, at p. 190.
77. Julian Bickmann, *Fact-Finding in International Arbitration: The Emergence of a Transnational Lex Evidentiae*, para. 3.55 (Kluwer Law International 2022); Landolt, *supra* n. 1, at pp. 189-190.
78. Frey, *supra* n. 65, at p. 52.
79. Siegfried H. Elsing, Procedural Efficiency in International Arbitration: Choosing the Best of Both Legal Worlds, 3 SchiedsVZ 114, 114 (2011).

authority. To offer practical guidance, it does so by revisiting different stages of the proceeding, from identifying and assessing the factual issues in dispute [*A*] to efficiently employing expert witnesses [*B*] and factual witnesses, as well as conducting evidentiary hearings [*C*] as investigative tools.

[A] Identifying Relevant Facts with Lists of Issues or Questions and Preliminary Assessments

There are several means to direct the parties' submissions to the (factual) issues that the arbitral tribunal considers relevant and material in deciding the dispute, including lists of issues or questions [*1*] and preliminary assessments by the arbitral tribunal [*2*].

[1] Fact-Finding Through Lists of Issues or Questions

Some institutional rules encourage the arbitral tribunal to determine a list of issues. For instance, the ICC Rules provide that the Terms of Reference shall include, 'unless the arbitral tribunal considers it inappropriate, a list of issues to be determined'.[80] Such an approach can also be adopted for non-ICC arbitration proceedings.[81] In a similar vein, the DIA Rules foresee that the arbitral tribunal and the parties identify which facts 'shall require the taking of evidence' during the preparatory meeting.[82] Given the early stage of the proceedings, it is within the arbitral tribunal's discretion to decide whether or not it considers that such a list of issues would streamline the process,[83] or whether, in contrast, a potential lack of agreement on its contents would rather cause delay.[84] In any event, an arbitral tribunal should indicate that the list of issues is non-exhaustive.

Further to identifying the issues in dispute, another approach is for the arbitral tribunal to pose targeted questions for the parties to address. For instance, under the LCIA Rules, the arbitral tribunal may require the parties to address specific questions or issues arising from the parties' dispute during the hearing.[85] Noting that the rules of this major arbitral institution seated in a traditionally adversarial common law jurisdiction grants such authority, this approach does not appear unduly inquisitorial.[86] Providing the parties with a list of questions is generally considered to contribute

80. Article 23(1)(d) ICC Rules 2021.
81. Cf. Thomas H. Webster, *Party Control in International Arbitration*, 19 Arb. Int'l 119, 134 (2003) https://doi.org/10.1093/arbitration/19.2.119 (accessed 1 October 2025).
82. Article 32(a) DIA Rules 2021.
83. Gabrielle Nater-Bass, The Initial Discussion with the Parties: How Should It Be Done? Which Topics Must Be or May Be Addressed?, p. 16 (Domitille Baizeau and Frank Spoorenberg (eds), Juris Publishing 2016).
84. Vijaya Kuma Rajah, *W(h)ither Institutional Terms of Reference?*, 39 J. Int'l Arb. 163, 174 et seq. (2022) https://doi.org/10.54648/joia2022007 (accessed 1 October 2025).
85. Article 19.2 LCIA Rules 2020.
86. *But see* Michael Kerr, *London Court of Arbitration*, p. 215 (Albert Jan van den Berg (ed.), ICCA & Kluwer Law International 1996), noting that this approach 'demonstrates the closeness of the letter of the LCIA Rules to the spirit of "inquisitorial" arbitrations under civil law systems'.

to increased efficiency.[87] On the condition that the questions are treated as non-exhaustive and the parties have sufficient and equal opportunity to address them, none of the fundamental principles identified above[88] conflicts with such a list.

The benefits of providing the parties with a list of questions are further increased if the list is not shaped as a single document, issued shortly before the hearing. Instead, efficient guidance on the relevant issues is best achieved if the arbitral tribunal provides the parties with selected questions at different stages of the proceedings. For instance, an arbitral tribunal could provide the parties with preliminary questions after the first round of written submissions and update its questions prior to the hearing. For the sake of legal certainty, an arbitral tribunal intending to do so should add a section along the following lines to its first procedural order:

> The Tribunal is at liberty to pose questions to the parties at any time during the proceedings. The parties will be given sufficient opportunity to respond and, where appropriate, to comment on each other's responses.

[2] Preliminary Assessment as a Fact-Finding Tool

By means of a preliminary assessment, the arbitral tribunal provides the parties with a non-binding evaluation of the merits of the dispute. Such preliminary assessments are regularly discussed in the context of facilitating settlements between the parties[89] and, for instance, listed as a potential measure for increasing procedural efficiency in Annex 3 to the DIS Rules. At the same time, they may also serve as a potent investigative tool by accentuating disputed facts and their potential impact on the outcome of the dispute.[90] If the parties principally appreciate this approach, we suggest that the procedural timetable reflect this scenario, and the first procedural order include a section such as:

> The Tribunal has the power to give its preliminary views on the case after the first round of written submissions if it considers this appropriate. These preliminary views are indicative and non-binding and cannot give rise to any impression of partiality or lack of independence on the part of the arbitral tribunal.[91]

Irrespective of the applicable institutional rules, recording the parties' express agreement with the arbitral tribunal sharing its preliminary views is vital. This is because, to some, communicating such assessment may, at first glance, cause parties to doubt an

87. *See, e.g.*, Nater-Bass, *supra* n. 83, at p. 21.
88. *See* section §4.02[D], *supra*.
89. *See* Klaus Peter Berger, The Direct Involvement of the Arbitrator in the Amicable Settlement of the Dispute Offering Preliminary Views, Discussing Settlement Options, Suggesting Solutions, Caucusing, 35 J. Int'l. Arb. 501, 510 (2018) https://doi.org/10.54648/joia2018027 (accessed 1 October 2025).
90. Christopher Harris, *Arbitrators and Settlement: A Common Law Perspective*, p. 90 (Domitille Baizeau and Frank Spoorenberg (eds), Juris Publishing 2016); cf. Elsing, *supra* n. 79, at pp. 118 et seq.
91. Oliver Caprasse and Nina Lauber-Thommesen, *Management of Construction Arbitrations*, p. 175 in fn. 10 (Patrick Baeten et al. (eds), Kluwer Law International 2024).

arbitrator's impartiality.[92] This does not mean that the arbitral tribunal is per se prevented from proposing this tool on its own motion.[93] But before moving forward with this initiative, it should assure itself of the parties' consent.[94] Instead of relying on the arbitration clause, it is prudent to obtain the parties' informed (written)[95] consent during the arbitration.[96] In recording the parties' consent, the arbitral tribunal should also ensure that the parties commit to not challenging an arbitrator on the basis of the preliminary assessment. From the authors' practical experience, the parties' waiver preceding a preliminary assessment may include the following:

> The Parties have expressed their wish for the Tribunal to inform the Parties of its preliminary, non-prejudicial assessment of the matter, first orally and then in writing. By signing this declaration, the Parties acknowledge that they have been advised that any views expressed by the Tribunal orally or in writing are preliminary, non-prejudicial and in no way binding and may thus subsequently be revised during the further course of the arbitral proceedings. The Parties confirm that they will not, based on the preliminary and non-prejudicial assessment of the Tribunal, and any views expressed by the Tribunal in this context orally or in writing, file a challenge against a member of the Tribunal, nor will they contest or challenge an arbitral award on this basis. Finally, the Parties, by signing this declaration, confirm that they will not record the Tribunal's preliminary, non-prejudicial assessment as presented orally.

As to the format, some commentators recommend that an arbitral tribunal should not issue its preliminary assessment in writing or put it otherwise on record (although the parties will likely and permissibly take written notes).[97] We suggest deciding this on a case-by-case basis,[98] provided that the waiver covers the format that is ultimately selected.

Limiting the assessment to an oral preliminary views conference reflects its preliminary nature and prevents the parties from employing the preliminary views as an argument in the course of the proceeding.[99] The latter aspect reflects the goal of this

92. Cf. Daniel Busse, *Art. 26 DIS Rules*, para. 10 (Gustav Flecke-Giammarco et al. (eds), Kluwer Law International 2020); Michael E. Schneider, *The Art of Blending Arbitration and Other ADR Methods: Some Examples from International Practice*, p. 317 (Arnold Ingen-Housz (ed.), Kluwer Law International 2010); contra Jeffrey Maurice Waincymer, *Procedure and Evidence in International Arbitration*, p. 407 (Kluwer Law International 2012).
93. Paolo Marzolini, The Arbitrator as a Dispute Manager: The Exercise of the Arbitrator's Power to Act as Settlement Facilitator, p. 115 (Domitille Baizeau and Frank Spoorenberg (eds), Juris Publishing 2016).
94. Berger, *supra* n. 89, at pp. 513 et seq.; Ugo Draetta, *Leveraging the Arbitral Process to Encourage Settlement: Some Practical and Legal Issues*, p. 372 (Miguel Àngel Fernàndez-Ballesteros and David Arias Lozano (eds), Kluwer Law International 2024); Hilmar Raeschke-Kessler, *The Arbitrator as Settlement Facilitator*, 21 Arb. Int'l. 523, 530 (2005) https://doi.org/10.1093/arbitration/21.4.523 (accessed 1 October 2025).
95. Hermann Bietz, *On the State and Efficiency of International Arbitration: Could the German 'Relevance Method' Be Useful or Not?*, 12 SchiedsVZ 121, 132 (2014); Busse, *supra* n. 92, at para. 11; Marzolini, *supra* n. 93, at p. 116.
96. *See* Berger, *supra* n. 89, at pp. 513 et seq.
97. Berger, *supra* n. 89, at p. 512.
98. Cf. Harris, *supra* n. 90, at p. 91.
99. Berger, *supra* n. 89, at p. 512.

tool, which intends to facilitate fact-finding but not to strengthen one party's substantive position.

There are, however, scenarios in which an (additional) written preliminary assessment best facilitates fact-finding or settlement negotiations. Parties may even expressly request such written assessments. Mindful of the additional work required on the part of the arbitral tribunal, such a document allows for pinpointing factual issues. In practice, depending on the volume of the preliminary assessment, it also ensures thorough consideration by the parties and expedites in-house coordination. This benefits both the preparation of upcoming submissions and the identification of further evidence, while also creating a solid foundation for potential settlement talks.

Regarding the content and delivery, some observe that preliminary assessments are 'most often' issued without reasoning.[100] To serve as a fact-finding tool, however, at least a limited reasoning is necessary when issuing preliminary assessments. Only if the parties can understand which factual circumstances the arbitral tribunal considered vital (and potentially in relation to which facts it considers further briefing necessary), they will put the necessary emphasis on clarifying such uncertainties in their remaining submissions. Parties need this clarity to make an informed assessment of their chances and risks in pursuing the arbitration instead of seeking an amicable settlement. It is for this reason that arbitral tribunals should explain for which issues additional evidence is required.[101] To advance preliminary assessments as a fact-finding tool, arbitrators might also consider the use of visualizations, such as a decision-tree analysis or Excel sheets indicating certain risk factors or prospects of success for individual claims. This may illustrate the impact of disputed facts on the outcome of the case.[102]

The opinions on the right timing for indicating preliminary views differ. It is a truism that a preliminary assessment requires a thorough understanding of the dispute, its factual and legal backgrounds as well as its commercial context. While some conclude that, therefore, giving a preliminary view is sensible after (the first round of) written submissions by the parties,[103] others submit that a reasonable assessment of the dispute is often possible only after the taking of evidence.[104]

To serve as an investigative tool and to increase the efficiency of the proceedings, naturally, the arbitral tribunal has to provide the parties with its preliminary views prior to the taking of evidence. It is only in this scenario that the parties may clarify factual ambiguities in a pre-hearing submission and in a subsequent evidentiary

100. Caprasse and Lauber-Thommesen, *supra* n. 91, at p. 175.
101. Manuel Liatowitsch and James Menz, *Alternative Dispute Resolution*, p. 326 (Elliott Geisinger and Nathalie Voser (eds), 2nd ed., Kluwer Law International 2013).
102. Cf. Berger, *supra* n. 89, at p. 511; Rouven Bodenheimer, *The Tribunal Visualized Approach: Improving Proceedings by Visualized Case Introduction*, 41 J. Int'l. Arb., 461, 474-477 (2024) https://doi.org/10.54648/joia2024020 (accessed 1 October 2025).
103. Cf. Caprasse and Lauber-Thommesen, *supra* n. 91, at p. 175.
104. Berger, *supra* n. 89, at pp. 515 et seq.; Harald Rieger, *Alternative Dispute Resolution Versus Schiedsgericht*, 14 ASA Bull. 190, 195 (1996) https://doi.org/10.54648/asab1996013 (accessed 1 October 2025).

hearing. The exact timing of the preliminary assessment is best decided case-by-case.[105] Whether to issue it after a first[106] or second[107] round of written submissions depends on several factors. These include the dispute's complexity, the submissions' thoroughness, and the quality of evidence offered.

If the case so allows, sharing preliminary views as part of a midstream conference enables the arbitral tribunal to efficiently guide the parties as to which facts and issues the next rounds of submissions should, *inter alia*, address.[108] In any event, when integrating a preliminary assessment into the procedural timetable, arbitrators should consider that its outcome might incentivize parties to (re-)enter settlement negotiations.[109]

It is a distinct question whether the assessment should also address issues that had not been raised by the parties and on which evidence such issues depend. Here, a cautious approach is advised.[110] Conceptually, it appears more intrusive to raise additional issues sua sponte than to request the parties to further substantiate issues that have already been brought forward. It seems hardly possible for the arbitral tribunal to assess in advance if parties refrained from addressing issues by neglect or deliberate choice, for instance, for strategic reasons.[111]

Are there particular risks that should categorically prevent arbitrators from sharing preliminary views? We do not think so.[112] If the parties' express consent is recorded and the arbitrators stress the merely preliminary nature of their views, the risks of successful challenges are minimal. The same applies to subsequent applications to have the award set aside. Less of a legal but a subjective risk is that a preliminary assessment naturally 'shows how much or how little the arbitrator has understood the case'.[113] Still, this should not deter arbitrators from resorting to this tool. It should rather encourage the arbitral tribunal to get ahead of the case file at an early stage of the proceedings, not least because this maximizes time and cost efficiency.[114] In particular, if merged with a list of questions,[115] sharing preliminary views is an effective tool to further investigate the facts. The two approaches are not mutually exclusive but should rather be understood as complementary tools. In any

105. Cf. Harris, *supra* n. 90, at p. 90; Rolf Trittmann and Ramona Schardt, *Art. 27 DIS Rules*, para. 65 (Gustav Flecke-Giammarco et al. (eds), Kluwer Law International 2020).
106. Cf. Harris, *supra* n. 90, at p. 90; cf. Klaus M. Sachs, *Do We Deliver: How to Make International Arbitration More Efficient*, pp. 225 et seq. (Neil Kaplan et al. (eds), Kluwer Law International 2020).
107. Cf. Alexander Gee and Olesya Bulka, *How to Make Arbitration Efficient: Practice Examples*, 20 SchiedsVZ 27, 29 (2022); Raeschke-Kessler, *supra* n. 94, at p. 528.
108. Sachs, *supra* n. 106, at p. 225.
109. Cf. Caprasse and Lauber-Thommesen, *supra* n. 91, at p. 175; Raeschke-Kessler, *supra* n. 94, at p. 534.
110. *But see* Raeschke-Kessler, *supra* n. 94, at p. 529, noting that '[t]here are no restrictions on the issues that the arbitral tribunal may wish to discuss with the parties, except that they should be relevant to the outcome of the case'.
111. Friedland, *supra* n. 70, at pp. 43 et seq.
112. *See also* Klaus Peter Berger and Jan Ole Jensen, *The Arbitrator's Mandate to Facilitate Settlement*, 13 Int'l Commercial Arb. Rev. 58, 71 (2017), who agree but also reference more cautious voices.
113. Schneider, *supra* n. 92, at p. 318.
114. Berger and Jensen, *supra* n. 112, at p. 72; cf. Draetta, *supra* n. 94, at p. 373.

event, even if indeed the arbitrator had understood little at this stage – a risk which can, of course, be limited or avoided by meticulously studying the case file – both approaches provide an opportunity to educate the arbitral tribunal.

[B] Employing Experts for Effective Fact-Finding

According to a 2020 report, expert witnesses were involved in 85% of the surveyed ICC proceedings with claims exceeding USD 25 million.[116] This reflects the vital role experts play in arbitral proceedings, particularly in assessing and explaining complex factual issues. Whereas (perceived) partiality, among other issues, is discussed as a detrimental consequence of party-appointed experts,[117] they are nonetheless employed in the vast majority of cases.[118] Rightly so: appointing experts forms part of a party's fundamental right to submit evidence,[119] which it, understandably, does not relinquish lightly.

Yet, the ensuing reports remain inconclusive at times, either due to irresolvable contradictions or because they miss crucial facts, speaking at cross purposes. This begs the question: do tribunal-appointed experts solve this conundrum? At first glance, there is reason to think so. First, the majority of the surveyed institutional rules provide for appointments by the arbitral tribunal.[120] Second, a tribunal appointment shelters the expert's independence.[121] Third, in theory, it reduces costs to the extent that it avoids multiple rounds of submissions in a 'battle of experts' appointed by the parties.[122] However, as arbitral tribunals tend to appoint experts at a late stage and in

115. On this, Waincymer, *supra* n. 92, at p. 407 notes: 'Inclinations can usually be framed as more neutral two-way questions. For example, the tribunal might ask, "should it take the contextual view on the evidence that … or conversely should we adopt a literal interpretation because … ?"'.
116. Queen Mary University of London, *Damages Awards in International Commercial Arbitration: A Study of ICC Awards*, p. 18, www.qmul.ac.uk/arbitration/media/law/docs/research/Queen-Mary-research-paper-December-2020.pdf (accessed 1 October 2025).
117. *See, e.g.*, Mohamed S. Abdel Wahab, *Party-Appointed Experts in International Commercial Arbitration: A Necessity or a Nuisance?*, pp. 194 et seq. (Franco Ferrari and Friedrich Rosenfeld (eds), Kluwer Law International 2022); Mark A. Kantor, *A Code of Conduct for Party-Appointed Experts in International Arbitration: Can One be Found?*, 26 Arb. Int'l 323, 333-336 (2010) https://doi.org/10.1093/arbitration/26.3.323 (accessed 1 October 2025).
118. Cf. Queen Mary University of London, *2012 International Arbitration Survey: Current and Preferred Practices in the Arbitral Process*, p. 29, www.qmul.ac.uk/arbitration/media/arbitration/docs/2012_International_Arbitration_Survey.pdf (accessed 1 October 2025), noting that expert witnesses were party-appointed in 90% of the proceedings considered for the survey.
119. *See, e.g.*, Bickmann, *supra* n. 77, at para. 3.103; Kantor, *supra* n. 117, at p. 336; Waincymer, *supra* n. 92, at p. 936.
120. *See* section §4.02[B], *supra*.
121. *See* Born, *supra* n. 61, at p. 2452.
122. Cf. Tobias Zuberbühler et al., IBA Rules of Evidence: Commentary on the IBA Rules on the Taking of Evidence in International Arbitration, Art. 8 para. 47 (2nd ed., Schulthess Juristische Medien 2022).

addition to – and seldom instead of – party-appointed experts, in practice, such considerations often remain a pipe dream.[123]

Besides, legal considerations as well as practicalities will often weigh against an appointment by the arbitral tribunal. From a legal perspective, appointing experts entails the risk that the arbitral tribunal is perceived to unduly delegate its decision.[124] From a practical perspective, one may doubt whether the arbitral tribunal is able to instruct the expert with sufficient precision and provide it with all relevant information.[125] This might explain why, for example, arbitral tribunals may appoint an expert to reconcile contradictory opinions of party-appointed experts under the DIS Rules[126] but rarely use this authority without the parties' prior requests.[127]

In light of this, the present contribution outlines three alternative tools to facilitate the use of experts: joint appointments by the parties upon the arbitral tribunal's instruction and supervision [*1*], expert teaming [*2*], and expert conferencing [*3*].

[1] Jointly Appointed Party Experts

We propose a different approach that combines the advantages of party- and tribunal-appointed experts in appropriate cases: the joint appointment of an expert by the parties upon the arbitral tribunal's instruction and under its supervision.[128] Joint appointments are expressly recognized, for example, by the DIA Rules.[129]

This approach bestows the expert with a neutral position,[130] while avoiding the perception that the arbitral tribunal delegates parts of its decision-making. Their appointment and their terms of reference are monitored and authorized by the arbitral tribunal while, in the first place, remaining in the hands of the parties. This approach rests on careful instruction by the arbitral tribunal:[131] to initiate this format, it will instruct the parties to jointly nominate an expert or, absent such agreement, submit a joint list without identifying which party nominated which candidate. The arbitral

123. Cf. Nigel Blackaby and Alex Wilbraham, *Practical Issues Relating to the Use of Expert Evidence in Investment Treaty Arbitration*, 31 ICSID Rev. 655, 664 (2016) https://doi.org/10.1093/icsidreview/siw031 (accessed 1 October 2025).
124. Blackaby and Wilbraham, *supra* n. 123, at p. 664; Kantor, *supra* n. 117, at p. 336; Jonathan Lim, *Tribunal-Appointed Experts in International Arbitration*, p. 215 (Franco Ferrari and Friedrich Rosenfeld (eds), Kluwer Law International 2022); cf. Born, *supra* n. 61, at p. 2448; Queen Mary University of London, *2021 International Arbitration Survey: Adapting Arbitration to a Changing World*, p. 14, www.qmul.ac.uk/arbitration/media/arbitration/docs/LON0320037-QMUL-International-Arbitration-Survey-2021_19_WEB.pdf (accessed 1 October 2025).
125. Cf. Kantor, *supra* n. 117, at pp. 338 et seq.; Waincymer, *supra* n. 92, at p. 974.
126. Article 28(2) DIS Rules 2018.
127. Haller and Strack, *supra* n. 45, at para. 8.
128. *See, e.g.*, CRCICA Case No. 1314/2019 for a published award in which a tribunal ordered the joint appointment of an expert; *but see also* Michael E. Schneider, Joachim Knoll and Christophe Guibert de Bruet, *Expert Evidence*, para. 41 (Andreas J. Roquette and Tom Christopher Pröstler (eds), C.H. Beck 2022), who note that it is unclear how frequently this approach is used in construction disputes.
129. *See* Art. 35 DIA Rules 2021.
130. Schneider, Knoll and de Bruet, *supra* n. 128, at para. 42.
131. *See* Waincymer, *supra* n. 92, at p. 936.

tribunal will further instruct the parties to, first, jointly identify the subject matters on which the expert is to be appointed, second, provide a joint draft for the expert's mission, and, third, also provide a preferably jointly drawn up document with issues on which the parties have not been able to agree.

In instructing the parties, the arbitral tribunal should also clarify, for the avoidance of doubt, that the expert is appointed jointly and directly by the parties, but in consultation with the arbitral tribunal and under its supervision. This ensures that the arbitral tribunal retains some control over the selection and mandate of the expert while, at the same time, it has the following potentially desirable implications: First, the experts render their services to the parties. This means that liability and remuneration are matters solely between the expert and the parties, the latter subject to the cost decision in the final award. Second, the rules governing tribunal-appointed experts do not directly apply.

[2] Expert Teaming

If the parties seem reluctant or even opposed to jointly appointing an expert, the arbitral tribunal can, alternatively, explore teaming experts as a 'compromise'.[132] This concept was prominently advanced by *Sachs* and *Schmidt-Ahrendts* with their 'Protocol on Expert Teaming'. This protocol envisions the following steps:[133] First, the parties list individual suggestions for experts. Second, after inviting the parties' comments on each list (particularly on conflicts of interest), the arbitral tribunal, third, appoints an expert team, consisting of one expert suggested by each party. Fourth, the arbitral tribunal prepares the terms of reference in a meeting with the parties and the expert team. Fifth, in accordance with the arbitral tribunal's terms of reference, the expert team jointly prepares a draft report for the arbitral tribunal and the parties to comment on. Sixth, the expert team submits its final report and is subject to cross-examination in the hearing.

Both the jointly party-appointed expert and expert teams are modern variations of party-appointed experts, aimed at fostering independent expert assessments in a cost-efficient manner and at vesting the arbitral tribunal with a better understanding of the facts. With the arbitral tribunal and the parties being involved in selecting the experts, drafting their terms of reference and cross-examining them,[134] it is likely that the reports will clarify crucial factual issues as identified by the arbitral tribunal and the parties.[135] Conceptually, the approaches differ insofar as only the expert team is, strictly speaking, appointed by the arbitral tribunal. As a consequence, this implies among other things that Article 6.3 IBA Rules 2020 does not directly allow the jointly

132. *See* Bickmann, *supra* n. 77, at para. 3.105 with this characterization.
133. *See* Klaus M. Sachs and Nils Schmidt-Ahrendts, *Protocol in Expert Teaming: A New Approach to Expert Evidence*, pp. 144-146 (Albert Jan van den Berg (ed.), ICCA & Kluwer Law International 2010) for the following outline; *see also* Kantor, *supra* n. 117, at pp. 336-339 and Waincymer, *supra* n. 92, at pp. 974 et seq. for discussions of the protocol.
134. *See* Waincymer, *supra* n. 92, at p. 936, noting that both parties should be allowed to cross-examine the jointly appointed expert.
135. Sachs and Schmidt-Ahrendts, *supra* n. 133, at p. 147.

appointed expert to request a party to provide information or access to documents. The authors suggest clarifying in a procedural order that, to the extent the jointly appointed experts are unable to comprehensively answer a question based on the information on record, they are authorized to approach the arbitral tribunal with a corresponding request for information or documents. In doing so, the jointly appointed expert should: (i) set forth with specificity the questions, respectively requests for documents or information; (ii) for what reason they are relevant and material for the experts' findings; (iii) identify with precision what (type of) documents or information they require; and (iv) which party is, presumably, in their possession. It is then up to the arbitral tribunal to decide on such a request, considering the relevance and materiality of the request, the stage of and the impact on the proceedings, and how much burden the request places on the party which is asked to produce the requested documents or information. The arbitral tribunal should also have regard to the burden of proof and the implications this might have when deciding on the expert's request.

Whereas expert teaming has the advantage of 'internal checks and balances', it also depends on the experts' internal cooperation with a risk of methodological gridlocks.[136] In choosing between the approaches, the arbitral tribunal should consider the parties' willingness to jointly appoint an expert and balance the potentially increased thoroughness of having an expert team with the potentially increased efficiency of the joint appointment.

[3] Expert Conferencing

Both joint appointments and expert teaming, naturally, rest on a reasonable degree of cooperation, be it between the parties or the experts. Expert conferencing, however, is a more confrontational and increasingly prominent[137] tool that allows the arbitral tribunal to clarify points of contention between party-appointed experts. The IBA Rules provide for such technique,[138] although the arbitral tribunal's discretion is in itself a sufficient legal basis.[139]

Expert conferencing, ideally, follows a three-tier procedure,[140] which, of course, can be tailored to a given case: First, prior to the hearing, the party-appointed experts meet to jointly prepare a document identifying which findings of their written reports they agree on, which findings remain contested, and for what reasons. Both the IBA Rules and the CIArb Protocol for the Use of Party-Appointed Expert Witnesses in

136. Cf. Waincymer, *supra* n. 92, at p. 973.
137. Abdel Wahab, *supra* n. 117, at p. 205; Bickmann, *supra* n. 77, at para. 3.90.
138. Article 8.4(f) IBA Rules 2020.
139. Waincymer, *supra* n. 92, at p. 967.
140. *See, e.g.*, Martin Hunter, *Expert Conferencing and New Methods*, p. 822 (Albert Jan van den Berg (ed.), ICCA & Kluwer Law International 2006); Nigel Blackaby, Constantine Partasides and Alan Redfern, *Redfern and Hunter on International Arbitration*, paras 6.197 et seq. (7th ed., Oxford University Press 2023), who advocate the following steps; for further guidance on expert-conferencing, *see also* CIArb Guidelines for Witness Conferencing in International Arbitration.

International Arbitration provide for such an expert discussion,[141] which is also encouraged by the ICC.[142] Second, the arbitral tribunal prepares an agenda based on the contested findings and shares it with the parties. Third, based on this agenda, the arbitral tribunal examines both experts simultaneously in the witness dock during the hearing. Typically, this will happen after the experts' individual cross-examinations but can also replace individual examinations altogether.

Such conferencing enables the arbitral tribunal to probe the experts directly on the contested factual findings, alternating between them and inviting reciprocal comments and questions on their statements. Whereas experienced experts often succeed in deflecting counsel's questions in cross-examination, the direct confrontation with the opposing expert may allow the arbitral tribunal to identify factual inconsistencies.[143]

[C] Investigative Tools for the Evidentiary Hearing

Most arbitral proceedings involve an oral hearing. Regularly, the taking of evidence and, thus, the examination of witnesses and experts is part of the oral hearing. Traditionally, a distinct procedural order outlines the hearing's agenda and calls the witnesses and experts offered by the parties, indicating the order of their examination.[144] Yet, there are two other approaches by which arbitrators might employ this procedural order to facilitate fact-finding more efficiently: identifying and clustering topics and the witnesses which the arbitral tribunal considers relevant as well as calling witnesses on the arbitral tribunal's own motion.

First, the arbitral tribunal may identify which witness should address which critical factual issues in their testimony.[145] If included in the procedural order in preparation for the evidentiary hearing, it can assist the parties to prepare for the hearing, including their own questioning of such witnesses. To the extent that it non-exhaustively lists factual issues of particular importance to the arbitral tribunal and allows the parties to also engage in the examination of the witnesses, it does not infringe on the parties' right to be heard. If an arbitral tribunal finds that the subject of a given testimony is manifestly irrelevant or has already been proven by other evidence, it could even, after consulting the parties, limit the testimony to individual subjects or – potentially – refrain from hearing a witness at all. Such authority is expressly reflected in the LCIA Rules and the IBA Rules.[146] Beyond those provisions, this authority is also derived from an arbitral tribunal's discretion and does not per se conflict with the parties' right to be heard.[147]

141. Article 5(4) IBA Rules 2020 and Art. 6(2) CIArb Protocol for the Use of Party-Appointed Expert Witnesses in International Arbitration.
142. Cf. ICC Commission Report, *supra* n. 38, at para. 67.
143. Cf. Abdel Wahab, *supra* n. 117, at p. 205.
144. Bickmann, *supra* n. 77, at para. 3.81.
145. Cf. Elsing, *supra* n. 79, at p. 117.
146. Article 20.4 LCIA Rules 2020, Art. 8.3 IBA Rules 2020.
147. Levine, *supra* n. 1, at pp. 334-342; Waincymer, *supra* n. 92, at p. 888. Cf. Landolt, *supra* n. 1, at p. 178; Roman Mikhailovich Khodykin, Carol Mulcahy and Nicholas Fletcher, *A Guide to the*

Second, arbitrators may exceptionally exercise their discretion to call a witness on their own motion who has not been named by the parties.[148] Major institutional frameworks such as the ICC Rules and the DIS Rules grant such authority, and the IBA Rules underscore this power.[149] Notably, however, the SCC Rules expressly only provide for an arbitral tribunal's authority to appoint experts on its own motion.[150] Depending on the applicable rules, the arbitral tribunal may wish to clarify this authority at an early stage of the proceeding to increase predictability and legal certainty for the parties. By means of illustration, the procedural order in a case administered by the Permanent Court of Arbitration under the 1976 UNCITRAL Arbitration Rules was cited as follows:[151]

> The Tribunal may, after consulting with the Parties at a reasonable time in advance of the hearing, request a Party to make available for testimony at the hearing a witness whose appearance has not been requested by the other Party. The Tribunal may also request the Parties to provide for, or to use their best efforts to provide for, the appearance for testimony of a person for whom no witness statement has been submitted.

Generally, a cautious approach is advised as presenting witnesses of fact is considered to be the responsibility of the parties.[152] As indicated, the arbitral tribunal should limit calling witnesses on its own motion to exceptional scenarios.[153] Some scholars, for example, refer to the scenario that the arbitral tribunal feels obliged to revisit issues ex officio on which the parties did not sufficiently elaborate.[154] In any case, arbitrators should consult the parties on their initiatives as this minimizes the risk of having the award set aside for allegedly depriving a party of its right to be heard.[155] It also allows the parties to raise any objections they might have.[156]

§4.04 CONCLUSION

Across civil law and common law jurisdictions, as well as under prominent institutional rules, arbitral tribunals generally possess robust fact-finding powers. Arbitrators

IBA Rules on the Taking of Evidence in International Arbitration, para. 11.42 (Oxford University Press 2019); *see also* Zuberbühler et al., *supra* n. 122, at Art. 8 para. 24, advocating a cautious approach.

148. Born, *supra* n. 61, at pp. 2455 et seq.; Waincymer, *supra* n. 92, at p. 888; *see* for an opposing view Catherine Kessedijan, *Inherent and Discretionary Powers of Arbitrators*, p. 20 (Bernado M. Cremades and Patricia Peterson (eds), ICC Publishing 2023).
149. *See* section §4.02[B] and section §4.02[C], *supra*.
150. *See* Art. 34(1) SCC Rules 2023.
151. Levine, *supra* n. 1, at p. 328; cf. also Khodykin, Mulcahy and Fletcher, *supra* n. 147, at para. 7.229 with reference to the cited procedural order.
152. Khodykin, Mulcahy and Fletcher, *supra* n. 147, at paras 7.221, 7.225; Zuberbühler et al., *supra* n. 122, at Art. 4 para. 92.
153. Born, *supra* n. 61, at pp. 2455 et seq.; Waincymer, *supra* n. 92, at p. 888; *see* for an opposing view Kessedijan, *supra* n. 148, at p. 20.
154. *See* Zuberbühler et al., *supra* n. 122, at Art. 4 para. 93, who offer this scenario as the only 'exception' based on which a tribunal should hear person not offered as witnesses. *See also* Friedland, *supra* n. 70, at pp. 39-41.
155. Khodykin, Mulcahy and Fletcher, *supra* n. 147, at para. 7.225.
156. *See* Art. 9.2, 9.3 IBA Rules 2020.

are well-advised to integrate proactive yet carefully calibrated measures into their procedural arsenal. While arbitral tribunals should not unduly discharge the parties' burden of proof with their own investigations, the proper use of the illustrated tools can streamline arbitral proceedings and enhance the arbitral tribunal's ability to fulfil the ultimate purpose of international arbitration: to efficiently resolve disputes through decisions, or by enhancing settlements, that are both legally sound and commercially sensible.

CHAPTER 5

Revised Danish Arbitration Rules on Evidence: Balancing International Practice, Party Autonomy and Danish Pragmatism

*Jimmy Skjold Hansen & Peter Schradieck**

§5.01 INTRODUCTION

One of the most significant events in the Nordic countries in 2010 was arguably the eruption of the Icelandic volcano Eyjafjallajökull. On 14 April 2010, a massive cloud of ash blasted into the atmosphere, grounding aeroplanes across Europe for weeks – presumably also disrupting one or two hearings in international arbitration cases on the continent.

Neither as visible nor as influential was the subsequent launch of the Danish Arbitration Association's Rules on the Taking of Evidence in Arbitration of 28 October 2010 (2010 DAA Rules). Nevertheless, in Denmark, the publication of these rules on the practical management of evidence in arbitration was groundbreaking in another way; it was a push in the Danish arbitration community to break free from handling evidence like the ordinary courts and instead embrace international arbitration standards that had gained traction globally. The main 'inventions' in the 2010 DAA Rules were written witness statements, document production requests, and party-appointed expert testimony.

The concurrent revision of the IBA Rules on the Taking of Evidence in International Arbitration in 2010 (the rules of 29 May 2010 and 17 December 2020 are jointly referred to as the 'IBA Rules' herein) provided useful and substantial inspiration for the authors of the 2010 DAA Rules, but the idea was never to offer the world a purely

* Assistant Attorneys Sofie Stemann Beck and Hjalte Struve Selcuk, Plesner, have assisted in the preparation of this chapter, and we are grateful for their contributions.

'Danish version' of the IBA Rules. Rather, it was to provide a hybrid solution. That remains the objective today.

In the last fifteen years, much has happened both in the international and the Danish arbitration communities. And so, the fundamental purpose of the Danish Arbitration Association's revised Rules on the Taking of Evidence in Arbitration of 1 March 2025 (2025 DAA Rules) is to provide a *best practice* set of rules and tools for practitioners in relation to the taking of evidence in arbitration cases seated in Denmark by striking a balance between contemporary international arbitration practice and the desire to preserve party autonomy as well as the pragmatic Danish approach to case management (some of which are rooted in fundamental principles of Danish court procedure).[1]

After all, the taking of evidence remains one of the most important aspects of any arbitration. As with the eruption at Eyjafjallajökull fifteen years ago, there is still – and perhaps even more today – a fundamental need to manage the forces of nature, that is, the inherent tension between the parties' ability and responsibility to drive the arbitral process forward and the personal preferences of international arbitrators for having more control over the process.

Against this background, the following sections will address the general approach and the underlying idea behind the 2025 DAA Rules (§5.02), outline key provisions in the 2025 DAA Rules and the underlying rationales (§5.03), suggest how international arbitrators should approach an arbitration seated in Scandinavia – particularly in Denmark – in case of little prior knowledge of the local tradition (§5.04), and finally provide a conclusion on the observations made in this chapter (§5.05).

§5.02 GENERAL APPROACH AND IDEA BEHIND THE 2025 DAA RULES

Most arbitrations today follow evidentiary rules derived from the IBA Rules which represent a compromise between civil law and common law traditions but are predominantly influenced by common law. The Prague Rules were introduced as an alternative to the IBA Rules, emphasising civil law principles and based on a more formalistic and inquisitorial approach to the arbitral process. They have had a modest impact. However, both the IBA Rules and the Prague Rules remain somewhat imbalanced from a Danish perspective and may not always provide a fully pragmatic solution.

As set out in the 2025 DAA Rules themselves, the rules are based on the fundamental legal principles of party autonomy and the adversarial approach and are intended to be a best practice set of rules and tools for practitioners in relation to the taking of evidence in arbitration cases seated in Denmark, i.e., cases governed by the Danish Arbitration Act of 2005, and pending between: (1) only Danish parties; (2) a mix of Danish and foreign parties; or (3) only foreign parties. The 2025 DAA Rules may be adopted between the parties – with or without the tribunal's acceptance or

1. The 2010 and 2025 DAA Rules can be found here: https://www.voldgiftsforeningen.dk/regler/regler (accessed 1 October 2025).

intervention – as binding rules or as guidelines. If adopted as binding, the 2025 DAA Rules will be binding on the parties and the tribunal. The tribunal may also, on its own initiative, decide to use the rules as guidelines.

The fundamental principle of Danish civil court practice has for decades been uncovering the 'substantive truth'. That means content trumps form. It does *not* mean, though, that there is discovery and other kinds of forced taking of evidence practised such as those known from the US court system. As a result, and within reason, deadlines or a cut-off date are typically adjusted by the court if the submission of additional evidence is deemed necessary to ensure that the court will not be prevented from receiving potentially material evidence. That principle has lived on in arbitrations in Denmark. In consequence, Danish practitioners may still be surprised to experience the approach taken by some international arbitrators whereby form can trump content, and deadlines seem more important than ensuring a proper framework for allowing the 'substantive truth' to come out.

Since the 2010 DAA Rules were issued, arbitration has arguably moved towards more regulation and also conferred more explicit powers on the tribunal. There is an inherent tension between the detail of regulation and the maintenance of flexibility for both parties and the tribunal. This was an ever-present consideration when working on the 2025 DAA Rules. The fundamental approach in the 2025 DAA Rules is set out in Article 8.1 which emphasises party autonomy: It is *the parties* who are responsible for providing the evidence in the case, while the tribunal may 'urge' the parties to present certain evidence (Article 8.2 of the 2025 DAA Rules). In some cases, the tribunal may step in and order certain evidence to be produced or in a certain form. Furthermore, reflecting the significant influence of the parties on the arbitral process in Denmark, Article 8.4 of the 2025 DAA Rules sets out the main – albeit non-exhaustive – objections to the production of evidence, etc. This stands in contrast to Article 9(2) of the IBA Rules which stipulates that objections to document production or a request for exclusion of evidence must be based on specific, predefined (exhaustive) grounds.

§5.03 KEY CHANGES AND PROVISIONS OF THE 2025 DAA RULES

[A] Focus on Efficiency: Written Witness Statements

Written witness statements are virtually not used in Danish court proceedings. Instead, oral testimony is presented directly and in full before the court at the oral hearing. The philosophy is that this allows the most credible testimony to be provided. While this may be the case in some situations (but certainly not all), it also carries risks. Witnesses often struggle with their memory under pressure, potentially leading to the very outcome that is undesired – unreliable testimony. Written witness statements mitigate the risk of such 'memory loss', and provide a better opportunity to properly contextualise key factual circumstances in addition to reducing the time required for witness examination at the oral hearing.

For these reasons, the 2010 DAA Rules formally introduced written witness statements in arbitrations seated in Denmark. There are no material changes in the

2025 DAA Rules to the concept. The parties are generally permitted to submit written witness statements (Article 3.2). However, to reflect the international direction over the last decade or more and the increasing use of written witness statements in arbitrations in Denmark, the 2025 DAA Rules now empower the tribunal to *order* the production of written witness statements, rather than merely encouraging a party to provide them, as was the case under the 2010 DAA Rules. In this respect, the balance between party autonomy and the tribunal's powers has tipped towards the tribunal. Given that a more widespread use of written witness statements may streamline the oral hearing and allow the oral hearing to be scheduled sooner, there could be a reduction in the overall runtime of arbitrations.

[B] Out of the Fire: Oral Testimonies of Witnesses and Party-Appointed Experts

While oral testimony given directly before the court has traditionally been the cornerstone of witness and expert evidence in Danish court proceedings, the 2010 DAA Rules sought to modify this approach by introducing written witness statements to allow the oral hearing to primarily focus on cross-examination. In practice, substantial examinations-in-chief have still been seen even in cases with written witness statements. In line with prevailing international practices, Articles 3.4 and 4.3 of the 2025 DAA Rules specifically address this dynamic by now making it the *default rule* that a witness or party-appointed expert should *not* testify at the oral hearing, unless requested to do so by either of the parties. At the same time, the arbitral tribunal no longer has the authority to request the appearance of a witness or a party-appointed expert, unless in cases of exceptional circumstances. This means that written witness statements or party-appointed expert reports can now be left self-standing, thereby potentially limiting the amount of time allocated to the oral hearing and the overall runtime of an arbitration.

Another significant change in the 2025 DAA Rules concerns the modification of the rules on the tribunal's power – subject to comments from the parties – to order expert conferral and/or expert conferencing for both party-appointed and tribunal-appointed experts (Articles 4.4, 4.5 and 5.7). The concepts are used to some extent internationally to facilitate a more structured and efficient evaluation of expert evidence by allowing experts to engage in direct discussions before or during the oral hearing to clarify agreement and disagreement on key technical issues. Conferral is now confined to a pre-hearing exercise that must be deemed 'necessary to ensure the efficient preparation of the arbitration proceedings and shall be conducted in an appropriate manner'. Similarly, conferencing is now confined to a supplementary oral exercise during the oral hearing that 'shall relate to one or more specified facts at issue'. These new limitations intend to make sure that the tribunal does not order conferral and/or conferencing without having thoroughly considered whether it may be beneficial to the overall process. As such, the limitations are intended to take back some control from the tribunal and give it back to the parties.

[C] Helping Hands: Tribunal-Appointed Experts

Danish civil court practice relies heavily on court-appointed expert testimony on technical (non-legal) matters, so-called syn og skøn (inspection and assessment), whereas party-appointed expert testimony has only in recent years gained some traction. 'Syn og skøn' is a unique Danish concept that is foreign to international arbitration practice but is still used in certain arbitrations in Denmark with construction disputes being the main example.

With the 2010 DAA Rules, party-appointed expert testimony was formally introduced to the wider Danish arbitration community, but the tribunal still had the possibility to order tribunal-appointed expert testimony at any stage of proceedings.

The 2025 DAA Rules take a step further away from the Danish court-inspired tradition and now stipulate that the tribunal may *only* appoint an expert itself if it determines that the existing evidence provided by party-appointed experts is insufficient to resolve one or more specific issues in dispute. In other words, tribunal-appointed experts can only be a subsidiary form of evidence, thereby reflecting prevailing international practice. In making its determination on whether to order such additional taking of evidence, the tribunal must consider the potential delays which a tribunal-appointed expert may cause and ensure that the parties are heard. In this respect, the power balance between the parties and the tribunal has also been tipped in favour of the parties. Less expert evidence will also reduce the time required for the oral hearing, although it may not reduce the overall runtime of arbitrations if the tribunal struggles to decide the case in the absence of such additional evidence that could bridge opposing views between party-appointed experts.

[D] Staying Humble and Pragmatic: Avoiding Potentially Prejudicing the Final Award

As mentioned, the fundamental principle of the 2025 DAA Rules is that the parties bear the primary responsibility for the arbitral process, including the presentation of relevant evidence to the tribunal. This builds on the Danish tradition of finding the 'substantive truth'. The tradition inspires arbitral tribunals to avoid taking procedural decisions along the way that may have a pre-emptive effect on how they may ultimately be able to decide the case at hand. In other words, the idea of 'keeping one's options open' in relation to the specific reasoning and result in the final award carries substantial weight. However, in some cases in Denmark, headed by international arbitrators, there has been a deviation from this fundamental principle, based essentially on the relevant arbitrators' own cultural or legal heritages.

A main example of form trumping content in an international arbitration was a case decided in 2017 that became subject to setting aside proceedings decided by the Danish Supreme Court in 2022 (the authors represented the claimant in the arbitration).[2] Throughout this arbitration, the tribunal had imposed very strict procedural measures, including tight deadlines and rigid evidentiary rules, deviating from Danish practice and certainly from Danish pragmatism. The claimant requested document production to substantiate its allegations of fraud on the part of the respondent under Danish law, but the tribunal denied the request, deeming it 'irrelevant to this dispute'. This view was simply mirroring an allegation from the respondent.

In the humble opinion of the authors (who have ongoing self-reflections on this point), the majority of the tribunal (from continental Europe) had not *then* understood the relevance of the fraud allegations under Danish law to the contract in dispute. When the claimant submitted party-appointed expert evidence obtained subsequently demonstrating fraud as alleged, the tribunal struck this evidence from the record, arguing that such evidence went beyond the – very unclearly defined – framework for what the claimant could file at the time, which was around one month before the oral hearing. In the final award, the tribunal then decided that the claimant *had not discharged its burden of proof* regarding fraud under Danish law. This point was subject to a 40-page dissenting opinion from the only Scandinavian in the tribunal (an esteemed Norwegian professor) who would have ruled in favour of the claimant.

It is still beyond the authors how the (majority of) the tribunal could both dismiss the document production requests concerning fraud for lack of relevance and dismiss the subsequent evidence provided by the claimant showing fraud only then to decide on the merits that fraud had not been proven by the claimant. Seemingly, by taking the strong stance on document production claiming that fraud was irrelevant in the specific contractual relationship in dispute, the majority of the tribunal had already cornered itself when the claimant late in the process managed to obtain and provide evidence itself going to the same point; given that arbitration is a one-shot process, the rationale of the majority must have been that the new evidence 'would not change anything anyway'. But after the oral hearing, it must have been clear also to the majority that fraud was indeed relevant, but by then it was too late to rule in favour of the claimant because of the prior procedural decisions made.

This case and the approach taken by two of the arbitrators to controlling the arbitral process has led to this addition in Article 8.1 of the 2025 DAA Rules: 'The Arbitral Tribunal shall not, in its procedural decisions during the arbitration proceedings, including in connection with the processing of a request for production of documents under Article 2.6, prejudge the final assessment of evidence in the arbitration.' In other words, to reflect the desire for 'material truth' and pragmatism, the tribunal should generally avoid taking decisions on evidence that may limit its options in deciding the case later.

2. Judgment of the Danish Supreme Court of 17 January 2022 in case 92/2020 between IMSPL Pte. Ltd (Singapore; claimant in the arbitration) and MAN Energy Solutions SE (Denmark/Germany; respondent in the arbitration) concerning the setting aside of the final award of 4 April 2017 rendered in Danish Institute of Arbitration Case No. E-2230 between the parties. The rejection of setting aside in this case has generated substantial debate in the Danish arbitration community.

§5.04 HOW SHOULD ARBITRATORS PLAY THE 'AWAY-GAME' IN SCANDINAVIA?

As one of the authors advocated at a GAR Live conference at the SCC some years ago, international arbitrators taking appointments in arbitrations seated in Scandinavia – and particularly in Denmark – would be well advised to preserve a certain degree of humility in the way in which they approach the arbitral procedure, including the taking of evidence.[3] The *evidence* offered to the audience at that conference was the fundamentally different outcomes of the arbitration mentioned in section [D] above (in which the client predominantly lost the case) and a very similar arbitration within the same case complex decided within months of the first case. The latter case was a full win for the client with an award describing the counterparty's behaviour before and during the arbitration as 'covert' and 'deceptive' (i.e., fraudulent). The main difference between the two cases seemed to be *the nationality and legal/cultural heritage of the two presidents* (the nationalities of the two respective co-arbitrators were the same in the two cases), and the difference in approach by the two presidents had a fundamental impact on the management of the cases and ultimately on the outcome on the merits.

It must be recognised – particularly by international arbitrators – that the balance between the tribunal's duty to ensure fairness and efficiency, including rendering a final award within a reasonable time, and the fundamental principle of party autonomy is simply struck differently in different jurisdictions.

Based on our experience and the changes made in the 2025 DAA Rules attempting to strike the said balance, at least as seen from a Danish perspective, we would suggest that international arbitrators consider the following in relation to general case management and chiefly with respect to the taking of evidence:

> *The first Case Management Conference (CMC):* Since this is ordinarily the first occasion where the parties (their counsel) and the tribunal will meet, this should be treated as a session in which the tribunal is very much in 'listening mode' and stays away from imposing the tribunal's – or perhaps only the president's – own agenda on the parties, unless this is necessary. Instead of circulating a 60-page draft Procedural Order No. 1 before the CMC, the tribunal should try to get an understanding of the parties' expectations as to the case management and evidence taking. For instance, if neither of the parties seems to desire document production, it would seem counterproductive for the tribunal to suggest a formal document production procedure (phase), including by having introduced language to that effect in a (prior) draft Procedural Order No. 1.
>
> *Procedural orders:* While procedural rules are usually helpful, tribunals should think about the pragmatism and flexibility that are normally associated with arbitrations in Scandinavia, and at least in Denmark. This should

3. 'Are Oral Hearings Too Short?: Tribunal's Perspective', Jimmy Skjold Hansen, GAR Live Stockholm, 21 May 2019.

guide the level of detailed rules that are set out, as the more detailed rules may constrain both the parties and the tribunal in the end.

Framework for taking evidence: While at least the Danish arbitration community could certainly need a push towards more frontloading of cases, tribunals should appreciate that a dispute and the availability of relevant evidence may develop over time, especially in cases with an imbalance between the parties regarding access to information. Allowing for document production requests on a more continuous basis in the arbitration (within reason) rather than having a single confined document production phase would probably assist the disadvantaged party in cases of unequal access to relevant information. Further, 'provocations' are often used in Danish court and domestic arbitration proceedings, that is, document or information requests made to the other party in written submissions. In case the other party does not comply, there may be an argument for the tribunal to draw adverse inferences. These measures can also be beneficial in cases where parties have equal access to relevant information, as they might prefer to avoid document production, a concept that is largely unfamiliar in Denmark.

Evidence 'out of turn': The starting point in relation to a request for submitting evidence, which potentially may be seen as 'out of turn' under the procedural calendar, should not simply be a denial of such evidence because it was not envisaged. At least sometimes, it will be helpful to everyone involved to have the evidence come at the time requested, and so such requests should not be perceived as dilatory per se, while the tribunal should of course consider whether they are likely ill-founded.

§5.05 CONCLUSION

The 2025 DAA Rules on the taking of evidence in arbitration represent a thoughtful evolution of Denmark's arbitration practices, balancing international standards with the country's unique legal traditions. Based on the last fifteen years of development of arbitration in Denmark since the 2010 DAA Rules were established, the revised rules of 2025 specifically address the balance of power between the parties and the arbitral tribunal in relation to the process around the taking of evidence. In doing so, the 2025 DAA Rules serve as a guide for international arbitrators – especially those unfamiliar with Scandinavian arbitration practices – emphasising a need for humility and adaptability to local procedural heritage when sitting as arbitrator, particularly in Denmark.

As the chapter showcases, successful arbitration in Denmark requires an appreciation of the flexible approach to arbitration applied in the country, fostering an environment where the 'substantive truth' may prevail without undue procedural constraints along the way.

CHAPTER 6

Unilateral Party-Appointment and Affiliation Bias: Is Joint Appointment the Solution?

Anne-Karin Nesdam & Marie Nesvik[*]

§6.01 INTRODUCTION

The principle of an arbitrator's impartiality and independence from the parties is a bedrock of international arbitration. Over the years, the impartiality and independence of unilaterally party-appointed arbitrators - and, by extension, the legitimacy of party-appointments on international tribunals - have been subject to scrutiny and discourse among scholars and practitioners alike. The opposites of the scholarly discourse may be summarized as follows: While critics of unilateral party-appointment argue that this in itself prevents impartiality, supporters claim that the parties' ability to unilaterally appoint an arbitrator ensures so-called representativeness and structural counterbalance on the arbitral tribunal, thereby ensuring fairness in the decision-making process. At the core of this discourse lies a number of empirical studies that seem to confirm that party-appointed arbitrators have an affiliation bias in favour of the party that appoints them, affecting their decision-making. As a consequence, several initiatives have aimed to eliminate the practice of party-appointment of arbitrators.

This chapter discusses affiliation bias and potential solutions that ensure impartiality and contribute to the legitimacy of the arbitral tribunal and it's decision-making. To provide the necessary backdrop for this discussion, §6.02 provides an overview of the arguments for and against party-appointments, by presenting two well-known empirical studies seemingly confirming affiliation bias, i.e., the study by Albert Jan van den Berg and the study by Sergio Puig and Anton Strezhnev,[1] as well as Catherine A.

* We are grateful to associates Kanwarjot Kaur and Hugo C. Pignol for assisting us in our drafting, *inter alia*, by doing research and proof reading.

1. Albert Jan van den Berg, *Dissenting Opinions by Party-Appointed Arbitrators in Investment Arbitration*, in Mahnoush Arsanjani et al. (ed.): *Looking to the Future: Essays on International*

Rogers' article criticizing these studies,[2] addressing their weaknesses and making the case in favour of why party-appointed arbitrators function as a 'structural check against various forms of cognitive bias that necessarily exist among all arbitrators on all arbitral tribunals'.[3] It should be noted from the outset that while the studies by both van den Berg and Puig/Strezhnev are based on investment arbitration cases (for the obvious reason that such awards to a greater extent are publicly available), the perspective of this chapter is commercial arbitration. It is therefore important to note that affiliation bias appears to be considered a more extensive problem in investment arbitration than in commercial arbitration. For instance, commenting on certain criticisms of his 2009 study, van den Berg notes that 'the percentage of dissenting opinions in commercial arbitration is much less than in investment arbitration and that the percentage was decreasing in the former, but increasing in the latter'.[4] Nevertheless, affiliation bias remains an issue also in commercial arbitration. Then, in §6.03, we present alternative solutions to party-appointment. In this context, we also address the advantages and disadvantages of the Norwegian model of joint appointment of the arbitral tribunal and consider certain aspects which may affect the suitability of this model in other jurisdictions.

§6.02 ARE PARTY-APPOINTED ARBITRATORS DEPENDENT ON THE APPOINTING PARTY?

[A] Critics of Party-Appointment

[1] The Root Cause of Affiliation Bias

Party-appointment has been characterized as an 'ill-conceived' and 'unprincipled tradition' that creates a 'moral hazard'.[5] It has been asserted that the 'root of the problem is the appointment method' and that unilateral party appointment 'may create

Law in Honor of W. Michael Reisman, 2011 ('van den Berg'), pp. 821-843; and Sergio Puig and Anton Strezhnev, *Affiliation Bias in Arbitration: An Experimental Approach*, Journal of Legal Studies, vol. 46 (June 2017) https://doi.org/10.1086/694416 (accessed 1 October 2025) ('Puig/Strezhnev'), pp. 371-398. The main focus of this article is the available solutions to mitigate affiliation bias and, as such, we have not exhaustively reviewed all available research on affiliation bias. When selecting the van den Berg study and the Puig/Strezhnev study as examples for the purposes of this article, we have done so on the basis that they are relatively well known among the practitioners in the field of arbitration.

2. Catherine A. Rogers, *Reconceptualizing the Party-Appointed Arbitrator and the Meaning of Impartiality*, Harvard International Law Journal, vol. 64, No. 1 (Winter 2023) ('Rogers'), pp. 137-202.
3. *Ibid.*, p. 137.
4. Albert Jan van den Berg, *Charles Brower's Problem with 100%: Dissenting Opinions by Party-Appointed Arbitrators in Investment Arbitration*, in David D. Caron et al. (eds), *Practising Virtue Inside International Arbitration* ('van den Berg 2015'), pp. 504-513, on p. 504. This observation is based on van den Berg comparisons against statistics from the International Chamber of Commerce (ICC) for the years 2004 through to 2008, *see* van den Berg, p. 832.
5. Jan Paulsson, *Moral Hazard in International Dispute Resolution*, ICSID Review, vol. 25 (2010), pp. 339, 340, 349, 354 https://doi.org/10.1093/icsidreview/25.2.339 (accessed 1 October 2025).

arbitrators who may be dependent in some way on the parties that appointed them'.[6] Critics of party-appointment distinguish between so-called selection bias on the one hand and affiliation bias on the other hand.[7] Selection bias refers to the fact that the parties seek to select arbitrators with views similar to theirs and are likely to view their case favourably,[8] for instance, based on the parties' knowledge of the arbitrator's legal expertise and experience and the arbitrator's positions on the relevant issues in dispute that may be discerned from his or her writing or similar. Affiliation bias goes beyond selection bias, describing arbitrator bias caused by implicit preferences for the appointing party.[9] Critics of party-appointment typically point to structural features resulting in affiliation bias, such as party-appointed arbitrators' alleged financial incentive to rule in favour of the party or the class of parties that appointed them in hopes of securing future appointments.[10] Both the van den Berg study and the Puig/Strezhnev study were designed to isolate affiliation effects in an attempt to empirically ascertain whether and to what extent such effects are factors in the decision-making of party-appointed arbitrators.

[2] Key Take-Aways from the Van Den Berg Study

The van den Berg study was undertaken in relation to the debate of dissenting opinions in international arbitration. Prior to conducting his study, van den Berg was a proponent for allowing dissenting opinions only in specific and limited circumstances, i.e., in case of fundamental flaws with the arbitral process, such as serious violations of due process, or in instances where the arbitrator is threatened with physical harm if not dissenting.[11] According to van den Berg, the study vindicated his view.[12] Of greater interest for the purposes of this chapter, however, is what van den Berg's analysis of arbitral decisions in investment cases revealed about affiliation bias among party-appointed arbitrators. The study may be summarized as follows: In his analysis, van den Berg looked at '150 publicly reported decisions, whether jurisdictional or on the merits, in investment cases', drawn from 'the Investment Treaty Arbitration (ITA) and ICSID websites'.[13] The study covers decisions reported on the aforementioned websites until June 2009.[14]

According to van den Berg, most of these decisions were made by three-member tribunals. In his article, van den Berg notes that the presiding arbitrator rarely dissented. However, of the 150 decisions analysed, dissenting opinions were issued by

6. van den Berg, pp. 824-825.
7. *See, e.g.*, van den Berg, p. 824; and Puig/Strezhnev, pp. 372-373.
8. van den Berg, p. 824; and Puig/Strezhnev, p. 373.
9. *See, e.g.*, Puig/Stezhnev, p. 373.
10. *See, e.g.*, Rogers, pp. 149-150.
11. van den Berg, p. 831.
12. *Ibid.*
13. *Ibid.*, p. 824.
14. *Ibid.*, footnote 11 and pp. 824 and 834. The annex the van den Berg article contains an overview of cases through 2008, but van den Berg stresses that the subsequent decisions reported until June 2009 do not differ from those to listed in the annex, *see* p. 834.

a party-appointed arbitrator in 34 cases, i.e., in 22% of the cases, and nearly all of the dissenting opinions were issued by the arbitrator appointed by the party that lost the case in whole or in part.

Taking selection bias into account, van den Berg concludes that the statistics show that dissenting opinions were universally issued in favour of the party that appointed the dissenter and points out that this raises concerns about neutrality.[15] In a later article, while maintaining that affiliation bias raises neutrality concerns, van den Berg seemingly modifies his position somewhat, toning down the scope of the problem: He clarifies that, in his opinion (and contrary to that of his critics), the crucial question is not the relative percentage of cases in which dissenting opinions are issued.[16] Rather, he queries why dissenting opinions were issued by the arbitrator appointed by the party that had lost the case and, after reviewing the dissents and opining that they were not made on a principled basis, why they were issued at all.[17] Van den Berg expresses concern that the practice of dissents in investment arbitration may have reached a point where a party-appointed arbitrator is expected to dissent if the party that appointed him or her has lost the case (so-called mandatory dissent).[18]

[3] Key Take-Aways from the Puig/Strezhnev Study

Puig and Strezhnev's study deals directly with the assertion that party-appointed arbitrators tend to be biased in favour of their appointers and seeks to measure this alleged effect using survey experiments with arbitration experts around the world.

More specifically, Puig and Strezhnev conducted an e-mail study, recruiting participants by collecting publicly available e-mail addresses of arbitrators and lawyers specializing in arbitration (the 'arbitrators'), primarily from lists published on the websites of arbitration institutions and in the directories of other professional organizations.[19]

The Puig/Strezhnev study consists of two e-mail surveys, the first conducted in the fall of 2015 and a replication study conducted in the spring of 2017. The participants in the study were presented with a brief vignette describing a hypothetical arbitration between an investor and a state. Elements of the vignette were randomized for each participant to study how the responses might vary across different scenarios.[20]

In the first e-mail survey in the fall of 2015, participants were told that they were appointed either by the respondent, by the claimant, by agreement of the litigating parties or simply that they were appointed to the tribunal, without any mention of the appointing method (i.e., so-called blind appointment, *see* §6.03[B] below). The vignette varied the implied resource endowment of the claimant and the respondent. Furthermore, the vignette varied the type of ruling across the outcome of the case, i.e.:

15. *Ibid.*, pp. 824-825.
16. van den Berg 2015, pp. 507-508.
17. *Ibid.*, p. 508.
18. *Ibid.*, p. 504. *See also* van den Berg, p. 830.
19. Puig/Strezhnev, p. 379.
20. *Ibid.*, pp. 376-377.

(i) claimant wins; (ii) respondent wins; (iii) respondent wins on technical grounds due to lack of jurisdiction of the tribunal; and (iv) the case is dismissed because the claimant's claims are manifestly without legal merit. The participants were then asked how they thought the parties' expenses in the dispute, including the cost of legal representation, should be apportioned. The choices available were to have one party reimburse the other for all or some of its expenses or to have each party bear its own expenses.[21] The participants were also asked to briefly discuss the reasoning behind their decision.

According to Puig and Strezhnev, 538 individuals responded to this e-mailed survey.[22] However, not all of these individuals completed the survey or answered all of the relevant questions, meaning that they received only 257 complete responses.[23] Puig and Strezhnev report that, on average, arbitrators were about 18 percentage points more likely to award all costs to the winning party when they were appointed by the winner rather than the loser.

In the replication study in the spring of 2017, Puig and Strezhnev sought to evaluate how the participants would reason through a decision on damages, i.e., how much the claimant should be awarded given that the tribunal has found the respondent at fault.[24] The participants were constrained to choose exclusively between the claimant's proposal and the respondent's proposal for the amount to be awarded in damages.[25] This study also retested the original question about the allocation of costs.[26] While 644 consented to participate in the study, only 248 of the participants responded to the questions on damages, and 252 participants answered the replication of the question about costs. Puig and Strezhnev found that with respect to the question of awarding damages, on average, arbitrators appointed by the claimant were about 15 percentage points more likely to choose the claimant's damages proposal compared with arbitrators appointed by the respondent. With respect to the question of cost allocation, arbitrators appointed by the claimant (winner) were about 15% more likely to have the respondent reimburse all of the claimant's costs.

[B] Defenders of Party-Appointment

[1] Arbitration as a Private Dispute-Resolution Process Subject to Party Control

Arbitration is a private dispute-resolution process subject to party control. The purpose of this dispute resolution mechanism is to give the parties more autonomy over the dispute-resolution process as compared to ordinary court proceedings. Arguably,

21. The relevant arbitration rules – ICSID 2006 – grant complete discretion to the arbitrators on costs and there is little precedential guidance for how the arbitrators should use such discretion. *See* Puig/Strezhnev, p. 379.
22. *Ibid.*
23. *Ibid.*
24. *Ibid.*, p. 383.
25. *Ibid.*, p. 384.
26. *Ibid.*, pp. 383 and 385.

party-appointment is a primary tool for exercising control and giving a party greater ownership of the dispute.[27] For instance, as observed by Rogers, party-appointments in international arbitration were originally implemented to obviate, and not introduce, bias in the decision-making process:[28] Arbitration as a dispute-resolution mechanism allows the parties to avoid the real or perceived biases of the opposing party's national courts. Furthermore, by allowing each party to appoint an arbitrator, no single party's nationality or legal culture dominates or is excluded from the tribunal. Consequently, party-appointments are well established in practice and an expected feature of arbitral proceedings. Proponents of party-appointments argue that active party participation in constituting the tribunal increases confidence in arbitral outcomes and, therefore, the perception of international arbitration legitimacy.

While it may be tempting to identify Rogers as a proponent of party-appointments, it is clearly stipulated in Rogers' article that her article 'neither supports the critics nor the defenders' of party-appointment.[29] Traditionally, proponents of party-appointments focus on either the usual practical defence of parties being used to party-appointments and unwilling to give them up, or the perceived legitimacy defence that active participation in constituting the tribunal supposedly lends to the arbitral process. According to Rogers, however, neither of these traditional defences addresses the core criticism that party-appointed arbitrators inject bias into a tribunal that is supposed to be impartial.[30] In her article, Rogers takes the starting-point that 'various forms of cognitive bias ... necessarily exists among all arbitrators on all arbitral tribunals', that '[a]rbitrators' cognitive bias cannot be eliminated, even by eliminating party-appointed arbitrators', but that '[t]hey can, however, be bounded and counter-balanced by reconceiving party-arbitrators as a type of Devil's Advocate that guards against the cognitive biases that distort tribunal decision making'.[31] Consequently, and as mentioned in the introduction of this chapter and as elaborated on directly below, Rogers concludes that party-appointments is a structural check against various forms of cognitive bias.

[2] Key Take-Aways from the Rogers Article

According to Rogers, the question at issue is not whether party-appointed arbitrators are biased or not, but rather: (i) which forms of bias are legitimate; (ii) who decides which forms of bias are legitimate; and (iii) how to police the boundary between legitimate and illegitimate forms of bias. In order to address these questions, Rogers examines 'what various empirical studies have revealed about the individual biases that affect all decisionmakers and all adjudicators',[32] addressing, *inter alia*, the van den Berg study and the Puig/Strezhnev study.

27. Similarly, *see ibid.*, p. 371.
28. Rogers, p. 145, with further references.
29. *Ibid.*, p. 142.
30. *Ibid.*
31. *Ibid.*, p. 137 (summary).
32. *Ibid.*, p. 142.

With respect to the van den Berg study, Rogers agrees that separate and dissenting opinions can provide valuable insights regarding individual arbitrators, who otherwise act as part of a three-person tribunal, but opines that flawed methodologies cause the study to significantly overstate its conclusion. Rogers' criticism may be summarized as follows: First, van den Berg classifies all separate opinions as dissenting opinions.[33] In other words, the study did not take into account that not all separate opinions necessarily disagree with the outcome.[34] Second, van den Berg seems to assume that separate opinions by party-appointed arbitrators necessarily benefit the appointing party.[35] Rogers notes that even if a separate opinion can be characterized as consistent with an appointing party's position on particular issues, it does not necessarily follow that the opinion favours that party, or by extension, undermines legitimacy.[36] Third, Rogers argues that it is inaccurate to assume that a separate opinion that concurs only in the final outcome is more favourable to the appointing party than a unanimous award.[37] Here, Rogers basically observes that an opinion that concurs in the outcome confirms the losing party's loss and underscores that this loss may, in fact, be justified by more than one reason.[38] Similarly, other authors, such as Brower and Rosenberg, have also argued that a number of the dissents in van den Berg's study 'are benign or actually disfavour the party that appointed the dissenter'.[39]

In addition to the methodological issues regarding classification, Rogers observes that van den Berg 'ignore[s] the baseline rate of separate decisions'.[40] Rogers' point is simply that while van den Berg contends 'that dissents by party-appointed arbitrators are a big problem', separate opinions were issued 'in only 22% of arbitrations in [his] sample ...'.[41] Rogers notes that this means that 'tribunals rendered unanimous decisions in 78% ... of cases', concluding that such a 'rate for unanimous awards suggests a surprisingly high degree of consensus on investment tribunals'.[42] This point – and that this fact alone undermines the worst impartiality concerns – has also been made by Brower and Rosenberg.[43] In addition, both Rogers and Brower/Rosenberg emphasize that it is also reasonable to assume that most separate opinions make awards more difficult to challenge and, as pointed out by Rogers, this 'may even increase party confidence in awards'.[44]

As for the Puig/Strezhnev study, Rogers observes that Puig and Strezhnev's observations are important 'because they suggest that the mere fact that an arbitrator

33. *Ibid.*, p. 152.
34. *Ibid.*
35. *Ibid.*, p. 153.
36. *Ibid.*
37. *Ibid.*, p. 154.
38. *Ibid.*
39. Charles N. Brower and Charles B. Rosenberg, *The Death of the Two-Headed Nightingale: Why the Paulsson-van den Berg Presumption that Party-Appointed Arbitrators are Untrustworthy is Wrongheaded*, in William W. Park (ed.), *Arbitration International*, 2013, vol. 29, No. 1 ('Brower et al'), pp. 7-44, on pp. 32-34.
40. Rogers, p. 154.
41. *Ibid.*
42. *Ibid.*, p. 155.
43. *See also* Brower et al., p. 28.
44. Rogers, p. 156 and Brower et al., pp. 41-42.

was appointed by a particular party may have a measurable influence on that arbitrator's decisionmaking and that bias arises even when the stakes are extremely low'.[45] However, Rogers also points out that experimental research about decision-maker bias has inherent limitations:[46] For instance, she highlights that writing neutral vignettes is difficult. Moreover, she points to the difference between answering a hypothetical question during a time-limited study and living through a case for two or three years as a party-appointee. Rogers also notes that 'the essential methodological feature of this type of research – the ability to isolate one specific aspect of decision-making – can itself distort outcomes'.[47] In essence, her argument is that adjudicators are subject to a wide range of cognitive biases, 'some of which collide with, overlap, intersect, amplify and even cancel out other biases'. This 'push-and-pull effect … would be impossible to measure and, if measurable, may only confirm that arbitrators are subject to the same foibles as all humans'.[48] Finally, Rogers observes that Puig/Strezhnev's study 'aims to measure the extent to which extra-legal factors produced outcomes that differ from the "correct" outcomes in particular cases'. According to Rogers, however, 'it is not only impossible to identify the correct legal outcome for a particular case, but also inappropriate to assume there is only correct legal outcome for a case'.[49]

Rogers makes it clear that her criticism (as summarized above) is not intended to detract from the valuable contributions of the studies, but merely to warn against drawing too strong conclusions from their results and basing proposed reforms on those conclusions.[50] She observes that decision-makers are not only affected by individual bias (such as party-appointment-related biases) but also group-based biases, such as influences from personal relationships among panel members or an inclination to defer to more prominent panel members. Pointing out that the van den Berg study confirms that the vast majority of international arbitral awards are unanimous, she suggests that this high degree of unanimity may indicate that collegiality in tribunals encourages cohesive decision-making and discourages dissent (so-called groupthink).[51] Rogers then goes on to discuss research suggesting introducing a devil's advocate to safeguard against potential group-based bias or 'groupthink'. The devil's advocate idea is to systemize challenge within a tight-knit group of decision-makers whenever consensus emerges within this group.[52] Observing that 'arbitrators have little financial gain from policing tribunal decisionmaking or insisting that a tribunal second-guess its intuitive decisionmaking',[53] Rogers emphasizes that party-appointed arbitrators are well placed to function as a devil's arbitrator. Her point is that party-appointed arbitrators, by the very fact that they are party-appointed, are

45. Rogers, p. 157.
46. *Ibid.*, p. 159.
47. *Ibid.*
48. *Ibid.*
49. *Ibid.*, pp. 159-160.
50. *Ibid.*
51. *Ibid.*, p. 167.
52. *Ibid.*, p. 170.
53. *Ibid.*, p. 169.

able to 'provide real-time, on-site, constructive quality control in tribunal decisionmaking' and 'serve as a structural counter-balance to the opposing party's appointed arbitrator'.[54] Also, Brower and Rosenberg have underscored how dissenting opinions between the arbitrators may ease the deliberative process and contribute to producing a better award.[55]

Rogers points to three aspects of the party-appointed arbitrator's role which facilitate their function in this regard:[56] The ability of parties to appoint an arbitrator ensures representativeness on the tribunal, in the sense that 'the tribunal includes among its members arbitrators who are influenced by those extra-legal factors that are aligned with extra-legal factors considered most important by the parties'.[57] Further, the party-appointed arbitrator serves as a check against decision-making shortcuts by the tribunal as a result of individual and collective cognitive biases. Finally, the party-appointed arbitrator serves as a counterbalance to the opposing party-appointed arbitrator, ensuring structural impartiality on the tribunal. Against this background, Rogers points out that '[t]he risk of bias from the party-appointment process may be less concerning compared to various other forms of cognitive bias' and argues that, '[w]hen outcomes cannot be corrected on appeal, structural counterbalance and representativeness on tribunals are essential to ensure fairness and predictability in the decision-making process'.[58] While recognizing that unilateral party-appointment may not be ideal, Rogers concludes that when evaluating whether to permit or prohibit party-appointment it might be useful to consider the internal role to counter bias that the party-appointed arbitrators play on a tribunal.[59]

[C] Preliminary Conclusions

The empirical studies conducted, *inter alia,* by van den Berg and by Puig and Strezhnev seem to confirm the anecdotal stories from experienced and highly respected arbitrators and practitioners alike of party-appointed arbitrators not acting impartially. While Rogers in her article challenges certain aspects of the methodologies underlying the van den Berg study and the Puig/Strezhnev study, she does not challenge the existence of affiliation bias as such. Rather, Rogers queries whether the scope of the problem is as extensive as van den Berg and Puig/Strezhnev indicate – and, more importantly, whether affiliation bias in fact may serve to counteract other biases arbitrators inevitably have and thus may secure the quality of the arbitral tribunal's decision-making.

Irrespective of where one stands on this issue, it is important to be aware of the potential for affiliation bias and to mitigate any negative impacts of such potential bias

54. *Ibid.*, p. 174.
55. Brower et al., pp. 33-34.
56. Rogers, p. 190.
57. *Ibid.*, pp. 191-192.
58. *Ibid.*, p. 201.
59. *Ibid.*

when possible. In the next section, we will look at the available alternatives to party-appointment and their advantages and disadvantages in mitigating bias.

§6.03 ALTERNATIVE SOLUTIONS

[A] Appointment by an Arbitral Institute

One alternative approach to unilateral party-appointment is appointment by an independent authority, such as an arbitral institute.

Appointments by arbitral institutes are quite frequently used when it comes to selecting the chairperson. Among the Nordic institutes, both the SCC and the NAC opt for this solution.[60] Other well-established institutes such as the ICC and the SIAC also refer to the appointment of the chair by the institute.[61]

Appointment by arbitral institutes of sole arbitrators or co-arbitrators seems to be less common – but does occur. Here, the rules of the London Court of International Arbitration serve as an example. Pursuant to Article 5 of these rules, the LCIA Court is solely responsible for the appointment of the arbitral tribunal, irrespective of the number of arbitrators.[62]

The limited use of this approach in the appointment of sole arbitrators or co-arbitrators is not very surprising: While appointment by arbitral institutes or other independent authorities may resolve some of the concerns emanating from the party-appointment system, such as affiliation bias, it completely ignores the principle of freedom of choice of the parties.[63] The latter principle is of particular importance as the selection of arbitrators is frequently seen as one of the most valuable characteristics of arbitration in comparison to conventional court litigation.[64]

---

60. The SCC Arbitration Rules, 2023 (SCC Rules) Art. 17(4): 'Where the Arbitral Tribunal is to consist of more than one arbitrator … the Board shall appoint the chairperson', and the Nordic Arbitration Centre of the Iceland Chamber of Commerce Arbitration Rules, 2013 (NAC Rules) Art. 12(4): 'Where the dispute is to be referred to three arbitrators, … the third arbitrator, who will act as the Presiding Arbitrator, shall be appointed by the NAC Board …'.
61. The ICC Rules of Arbitration, 2021 (ICC Rules) Art. 12(5): 'Where the dispute is to be referred to three arbitrators, the third arbitrator, who will act as president of the arbitral tribunal, shall be appointed by the Court …', and the Arbitration Rules of the Singapore International Arbitration Centre, 2025 (SIAC Rules) Art. 22.3: 'The presiding arbitrator shall be appointed by the President', i.e., the President of the SIAC Court.
62. *See also* the Rules of the Milan Chamber of Commerce, 2023 Art. 15, 2: 'Unless otherwise agreed in the arbitration agreement, the sole arbitrator shall be appointed by the Arbitral Council'; and the Rules of the Dubai International Arbitration Centre, 2022 Art. 12.1: 'All arbitrators shall be appointed by the Arbitration Court …'.
63. *See*, for instance, Sergio Puig, *Blind Appointments in Arbitration*, in Aaron S. Kesselheim and Christopher T. Robertson (eds), *Blinding as a Solution to Bias, Strengthening Biomedical Science, Forensic Science and Law, Academic Press, 2016* ('Puig'), pp. 307-318, on p. 309.
64. *See, e.g.*, the Queen Mary/White & Case surveys. In the 2015 International Arbitration Survey: Improvements and Innovations in International Arbitration, pp. 18-19 'free choice of arbitrators' was ranked fourth among the most valuable characteristics of arbitration. In the 2018 International Arbitration Survey: The Evolution of International Arbitration, Chart 3, on p. 7, the ability of parties to select arbitrators was still ranked fourth. *See also* the International Dispute Resolution Surveys from Singapore Management University (SIDRA Survey). In the 2024 SIDRA

Furthermore, appointment by arbitral institutes grants the institute a great deal of control over the proceedings.[65] The effect of this transfer of power from the parties to the arbitral institute will of course depend on the institute in question, including its policies, bureaucracy and pool of available arbitrators. However, the interests of the arbitral institutes may not always align and coincide with the interests of the parties, which could potentially complicate matters. For these reasons, appointment by arbitral institutes might not appear as an attractive alternative for the users of arbitration.

[B] 'Blind' Appointments

A second alternative approach, which does maintain the fundamental feature of party control, is 'blind' appointments. Blind appointments allow parties to appoint arbitrators, but prevent the arbitrators from knowing which party appointed them, which should mitigate bias and adversarial influence of explicitly known party appointments.[66]

To our knowledge, the use of blind appointments is limited in practice. We are only aware of one arbitral institute that has adopted this as the default method of appointing arbitrators: the New York-based International Institute of Conflict Prevention and Dispute Resolution.[67] However, there are scholars arguing for more broadly introducing blind appointments as a useful approach to reduce bias. Among these are Puig and Strezhnev, who conclude that the results of their study provide support for implementing blind appointments in arbitration proceedings.[68]

We agree that blind appointments are an interesting alternative to unilateral party appointment. Blind appointments have multiple benefits, the chief of which is that they resolve some of the concerns latent in unilateral party appointment without eradicating the practice of party appointments, which parties value highly.[69] This approach ensures the legitimacy of the appointment and the resulting arbitral award without going against the firmly rooted traditions of party autonomy in commercial arbitration.[70]

However, blind appointments are not without their own challenges, as Puig and Strezhnev acknowledge.[71] Certain difficulties are the practical matters involved, which

---

Survey, exhibit 5.2, on p. 15, the factor of flexibility in choice of arbitrators ranked as fifth out of fourteen in preferences for arbitration as a dispute resolution mechanism. In addition, the 2020 SIDRA Survey, p. 11, notes that '[i]n relation to impartiality and neutrality, satisfaction with international litigation (59%) ranks lower than that of arbitration (68%) and mediation (72%). This may stem from greater flexibility with regards to the choice of arbitrator and mediator in arbitration and mediation'.

65. Puig, p. 314.
66. Puig/Strezhnev, p. 375.
67. CPR Rules for Administered Arbitration of International Disputes, 2019 Art. 5.1(c) and 5.4.
68. Puig/Strezhnev, p. 394.
69. *See supra* n. 65.
70. *See, e.g.*, Puig/Strezhnev, p. 375.
71. Puig/Strezhnev, pp. 393-394. *See also* Sergio Puig, *Blind Appointments in Arbitration, in Blinding as a Solution to Bias: Strengthening Biomedical Science, Forensic Science, and Law,* 2016, Elsevier (Chapter 20, pp. 307-318), on pp. 315-316.

require involving an additional step – namely, the arbitral institute – with the potential of delay this might entail. The crucial role played by the institute in blind appointments is also a reason why this approach might not work in countries such as Norway, where ad hoc arbitration without institutional involvement remains the preferred and utilized form of arbitration. While the first concern of time can be mitigated by stringent time limits for the arbitral institution to make its choice, shifting the long-standing habits of parties accustomed to ad hoc arbitration to a mechanism involving greater institutional involvement may prove more challenging.

[C] 'The Norwegian Approach':[72] Joint Appointment of the Whole Tribunal

A third potential approach is joint appointment, i.e., that the parties agree on who to appoint.

Joint appointment is often used for the appointment of sole arbitrators. All of the Nordic institutes opt for this approach,[73] as do numerous institutes outside of the Nordics.[74] Joint appointment is sometimes also used for appointing the chair. This

72. Borgar Høgetveit Berg, *Appointment of Arbitrators: The Norwegian Approach, Scandinavian Studies in Law*, vol. 63, 2017 ('Berg'), pp. 13-22.
73. *See* the SCC Arbitration Rules Art. 17(3): 'Where the Arbitral Tribunal is to consist of a sole arbitrator, the parties shall be given ten days to jointly appoint the arbitrator …'; the DIA Rules Art. 19(2): 'Where the case is to be decided by a Sole Arbitrator, the parties may jointly appoint the Sole Arbitrator …'; the FAI Rules Art. 18.1: 'Where the parties have agreed that the dispute shall be referred to a sole arbitrator, the claimant and the respondent may jointly nominate the sole arbitrator …'; the NAC Rules Art. 12(2): 'The parties may jointly nominate a sole arbitrator for confirmation'; the Rules of the Arbitration and Dispute Resolution Institute of the Oslo Chamber of Commerce, 2017 (OCC Rules) Art. 8(2): 'To the extent possible, the parties shall jointly appoint the arbitral tribunal'; and the NOMA Arbitration Rules, 2024 (NOMA Rules) Art. 6(1): 'If the parties have agreed that a sole arbitrator is to be appointed, the parties shall, as far as possible, appoint the sole arbitrator jointly'.
74. *See, e.g.*, the ICC Rules of Arbitration Art. 12(3): 'Where the parties have agreed that the dispute shall be resolved by a sole arbitrator, they may, by agreement, nominate the sole arbitrator…'; the SIAC Rules Art. 21.1: 'Where a sole arbitrator is to be appointed, the parties may jointly nominate the sole arbitrator…'; the Rules of the Hong Kong Arbitration Centre, 2024 Art. 7.1(a): 'where the parties have agreed before the arbitration commences that the dispute shall be referred to a sole arbitrator, they shall jointly designate the sole arbitrator …'; the Asian International Arbitration Centre, 2023 Rule 3(4): 'the Parties are free to nominate the sole arbitrator …'; the Rules of the Saudi Centre for Commercial Arbitration, 2023 Art. 16: 'If the matter is to be resolved by one arbitrator, the parties should attempt to nominate the arbitrator jointly …'; the Rules of the Istanbul Arbitration Centre, 2015 Art. 14(1): 'In cases where the dispute shall be resolved by a Sole Arbitrator, the parties shall choose the Sole Arbitrator together'; the Rules of the Swiss Arbitration Centre, 2021 Art. 10(1): 'Where the parties have agreed that the dispute shall be referred to a sole arbitrator, they shall jointly designate the sole arbitrator …'; the Rules of the Vienna International Arbitration Centre, 2021 Art. 17(3): 'If the dispute is to be resolved by a sole arbitrator, the parties shall jointly nominate a sole arbitrator…'; the Rules of the German Arbitration Institute, 2018 Art. 11: 'If the arbitral tribunal is comprised of a sole arbitrator, the parties may jointly nominate the sole arbitrator'; and the UNCITRAL Rules, 2021 Art. 8: 'If the parties have agreed that a sole arbitrator is to be appointed and if within 30 days after receipt by all other parties of a proposal for the appointment of a sole arbitrator the parties have not reached agreement thereon …'.

latter approach is adopted by all the Nordic institutes, except for the SCC and the NAC,[75] but we have not been able to identify this approach outside the Nordics.

However, when it comes to the appointment of *co-arbitrators*, or the whole arbitral tribunal (if it consists of more than one arbitrator), joint appointment is a mechanism that is rarely used. In this respect, Norway is the exception.

In Norway, with the entry into force of the Norwegian Arbitration Act in 2005,[76] the following rule was introduced: 'The parties shall, to the extent possible, jointly appoint the arbitral tribunal'.[77] Prior to the implementation of the Arbitration Act, the Dispute Resolution Act of 1915 adopted the traditional approach of unilateral party appointment, with the co-arbitrators appointing the chair.[78] While the Arbitration Act kept this rule as a fall-back rule, it implemented joint appointment as the new main rule. According to the preparatory works of the Arbitration Act, the reason for the implementation of this rule was to ensure an independent and impartial tribunal, which in turn would increase trust in the tribunal.[79]

Even if there are no available statistics on the topic, it seems that the rule on joint appointment has been very well received in the Norwegian arbitration community.[80] In addition to the fact that joint appointment actually seems to work quite well in practice, the smooth transition from unilateral party appointment to joint appointment as the main rule may also be explained by its widespread usage in the arbitral traditions of Norway even prior to its legislative implementation. Already in the 1980s, joint appointment was referred to in standard shipbuilding contracts.[81] Furthermore, in 2001, the starting point in the Rules of the Oslo Chamber of Commerce was that parties should be given the opportunity to agree on who should serve as arbitrators. Unilateral party-appointment, with the institute appointing the chair, was the fall-back option if the parties were not able to agree.

Following the implementation of joint appointment of the tribunal in Norwegian law, the wording of the OCC Rule on appointment of the arbitrators was aligned with the Norwegian Arbitration Act. The current rule, Article 8(2), which was introduced with the revision of the OCC Rules in 2017, now uses the same formulation as section 13(2) of the Arbitration Act.[82] Later that same year, the Nordic Offshore and Maritime

75. *See* the DIA Rules Art. 19(3): 'The third arbitrator, who shall be the President of the Arbitral Tribunal, may be appointed jointly by the parties ...'; the FAI Rules Art. 19.1(d): 'the claimant and the respondent may jointly nominate the third arbitrator, who shall act as the presiding arbitrator ...'; the OCC Rules Art. 8(2): 'To the extent possible, the parties shall jointly appoint the arbitral tribunal'; and the NOMA Rules Art. 7(1): 'If the parties have agreed on appointing a tribunal of three arbitrators, the parties shall, as far as possible, appoint the arbitrators jointly.'
76. Lov om voldgift 14. mai 2004 nr. 25.
77. Section 13(2).
78. Lov om rettergangsmåten for tvistemål (tvistemålsloven) 13. august 1015 nr. 6.
79. NOU 2001: 33 Voldgift p. 65.
80. Berg, p. 16.
81. *See, inter alia,* 'den norske standardkontrakt for bygging av skip' (1981) § 17 and 'den norske standardkontrakt for reparasjon av skip m.v'. (1985) § 16, referred to in Sjur Brækhus, Voldgift: erfaringer og refleksjoner, Lov og Rett, 1999, pp. 259-282 on pp. 265-266. *See also* Berg, p. 16.
82. The OCC Rules Art. 8(2): 'To the extent possible, the parties shall jointly appoint the arbitral tribunal.'

Arbitration Association was established, incorporating joint appointment as the starting point in the NOMA Rules.[83] However, to our knowledge, no other arbitral institutes have adopted a similar approach.

Joint appointment as a method for appointing arbitral tribunals has many of the same advantages as blind appointments. In the same way as blind appointments, it relieves the proceedings from the effects of unilateral party appointments while retaining the benefits of party-involvement in the appointment process. However, as the Norwegian rule on joint appointment covers the whole arbitral tribunal, it actually gives the parties *more* control than the traditional system of unilateral party-appointment. Not only are the parties in charge of appointing the co-arbitrators, but they also retain the power of appointing the chair.

It may also be argued that joint appointment makes it easier to take a more holistic approach to the composition of the tribunal, ensuring that it has the necessary skills required by the case in question and safeguarding diversity. However, while we agree that joint appointment undoubtedly creates a potential for increasing diversity on tribunals in theory, this has only to a limited extent been achieved in practice.[84] With respect to safeguarding diversity on tribunals, the involvement of arbitral institutes seems to achieve better results.[85] That being said, the more limited success regarding diversity on tribunals cannot be seen as a downside of joint appointment as such. Rather, as most arbitrations in Norway are ad hoc, not institutional, there is no public scrutiny to incentivize the safeguarding of diversity.

When it comes to potential downsides, Puig argues that 'in practice not only is agreement between the parties difficult to achieve, but also these types of appointments are often disguised party appointments ("I agree to your arbitrator, if you agree to mine")'.[86] However, our experience from a Norwegian context is the opposite: The model works well, and it is not particularly 'difficult to achieve' an agreement on appointment of the whole tribunal between the parties.

Having said that, a party could undoubtedly seek to delay the arbitral proceedings by drawing out the joint appointment process and refusing to achieve unanimity. To counteract such behaviour, the Norwegian Arbitration Act provides for unilateral

83. NOMA Rules, 2017 Art. 6(1): 'If the parties agree a sole arbitrator is to be appointed, a sole arbitrator shall at the request of a party be appointed by NOMA, unless a sole arbitrator is appointed jointly by the parties'; and Art. 7(1): 'The parties shall, as far as possible, appoint the arbitrators jointly'. Articles 6(1) and 7(1) were continued in the 2021 and 2024 updates of the NOMA Rules, however with a slightly updated wording in the 2024 update.
84. In a survey on diversity in arbitration in a Norwegian context, conducted by the law firms BAHR and Wikborg Rein in 2021, the respondents reported that a female arbitrator had been appointed in 16.9% of the arbitrations they had participated in and more than one female arbitrator had only been appointed in 2.8% of the cases.
85. For instance, the SCC's statistics for 2023 show that of the arbitrators appointed by the SCC, the parties and the co-arbitrators, 39% were female and 61% were male. The arbitral institute generally appoint a larger number of female arbitrators than parties and co-arbitrators. The SCC's 2023 statistics show that of the arbitrators appointed by the SCC, 55% were female and 45% were male. By comparison, the parties appointed 31% female arbitrators and 69% male arbitrators and the co-arbitrators appointed only 10% female arbitrators.
86. Puig, pp. 313-314.

party-appointment as a fall-back rule.[87] This, in turn, raises the question of how the qualification 'to the extent possible' in Article 13(2) of the Norwegian Arbitration Act should be understood, as this directly impacts how quickly a party may trigger the fall-back rule of unilateral party appointment.[88] According to Berg, '[t]here are good arguments for a party being entitled to demand that the opposing party makes a loyal and genuine effort to reach an agreement, for example, that one at least should require both parties to contribute by exchanging suggestions for candidates to the appointment of arbitrators. Such a duty is found in the wording "unable to agree" in Section 13 Subsection 3 – and can also be derived from the purpose of the provision.'[89]

As for the concern of 'disguised party appointments' referred to by Puig, this is in our experience virtually non-existent in the context of joint appointment pursuant to the Norwegian Arbitration Act. The fact that the parties jointly appoint the *whole* tribunal, and not only the co-arbitrators who otherwise would be subject to unilateral party-appointment, minimizes the potential of this problem.

§6.04 CONCLUSIONS

Both anecdotal evidence and empirical studies seem to confirm that party-appointed arbitrators have a tendency to rule in favour of the party that appointed them – and thus are subject to affiliation bias. While the extent of this problem is subject to further debate, one should nevertheless be aware of and seek to mitigate affiliation bias if possible. It is in our view important to have sufficient safeguards against affiliation bias becoming a problem that would threaten the legitimacy of the arbitral process.

This chapter points to both blind appointments and joint-party appointments as solutions that balance the parties' well-established expectation of being able to appoint the tribunal – and the need to ensure that the arbitrators are in fact impartial and independent. Based on our own experience as well as discussions with colleagues in the Norwegian arbitration community, joint-party appointments work well in practice and are well-regarded, also with respect to the legitimacy of the outcome of the arbitral process. We note that joint-party appointments may be successful in a Norwegian context because the legal community is fairly small and easy to oversee – as well as generally characterized by trust and pragmatism. These characteristics are something the Nordic countries share, and we would therefore expect the shared characteristics of the Nordic arbitration environments to be conducive to making joint-party appointments a viable and valuable method. In circumstances where these factors are lacking, however, blind appointments might be the better option.

87. *See also* the OCC Rules Art. 8(2) and the NOMA Rules Art. 7(1).
88. *See also* the NOMA Rules Art. 7(1) ('as far as possible') and the OCC Rules Art. 8(2) ('to the extent possible'). However, the OCC Rules expressly provides the parties with two weeks to agree: 'If the parties fail to agree on the composition of the arbitral tribunal within two weeks after the Institute has notified the respondent of the request for arbitration in accordance with Article 6 …'.
89. *See* Berg, section 16. *See also* Borgar Høgetveit Berg (ed.), Voldgiftsloven med kommentarer (Gyldendal, 2006) p. 172, and Geir Woxholth, Voldgift (Gyldendal, 2013), p. 391.

CHAPTER 7

Boxed in by the "Four Corners" Approach: A Review of the *Save Mart* Acquisition and the Subsequent Arbitration Proceedings, with a Comparative Lens

Michael F. Decker & Erlend Haaskjold[*]

§7.01 INTRODUCTION

When drafting contracts, some transactional lawyers pay careful attention to the choice of substantive law governing their contracts. Many deprioritize the matter.[1] The latter group may assume that the choice among several developed legal systems for a contract's governing law only makes a difference "at the margins." The *Save Mart* case is a recent post-M&A dispute resolved in a Delaware-seated arbitration, with Delaware law governing the parties' contract. This case is a reminder to every lawyer that it is worth attending thoughtfully to the question of which country's law will govern a contract: When a dispute does fall "at the margins," the deviation in outcomes under different legal systems can be enormous.

* The authors are partners at Advokatfirmaet Schjødt in Oslo, Norway. Michael F. Decker is qualified as an attorney in New York state, as a solicitor in England & Wales, and as a lawyer (advokat) in Norway. He is the Chair of Young Arbitration Practitioners Norway. Erlend Haaskjold is qualified as a lawyer (advokat) in Norway and as a barrister in England & Wales. He is also the author of multiple leading treatises on topics related to Norwegian contract law. The authors are deeply grateful to Tore Fjørtoft, Sujeet Indap, Asade Pourmand, Amund Bjøranger Tørum, Glenn West, Paul MacMahon, and the editorial committee of the Stockholm Arbitration Yearbook for their helpful advice and input regarding this chapter. All errors within remain our own.

1. *See, e.g.*, Giuditta Cordero-Moss, *International Commercial Contracts*, p. 135 (2nd ed., Cambridge 2024).

In *Save Mart*,[2] the seller parted with a profitable grocery store chain. Based on the buyer's offer letter and other preliminaries, the seller expected to walk away with around USD 40 million. Instead, during a post-closing purchase price calculation exercise, the buyer included an additional USD 100+ million debt item based on a literal reading of the contract's text. In a subsequent dispute centering on this point, the sole arbitrator, taking an exceedingly textualist approach, endorsed the buyer's approach, overlooking the squarely contrary extrinsic evidence, including that the economics of the deal were being turned on their head. In 2024, the Delaware courts reluctantly confirmed the arbitral award, leaving the private equity community "gob-smacked"[3] at this "obviously shocking" turn of events.[4]

The apparently erroneous outcome in the case can potentially be laid at the feet of several actors and institutions: (1) the arbitrator, who may have incorrectly applied Delaware law; (2) the seller's lawyers, who may have drafted the contract sloppily; (3) the seller's side again, which preferred arbitration with its narrow opportunity for review, and agreed to use a sole arbitrator; (4) the buyer and/or its lawyers, who may have improperly withheld knowledge of an important drafting error; (5) some combination of the foregoing, or other factors; or (6) no one—as this case may have been a correct application of a particularly rigid approach to contract interpretation.

This chapter reviews the *Save Mart* proceedings mainly with a comparative law lens—not only focusing on item (1) above but also considering how the matter might have been decided differently both in Delaware and in other common-law[5] jurisdictions, as well as in Scandinavia. This comparison is more relevant than ever, with powerful investors from common-law jurisdictions appearing more and more frequently in Scandinavia. For example, in recent years, parties from common-law countries represent the biggest contingent of M&A counterparties from outside of the region—which in turn is an M&A hotspot, far outstripping the rest of Europe when compared, e.g., to the respective nations' GDP levels. And, in our experience, it is a question that regularly comes up whether international commercial contracts with a Scandinavian connection should be governed by the law of a common-law country or that of a Scandinavian country. As the authors believe the *Save Mart* case demonstrates, both foreign investors and their Scandinavian partners must make this choice with care.

In the following sections, this chapter first provides background on the approaches to contract interpretation in the legal systems discussed in this chapter (§7.02), then reviews the *Save Mart* case itself (§7.03), and finally considers how the case might have been decided differently (§7.04), before briefly reviewing the other

2. The full case citation and a more detailed description of the case are found in §7.03 *infra*. *See also infra* n. 79.
3. Glenn D. West, *Post-Closing Purchase Price Adjustments Gone Wrong: The Save Mart/Kingswood Capital Dispute*, https://businesslawtoday.org/2024/05/post-closing-purchase-price-adjustments-gone-wrong-the-save-mart-kingswood-capital-dispute/ (accessed March 29, 2025).
4. David I. Albin, *Lessons from the Save Mart Case*, https://chambers.com/content/item/5862 (accessed March 29, 2025).
5. We focus on English and American law, these being the jurisdictions where we are qualified, and the common-law jurisdictions whose actors have the greatest involvement in Scandinavia.

potential drivers of the result in this case (items (2) through (6) above) and concluding (§7.05).

§7.02 COMPARATIVE LAW BACKGROUND

[A] Introduction and Caveat

Before reviewing the *Save Mart* proceedings in §7.03 below, we will first discuss some relevant points about the common-law and Scandinavian approaches to contract interpretation. Of course, it would be virtually impossible to summarize in this chapter all of the key points under either of these systems, for reasons including: (1) the volume of material to be covered;[6] (2) heterogeneity of approaches between different jurisdictions in a single legal system;[7] (3) heterogeneity of approaches between different judges within a single jurisdiction;[8] (4) movement over time, reflecting the plodding development of the law, sometimes even in ways that lead to reversals in prevailing doctrines;[9] and (5) heterogeneity within individual cases.[10]

Overall, we consider apt the observation that "[i]n virtually every jurisdiction, one finds irreconcilable cases, frequent changes in doctrine, confusion, and cries of despair."[11]

---

6. Given that "contract interpretation remains the largest single source of contract litigation between business firms," (Alan Schwartz and Robert E. Scott, *Contract Interpretation Redux*, 119 Yale L.J. 926, 928 (2010)), there are not only countless judicial opinions but also scholarly articles and books on the topic, whose essence we could hardly hope to summarize even if we used much more space.
7. The common law covers many countries, and Nordic law a handful. Despite sharing traditions and certain core elements of the approach to contract interpretation, different jurisdictions will still vary within a given system. In fact, even within Great Britain there can be substantial variation. "Sometimes the rules of contract law in England and Scotland may be very similar, if not identical ([e.g., for] contractual damages); sometimes the conceptual analyses of the law may differ ([e.g.,] the law of agency, or ... [the Scottish] separate obligation of unilateral promise distinct from contract); sometimes its substantive rules will differ (as in differing analyses of the nature of breach of contract, and the classification and availability of remedies)." *Comparative Contract Law: British and American Perspectives* (Larry A. DiMatteo & Martin Hogg eds, 2016), 4-5.
8. Various courts/jurisdictions will have internally inconsistent judicial commentary on the same topic, whether from genuine disagreement among judges, from misunderstanding of the law, or for other reasons. *See, e.g.*, Eric A. Posner, *The Parol Evidence Rule, The Plain Meaning Rule, and the Principles of Contract Interpretation*, 146 U. Pa. L. Rev. 533, 540 (1998) https://doi.org/10.2307/3312625 (accessed October 1, 2025).
9. *See* Posner, *supra* n. 8, at 539-540 ("[W]ithin a single jurisdiction, the parol evidence rule may vary considerably over time. In Pennsylvania, for example, hard-PER prevailed from the 1920s to the 1950s, confusion that gradually resolved itself into soft-PER prevailed from the late 1950s through the 1970s, and hard-PER has made a comeback in the late 1980s and 1990S. In California, hard-PER prevailed until the 1960s, and soft-PER thereafter.").
10. Sometimes, a judge's confusion or the utter complexity of the legal issues leads to seemingly inconsistent legal commentary within a single case. *See* Joshua M. Silverstein, *The Contract Interpretation Policy Debate: A Primer*, 26 Stan. J.L. Bus. & Fin. 235 (2021) ("courts often set forth inconsistent principles within a single opinion").
11. Posner, *supra* n. 8, at 539-540. *See also* Silverstein, *supra* n. 10, at 222 n.82 (collecting citations of other sources reflecting the confused state of the law in various U.S. jurisdictions).

We are also mindful of space limitations. Therefore, what we venture here are instead some limited comments which we feel may inform the discussion that follows. We hope that these comments may be especially useful to those less familiar with either the common law's approach or the Scandinavian approach to interpreting contracts. In section [B] below, we consider some common-law questions, in section [C] below the Scandinavian angle, and in section [E] below some overarching considerations about "textualist" versus "contextualist" approaches to contract interpretation.

[B] Common-Law Approaches

[1] "Objectivity" and the "Four Corners of the Contract"; Textualism and Contextualism

Common-law jurisdictions are sometimes caricatured as following a quite strictly text-based approach to contract interpretation.[12] According to this account, a judge reviewing a dispute over the meaning of a contract will, in order to decide how a particular clause should be understood, look to nothing other than the disputed text itself and potentially some apparently neutral sources such as dictionaries. Thus, it is said, a common-law judge restrains the analysis to the "four corners of the contract."

This account of common-law contract interpretation is oversimplified and ultimately incorrect—but it contains a kernel of truth: in common-law jurisdictions it is traditionally understood that the starting point for interpreting contracts is the text itself, whose meaning is determined based on an "objective" view of the material to be interpreted, rather than a view particular to the parties' subjective intentions about the contract. And the text is often the decisive matter, and ideologically it is the favored source of meaning.

As a shorthand, judges, academics, and even whole legal systems leaning most in the direction of this restrictive approach are said to be (contractual)[13] "textualists," "contractarians," or "literalists." This group has been described as "tak[ing] the view both that words have plain meanings and that courts should apply that plain meaning even if it leads to absurd results," and as preferring "a rigid objectivism that relies

12. When speaking about treatment of contracts in common-law jurisdictions, we refer generally to contracts purporting to be "fully integrated." An "integration clause" purports to define the contracts as the parties' exclusive agreement, rendering prior agreements on the same matter, and prior inconsistent agreements, superseded and ineffective. *See* American Law Institute, *Restatement (Second) of the Law of Contracts* (1981), § 213 (hereinafter "Restatement"). Written contracts that are not fully integrated—where the written contract does not reflect the parties' full agreement on the topic at hand—by definition require reference to evidence beyond the written contract document itself, including potentially testimony from the parties, to establish the content of the agreement. International commercial contract pertaining to a significant value normally contain an integration clause, sometimes alternatively called a "merger clause" or an "entire agreement clause."
13. This is as opposed to textualists with respect to, e.g., constitutional or statutory interpretation.

almost wholly on applying a semantic interpretative approach."[14] However, those who are more open to considering extrinsic evidence—"the background or context in which the agreement operates,"[15] sometimes referred to as the "matrix of facts"—have been called "contextualists" (or sometimes "purposivists"), with these two approaches conceived as the respective ends of a spectrum.

[2] Nuances in the Textualist Approach

An "objective" interpretation does not entail a myopic focus on a word or phrase to the exclusion of all else. Thus, even in the most "textualist" jurisdictions, judges tend to approach contract interpretation with more nuance than might be believed based on a quick caricature. One fundamental principle of contract interpretation under the common law—applicable in "textualist" common-law jurisdictions as well as in "contextualist" ones—is that a contract's text shall be interpreted as a whole, with any word or sentence being interpreted in light of its location in a broader paragraph and a section, each of which is adjacent to and in some respects related to others, and ultimately part of a contract text as a whole.[16]

In a regime focused on the contract text, this general principle justifies certain narrower principles designed to ensure consideration of context, such as: (i) the *presumption of consistent usage*: when a word or phrase is used multiple times in a single document, the starting presumption should be that the individual usages share a single meaning; and (ii) *the rule against superfluity*: an interpretation that renders one or more words or parts of a contract superfluous should be avoided; and even (iii) the *lex specialis*, meaning that specific terms should be given greater weight than, or prevail over, general terms.[17]

Even the most obscure-sounding contract interpretation principles, which often go by their Latin names, boil down to a requirement that words be understood in context. For example, the *ejusdem generis* rule provides that a catch-all at the end of a list should be interpreted as being of the same kind as the words in the list.[18] This canon was at play in *McBoyle v. United States*, a 1931 U.S. Supreme Court case in which Justice Oliver Wendell Holmes, Jr. authored an opinion overturning the conviction of a man who had stolen an aircraft under a statute forbidding theft of "motor vehicles," with a definition providing that the "term 'motor vehicle' shall include an automobile,

14. Catherine Mitchell, "Interpreting Commercial Contracts: The Policing Role of Context in English Law" in Comparative Contract Law, *supra* n. 7, at 233.
15. *Ibid.*
16. Restatement, *supra* n. 12, § 202(2) and comment d.
17. *Ibid.*, § 203(c).
18. The rule (and many others of these rules) applies to statutes, contracts, and wills, among other documents. "[F]or example, where a will leaves to a particular devisee 'my furniture, clothes, cooking utensils, housewares, motor vehicles, and all other property', the general phrase 'all other property' will, absent contrary signals, be construed in light of the specific items previously named to include not *all* types of property, including real estate, but only other items of personal property." *Citizens Ins. Co. of Am. v. Wynndalco Enterprises, LLC*, 70 F.4th 987, 1000 (7th Cir. 2023) (quoting A. Scalia and B. Garner, *Reading Law: The Interpretation of Legal Texts*, at 199 (2012)).

automobile truck, automobile wagon, motor cycle, or any other self-propelled vehicle not designed for running on."[19] Among other points, Justice Holmes reasoned:

> No doubt etymologically it is possible to use the word ["vehicle"] to signify a conveyance working on land, water or air … . [Here], after including automobile truck, automobile wagon, and motor cycle, the words "any other self-propelled vehicle not designed for running on rails" still indicate that a vehicle in the popular sense—that is, a vehicle running on land—is the theme. It is a vehicle that runs, not something, not commonly called a vehicle, that flies.

Similar is *noscitur a sociis*, which provides that, among several possible meanings of a term, that which aligns with the context should be preferred.[20] There is also *expressio unius est exclusio alterius*: the affirmative inclusion of one item can indicate the exclusion of another item not mentioned.[21] This canon is recognized to apply only sometimes, with the pragmatic context being determinative. If sitting in a restaurant, one is asked by a waiter if one would like coffee or orange juice, and the answer is "orange juice, please," it is not necessary to say "and not coffee (or tomato juice)." The latter is impliedly excluded based on the context. (Then again, should the waiter not bring water? This will of course depend on context—and is a hint to the limitation in this rule's guidance.) In a contract, then, where the parties write a clause invoking certain items, other items are (often) implied to be excluded from the same clause.

Because textualists attach great weight to the text in the contract, rules such as these are valuable to elucidate the likely meaning of the parties as implied from the contract's text, and it is not surprising that one sees comparatively frequent references to rules such as these in common-law contract decisions, whereas these rules are hardly mentioned by name (although implicitly used now and again) in Scandinavian case law. Yet, these interpretive principles are not really rules of law, but rather pragmatic rules of language—heuristics which remind lawyers and judges how language is ordinarily used. They are therefore also useful to the extent that an objective approach is prioritized in the Scandinavian context—which, as we shall see, occurs quite regularly.

[3] Extrinsic Evidence in Common-Law Contract Interpretation

There are in theory also a number of opportunities for extrinsic evidence of one kind or another to come into consideration in the determination of a contract's contents under the common law—in limited respects (and depending on what is defined as extrinsic

---

19. *McBoyle v. United States*, 283 U.S. 25, 26 (1931).
20. *See, e.g.*, *Severstal Dearborn, LLC v. Praxair, Inc.*, 899 F. Supp. 2d 667, 672 (E.D. Mich. 2012) (concluding, based on noscitur a sociis canon, that a term in a contract barring recovery of "incidental, consequential, [etc.] damages" was not a general bar, but only applied to harms arising from noxious gases, based on location of this term within provision pertaining to noxious gases).
21. *See, e.g.*, *Murphy v. DirecTV, Inc.*, 724 F.3d 1218, 1234 (9th Cir. 2013) (in deciding whether a particular party was intended as a third-party beneficiary under a contract, noting that a different party was mentioned, but the party in question was not, leading to the inference that the party in question was not intended to be included as a third-party beneficiary).

evidence) even in the most "textualist" jurisdictions. For example, it is well accepted that, if the context in a common-law contract implies that a technical term is being used, then the term should be given its technical meaning.[22] The same is of course recognized in other legal systems around the world.[23]

And it is generally not disputed that, after a contract term is determined to be ambiguous, the door is opened to the use of extrinsic evidence, including evidence regarding the parties' subjective understandings, to inform the meaning of the ambiguous term.

But what sources can be used in the threshold determination of whether the contract clause is ambiguous in the first place? This question and related ones are the subject of some controversy—so much, in fact, that debates over what sorts of extrinsic evidence should be allowed to be considered in various contexts have been called "[t]he central policy issue in the field of contract interpretation."[24] Perhaps the key point of disagreement related to extrinsic evidence relates to how contract terms should be determined as ambiguous. Those who lean "textualist" prefer the narrowest approach, limited largely to finding ambiguities in the text itself, while those who lean "contextualist" prefer a freer inquiry even for this threshold question. As we shall see in the following subsection, and yet more in section [D] below, the respective sides of this debate have long and freely exchanged critiques of each other's approaches.

[4] Textualist and Contextualist Approaches in Selected Common-Law Jurisdictions

In the United States, it has been said that the textualist view is "the traditional rule."[25] Yet, already more than one hundred years ago, Benjamin Cardozo (1870-1938), then sitting on the New York Court of Appeals,[26] and later a U.S. Supreme Court justice, expressed support for a context-based, and potentially even intersubjective, interpretation of contracts, writing:[27]

---

22. Restatement, *supra* n. 12, § 202(3)(b).
23. *See, e.g.*, Judgment by the Supreme Court of Norway, Rt-1920-890 (The Damptran Decision) ("Regarding the meaning of the term 'non-clarified steam liver oil', I must, based on the statements from a number of well-known and respected companies ..., etc., consider it fully proven that when the term 'steam liver oil' is used without further specification, it refers, according to established business language, only to steam-purified medicinal liver oil made from cod liver. If another type of steam-purified oil is meant, designations such as 'saithe oil', 'shark liver oil', 'seal oil', 'whale oil', etc., must be explicitly added.") (office translation).
24. Silverstein, *supra* n. 10, at 224.
25. *See, e.g.*, *Trident Center v. Connecticut General Life Insurance Co.*, 847 F.2d 564, 568 (9th Cir. 1988).
26. The Court of Appeals is the somewhat unconventional name used for the highest court in the state of New York.
27. *See Utica City National Bank v. Gunn*, 222 N.Y. 204, 207-8 (N.Y. 1918) (citations omitted). This is not to say that contract interpretation under New York law today matches this approach. Generally New York law is now perceived to be more textualist than California. *See* Geoffrey P. Miller, *Bargains Bicoastal: New Light on Contract Theory*, 31 Cardozo L. Rev. 1475, 1478 (2010).

> To ascertain the meaning of this contract, we must recall the surrounding circumstances. ... We may concede that the words, when viewed alone, apart from the setting of the occasion, give support to the defense. ... The [so-called] proper legal meaning, however, is not always the meaning of the parties. Surrounding circumstances may stamp upon a contract a popular or looser meaning. The words ["]loans["] and ["]discounts["] are not so clear and certain that circumstances may not broaden them to include renewals. They often have that meaning in the language of business life. ... To take the primary or strict meaning is to make the whole transaction futile. To take the secondary or loose meaning, is to give it efficacy and purpose. In such a situation, the genesis and aim of the transaction may rightly guide our choice.

And close to sixty years ago, in an opinion that is perhaps even better known than Cardozo's, Justice Roger Traynor (1900-1983), sitting on the California Supreme Court, confirmed that under California contract law,[28] extrinsic evidence can be used to establish ambiguity.[29]

This opinion was followed in 1981 by the Restatement (Second) of the Law of Contracts, which endorsed the same approach from the perspective of American legal academics.[30]

Then again, these contextualists approaches have also faced sharp criticism in the U.S.A. Judge Alex Kozinski (1950), sitting on the federal appeals court, wrote in the 1980s that Justice Traynor's opinion "casts a long shadow of uncertainty over all transactions negotiated and executed under the law of California," and that while this approach "creates much business for lawyers and an occasional windfall to some clients, it leads only to frustration and delay for most litigants and clogs already overburdened courts."[31]

If we were to sum up the situation in the most recent period in the U.S.A. on this question, we could say that, while some states have moved in the contextualist direction, the textualist approach remains the dominant view across the United States—including, as we shall see, in Delaware.[32]

* * *

---

28. Contract law is a matter of state law in the United States, meaning there is no single contract law, but rather a separate contract law in each state within the United States. However, in practice contract law is for the most part (the present topic being one exception) quite similar across state lines.
29. *Pacific Gas & Electric v. GW Thomas Drayage*, 69 Cal. 2d 33, 40 (1968).
30. *See* text accompanying n. 77 *infra*. This Restatement is one of a series of books published by the American Law Institute, written with the goal of summarizing the principles of a given area of U.S. law, even where there are differences across individual jurisdictions within the United States.
31. *Trident Center, supra* n. 25.
32. *See, e.g.*, Peter Linzer, *The Comfort of Certainty: Plain Meaning and the Parol Evidence Rule*, 71 Fordham L. Rev. 799, 800 (2002). *See also* Schwartz and Scott, *supra* n. 6, at 928 n.1 ("A state-by-state survey of recent court decisions shows that thirty-eight states follow the textualist approach to interpretation. Nine states, joined by the Uniform Commercial Code for sales cases (UCC) and the Restatement (Second) of Contracts, have adopted a contextualist or 'antiformalist' interpretive regime. The remaining states are indeterminate.").

As for other common-law jurisdictions, it has likewise been argued that "the general trend ... is towards adoption of the contextualist approach."[33] For example, in England, the home of the common-law system, while traditionally there has been a "general rule that extrinsic evidence was inadmissible to explain or interpret a writing,"[34] more recently, the courts have moved toward a more flexible approach. England's "basic rule," which is still considered an "objective approach to contractual interpretation," thus makes allowance for "look[ing] to the surrounding circumstances, because the contract is not made in a vacuum," but the relevant facts are generally those "which both (or all) parties knew or would reasonably be taken to have known"—thus "[t]he knowledge of one party, which he or she has not disclosed to the others, is irrelevant."[35]

Lord Hoffmann's 1998 opinion in *Investors Compensation Scheme* observed, among other points, the importance of interpreting language against "the background knowledge which would reasonably have been available to the parties," which "includes absolutely anything which would have affected the way in which the language of the document would have been understood by a reasonable man," apart from declarations of subjective intent and evidence of prior negotiations.[36] This opinion endorses the core contextualist principle that "it [i]s not necessary to find an 'ambiguity' before one c[an] have any regard to background."[37]

Lord Hoffmann's comments in *Investors Compensation Scheme* have by some been regarded as a "watershed" for the English law of contract interpretation.[38] The case was even "viewed with alarm by some distinguished commercial lawyers as having greatly increased the quantity of background material which courts or arbitrators would be invited to consider."[39]

Then again, some of Lord Hoffmann's colleagues have "suggested that the case did not articulate a fundamental change in the law of contractual interpretation but rather involved a change of emphasis."[40]

And, more recently, many argue that the pendulum has swung back away from contextualism, with the leading cases—such as *Arnold v. Britton* in 2015—suggesting that the English courts have taken at least a significant step back in the direction of a textualist approach. In this case, it was commented, for example, that "[t]he mere fact that a contractual arrangement, if interpreted according to its natural language, has

33. Schwartz and Scott, *supra* n. 6, at 928 n.1, citing Gerard McMeel, *The Construction of Contracts: Interpretation, Implication, and Rectification* (2nd ed. Oxford, Oxford University Press, 2011) at para. 2.01.
34. Lord Hodge, "Can Judges Use Business Common Sense in Interpreting Contracts?" in Comparative Contract Law, *supra* n. 7, at 273.
35. *Ibid.*, at 274 (quoting and discussing *Rainy Sky SA v. Kookmin Bank* [2011] 1 WLR 2900, [21], among other decisions).
36. *Investors Compensation Scheme v. West Bromwich Building Society*, [1997] UKHL 28; [1998] 1 All ER 98; [1998] 1 WLR 896 (June 19, 1997).
37. *Chartbrook Ltd v. Persimmon Homes Ltd & Ors*, [2009] UKHL 38 (July 1, 2009) at [37] (describing *Investors Compensation Scheme*).
38. *See, e.g.*, McMeel, *supra* n. 33, at para. 1.101.
39. *Chartbrook*, *supra* n. 37, at [37].
40. Hodge, *supra* n. 34, at 273.

worked out badly, or even disastrously, for one of the parties is not a reason for departing from the natural language."[41]

Ultimately, in English legal circles, much as in the United States, there are stark differences of opinion on how and to what extent various kinds of extrinsic evidence can or should be allowed to influence the interpretation of a contract.[42]

There are endless variations along the textualist-contextualist spectrum in various common-law countries. For example, on the specific question whether extrinsic evidence in the form of post-contracting conduct can be used to aid in interpreting a contract's terms, in England "it remains a general rule that the court does not look to the post-contractual behavior of the parties in construing their contract"—but that "Canada, New Zealand, [and] South Africa," among other jurisdictions, do allow the consideration of such evidence.[43]

It is difficult to give a "weighted" consideration to the dominance of textualist versus contextualist approaches to contract interpretation based on the relative prevalence of different jurisdictions' laws as governing in commercial contracts around the world. However, we can at least observe that, notwithstanding the economic power of the U.S. and its actors in the legal market, English law seems to have an undeniable dominance in the realm of international commercial contracts across the globe.[44]

[5] Further Relevance of Extrinsic Evidence

Beyond interpreting (arguably) ambiguous terms, extrinsic evidence can also be relevant for other purposes. Typical examples are claims of fraud and claims for rectification (reformation)[45] of a contract's text based on a mistake, whether committed by both parties (mutual mistake) or by just one (unilateral mistake).[46]

The basic requirements for establishing entitlement to rectification under *mutual mistake* are that: (i) the written contract document does not express the content of the parties' actual agreement at the time the contract was entered; and that (ii) this failure to express the agreement adequately is due to a mistake of both parties.[47]

The requirements are similar for *unilateral mistake*, a doctrine whose rationale "is consistent with the traditional rationale of rectification for common mistake and gives effect to the same underlying equity."[48] The requirements are that: (i) the written

41. *Arnold v. Britton* [2015] UKSC 36 [19].
42. *See, e.g.*, Lord Sumption, *A Question of Taste: The Supreme Court and the Interpretation of Contracts*, https://supremecourt.uk/uploads/speech_170508_368f616b7d.pdf (accessed March 29, 2025) (identifying and discussing "a number of problems about the approach to construction which they adopted").
43. Hodge, *supra* n. 34, at 281 & n.42. *See also Lloyds TSB Foundation for Scotland v. Lloyds Banking Group plc*, [2013] UKSC 3, [2013] SC (UKSC) 169.
44. *See* Miller, *supra* n. 27.
45. What is otherwise typically called "rectification" is in the United States termed "reformation." In this chapter, we will ordinarily refer to the doctrine as "rectification."
46. *Investors Compensation Scheme, supra* n. 37.
47. *See* Restatement, *supra* n. 12, §155.
48. *FHSC Group Holdings Ltd v. Glas Trust Corp Ltd*, [2019] EWCA Civ 1361 at [105].

contract document does not express the content which party A erroneously believed it did; and that (ii) party B knew of, or had reason to know of Party A's mistake.

As can be expected, the precise borderlines of this doctrine will vary from one jurisdiction to another—or even from judge to judge, as well as over time and perhaps on other dimensions. For example, what level of knowledge of the mistake by Party B is required to justify rectification—actual knowledge, reason to know, or something else?[49] However, in our view, these basic outlines give a good indication of the general principles at play. In terms of examples, the Restatement (Second) of the Law of Contracts provides the following two as instances where rectification could be available:

- As an example of mutual mistake: "A and B agree that A will sell and B will buy a tract of land for $100,000, payable by $50,000 in cash and the assumption of an existing mortgage of $50,000. In reducing the agreement to writing, B's lawyer erroneously omits the provision for assumption of the mortgage, and neither A nor B notices the omission. ... [A]t the request of either party, the court will decree that the writing be reformed to add the provision for assumption of the mortgage."[50]
- As an example of unilateral mistake: in response to B's solicitation of construction bids, "according to stated specifications, A submits an offer to do the work for $150,000. A ... has made an error by inadvertently omitting a $50,000 item, and in fact [B's offer should have been for] $200,000. ... B had estimated the expected cost as $180,000 before advertising for bids, and the ten other bids were all in the range between $180,000 and $200,000. ... [T]he discrepancy between A's bid ... and B's estimate and the ten other bids [may justify concluding] that B had reason to know of A's mistake."[51]

The boundaries between some "substantive" contract-policing doctrines (such as mistake) and supposedly "pure" interpretation are sometimes difficult to delineate.[52]

49. In some jurisdictions, for instance, it has at times been prevailing law that Party B's behavior must have been unconscionable for Party A to obtain relief, or that other requirements must be met. *See, e.g.*, *Scion Breckenridge Managing Member, LLC v. ASB Allegiance Real Est. Fund*, 68 A.3d 665, 679 (Del. 2013) (overruling earlier Delaware requirement to show fraud in order to obtain rectification of a contract based on unilateral mistake); *Matter of ENSTAR Corp.*, 604 A.2d 404, 411 (Del. 1992) (holding that only rescission, not rectification, is available in case of unilateral mistake, and requiring unconscionability to obtain this relief).
50. Restatement, *supra* n. 12, §152, illustration 10.
51. *Ibid.*, §155, illustration 9 (based on illustration 1 to same §).
52. "[T]here are occasions where a conclusion presented by a judge as derived from an interpretative enquiry into the meaning of the contract text (in context) could just as easily be presented as the result of imposing an external standard directly to the agreement." Mitchell, *supra* n. 14, at 232. *See also ibid.*, at p. 235 ("[T]he lines between what is an exercise of contextual interpretation and what is an exercise of something else, whether the application of contract law doctrine or an exercise of judicial discretion, are easily blurred."). *See also* Amund B. Tørum, *Interpretation of Commercial Contracts*, §1-009 (Universitetsforlaget, 2019) ("[W]here the contract is unclear or silent on the disputed issue, there may be a complex interaction between interpreting the contract and supplementing the contract with the background law (gap-filling). It is difficult to define clear and precise guidelines for this interaction.").

Judges may sometimes appear drawn to handle through interpretation what might more properly have been evaluated through the lens of mistake or another doctrine—perhaps to avoid appearing to engage in the distasteful activity of "meddling with" a contract, least of all by probing extrinsic evidence.[53] We will return to the question of "mistake" later, in the context of the *Save Mart* arbitral award's reasoning and our own analysis of how the case might have been resolved.

[C] The Scandinavian Approach

[1] Intersubjectivity as the Basic Principle

The law of contract interpretation is for present purposes (and many others) quite similar in Denmark, Norway, and Sweden.[54] In the present chapter, we will refer to this as the Scandinavian approach to interpretation of contracts. The nominal starting point under the Scandinavian approach is that contracts "shall be interpreted according to the common intention of the parties."[55] In an oft-cited case from 1993, the Supreme Court of Norway stated that the primary purpose of contract interpretation is to find the parties' intention.[56] As a main rule, this common intention is however understood to be expressed by the words in the contract.

The underlying rationale of this "common intention" starting point is that the parties shall be bound to what they have actually agreed upon. The courts will thus seek to establish the parties' shared understanding. If agreement on a particular point may be proved, it is not in itself essential that this agreement is not reflected in the written contract. Based on the evidence, courts may even conclude that the real

---

53. *See, e.g.*, Mitchell, *supra* n. 14, at 236-237; *Credential Bath Street Ltd. v. Venture Investment Placement Ltd.*, [2007] CSOH 208 ("[I]t is inherent in the contextual approach to interpretation that mistakes in a document which are apparent in the light of the surrounding circumstances can be corrected through the process of construction in the same way as mistakes which are apparent on the face of the document"); *Chartbrook*, *supra* n. 37, at [36] ("There is certainly a view in the profession that the less one has to resort to any form of background in aid of interpretation, the better."); Mitchell, *supra* n. 14, at 237 ("[C]ourts can, motivated by policy, adjust a bargain through the auspices of interpreting a contract."); *ibid.*, at 241 (observing that even where "interventionist approaches may be warranted, ... pursuing such outcomes through interpretation rather has a tendency to obscure more than illuminate").—Furthermore, arguing from the doctrine of mistake can potentially be seen as going some way toward admitting legal malpractice liability, which might lead some lawyers to be less comfortable arguing this approach, especially if they are the same lawyers (or law firm) who was involved in negotiating the underlying transaction.
54. *See, e.g.*, K. Zweigert & H. Kötz, *An Introduction to Comparative Law*, 277–285 (3rd ed. Oxford, 1998).
55. UNIDROIT Principles of International Commercial Contracts (hereinafter "UNIDROIT PICC"), Art. 4.1.1.
56. Judgment by the Supreme Court of Norway, Rt-1993-564. *See also* Tørum, *supra* n. 52, at §1-004 ("[T]he traditional point of departure in Nordic and Civil law has been to search for what the parties intended—their 'common understanding'."). *See also* some similar illustrations from the jurisprudence of the Supreme Court of Denmark: U 1985 p. 14; U 1987 p. 636; U 2003 p. 23.

agreement between the parties differs from what is written in the contract.[57] In Scandinavian legal theory, this is often referred to as the "principle of intersubjectivity." The starting point in Scandinavia is therefore—at least nominally—somewhat different from that in any common-law jurisdictions.

However, the legal effect of this theoretical difference in approach should not be exaggerated. When the parties have formulated their agreement in a written contract document, it is fair to assume that the written text accurately reflects the common intention of the parties.[58] The written words of the contract will therefore—as the main rule—be the true natural starting point in the interpretation process, at least in commercial contracts.

Scandinavian courts are, moreover, typically reluctant to find a common understanding which deviates from the written words of the contract. And it is only in some exceptional cases that a party asserts that the contracting parties' common intention is not reflected in the written contract, anyhow. However, it may be that the contract is alleged not to be complete, so that the common intention on a certain point is not regulated in writing at all, or that the words used in the contract allegedly do not reflect the parties' actual (intersubjective) agreement.

In a case reported in Rt. 1910 p. 38, the Norwegian Supreme Court had to interpret a contract for the sale of land, which provided that the buyer should assume liability for certain "taxes and public charges." The issue in dispute was whether a ground fee could be characterized as a "public charge." The Supreme Court stated that both parties, at the time of entry into the contract, had the understanding that the buyer should pay the ground fee in question. It was, therefore, not necessary to analyze the linguistic meaning of the expression "public charges." In the more recent case in Rt. 2011 p. 1553, the Supreme Court noted that if the parties have a mutual understanding of the words used in a contract, it is not necessary to examine the "normal" meaning of the language.

A number of similar decisions may be found in Denmark and Sweden. In the Danish case reported in U 1974 p. 783 V, the parties were in agreement that a land charge should be without personal liability. The fact that the signed documents contained an express provision to the effect that there was personal liability did not overrule the common understanding of the parties. Likewise, the Swedish Supreme Court in NJA 1984 p. 288 held that the wording of an index clause could not be decisive, as the parties discussed the contents of the clause prior to the conclusion of the contract.

The principle of intersubjectivity is first and foremost decisive when there is evidence that the contents of the written contract do not reflect the actual intention of the parties at the time of the conclusion of the contract. When the common intention

57. *See*, for instance, Judgment by the Supreme Court of Sweden, NJA 2021 p. 643, expressly stating that a "common intention of the parties even takes precedence over clear wording in a written agreement."

58. Haaskjold, *Kontraktsforpliktelser*, 199; Jan Ramberg and Christina Ramberg, *Allmän avtalsrätt*, 148-149; Lennart Lynge Andersen and Palle Bo Madsen, *Aftaler og mellemmænd*, section 369. A recent example is the decision of the Danish Supreme Court in U 2005 p. 2218.

can be established from relevant sources, this intention will—as noted above—supersede the written words of the contract. As the written words do not reflect the intention of the contracting parties, there is no justification in looking at the text in the contract: *falsa demonstratio non nocet*. This doctrine resembles somewhat the common-law doctrine of mutual mistake, but, as noted above, it is an ideological starting point in Scandinavia, rather than an exception.

The principle of intersubjectivity is also relevant when the parties have a common understanding *in addition to*, but not inconsistent with, what is written in the contract. Typically, this will be a definition, an assumption, or a certain understanding of how the contract will work. Used in this sense, the common understanding may be used as a source for contractual gap-filling.

[2] Extrinsic Evidence in Scandinavian Law Contract Interpretation

Whereas the textualist common-law approach is to focus on the contract text to divine the parties' common intention, the Scandinavian approach is to evaluate the text and all of the potentially relevant surrounding circumstances to arrive at the common intention.[59] The use of extrinsic evidence is indeed a necessary consequence of the principle of intersubjectivity: Courts will look at all factors that may shed light on the common intention of the parties at the time of entry into the contract. The Scandinavian approach, even for highly detailed, professionally-drafted contracts, can sometimes be said to resemble the common-law approach to partially-integrated contracts, in which the courts will allow a wider range of evidence to demonstrate the contents of the oral part of the contract.

In Scandinavian law, there are *no formal restrictions* on what evidence may be taken into account. Parties are free to present whatever may be considered relevant to reflect the content of the parties' agreement. Scandinavian case law shows that the courts—in order to establish the common intention—often look to evidence such as preliminary drafts and negotiations between the parties, their conduct subsequent to the conclusion of the contract, and evidence reflecting the nature and purpose of the contract. The courts may even hear testimony from each side regarding what was said and discussed during negotiations leading up to the contract, and what was internally intended on one side with the words chosen (or not chosen). Then again, although this form of evidence is in principle permissible, the case law reflects a reluctance to attach (much) weight to such testimony in hindsight.

Finally, it should be mentioned that extrinsic evidence is often used when it is asserted that a party knew or ought to have known that the other party had a different understanding of the words used in the contract—in which case a duty of care falls on this party. It is well established that in such circumstances, the understanding of the other party shall prevail. In Swedish law, this principle of interpretation is sometimes

59. *See* Haaskjold, *Kontraktsforpliktelser*, 195-197; Tørum, *supra* n. 52, at §1-004 (noting that the Scandinavian approach "invites the judge to consider a broad spectrum of facts beyond the four corners of the contract: in particular, the purpose and the negotiation phase, but also subsequent events that may reveal what the parties intended at the time the contract was entered into").

referred to as the "dolus doctrine."[60] While the Scandinavian intersubjective approach can be compared with the common-law doctrine of "mutual mistake," the dolus rule more resembles the common-law doctrine of "unilateral mistake."

[3] The Objective Approach, Particularly Relevant in Professional Contexts

Assuming there is no basis to determine a contract's content via the "common understanding" approach, courts applying Scandinavian law will adopt an objective approach to the interpretation of contracts. The objective approach aims to arrive at the intention of the parties, with the point of departure being the written words of the contract. Then again, this approach can, like contextualist common-law jurisdictions, involve sources beyond the text, including sources well beyond those allowable in such contextualist common-law jurisdictions, such as the parties' negotiations, previous dealings, and post-contracting behavior. These and other sources make up what we might call "the Scandinavian factual matrix."[61]

Although under this approach a court can consider far more evidence than would be considered in common-law jurisdictions' own "objective" approaches, including some material that common-law lawyers might consider "subjective," it is still considered "objective" under Scandinavian contract law in particular, by contrast to the intersubjective approach described above. (Interpretation is a process, and some of the same elements may have an impact at different stages of the interpretation process.)

Especially in the most professional and commercial settings, Scandinavian courts tend toward an objective approach to interpretation. Therefore, much as in the common-law countries, in Scandinavia "the wording of the contract is the centre of gravity."[62] Professional parties are presumed to have expressed their agreement in the written contract, and the party whose position is not correctly or adequately reflected in the contractual terms will have to bear the risk. In the *Scanvest* case, for example, the Supreme Court of Norway refused to imply terms into a shareholder agreement on the basis of the purpose of the agreement, notwithstanding some apparently weighty arguments in favor of such implication.[63]

[4] Legal Guidelines

The Scandinavian courts will often make use of certain *legal guidelines* when they interpret contracts. Such legal guidelines may be seen as a parallel to the linguistic

60. *See* Judgment of the Swedish Supreme Court, NJA 2021 p. 643. *See also* UNIDROIT PICC, *supra* n. 55, Art. 4.2.1: "The statements and other conduct of a party shall be interpreted according to that party's intention if the other party knew or could not have been unaware of that intention."
61. *See* UNIDROIT PICC, *supra* n. 55, Art. 4.1.2, stating that "the contract shall be interpreted according to the meaning that reasonable persons of the same kind as the parties would give to it in the same circumstances."
62. Tørum, *supra* n. 52, at p. XIV. *See also ibid.*, § 2-001 ("The 'objective' interpretation is the golden rule of the interpretation of commercial contracts.").
63. Rt. 1994 p. 581.

guidelines—or canons of interpretation—often used by the common law courts, cf. section [B][2] above. The legal guidelines are based on what the parties would normally be taken to have agreed upon, and, however, what typical parties would not have agreed unless the intention is made clear in the contract. For example, a contract is presumed to be in conformity with the law, so that no contractual provision should be taken to contravene the law.[64] Moreover, there is a general presumption that the parties have meant all terms of their contract to have effect, so that no provision is superfluous or meaningless. Finally, there is a general presumption that the agreed terms are fair and balanced. The courts will therefore avoid arriving at a result that is unreasonable or contrary to business common sense.

[5] The Role of Section 36 in the Scandinavian Contract Acts

A particular feature of the Scandinavian countries' Contract Acts is a provision to the effect that a contractual term may be altered or set aside to the extent that its application will lead to an "unreasonable" result. The courts are thus given the power to assess the "reasonableness" of contractual terms, or indeed the entire contract as such. To common-law lawyers, this provision can be surprising. However, it is generally assumed that the provision is a safety valve, primarily in instances of abuse of the freedom of contract, and it is meant to be used only as a safety valve to avoid the most extreme results. It is therefore important to note that the courts will not assess the fairness of a contractual term. In the common law context, it could perhaps be said that the provision prevents results that the courts find "unconscionable."

Even though the threshold for application of section 36 is very high, the statutory provision seems to have had a certain effect on the way the courts interpret contracts. Even without citing section 36, courts seem generally to avoid arriving at a result that would imply the parties agreed on a system that would be described as "unreasonable" (or perhaps "unconscionable"), or contrary to what might be expected from the application of basic business common sense.[65] As we have seen in section [C][4] above, the use of "fairness and balance" as a guideline in the interpretation process is well established in Scandinavian law. In practice, section 36 has also had a preventive effect, in that parties often refrain from contract terms that will lead to an unreasonable result.

Yet, the general impression is that the courts have been quite reluctant to apply section 36 directly when it is relied upon in a dispute. The parties' freedom of contract is there to be used, and the principle of sanctity of contract is still fundamental. Section 36 is thus typically only used to set aside terms which appear to be the result of abuse of this freedom, and terms which turn out to have an unintended effect because of supervening facts.

---

64. Haaskjold, *Kontraktsforpliktelser*, 279-286; Andersen and Madsen, *supra* n. 58, at 396-397.
65. *Ibid.*, at pp. 398-406.

[D] Overarching Considerations Regarding the Common-Law and Scandinavian Systems

Overall, in the authors' views, there will be many ways in which the common-law and Scandinavian approaches to contract interpretation—and adjacent doctrines such as mistake—will resemble one another. In commercial contexts in particular, the text is of great (or the greatest) importance, but other factors can come into play. In both approaches, there are various alternatives to deciding an interpretation squarely from the text, but the availability of these alternatives is somewhat limited—to different extents and in different ways in different systems and jurisdictions. Some have even argued that these legal systems' approaches are, on the whole, slowly converging.[66] And there is probably some truth to this. The reasons are likely complex and multifaceted, with contributions from such factors as the prevalence of intercontinental trade. Yet, we would not want to overstate the extent of any similarities or resemblances. In reality, there will be many cases where the legal systems will arrive at quite different results—not to mention that one can find different results even within different jurisdictions under the umbrellas of each of these legal systems.

[E] Contextual or Textual Approaches to Interpretation: Some Policy Considerations

The policy arguments in favor of the textualist and contextualist (including both Scandinavian and common-law) sides of the contract interpretation debate are many—and in any given jurisdiction across the globe, one will find both defenders and critics of the prevailing local approach. However, in the authors' experience, one tends to find a certain bias of each lawyer in favor of the approach taken in his or her home jurisdiction—or, perhaps more precisely—in favor of the approach that the lawyer learned in law school.

One main area of disagreement between textualism and contextualism relates to the concern for transaction costs (contract drafting, etc.), on the one hand, versus enforcement costs (litigation, etc.), on the other hand.[67] It is typically argued that a contextualist approach would seem to encourage lower transaction costs, given that under contextualist regimes, there is more openness to "verifying" the parties' intentions later, and thus perhaps less need to refine the language in the written contract in order to reflect the parties' true agreement.[68] A textualist approach, however, would seem to encourage lower enforcement costs, since fewer sources available for or relevant to interpretation should imply less material available to mine for arguments, and potentially also less uncertainty as to a contract's meaning, with, consequently, less role for the courts to fill.[69]

66. *See, e.g.*, Tørum, *supra* n. 52, at p. XIII.
67. These various arguments and more are summarized in Silverstein, *supra* n. 10, at 253-271.
68. *See* Silverstein, *supra* n. 10, at 253-254.
69. *See Chartbrook*, *supra* n. 37, at [35] (noting the argument that "the admission of pre-contractual negotiations would create greater uncertainty of outcome in disputes over interpretation and add to the cost of advice, litigation or arbitration"). This point is also argued, for example, in Hodge, *supra* n. 34, at 280-281.

However, these arguments may be turned around. Some textualists seem to think that the openness to reinterpretation of otherwise-clear terms actually raises transaction costs in contextualist regimes, as parties may feel the need to use especially clear language to reduce the risk of being overridden by judicial reliance on extrinsic evidence later; thus, a textualist approach is supposed to "minimiz[e] transactional costs by promoting certainty and predictability."[70] Similarly, some contextualists argue that, for example, the availability of extrinsic evidence tends to render facially-ambiguous terms *more* certain, leading to lower enforcement costs, while the longer, more complex contracts which prevail in textualist regimes will lead to yet more potential areas for dispute. There is also a middle-ground argument from the contextualists:

> [W]hen a dispute over construction is litigated, evidence of the pre-contractual negotiations is almost invariably tendered in support of an alternative claim for rectification ... or an argument based on estoppel by convention or some alleged exception to the exclusionary rule. Even if such an alternative claim does not succeed, the judge will have read and possibly been influenced by the evidence. The rule therefore achieves little in saving costs and its abolition would restore some intellectual honesty to the judicial approach to interpretation.[71]

There are various ancillary considerations here—for example, when considering the balance of transaction costs and litigation costs, it would be relevant also to keep in mind that only a fraction of written contracts entail litigation costs in any jurisdiction, while all written contracts must of course be drafted. In other words, enforcement costs (in particular litigation) occur sometimes, while transaction costs occur always, so that a small improvement in per-contract transaction costs can weigh much more heavily than a per-dispute improvement in enforcement costs.[72]

The other main policy debate between textualists and contextualists pertains to which system does a better job of achieving a substantively better (i.e., more correct) result.[73] The textualists would argue, among other points, that the contract text provides more reliable evidence of the parties' intentions than extrinsic evidence. It hardly needs mentioning that, to the extent one considers the input of witnesses relevant, the types of accuracy failures can be numerous—(1) witnesses may have misperceived things in the moment; (2) may remember matters unreliably; or (3) may intentionally misrepresent their memories—among other problems. Also, witnesses can be unavailable—for example, because they are not on friendly terms with the people or entities on "their side" of the dispute (anymore)—or, to take a simpler example, because they are dead. It hardly seems intuitive that a contract's meaning should change if a key negotiator becomes unavailable.

---

70. Hodge, *supra* n. 34, at 272.
71. *See Chartbrook, supra* n. 37, at [35].
72. *See* George M. Cohen, *Interpretation and Implied Terms in Contract Law* (Virginia Law and Economics Research Paper No. 2009-12), https://ssrn.com/abstract=1473854 (accessed March 29, 2025) 8.
73. This then assumes that there *is* a "correct" result in every case as to what the parties' agreement was—which is far from a certainty. *See Tørum, supra* n. 52, at XI.

And as for the contextualists, their main argument may be that their more flexible approach "giv[es] effect to the reasonable expectations of honest business people by avoiding a legalistic and overly literal approach to commercial contracts."[74] For example, "skilled lawyers may have been working against very tight deadlines and may have run out of time or energy after burning the midnight oil for several nights," so that to take "too literal an approach to construction" may not match the parties' *actual* expectations.[75] Contextualists can also point to the more philosophical argument about the meaning of language presented in the Restatement (Second) of Contracts:

> It is sometimes said that extrinsic evidence cannot change the plain meaning of a writing, but meaning can almost never be plain except in a context. Accordingly, the [consideration of circumstances surrounding the agreement] is not limited to cases where it is determined that the language used is ambiguous. Any determination of meaning or ambiguity should only be made in the light of the relevant *evidence of the situation and relations of the parties*, the subject matter of the transaction, *preliminary negotiations and statements made therein*, usages of trade, and the course of dealing between the parties.[76]

Proponents of both approaches express concern for manipulation by the other approach. For example, textualists express concern that parties in a contextualist system will manipulate extrinsic evidence even while contract negotiation is underway, in order to lay the groundwork for later potential contract disputes.[77] Contextualists argue that "[t]extualism incentivizes parties to stand on express terms that are inconsistent with the other side's reasonable expectations more than contextualism does because the former system prevents litigants from submitting extrinsic evidence regarding their expectations when the contested language of an agreement is clear."[78]

* * *

We will not here settle—or even come close to fully laying out—this debate, but have tried here to highlight a few aspects of the substantial disagreement on this topic, not only as a matter of textualist versus contextualist jurisdictions but also within each jurisdiction.

§7.03 CASE STUDY: *SM BUYER V. RMP SELLER HOLDINGS*

[A] Introduction and Description of the Case

We will now review some key facts and the procedural history of the *Save Mart* case, which is, we believe, an excellent vehicle for considering the relative merits of contextual versus textual approaches to contract interpretation.

74. *See* Hodge, *supra* n. 34, at 272.
75. *Ibid.*, at 277.
76. Restatement, *supra* n. 12, §212, comment b (emphases added). It should be noted that, even according to such a more liberal approach, "after the transaction has been shown in all its length and breadth," then "the words of an integrated agreement remain the most important evidence of intention." *Ibid.*
77. Silverstein, *supra* n. 10, at 242.
78. *Ibid.*, at 267.

The dispute in question arose out of the sale of Save Mart Supermarkets, LLC ("Target") from RMP Seller Holdings, LLC (f/k/a New Save Mart Corporation) ("Seller") to SM Buyer LLC ("Buyer"), associated with Kingswood Capital Management, LP, a California private equity firm with multiple billions of USD under management.[79] At the time of the transaction, the Target "operate[d] more than 200 stores across California and northern Nevada"[80] "under the brands Save Mart, Lucky California, and FoodMaxx."[81] The Target also owned a slight majority stake[82] in Super Store Industries (SSI), a wholesale grocery distributor organized as a general partnership under California law. SSI's debt around the time of the transaction was USD 109 million, consisting of a revolving line of credit and a real estate loan.

Negotiations related to the acquisition began in 2021, with a draft transaction agreement being circulated at least as early as December 2021.[83] In an initial letter of intent ("LOI"), the Buyer valued the Target at USD 270 million.[84] This LOI, but not the contract itself, described the transaction as a cash-free, debt-free transaction, implying that excess cash would be swept from the Target, but that debt would also be paid off or otherwise deducted from the purchase price.[85] The LOI referred to a list of debt items that would be accounted for in such adjustment, and the SSI debt was not in that list.[86] However, the SSI interest as a whole was among the assets valued within the USD 270 million total.

The Buyer later revised its LOI valuation down to USD 245 million. This valuation was reflected in the parties' Equity Purchase Agreement ("EPA"), which was signed on March 7, 2022, and in the Amended EPA of March 25, 2022.[87] Both the USD 245 million and USD 270 million valuations seem to have been inflated because they included around USD 205 million in excess cash on the Target's balance sheet, which the Seller swept out before the transaction went through.[88] Of the remaining circa USD 39 million valuation, the Target's stake in SSI was a net positive contributor, "arguably the

79. *See RMP Seller Holdings, LLC v. SM Buyer LLC*, Final Award (September 5, 2023) (hereinafter "Final Award") 4.
80. *SM Buyer LLC v. RMP Seller Holdings, LLC*, No. 2023-0975-JTL, 2024 WL 865918, at *1 (Del. Ch. February 28, 2024) (hereinafter "Chancery Court Decision").
81. Final Award, *supra* n. 79, at 5.
82. *Ibid.*, at 4.
83. *Ibid.*, at 5. *See also* Sujeet Indap, *The Inequity Method of Accounting* (Financial Times April 11, 2024), https://www.ft.com/content/7ef1559a-0b7c-48cd-80dc-084081bea8ad (accessed March 30, 2025).
84. Indap, *supra* n. 83.
85. *See* Appellant's (Seller's) Opening Brief, *RMP Seller Holdings, LLC v. SM Buyer LLC*, Civil Action No. No. 2023-0957-JTL (Delaware Supreme Court) 23.
86. *Ibid.*, at 10-11.
87. Final Award, *supra* n. 79, at 5.
88. *Ibid.* Before the transaction process began, the seller also had previously divested the target of real estate holdings (dozens of *Save Mart* locations), netting USD 1.15 billion in proceeds from that sale. This fact does not appear to be of particular legal relevance, especially as the transaction was earlier and not with the buyer as counterparty, although it would presumably tend to reduce the perceived sympathy value of the seller.

crown-jewel of the sale,"[89] in the end being valued at circa USD 90 million net valuation (i.e., an equity valuation, after subtracting debts).[90]

As the arbitral award recognized, "Kingswood's original letter of intent did not include any SSI Debt in its sample Indebtedness calculation."[91] The transaction used a completion accounts approach. According to this approach, the transaction price is determined based on the actual value of the company as of when the target changes hands, i.e., at closing. Thus, the intended purchase price as offered in the LOI or reflected in the transaction documents at signing is only an estimate. Then, just before closing, the seller calculates a tentative purchase price based on the company's financials at that moment, which the buyer pays. After a short period, the buyer then makes its own refined calculation of the purchase price based on the target's status as of the actual time of closing. If there is disagreement over the purchase price at this stage, then the parties resolve this via a dispute resolution mechanism, which would ordinarily be described in the contract. This was, as the court wrote in the context of the arbitration award confirmation proceedings, "a standard purchase price adjustment mechanism designed to capture the Company's value at closing."[92]

In the case of this transaction, the parties closed on March 28, 2022. At this point, the Buyer paid the aforementioned circa USD 39 million, with USD 32.6 million going straight to the Seller, and another circa USD 7 million being deposited in escrow.

What happened next triggered the dispute. When it came time for the Buyer to make its own calculation of the purchase price based on the completion accounts, on June 27, 2022, the Buyer added into the mix an item that was never accounted for in the purchase price calculation discussions before: the SSI debt. And it added not just the Seller's proportionate share based on its partial ownership of SSI,[93] but all USD 109 million of it. Together with other (much smaller) adjustments made, the Buyer's position was now that the Seller owed it USD 87.4 million.[94]

89. Appellant's (Seller's) Reply Brief, *RMP Seller Holdings, LLC v. SM Buyer LLC*, Civil Action No. 2023-0957 JTL (Delaware Supreme Court) 15 n. 10.
90. The remainder of the Target group must then have had a net negative value of around USD 50 million, although it is difficult to verify from the quite limited documentation available.
91. Final Award, *supra* n. 79, at 48.
92. Chancery Court Decision, *supra* n. 80, at *1 (para. 2.b).
93. Although the case has been much commented upon, the proportion question has not been addressed insofar as the authors have seen. The arbitral award and the key decision in the confirmation proceedings here confirm that the Seller only ever held a partial stake in SSI. It is unclear why the parties' contract should not have taken the pro-rata portion of the debt into account. Of course, by law, partnership members are jointly liable for partnership debts. Yet, ordinarily, partners would be responsible only for a portion of a company's debt, just as they are entitled only to a portion of its profits. And the latter sort of proportionality is reflected in the Seller's equity accounting for its SSI stake on its balance sheet. But it was not reflected in the Buyer's adjustment or in the arbitration award, since the definitions in the contract referred to debt as a whole, not making any adjustment for proportional liability for debt held by JVs of the Target and another company. This might have been a (further) ground to consider potential ambiguity in the contract's text.
94. *See* Chancery Court Decision, *supra* n. 80, at *2 (para. 2.f) and *3 (para. 2.m).

[B] The Arbitral Award

Delaware law governed the transaction. After the dispute arose, the parties opted to resolve their dispute over the treatment of the SSI Debt via arbitration rather than by another method, e.g., via the ordinary courts.[95] The parties appointed a sole arbitrator to decide the matter—a former judge who had served more than twenty years in the Delaware court system, including a number of years as a Vice Chancellor of the Delaware Court of Chancery.

The award was ultimately issued on September 5, 2023. As the arbitrator characterized the dispute therein:

> the issues ... distill down to a choice between two arguably unsatisfying outcomes: apply the clear and unambiguous terms of the operative contract and reach a result that is in tension with the extrinsic evidence; or follow that extrinsic evidence to a result that cannot be squared with the clear and unambiguous contract as written.

The Buyer's approach in the arbitration was apparently to focus on the specific language used in the operative clauses: the EPA's purchase price adjustment mechanism included an adjustment for "Closing Date Indebtedness" ("CDI").[96] CDI was defined to include "the aggregate amount of all Indebtedness of the Group Companies."[97] SSI was in turn defined as one of the "Group Companies."[98] In the arbitrator's view, these circumstances alone were adequate to justify including the additional USD 109 million of SSI debt in the purchase price.[99]

The Seller raised a number of arguments against the inclusion of the SSI debt. Framing its arguments with a focus on objective contract interpretation, as required and prudent[100] under the applicable approach to contract interpretation, it first attempted to argue that other clauses in the contract required the opposite result—so that even without looking to extrinsic evidence, the arbitrator would have to conclude in favor of the seller's interpretation; and alternatively argued that the contract was ambiguous in the relevant respect, such that the arbitrator could resort to extrinsic evidence (which, as the arbitrator did not dispute, firmly supported the Seller's position).[101]

---

95. There was also a smaller dispute which was referred to an accountant for expert determination. Chancery Court Decision, *supra* n. 80, at *2 (para. 2.k).
96. Final Award, *supra* n. 79, at 6.
97. *Ibid.*, at 12.
98. *Ibid.*, at 13.
99. *See ibid.*, at 14 (first paragraph especially) through 16 (especially last paragraph on this page, which reiterates the conclusion).
100. As we have noted, the starting point in common-law jurisdictions tends to be the objective approach. Therefore, to the extent it is possible to argue from this perspective, it will generally be beneficial to do so—at least partly because, when the same "problem" in a contract can be resolved arguably *either* through interpretation *or* through the application of "substantive" rules, courts will prefer the former. *See supra* n. 54 and text accompanying note.
101. This position is summarized in the Final Award, *supra* n. 79, at 1-2, and addressed in more detail in most of the remainder of the award. These arguments are fleshed out in some detail, and commented further upon, in West, *supra* n. 3.

The arbitrator rejected these arguments categorically, finding no basis to conclude that the contract text was ambiguous, let alone plainly in the Seller's favor.[102] Therefore, according to the arbitrator, there was no basis to introduce consideration of extrinsic evidence as part of the interpretive process.

The arbitrator also rejected the Seller's alternative arguments, for example, that essentially, the Buyer's approach would lead to an absurd result.[103] To do this, the arbitrator distinguished certain lines of Delaware court cases where the court had evidently been willing to bend the apparent plain meaning of a contract's text in light of "the basic business relationship between the parties."[104] In rejecting these "absurdity"-type arguments, the arbitrator again considered how the question of extrinsic evidence was decisive:

> Seller's most persuasive points are found outside the EPA and in the extrinsic evidence it presented. I acknowledge that some of these facts might appear to be at odds with my plain meaning construction. But when faced with tension between unambiguous contract terms supporting one result and extrinsic evidence supporting another, Delaware courts have consistently and reliably resolved the dispute based on the contract's plain language.[105]

Among other arguments raised by the Seller, the arbitrator also rejected the argument that there was a "mistake." The arbitrator described here, again, Delaware's approach as rather strict, observing that "Delaware law is clear that claims for mistake are not supported by 'poor contract drafting' and 'cannot save a party from its agreement to unambiguous contract provisions that later prove disadvantageous'."[106]

In general, the impression that the arbitral award gives is that extrinsic evidence firmly supported the Seller's approach, while the contract document's text, if not absolutely clear, weighed firmly in favor of the Buyer—especially based on a narrow focus on the straightforward apparent meaning of the "Closing Date Indebtedness" clause, and the definitions of the words in that clause.

[C] The Decision from the Confirmation/Challenge Proceedings

The parties initiated confirmation/challenge proceedings in the Delaware courts immediately after the arbitral proceedings concluded. The substantive decision in such proceedings was issued less than six months after the arbitration award, on February 28, 2024, with a final judgment being issued on March 17, 2024.

The court squarely disagreed with the arbitrator's conclusion. It reasoned, in relevant part, that the EPA's definition of Closing Date Indebtedness "sought to capture all of the debt that the Company owed. It therefore logically included subsidiary-level debt. Under a literal reading of the Agreement, the Other Business was a subsidiary, so

102. Final Award, *supra* n. 79, at 17-39.
103. *See ibid.*, at 40-47.
104. *Ibid.*, at 40 et seq.
105. *Ibid.*, at 44.
106. *Ibid.*, at 48.

the Other Business Debt fell within the definition of Closing Date Indebtedness."[107] However, while this approach was a correct "literal reading"—i.e., as the court also observed, it "hewed strictly to the definition of Closing Date Indebtedness"—in the court's view, "that adjustment had nothing else to commend it."[108] The court noted that "the adjustment disregarded the need to prepare the Pre-Closing Balance Sheet and the Post-Closing Balance Sheet on a consistent basis."[109] "From the standpoint of economic substance, the adjustment made no sense. Nothing changed about the Company, the Other Business, or the GP Interest"—and yet the Buyer relied on its literal reading of the agreement to "radically change[] the economics [of the deal] in its favor."[110] Ultimately, the judge stated:

> I would have ruled differently than the Arbitrator. I think the agreed-upon accounting principles and the mandate to prepare the reference statement and the final statement consistently meant that the Buyer's adjustment was contrary to the plain meaning of the Agreement. At a minimum, I think the Agreement, read in conjunction with the Amendment and the separate treatment of the GP Interest, rendered the parties' treatment of Closing Debt Indebtedness ambiguous.[111]

The seller ultimately relied on one avenue available under Delaware law that begins to approach a degree of substantive review—"manifest disregard for the law."[112] A finding of "manifest disregard for the law" requires "that the arbitrator (1) knew of the relevant legal principle, (2) appreciated that this principle controlled the outcome of the disputed issue, and (3) nonetheless willfully flouted the governing law by refusing to apply it." Here, the court was unable to conclude that there was manifest disregard. To the contrary, the arbitrator's award:

> flows entirely from the language of the Agreement, with particular emphasis on one definition in the Agreement. That means the Award is grounded in the Agreement. The Arbitrator also did not willfully flout the governing law. To the contrary, the Arbitrator cited and followed many Delaware precedents that set out principles of contract interpretation which, when applied strictly, support the result he reached.

Thus, the court confirmed the award.

There was then an appeal to the Delaware Supreme Court which, after oral argument, affirmed the Court of Chancery's decision with a one-page ruling on November 8, 2024, "on the basis of and for the reasons stated" in the February 28, 2024 and March 17, 2024 decisions discussed above.[113]

107. Chancery Court Decision, *supra* n. 80, at *2 (para. 2.g).
108. *Ibid.*, at *2 (para. 2.h).
109. *Ibid.*, at *2 (para. 2.i).
110. *Ibid.*, at *2 (para. 2.j). The "GP Interest" here refers to the stake in SSI.
111. *Ibid.*, at *4 (para. 9.e).
112. *Ibid.*, at *3 (para. 7). It should be noted that the legitimacy of this ground for an award challenge under United States law is hotly debated.
113. *RMP Seller Holdings, LLC v. SM Buyer LLC*, 329 A.3d 1044 (Del. November 8, 2024).

§7.04 HOW *SAVE MART* MIGHT HAVE BEEN DECIDED DIFFERENTLY

[A] Introduction

As noted in the introduction, the result in the *Save Mart* case could have come out differently if not for several different factors, including, for example:

(1) the arbitrator's potentially incorrect application of Delaware law;
(2) the seller's (lawyers') poor contract drafting;
(3) the seller's (lawyers') preference for arbitration over litigation and use of a sole arbitrator; and/or
(4) the buyer's (lawyers') possible withholding of knowledge of an important drafting error.

Other authors have already written at least to some extent on items (2), (3), and (4) above. For this reason among others, in the remainder of this section, we primarily focus on item (1) above, as well as the adjacent question of how the matter might have been decided under the laws of other jurisdictions, or even another legal system—neither of which, to our knowledge, has been commented upon previously. Regarding the latter topic, notwithstanding that the arbitrator may have gotten the law wrong, the authors consider this case an apt vehicle for considering how a jurisdiction's place on the textualism-contextualism spectrum can affect the outcome in borderline cases.

In the following subsections, we explore first (section [B]) the "alternative explanations"—items (2) through (4) above; then (section [D]) how the matter might have been decided differently under Delaware law, or under the law of other common-law jurisdictions; and finally (section [E]) how the matter might have been decided if Scandinavian law governed the transaction.

[B] "Alternative Explanations" for the Surprising Outcome in This Case

Perhaps the most obvious overall "explanation" for the outcome in this case—one which multiple American lawyers commented upon shortly after this case became public—is that the seller (or more probably the seller's lawyers) may simply have engaged in sloppy contract-drafting practices. Prior commentators have raised a range of suggestions for how the sellers might have avoided the present outcome, typically focusing on the core of the apparent drafting error(s) and the arbitrator's actual reasoning (naturally, if one changes what was the foundation for the arbitrator's reasoning, then one would of course expect that the outcome might be different). Here, we highlight a few points which are, to varying degrees, inspired by or repeating what these commentators have noted:[114]

114. *See especially* West, *supra* n. 3, but also Albin, *supra* n. 4.

- The definition of Closing Date Indebtedness in an SPA should as a rule not include the debt of subsidiaries without qualifications. Naturally, a partly owned subsidiary should not have all of its debt attributed to the parent. A partnership interest (through which the target held SSI here) could present a special situation—but in any case, if the seller's lawyers used a nuanced template definition of Closing Date Indebtedness, they might have avoided this situation.
- SSI should not have been listed as a relevant company on the schedule of group companies, given the special way that this company was held and accounted for: (i) minority stake; (ii) held in a partnership; (iii) with the holding's value recognized through a single equity position on the target's balance sheet. Had this apparent mistake not been made, the SSI debt would again have been excluded from possible relevance in the purchase price adjustment process.
- A sample calculation of the purchase price could have been included with the EPA, and a requirement could have been inserted in the SPA that the purchase price calculation would have to use the same approach.[115] Had such a requirement been in place, the buyer's insertion of a new debt item which was known at the time of deal signing would have been foreclosed.
- Even a generous cap on the purchase price adjustment quantum—for example, equal to, or even double, the escrow amount of circa USD 7 million, could have saved the Sellers from virtually all of the consequences that they eventually faced.

A second overall "explanation" of this case's outcome is that it was a fluke enabled by a risky choice of dispute resolution format. In this light, the case can be seen as a warning regarding the perils of "rogue arbitrators"—particularly sole arbitrators—coming to outlier results.[116] One of the commonly cited arguments for the very existence of courts of appeal is that they allow for the correction of errors committed by trial courts. Typically, appeals courts consist of panels rather than individual judges (with deliberation perhaps improving the quality of decision-making), and their opinions are published, or at least not confidential (potentially increasing pressure on judges to get the reasoning and result correct). Resolving a dispute instead via a final award issued by a sole arbitrator introduces several risks of error (by which we would mean here: deviation from the final outcome that would be reached in the ordinary courts): (1) one lacks a panel of judges considering potential errors on appeal; (2) there is (effectively) no appeal available at all; (3) even in the first

115. *See* Vincent J. Cannizzaro, *Chancery Confirms Arbitration Award Resulting in Negative Purchase Price*, https://www.morrisjames.com/p/102jgqa/chancery-confirms-arbitration-award-resulting-in-negative-purchase-price/ (accessed March 29, 2025).
116. *See* West, *supra* n. 3 (alluding to this topic at a high level). *See also* John A. Kupiec et al., *Raw Deal: Seller Ordered to Pay Buyer Over Twice the Purchase Price in Post-Closing Purchase Price Adjustment Dispute*, https://www.clearymawatch.com/2024/03/raw-deal-seller-ordered-to-pay-buyer-over-twice-the-purchase-price-in-post-closing-purchase-price-adjustment-dispute/ (accessed March 29, 2025).

instance there is only one adjudicator deciding; and (4) the award is (as a rule) confidential, quite the opposite of being published/reported. The first three factors imply less opportunity for the adjudicator to deliberate, and the last would seem to imply less incentive to deliberate. Of course, these risks are hardly new—other commentators have discussed them in other cases, as well as (to some extent) in this particular case. And the risks of arbitration more generally have been discussed *ad nauseam* in the literature. But the issue is no less relevant for having been discussed before.

A third point to consider is that there may have been an ethical breach by the buyer's lawyers, or a choice that was imprudent in the long term by the buyer itself. We refer here especially to the text accompanying footnotes 126 to 128 *infra*. The ethical questions here can be complex and have not been the focus of the authors' investigation for this chapter. However, other commentators have questioned whether the circumstances of this case may have involved the buyer's lawyers "knowingly mak[ing] a false statement of material fact or law to" the seller side (American Bar Association Model Rules of Professional Conduct, Rule 4.1), or—at a more general level—"engag[ing] in conduct involving dishonesty, fraud, deceit or misrepresentation" (Rule 8.4(c)). Ultimately, the limited facts available to the authors, in particular about the buyer's lawyers' knowledge and actions, do not allow us to analyze the question in a fulsome manner.[117]

Even setting aside the question of whether the buyer's lawyers complied with applicable ethics rules, a related question is whether the buyer and its team made the right choice in pursuing the aggressive legal position that it did. It is possible that the buyer and/or the buyer's lawyer may face reputational or practical repercussions for the positions they took in this case. For example, it is not out of the question that future business partners might be skeptical about transacting with the buyer, or outright unwilling to deal with them.[118] Consequently, it can in some sense be said that potentially ethical, but at least prudential, concerns could or should have prevented the outcome that actually occurred in this case.

[C] How the Case Should Have Been Decided under Delaware Law or the Law of Another Jurisdiction—Initial Comments

As has been noted already, there is another topic of discussion related to the outcome in this case which in the authors' view is in many respects more important and interesting than the foregoing explanations, which has two elements: (1) did the arbitrator get the law wrong; and (2) how would the case have been decided under the laws of a different jurisdiction or even a different legal system? In the authors' view, this topic may provide a better explanation for the outcome here, and may also provide more generally useful guidance to lawyers and industry actors in future cases.

117. *See* Albin, *supra* n. 4.
118. *See* West, *supra* n. 3 (making this very point).

In the following section [D], we consider how the case may have been decided wrongly under Delaware law, which in our view should generally have aligned with other common-law jurisdictions in how it would resolve the case. In section [E], we consider how the case might have been decided if Scandinavian substantive (contract) law had been used instead.

[D] How the Arbitrator Might Have Decided Differently under a Common-Law Approach

[1] Introduction

The arbitrator in this case characterized the matter as hinging on whether extrinsic evidence would be considered at all.[119] Delaware law, which governed here, sits far, or perhaps on the edge, on the textualist side of the spectrum discussed earlier in this chapter—that is, it is quite exceptional that extrinsic evidence can be considered when interpreting contracts under Delaware law.[120]

The arbitrator may, however, have overstated the extent of Delaware's textualism, leaning practically into a caricature of literalism. Perhaps the best evidence of possible error in this regard is that, in the confirmation/challenge proceedings, the Chancery Court commented that it would have decided the case differently.

Yet in the authors' view, there was an even more striking apparent error in the award: that the doctrines of mistake were given such short shrift.

In any case, that the actual outcome occurred as it did seems to indicate a certain likelihood of reaching this sort of outcome when using Delaware law.

In our view, there are at least three ways that the case should have been resolved differently under a Delaware law (or more generally common-law) approach: (1) a straightforward or objective interpretation; (2) interpretation based on extrinsic evidence in light of textual ambiguity; or (3) the doctrine of mistake—this last approach having been more or less overlooked by the arbitrator.

[2] The Ordinary Interpretive Approach

First, the matter might have been resolved as a *straightforward question of interpretation*, without concluding that any terms were ambiguous and thus evaluating the full range of extrinsic evidence. This is in a sense the simplest solution, insofar as it avoids some of the potential doctrinal complexities involved with the other routes discussed below. And this is in fact what the Delaware Court of Chancery said it would have done.[121]

119. *See* quotation from the Final Award at the beginning of §7.03[B] *supra*.
120. *See, e.g.*, Final Award, *supra* n. 79, at 2 ("Delaware law is more contractarian than most.").
121. *See* text accompanying *supra* n. 107.

From a comparative perspective, we can recall[122] in passing here that, in contextualist jurisdictions, a "straightforward interpretation" can in fact consider some extrinsic evidence. Given that (as the arbitrator recognized) the extrinsic evidence decisively favored the seller's approach to interpreting the contract, insofar as the parties relied on the laws of another jurisdiction (which would typically be more open to considering extrinsic evidence at this stage), a pro-buyer result would have been much more likely here.

Yet, perhaps this "straightforward" approach is not the approach that best matches the circumstances.

[3] Interpretation Relying on Extrinsic Evidence after a Finding of Textual Ambiguity

A *second approach* would be to determine that the *agreement's text was ambiguous*, and therefore to resolve the matter by explicit resort to extrinsic evidence to clarify the content of the parties' agreement. This approach is what the Chancery Court was referring to when it noted that "the Agreement, read in conjunction with the Amendment and the separate treatment of the GP Interest, rendered the parties' treatment of Closing Debt Indebtedness ambiguous."[123]

In a textualist jurisdiction such as Delaware, an intermediate conclusion that the text was ambiguous would allow the consideration of extrinsic evidence. In more contextualist jurisdictions (where some extrinsic evidence might already have been considered to establish ambiguity), such an intermediate conclusion (that the text was ambiguous) would have opened for the consideration of even more forms of extrinsic evidence.[124] In any case, as the arbitrator himself recognized, considering the extrinsic evidence would have led to a pro-buyer result here.

For reasons similar to those already stated in respect of the first approach above, the same result would presumably obtain in other jurisdictions as well.

[4] Rectification of Contract Text Based on Mistake

A *third approach* was unfortunately barely touched upon in the *Save Mart* arbitral award—with the law being laid out inadequately there—and was not at all mentioned in the subsequent court decisions. Nor, to the authors' knowledge, have other commentators addressed it. Yet, from what we can see of the facts, this seems to be the most legitimately applicable of all: mistake.[125] Either the "mutual mistake" or "unilateral mistake" doctrines probably could have been invoked and established here. We focus on unilateral mistake below.

122. *See supra* §7.02[B][1] and §7.02[B][4].
123. Chancery Court Decision, *supra* n. 80, at *4 (para. 9.e).
124. *See, e.g., Eagle Indus., Inc. v. DeVilbiss Health Care, Inc.*, 702 A.2d 1228, 1232 (Del. 1997) (noting that in case of ambiguity extrinsic evidence may be considered, citing specifically, e.g., "evidence of prior agreements and communications of the parties").
125. We have commented generally on the mistake doctrines above. *See* §7.02[B][5].

[a] Under Delaware Law: A Fresh Analysis of the Facts and Law

Earlier, we addressed the doctrine of mistake at a high level.[126] The doctrine's nuances can vary from one common-law jurisdiction to another. We therefore first consider Delaware law specifically.

Under Delaware law, a party can obtain rectification of a contract if it establishes a unilateral mistake.[127] The requirements are that: (i) the parties came to a specific prior understanding that differed materially from the written agreement (established with "clear and convincing evidence");[128] (ii) the rectification-seeker was mistaken; and (iii) the other party knew of the rectification-seeker's mistake but remained silent. Here, the available material indicates:

- The transaction discussion started with the buyer providing the seller an LOI which indicated that the circa USD 110 million SSI debt would only be part of the purchase price calculation insofar as it affected the total equity value of the Target's stake in SSI.
- The communication between the parties along the way never indicated any deviation from this understanding, resulting in an expected purchase price of around USD 40 million to be paid by the buyer.
- The seller apparently provided a draft of the SPA in December 2021 which (according to the buyer's eventual calculation and the arbitrator's conclusion) *did* define the SSI debt as included for adjustment in the purchase price calculation.[129]
- The seller never seemed to be aware of the debt-definition issue with the SPA draft, through and including when: (a) the seller made its draft calculation of the purchase price at closing, and (b) the buyer paid according to that draft calculation and did not object, up until (c) the buyer finally provided a new calculation.
- As later quoted in reporting by the Financial Times,[130] the buyer was aware of this discrepancy between its LOI and the SPA's text, but did not alert the seller: "[W]e had had a draft purchase agreement from [the Seller] dating back to, you know, December [2021] that clearly laid out" that indebtedness for purposes of the transaction would include the USD 109 million in debt held by SSI.[131] And "we assumed that they had read their own document that they drafted."[132] "For some reason, which we don't know why, [it] appeared not to

126. *See supra* §7.02[B][5].
127. *See Scion Breckenridge Managing Member, LLC v. ASB Allegiance Real Est. Fund*, 68 A.3d 665, 679 (Del. 2013) (laying out elements, and rejecting the suggestion that the situation must be "exceptional").
128. This is a higher-level burden of proof than merely preponderance of the evidence. *See Cerberus Int'l, Ltd. v. Apollo Mgmt., L.P.*, 794 A.2d 1141, 1151 (Del. 2002).
129. *See* Indap, *supra* n. 83.
130. *Ibid.*
131. *Ibid.*
132. *Ibid.*

be the perspective of the seller" that the SSI debt would be accounted for in an adjustment to the purchase price.[133]
- The result of adding the whole SSI debt separately in the purchase price adjustment process rendered the transaction one where a profitable business was "sold," for a hefty price paid *by the seller, to the buyer*, in a manner contrary to any expectations of the parties reflected in their written (or oral) communications up to that point—only (perhaps) in the text of the contract itself.

In the authors' view, under the Delaware doctrine of unilateral mistake, the requirements for providing relief to the buyer in this case are met based on the above facts.[134] In particular:

- the LOI (and absence of any indication of change of position in the subsequent negotiations) constitutes an adequate "specific prior understanding";
- the absence of evidence that the seller was aware of the meaning of the text later invoked by the buyer—through the signing of the SPA and its calculation of the purchase price—shows that the seller was mistaken about the contents of the contract's text;
- the buyer has admitted that it was aware of the relevant discrepancy between the text of the contract and the seller's expectations about the content of the parties' agreement.

At a high level, we also note that, looking to the illustrations cited earlier from the Restatement (Second) of the Law of Contracts, this case resembles both illustrations in the critical respects.[135] The requirements for rectification according to the doctrine of unilateral mistake thus appear to be met here.

Of course, we cannot be completely sure about this analysis, since much of the evidence is simply not directly available outside of the confidential arbitration proceedings. But it seems quite probable.

[b] The Arbitrator's Summary Rejection of "Mistake" Seems to Have Misstated and Probably also Misapplied the Law

The arbitrator denied the seller's rectification argument in summary fashion. Admitting that "Kingswood's original letter of intent did not include any SSI Debt in its sample Indebtedness calculation,"[136] the arbitrator nonetheless characterized the LOI—which apparently, apart from the SSI debt question, was reflected in the parties' eventual agreement—not as a "specific prior understanding" on the SSI debt question, but

133. *Ibid.*
134. The same probably also applies for mutual mistake, as well as for *both* unilateral mistake and mutual mistake under the laws of many common-law jurisdictions around the world, not just in Delaware.
135. *See* text accompanying *supra* nn. 51 and 52.
136. Final Award, *supra* n. 79, at 48.

merely as being silent on that question. This, in our view, was not the right conclusion. While the LOI may not have explicitly spelled out that the SSI Debt would not be added separately, by arriving at a total valuation based on omitting that item (or, more precisely, integrating a pro-rata portion of it as part of the total equity value of the SSI interest), it *did* include this item. In reality, the valuation in the LOI could *only* be reached if the SSI Debt was included in this way.[137]

The arbitrator concluded his very short analysis of the "mistake" question with two quotations from another Chancery Court case, with no further elaboration:

> Delaware law is clear that claims for mistake are not supported by "poor contract drafting" and "cannot save a party from its agreement to unambiguous contract provisions that later prove disadvantageous."[138]

These quotations are both *dicta*[139] in the decisions in which they respectively appear. Moreover, to the extent considered legal rules, they directly contradict Delaware Supreme Court precedent, which confirms that the mistake doctrine absolutely can save a party "from its agreement to unambiguous contract provisions"—as long as the actual elements of a claim for mistake are established.[140]

Likewise, "poor contract drafting"—the suggestion here is negligent legal work—is no bar to recovery for mistake, although it is, to be sure, not sufficient *standing alone* to obtain relief under the doctrine. In fact, mistake practically by

137. While we thus do not consider this an instance of silence, the following English commentary is also informative: "It would be inconsistent with the objective of rectification for common mistake if the court were precluded from considering, as a part of that assessment, understandings that the parties thought so obvious as to go without saying, or that were reached without being spelled out in so many words." *FSHC Group Holdings Ltd v. Barclays Bank Plc*, [2018] EWHC 1558 at [35].

138. Final Award, *supra* n. 79, at 49 (quoting *Frontline Techs. Parent, LLC v. Murphy*, No. 2023-0546-LWW, 2023 WL 5424802, at *5 (Del. Ch. August 23, 2023)). As the *Frontline Technologies* decision is written, it appears to reject the mistake claim in large part simply because it is pled in the alternative, which appears not to be a legitimate reason to reject such a claim.

139. *Obiter dicta*, "said in passing," are comments in a judicial opinion which do not form part of the basis of the relevant ruling, and are therefore not treated as establishing a rule for future cases. *See, e.g.*, *King v. Erickson*, 89 F.3d 1575, 1582 (Fed. Cir. 1996).

140. *See Interactive Corp. v. Vivendi Universal, S.A.*, No. CIV.A. 20260, 2004 WL 1572932, at *15 (Del. Ch. June 30, 2004), which comments as follows (emphasis added):

> [I]n order for a dispute centered on the interpretation of a contract to move beyond the pleading stage [i.e., to establish a question of fact rather than legal interpretation], a court must find that a contract's terms are ambiguous or susceptible of different meanings. If the court finds the terms are not ambiguous, the court will enforce those terms as written, and the case will not move to the expensive, time-consuming stages of discovery and trial. ... Mistake is a claim that *disregards this framework*. One claiming mistake assumes that the contract is clear on its face. The claimant must argue that, notwithstanding this clarity, the court should enforce another meaning of the contract. The argument is that the contract's "clear meaning" is not *really* the meaning the parties intended.

See also, for example, *Alvarez v. Castellon*, 55 A.3d 352, 354 (Del. 2012) ("A court may, however, set aside a clear and unambiguous release where there is fraud, duress, coercion, or mutual mistake concerning the existence of a party's injuries.").

definition captures a range of circumstances that could be described as "poor contract drafting"—from correcting typos, to referring to incorrect locations and movable property, to misstating a price, to (as here) erroneously inserting or omitting terms.

In the authors' view, the arbitrator's selection of these quotations is informative as a sign of ideology. Both quotations underscore that the exclusively "contractarian" approach which underpinned the arbitrator's rejection of the seller's positions regarding contract interpretation may also have been a key driver behind the arbitrator's rejection of the claim for mistake.

[5] Concluding Considerations

In other common-law jurisdictions, the same results would, in our view, be quite likely. As has been noted already, other common-law jurisdictions tend to sit on the more contextual side of the spectrum compared to Delaware.

Meanwhile, their mistake doctrines are hardly very different from Delaware's. For example, in England, the law regarding rectification for unilateral mistake has been summed up to require as follows:[141]

> *first*, that one party (A) erroneously believed that the document sought to be rectified contained a particular term or provision ... *secondly*, that the other party (B) was aware of the omission or the inclusion and that it was due to a mistake on the part of (A); *thirdly*, that (B) has omitted to draw the mistake to the notice of (A) ... *fourth* ... that the mistake must be one calculated to benefit (B).

These grounds, being quite similar to those expressed by the Delaware Supreme Court, seem to be met here as well. And judges from England or other jurisdictions, conversely to the arbitrator here, would probably be more open to arguments regarding mistake.

In sum, there are several ways that the arbitrator, applying Delaware law, could and probably should have arrived at a conclusion in favor of the seller instead of the buyer. To the extent that a different common-law jurisdiction's substantive law applied to the case, such background law would be more likely to be applied in a contextualist fashion, and therefore would be even more likely to have been decided in favor of the seller.

[E] How This Case Might Have Been Approached under Scandinavian Contract Law

[1] Introduction

The likely outcome of the *Save Mart* case would, in the authors' view, have been somewhat more doctrinally straightforward under Scandinavian law than under a

141. *Thos. Bates v. Wyndhams (Lingerie)* [1981] 1 WLR 505 at 516A-B, as quoted in *Littman & Anor v. Aspen Oil (Broking) Ltd* [2005] EWCA Civ 1579 (December 19, 2005) at [20] (emphases added). It may be that the last requirement here simply should be taken to mean that the mistake harms (A), as indicated by, e.g., Lord Justice Everleigh in *Thomas Bates*.

common-law approach. We consider in this section some alternative scenarios for how a Scandinavian court or tribunal might have resolved the dispute. In addition to the plain interpretive approach (section [E][2]), we shall also consider the possibility of relying on section 36 of the Scandinavian Contract Acts (section [E][3]).

[2] Ordinary Interpretive Approaches

First, we recall that the principle of intersubjectivity is the natural starting point for any contract interpretation under Scandinavian law. Thus, before anything else, a Scandinavian court or arbitral tribunal would need to decide here whether the parties at the time of making the contract had a common understanding of the contract clause(s) in question. In order for a court or arbitral tribunal to conclude that there was, in fact, a common understanding, there must be clear evidence.[142] Then again, under Scandinavian law, the full range of evidence would be available to a court or arbitral tribunal—including, for example, testimony from the relevant individuals—which would then freely evaluate the most likely shared intention of the parties.

On the facts available to us, and as described above (e.g., in section [D][4][a]), we believe a court or arbitral tribunal applying Scandinavian background law would be likely to conclude that the parties had a mutual understanding that the SSI debt would not properly be added separately to the purchase price calculation, so that the seller and not the buyer would prevail. In the evaluation of the evidence, the respective parties' testimony might play some part, but the documents would have more significant weight. Here, it would be especially significant that the LOI did not indicate that the SSI debt should be separately included, and that the seller's calculation of the purchase price in connection with closing, which was in line with the LOI, went uncommented at the time by the buyer. It would also be notable that there was evidently no documentary evidence that the parties intended to change their approach from the approach used in the LOI, and that the difference in the price effected by including the SSI debt separately was so extreme as would presumably warrant some kind of written discussion.[143] Again, since much of the evidence is not available, we cannot confirm this view with great certainty—so these conclusions are instead based on what we believe the evidence would show based on the descriptions in the relevant decisions and filings.

Second, it could be considered whether this matter should have been resolved by application of the dolus doctrine.[144] The question to be decided would then be whether the buyer ought to have understood that the seller did not share the understanding, supposedly held by the buyer, that the SSI debt would be separately added to the

142. *See supra* §7.02[C][1], noting the reluctance of Scandinavian courts to apply the intersubjective approach to resolve contract disputes, notwithstanding the ideological primacy of this principle.
143. Overall, the reader may observe a similarity between how the case might have been resolved under the (mutual) mistake doctrine under the common law and under this intersubjective approach under Scandinavian contract law.
144. *See supra* §7.02[C][2].

purchase price calculation. Although subsidiary to the principle of intersubjectivity, the dolus doctrine has the obvious advantage that it does not require a court to find that, as a matter of fact, there was a common understanding between the parties. Instead, the dolus doctrine allows a court to reach an equivalent result based purely on a legal assessment of the behavior of the contracting parties. That is, to apply the doctrine here, a court would conclude as a legal matter that the buyer had a duty of care which it did not fulfil. Given the extreme position taken by the buyer in comparison to the background assumptions (we refer again here in particular to the LOI), and insofar as it would mean the seller would, contrary to one's ordinary expectation, be paying the buyer to accept its company, in our view, there are good arguments for the application of this doctrine.

Third, we should consider the objective approach to contract interpretation. In contracts between highly professional parties, the presumption that the parties have expressed their intention in the text of their written contract is particularly strong. Then again, the Scandinavian "objective approach" involves a much broader conception of the "factual matrix" than even in the more contextualist common-law jurisdictions—even for professional parties. Yet, although a deviation from the formal contract's text is thus available in this approach, in particular if there is evidence to suggest that the wording does not reflect the will of the parties,[145] there must be sufficient evidence to justify a deviation. In the present case, the seller would essentially argue that the LOI should be read as part of the contract's broader contents. Doing so, the seller would in practice be arguing that the potential deviation from the LOI's clearer contents in the details of the definitions in the SPA that were eventually relied upon by the arbitrator did not override the obvious intention of the parties in the LOI.

Also, under this Scandinavian objective approach, then, we consider it very likely that the seller would have prevailed.

Overall, then, in our view, the Scandinavian approach to contract interpretation would likely have led to results similar to those of a common-law contextualist approach, but with more ease, without any ideological resistance that can arise when considering extrinsic evidence or evaluating the apparent shared intention of the parties "outside the four corners of the contract" under the common law.

[3] Revising the Contract's Text under Section 36

In the authors' view, this is not a case where application of section 36 of the relevant Scandinavian Contract Act would be relevant to resolve the matter. As noted in §7.02[C][5] above, section 36 is a statutory provision which has been applied most often in contexts where, for example: (1) there is some defect in the making of the contract; (2) a longer-term contract ends up putting one party in a commercially impracticable situation; or (3) some unforeseen event makes the contract imbalanced or inoperative.

---

145. Section 32 of the respective Scandinavian Contract Acts is an example of this attitude.

Before its enactment, section 36 was considered by some commentators to have a potential erosive force on the binding power of contracts and ultimately on the rule of law. Perhaps as a consequence, then, despite its enactment, courts have historically construed section 36 relatively narrowly, avoiding relying on it to amend a contract's objective text.

Yet, it has been commented that section 36 has had an indirect effect on the way that courts interpret contracts (i.e., beyond its actual scope), in that there is a pressure to discard unreasonable results by way of the ordinary interpretation process. Section 36 then provides an additional pressure on courts to rely doctrinally on an intersubjective approach that deviates from an objective textual reading if such an approach will appear more commercially balanced. This phenomenon can be compared to the equivalent preference of common-law judges to prefer to decide cases as matters of interpretation rather than policy.[146]

§7.05 FINAL REFLECTIONS

As noted in the introduction, there are several different factors that could be described as explanations or lessons to draw from the *Save Mart* case. In the foregoing, we have focused on: (i) whether the arbitrator applied Delaware law incorrectly; and (ii) how the case might have been (more likely to be) decided differently under the laws of other jurisdictions, including in particular Scandinavian law.

While—as discussed in §7.04[B]—there are other possible explanations or lessons to draw from the *Save Mart* case, in the authors' view the factors that we have focused on are of particular interest, as: (i) they have not been discussed before in connection with this case; (ii) this dispute is a particularly good example of how "edge cases" can produce opposite results in different legal systems; and (iii) the actual lesson(s) to be learned from an edge case such as this one can be of great relevance for commercial actors with global presences, and therefore frequent opportunities to choose which law applies to their commercial interactions.

Perhaps above all else, the *Save Mart* case underscores the oversimplicity of the traditional view that textualism is the best choice for actors who favor predictability. In fact, in our view, both parties in this transaction seem to have expected the transaction to turn out the way that the seller claimed was correct, until at some point a drafting error was introduced, which the buyer probably knew about and withheld. Having the contract governed by Delaware law rather than, e.g., Scandinavian law substantially increased the possibility that the agreement's interpretation would be infected by this error. As a corollary to this observation, then, this case reflects that, in important respects, one may find more predictability in contextualist jurisdictions and legal systems—especially in Scandinavia, where a more flexible and holistic approach to contract interpretation reigns—than in textualist ones.

Parties engaged in commercial transactions should thus, in addition to other factors, evaluate carefully which jurisdiction's law may best serve them. And then,

146. *See supra* n. 54 and text accompanying note.

having chosen a set of background laws to apply to their contract(s), they must govern their behavior accordingly, not only in terms of the clauses inserted into the contract, but even in terms of the trail of evidence they create and leave along the way.

CHAPTER 8

A Practitioner's Guide to Decision Analysis: Strengthening Strategy and Decision-Making in Arbitration

Anna Bladh Redzic & Olof Heggemann

In the high-stakes world of international arbitration, decisions are often shaped by instinct, experience, and persuasion. But what if there were a more structured way to navigate complexity and assess risk? Decision analysis offers just that – a powerful framework that helps counsel and their clients to clarify options, weigh outcomes, and make choices with greater confidence. It may also assist arbitrators in reaching better decisions.

Rooted in eighteenth-century mathematics[1] and refined by advances in negotiation theory and behavioural psychology,[2] decision analysis has gained increasing attention in litigation and arbitration.[3] It focuses on how decisions are made under uncertainty and, crucially, how they can be improved by defining objectives, mapping

1. Including the work of Blaise Pascal, Daniel Bernoulli, Thomas Bayes, and Pierre-Simon Laplace on probability theory and the expected value.
2. Some notable works include: Ronald A. Howard and James E. Matheson, The Principles and Applications of Decision Analysis (Menlo Park, CA: Strategic Decisions Group, 1989), Howard Raiffa, The Art and Science of Negotiation: How to Resolve Conflicts and Get the Best Out of Bargaining (Cambridge, MA: Belknap Press, 1982), and Roger Fisher, William Ury and Bruce Patton, Getting to Yes: Negotiating Agreement Without Giving In (New York: Penguin Books, 1991).
3. *See*, for example: Marjorie Corman Aaron, Risk & Rigor: A Lawyer's Guide to Decision Trees for Assessing Cases and Advising Clients (New York: American Bar Association, 2019), John Celona, Winning at Litigation through Decision Analysis (Cham: Springer, 2016), Michaela Keet, Heather Heavin and John Lande, Litigation Interest and Risk Assessment: Help Your Clients Make Good Litigation Decisions (New York: American Bar Association, 2020), Robert H. Mnookin, Scott R. Peppet and Andrew S. Tulumello, Beyond Winning: Negotiating to Create Value in Deals and Disputes (Cambridge, MA: Harvard University Press, 2000) and Jörg Risse, Prozessrisikoanalyse: Erfolgsaussichten vor Gericht bestimmen (Munich: Verlag C.H. Beck, 2014). *See also* the many articles written by the American attorney Marc B. Victor.

scenarios, and quantifying risks. Widely used in fields such as medicine, pharmaceuticals and energy, decision analysis is equally well-suited to dispute resolution.

This chapter examines how arbitration practitioners can apply decision analysis to improve strategic planning and client communication, support settlement negotiations, and enhance adjudicative decision-making. Through practical examples - drawn primarily from the authors' experience in technology-related disputes - it illustrates how decision analysis can offer valuable insights across a wide range of cases.

§8.01 INTRODUCTION TO DECISION-TREE ANALYSIS: BASIC CONCEPTS EXPLAINED

The following section will explain the basic concepts of decision-tree analysis through the simplified case example below.

A software developer is considering pursuing a claim of EUR 1 million through arbitration. The developer performed a significant amount of additional work in a project, but the customer now objects that this work was included in the initial scope of the project and therefore rejects the claim for additional compensation. If brought to arbitration, the arbitral tribunal would need to determine:

(a) whether the developer is entitled to additional payment; and
(b) if the claimed amount is reasonable compensation for the additional work.

Resolving the case through arbitration would cost each party approximately EUR 200,000 covering counsel and arbitration fees. The losing party would bear the total costs for both parties.

The customer has made a final offer of EUR 100,000 to settle the dispute. Would it make sense for the developer to accept this settlement if the goal is to maximize the monetary value of the claim?

After reviewing the case, the developer's legal counsel assesses that an arbitral tribunal is *more likely than not* (60% chance) to find that the work merits additional payment, that the full amount could *perhaps* (25% chance) be awarded, albeit will *probably* (50% chance) be reduced to EUR 750,000 and *perhaps* even (25% chance) to half the amount claimed. The outcomes and subjective probabilities can be illustrated in a tree structure and a cumulative probability graph as follows.

Figure 8.1 Tree-Model and Table Showing the Four Possible Outcomes of a Disputed Claim, Their Probabilities, Probability-Weighted Values, and the Total of These Weighted Values (The Expected Value)

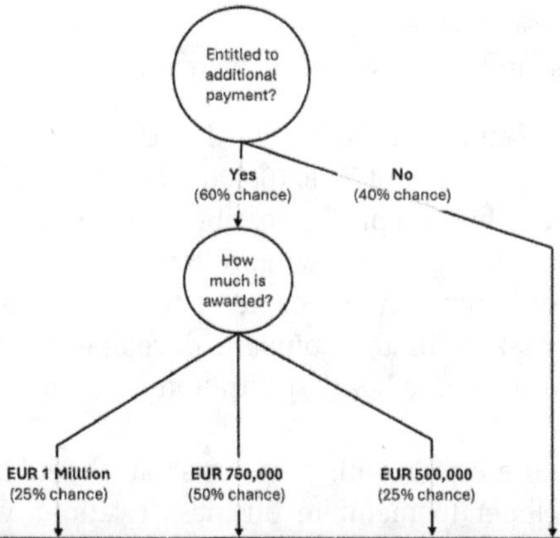

	Full win	Medium win	Low win	Loss	Total
Probability	15%	30%	15%	40%	100%
Outcome (EUR)	1,000,000 (award)	750,000 (award)	500,000 (award)	-400,000 (legal costs)	
Weighted value (EUR)	150,000	225,000	75,000	-160.000	290,000 (Expected value)

Figure 8.2 Graph Based on the Table in Figure 8.1, Showing the Probability–Value Distribution of the Possible Outcomes

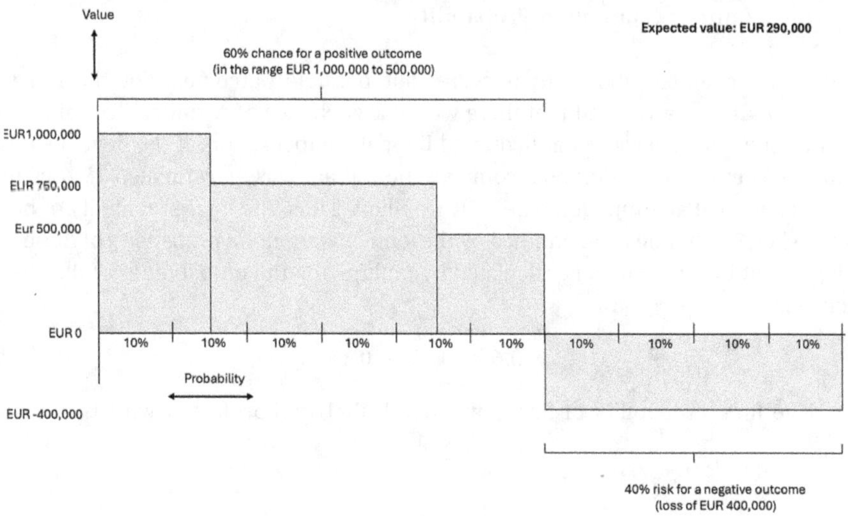

The decision-tree analysis above shows that arbitration could result in one of four outcomes:[4]

- a EUR 1 million award (15% chance);
- a EUR 750,000 award (30% chance);
- a EUR 500,000 (15% chance); or
- a EUR 400,000 loss in legal costs (40% chance).

The expected value of pursuing arbitration is EUR 290,000. That is a clearly higher value than the settlement offer of EUR 100,000. In essence, if the developer can financially (and psychologically) accept the possibility of losing and paying the full legal costs, the best decision is to proceed with arbitration.

The developer cannot control the outcome of the case, but with a structured assessment, the decision-makers in the software developer's organization can be confident that the decision to proceed with arbitration is reasonable and withstands scrutiny.

This is assuming that there are no other interests that should be considered, such as the value for the developer to maintain business relations with the customer, internal costs and more. Such aspects may be commercially valid to consider and can also be included in a decision analysis model, as will be further explored below.

§8.02 BASIC CONCEPTS EXPLAINED

The example above includes some highlighted terms and calculations that may not be familiar to all readers. The following section provides explanations for these terms.

[A] Joint or Compound Probability

In the case example above, there were four possible outcomes. For the full win alternative, it was estimated that there was a 60% chance of winning the main issue; whether the developer was entitled to additional compensation. If the developer was found to be entitled to additional compensation, there was an estimated 25% chance that the awarded amount would be EUR 1 million. Thus, the total probability of being awarded EUR 1 million is determined by the joint or compound probability of these two independent events, which is calculated by multiplying the probabilities of the events occurring.

$$0.6 \times 0.25 = 0.15$$

The final probability of being awarded EUR 1 million (a full win) is therefore 15%.

4. Interest has been excluded to simplify the example.

The same calculations are made to assess the likelihood of a medium win, a low win, and a loss, as shown in the table below:

Probability of full win	=	0.6 × 0.25	=	0.15 (15%)
Probability of medium win	=	0.6 × 0.5	=	0.30 (30%)
Probability of low win	=	0.6 × 0.25	=	0.15 (15%)
Probability of loss	=	0.4	=	0.4 (40%)
Total probability			=	1.0 (100%)

[B] Expected Value

The expected value represents the probability-weighted average of all possible outcomes.[5] To calculate the expected value, one simply multiplies the value of each outcome by its likelihood to occur and then sums these values.

To illustrate, a person has the option to participate in a game, free of charge. A coin is flipped:

- heads (50% chance) → win EUR 1 million;
- tails (50% chance) → win nothing.

The expected value of the game can therefore be calculated as follows:

Heads:	0.5 × EUR 1,000,000	=	500,000	(weighted value)
Tails:	0.5 × EUR 0	=	0	(weighted value)
Total:		=	500,000	(expected value)

While the actual outcomes are either EUR 1 million or 0, the expected value of the bet is EUR 500,000. The expected value can be more easily understood when connected to a graph that shows the probability distribution of the outcomes, as seen in the case example above.

[C] Risk Tolerance and Risk Neutrality

Given the option to either flip the coin in the example above or instead accept EUR 500,000 directly, a truly risk-neutral person would be completely indifferent. Both choices have an expected value of EUR 500,000, making them equally valuable.

5. A famous example of expected value reasoning comes from US negligence law. The Learned Hand rule holds that a party may be negligent for failing to prevent harm, if the cost of prevention is lower than the expected value of harm (the risk of harm multiplied by the potential damages).

However, research shows that most people are risk-averse. For many, the possibility of winning EUR 1 million is not worth the risk of ending up with nothing. Instead, when faced with a decision, most people are likely to choose the secure amount of EUR 500,000. Many would also accept an even lower amount, perhaps as low as EUR 400,000, to avoid the uncertainty involved with flipping the coin. This is essentially the same as paying a premium of EUR 100,000 to insure against the possibility of walking away empty-handed.

Large companies that can afford the risk involved with commercial decisions are in the long run better off being risk neutral. It makes little sense to pay a premium to insure against losses they can manage, or to take financial risks that are greater than the potential upside. Actors, such as smaller companies or private persons, might be better off by paying an extra 'risk premium' to avoid the risk of facing a significant financial loss.

§8.03 THE PSYCHOLOGY OF DECISION-MAKING

The concept of decision analysis is not only confined to answering the question of how decisions *should* be taken, which a prescriptive approach such as decision-tree analysis seeks to answer. Another equally important approach to decision analysis is the behavioural decision-making side – the study of how real people *actually do* make decisions.[6]

Legal formalism assumes that judges and arbitrators apply legal reasoning to the facts of the case in a completely rational, mechanical and intentional manner.[7] Unsurprisingly, however, research has shown that this is not the case. Thus, an alternative view of the law – encapsulated in the influential twentieth-century legal realist movement – is that judicial decisions cannot be explained by legal reasoning alone since they are also influenced by psychological, political, and social factors. This theory was expressed as early as the 1930s by the US Supreme Court Justice Oliver Wendell Holmes, who stated that 'the life of the law has not been logic; it has been experience'.[8]

The psychologist and Nobel laureate Daniel Kahneman and cognitive and mathematical psychologist Amos Tversky have based on their research presented a thesis that human thinking can be understood as operating through two systems. System 1 is fast, intuitive, and automatic, while System 2 is slow, deliberate, and analytical. Most decisions are made using System 1, which relies on mental shortcuts and instincts, but it is prone to biases and errors. System 2 steps in when more careful, logical thinking is required but demands more effort and energy.

6. Howard Raiffa, John Richardson and David Metcalfe, *Negotiation Analysis: The Science and Art of Collaborative Decision Making* (Cambridge, MA: Belknap Press of Harvard University Press, 2002) 33.
7. Brian Leiter, 'American Legal Realism' in William A. Edmundson and Martin P. Golding (eds), *The Blackwell Guide to the Philosophy of Law and Legal Theory* (Blackwell 2005) 50-66.
8. Jerome Frank, *Law and the Modern Mind* (Transaction Publishers 1930) 1.

Through their research, Kahneman and Tversky illustrate how the two systems influence judgments and behaviours, often in ways not realized.[9] A large body of cognitive psychological work has shown that where either complexity or uncertainty is present (and especially if both are present), which is common in legal disputes, intuition (System 1) reliably fails. In this respect, 'failing' means that people intuitively make decisions that, upon further scrutiny, they no longer believe are the best decisions.

Recent research shows that even structured legal decisions by professionals are affected by irrelevant, but very human factors. Studies in the field of criminal law indicate that an unexpected loss by the local football team leads to, on average, one month longer sentences for juveniles the subsequent week.[10] Another study showed that hunger or fatigue after long court sessions leads judges to make decisions that maintain the status quo, which in the study meant that judges rejected requests for early release on parole.[11]

In the following, some of the most common decision traps that may arise in decision-making will be explained. This will be followed by a review of how this knowledge may be used by stakeholders in arbitration.

[A] The Anchoring Trap: First Impressions

The anchoring bias is likely one of the most well-known cognitive traps in decision-making. It provides that people give disproportionate weight to an initial anchor point of reference, even though subsequent information warrants that the initial assessment should be revised.[12]

To exemplify, a party to a contractual dispute, Party A, claims damages of EUR 5 million, while Party B argues that the damages should not exceed EUR 500,000. During the course of the arbitration, Party A's counsel presents the EUR 5 million figure early and emphasizes it repeatedly. Even though the evidence suggests that the damages are closer to EUR 1 million, the arbitrator's final award comes out at EUR 2.5 million, influenced by the initial EUR 5 million anchor, despite the lack of support for that figure.

One might assume that experienced lawyers would be more resistant to the cognitive errors caused by the anchoring trap. However, this is not necessarily the case. In one study, German judges with an average of over ten years of experience were found to be influenced by a seemingly random dice roll when assessing sentencing

9. As originally developed with Amos Tversky, the concept is explored in Daniel Kahneman, *Thinking, Fast and Slow* (Farrar, Straus and Giroux 2011) Part II.
10. Ozkan Eren and Naci Mocan, 'Emotional Judges and Unlucky Juveniles', (2018) 10(2) *American Economic Journal: Applied Economics*, 171-205 https://doi.org/10.1257/app.20160390 (accessed 1 October 2025).
11. Shai Danziger, Jonathan Levav and Liora Avnaim-Pesso, 'Extraneous Factors in Judicial Decisions' (2011) 108(17) *Proceedings of the National Academy of Sciences of the United States of America* 6889-6892 https://doi.org/10.1073/pnas.1018033108 (accessed 1 October 2025).
12. Kahneman, *supra* n. 9, Chapter 11.

length. Those who rolled a high number recommended prison sentences that were, on average, nearly 50% longer than those who rolled a low number on the dice.[13]

[B] The Framing Trap: Solving the Wrong Problem

Rational decision-makers should make the same choices irrespective of the way the problem is described. However, experiments have shown that framing a given problem in various ways can yield different decisions and responses.

Kahneman and Tversky evidenced the so-called framing trap by phrasing questions in terms of lives saved or deaths caused.[14] They created two groups of respondents who were presented with one problem each. The first group of respondents were given the following Problem 1:

Imagine that the US is preparing for the outbreak of an unusual Asian disease, which is expected to kill 600 people. Two alternative programmes to combat the disease have been proposed. Assume that the exact scientific estimates of the consequences of the programmes are as follows:

> Problem 1:
>
> If Programme A is adopted, 200 people will be saved.
>
> If Programme B is adopted, there is a 1/3 probability that 600 people will be saved, and a 2/3 probability that no people will be saved.
>
> Which of the two programmes would you favour?

The second group of respondents was given the same cover story, but with a different wording of the alternative programmes, as follows:

> Problem 2:
>
> If Programme C is adopted, 400 people will die.
>
> If Programme D is adopted, there is a 1/3 probability that nobody will die, and a 2/3 probability that 600 people will die.
>
> Which of the two programmes would you favour?

Although both versions of the same problem share the same expected value, the results showed that framing the given problem in terms of either gains or losses yields different risk-behaviour. For the respondents faced with Problem 1, the majority chose the risk-averse option: Certainly saving 200 lives is more attractive than the risky prospect of equal expected value, i.e., a one-in-three chance of saving 600 lives. However, the majority of the participants faced with Problem 2 chose the risk-seeking option: The certain prospect of 400 deaths is less acceptable than a two-in-three chance of losing 600 lives.

---

13. Birte Englich, Thomas Mussweiler and Fritz Strack, 'Playing Dice with Criminal Sentences: The Influence of Irrelevant Anchors on Experts' Judicial Decision Making' (2006) 32(2) *Personality and Social Psychology Bulletin*, 188-200 https://doi.org/10.1177/0146167205282152 (accessed 1 October 2025).
14. Kahneman, *supra* n. 9, at 412-414.

Framing effects can have a significant impact on arbitration, as the requests for relief brought by the claimant, and possible counterclaims filed by the respondent, create a frame for the possible outcomes. Also, the framing trap may cause a claimant to be more prone to an early settlement than a respondent. Claimants typically face the choice between accepting a guaranteed gain in the form of a settlement or accepting an uncertain but potentially more beneficial outcome by pursuing a trial. By contrast, respondents must choose between a certain loss by settling the dispute or an uncertain and potentially worse outcome when proceeding to trial.[15]

Experiments conducted on judges also suggest that framing effects induce judges (and arbitrators if they are involved in settlement discussions) to perceive settlement decisions differently when adopting either the claimant's or the respondent's view.[16] Guthrie et al. conducted an experiment where US judges were presented with identical case facts involving a USD 200,000 copyright dispute. The participants were randomly assigned to one of two conditions: in the 'Plaintiff/Gains' group, judges assessed whether a plaintiff should accept a USD 60,000 settlement, an amount which was higher than the expected trial value of the case which was USD 50,000.[17] The other half of participating judges, who were assigned to the 'Defendant/Losses' group, were asked whether they deemed that the defendant should be willing to pay USD 140,000 to settle the case, an amount lower than the expected cost of pursuing litigation, which was USD 150,000.[18] Even though the judges evaluated choices that were economically the same, 39.8% of the judges in the 'Plaintiff/Gains' group thought the plaintiff should accept the USD 60,000 settlement (i.e., showing risk-averse behaviour), while only 25% of those in the 'Defendant/Losses' group indicated that the defendant should pay USD 140,000 to settle the case instead of starting a lawsuit with a negative value of USD 150,000 (i.e., the majority showed risk-seeking behaviour), thus confirming behavioural insights as suggested by framing theory.

[C] Myside Bias, Confirmation Bias and the Overconfidence Trap: Seeing What You Want to See

Myside bias is explained as the phenomenon when people evaluate evidence and test hypotheses in a way that is biased towards their own prior beliefs, opinions and

15. Jan-Philip Elm, 'Behavioral Insights into International Arbitration: An Analysis of How to De-Bias Arbitrators' (2017) 1 *University of St Gallen Law and Economics Research Paper Series*, 33.
16. Chris Guthrie, Jeffrey J Rachlinski and Andrew J Wistrich, 'Inside the Judicial Mind' (2001) 86(4) *Cornell Law Review*, 777-829.
17. There was an estimated 50% chance of the plaintiff recovering the full USD 200,000 if the case went to trial, but each party would then pay its own legal costs of USD 50,000, reducing the expected value of USD 100,000 to USD 50,000.
18. With an estimated 50% chance of the defendant being held to pay the full amount of USD 200,000 and an estimated 50% chance of winning on the merits but still having to pay its own legal costs, the estimated negative value for the defendant is 150,000 = (0.5 × 200,000 + 50,000).

attitudes.[19] For example, when asked to rank the quality of arguments, smokers are less likely to agree that second-hand smoke presents health hazards, religious people are more likely to believe religiosity correlates with honesty, and people who drink a lot are less likely to acknowledge the risks of alcohol consumption.[20] Myside bias is closely linked to confirmation bias – the tendency to seek out, interpret, and recall information in ways that confirm pre-existing beliefs, while ignoring or downplaying contradictory evidence. Together, these biases may reinforce flawed assessments and make it difficult to update views even when new, objective information becomes available, something that can lead to overconfidence.

Specific research and experiments conducted in a legal setting further point to the average lawyer being roughly 11%-15% points overconfident in his or her assessment of the likelihood of reaching a set goal (e.g., winning a case in court or receiving a certain settlement).[21] Notably, the study indicates that female lawyers are slightly less prone to overconfidence bias than their male counterparts.[22] Studies suggest that, although overconfidence bias can be reduced, it is very difficult, if not impossible, to eliminate it entirely.[23]

[D] Sunk Cost Trap: Wanting to Recoup Previous Costs

Another cognitive trap that can arise in the context of decision-making is the sunk cost trap. The sunk cost trap (or fallacy) is the tendency to continue with an endeavour that a person has invested money, effort, or time in – even if the current costs outweigh the benefits.[24]

Imagine that a company has already invested EUR 50 million in a project. The project is behind schedule, and the yield forecasts are no longer as favourable as they were at the beginning of the planning. An additional investment of EUR 60 million is needed for the project to be successful. The alternative is to invest the same amount in a completely new project, which currently seems to offer higher returns. What does the company do? As expressed by Kahneman, all too often, a company that has already invested heavily in a project will choose to head out into the blizzard, throw the money

19. K.E. Stanovich, R.F. West and M.E. Toplak, 'Myside Bias, Rational Thinking, and Intelligence', (2013) 22(4) *Current Directions in Psychological Science*, 259-264 https://doi.org/10.1177/0963721413480174 (accessed 1 October 2025).
20. Keith E. Stanovich and Richard F. West, 'Natural Myside Bias Is Independent of Cognitive Ability' (2007) 13(3) *Thinking & Reasoning* 225-247 https://doi.org/10.1080/13546780600780796 (accessed 1 October 2025).
21. Mihael A Jeklic, 'Can You Trust Your Lawyer's Call? Legal Advisers Exhibit Myside Bias Resistant to Debiasing Interventions' (2023) 20(2) *Journal of Empirical Legal Studies* 409-433 https://doi.org/10.1111/jels.12350 (accessed 1 October 2025); Jane Goodman-Delahunty et al., 'Insightful or Wishful: Lawyers' Ability to Predict Case Outcomes' (2010) 16(2) *Psychology, Public Policy, and Law* 133-157 https://doi.org/10.1037/a0019060 (accessed 1 October 2025).
22. Goodman-Delahunty et al., *supra* n. 21, *Insightful or Wishful.*
23. Douglas N Frenkel and James H Stark, 'Improving Lawyers' Judgment: Is Mediation Training De-Biasing?' (2015) *Harvard Negotiation Law Review* 1; Robert S Adler, 'Flawed Thinking: Addressing Decision Biases in Negotiation' (2005) 20 *Ohio State Journal on Dispute Resolution* 683, 725-727.
24. Kahneman, *supra* n. 9, Chapter 32.

in the lake, and finally resign itself to the humiliation of liquidating the account as a costly failure.

The sunk cost fallacy can sometimes be linked to or reinforced by the so-called principal-agent problem. Although ploughing additional money into a failing project does not benefit the company, it is not necessarily a disadvantage for the manager in charge of the faltering venture. Shutting down a project forever could tarnish the manager's record, and his or her personal interests may be best served by continuing to play with the organization's resources in the hope of either recouping some of the initial investment or postponing the moment of truth.

When large sums have already been invested, the project manager's interests diverge from those of the company and shareholders. A prudent board of directors is well aware of the conflicts and often replaces a CEO who is hampered by past decisions and unwilling to curb losses.

In essence, the money and time spent are sunk and should not affect the decision to proceed or not. The only relevant question is whether investing further - both financially and reputationally - makes sense in light of the current prospects of the case.

Recognizing the trap requires discipline. A board or management team removed from the emotional investment may be better positioned to make an objective decision rather than a project lead or legal manager, whose judgment may be clouded by the time and resources already sunk into the dispute. Protracted disputes may therefore more often be resolved when a new individual assumes responsibility for the management of the dispute, as they find it easier to disregard sunk costs.

[E] Representation Bias: What You Have Seen Before Is What You See

Representation bias (also called representation heuristics or availability bias) is a mental shortcut used when judging the likelihood of something based on how much it resembles something we already know, even if that resemblance is superficial and the actual statistics or facts do not support the conclusion. Representation bias means that one question is substituted by another: the question to be answered is the size or frequency of a certain category, but instead it is answered by how easy it is to recall cases that fall into the category.[25]

In the context of arbitral proceedings, representation bias can cause skewed risk assessments, create blind spots to the unique features of a case or affect tribunal strategy, such as arbitrator selection. Also, arbitrators may be unconsciously affected by representation bias, especially when under time pressure or faced with complex factual records. An arbitrator might compare the current dispute to a previous case he or she has seen that resembles it, consciously or not, and let that perceived similarity guide his or her thinking without taking sufficient account of the facts and evidence of the case.

25. This phenomenon, originally researched by Kahneman and Tversky, is described in *Thinking, Fast and Slow*. *See* Kahneman, *supra* n. 9, at 149.

[F] Authority Bias and Priming: Listening to the Messenger, Not the Message

Another phenomenon is authority bias, which refers to placing undue confidence in the judgments of individuals with formal or informal authority, thereby allowing their views to exert more influence than warranted. Notably, the Norwegian Supreme Court has followed a practice whereby the most senior judge begins the deliberations and presents their view first, with the remaining judges following in order of seniority – a method that has drawn criticism.[26] In contrast, Sweden follows the opposite approach: the Procedural Code has long prescribed that deliberations should proceed in reverse order of seniority.[27]

A similar notion is the priming effect, as described by Kahneman, which refers to how subtle cues can unconsciously influence thoughts, feelings, and behaviours. Priming influences how people interpret messages based on who delivers them, especially with regard to appearance-related cues like age, race, gender, attractiveness, or even clothing. For example, attractive people are often primed with traits like competence or honesty – known as the 'halo effect' – making their message seem more convincing.[28]

§8.04 BENEFITS, LIMITATIONS AND COMMON MISCONCEPTIONS AROUND DECISION ANALYSIS

Before turning to the example case, some of the typical concerns and perceived limitations that are often raised in relation to decision analysis will be addressed. These concerns highlight common misunderstandings about the method and provide useful context for the example that follows.

[A] Using Percentages as Opposed to Words Implies a Certainty That Simply Is Not There

Legal practitioners are experienced in assessing outcomes and risks and communicating their views in memos and meetings. However, communicating the result of a decision-tree analysis requires going beyond verbal estimates and instead using numerical equivalents to express probabilities as percentages.

A criticism sometimes heard towards using numbers when communicating an assessment is that it implies certainty, while words convey a 'softer' meaning that better explains the inherent uncertainty of the assessment. While this may be true, there are several historical examples of how words of estimative probability have led decision makers astray. One example is when the US military, prior to the US-

26. Jan-Ole Hesselberg and Margrete Malmgård, 'Hvem får ordet først? Og hva gjør det med møtet: og med beslutningen?', *Dagens Næringsliv*, 17 January 2025.
27. Chapter 16 section 1 of the Swedish Procedural Code, with one exception: The judge responsible for the case always starts.
28. Kahneman, *supra* n. 9, 25-55, 82.

sponsored invasion of the Bay of Pigs in Cuba in 1961, internally assessed the likelihood of success of an invasion at around 30% but described it to the newly elected President John F. Kennedy as having a 'fair chance of success'. The vague phrasing led Kennedy to interpret the odds as favourable, likely contributing to a strategic miscalculation.[29]

Studies show that qualitative expressions can have a margin of misunderstanding of more than 50%. As seen in Figure 8.3,[30] some may interpret the term 'likely' as close to a 50% chance, while others may see it as closer to 90%.

---

29. Jeffrey A Friedman et al., 'The Value of Precision in Probability Assessment: Evidence from a Large-Scale Geopolitical Forecasting Tournament' (2018) 62 *International Studies Quarterly* 410 https://doi.org/10.1093/isq/sqx078 (accessed 1 October 2025).
30. The data presented is inspired by the work of CIA analyst Sherman Kent, who introduced the term 'words of estimative probability' in a now declassified 1964 report with this title. The graph shown is in turn based on a replication of a CIA study on how NATO officers interpret such terms, published 1977 in the declassified *Handbook for Decision Analysis*, itself influenced by Kent's earlier work. The chart and its underlying data from an internet poll is available at https://github.com/zonination/perceptions (accessed 1 October 2025), and credit is due to the contributor zonination.

Figure 8.3 Chart Illustrating How People Interpret Verbal Expressions of Probability, Showing the Wide Variation in Numerical Values Assigned to Terms such as 'Likely,' 'Improbable,' and 'Unlikely'

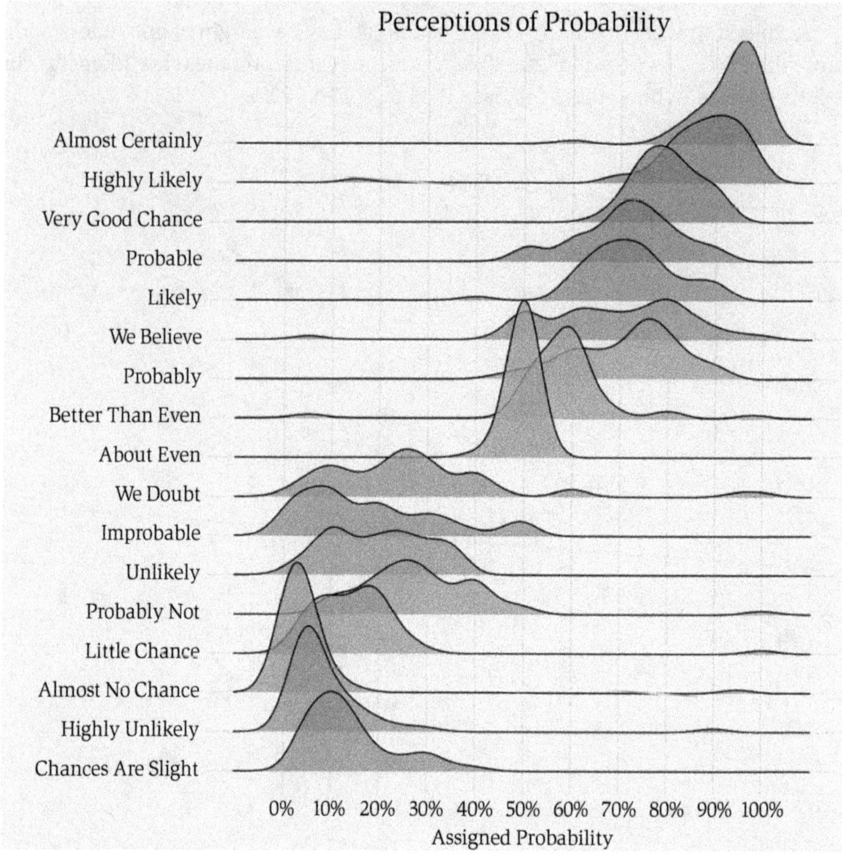

A quantitative assessment, however, is difficult to misinterpret and has the benefit that it can be relied on to better understand how the uncertainty affects the bigger picture.

The inherent uncertainty in assessments can be managed by reassessing the case using different assumptions. Showing alternative scenarios can illustrate how 'sensitive' various factors are in the overall evaluation. This technique is known as sensitivity analysis, sometimes described as 'what-if' analysis. It involves re-running the assessment with alternative inputs – for example, analysing how the case value changes if the estimated chance of success is set lower. Running the numbers this way can help confirm how robust a proposed course of action is. In many cases, a 'what-if' becomes an 'even-if': even if the case is 20% stronger than estimated, settlement is still the better option.

[B] Quantifying the Monetary Value of a Case Does Not Factor in the Other Values Associated with the Dispute

A common objection to decision analysis is that it overlooks other aspects of arbitration or disputes, such as the value of, for example, good relationships or reputation. Consider, for example, the following scenario: an arbitration involving a EUR 100 million claim has an expected value of EUR 50 million. However, the claimant insists on receiving EUR 60 million, a difference of EUR 10 million.[31]

A respondent faced with deciding whether to pay EUR 60 million to settle the case should therefore ask itself whether it is worth paying EUR 10 million more than the expected value of pursuing arbitration to maintain a good relationship and avoid arbitration. Without knowing the claim's expected value, this comparison would be impossible. It is like basic algebra; if you know A, assessing B becomes easier.

Moreover, other factors involved in a dispute, such as negative PR in case of a potential loss, or internal costs for a party to manage the dispute, can be included in a decision-tree analysis. This can be done by quantifying the potential good or bad PR value as a monetary value and tying those estimated values to the potential outcomes.[32]

Arguments such as 'we cannot let the customer get away with this' may be a commercially legitimate reason to pursue arbitration. To determine whether this is the case, however, it makes sense to follow through on that thought and ask whether a 'win' in the arbitration will improve future business opportunities in a meaningful way. Conversely, the question should be posed whether a potential loss in the arbitration affects future opportunities in a negative way.

Framed correctly, external values associated with a dispute can be included in the assessment of whether arbitration is worth pursuing.

[C] 'The Case Value Always Comes Out Too Low in These Types of Models'

One common criticism of decision tree models is that the expected value of cases comes out 'too low' for a claimant. There can be several reasons for this, which will be examined in the following.

[1] Treating Factors as Independent That Are Directly or Indirectly Linked

If a claimant 'might' (50% chance) prove breach of contract, 'might' (50% chance) prove causation, and 'might' (50% chance) establish the claimed loss, the mathemati

31. These thoughts were well expressed by the lawyer Patrick Shroeder, attending a panel discussion on the topic of decision analysis on hosted by the law firm Wiersholm in Norway, 2025.
32. John Celona, *Winning at Litigation through Decision Analysis: Creating and Executing Winning Strategies in Any Litigation or Dispute* (Springer 2016) 267.

cal joint probability of succeeding with all three factors is calculated as 0.5 × 0.5 × 0.5 = 0.125, resulting in a mere 12.5% chance of success.

If the three liability requirements are completely independent, and the assumptions are correct, it is a mathematical fact that the probability of winning is 12.5%. However, the estimated probability assumes that an arbitral tribunal will handle the issues completely independently (as theorized in the above-mentioned school of legal formalism). In the example with the three liability requirements set out in the above paragraph, it may be more reasonable to assume that the topic of breach of contract may spill over to the following, perhaps technically unrelated questions and that the overall chance of success is significantly higher than 12.5% (but still less than 50%). Factors that cause the arbitral tribunal to find that there was a breach of contract may cause the arbitral tribunal to be more likely to find that there was a causation between the loss and the contract breach.

In many cases, it does not make sense to 'model the briefs' – that is, to attempt to map out every argument made by both parties in a decision tree. The goal of creating a structured model is not to make a map that accurately reflects everything that can occur, but to serve as a tool to provide an understanding of what paths a case can take, how likely they are and what the financial implications of each outcome are.

[2] Overly Cautious Probability Expressions

From the authors' experience, lawyers can be reluctant to provide their true understanding of the likelihood of success. Even if they 'strongly' (in numbers around 90%) believe their client's case will be successful, counsel may still communicate a lower estimated success chance. A worry around potentially being held liable for adverse outcomes could be the reason behind this, or perhaps a will to 'underpromise and overdeliver'.

A caution in assessments will naturally reduce the overall value of a case. If the caution is repeated over several factors required to establish liability, it will substantially reduce the overall likelihood of success.

The attentive reader may find that such caution would be warranted as a means to offset overconfidence bias. This may be true, but decision analysis is about communicating clearly the real assessment by taking into account the science regarding cognitive traps. Thus, the first question to ask should be: What is my assessment of the chances of success? The second question should then be: Should I revise this assessment in the light of what I know about the existence of overconfidence bias?

Decision analysis requires lawyers to say what they mean and mean what they say. Ultimately, it should then be up to the decision-maker – the client – to evaluate the advice and make the decisions. An assessment that is silently overcautious will not provide a good understanding of the overall risk and value of the case for a client.

[3] Anchoring Bias

A third reason behind a 'low case value' relates to the above-mentioned issue of anchoring bias. For example, if a claimant has an extremely strong argument (an estimated probability of establishing breach of contract exceeding 90%), claims EUR 100 million in damages, but is most likely to receive a significantly lower amount upon success, the expected value of the proceeding with arbitration will be nowhere near the full claim amount. If the decision-maker anchors around the high claimed amount in its assessment of what is a fair solution, a settlement offer of less than half the claimed amount may appear low. Relying on a structured assessment can help to explain that a high claim amount that is unlikely to be awarded has little relevance when determining the overall value of a case. It can be surprisingly difficult to cast off a high anchor point, no matter how unlikely the outcome is.

[4] The Other Party's Risk Is Not Examined

A fourth reason that may result in being confounded by an unexpectedly 'low value' can come from not also examining the other party's position.

For example, the claimant has a decent (65%) chance of winning 10 million if pursuing arbitration. The legal fees per party are projected to be 2 million, and the principle that the losing party is responsible for the costs applies. This means that there are two possible outcomes in an arbitration for the claimant:

- A 65% chance of winning 10 million, which has a weighted value of 6.5 million.
- A 35% risk of getting nothing and paying legal fees of 4 million, which has a weighted value of negative 1.4 million.

The expected value of the case is therefore 5.1 million (6.5 million – 1.4 million), close to half of the claim amount of 10 million. A decent chance to win fully that has an expected value of only half the claimed amount may feel disheartening to the claimant.

But if the case assessment is done from the view of the respondent, the case value for the respondent is negative 9.1 million.[33] Accordingly, despite having at least a 'fair chance' (35%) of winning, it is rational for the respondent to pay more than 90% of the claim amount to settle the dispute.[34] This could also be a disheartening truth for the respondent.

Conducting an assessment from both parties' perspectives can therefore help a claimant to understand that a settlement of 5.1 million is at least acceptable. If the claimant's counsel manages to use the leverage of arbitration towards the respondent to achieve a settlement closer to the respondents' estimated cost of letting the case be resolved through an arbitral award (9.1 million), the claimant could reach an outcome that is *better* than the value of proceeding with arbitration.

33. A 65% chance of paying 14 million (award and legal costs) has a weighted value of negative 9.1 million, a 35% risk of paying nothing and being compensated for legal cost has a weighted value of 0. The negative expected value is thus 9.1 million + 0 = 9.1 million.
34. The range within which it would be reasonable for both parties to settle equals the legal costs that could be avoided through a settlement (4 million) and is sometimes known as the Zone of Potential (or possible) Agreement (ZOPA).

[D] The Detailed Structures in Models Do Not Reflect How Arbitrators Make Decisions

Many academic articles and example cases detailing decision-tree models in dispute resolution strictly follow the legal questions that will be tried, such as 'will the arbitral tribunal find causation'? Some experienced counsel raise a healthy concern with respect to such decision-tree models. They point out that there are also other factors in play when the tribunal decides on the case. Thus, the objection is raised that the model does not reflect reality.

When modelling is decided by humans, there is really one rule. The reasoning, and the probability assessments behind the reasoning, should be mapped as one would expect the way the jury, judges or arbitrators will approach the matter. If there is a concern that arbitrators will be hesitant to award high damages to be known as careful and conservative arbitrators, such concerns can be accounted for when estimating the probabilities of different outcomes.

If the claimant has the 'overall moral high ground' in a case, and there is 'enough room in the legal issues on the table' to allow for the claimant to succeed, then this overarching matter can and should be factored into the model.

§8.05 APPLYING DECISION ANALYSIS TO ARBITRATION: AN EXAMPLE FROM A TECH DISPUTE

Using the concepts explained above, the following section will describe how decision analysis can be applied to an example dispute from start to finish.

The analysis will first be made from a party's and a counsel's perspective, exploring how decision analysis may be applied to a party's strategic advantage from the initial decision whether to pursue arbitration until the oral hearing and rendering of the final award.

This will be followed by an exploration of how decision analysis may be used to improve arbitrators' decisions throughout the arbitration.

§8.06 BASIC FACTS EXPLAINED

The example case is drawn from a recurring type of dispute in the tech industry, which arises when a company has contracted a software developer to build or modify software for its operations. To clearly define the requirements for such a project appears to be very challenging, not least given the complexity of the projects and the unexpected problems that may appear during the implementation phase. This often results in disagreements that arise from differing interpretations of the initial scope of work and subsequent requests for changes, not unlike the challenges of large construction projects.

The facts are the following.

A large project for the development of a logistics software solution has failed, and the customer has terminated the agreement with the software developer contracted to build the system.

The customer is now contemplating initiating arbitration proceedings to recover its losses. If the arbitral tribunal were to find that the customer had cause for termination, the agreement provides that the developer would need to return the EUR 5 million already received under the contract. In this scenario, the developer would potentially also be liable for damages caused when the customer had to contract another firm to urgently implement a working system – at an increased cost that the customer estimates to be EUR 10 million. The customer's total claim therefore amounts to EUR 15 million.

However, if the arbitral tribunal found that the customer did not have cause for termination, the customer would be liable to pay the outstanding invoices of EUR 1.5 million. The customer would potentially also have to compensate the developer for the loss of profits that the contract would have generated. According to the developer, such losses amount to EUR 4 million. The total claim from the developer is therefore EUR 5.5 million.

The customer's counsel estimates that the case would cost EUR 2 million per party in legal costs. Approximately 80% of these costs would be recoverable by the successful party, but the same amount would need to be paid to the opposing party in the event of a loss.

No full discovery of the evidence has been made, but certain facts point towards the developer having failed to hold up its part of the contract. One such fact is that the software developer replaced the head of the project several times during the project period. The group of software developers working with the project also had a quick turnover. Moreover, the developer has been behind schedule during all the projected milestones listed in the initial project plan.

However, the customer has introduced some revisions during the project, which might have made it more challenging for the developer to follow the initial plan.

According to the customer's legal counsel, the overall picture from the available evidence points very strongly towards the customer having had cause for termination. After listing all the reasons for and against, the customer's legal counsel assesses that the average arbitrator would most likely (75% chance) find in favour of the customer on the question of termination for cause.

The contract does not clearly state under which conditions a party should be compensated for damages or loss of profits due to a breach of contract. In both scenarios, it 'could go either way' (a 50/50 chance). The estimates and assumptions for assessing damages for the company and loss of profits for the developer will also be challenged, which could lead to a reduction of the amount awarded. The customer's legal counsel therefore assesses that the high values are possible, but less likely (25% chance), that being awarded a moderate amount is more likely (50% chance) and that there is a remaining 25% risk that the customer's damages claim is reduced further.

§8.07 INITIAL CASE ASSESSMENT

By setting up a model, the claimant's counsel can visualize the different outcomes in a tree model as follows.

Figure 8.4 Tree Model with Corresponding Outcome Table, Illustrating the Possible Awards, Probabilities, and Costs in the Dispute. The Combined Probability-Weighted Outcomes Yield an Expected Value of EUR 4.6 Million

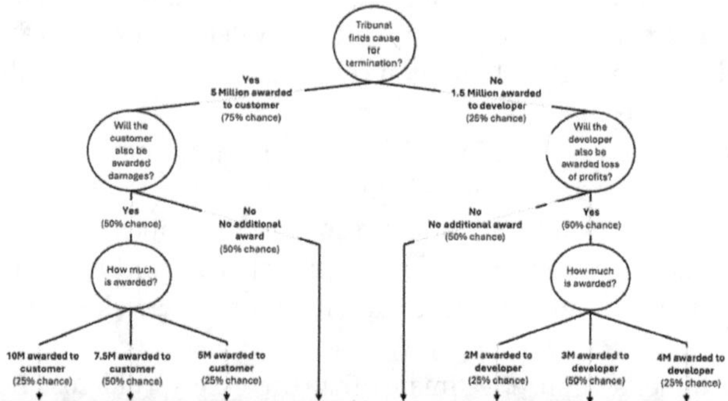

Outcome description	Max damages awarded	Medium damages awarded	Low damages awarded	Only repayment awarded	Only outstanding payment awarded	Low loss of profits awarded	Medium loss of profits awarded	High loss of profits awarded	Total
Probability of outcome	9.38%	18.75%	9.38%	37.5%	12.5%	3.13%	6.25%	3.13%	100%
Amount awarded	15M	12.5M	10M	5M	-1.5M	-3.5M	-4.5M	-5.5M	
Future legal costs	-2M	-2M	-2M	-2M	-2M	-2M	-2M	-2M	
Costs recovered/paid	1.6M	1.6M	1.6M	1.6M	-1.6M	-1.6M	-1.6M	-1.6M	
Net outcome (total)	14.6M	12.1M	9.6M	4.6M	-5.1M	-7.1M	-8.1M	-9.1M	
Weighted value	1.37M	2.27M	0.9M	1.73M	-0.64M	-0.22M	-0.51M	-0.28M	4.61M (Expected value)

Figure 8.5 Graph Based on the Previous Figure, Showing the Probability–Value Distribution of the Possible Outcomes

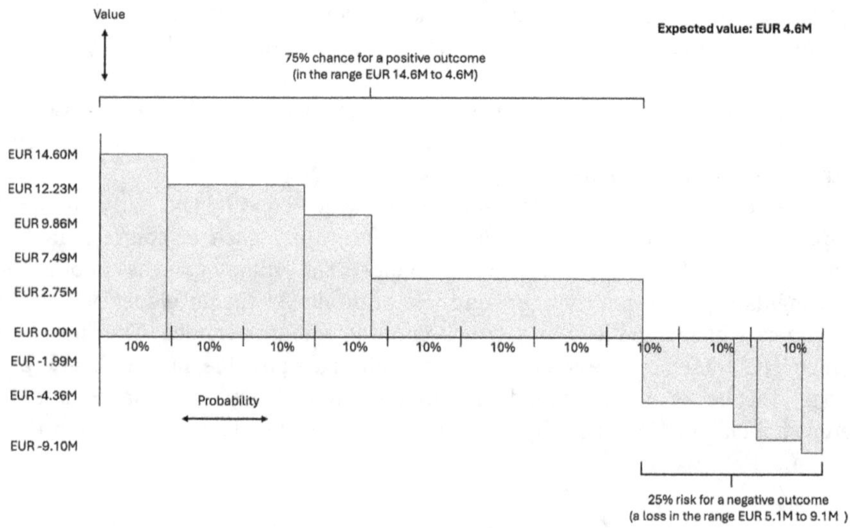

The assessment and the graph produced provide that the expected value for the customer of proceeding to arbitration is EUR 4.6 million. Pursuing arbitration could at best generate a gain of EUR 14.6 million and at worst a loss of EUR 9.1 million.

For a risk-neutral company, it would make sense to pursue arbitration. However, before presenting the assessment to the client, the legal counsel representing the customer sense-checks the model and also considers the psychological biases that could affect the counsel's analysis.

[A] Accounting for Cognitive Biases

[1] Overconfidence and Confirmation Bias

The research described above shows that counsel and parties are likely to be overly optimistic about the prospect of success. As mentioned, some research indicates that this could be around 15% points. From experience, the counsel also knows that legal cost often ends up significantly higher than first anticipated.

Therefore, the customer's counsel asks: 'what if' the assessment on the probability of success is too optimistic? And also, what if our projections on legal costs are too low?

The probability of success on the main issue of breach of contract is reduced by 15% points. The projected legal costs is also increased from EUR 2 to EUR 3 million per party. As shown in the table below, even if these changes are made, the value of arbitration still comes out as a positive value of EUR 1.5 million.

Figure 8.6 Outcome Table, Illustrating the Possible Awards, Probabilities, and Costs in the Dispute after Considering Potential Overconfidence and Potentially Higher Costs

Expected value: 1.5M

Outcome description	Max damages awarded	Medium damages awarded	Low damages awarded	Only repayment awarded	Only outstanding payment awarded	Low loss of profits awarded	Medium loss of profits awarded	High loss of profits awarded	Total
Probability of outcome	7.5%	15%	7.5%	30%	20%	5%	10%	5%	100%
Amount awarded	15M	12.5M	10M	5M	-1.5M	-3.5M	-4.5M	-5.5M	
Future legal costs	-3M	-3M	-3M	-3M	-3M	-3M	-3M	-3M	
Costs recovered/paid	2.4M	2.4M	2.4M	2.4M	-2.4M	-2.4M	-2.4M	-2.4M	
Outcome (Total)	**14.4M**	**11.9M**	**9.4M**	**4.4M**	**-6.9M**	**-8.9M**	**-9.9M**	**-10.9M**	
Weighted value	1.08M	1.79M	0.71M	1.32M	-1.38M	-0.45M	-0.99M	-0.55M	1.53M (Expected value)

Consequently, even with reduced chances of success and increased costs projections, it is still rational for the customer to pursue arbitration rather than just abandoning the claim, which has a value of nothing, since the developer has not made any settlement offers so far.[35]

[2] Considering Arbitrators' Possible Representative/Availability Bias

The phenomenon of representative bias explained above may also influence how the arbitrators resolve the main question of breach of contract. The legal aspect around breach of contract is usually clear. Pacta sunt servanda: the software developer should deliver its services in accordance with the contract.

However, the counsel who is aware of the representative bias considers how the arbitrators' past experiences may affect their decision-making. The arbitrators chosen for the task are well-versed in software disputes. Ideally, most software development projects finish without reaching a critical failure or a termination of the contract. Nevertheless, major failures of large software projects have recently been much discussed in Sweden. The customer's counsel knows that the dispute resolution lawyer acting as the chairman has probably seen more failed projects than successful ones. Thus, the counsel considers whether the arbitrators' experience of challenges involved in executing complex IT projects will colour their understanding of the challenges in delivering complex software. If such past experiences are readily available, it may lead to an arbitrator thinking that software projects are inherently difficult and that the threshold for asserting that a material breach of contract has been committed must necessarily be set high.

By again conducting a sensitivity analysis, the counsel concludes that even if availability/representative bias would make it more challenging to successfully argue breach of contract, a reduction from 75% to 50% on the estimated chances of succeeding on the breach of contract issue would still mean that the decision to initiate arbitration is justified.

[B] Pre-arbitration Settlement Discussions

Before pursuing arbitration, the developer and customer initiate discussions to see if they can reach an agreement. At this stage, a decision-tree analysis may be used to a party's strategic advantage.

The customer's legal counsel advises the customer to change perspective and assess the case from the developer's perspective. The model will then look as follows.

35. This is a simplified version of what is known as two-way sensitivity analysis. The input on two key variables is changed to see how these changes affect the value of the case.

Figure 8.7 Outcome Table, Illustrating the Possible Awards and Probabilities from the Perspective of the Developer, Showing an Expected Value of Negative EUR 8.6 Million

Expected value: -8.6M

Outcome description	Max damages awarded	Medium damages awarded	Low damages awarded	Only repayment awarded	Only outstanding payment awarded	Low loss of profits awarded	Medium loss of profits awarded	High loss of profits awarded	Total
Probability of outcome	9.38%	18.75%	9.38%	37.5%	12.5%	3.13%	6.25%	3.13%	100%
Amount awarded	-15M	-12.5M	-10M	-5M	1.5M	3.5M	4.5M	5.5M	
Future legal costs	-2M	-2M	-2M	-2M	-2M	-2M	-2M	-2M	
Costs recovered/paid	-1.6M	-1.6M	-1.6M	-1.6M	1.6M	1.6M	1.6M	1.6M	
Outcome (Total)	18.6M	16.1M	13.6M	8.6M	1.1M	3.1M	4.1M	5.1M	
Weighted value	-1.75M	-3M	-1.28M	-3.23M	0.14M	0.1M	0.25M	0.16M	8.61 M (Expected value)

The above table shows that if the developer had the same understanding around the probabilities of success (although this is unlikely), it would make sense for the developer to settle by paying any amount less than EUR 8.6 million.

It would not be uncommon for a party in the customer's position, claiming EUR 15 million with a strong case, to request that the other party settle by paying 'at least EUR 10 million'. This may appear reasonable from intuition or gut feeling. However, even with the customer's counsel's own estimates, such a settlement would not be rational from the developer's perspective.

Based on the available information, pursuing arbitration is a reasonable decision for the customer. However, if the developer were to offer a settlement of EUR 4.6 million or more, it would be rational to accept that offer. The customer could naturally aim somewhat higher, perhaps towards EUR 8.61 million, which is the (negative) expected value for the developer. The analysis therefore helps the customer to understand the other party's position and may be used to find arguments to reach a favourable settlement.

Negotiation fails as the developer's case manager refuses to pay anything, stuck in the sunk cost trap and reluctant to acknowledge a loss at an early stage (the framing trap). Thus, the customer decides to initiate arbitral proceedings.

[C] Initiating Arbitration and the Advantages and Risks of Anchoring High

Since the expected value of the dispute for the customer is EUR 4.6 million, it is rational to proceed with arbitration if the customer is risk-neutral and can afford a loss.

However, before filing the request for arbitration, the customer's counsel considers whether any steps taken could improve the value of the case. One factor that could have a significant impact is the size of the damages claimed.

The counsel considers whether it would be reasonable to claim EUR 10 million in damages, even if the likely outcome is a lower value. A more aggressive claim may help increase pressure on the developer through the anchoring effect. However, a high claim amount could allow the developer to argue strongly regarding the flaws of the customer's claim by arguing that it is inflated, which may spill over onto the overall credibility of the case and thus increase the risk for the customer.

Another thing to consider is that a high claim that is not fully successful can mean that an arbitral tribunal is less likely to award full compensation for legal costs. In the example case, the experience of the customer's counsel is that the arbitral tribunal usually handles legal costs in relation to the main question of liability, and not so much connected to the proportionate success in relation to the claimed amount. Thus, the claimant's counsel advises the customer that choosing to file the higher claim of EUR 10 million in damages should not be a major risk.[36]

[D] Framing the Case: Using Decision Analysis as a Tool for Advocacy

In some cases, a decision tree mapping the legal issues can be used not only for assessing the case but also as a tool for advocacy. In practice, we have seen several examples of respondents wanting to steer an arbitral tribunal to follow a decision-tree type for resolving a case. In some cases, it might be sufficient for the tribunal to reject just one argument in the tree for the claimant's claim to be completely rejected. As discussed above, the more hurdles a claimant needs to overcome to win, the greater the risk of losing the arbitration.

Conversely, a claimant may wish to steer an arbitral tribunal away from such a 'bottom-up approach' and instead argue that the arbitral tribunal should take a more holistic, or 'top-down' approach.

In the example case, the legal questions involved in the example case are similar for both parties. Whether damages or loss of profits should be awarded hinges on the same contractual clauses. Thus, there is no clear benefit of framing the legal issues in a detailed tree as opposed to adopting an overarching approach when framing the disputed issues.

[E] Updating a Previous Assessment and Considering Incurred Costs

The arbitration proceeds, and the parties have submitted their written briefs and evidence. Eight months have passed, 2 million in legal costs have already been spent per party, and it appears that an additional million per party will be required until the rendering of the award.

During the document production phase, the customer has obtained written evidence in the form of internal memos and notes showing internal challenges and problems in the developer's organization of the project, which support the customer's case.

36. In some jurisdictions, settlement offers that are not 'beaten' can affect cost decisions (so-called Calderbank offers). If so, it may be worth considering whether a settlement offer could enhance the case's value. A similar principle is found in the Norwegian Dispute Act (Tvisteloven), section 20-2(3)(b), which allows the court to consider whether a party has rejected a reasonable offer of settlement when allocating costs.

However, a key witness for the customer, Mr Born, who managed the project for the customer has left for a competitor and is now reluctant to testify. Even if Mr Born were to testify, the customer's legal counsel does not expect him to be as good a witness as first anticipated.

As the customer and its legal counsel are preparing for the oral hearing, the software developer's counsel reaches out and indicates that the developer might be willing to pay something to resolve the case after all. But what would be a reasonable amount to accept?

Before conducting an updated assessment, the customer's legal counsel should consider the risk of being overly influenced by impressions formed earlier in the case due to confirmation bias. For simplicity and to avoid recalculating the model with new inputs, the example case will assume that the customer's counsel concludes that the initial assessments of probabilities and damages are still valid.

Although new information still supports the original estimates regarding the probability of success and potential damages, this does not automatically justify relying on the initial expected value of EUR 4.6 million. The assessment should be updated to reflect the current situation regarding costs. A question that often comes up at this stage is how to manage the situation with already incurred legal costs.

The EUR 2 million already spent cannot be unspent. To avoid the sunk cost trap, past costs should generally be excluded from the decision-making process. The focus should instead be on the potential outcomes and the additional costs required going forward.

However, as in this case example, excluding the already incurred legal costs entirely would be incorrect. This is because 80% of these costs may still be recovered if the customer wins. At the same time, the projected increase of EUR 1 million per party in additional costs will reduce the overall value of the case, mainly because a loss will now be more costly.

When the customer's counsel recalculates the decision tree, only the future costs are considered a negative value, but 80% of the full EUR 3 million should be considered when assessing the potential cost recovery. As projected in the table below, the updated outcomes are as follows.

Figure 8.8 Outcome Table, Illustrating the Possible Awards, Probabilities, and Costs after Part of the Legal Costs Have Been Incurred

Expected value: 6.0M

Outcome description	Max damages awarded	Medium damages awarded	Low damages awarded	Only repayment awarded	Only outstanding payment awarded	Low loss of profits awarded	Medium loss of profits awarded	High loss of profits awarded	Total
Probability of outcome	9.38%	18.75%	9.38%	37.5%	12.5%	3.13%	6.25%	3.13%	100%
Amount awarded	15M	12.5M	10M	5M	-1.5M	-3.5M	-4.5M	-5.5M	
Future legal costs	-1M	-1M	-1M	-1M	-1M	-1M	-1M	-1M	
Costs recovered/paid	2.4M	2.4M	2.4M	2.4M	-2.4M	-2.4M	-2.4M	-2.4M	
Outcome (Total)	**16.4M**	**13.9M**	**11.4M**	**6.4M**	**-4.9M**	**-6.9M**	**-7.9M**	**-8.9M**	
Weighted value	1.54M	2.60M	1.07M	2.4M	-0.61M	-0.22M	-0.49M	-0.28M	6.01M (Expected value)

The expected value is now EUR 6 million, which is higher than the initial net assessment of EUR 4.6 million. This is not because the case has improved, but because the remaining costs required to produce an award is now less than before. The customer must pay more in total to reach the final stage of arbitration and get an award. However, if the customer wins, it can anticipate recovering not only 80% of that additional million but also 80% of the already incurred costs of EUR 2 million.

In essence, if the customer accepts a EUR 6 million settlement, but has already used EUR 2 million to pay its legal counsel, the customer is left with EUR 4 million net. This sum is less than the initial assessment of a net recovery of EUR 4.6 million, which is only due to the increased legal costs.

The developer's counsel reaches out and conveys that she has a mandate to settle the dispute immediately with the offer that the developer pays EUR 5 million.

The customer's counsel compares the settlement offer of EUR 5 million with the estimated expected value of EUR 6 million and notes that it is EUR 1 million less. The counsel then asks the customer: How much would you pay just to get rid of the dispute. The answer comes quickly: About EUR 1 million. There are other matters that require management's time and effort.

Based on this, the counsel advises the customer that the EUR 5 million offer makes commercial sense to accept. The customer accepts the offer. Having paid legal costs of EUR 2 million, the net reward from the settlement ends up at EUR 3 million.

Although the EUR 3 million net reward is less than what the customer had initially hoped for, it is not at an awful distance away from the EUR 4.6 million that was the estimated value of the case before initiating arbitration. It is also more than the EUR 1.5 million that was the estimated value when accounting for potential overconfidence and increased legal cost. It is also a clearly better outcome than not having initiated arbitration at all and ending up with nothing.

By relying on decision analysis, the customer has made informed decisions every step of the way.

[F] Using Decision Analysis to Improve Arbitrators' Decisions

For arbitrators, decision analysis can be relevant in two ways: first, as a tool for the arbitrator when assisting in settlement discussions, and second, as a tool to try to avoid or mitigate cognitive traps and make better decisions. In the example case, the parties might have ended up with the same settlement less legal fees, already eight months earlier if the respondent had applied decision analysis from the onset.

[G] Decision Analysis as a Tool for Facilitating Settlement

[1] The Debate Regarding Whether Arbitrators Have the Mandate to Assist in Settlement Negotiations

Historically, it has been a highly controversial issue whether an international arbitral tribunal should be involved in the facilitation of an amicable settlement of the parties' dispute and, if so, how active they should be in promoting settlement.[37]

The debate brings to light two basic models which conscientious arbitrators look to when reflecting on their proper function in an international arbitration: The arbitrator as a 'decision-maker' versus the arbitrator as a 'dispute-resolver'.[38]

The traditional viewpoint has been that the role of the arbitral tribunal is to be a decision-maker and decide the case in an enforceable award. This view is more pertinent not only among practitioners from common law jurisdictions but also from Latin America and other parts of the world.[39] Proponents of the traditional approach consider that the parties remained free to negotiate and settle their dispute should they wish to do so, but that this is not something the arbitral tribunal should seek to encourage, facilitate or, least of all, become directly involved with. This view was motivated by concerns that taking on such a role would negatively impact the arbitral tribunal's neutrality vis-à-vis the merits of the dispute or the parties' perception of it.[40]

The other approach, more common in 'Germanic' jurisdictions such as Germany, Switzerland and Austria, adopts a wider view of the arbitrator's role as a 'dispute-resolver'. The more proactive role of the arbitrator as helping the parties to resolve their dispute in a wider sense is deeply rooted in the traditional role of domestic judges in those jurisdictions. In these countries, as well as in Sweden, procedural laws provide the courts with a mandate to go beyond the decision of the dispute and promote an amicable settlement.[41] In some jurisdictions, such as Germany, the arbitrator's broader

37. Klaus Peter Berger, 'The Direct Involvement of the Arbitrator in the Amicable Settlement of the Dispute: Offering Preliminary Views, Discussing Settlement Options, Suggesting Solutions, Caucusing' (2018) 35(5) *Journal of International Arbitration* 501-516 https://doi.org/10.54648/joia2018027 (accessed 1 October 2025); Pierre Lalive, 'The Role of Arbitrators as Settlement Facilitators: A Swiss View', in Jan van den Berg (ed.), *New Horizons in International Commercial Arbitration and Beyond,* International Council for Commercial Arbitration Congress series no. 12 (Kluwer Law International 2005) 556; Steven P Finizio and Duncan Speller, *A Practical Guide to International Commercial Arbitration: Assessment, Planning and Strategy* (Sweet & Maxwell 2010) para. 9.4.3.
38. Berger, *supra* n. 37, at p. 505.
39. Matthias M Pitkowitz and Marie-Therese Richter, 'May a Neutral Third Person Serve as Arbitrator and Mediator in the Same Dispute?' (2009) *SchiedsVZ* 225, 227; Michael Hwang, 'The Role of Arbitrators as Settlement Facilitators: Commentary', in Jan van den Berg (ed.), *New Horizons in International Commercial Arbitration and Beyond,* International Council for Commercial Arbitration Congress series no. 12 (Kluwer Law International 2005) 571-581.
40. International Chamber of Commerce (ICC) Commission on Arbitration and ADR, *Facilitating Settlement in International Arbitration* (ICC Publication DRS900 ENG, 2023).
41. *See* section 278(1) of the German Code of Civil Procedure (Zivilprocessordnung, ZPO): 'The court shall, at any stage of the proceedings, seek to promote an amicable settlement of the dispute or of individual disputed issues, Austrian Code of Civil Procedure: 'At the oral hearing, the court may, either at the request of a party or ex officio, attempt an amicable settlement of the

mandate to facilitate settlements is explicitly provided in institutional arbitration rules.[42]

Interestingly, although Swedish courts have a long-standing tradition of actively encouraging and helping parties try to reach an amicable settlement of disputes, the norm among Swedish arbitrators seems to be that they do not actively explore or encourage the parties to engage in settlement negotiations with the arbitrator's assistance. The SCC Arbitration Rules (2023) contain a rule that allows the arbitrator to make a consent award recording a settlement reached between the parties[43] but otherwise remain silent on whether an arbitrator should seek to encourage an amicable settlement of the dispute.

The fact that the topic is not mentioned at all in the otherwise comprehensive project of documenting Sweden's arbitration which in 2024 resulted in the book High-Quality Arbitration in Sweden, is a sign that facilitating settlement is not seen as a fundamental part of an arbitrator's duties among Swedish arbitrators.[44]

Today, the notion that the arbitrator's mandate also includes facilitating settlement has gained more acceptance within the international arbitration community. As reported by the ICC Commission on Arbitration and ADR, several institutional rules, such as the ICC Arbitration Rules, include provisions whereby arbitrators, subject to the parties' consent, are encouraged to explore the possibilities of reaching an amicable settlement of their dispute.[45] A pilot study made by the ICC Commission on Arbitration and ADR also shows that almost 70% of participants were of the view that arbitrators should inform the parties about ADR options during the first case management conference. A similar survey has shown that almost 80% of the participants asked think that arbitrators have a role in fostering settlement.[46] The idea that arbitrators may act as settlement facilitators is increasingly accepted even in common law jurisdictions.[47]

---

entire dispute or certain aspects thereof,' and Swiss Civil Code, Art. 197: 'Litigation shall be preceded by an attempt at conciliation before a conciliation authority,' Swedish Code of Civil Procedure Chapter 42 section 6 item 5 and section 17 stipulates that the court during the proceedings shall seek to clarify whether there is a possibility to reach a settlement or any other amicable solution.

42. *See* Art. 26 of the 2018 Arbitration Rules of the German Arbitration Institute (DIS) stipulating that the arbitral tribunal shall at every stage of the arbitration seek to encourage an amicable settlement of the dispute, albeit with the very important clarification of a veto right of the parties.
43. Article 45 in the SCC Arbitration Rules (2023), a corresponding provision is found in Art. 45 of the SCC Expedited Arbitration Rules.
44. Högkvalitativa skiljeförfaranden i Sverige – En samling av de fem första rapporterna inom projektet SAA Arbitration Reports, Kristoffer Löf, red. SAA Arbitration Reports 2024: 1-5.
45. *See* Appendix IV – Case Management Techniques, item h, *see also* the report of the CEDR Commission on Settlement in International Arbitration (www.cedr.com, November 2009) (the CEDR Report) which sets out several recommendations to parties, arbitrators and arbitral institutions, all aimed at increasing the prospects of parties to arbitration proceedings being able to settle their disputes without the need to proceed through to the conclusion of arbitral proceedings. The CEDR Commission was co-chaired by the English Judge Lord Woolf and the Swiss arbitrator Professor Gabrielle Kaufmann-Kohler and its members were leading arbitration and ADR practitioners from around the world. The report was accompanied by a set of rules for the facilitation of settlement in international arbitration.
46. *See* ICC Commission on Arbitration and ADR, *supra* n. 40, 6.
47. Berger, *supra* n. 37, at 507.

Understandably, what has not changed is the concern that whatever steps are taken by an arbitral tribunal to facilitate settlement, such steps should not expose the arbitrators to challenge or jeopardize the enforceability of their award. Thus, an essential prerequisite for an arbitrator's involvement in settlement discussions, whether it is by chairing a settlement meeting, providing a preliminary view on certain matters or taking any other steps to facilitate settlement, is that this is always based on the informed and uncoerced consent of the parties, i.e., an agreement by the parties during (not before) the arbitration.[48] Further, it has been highlighted that while caucus sessions (meeting with the parties separately) may be an efficient method in the context of settlement discussions, this should be avoided. The CEDR Report identified the chairing of settlement conferences as a potential role for an arbitral tribunal but states that arbitrators should not meet with the parties separately or obtain any information from one party which is not shared with the other parties. As explained by Klaus Peter Berger, the absence of caucusing will 'do away' with many of the objections raised by opponents of the arbitrator's mandate to facilitate settlement.[49]

[2] How Decision Analysis Can Be Used by Arbitrators to Facilitate Settlement

Assuming that the parties provide their informed and uncoerced consent, decision analysis can serve as a useful tool for an arbitrator or arbitral tribunal when they seek to facilitate settlement of the parties' dispute. To do this, the arbitrator should be well acquainted with both the factual and legal aspects of the case. As expressed by one scholar, a proactive settlement facilitation is incompatible with the 'reality of the hands-off arbitrator'.[50]

An arbitrator may, either in connection with the case management conference (CMC) or at a later stage, encourage parties to do a decision-tree analysis of their case, both from their own perspective and from the other parties' perspective. As separate meetings with the parties should be avoided, it will be challenging for the arbitrator to reality test a party's assessment (as is usually done in mediation through private sessions), to reduce the parties' usually overoptimistic assessment of their prospects of success (in line with the overconfidence bias accounted for above). However, nothing

48. The 2024 IBA Guidelines on Conflicts of Interest in International Arbitration, General Standard 4(d) provides that 'An arbitrator may assist the parties in reaching a settlement of the dispute, through conciliation, mediation, or otherwise, at any stage of the proceedings. However, before doing so, the arbitrator should receive an express agreement by the parties that acting in such a manner shall not disqualify the arbitrator from continuing to serve as arbitrator. Such express agreement shall be considered to be an effective waiver of any potential conflict of interest that may arise from the arbitrator's participation in such a process, or from information that the arbitrator may learn in the process.', the same effect of the parties' informed consent is accorded in Article 9 of the Rules on Conduct on the Taking of Evidence in International Arbitration ('Prague Rules').
49. Berger, *supra* n. 37, at 513.
50. Michael E Schneider, 'The Art of Blending Arbitration and Other ADR Methods: Some Examples from International Practice' in Arnold Ingen-Housz (ed.), *ADR in Business: Practice and Issues across Countries and Cultures*, vol. II (Kluwer Law International 2011) 313.

prevents the arbitrator from expressing in general terms the notions of overconfidence bias to help the parties in reaching more realistic case assessments. Further, taking our example dispute between the software developer and its customer, the arbitrator can use decision analysis to aid the parties in mapping out the possible outcomes, assigning probabilities and costs and calculating expected values. This allows the arbitrator to engage in structured reasoning and aid the parties in systematically evaluating the possible outcomes. For example, the arbitrator may ask the parties: Is this a realistic assessment of the case? This may help to unlock impasses when parties seem to be entrenched in their respective positions regarding what they deem a 'fair' solution of the dispute.

If the parties' wish and consent to the arbitrator or arbitral tribunal expresses a preliminary opinion on certain aspects of the case, the arbitral tribunal may also illustrate its preliminary views using a decision-tree analysis. Unlike the parties' giving of 'informed consent' and waiver of their right to challenge the arbitrators, the arbitral tribunal's preliminary views and further facilitation activities are best served without a transcript being taken (i.e., off the record). This serves two significant purposes: First, it shows the preliminary and non-binding nature of the arbitral tribunal's considerations. At the same time, it takes into account the fact that if the arbitration continues, a party may otherwise feel inclined to refer to recorded statements made by arbitrators to the other party during the settlement conference. Thus, all statements made by the parties during this process should be subject to the transnational principle of 'settlement privilege' to preserve the parties' confidence in such negotiation-driven alternative dispute resolution processes.[51]

[H] Using the Knowledge of Cognitive Biases and Traps to Make 'Fairer' Decisions

With the example case used above, it will now be explored how arbitrators can use the knowledge of cognitive biases and traps, i.e., knowledge of how decisions are *actually* taken, to mitigate or avoid making bad decisions.

[1] The Initial Phase of the Arbitration: Consider the Opposite

When the case is referred to the arbitral tribunal, the parties have only presented a limited number of facts and evidence in the customer's request for arbitration and the software developer's answer and counterclaim. The arbitral tribunal reviews the case file to get an idea of what the case is about and to decide how best to proceed. Already at this stage, the risk of framing or anchoring effect and representation bias arises.

The claimant (the customer) has requested EUR 15 million from the software developer, who in turn has requested EUR 5.5 million in the reply and counterclaim.

51. Klaus Peter Berger, 'The Settlement Privilege: A General Principle of International ADR Law' (2008) 24(2) *Arbitration International* 265, 274 https://doi.org/10.1093/arbitration/24.2.265 (accessed 1 October 2025).

According to the presiding arbitrator, the documents submitted initially indicate that the customer probably had a fairly strong basis for terminating the agreement. When the arbitrators have their initial meeting before the CMC, one of the younger co-arbitrators asks the presiding arbitrator what he thinks of the case so far. The chairman has sat on many similar cases and knows from experience that when software developers change the lead manager several times as has been done in this case, when in fact it is 'accepted' that a customer often requests in the contract that certain key people be included, then it is a clear sign that the software developer cannot fulfil its obligations. The arbitrator's first impression is reinforced by what the customer has stated in the request for arbitration about the software developer not meeting some of its agreed milestones.

The arbitrator makes an initial assessment based on how similar this is to previous cases the arbitrator has encountered, and risks ignoring the facts pointing to the customer's right to terminate the contract. This is representation bias. The arbitrator may also, unconsciously be disinclined to reconsider his position even if it is revealed later in the process, e.g., during the testimony of the customer's project manager Mr Born that the customer did not in fact provide the software vendor with all the necessary information for the implementation of the system to go according to plan.

However, there are some strategies that can be used as a de-biasing method to avoid or at least mitigate parts of the cognitive traps that all arbitrators are exposed to.

One basic rule that many conscientious arbitrators follow is not to express any value judgments about the case or the strength of the parties' positions until deliberation (after the oral hearing). When asked by the junior co-arbitrator for a preliminary opinion of the case, the conscious chairman tells the junior co-arbitrator 'I will keep my initial thoughts to myself at this stage until we have heard all the facts and evidence. Otherwise, we will risk jumping to a premature conclusion.'

Furthermore, the so-called consider the opposite method is a strategy that has proven to be an effective de-biasing mechanism in arbitration.[52] In simple terms, the strategy boils down to asking the following question.

What are the reasons that my initial judgment might be wrong?

Asking this question redirects the arbitrator's attention towards contrary evidence that would not have been considered otherwise. Even if the method seems trivial, posing the question is necessary as it results in a conscious thought process. Making the question explicit primes stimuli other than the ones that are normally triggered by the very same mechanism that gives rise to association-based errors, thus broadening the sample subject to scrutiny and making it more representative. In our example, posing the question causes the arbitrator to consciously recall that he does not actually have the whole picture yet and that the software developer may have a justified position that

52. Charles G Lord, Mark R Lepper and Elizabeth Preston, 'Considering the Opposite: A Corrective Strategy for Social Judgment' (1984) 47 *Journal of Personality and Social Psychology* 1231-1243 https://doi.org/10.1037//0022-3514.47.6.1231 (accessed 1 October 2025); Jan-Philip Elm, 'Behavioral Insights into International Arbitration: An Analysis of How to De-Bias Arbitrators' (2017) 1 *University of St Gallen Law and Economics Research Paper Series*, 54.

the system was more complex to implement than either party could reasonably have anticipated at the outset of the project. Thus, 'consider the opposite' may successfully counteract anchoring, the hindsight bias, and the egocentric bias.

[2] The Oral Hearing: When Are We Having Lunch?

After a fairly smooth written phase of the arbitral proceedings, during which the arbitral tribunal has only been required to decide on a few document production requests, it is time for the oral hearing. Both parties have invoked several witnesses. Although written witness statements have been submitted, the parties have agreed to allow for a shorter direct examination followed by cross-examination. There are also quantum experts invoked on both sides regarding the calculation of the respondents' claimed damages for lost profits (amounting to EUR 4 million) and what a reasonable estimate of the customer's cost of implementing an equivalent system by a third party amounts to (EUR 10 million damages claim).

The parties, who want to maximize the possibility that the arbitrators listen attentively to their experts and minimize the possibility that the arbitrators take into account what the other side's experts say, both want their expert to be heard on the morning of the second day, when the arbitrators are expected to be most alert.

Arbitrators often allow the parties to plan the schedule as far as possible and reasonable. The chairman is aware that research shows (and he knows from experience) that arbitrators generally find it harder to absorb complex reasoning later in the day than just before lunch. At that time, although trying to stay attentive, the arbitrator cannot help but let the attention slip and instead think about when lunch is served. Many arbitrators would probably be reluctant to change the schedule the parties have agreed on and suggest that both sides' experts be heard first thing in the morning on days 2 and 3. An alternative might then be to listen to the hearing of the expert heard in the late afternoon, also at a later date, so that the arbitrators do not risk overlooking important observations made during the hearing.

During the parties' oral presentation, the customer's closing argument is presented by the customer's lead counsel, a very senior partner from one of the largest law firms in the country. The partner, who is male, is attractive and has a lot of authority. The lawyer presenting the software developer's closing argument is considerably younger, female, and although she presents strong arguments, she speaks more quietly and not with the same confidence as the opposing counsel.

All the arbitrators are on a conscious level focused on basing their assessment on the strength of each party's argument, and not the appearance or presentation skills of their counsels. However, the priming effect explained above has proven that the decision makers (arbitrators not excluded) may unconsciously consider a message more trustworthy if delivered by a person with certain physical features. Thus, it may be advisable for an arbitral tribunal, if not already required by the case's complexity, to have several deliberations where the arbitral tribunal revisits the written submissions and evidence when the impressions from the oral presentations have faded.

[3] The Deliberations and Reaching a Reasoned Award

During the deliberations, the chairman lets the most junior co-arbitrators speak first and express their views about the case. This mitigates the authority bias, which risks letting a decision maker be unduly influenced by what a person with more seniority or authority thinks.

Further, the arbitral tribunal can also during the deliberations return to the 'consider the opposite' strategy as a de-biasing mechanism. Further, as many arbitrators are well aware, assessments made during deliberations may turn out not to hold up for scrutiny when the reasoning of the award is drafted. Thus, a prudent presiding arbitrator will tell his co-arbitrators during deliberations that he or she will follow up should any new insights come to light during the drafting of the award.

§8.08 CONCLUSION

Any stakeholder in an arbitration, be it a party representative, counsel, or arbitrators, benefits from having knowledge of decision analysis. For parties and their counsel, decision analysis can be used in two important ways. First, the knowledge can help to avoid or at least mitigate the most common traps that result in counsels making, or recommending a client to make, intuitive but non-rational decisions. Second, they can shed light on how to exploit others' mistakes to the client's advantage in the arbitration.

For an arbitrator, it can assist him or her in raising awareness and avoid or at least mitigate certain unconscious biases and cognitive errors with the aim of rendering 'fairer' decisions.

The quality of decisions is often judged by their outcome. This hindsight can however be an unfair way of judging if an individual decision was good or bad. Most people buying a lottery ticket and winning would describe the decision as a good decision, when it in fact was, from a pure dollar perspective, a bad decision with a good outcome. If one could choose, one would of course choose good outcomes – but outcomes in arbitration are never guaranteed. Even if good outcomes cannot be guaranteed, it is possible to optimize for good outcomes by making good decisions.

A quote that is often attributed to the statistician George E. P. Box summarizes the value of decision analysis very well.

'All models are wrong, but some models are useful.'

Decision analysis models will always be flawed in some way. It is not possible to account for every factor of a dispute. This does not mean that the models cannot be immensely powerful.

CHAPTER 9

Acting as a Legal Representative in Front of the Court of Arbitration for Sport

Malin Stenberg & Marie-Anne Lindhardt

§9.01 INTRODUCTION AND LIMITATIONS OF THE ARTICLE

This chapter aims to provide the reader with an insight into the specifics of commercial[1] dispute resolution within the sports community.

To clarify the context, the first part will introduce the rationales behind arbitration as the primary dispute resolution mechanism in sports. This will be followed by an overview of the world's Supreme Court for sport, the Court of Arbitration for Sport (CAS), and various types of disputes adjudicated by the CAS.

The second part will address appeal proceedings before the CAS, including certain aspects that add extra complexity and require special procedural strategies by the legal representatives. This part will also address differences compared to ordinary arbitration proceeding.[2] The majority of proceedings before the CAS are football-related, and references to relevant football regulations will therefore be made when describing and elaborating on the characteristics of appeal proceedings before the CAS.

The third part will address some potential changes to the dispute resolution mechanisms in sports due to recent jurisprudence that might challenge the previously protected environment in which sports have long operated. In recent years, criticism has been directed at CAS regarding its credibility as an institution and its overall structure, *inter alia,* concerning its compliance with EU law and the European Convention on Human Rights. Critics also point to its (non-)contribution to the development of law, governance issues, and concerns over athletes' rights due to a

1. For avoidance of doubt, when refereeing to 'commercial' or 'commercial disputes' this also includes employment law matters.
2. For example, in accordance with the Arbitration Rules of the SCC Arbitration Institute.

perceived lack of transparency. Although jurisprudence in these areas is growing, there is still a great deal to address.

In this chapter, we focus on certain disputes before the CAS, which naturally restricts our examination of every possible criticism against CAS as an institution. The third part will therefore focus on the criticism that has arisen in light of EU law.

Finally, this chapter does not aim to cover all the differences between appeal proceedings before the CAS and other arbitration proceedings. It seeks solely to provide the reader with an understanding of questions a legal representative may encounter when presenting a case before the CAS.

[A] The Rationale Behind Arbitration as the Principal Means of Resolving Sports-Related Disputes, and the Safeguarding of That Principle

Within the world of sport, sports arbitration has long been considered to offer several benefits for resolving sports-related disputes.

In addition, the general stance of courts in Europe, as well as in most other parts of the world, has been – at least historically – to refrain from intervening in sports disputes, except under very specific and limited circumstances. This is due to the common understanding that sports bodies are much better positioned to assess sports-related issues than the courts, and that it is preferable to resolve legal disputes 'within the sports community'.[3]

Moreover, the notion that arbitration shall be given preference over court litigation is closely related to the inherent nature of sports – arbitration panels are simply seen as more suitable for applying the various rules and principles found across different countries and different sports.[4] This also provides for a consistent worldwide jurisprudence in relation to the application of the respective rules and regulations of each sport.

To uphold and safeguard the principle of arbitration as the preferred and mandatory dispute resolution mechanism within the sports community, the rules and regulations of international sports federations provide for arbitration as the method for resolving disputes. Each international sports federation has established its own dispute resolution system, which stipulates an obligation to refrain from ordinary courts of law and submit any dispute to a designated decision-making body or an arbitration tribunal. In addition, the statutes and regulations of international sports federations also include an obligation for the national member associations to include a corresponding dispute resolution mechanism in their own national regulation. By doing so, arbitration is secured worldwide as the method for resolving disputes 'within the sports community' in each respective sport.

---

3. Ian Blackshaw, *The Court of Arbitration for Sport: An International Forum for Settling Disputes Effectively 'Within the Family of Sport'*, Entertainment Law 2, no. 2, 61-83, 61-62 (Summer 2003) https://doi.org/10.16997/eslj.139 (accessed 1 October 2025).
4. Richard H. McLaren, *The Court of Arbitration for Sport: An Independent Arena for the World's Sports Disputes*, Valparaiso University Law Review 35, 379-405, 381 (2001).

As an example, Article 51 paragraphs 2 and 3 of the FIFA[5] Statutes read as follows:

> 2. Recourse to ordinary courts of law is prohibited unless specifically provided for in the FIFA regulations. Recourse to ordinary courts of law for all types of provisional measures is also prohibited.
> 3. The associations shall insert a clause in their statutes or regulations, stipulating that it is prohibited to take disputes in the association or disputes affecting leagues, members of leagues, clubs, members of clubs, players, officials and other association officials to ordinary courts of law, unless the FIFA regulations or binding legal provisions specifically provide for or stipulate recourse to ordinary courts of law. Instead of recourse to ordinary courts of law, provision shall be made for arbitration. Such disputes shall be taken to an independent and duly constituted arbitration tribunal recognised under the rules of the association or confederation or to CAS.
>
> The associations shall also ensure that this stipulation is implemented in the association, if necessary by imposing a binding obligation on its members. The associations shall impose sanctions on any party that fails to respect this obligation and ensure that any appeal against such sanctions shall likewise be strictly submitted to arbitration, and not to ordinary courts of law (emphasis added).

Similarly, the statutes of the Swedish Football Association (SvFF) include the following provisions:

> Art. 11 para. 9 of the SvFF Statutes
>
> By virtue of their membership, both association and individual member have committed themselves to not initiate proceedings in an ordinary court of law concerning matters related to the application of the statutes or the Federation's competition rules (emphasis added).
>
> Art. 49 of the SvFF Statutes
>
> The Arbitration Tribunal shall, except in cases where 52 § is applicable or when another specific procedure is prescribed in the competition regulations or rules of the SvFF, adjudicate disputes where the parties are directly or indirectly members of FIFA, UEFA, the Federation, District Football Associations (SDF), or clubs within these organisations. The Arbitration Tribunal shall also adjudicate disputes where one of the parties is directly or indirectly a member of any of the aforementioned organisations and the parties have specified in an arbitration agreement that the dispute shall be adjudicated by the tribunal. Disputes under this provision may not be brought before an ordinary court of law but shall be resolved by the Federation's Arbitration Tribunal. The Federation's board of directors establishes the rules concerning the Arbitration Tribunal (emphasis added).
>
> Art. 52 of the SvFF Statutes
>
> Actions in disputes concerning the statutes and other regulations of FIFA or UEFA, as well as decisions made by FIFA or UEFA, may not be brought before an ordinary court of law but shall be referred to the appropriate body within FIFA or UEFA, or, where applicable, the Court of Arbitration for Sport (CAS) in Lausanne; all in

5. Federation Internationale de Football Association.

accordance with the provisions of FIFA's and UEFA's statutes in force at any given time (emphasis added).

Hence, through the international and national regulations of sports, the principle that the members of the sports community shall refrain from ordinary courts of law and refer any dispute to arbitration is upheld, and a system created by which sports disputes are handled within the sports community.

Thus, there is no doubt that arbitration is the preferred, and from the contributors' perspective, the necessary choice for dispute resolution across all types of sports worldwide. Given the international nature of high-level sports, the development of a global Supreme Court for sport was likely both necessary and inevitable.

Moreover, the idea of political neutrality and autonomy of sport[6] requires that there is an independent and neutral institution which takes on the responsibility of resolving sports disputes.

[B] The World's Supreme Court for Sport

The global Supreme Court, known as the CAS, was established in 1984 by the International Olympic Committee (IOC) to resolve the increasing number of sports-related disputes in a flexible, quick and inexpensive manner. Since then, the CAS, based in Lausanne, Switzerland, has provided an international forum for athletes, clubs, sports federations, etc., to resolve disputes. The CAS is an independent and proficient sports adjudication body that can uphold and apply the rules of different sports organisations.[7]

With nearly 300 arbitrators from 87 countries and over 900 registered cases in 2023 and 2024,[8] the CAS has over the years consolidated its position as the world's 'Supreme Court for sport'.[9] The route the CAS has taken to get where it is today has, however, been far from straight. A major reason for this, *inter alia*, was that the big wave of doping scandals did not arise until the second half of the 1980s. Moreover, for many years, international federations – such as the International Association of Athletics Federations (IAAF) – had their own adjudicating bodies. As a result, the CAS rendered only a small number of decisions during the years following its establishment.[10]

6. *See* IOC Code of Ethics, Art. 1.2-1.3 and the 'Fundamental Principles of Olympism' set forth in the Olympic Charter.
7. Richard H. McLaren, *The Court of Arbitration for Sport: An Independent Arena for the World's Sports Disputes*, Valparaiso University Law Review 35, 381 (2001).
8. CAS, *Frequently Asked Questions Frequently Asked Questions: Tribunal Arbitral du Sport / Court of Arbitration for Sport*, https://www.tas-cas.org/en/general-information/frequently-asked-questions.html (accessed 9 November 2025) and FIFA, *CAS Football Annual Report*, 25 (2024).
9. Matthew J. Mitten, *The Court of Arbitration for Sport and its Global Jurisprudence: International Legal Pluralism in a World without National Boundaries*, Ohio State Journal on Dispute Resolution 30, no. 1, 1-44, 9 (2014).
10. Lorenzo Casini, *The Making of a Lex Sportiva by the Court of Arbitration for Sport*, German Law Journal 12, no. 5, 1317-1340, 1321-1322 (2011) https://doi.org/10.1017/s2071832200017326 (accessed 1 October 2025).

Furthermore, in its early days, the CAS was set up as a judicial arm of the IOC, with the IOC holding both political and financial authority over it. As the Swiss Federal Tribunal (SFT) highlighted in a judgment from 1993, this raised some concerns over the CAS' independence from the IOC.[11] This judgment later became a strong contributing factor to the creation of a new administrative body in 1994 – the International Council of Arbitration for Sport (ICAS) – whose purpose is to facilitate the resolution of sports-related disputes and to safeguard the independence of the CAS and the rights of the parties. The ICAS is likewise responsible for the administration and financing of the CAS, a responsibility that previously belonged to the IOC.[12]

Fast forward to today, the jurisdiction of the CAS has been recognised by all Olympic sports federations and several non-Olympic federations,[13] and the CAS' role as an independent arbitral body and the world's Supreme Court for sport has also been affirmed by the SFT.[14]

In line with this view of the CAS as a legitimate arbitral institution, the CAS Code of Sports-related Arbitration (CAS Code) enshrines that the CAS' mission is to constitute panels which have the responsibility of resolving disputes arising in the context of sport by arbitration and/or mediation pursuant to the CAS Code's procedural rules.[15] To fulfil this mission, the CAS is divided into three divisions:[16] an Anti-Doping Division, an Ordinary Arbitration Division and an Appeals Arbitration Division.[17]

The Anti-Doping Division was established to hear and decide anti-doping cases as a first-instance authority,[18] and the Ordinary Arbitration Division consists of panels whose task it is to resolve disputes which may arise out of an arbitration clause contained in a contract or regulations or by reason of a later arbitration agreement

11. Lorenzo Casini, *The Making of a Lex Sportiva by the Court of Arbitration for Sport*, German Law Journal 12, no. 5, 1317-1340, 1322 (2011) https://doi.org/10.1017/s2071832200017326 (accessed 1 October 2025) with reference to judgment of the Swiss Federal Tribunal, *Gundel v. Fédération Equestre Internationale*, BGE 119 II 271 (15 March 1993).
12. CAS, *the CAS Code*, Art. S2 (2023).
13. FIFA, *FIFA Statutes*, Art. 49 para. 1 (May 2024).
14. Lorenzo Casini, *The Making of a Lex Sportiva by the Court of Arbitration for Sport*, German Law Journal 12, no. 5, 1317-1340, 1321 (2011) https://doi.org/10.1017/s2071832200017326 (accessed 1 October 2025) with reference to judgment of the Swiss Federal Tribunal, *A. et B. v. Comité International Olympique, Fédération Internationale de Ski et Tribunal Arbitral du Sport*, BGE 129 III 445 (27 May 2003).
15. CAS, *the CAS Code*, Art. S12 (2023).
16. Additionally, during sports events such as the Olympics or the FIFA World Cup, a CAS Ad Hoc Division is installed by the ICAS for the arbitration of disputes arising in connection with the specific event. One notable example in a Swedish context that illustrates the ad hoc Division's role in delivering prompt decisions, is the conflict between six Swedish athletes and the Swedish Olympic Committee (SOK) which garnered significant attention leading up to the Paris Olympics 2024. Six Swedish athletes who were not selected for the Swedish Olympic team, and who were of the opinion that the SOK had acted in violation of the IOC's Olympic Charter by not selecting the athletes despite them (according to their opinion) being qualified, initiated a procedure before the CAS ad hoc Division for the Olympics in Paris during the second half of July 2024. The CAS Ad hoc Division rendered its decision as early as on 26 July 2024. However, to the athletes' disappointment, the CAS sided with the SOK and found no reasons to support the view that the SOK's eligibility requirements were in conflict with the IOC's Olympic Charter.
17. CAS, *the CAS Code*, Art. S20 (2023).
18. CAS, *the CAS Code*, Art. S20b (2023).

(ordinary arbitration proceedings). The task of the latter – the Appeals Arbitration Division – is to resolve appeals against decisions rendered by a federation, association or sports-related body where the statutes or regulations of such bodies, or a specific agreement, provide for an appeal to the CAS (appeal arbitration proceedings).[19]

It is worth emphasising that regardless of which CAS division resolves a dispute, the seat of CAS arbitration is Switzerland.[20] This means that the Swiss Private International Law Act (PILA) which governs all arbitration proceedings held in Switzerland, is applicable to all CAS proceedings.

When it comes to the law applicable on the merits, it differs between ordinary proceedings, appeal proceedings and doping proceedings. The merits of an ordinary proceeding are assessed on the basis of the law chosen by the parties or, in the absence of such choice, Swiss law.[21] The merits of an appeal proceeding are primarily assessed on the basis of the regulations of the relevant sport governing body, and subsidiarily on the basis of the law chosen by the parties. If the parties have not chosen which law to apply, the law of the country where the governing body is based will be applied. Alternatively, the panel can apply whichever legal rules it considers appropriate.[22] In doping proceedings, the CAS panel shall apply the applicable anti-doping regulations or the laws of a particular jurisdiction chosen by agreement of the parties or, in the absence of such choice, Swiss law.[23]

It is evident that the CAS has assumed the role of the Supreme Court by developing a transnational sports law known as 'lex sportiva'.[24] In the next section, we will delve further into some statistics that provide an idea of the most common disputes before the CAS.

[C] Proceedings Before the CAS: The Most Common Types

Of the disputes that are brought before the CAS, the appeal proceedings account for the majority, or over 70%, of all proceedings.[25]

---

19. CAS, *the CAS Code*, Art. S20 (2023) and CAS, *the CAS Code*, Art. R27 (2023).
20. CAS, *the CAS Code*, Art. R28 (2023). The option mentioned in the provision to hold a hearing in another place does not affect the seat of CAS and its arbitration panels. It should though be noticed, that UEFA has, as a result of the decision in the ISU case (*see* section §9.03[A][2] below), amended the UEFA Authorization Rules governing International Club Competitions and provides the party filing the statement of appeal and/or a request for provisional measures the possibility to decide whether the seat of the CAS arbitration shall be Lausanne (Switzerland) or Dublin (Ireland), *see* Art. 16 para. 3 of the UEFA Authorization governing International Club. The amendment is a derogation of Art. R28 of the CAS Code, and whether it will be deemed compatible with the CAS Code or not, has not yet been decided upon.
21. CAS, *the CAS Code*, Art. R45 (2023). The parties may also authorise the panel to decide ex aequo et bono.
22. CAS, *the CAS Code*, Art. R58 (2023). In practice, in most proceedings before the CAS, Swiss substantive law is applied since many of the international sports governing bodies have their headquarters in Switzerland.
23. CAS, *Arbitration Rules CAS Anti-Doping Division*, Art. A20 (2024).
24. Lorenzo Casini, *The Making of a Lex Sportiva by the Court of Arbitration for Sport*, German Law Journal 12, no. 5, 1317-1340, 1321 and 1326-1327 (2011) https://doi.org/10.1017/s2071832200017326 (accessed 1 October 2025).
25. CAS, *CAS Statistics* (accessed 1 April 2025).

As mentioned above, an appeal against a decision of a federation, association or sports-related body may be filed with the CAS if the statutes or regulations of the said body so provide, or if the parties have concluded a specific arbitration agreement. It is also specified that the appellant must have exhausted the legal remedies available to it prior to the appeal, in accordance with the statutes or regulations of the body whose decision is appealed.[26]

A significant portion of the disputes that arise 'in the context of sport' are related to football. Consequently, it is unsurprising that football-related disputes represent a clear majority of the cases brought before the CAS.

In 2024, 72% of the 916 cases that were registered at the CAS were related to international, continental and national football.[27] Out of the 657 football-related proceedings, 72% were appeal proceedings and 28% ordinary proceedings.[28]

Appeals against final decisions passed by the different bodies of FIFA constituted 68% of the total number of football-related appeals before the CAS in 2024. The remaining appealed decisions were issued by confederations, national or regional football associations.[29] About half of the appealed decisions were related to employment law matters followed by disciplinary matters which accounted for nearly 20% of the football-related appeals in 2024.[30]

With the above in mind, we proceed to the next part of this chapter, where we will address certain aspects of appeal proceedings before the CAS and further elaborate on what such aspects entail for legal counsels presenting a case before the CAS.

§9.02 APPEAL PROCEEDINGS BEFORE THE CAS

[A] Introduction

Based on the aforementioned statistics, it is evident that most disputes before the CAS are appeal proceedings and football-related disputes.

In order to compare appeal proceedings in front of the CAS with other commercial arbitration proceedings, from the legal representative's perspective, we find it most interesting to look at commercial disputes.

With this in mind, this part will focus on selected characteristics of appeal proceedings in commercial disputes before the CAS that, in the contributors' opinion, affect the considerations of legal representatives.

26. CAS, *the CAS Code*, Art. R47 (2023). *See also*, for example, *Club Salernitana Calcio 1919 S.p.A v. Club Atlético River Plate & Cesar Costa*, CAS 2009/A/1919 (7 May 2019).
27. FIFA, *CAS Football Annual Report*, 26 (2024).
28. FIFA, *CAS Football Annual Report*, 27 (2024).
29. FIFA, *CAS Football Annual Report*, 28 (2024).
30. FIFA, *CAS Football Annual Report*, 29 (2024).

[B] Appeal Proceedings in the CAS Are a Hybrid form of Arbitration Proceedings

The rationales behind arbitration in sports are in one way similar to those for commercial parties. However, some principles have fallen into obscurity when discussing arbitration in sports.

Arbitration is based on the principle of the parties' free will, and the parties must mutually agree to take a dispute to arbitration. Consequently, one of the foundations of both domestic and international arbitration is party autonomy. In the sport community, as mentioned above, athletes, clubs and associations are in general bound by arbitration clauses, directly or indirectly, through their membership in the national or international sports association. Within the sports community, this commitment is seen as an agreement on arbitration, something which is also reflected in the CAS Code:

> Art. R27 of the CAS Code
>
> These Procedural Rules apply whenever the parties have agreed to refer a sports-related dispute to CAS. Such reference may arise out of an arbitration clause contained in a contract or regulations or by reason of a later arbitration agreement (ordinary arbitration proceedings) or may involve an appeal against a decision rendered by a federation, association or sports-related body where the statutes or regulations of such bodies, or a specific agreement provide for an appeal to CAS (appeal arbitration proceedings) (emphasis added).

This constitutes a kind of hybrid, as participants in sport are often bound by arbitration clauses despite the absence of a specific contractual clause in the agreement at the centre of the dispute. Therefore, it can scarcely be argued that CAS proceedings are based on party autonomy.

The party autonomy is also affected by the fact that the CAS is serving as second instance in appeal proceedings before the CAS. It does so, not only in relation to decisions taken by a decision-making body of a sports federation against a direct or indirect member – such as in disciplinary matters – but also in commercial disputes. In football, for example, the decision-making bodies of FIFA have jurisdiction as first instance in several different types of disputes related to international transfers of players,[31] such as employment-related disputes and contractual disputes. The decisions taken by the relevant FIFA bodies in these types of disputes can, based on the statutes and regulations of FIFA, be appealed to the CAS.

The fact that the CAS serves as an appeal arbitration body affects the parties' possibility to determine the procedure to be followed by the CAS panel in conducting the proceedings, as well as the scope of the panel's review.

31. Under the precondition that there is an international dimension to the dispute, *see* FIFA, *Regulations on the Status and Transfer of Players*, Art. 22 (January 2025 Edition).

[C] The Parties Do Not Decide the Scope of the CAS' Review

One of the most distinctive features of presenting a case in an appeal proceeding before the CAS is that the process before the CAS is not restricted by what the parties presented or invoked at the first instance.[32] We will elaborate on this theme in the following two sections of this chapter.

[1] The CAS' Full Power of Review of the Case

If there is support for an appeal, and it subsequently occurs, the CAS' review of the case will not be limited to the arguments and issues presented in the decision or the decision's compliance with applicable law and regulations. Instead, it is a well-established and fundamental principle for the CAS that decisions issued by internal sports bodies and appealed to the CAS will undergo a complete and independent review on the merits (*the de novo principle*).

This distinctive feature of the CAS appeal proceedings is found in Article R57 of the CAS Code which states that:

> The Panel has full power to review the facts and the law. It may issue a new decision which replaces the decision challenged or annul the decision and refer the case back to the previous instance.

Thus, the CAS has full authority to re-examine the case (de novo). Moreover, this is not only a possibility but also an explicit obligation for the CAS arbitration panels, as clearly demonstrated by CAS jurisprudence.[33]

However, there is naturally an ultimate limit to the panel's review. The arbitration panel must not exceed the requests that were subject to review in the previous handling of the case or that were addressed within the framework of the appealed decision, nor exceed the requests presented before the CAS.

In the legal doctrine, it has been argued that the necessity of the full power to review:

> [is] due to the fact that the appeal to CAS is, in principle, the first opportunity for the parties to bring their case before an independent arbitral tribunal, since the jurisdictional organs of sports organizations do not meet the criteria to be considered as independent arbitration tribunals.[34]

32. *See* for some limitations in §9.02[A][3][a] below.
33. *FC Sion v. Fédération Internationale de Football Association (FIFA) & Al-Ahly Sporting Club & CAS 2009/A/1881 E. v. Fédération Internationale de Football Association (FIFA) & Al-Ahly Sporting Club*, CAS 2009/A/1880-1881 (1 June 2010) and *FC Otelul Galati S.A. v. Romanian Football Federation (RFF) & Codoban Tatar Ionel*, CAS 2012/A/2900 (12 June 2013).
34. D. Mavromati and M. Reeb, *The Code of the Court of Arbitration for Sport: Commentary, Cases and Materials*, 507 (2015).

The essence of the *de novo principle* is also found in Article R57 paragraph 2 of the CAS Code:

> After consulting the parties, the Panel may, if it deems itself to be sufficiently informed, decide not to hold a hearing (emphasis added).

It is not the possibility to refrain from holding a hearing that is of interest - but the expression of the panel being sufficiently informed.

The requirement of the panel being sufficiently informed is closely related to the *de novo principle* and is an expression of the fact that it is important for the CAS arbitrators to give an accurate award. The outcome of the case must not depend on the parties' economic or practical ability to manage the proceeding in front of the CAS.

With the *do novo principle* at the centre of each appeal proceeding before the CAS, the legal representatives acting before the CAS must ensure that the case presented, especially if representing the appellant, will be accepted based on all circumstances, regardless of whether they are highlighted by a party or not. This, since the *de novo principle* gives the panel authority to base its assessment on legal facts that are not invoked by the parties. The CAS panel can base its award on circumstances it deems relevant, and it is therefore crucial for a legal representative to take a step back to reevaluate the case and identify the circumstances that will be considered by the panel. The aim is, of course, for the CAS to make accurate decisions, but this environment results in complex strategic decisions and sometimes uncertain outcomes.

Historically, the CAS' obligation to fully review cases led to a more lenient stance on the admission of new evidence. Although this leniency has been modified and clarified in CAS jurisprudence, it remains permissible in appeal proceedings to a degree that is distinctive from commercial disputes. This is a notable feature of appeal proceedings before the CAS. Since it is not directly comparable to other commercial arbitration proceedings or to litigation in ordinary courts of law, it requires a different approach to managing the appeal procedure as a legal representative.

[2] The Possibility of Invoking New Evidence in an Appeal Proceeding in Front of the CAS

A common reason for not succeeding with its requests in the first instance is the party's failure to fulfil its burden of proof. When this occurs, it is very common that the appellant attempts to secure a change in the outcome by introducing new evidence before the CAS.

As a consequence of the CAS' right and obligation to review each appeal de novo, each party is generally entitled to present new evidence before the CAS. Additionally, the CAS has the authority to request additional evidence in the case ex officio. According to Article R44 paragraph 3 of the CAS Code:

> the Panel may at any time order the production of additional documents or the examination of witnesses, appoint and hear experts, and proceed with any other procedural step ... .

In recent years, however, an exception to the general rule allowing parties to submit new evidence has developed. Initially, through case law and subsequently through the introduction of the explicit provision in the current Article R57 paragraph 3 of the CAS Code:

> The Panel has discretion to exclude evidence presented by the parties if it was available to them or could reasonably have been discovered by them before the challenged decision was rendered.

Therefore, there is a risk that new evidence will not be considered if the arbitration panel determines that the evidence could have been presented already in the first instance.

It is though important to note that Article R57 paragraph 3 of the CAS Code does not prohibit new evidence; it merely provides the arbitration panel *with the discretion to exclude it*. The rationale behind the provision is to balance the CAS' full power of review (i.e., judicial truth) and the economy of procedure. Hence, the provision was inserted to avoid evidence submitted in an abusive way, to hinder parties acting in bad faith in first instance and to increase parties' procedural behaviour.[35]

The possibility to exclude such evidence that a party knew, or should have known about, before the challenged decision was rendered affects the CAS' role as an appeal instance.[36] In conjunction with the introduction of the exception in Article R57 paragraph 3 of the CAS Code, several clear positions were taken in the doctrine advocating for a restrictive application of the provision,[37] which has also been reflected in the CAS jurisprudence. The CAS has clarified, based on the *de novo principle*, that new evidence should not be excluded more than necessary and that this option should be used with caution. The caution exercised by a CAS panel when excluding evidence is a consequence of its overall aim to be sufficiently informed.

This fundamental view on the admissibility of new evidence before the CAS is a parameter that affects the strategic considerations of a legal representative. The possibility of success in the case of an appeal cannot merely be based on what has been presented in the first instance, but must also take into account the possibility of how the counterparty chooses to present the case and additional evidence in front of the CAS.

At the same time, in cases where you are first assigned as a legal representative when your client is facing an appeal (which is not an unusual situation, since it is not

35. D. Mavromati and M. Reeb, *The Code of the Court of Arbitration for Sport, Commentary, Cases and Materials*, 519-520 (2015).
36. Note that Art. R57 para. 3 of the CAS Code should not be confused with Art. R56 of the CAS Code. The latter provision regulates cases where additional evidence, regardless of whether it was subject to be reviewed in a previous instance or not, is presented before the CAS only after both the appeal brief and the answer have been exchanged. To present additional evidence so late in the process requires an agreement between the parties or the arbitration panel's determination that there are exceptional circumstances.
37. D. Mavromati, *Bulletin TAS CAS Bulletin no. 1 (2014), The CAS Panel's Right to Exclude Evidence Based on Art. R57 Para. 3 CAS Code: A Limit to CAS' Full Power of Review?* (2015) and Roy Levy, *CAS 2014/A/3846 MFK Dubnika*, p. 179. A. Duval, and A. Rigozzi, *Yearbook of International Sports Arbitration 2015* (Springer 2016).

uncommon that a party acts without a legal representative before the first instance), the possibility of invoking new evidence before the CAS is often advantageous. As the legal advisor, you have better opportunities to formulate the case in a favourable way for the client.

An additional dimension is that each party is typically allowed to present only one submission in the appeal proceeding, necessitating further considerations and strategic decisions. In the following chapter, we will elaborate on the challenges and considerations required due to the formalistic nature of the appeal proceedings.

[D] CAS Proceedings Are Formalistic, and Procedural Rules Are Unwavering

An appeal proceeding in front of the CAS is initiated when the appellant submits its 'Statement of Appeal' to the CAS.[38] Thereafter, the appellant has ten days, counted from the expiry date of the time limit for the appeal, to file its 'Appeal Brief'.

In the Appeal Brief, the appellant must give a brief statement of 'the facts and legal arguments giving rise to the appeal, together with all exhibits and specification of other evidence upon which he intends to rely on'.[39] The Appeal Brief shall also contain a list of names of witnesses and experts that the appellant intends to hear. Any witness statements shall also be filed together with the appeal brief.[40] Once the Appeal Brief is submitted, the respondent shall within twenty days from the respondent's receipt of the ground for the appeal submit its answer.[41]

Except in cases of exceptional circumstances or if the parties agree otherwise, the parties are not allowed to supplement or amend their requests or their arguments or add supporting evidence once the Appeal Brief and the answer have been submitted.[42] Practically, this means that the mentioned submissions will, in most cases, be the sole written submissions in the case. Although the panel has the possibility to allow a second round of submissions, it is an exception rule. Since an oral hearing is not mandatory in CAS appeal proceedings, the panel has discretion to allow a second round of submissions for various reasons.[43] For example, the panel has the discretion to allow or require a second round of submissions to replace a hearing. Additionally, if national law is applicable, a second round can be appropriate for the parties to further elaborate on the relevant legislation.

---

38. CAS, *the CAS Code*, Art. R48 (2023). D. Mavromati and M. Reeb, *The Code of the Court of Arbitration for Sport: Commentary, Cases and Materials*, 405 (2015) regarding the starting point of appeal proceedings.
39. CAS, *the CAS Code*, Art. R51 (2023).
40. CAS, *the CAS Code*, Art. R51 para. 2 (2023).
41. CAS, *the CAS Code*, Art. R55 (2023) and D. Mavromati and M. Reeb, *The Code of the Court of Arbitration for Sport: Commentary, Cases and Materials*, 485 (2015). There are ways for a Respondent to obtain an extension of filing the answer, for example, it can be requested that the time limit be fixed after the payment by the appellant of its share of the advance of costs, *see* CAS, *the CAS Code*, Art. R64 para. 2 (2023).
42. CAS, *the CAS Code*, Art. R56 (2023).
43. D. Mavromati and M. Reeb, *The Code of the Court of Arbitration for Sport: Commentary, Cases and Materials*, 496-497 (2015).

The time limits accounted for above are fixed, and official holidays and non-working days are normally included in the deadlines you are obliged to adhere to.[44] In accordance with Article R32 of the CAS Code, time limits are respected if the submission is sent before midnight (local time),[45] on the last day on which such time limits expire (if the last day is a national official holiday or a non-business day, the time limit expires on the first subsequent business day).

When reviewing the applicable rules in the CAS Code, it becomes clear that extensions of the fixed time limits are an exception to the main rule.[46] Anyhow, you can normally assume that an extension of ten days will be granted if it is the *first* request for an extension of time (apart from the time limit for the Statement of Appeal). This is due to a procedural rule that simplifies the procedure, namely that the CAS Secretary General is entitled to grant such first request for extension, without submitting a request to the relevant division and without consulting the other party.[47] In case of further requests for extension, the main rule is that the party that submits the request must present justified grounds and that the other party will be given the opportunity to give its opinion on whether or not the request shall be granted. Hence, even though one can request an extension of time, the possibility of being granted such an extension is more restricted than in other dispute resolution proceedings. Furthermore, the request must be made prior to the initial time limit having expired.

The consequence of non-respect for the time limit for the Statement of Appeal does not differ from other proceedings, i.e., the appeal shall be deemed inadmissible.[48] The same applies to the Appeal Brief, if the Appellant has not been granted an extension of time or clarified that the Statement of Appeal shall be considered the Appeal Brief.[49]

Regarding other submissions or evidence that are not submitted on time, the CAS would normally invite the other party to express its view on the circumstances. For example, if the answer is submitted in a timely manner, but the evidence attached to the answer is submitted after midnight of the date the time limit expires, there is no guarantee that the evidence will be submitted to the file.

Deadlines for submissions are short, and you have only one opportunity to present your case. Based on experience, aside from the initial request for a ten-day extension, the possibility of being granted further extensions is dependent on the circumstances of the case, as well as the willingness of the other party/parties to not object to the request for extension. There are, of course, situations and circumstances that may allow for further extensions, but the contributors' understanding is that the

44. This is consistent with Swiss law, D. Mavromati and M. Reeb, *The Code of the Court of Arbitration for Sport: Commentary, Cases and Materials*, 125 (2015).
45. If the party is represented, the local time at the domicile of the party's main legal representative applies.
46. *See* the general rule in the CAS, *the CAS Code*, Art. R32 (2023).
47. D. Mavromati and M. Reeb, *The Code of the Court of Arbitration for Sport: Commentary, Cases and Materials*, 128 (2015).
48. CAS, *the CAS Code*, Art. R49 (2023).
49. CAS, *the CAS Code*, Art. R51 (2023).

CAS regulations provide less flexibility for extensions than arbitration under the Arbitration Rules of the SCC Arbitration Institute.

Thus, the fixed time limits set out in the CAS Code are not something you take lightly if you act as legal representative in front of the CAS.

The strict procedural rules, the time limits and the limitations in supplementing or amending requests or arguments after the Appeal Brief and the answer must be seen in light of the principle of *de novo* and the parties' extensive possibilities to invoke new arguments and evidence in the appeal proceedings. The formalistic procedure and the short time limits are balanced by the fact that the CAS creates the frame of the proceeding with the aim of being sufficiently informed.

Apart from the procedural structure of CAS proceedings, there are certain questions relating to the parties involved that differ from other arbitration proceedings, such as arbitration proceedings under the Arbitration Rules of the SCC Arbitration Institute, and that adds an extra dimension in working as a legal representative in front of the CAS. This will be addressed in section [5] below.

[E] The Impact of the Parties Involved

In commercial appeal proceedings before the CAS based on, for example, the FIFA Regulations on the Status and Transfer of Players (RSTP),[50] the legal representative must consider the necessity of addressing the appeal not only against the opposing party but also against the decision-making body that issued the decision subject to appeal.

This is a result of the horizontal and vertical nature of decisions from the decision-making bodies of FIFA. The dispute between the parties involved in the commercial dispute is of horizontal nature. The sanctions that might be imposed against a party by FIFA in first instance, due to that party's breach of the regulations, create a vertical relationship that according to CAS jurisprudence requires the appellant to appeal against both the parties involved in the commercial dispute, as well as FIFA (if the party appeals against the imposed sanctions). If FIFA has not been addressed as a respondent in the appeal, and the appeal in whole or in part concerns the imposition of sanctions, the part of the appeal that concerns the imposed sanctions will be deemed inadmissible and not accepted for review by the CAS.

In contractual disputes that are subject to other forms of commercial arbitration, it is an unusual situation to have to deal with the authority of the lower court. For sport governing bodies, such as FIFA, the stakes often involve maintaining the integrity and enforceability of regulations. Inevitably, this means that there is a party involved in the appeal proceeding that will take the role of defending its decision. The parties involved will profoundly influence the strategies and considerations of legal representatives in these cases.

The presence of FIFA or similar decision-making bodies as a party in the CAS proceeding not only introduces additional layers of complexity in the proceedings of

50. FIFA, *FIFA Regulations on the Status and Transfer of Players* (January 2025 Edition).

the actual case but also for the possibility of reaching a settlement that ends the arbitration. Decision-making bodies normally have less interest in finding a solution than the parties involved in the commercial dispute, but the parties in the commercial dispute cannot agree on the disciplinary aspect of the proceeding. Legal representatives must be prepared to engage with FIFA's established procedures and navigate the potential political and regulatory implications of the dispute. This often involves addressing issues that extend beyond the immediate parties, impacting the sport's global governance and regulatory landscape.

In order to navigate the regulatory landscape with the CAS as the Supreme Court, the jurisprudence of the CAS becomes a vital part of a legal representative's ability to assess the likelihood of a positive outcome in a case. This leads us to the next chapter.

[F] The Question of Transparency Versus Confidentiality

Confidentiality is typically one of the reasons commercial entities opt for arbitration agreements in the event of a dispute, and commercial arbitrations are therefore generally confidential. The CAS is a hybrid also in this regard.

As elaborated above, CAS appeal proceedings are not based on party autonomy as we normally know it, and therefore, the arguments for confidentiality do not bear the same weight as in other forms of arbitration. The role of the CAS as a lawmaker within the global sport community implies increased authority and power for this institution, which calls for increased transparency to ensure its legitimacy.

The main rule for ordinary proceedings before the CAS is that the arbitration process is conducted confidentially, requiring the parties involved, arbitrators, and the CAS personnel to refrain from disclosing any information related to the dispute, and the awards are typically kept confidential. In contrast, the appeal procedure generally favours transparency. On its website, the CAS publishes information about upcoming hearings in appeal proceedings, and the awards, along with a summary and/or a press release detailing the outcome of the proceedings, can be publicly disclosed by the CAS unless the parties to the specific arbitration proceeding agree to maintain confidentiality.[51]

The reasoning behind the differing approaches between the ordinary procedure and the appeal procedure is based on the nature of the disputes handled. While the ordinary procedure often involves commercially oriented disputes requiring confidentiality, appeal proceedings typically address decisions with both contractual, regulatory and disciplinary aspects, which are of – more – public interest. This adds an extra dimension to the question of transparency or confidentiality.

In cases of commercial nature and with elements of regulatory framework application, there is a broader interest in guidance on how the relevant sports regulations should be interpreted and applied. In those cases, transparency is important. Hence, the question arises as to which interest should weigh heaviest: the

51. CAS, *the CAS Code*, Art. R59 para. 7 (2023).

commercial parties' interest in confidentiality or the importance of transparency due to the CAS' role as a lawmaker.

With reference to the reasons outlined above, there is an interest for the parties involved, as well as for the sport community as a whole, that the CAS clarifies its position on disputed questions. There is an ongoing discussion regarding the transparency of the CAS, and it is often highlighted that too few awards are published.

The CAS frequently publishes recent CAS awards on its website, but searching the CAS website reveals that during 2023, only 70 awards were published and searchable in the website's database, compared to the 695[52] appeals submitted to the CAS in 2023. However, it is said that the CAS has started to publish awards a week after they are issued, and that these can be found under 'Recent Decisions' on the CAS website. It is noted, however, that the awards are not yet searchable, but it is at least a positive development in terms of transparency. Historically, the proportion of awards published has been modest and probably insufficient to provide the guidance required for a court that establishes the framework for a global regulatory system.

The scarce availability of relevant jurisprudence sometimes contributes to uncertainties in the application of rules, leading to increased work and consequently higher costs for legal representation in appeal proceedings.

The aspect of cost is always present in commercial arbitration. However, when deciding whether to bring a case before the CAS, the cost parameter typically requires considerable thought for the following reasons.

[G] Costs: A Parameter That Might Affect the Willingness to Appeal to the CAS

Unlike commercial arbitration proceedings, the main rule in proceedings before the CAS is that each party bears its own costs for legal fees, regardless of the outcome of the dispute.

The allocation of costs in proceedings before the CAS is governed by specific provisions within the CAS Code, which outline how costs are determined and distributed among the parties involved.

Under the CAS Code, the term 'costs' typically encompasses the arbitration costs, which include the fees and expenses of the arbitrators, the administrative costs of the CAS, and any other expenses incurred in connection with the arbitration proceedings. Additionally, costs may also cover the legal fees and expenses of the parties, although these are subject to specific rules regarding their recoverability.

Article R64 paragraph 4 of the CAS Code provides that the CAS Court Office shall determine the final amount of the cost for arbitration at the end of the proceedings. According to Article R64 paragraph 5 of the CAS Code, the panel shall determine the distribution of the arbitration costs in the arbitral award, and the Panel generally decides that the unsuccessful party shall bear the arbitration costs.

52. CAS, *CAS Statistics* (accessed 9 November 2025).

Regarding the legal and other costs incurred by the parties, the panel has, in accordance with Article R64 paragraph 5 of the CAS Code, discretion to 'grant the prevailing party a contribution towards its legal fees and other expenses incurred in connection with the proceedings and, in particular, the costs of witnesses and interpreters'.

The background of the use of the notion *contribution* is to clarify that the costs shall not be the focus for a party that found itself in need of bringing a case to the CAS. The distribution of costs is well in line with the philosophy of the International Council of Arbitration for Sport (ICAS), which is to encourage parties to invest reasonable and proportionate costs to present their case or defence, since the potential contribution granted will be reasonable.[53] Hence, it is also a clear signal to the parties and legal representatives involved in CAS proceedings.

According to the above-mentioned article, the panel may consider various factors, such as the complexity of the case, the reasonableness of the costs incurred, and the conduct of the parties during the proceedings. Article R64 paragraph 5 of the CAS Code allows the Panel to ensure that the distribution of costs is fair and equitable, reflecting the nature and outcome of the dispute. A contribution is, though, by definition, only a proportion of the costs incurred by the party, so the prevailing party cannot expect full cover for legal costs.

The contributions awarded are relatively modest, and commonly between CHF 0 and CHF 20,000.[54] In a very complex and lengthy case, a contribution of up to USD 100,000 was awarded. In that particular case,[55] the CAS granted a higher contribution towards the attorney's fees due to the other party's bad behaviour and misconduct during the proceedings.

The rules regarding cost distribution are a factor that will affect the decision on whether or not a case should be appealed to the CAS. It will also have an impact on the strategy of the legal representative presenting the case to the CAS.

[H] Conclusion

The characteristics we have focused on above all contribute to the unique legal landscape that we, as legal representatives in proceedings before the CAS, need to navigate. The *de novo principle* imposes high demands on the representatives but simultaneously provides a sense for both the representatives and the parties involved that the purpose of a review by the CAS is to ensure justice. This fundamental aspect is evident in several respects, including the special procedural rules that govern the proceedings.

53. D. Mavromati and M. Reeb, *The Code of the Court of Arbitration for Sport: Commentary, Cases and Materials*, 628 (2015).
54. D. Mavromati and M. Reeb, *The Code of the Court of Arbitration for Sport: Commentary, Cases and Materials*, 629 (2015).
55. *F. Landis v. USADA*, CAS 2007/A/1394, para. 289 (30 June 2008).

As representatives, it is motivating to work in an environment that demands high standards of efficiency and accuracy, among other things, when the goal for the arbitration panel is to arrive at a correct decision based on the aspect of truth.

§9.03 WILL EU LAW MAKE THE CAS IRRELEVANT FOR EU-RELATED SPORTS DISPUTES?

[A] Introduction

'Sports law is not just international; it is nongovernmental as well, and this differentiates it from all other forms of law.'[56] This sentence captures not only the essence of sports law but also the nature of the entire sporting community, encompassing all sports, from fencing to football, and everything in between. Historically, the sporting community has been allowed to develop within its own protected environment, and due to its special nature, it has been somewhat accepted as a parallel world to the rest of the society.

It has also been recognised as such through judgments from the European Court of Justice (ECJ), which have clarified that sport federations possess legal autonomy, entitling them to adopt rules relating, *inter alia*, to the organisation of competitions, their proper functioning, and the participation of athletes in those competitions. This 'protected world' has been somewhat accepted by society. However, it has also been stated that sports associations cannot limit the exercise of rights and freedoms conferred on individuals by EU law.[57]

The protected sphere of sport has been brought to light and is beginning to be scrutinised from a broader perspective. In December 2023, the ECJ delivered judgments in three distinct cases addressing the discretionary authority of sports federations to restrict alternative competitions and to impose requirements potentially at odds with European law.[58] The outcome of these three cases is that the primacy of EU law is upheld in the organisation of sport.

Of particular interest for this chapter is the case between the International Skating Union (ISU) and the European Commission, as the ECJ sheds light on the role of the CAS and the Swiss Federal Tribunal in matters related to EU competition law. It is also relevant for all sports associations that have an arbitration mechanism involving arbitration before the CAS.

56. Lorenzo Casini, *The Making of a Lex Sportiva by the Court of Arbitration for Sport*, German Law Journal 12, no. 5, 1317-1340, 1317 (2011) https://doi.org/10.1017/s2071832200017326 (accessed 1 October 2025).
57. *International Skating Union v. Commission ECLI:EU:C:2023:1012*, para. 196 (C-124/21 P) (2023).
58. *International Skating Union v. Commission ECLI:EU:C:2023:1012* (C-124/21 P), (2023), *Royal Antwerp Football Club ECLI:EU:C:2023:1010* (C-680/21l), (2023) and *European Superleague Company ECLI:EU:C:2023:1011* (C-333/21), (2023).

The legitimacy of the CAS has been further questioned, and one might say attacked, in the Opinion of the Advocate General delivered on 16 January 2025[59] in the *Seraing* case, following a request for a preliminary ruling from a court in Belgium. On 1 August 2025, the ECJ delivered its judgment in the *Seraing* case, which had a more moderate approach than the Advocate General but clearly establishes the principle of EU public policy, in mandatory arbitration, having precedence over CAS jurisdiction.

Since the issuance of the judgment in the ISU case, its practical implications for the sports movement and the CAS as the Supreme Court of sports have been discussed. A discussion that accelerated even more after the delivery of the Advocate General's Opinion, and the subsequent ECJ judgment, in the *Seraing* case. But are the practical consequences for the sport resolution system and the CAS as large as they seem at first glance?

[B] Case C-124/21, *P International Skating Union v. European Commission*

The case of *International Skating Union v. European Commission* (C-124/21 P), decided by the ECJ on 21 December 2023, revolves around the ISU's practices of its eligibility rules, which were challenged by the European Commission as being anti-competitive. The case is of particular interest in the context of arbitration in the sport context, since the ECJ made statements regarding the CAS as a legitimate court in cases that involve competition law within the EU.

The ISU rules in the centre of the dispute stated that an organiser of an international skating competition required ISU's prior approval, and athletes who took part in a skating competition that had not been authorised by the ISU would be exposed to severe penalties under the ISU rules. In addition, any decision by the ISU applying the prior authorisation and eligibility rules could only be challenged before the CAS.

The ECJ upheld the European Commission's decision, affirming that the ISU's eligibility rules constituted a restriction of competition, because they were not subject to any guarantee ensuring that they were transparent, objective, non-discriminatory and proportionate. In addition, the ECJ also questioned the ISU's arbitration rule, which is of relevance for this chapter.

In its judgment, the ECJ limited its finding regarding the arbitration rules imposed by the ISU to two types of disputes, more precisely: (i) the organisation and marketing of international skating events; and (ii) the right to take part in such competitions as a professional athlete. Arbitration rules which thereby applied to disputes concerning economic activity, and thereby, in the territory of the EU, came under EU competition law.[60]

59. Opinion of the Advocate General, *Royal Football Club Seraing v. Fédération Internationale de Football Association (FIFA), Union Royale Belge des Sociétés de Football Association ASBL (URBSFA), Union européenne des Sociétés de Football Association (UEFA), joined party: Doyen Sports Investment Ltd* (C-600/23) (2024).
60. *The case of International Skating Union v. European Commission* (C-124/21 P), para. 189 (2023) 'concerning the exercise of a sport as an economic activity and, on that basis, come under EU competition law' and para. 190.

The ECJ observed that Articles 101 and 102 of the TFEU, articles relevant in the dispute, have direct effect, which can create rights for individuals that national courts are held to protect. The rights under these articles need to be protected, and the ECJ pointed out that arbitral awards concerning these articles require the possibility for effective judicial review, including a review on the basis of the fundamental provisions that are a matter of EU public policy. Especially when an arbitration clause has been imposed by an international sports association on an athlete.[61]

Thus, according to the ECJ's judgment, disputes concerning sports as an economic activity, which fall under EU competition law, cannot be subject to mandatory arbitration before the CAS because its decisions are only reviewed by the Swiss Federal Tribunal, i.e., a third state court outside of the EU legal system that is not empowered to refer a question to the ECJ for a preliminary ruling.

In the words of the ECJ:

> In the absence of such judicial review, the use of an arbitration mechanism is such as to undermine the protection of rights that subjects of the law derive from the direct effect of EU law and the effective compliance with Articles 101 and 102 TFEU, which must be ensured – and would therefore be ensured in the absence of such a mechanism – by the national rules relating to remedies.[62]

Despite the ECJ's statements above, in the end, it did not question the existence or operation of the CAS as such. The ECJ merely sided with the Commission's statement that the inherent problem with the procedure imposed by the ISU's mandatory arbitration mechanism was 'the legal immunity enjoyed by the ISU' in the light of EU competition law.[63]

The ISU ruling is not entirely clear regarding its effects for the mandatory CAS arbitration mechanism found in the statutes of many international sports federations. Nevertheless, it is clear that national courts examining the economic aspects of sport that intersect with EU competition law will have an opportunity to adjudicate the dispute, even if a party refers to a mandatory arbitration clause stipulating that the dispute should be resolved by the CAS.

[C] Case C-600/23, *Royal Football Club Seraing v. FIFA Among Others: Preliminary Reference*

As initially mentioned, the role of the CAS has been further questioned by the Advocate General in an Opinion given on 16 January 2025.

Royal Football Club Seraing challenged certain regulations imposed by FIFA, UEFA, and the Royal Belgian Football Association (URBSFA), arguing that these regulations infringe upon EU law principles, particularly concerning competition law and free movement. Due to a prior CAS Award in the matter at hand, one of the

61. *The case of International Skating Union v. European Commission* (C-124/21 P), paras 192-193 (2023).
62. *The case of International Skating Union v. European Commission* (C-124/21 P), para. 194 (2023).
63. *The case of International Skating Union v. European Commission* (C-124/21 P), para. 184 (2023).

questions referred to the ECJ for a preliminary ruling concerns the res judicata effect of a CAS award in a follow-up proceeding before a national court in an EU-law matter.

With the judgment in the ISU case as starting point, the Advocate General distinguish arbitration proceedings before the CAS on the basis of the statutes and regulations of FIFA from 'ordinary' commercial arbitration on two grounds: (i) arbitration before the CAS is mandatory; and (ii) the self-enforcing nature of CAS awards under the rules and regulations of FIFA.[64]

Based on these two characteristics, the Advocate General argues for the ECJ to expand on its judgment in the ISU case and 'develop a separate approach to the judicial review of arbitral awards resulting from mandatory arbitration, such as the one before CAS on the basis of the FIFA Statutes'.[65]

The Advocate General further stated with emphasis that:

> Direct access to challenge FIFA's rules, despite a CAS award confirming their validity, should be available to subjects who claim that their rights guaranteed by EU law have been infringed. The scope of review should not be limited to public policy, but should include all relevant EU law provisions. It should be possible to exercise such review in all judicial proceedings, be they initiated as a direct challenge to FIFA's rules, in enforcement proceedings of a CAS arbitral award, or incidentally in a different type of procedure, such as the one initiated by an action for damages.[66]

Hence, the Advocate General are of the opinion, and argues, that a CAS award on the basis of the rules and regulations of FIFA cannot be given res judicata effect and thereby hinder the national court's power to review such rules and regulations conformity with EU law, and the national court's possibility to refer the question of interpretation to the ECJ.[67]

It is clear that the Advocate General's intention was to make a statement expanding the scope of the ECJ's clarifications in the ISU case even further, but in our opinion, as well as the ECJ's, the Advocate General went too far.

[D] Case C-600/23, *Royal Football Club Seraing v. FIFA Among Others*: Judgment of the ECJ

As clarified in the previous chapter, the Advocate General favoured a far-reaching review of CAS awards by national courts when any kind of EU law is applicable.

The ECJ is more restrained in its judgment and upholds the principles of the ISU case. The ECJ points out the mandatory nature of the arbitration mechanism in sports associations' rules and regulations, and it emphasises that effective judicial review

64. Opinion of the Advocate General, *Royal Football Club Seraing v. Fédération Internationale de Football Association (FIFA) amongst others* (C-600/23), para. 95 (2025).
65. Opinion of the Advocate General, *Royal Football Club Seraing v. Fédération Internationale de Football Association (FIFA) amongst others* (C-600/23), para. 123 (2025).
66. Opinion of the Advocate General, *Royal Football Club Seraing v. Fédération Internationale de Football Association (FIFA) amongst others* (C-600/23), para. 125 (2025).
67. Opinion of the Advocate General, *Royal Football Club Seraing v. Fédération Internationale de Football Association (FIFA) amongst others* (C-600/23), para. 105 (2025).

therefore is of particular importance in relation to the principles and provisions which form part of EU public policy.[68]

The ECJ thoroughly accounts for what is required to secure an effective judicial review under EU law and elaborates on the scope of the review, the tribunal/court's possibility to draw legal conclusions and the power to grant interim relief. Furthermore, the ECJ holds that a prerequisite for an effective judicial review is that the court is authorised to make a reference to the ECJ for a preliminary ruling.[69] The CAS obviously does not meet these prerequisites.

The ECJ concluded the following regarding the question of interest for this article:

> the second subparagraph of Article 19(1) TEU, read in conjunction with Article 267 TFEU and Article 47 of the Charter, must be interpreted as precluding:
>
>> the authority of res judicata from being conferred within the territory of a Member State on an award made by the CAS, in the relations between the parties to the dispute in the context of which that award was made, where that dispute is linked to the pursuit of a sport as an economic activity within the territory of the EU and the consistency of that award with the principles and provisions of EU law which form part of EU public policy has not first been subject to effective review by a court or tribunal of that Member State that is authorised to make a reference to the Court of Justice for a preliminary ruling.[70]

Hence, a CAS award involving an economic activity related to EU public policy does not hinder a review by a national court within a Member State. The consequence is that European parties in proceedings before the CAS, under these circumstances, will have the opportunity for a second trial before a national court if the outcome of the CAS award is unsatisfactory. In a broader context, this means that there is scope for EU public policy to influence the sports associations' drafting of their future regulations.

[E] Conclusions

The ECJ's statements regarding mandatory sports arbitration clearly question the applicability and relevance of referring disputes to the CAS for arbitration in cases where EU public policy is applicable.

The question is to what extent the ECJ's statements will affect the ability of sports organisations to include such clauses in their rules and whether the judgments in the *ISU* case and the *Seraing* case will open the door to a reform of the sports dispute resolution system or for parallel practices outside the sporting sphere, which would be determinant and risk creating legal uncertainty within the sports community. There is a risk that the approach to issues fundamentally governed by sports regulations will differ depending on where the parties are domiciled.

68. The case of *Royal Football Club Seraing v. Fédération Internationale de Football Association (FIFA) amongst others* (C-600/23), paras 90-91 (2025).
69. The case of *Royal Football Club Seraing v. Fédération Internationale de Football Association (FIFA) amongst others* (C-600/23), para. 105 (2025).
70. The case of *Royal Football Club Seraing v. Fédération Internationale de Football Association (FIFA) amongst others* (C-600/23), para. 125 (2025).

An intriguing aspect of this matter is whether the ECJ intended to categorise all types of sports disputes potentially subject to arbitration as 'mandatory arbitration'. It is unclear whether the ECJ has considered the distinctions between horizontal and vertical disputes, as well as the mix of those two. Upon reviewing the ECJ's judgment in the *Seraing* case, we lack the nuances in the conclusions, leading to the impression that the ECJ might have been somewhat broadly generalised. At this point, our opinion is that EU law will not make the CAS irrelevant for EU-related sports disputes. However, EU law, along with the *Seraing* case, will have a greater impact than previously on the development of sports regulations, and we will likely witness parallel dispute resolution procedures. In any case, an initial measure to pre-empt any such problem would be to adopt the approach implemented by UEFA in its Authorisation Rules governing International Club Competitions and amend the relevant provisions of the CAS Code, i.e., to provide for an alternative seat of arbitration within the EU for disputes in EU law matters. By revising the CAS Code and accommodating such an option, the most obvious obstacle for the continuation of the sports dispute resolution system as we know it today could be surmounted.

§9.04 CONCLUSION AND FUTURE PERSPECTIVE

Acting as a legal representative in appeal proceedings before the CAS is, to say the least, interesting. It requires a different approach to case presentation and argumentation than Swedish-educated and trained legal counsels are accustomed to. Furthermore, the underlying principles of the rules within the sports community, including procedural rules, contain elements that challenge the concept of procedural justice, which is commonly the objective in commercial disputes.

As previously elucidated, the sporting community has been allowed to develop within its own protected environment, and any deviations from established rules have been subject to review by its own decision-making bodies and, in the final instance, by the CAS. It is apparent that the sporting community's obligation to comply with broader societal rules (including EU law), along with the legitimacy of its own internally established rules, has opened the door to further scrutiny. We are likely witnessing a series of events that may influence future changes in how the sporting community is shaped in terms of regulations, and possibly even in the aspect of allowed dispute resolution mechanisms within sport.

Nonetheless, our opinions, beliefs, and hopes are that the CAS will continue to serve as a pivotal institution for creating and providing guidance on applicable regulations within the sporting community and for the resolution of sports-related disputes. For the CAS to maintain credibility in this regard, it is crucial to continue promoting transparency. It may also be worth considering the option of establishing a seat within the EU by adjusting the relevant rules to allow for that possibility. From a sports law perspective, the CAS remains the preferred forum for resolving disputes, and from our perspective, we would, without hesitation, rather bring such cases before the CAS than rely on a national court.

CHAPTER 10

Complexities of Foreign Arbitral Award Enforcement in Russia: *The Impact of the Lugovoy Law*

David Johansson, Miljana Bigović & Bohdana Sokoliuk

§10.01 INTRODUCTION

The process of recognition and enforcement of foreign arbitral awards in Russia currently poses significant challenges for arbitration practitioners. However, the landscape of foreign award enforcement in Russia has not always been as it is today. A study on the application of the New York Convention, conducted by the Russian Arbitration Association, revealed that, between the years 2008 and 2017, 80% to 97% of all recognition and enforcement applications made in Russia were approved.[1] In total, out of 472 applications, 378 were accepted, 45 were rejected, and 49 were not considered, primarily due to procedural reasons. Although similar comprehensive studies for subsequent years are lacking, reports indicate that, in 2020, Russian courts dismissed 87 out of 244 applications submitted to them, representing a staggering 35.6%.[2]

Grounds for refusal of the recognition and enforcement of foreign arbitral awards in Russia are enumerated in Article 244 of the Arbitrazh Procedural Code of the Russian Federation (APC). Notably, Article 244.1(3) of the APC provides that the recognition and enforcement of a foreign award may be refused if 'the consideration of a case, in

1. Russian Arbitration Association, *Application of the New York Convention in Russia,* https://arbitration.ru/en/press-centr/news/application-of-the-new-york-convention-in-russia/ (accessed on 10 December 2024).
2. Anastasia Cheredova, *Foreign Arbitral Awards in Russia: Public Policy Issue,* https://ceelegalmatters.com/russia/17285-foreign-arbitral-awards-in-russia-public-policy-issue (accessed on 10 December 2024).

accordance with a treaty of the Russian Federation or federal law, falls within the exclusive jurisdiction of a court in the Russian Federation'.[3] With the entry into force of the Federal Law of 8 June 2020 No. 171-FZ (Lugovoy Law) on 19 June 2020, this specific provision has taken on new dimensions. The Lugovoy Law extended the concept of 'the exclusive competence of a court in the Russian Federation' referred to in Article 244.1(3) to disputes involving persons in respect of whom restrictive measures are applied by a foreign state, a state association and/or a union.[4]

The wide personal scope of application of the newly introduced provision allows interested parties to apply for resolution of their dispute to the arbitration court in Russia, as well as to seek a prohibition to initiate or continue proceedings in a foreign court or international commercial arbitration outside the Russian Federation.[5] To achieve the latter, the Lugovoy Law explicitly empowered the Russian arbitration courts to issue anti-suit and anti-arbitration injunctions.[6] Further, the exclusive jurisdiction of Russian courts applies in cases where the parties' agreement to resolve their disputes in a foreign court or international commercial arbitration is unenforceable due to the imposed restrictive measures.[7]

In view of this legislative change, the chapter will examine the current situation in terms of enforcement of foreign awards in the Russian Federation. The chapter examines how considerations triggering the application of the Lugovoy Law relate to the enforcement decisions, focusing on judgments of the Russian courts enforcing, or rejecting the enforcement, of Swedish arbitral awards.

§10.02 IMPACT OF THE LUGOVOY LAW ON THE ENFORCEMENT OF SWEDISH AWARDS

In light of the recent enactment of the Lugovoy Law and its increasing significance amid expanding sanctions regimes against Russian entities, it is important to note the absence of precise statistics on its application in Russia. This section will therefore provide a case-by-case analysis of relevant court practices established to date.

[A] *UTM v. PESA*

The case of *UTM v. PESA* relates to a 2013 supply agreement concluded between Poland's largest manufacturer of railway vehicles, Pojazdy Szynowe PESA Bydgoszcz SA (PESA), and Russia's manufacturer of self-propelled artillery, UralTransMash (UTM). Under this agreement, PESA was to supply 120 trams to UTM in the period of 2014-2015, valued at EUR 149 million in total. The agreement contained an SCC arbitration clause.

3. Arbitrazh Procedural Code of the Russian Federation (4 July 2004), https://www.wipo.int/wipolex/en/legislation/details/21780 (accessed on 10 December 2024).
4. Article 248.1(1) of the APC.
5. Article 248.1(3) of the APC.
6. Article 248.2 of the APC.
7. Article 248.1(4) of the APC.

In 2014, following the annexation of Crimea, UTM's parent company Uralvagonzavod became sanctioned in the EU, the US, Liechtenstein, Switzerland, and Ukraine. In 2018, after UTM failed to pay the full amount for the trams, PESA commenced SCC arbitration seeking to claim around EUR 55 million from UTM.

UTM responded by filing several civil claims against PESA before the Russian courts. UTM's parent company requested the Arbitration Court of Sverdlovsk Oblast to recognise the arbitration clause in the mentioned supply contract as unenforceable, considering that UTM was a state-owned entity and thereby incapable of entering into arbitration agreements over matters involving a public element. The Court refused this motion, finding the contract to be a standard commercial supply contract between two commercial parties, not relating to the public interests or the interests of the Russian Federation.[8]

In 2020, following the adoption of the Lugovoy Law, UTM applied for an anti-arbitration injunction to the same Court. According to the Court's decision dated 24 November 2020, an anti-arbitration injunction under Article 248.2 of the APC could be granted only if the applicant were to prove that Russian courts have exclusive jurisdiction over a case under Article 248.1 of the APC. This would happen in cases when there is no arbitration agreement between the parties, or the arbitration agreement would be deemed unenforceable due to the application of measures restricting one of the parties' access to justice.[9]

The existence of the arbitration clause was not disputed in this case, but UTM argued that the restrictive measures imposed by the EU and the US hindered its access to justice in the pending SCC proceedings:

> the effect of these restrictive measures is manifested, for example, in the inability to pay the necessary expenses in the case, as banks block all payments, the inability to engage a certified legal representative (attorney) to participate in the case, as, in most cases, they (representatives) refuse to provide services, referring to the fact that cooperation with such Russian persons, or an e-mail sent to a person on the sanctions list from the territory of the United States or the European Union, or a telephone call may be interpreted as assisting such a person (included in the sanctions list) and, accordingly, the representatives bear the risk of being held liable. As a result, [UTM] is deprived of the right to a fair trial, has no opportunity to protect its interests properly, as well as incurs huge financial losses.[10]

The Court rejected the motion, finding that EU 'blocking' sanctions under Decision No. 2014/145/CFSP[11] and Regulation No. 269/2014[12] did not apply to UTM, whereas

8. Arbitration Court of Sverdlovsk Oblast, Judgment dated 4 October 2019 in Case No. A60-62910/2018.
9. Arbitration Court of Sverdlovsk Oblast, Judgment dated 24 November 2020 in Case No. A60-36897/2020 (unofficial translation), pp. 6-8.
10. *Ibid.*, p. 13.
11. Council Decision 2014/145/CFSP of 17 March 2014 concerning restrictive measures in respect of actions undermining or threatening the territorial integrity, sovereignty and independence of Ukraine.
12. Sanctions including a ban on entry to the EU and freezing of funds and economic resources of persons listed in the annexes to these acts.

applicable measures under Regulation No. 833/2014[13] and Decision No. 2014/512/CFSP[14] were limited in scope and did not extend to the existing contractual relations between the parties. Similarly, the Court rejected the argument that access to justice was restricted due to the US restrictive measures, as 'the applicant has not provided adequate evidence that the relevant laws or orders of the US President are part of the regulatory framework (binding) in the territory of Sweden or in the territory of the EU, where the arbitration proceedings are taking place'.[15]

The Court, *inter alia*, noted that UTM's claims about restrictions to access to justice were refuted by the actual circumstances of the case, concluding that 'it follows from the case materials that [UTM] has been actively participating in the SCC arbitration proceedings for more than two years, filing voluminous procedural documents, including counterclaims, and using the services of highly qualified Russian and Polish lawyers and economists'.[16] The Court took a pro-arbitration stance, further underscoring that 'the financial situation of the parties or the cost of participation in the proceedings is not in itself relevant to the question of enforceability of an arbitration clause'.[17]

This decision was subsequently upheld by the Court of Appeal.[18] Yet, in its decision dated 9 December 2021, the Supreme Court took a different stance on the interpretation of the Lugovoy Law, concluding that, within the meaning of Article 248.1(4) of the APC, 'the application of restrictive measures in itself already impedes the Russian party's access to justice, which is why the former's unilateral expression of will ... would be sufficient to transfer the jurisdiction over the dispute to Russian arbitration courts'.[19]

In its landmark 2021 decision, the Russian Supreme Court further noted that UTM already objected to foreign proceedings when it had applied for an anti-arbitration injunction and, in doing so, should not have been required to substantiate the restrictive measures' negative effect on its access to justice:

> The legislator's way of phrasing Article 248.2(2)(4) of the APC, according to which the circumstances confirming the impossibility of enforcing the arbitration clause shall be indicated by the applicant if they exist, also confirms that there is no need to prove the impact of restrictive measures on the enforceability of an arbitration clause. The wording of this provision emphasizes the optionality of proving these circumstances.[20]

13. Council Regulation (EU) No. 833/2014 of 31 July 2014 concerning restrictive measures in view of Russia's actions destabilising the situation in Ukraine.
14. Council Decision 2014/512/CFSP of 31 July 2014 concerning restrictive measures in view of Russia's actions destabilising the situation in Ukraine.
15. Arbitration Court of Sverdlovsk Oblast, Judgment dated 24 November 2020 in Case No. A60-36897/2020 (unofficial translation), p. 20.
16. *Ibid.*
17. *Ibid.*
18. Arbitration Court of Urals District, Judgment dated 10 March 2021 in Case No. A60-36897/2020.
19. Supreme Court of the Russian Federation, Judgment dated 9 December 2021 in Case No. A60-36897-2020 (unofficial translation), p. 6.
20. *Ibid.*

According to the Supreme Court, the courts of lower instances erred in rejecting UTM's application for an anti-arbitration injunction. However, considering that the final award in the dispute had already been rendered in May 2021, the Supreme Court dismissed UTM's motion:

> UTM's claim, aimed at prohibiting the claimant from performing certain actions, is preventive in its nature. Such an injunction, like, for example, an injunction imposed within the framework of interim measures, is relevant and effective only until such actions are performed. Once they have been committed, the injunction is no longer enforceable, does not provide the applicant with judicial protection and, as a consequence, loses all meaning.[21]

In light of the Supreme Court's interpretation of the Lugovoy Law, on 16 August 2024, the Arbitration Court of Sverdlovsk Oblast rejected PESA's application for enforcement of the already rendered SCC award.[22]

Unsurprisingly, in its decision, the Court heavily relied on the interpretation of the Law given by the Supreme Court and concluded that the recognition and enforcement of the award would have been contrary to the public policy of the Russian Federation, since the dispute between the two parties fell within the exclusive jurisdiction of Russian courts.[23]

The refusal, according to the Court, was also based on the possible consequences of the enforcement, taking into account the public importance of the award debtor for Russia:

> considering the importance of the Russian company – party to the dispute, its classification as a strategic enterprise, recognition and enforcement of the above decision in the territory of Russia in the situation of a legal aggression from a number of unfriendly countries may damage a major enterprise of the Russian industry, which is inadmissible and does not correspond to the interests of the Russian party, both in terms of private and public interest ...[24]

Furthermore, the Court took into account the existence of Russian countermeasures affecting the contractual performance:

> the award ... actually imposed penalties, while the interested party stated during the proceedings that the fulfilment of obligations under the contract was affected, among other things, by the ban imposed ... by the Government of the Russian Federation on the purchase of foreign-made trams for state and municipal needs, which, in turn, was Russia's countermeasure in response to the economic sanctions imposed by foreign countries against the Russian Federation.[25]

Finally, the Court also referenced the foreign nationality of two of the arbitrators, 'whose impartiality the interested party had reasonable doubts about, and one of

---

21. *Ibid.*, p. 7.
22. Arbitration Court of Sverdlovsk Oblast, Judgment dated 16 August 2024 in Case No. A60-24839/2024 (unofficial translation).
23. *Ibid.*, p. 12.
24. *Ibid.*
25. *Ibid.*, p. 13.

whom the disputing party also challenged during the arbitral proceedings, but the application was rejected'.[26]

The case, thus, revealed that a party initially succeeding in enforcing a foreign-seated arbitration clause before the Russian courts may not always rely on the same courts to preserve their pro-arbitration stance when faced with an enforcement application. The significant time lapse between the two sets of proceedings and the practice developed by the Russian Supreme Court in the meantime could have been indicative of such an outcome.

As will be shown below, subsequent rulings of Russian courts on anti-arbitration injunctions were considerably more consistent.

[B] *TNG v. FNPC*

On 1 March 2023, the Arbitration Court of Tyumen Oblast prohibited a US company First National Petroleum Corporation (FNPC) from continuing arbitration proceedings against Russian AO Tyumenneftegaz (TNG) before the SCC Arbitration Institute.[27]

The arbitral proceedings in question were part of a series of SCC-administered arbitrations that followed the liquidation of the Russian-American joint venture Tyumtex. The specific arbitration was commenced in 2021 by FNPC and concerned the recovery of approximately USD 150 million. This amount had been previously awarded to FNPC in the SCC Case No. V2015/178 as interest on damages, but was subsequently set aside by the Svea Court of Appeal on 2 June 2021.

Following the commencement of the war in Ukraine in 2022, TNG became subject to EU restrictive measures as its parent company PJSC Rosneft was sanctioned by virtue of Decision No. 2022/430.[28] Subsequently, according to TNG, TNG's representatives from Swedish and English law firms, as well as its legal expert, refused to continue providing legal services in the matter. Yet, despite TNG's repeated requests to discontinue or suspend the proceedings due to its issues with finding new representatives, on 5 May 2022, the tribunal rejected their application.

In the Russian Court's view, the existence of the restrictive measures was generally known and did not need to be proven, which, in turn, was enough to trigger the application of Articles 248.1-248.2 of the APC:

> the mere fact that restrictive measures have been imposed on a Russian legal entity involved in a dispute in an international commercial arbitration located outside the territory of the Russian Federation is presumed to be sufficient to conclude that such person's access to justice in the foreign state applying the restrictive measures is restricted.
>
> The introduction by foreign states of restrictive measures ... against Russian legal entities and individuals affects their rights at least reputationally and thus

26. *Ibid.*
27. Arbitration Court of Tyumen Oblast, Judgment dated 1 March 2023 in Case No. A70-26488/2022 (unofficial translation).
28. Council Decision (CFSP) 2022/430 of 15 March 2022 amending Decision 2014/512/CFSP concerning restrictive measures in view of Russia's actions destabilising the situation in Ukraine.

> knowingly puts them in an unequal position with other persons. In such circumstances, doubts are justified that a dispute involving a person located in a state that has applied restrictive measures, in the territory of a foreign state that has also applied restrictive measures, will not be considered to be in compliance with fair trial guarantees, including those relating to the impartiality of the court, which is one of the elements of access to justice ...[29]

According to this Court, the refusal to postpone the arbitral proceedings violated fair trial guarantees, as 'the Arbitration Institute of the Stockholm Chamber of Commerce, while invoking the right of access to justice, simultaneously violated [TNG]'s right of defence by not agreeing to postpone or suspend the proceedings allowing the latter to find new representatives'.[30]

Further, the Court noted that, arguably, EU sanctions gave rise to the following obstacles to TNG's participation in the arbitration:

- the impossibility of engaging qualified Swedish counsel, which was considered essential in a dispute with Swedish law governing both substantive and procedural issues;
- the inability to engage EU experts on Swedish and EU law;
- the impossibility of paying for legal services, even if they had been provided.[31]

Consequently, the Court considered that, in circumstances like these, fair trial procedure can be adhered to only within the Russian territory:

> the arbitration clause puts [FNPC] in an advantageous position compared to [TNG], since under the current sanctions regime in force with respect to this entity, its ability to protect its rights and economic interests is significantly limited, given that, in fact, the protection of the rights and interests of the company can now be exercised only within the territory and jurisdiction of the Russian Federation.[32]

Since FNPC did not participate in the proceedings, the Court accepted the alleged circumstances as uncontested.[33]

Notably, when granting TNG's request for an anti-arbitration injunction in March 2023, the Court considered the arbitration proceedings still pending. However, other sources indicate that the tribunal rendered its final award in favour of FNPC on 19 December 2022.[34] It could therefore be argued that, had FNPC actively participated in the Russian proceedings, as PESA did in the previously discussed case, the injunction may not have been granted, as the award was already issued.

29. *Ibid.*, p. 4.
30. *Ibid.*, p. 3.
31. *Ibid.*, p. 4.
32. *Ibid.*, p. 5.
33. *Ibid.*
34. Graham Butler, *Svea Court of Appeal: EU Restrictive Measures (Sanctions) Cannot Halt Commercial Arbitration as Parties to Disputes Continue to Have Access to Research and Legal Services Necessary for Arbitral Proceedings*, https://niels.institute/2024/08/20/svea-court-of-appeal-eu-restrictive-measures-sanctions-cannot-halt-commercial-arbitration-as-parties-to-disputes-continue-to-have-access-to-research-and-legal-services-necessary-for-arbitral-procee/ (accessed 11 December 2024).

Notwithstanding the injunction, on 28 June 2024, the Svea Court of Appeal dismissed TNG's application for the setting aside of the rendered award. In the challenge, TNG relied on its inability to find legal counsel in Sweden and argued that Regulation No. 833/2014 prohibited EU parties from engaging in any transactions with Russian parties, claiming that the dispute could not be deemed arbitrable under Swedish law. In the view of the Svea Court of Appeal, TNG failed to raise the argument concerning the inability to obtain legal counsel before the tribunal. Furthermore, TNG was deemed properly informed of the existing exemption for legal services under the mentioned Regulation, but deliberately chose not to participate in the arbitration. The Court also did not find that restrictive measures affected the arbitrability of the dispute.[35]

The dichotomy between the decisions of the Russian and Swedish Courts makes it unclear whether TNG indeed raised any objections to the arbitral proceedings before the tribunal. FNPC's participation in the Russian proceedings could indeed have shed more light on the actual circumstances. Nonetheless, it can be argued with a high degree of certainty that the arbitral award in the present case would not be enforced in Russia. At the same time, the Russian Court's injunction makes it unlikely that FNPC will ever attempt to pursue this track.

The decision on an anti-arbitration injunction that almost immediately followed this one, and which shall be discussed below, further shows that Russian courts quickly learned the ropes and began to use quite standardised reasoning when applying the Lugovoy Law.

[C] *RZhD v. VRG, KT, and CB*

On 20 March 2023, the Arbitration Court of Moscow City granted the application of JSC Russian Railways (RZhD) and issued an injunction prohibiting the Finnish-incorporated VR Group PLC (VRG), OY Karelian Trains Ltd (KT), and OP Corporate Bank PLC (CB) to initiate arbitration proceedings in accordance with the Arbitration Rules of the Finland Chamber of Commerce and the SCC Arbitration Institute.[36]

The contractual relations that preceded the ruling are reflected in multiple agreements that together define the procedure and conditions for freight and passenger traffic on the Russian-Finnish direct railway service, all containing arbitration clauses for either of the above arbitral institutions: fifteen agreements between RZhD and VRG,

35. Maria Fogdestam Agius and Natalia Petrik, *Swedish Court of Appeal Rejects Award Challenge Based on Arbitrability and Counsel Retention Issues in Russian Sanctions Case*, https://westerberg.com/wp-content/uploads/2024/08/Swedish-Court-of-Appeal-rejects-award-challenge-based-on-arbitrability-and-counsel-retention-issues.pdf (accessed 11 December 2024). *See also* Graham Butler, *Svea Court of Appeal: EU Restrictive Measures (Sanctions) Cannot Halt Commercial Arbitration as Parties to Disputes Continue to Have Access to Research and Legal Services Necessary for Arbitral Proceedings*, https://niels.institute/2024/08/20/svea-court-of-appeal-eu-restrictive-measures-sanctions-cannot-halt-commercial-arbitration-as-parties-to-disputes-continue-to-have-access-to-research-and-legal-services-necessary-for-arbitral-procee/ (accessed 11 December 2024).
36. Arbitration Court of Moscow City, Judgment dated 20 March 2023 in Case No. A40-222671/22-107-1477 (unofficial translation).

four agreements between RZhD and KT, and an agreement between RZhD and CB in respect of a loan agreement to KT.

In 2022, RZhD was sanctioned in the US, the UK, and the EU, including Finland. As a result, in March 2022, VRG discontinued passenger railway service under the agreements, unilaterally terminating them as of December 2022, and demanding early payment of leasing instalments for 2022-2023 in the amount of around EUR 10.9 million. This, according to RZhD, entailed the risk that VRG would invoke the arbitration clause present in the agreements, and affect RZhD's ability to perform under its parallel agreements with KT and CB.[37]

RZhD submitted an application under Article 248.2 of the APC in Russia on two grounds:

- impossibility of engaging qualified foreign lawyers and paying for arbitral and legal fees; and
- lack of impartiality and fair trial guarantees in international arbitrations seated in the EU.[38]

The Court, relying on the Supreme Court's ruling in *UTM v. PESA*, reiterated that the existence of sanctions is sufficient to conclude that a person's access to justice is restricted and does not require additional proof:

> The Court considers these circumstances to be an unconditional impediment to [RZhD's] ability to exercise due process in foreign jurisdictions, i.e. an obstacle to access to justice, which, given the sanctions imposed on it, is an absolute basis for granting the application ...[39]

It may seem that, as the existence of sanctions cannot be refuted, the defendant in the proceedings had no arguments to make. However, the Court's statement on the roles of the parties in the proceedings, in relation to Article 248.1 and 248.2 of the APC, suggests the existence of at least one avenue that a defendant may wish to pursue:

> the person applying for a prohibition [...] need only prove that it is subject to restrictive measures (sanctions) imposed by foreign public legal entities, while the other party to the arbitration, who is subject to a prohibition to initiate or continue the proceedings, needs to prove that the applicant is not prevented from exercising due process in the arbitration despite the sanctions imposed on it and that the international arbitral tribunal concerned observes the guarantees of fairness and impartiality of proceedings ...[40]

How easy (or difficult) it would be to prove such a fact in practice is yet to be seen.

37. *Ibid.*, p. 3.
38. *Ibid.*, p. 4.
39. *Ibid.*, p. 5.
40. *Ibid.*

[D] *GazE v. EurPolGaz*

Another injunction aimed at halting an SCC arbitration was issued on 26 October 2024 by the Arbitration Court of St. Petersburg and Leningrad Oblast, following an application of the Russian LLC Gazprom Export (GazE) against Polish JSC EurPolGaz Transit Gas Pipeline System (EuroPolGaz), set up as a joint venture between Gazprom and Poland's state-owned PGNIG.

On 9 May 2023, EurPolGaz commenced an SCC-administered arbitration as a result of GazE's halt on gas shipments to Poland, seeking around USD 285 million over payments for gas transmission between 2006 and 2009, and around PLN 5.36 billion for lost revenues between 2022 and 2045, as well as interest.[41]

As GazE's listing as a designated entity was not disputed, the Court proceeded with the sample reasoning on the application of the Lugovoy Law.[42] The Court also scrutinised the probability of fair trial proceedings in the SCC-administered arbitration, concluding that there was 'no prospect of an impartial, objective, comprehensive and fair trial administered by the Stockholm Chamber of Commerce against [GazE] at the present time'.[43]

According to the Court, this was substantiated by the following factors:

- impossibility to ensure the legal representation for GazE for 'objective technical, economic, as well as political reasons';
- SCC's refusal to suspend the proceedings due to 'the invalidity of the arbitration clause, the lack of competence of the arbitral tribunal formed by the SCC', and general due process concerns listed by GazE;
- EurPolGaz's 'advantageous position' compared to GazE in view of the current US sanctions regime.[44]

Interestingly, the extension of EU restrictive measures to GazE was not discussed in the ruling. Compared to *UTM v. PESA*, the Court did not elaborate on the relevance of US restrictive measures for Stockholm-seated arbitrations, which only underscores the sufficiency of Russian entities' listing for the applicability of the Lugovoy Law.

41. Arbitration Court of St. Petersburg and Leningrad Oblast, Judgment dated 31 October 2023 in Case No. A56-96787/2023 (unofficial translation). *See also* Jack Ballantyne, *More Claims Filed over Halted Gazprom Supplies*, https://globalarbitrationreview.com/article/more-claims-filed-over-halted-gazprom-supplies (accessed 11 December 2024). Jack Ballantyne, *Russian Court Restrains Billion-Dollar Claim Against Gazprom Unit*, https://globalarbitrationreview.com/article/russian-court-restrains-billion-dollar-claim-against-gazprom-unit (accessed 11 December 2024).
42. Arbitration Court of St. Petersburg and Leningrad Oblast, Judgment dated 31 October 2023 in Case No. A56-96787/2023 (unofficial translation), pp. 2-3.
43. *Ibid.*, p. 4.
44. *Ibid.*, pp. 4-5.

[E] *GazE v. Upiter and Metha*

The subsequent ruling on a similar matter concerning failure to supply gas further illustrates that the Lugovoy Law may be employed by Russian companies seeking to avoid foreign proceedings.

On 15 March 2024, the Arbitration Court of St. Petersburg and Leningrad Oblast granted the application for an anti-arbitration injunction submitted by GazE against a Stockholm-seated arbitration, initiated on 28 November 2022 by two German energy companies, Upiter Global Commodities SE (Upiter) and Metha-Methanhandel GmbH (Metha).[45]

Although there was no dispute between the parties as to whether GazE is subject to EU restrictive measures, the Arbitration Court of St. Petersburg and Leningrad Oblast decided to identify hostile jurisdictions in this decision:

> Pursuant to the Presidential Decree No. 95 dated 05.03.2022, the Government of the Russian Federation ... approved the list of foreign states and territories committing unfriendly actions against the Russian Federation, Russian legal entities and individuals. These states include, inter alia, member states of the European Union ... .[46]

In considering GazE's reasons for the application, the Court also referred to Article 5(n) of EU Regulation No. 833/2014, which, in its own interpretation, imposes a prohibition on 'lawyers and law firms in the European Union from providing legal services to Russian persons'.[47]

Accordingly, the Court found it sufficient that, in support of its application, GazE had submitted 'publicly available statements of foreign law firms, which contain an indication of refusal to act on behalf of individuals and legal entities controlled or influenced by the Russian State'.[48] Upiter's objection that GazE relied on the services of foreign lawyers in a number of proceedings abroad, did not, in the Court's opinion, 'refute the fact that [GazE's] ability to engage a qualified lawyer to defend its rights outside the Russian Federation [was] limited'.[49]

In imposing the measure, the Russian Court proceeded from the earlier established presumption that, by virtue of Article 248.2 of the APC, the application of sanctions by a foreign state in itself creates obstacles to access to justice for a Russian party. The Court thus rejected Upiter's argument that the impact of restrictive measures on the enforceability of the specific arbitration clause was not established.[50] Upiter's and Metha's subsequent appeals against the decision of the Court were dismissed.[51]

---

45. Arbitration Court of St. Petersburg and Leningrad Oblast, Judgment dated 15 March 2024 in Case No. A56-16212/2024 (unofficial translation).
46. *Ibid.*, p. 3.
47. *Ibid.*
48. *Ibid.*
49. *Ibid.*
50. Arbitration Court of St. Petersburg and Leningrad Oblast, Judgment dated 15 March 2024 in Case No. A56-16212/2024 (unofficial translation), p. 4.
51. Arbitration Court of North-Western District, Judgment dated 4 July 2024 in Case No. A56-16212/2024.

The fate of the EUR 13 million arbitral award rendered on 7 June 2024 in favour of Upiter is unknown at this stage.[52]

Overall, the above cases demonstrate that Russian courts seem to have established a distinct position on the interpretation of the Lugovoy Law, with the sole criterion for its application being the existence of sanctions against the relevant party. The reviewed court practice provides little basis to suggest that positive enforcement decisions may be rendered in Russia when injunctions under the Lugovoy Law have been or could have been granted. In light of the final rulings in *UTM v. PESA* and *GazE v. Upiter and Metha*, it is further doubtful whether a party initiating arbitration against a sanctioned entity in a foreign jurisdiction enforcing EU restrictive measures (such as Sweden) can successfully demonstrate the observance of fair trial guarantees and thereby challenge the relevance of the Lugovoy Law.

However, as will be shown below, the Russian courts' concerns about due process and fair trial in foreign jurisdictions cannot be deemed to extend to all Stockholm-seated arbitrations.

[F] *Sibur v. KC*

By its recent judgment dated 11 October 2024, the Arbitration Court of Moscow Oblast granted the application of an Austrian-incorporated company, Sibur International GmbH (Sibur), to enforce an SCC award rendered in its arbitration against the UK-based Kimberly-Clark Ltd (KC).[53]

The dispute arose out of KC's failure to pay for a part of the products supplied by Sibur under purchase orders from January to March 2022. In the arbitration, KC contended that the payment was prohibited because a company which was a member of the Sibur Group was subject to UK and EU sanctions. Thus, KC argued, payments to Sibur itself should be prohibited. In its award dated 9 August 2024, the tribunal rejected this argument and ordered KC to immediately pay around EUR 1.1 million in compensation plus contractually agreed-upon 8% interest.[54]

As KC did not comply with the award voluntarily, Sibur sought to recognise the award in Russia and, then, enforce the award against KC's Russian-incorporated subsidiary, Kimberly-Clark LLC.[55] After noting that the dispute was of a private nature, and thus, appropriately subject to arbitration, the Arbitration Court of Moscow Oblast held that KC does not fall within the Russian domestic jurisdiction, as it was not registered in Russia.[56]

52. Jack Ballantyne, *Uniper Reports €13 Billion Win Against Gazprom*, https://globalarbitrationreview.com/article/uniper-reports-eu13-billion-win-against-gazprom (accessed 11 December 2024). *See also* Upiter, *Uniper Terminates Russian Gas Supply Contracts*, https://www.uniper.energy/news/uniper-terminates-russian-gas-supply-contracts (accessed 11 December 2024).
53. Arbitration Court of Moscow Oblast, Judgment dated 11 October 2024 in Case No. A41-72465/24 (unofficial translation).
54. *Ibid.*, p. 2.
55. *Ibid.*, pp. 2, 7.
56. *Ibid.*, p. 5.

Despite KC's Russian subsidiary's objection that it was not a party to the arbitration,[57] the Court found that '[KC] and Kimberly-Clark LLC are part of the same group of companies and, accordingly, may be considered a single economic entity',[58] thus granting the enforcement of the award against the assets of KC's Russian subsidiary, Kimberly-Clark LLC.

As KC did not appear in the proceedings, the Court held that under Swedish law the award was final and not subject to appeal, as well as that no public policy violations or other grounds for refusing the enforcement were raised or found:

> Having assessed in the aggregate the evidence presented in the case file, the Court concludes that the application is justified, as no grounds for refusal to recognise the arbitral award in the territory of the Russian Federation have been established.[59]

This decision is distinct from the previous ones as the non-performing party attempted to justify its non-performance based on the claimant's alleged links with designated persons. The tribunal determined that the claimant was not subject to sanctions, which led the claimant to seek enforcement of the award in Russia. Thus, the argument of a foreign jurisdiction's unfriendliness may not be relied upon when the allegedly sanctioned party (ultimately deemed unaffected by the sanctions) initiates arbitration. It can also be speculated that the favourable decision may have been influenced by factors such as the Russian nationality of the claimant's parent company and/or the presence of a Russian arbitrator on the panel.

Given the limited number of Russian courts' judgments dealing with the enforcement of Swedish awards, it is also beneficial to examine a few landmark enforcement decisions concerning other foreign-seated arbitrations before drawing final conclusions about the interplay between the Lugovoy Law and the current enforcement climate in Russia.

§10.03 IMPACT OF THE LUGOVOY LAW ON THE ENFORCEMENT OF FOREIGN AWARDS: AN INTERNATIONAL PERSPECTIVE

To assess the prospects for the enforcement of foreign arbitral awards in the Russian Federation, the present part of the chapter will account for both positive and negative decisions, starting with a case where enforcement was refused. This case deserves particular attention, although it does not involve the application of the Lugovoy Law – the respondent was not subject to restrictive measures, or, at least, this question was not raised in the proceedings.

57. *Ibid.*, p. 3.
58. *Ibid.*, p. 6.
59. *Ibid.*, p. 7.

[A] *Thywissen v. NHP*

The dispute stems from a number of agreements concerning flaxseed supply between the Russian agricultural company JSC Novosibirskhlebprodukt (NHP) and the German food producer C. Thywissen GmbH (Thywissen). The agreements contained complementary dispute resolution clauses providing for London-seated arbitration under the FOSFA Arbitration Rules.

Following NHP's failure to supply produce due to an alleged force majeure circumstance (drought), Thywissen commenced arbitration seeking around USD 600,000 in damages, being the difference between the contractually agreed price of goods and the market value of similar goods at which Thywissen could have purchased them when the performance of the contract was due. On 16 November 2022, the tribunal rendered its award in favour of Thywissen, rejecting NHP's force majeure defence and awarding the sought compensation.

Following Thywissen's application, on 24 August 2023, the Arbitration Court of Novosibirsk Oblast granted the enforcement of the award.[60] NHP appealed the decision on various grounds, citing its alleged lack of knowledge of the proceedings and inability to present arguments in its defence, the lack of fair trial guarantees in a foreign jurisdiction, the impossibility of participating in the proceedings, prohibitions on international payments for legal services, and even difficulties obtaining the UK visas.[61]

On 14 December 2023, the Arbitration Court of West Siberian District upheld the decision of the lower court, finding that the actual circumstances of the case confirm that NHP was duly notified of the proceedings and actively participated in them, as evidenced by its numerous objections throughout the arbitration process.[62] The Court also restated the objectives behind the adoption of the Lugovoy Law, but noted that NHP had never sought any remedies under it.[63]

Finding no grounds for refusing enforcement of the award, the Court elaborated on one notable consideration influencing enforcement decisions in Russia, which was also discussed later by the Supreme Court:

> A decision of a foreign court may be recognised as contrary to the public order of the Russian Federation if, as a result of its execution, actions will be taken that are either expressly prohibited by law or are detrimental to the interests of large social groups, that are incompatible with the principles of the economic, political and legal system of the state, that affect the constitutional rights and freedoms of citizens, and that contradict the basic principles of civil law.
>
> Thus, it is not the decision of a foreign court but the result of its enforcement, i.e. the consequences of the application of foreign law norms in the territory of the Russian Federation, that is subject to the assessment. If the consequences of application are incompatible with the basic principles of the legal order of the

60. Arbitration Court of Novosibirsk Oblast, Judgment dated 24 August 2023 in Case No. A45-19015/2023.
61. Arbitration Court of West Siberian District, Judgment dated 14 December 2023 in Case No. A45-19015/2023 (unofficial translation), p. 2.
62. *Ibid.*, p. 8.
63. *Ibid.*, pp. 9-10.

> Russian Federation and affect the interests of large social groups, the court has the right to refuse to recognise and enforce a foreign arbitral award ...[64]

On 26 July 2024, the Supreme Court of the Russian Federation, considering that the lower courts materially breached the provisions of substantive and procedural law, annulled their decisions and referred the case back for renewed examination.[65] In doing so, the Supreme Court, remarkably, revisited the merits of the case.

The Supreme Court considered, *inter alia*, that Thywissen had neither proved sustained losses nor taken measures to mitigate such losses.[66] This, according to the Court, contradicted the principle of proportionality of civil liability as a cornerstone of Russian public policy. Further, the Supreme Court noted that the FOSFA tribunal rejected NHP's force majeure defence, yet, when recognising such an award, lower courts should have taken into account the local authorities' decrees on an emergency regime in NHP's region imposed due to unfavourable climatic conditions.[67]

Reflecting on the result of a possible enforcement, the Court critically addressed its effects on NHP and the social stability of its region, referencing the above-mentioned considerations made by the Arbitration Court of West Siberian District:

> The courts of the first and cassation instances did not assess the consequences of enforcing the FOSFA arbitration award in the Russian Federation, did not take into account the public importance of [NPH], and did not take into account the fact that enforcement of the FOSFA arbitration award would entail the risk of financial instability of the company and would have a significant impact on employment and social stability of the region. Instead of assessing the consequences of enforcing a foreign arbitral award, the courts assessed the transaction made by the parties and recognised it as valid.[68]

Further, the Court went on to evaluate the tribunal's adherence to the principle of objectivity and impartiality. Relying on the practice of the European Court of Human Rights, the Supreme Court noted that 'judicial impartiality in the objective sense implies that there are sufficient safeguards to exclude any doubt as to whether the judge has no interest or personal bias in the case'.[69] Considering that the arbitrators were nationals of Ukraine, the UK, and Denmark, and in view of Presidential Decrees No. 79 and No. 95 recognising 'the named countries as unfriendly countries with the purpose of damaging the Russian Federation, Russian legal and natural persons',[70] the Court concluded that 'the lack of impartiality and objectivity in the present case before the FOSFA Arbitral Tribunal is presumed by this composition of arbitrators until there is evidence to the contrary'.[71]

64. *Ibid.*, p. 10.
65. Supreme Court of the Russian Federation, Judgment dated 26 July 2024 in Case No. A45-19015-2023 (unofficial translation).
66. *Ibid.*, p. 8.
67. *Ibid.*
68. *Ibid.*
69. *Ibid.*, p. 9.
70. *Ibid.*
71. *Ibid.*

In this regard, it appears that NHP had previously unsuccessfully challenged the Ukrainian arbitrator, but that challenge was based on the arbitrator's alleged lack of independence due to a shared FOSFA committee membership with Thywissen's representative and procedural irregularities in the appointment process.[72]

The Court's decision also dispraised the lower courts' failure to assess NHP's arguments regarding the lack of clarity in the arbitration appeal process, as well as the adverse effect of Western sanctions on Russia and the accompanying difficulties for Russian entities in protecting their rights abroad.[73] Consequently, the findings of the Supreme Court in this matter seem to reflect partially already established case practice on the application of the Lugovoy Law in Russia.

Turning now to the positive decisions, at first glance, it is evident that they do not offer an alternative interpretation of the Lugovoy Law, but are either favourable to sanctioned Russian entities or do not concern the 'traditional' impact of sanctions on the parties' rights in the arbitral process.

[B] *Power Machines v. Petrovietnam*

On 2 October 2024, the Arbitration Court of Moscow City granted the application of a Russian engineering company Power Machines for the enforcement of a USD 500 million SIAC award against a Vietnamese national oil and gas group Petrovietnam.[74]

The dispute involved the Long Phú thermal power plant project in southern Vietnam, initiated by a joint venture between Power Machines, Petrovietnam's subsidiary PTSC, and Philippines' BTG Holdings, which secured an EPC contract in 2015 with Power Machines as the general contractor.[75] Due to Power Machines' inclusion in the US sanction list in 2017,[76] the company was unable to obtain key materials, leading to a suspension of work. Consequently, Petrovietnam halted payments, prompting Power Machines to terminate the contract and initiate arbitration to recover payments for the work it had already completed.

Following the arbitration, it appears that Petrovietnam filed a setting-aside application in the Singapore High Court based on the allegations that some of the tribunal's conclusions were beyond the scope of the parties' submissions.[77] Nevertheless, the Arbitration Court of Moscow City found that there were no grounds for refusing the recognition and enforcement of the award in Russia.

72. *Ibid.*
73. *Ibid.*, p. 10.
74. Arbitration Court of Moscow City, Judgment dated 2 October 2024 in Case No. A40-20468-24-19-154.
75. Tom Jones, *Russian Court Enforces Vietnam Power Plant Award*, https://globalarbitrationreview.com/article/russian-court-enforces-vietnam-power-plant-award (accessed 11 December 2024).
76. U.S. Department of the Treasury, *Treasury Sanctions Additional Individuals and Entities in Connection with the Conflict in Ukraine and Russia's Occupation of Crimea*, https://home.treasury.gov/news/press-releases/sm0266 (accessed 18 December 2024).
77. Tom Jones, *Singapore Court Asks Panel to Revisit Vietnamese Power Plant Award*, https://globalarbitrationreview.com/article/singapore-court-asks-panel-revisit-vietnamese-power-plant-award (accessed 11 December 2024).

In the Court's view, Petrovietnam's objections to the tribunal's excess of mandate and fundamental breaches of law remained unfounded and aimed at reviewing the award on the merits, which, in this case, was not deemed appropriate by the Court. Further, Petrovietnam's initiation of the setting-aside proceedings, according to the Court, 'is not a ground for refusal to recognise and enforce the award in the territory of the Russian Federation'.[78]

As Power Machines were subject to US sanctions not binding on a Singapore-seated tribunal, the case neither gave rise to due process concerns with regard to the sanctioned entity, nor did it concern an 'unfriendly jurisdiction'. Thus, the case demonstrates the circumstances under which an award involving a sanctioned entity may be enforced in Russia.

In a similar vein, although the following enforcement decision stems from an investment dispute, the case of *Belarus v. Grand Express* showcases the scenario in which a domestic entity's reliance on the lack of fair trial in an EU-seated arbitration may be rejected as well.

[C] *Belarus v. Grand Express*

On 5 November 2024, the Arbitration Court of Moscow City granted the enforcement application of the Republic of Belarus (Belarus) against an insolvent Russian railway company JSC Grand Express (Grand Express), for a debt of approximately USD 10.3 million.[79]

According to the Arbitration Court of Moscow City, Grand Express commenced an ICSID arbitration against Belarus in 2018, seeking investment protection related to the implementation of its joint project with a Belarusian state company in the territory of Belarus. In 2024, the tribunal dismissed a number of claims based on its lack of jurisdiction, while the remaining claims were considered inadmissible.[80]

Objecting to Belarus' application for the enforcement of the award granting its arbitration-related costs, Grand Express and its insolvency administrator referred to multiple grounds for refusal, including, *inter alia*, a violation of the principle of impartiality and objectivity of the court as well as the tribunal's excess of mandate.[81]

The Arbitration Court of Moscow City noted that the award was rendered in Geneva by a Bulgarian, a Canadian, and a dual Brazilian and Swiss national, while the secretariat was based in Washington, D.C. It further stated that, in such circumstances, the lack of impartiality is normally presumed. Yet, it considered that, in the case at hand, such arbitral composition did not put Grand Express in an unequal position:

78. Arbitration Court of Moscow City, Judgment dated 2 October 2024 in Case No. A40-20468-24-19-154 (unofficial translation), pp. 3-4.
79. Arbitration Court of Moscow City, Judgment dated 5 November 2024 in Case No. A40-46865/24-109-128. *See also* Sebastian Perry, *Belarus Enforces ICSID Award Against Claimant in Russia*, https://globalarbitrationreview.com/article/belarus-enforces-icsid-award-against-claimant-in-russia (accessed 12 December 2024).
80. Arbitration Court of Moscow City, Judgment dated 5 November 2024 in Case No. A40-46865/24-109-128 (unofficial translation), p. 3.
81. *Ibid.*, p. 3.

> However, the debtor does not take into account the fact that these countries are also unfriendly towards the Republic of Belarus. Resolution of the Council of Ministers of the Republic of Belarus No. 209 of 06.04.2022 'On the List of Foreign States Committing Unfriendly Actions against Belarusian Legal Entities and/or Individuals' approved the list of such countries. Among them are Member States of the European Union, Canada, the Swiss Confederation, the USA, etc. In the present case, it is fair to note the lack of impartiality and objectivity in the ICSID's consideration of the case, both with respect to the debtor (a subject of the Russian Federation) and the Republic of Belarus. In view of the above, there are no grounds to conclude that there is no impartiality in the present case, given the equal position of the parties.[82]

With regard to Grand Express's assertion that the award is based on a dispute not covered by the arbitration agreement, the Court held that such argument contradicts Grand Express's position in the arbitration, as it was the party initiating the proceedings. This confirmed the tribunal's competence to determine the dispute and displayed bad faith on the part of Grand Express.[83]

Indeed, the current attitude on enforcing foreign arbitral awards in Russia leaves a great leeway for Russian parties to invoke 'Western' sanctions towards the Russian Federation as a ground for resisting enforcement. However, when both parties are at the same 'risk' of being treated unfairly, the Russian courts resort to simple math, where injustice to both sides corresponds to equal treatment towards them.

§10.04 CONCLUSION

The introduction of the Lugovoy Law has significantly reshaped the enforcement landscape of foreign arbitral awards in Russia. By extending the exclusive jurisdiction of Russian courts to disputes involving parties subjected to foreign restrictive measures, the law aims to protect Russian entities from legal actions perceived as hostile or unfair due to international sanctions. This legislative shift has profound implications for arbitration practitioners and international businesses engaging with Russian counterparties.

The cases examined, such as *UTM v. PESA*, *GazE v. EurPolGaz*, and *GazE v. Upiter and Metha*, demonstrate a consistent judicial approach where Russian courts readily apply the Lugovoy Law. The mere existence of foreign sanctions against a Russian party suffices to invoke exclusive jurisdiction, leading to the refusal to enforce foreign arbitral awards. The courts have emphasised that sanctions inherently impede access to justice for Russian entities in foreign jurisdictions, justifying the transfer of disputes to Russian courts regardless of existing arbitration agreements.

This stance undermines the reliability of arbitration clauses and the enforceability of awards involving Russian parties, especially when proceedings are seated in countries applying sanctions against Russia. The presumption of bias and lack of impartiality in foreign arbitral tribunals, as highlighted by the Russian Supreme Court,

82. *Ibid.*, pp. 3-4.
83. *Ibid.*, pp. 4-5.

further complicates the situation. The courts' willingness to scrutinise arbitrators' nationalities and question the fairness of international arbitration proceedings poses additional challenges.

However, not all decisions have led to refusals of enforcement. The case of *Sibur v. KC* illustrates that Russian courts may enforce foreign arbitral awards when the award debtor is a non-sanctioned foreign counterparty. Similarly, in *Power Machines v. Petrovietnam*, the enforcement was granted despite the claimant being subject to US sanctions, possibly due to the neutral seat of arbitration in Singapore. The fact that the enforcing party in both cases was a Russian-controlled entity may have influenced the decisions.

For international arbitration practitioners, these developments necessitate a cautious and strategic approach. It is essential to consider the potential impact of the Lugovoy Law when encountering arbitration agreements with Russian entities. Selecting arbitral seats in neutral jurisdictions, understanding the nuances of Russian enforcement proceedings, and assessing the enforceability of awards in alternative jurisdictions where the counterparty holds assets become critical considerations.

In conclusion, the Lugovoy Law has introduced complexities that fundamentally alter the enforcement of foreign arbitral awards in Russia. The Russian courts' prioritisation of national interests and protective legal measures in response to international sanctions challenge the effectiveness of traditional arbitration mechanisms. As the legal environment continues to evolve, parties that find themselves in a situation where they need to engage with Russian entities must remain vigilant, adapting their dispute resolution strategies to mitigate risks associated with enforcement uncertainties.

CHAPTER 11

Navigating Interest in Arbitration: Legal, Economic, and Cultural Dimensions

Elena Koch & Narmin Abdulova[*]

§11.01 INTRODUCTION

Significant standardization in many aspects of arbitration law and procedure has generated a great deal of interest among transnational parties in arbitration as a dispute resolution mechanism and has driven the growing prominence of this field. However, interest in arbitration has remained one of not many aspects of arbitration, which firmly reflects cultural and economic diversity in arbitration. This article considers different perspectives of interest in arbitration, focusing on cultural variations and economic reality.

First, the focus is on the merits of the dispute – interest on the amounts claimed and costs. The award of interest in international arbitration remains a crucial but underexplored aspect within this framework. While interest serves to compensate for the time value of money and to ensure full compensation, its determination is often ambiguous in the absence of uniform guidelines. This complexity arises not only from the variety of applicable interest rates, types of interest and accrual periods, all of which are influenced by the parties' agreements, statutory rules and different jurisdictional practices, but also from the peculiarities of the legal culture of the parties to the arbitration. This article investigates the main factors influencing arbitral tribunals' decisions on granting interest and the mechanisms of determination of applicable interest types, rates and periods. It also examines recent trends in arbitral practice, including the increasing use of compound interest and the emphasis on aligning

* We are grateful to Professor Albert Jan van den Berg for his inspiration and encouragement during the 11th cycle of the Young ICCA Mentoring Programme, which led to the development of this article. The views expressed in this chapter are solely those of the authors.

interest rates with commercial realities. In order to provide practical insights, the article reviews landmark cases that illustrate the process of deciding on interest at two different stages: (i) the pre-award period (i.e., from the date of the loss until the date of the award); and (ii) the post-award period (i.e., from the entry of a judgment, including any appeals, until payment is made in satisfaction of the judgment). These examples highlight the complexity of establishing a harmonized approach to ensuring predictability of arbitral awards, taking into account both the commercial realities and the specific circumstances of the parties involved.

Second, the article analyses the procedural role of interest in arbitration from an institutional perspective, in particular: (i) the role of arbitral institutions in harmonizing the regulation on decision-making on interest in disputes on the merits, (ii) the applicability of interest on arbitration costs from the perspective of the economic interest of the parties, arbitral tribunals and arbitral institutions, and, finally, (iii) alternative view on interest to be taken into consideration for calculation of the amount in dispute and, subsequently, for calculation of the costs of the arbitration. Attention is drawn to the treatment of interest in the arbitration rules of the major arbitral institutions, providing insights into their implications. The goal of the analysis of the procedural aspects of interest in arbitration is to demonstrate the role of arbitral institutions in shaping the legal and economic environment of arbitration.

The article also focuses on changes in the national legislation of certain jurisdictions in relation to issues of interest in arbitration, which also reflect the general pro-arbitration trend.

In conclusion, the article emphasizes the multifaceted challenges posed by interest in arbitration and evaluates approaches to addressing them from diverse legal, economic and cultural perspectives. The authors consider whether a comprehensive standardization or harmonization of interest-based practices is necessary, or whether a certain degree of flexibility is essential to ensure the transnational nature of arbitration.

§11.02 UNDERSTANDING LEGAL FOUNDATIONS AND MATH BEHIND INTEREST

The award of interest is a fundamental yet complex element of international arbitration, bridging legal principles and economic realities to ensure that the prevailing party receives full and fair compensation. While often treated as a technical afterthought, interest directly impacts the value of awards, raising critical questions of fairness, enforceability and commercial practicality. First section of the article analyses two pillars of interest in arbitration: the legal framework governing interest and the methodologies for calculating it, with particular attention to commercial arbitration, while drawing comparative insights from investment arbitration where relevant.

The discussion begins by examining the concept of interest in arbitration and its significance in preserving the value of an award over time. The discussion then moves to the legal and economic rationales that support awarding interest on damages and costs. Attention is also given to the different sources authorizing tribunals to award interest ranging from national laws and institutional arbitration rules to general principles of international law. Equally important is the practical question of how interest is calculated. This includes the choice of interest rates, the distinction between simple and compound interest, and the timing of accrual – pre-award and post-award. The section further addresses observations on the treatment of interest in commercial versus investment arbitration. Taken together, these elements illustrate how tribunals balance legal principles and economic considerations in awarding interest as part of fair and effective dispute resolution.

Finally, reference will be made to landmark cases that have shaped the guiding principles governing the award of interest in arbitration, providing practical insights into how tribunals have approached this issue in the ruling of cases.

[A] Legal Framework of Interest in Arbitration

[1] What Is Interest in Arbitration?

The concept of interest has historical roots, originating from Roman Law, where it was a sum 'due from a debtor who delayed or defaulted in repayment of a loan. The measure of the amount due for the default or delay was the difference between the claimant's current position and what it would have been had the loan been timely and fully repaid'.[1]

In today's legal and financial system, interest serves a similar purpose: it compensates for the loss of use of money. It is a sum paid or payable for temporary withholding of the invested funds to which a party is legally entitled.[2] This principle is also well established in arbitration practice. For instance, in the case, *Yukos Universal Limited v. The Russian Federation*,[3] the tribunal has emphasized that interest is intended to compensate for the harm caused by the debtor's non-payment, during which the creditor was deprived of the ability to use and manage the funds they were entitled to receive.

This compensatory function becomes particularly critical in high-value international arbitration cases that frequently span a decade or more when accounting for the full dispute lifecycle. Complex proceedings typically begin with extended pre-arbitration negotiations, followed by multi-year adjudication and often conclude with lengthy enforcement efforts against reluctant parties. Given such prolonged timelines, a tribunal's award of interest may be as large as the principal claim itself;[4] therefore, appropriate interest calculations are essential to preserve the economic value of an award, ensuring that the prevailing party receives compensation that reflects the true

1. Liu Chengwei, *Recovery of Interest*, 1 Nord. J. Commer. Law 2, 2 (2003).
2. Thierry J. Senechal and John Y. Gotanda, *Interest as Damages*, 47 Colum. J. Transnat'l L, 491, 495 (2009).
3. *Yukos Universal Limited (Isle of Man) v. The Russian Federation*, PCA No. 2005-04/AA227, para. 1657.
4. *Compalia del Desarrollo de Santa Elena v. Costa Rica*, 15 ICSID Rev., Foreign Investment L.J. 169, 200 (2000), an arbitral tribunal awarded USD 4.15 million in damages and USD 11.85 million in interest.

cost of delay – accounting for the significant passage of time between the original breach and ultimate enforcement of the award.

[2] Economic and Legal Rationale for Award of Interest

The issue of interest as compensation is as essential as the main claim for damages or payment of principal and should be given the same level of careful consideration both by counsel and tribunals.[5] In arbitration, the award of interest is not merely a discretionary remedy – it is a compensatory mechanism for claimant's loss of the use of money during the period of non-payment.[6] When a party suffers financial loss due to delayed payment or prolonged dispute resolution, interest serves to compensate for the time value of money and the opportunity cost of capital. Without it, even a successful claimant may fall short of full reparation. As such, awarding interest has both legal and economic justifications grounded in principles of fairness and efficiency.

The selected interest rate must reflect economic principles and provide fair compensation. Fair compensation is referred to as an interest rate marked as it compensates for the risks and preserves the fair market value of the award. The interest awarded should address two of the most basic concepts in finance: time value of money and the risk of the cash flows at issue.[7]

The first component refers to having a given amount of money today over receiving the same amount of money at a later point in time. The time value of money reflects the impact of inflation and, therefore, compensates for the expected change in purchasing power between the date of breach or injury and the date of eventual payment. While arbitral tribunals rarely include inflation separately (as ruled in the case *Aminoil v. Kuwait*, where the tribunal applied an interest rate of 7.5% and an inflation rate of 10%), this component remains an essential, though often implicit, element of interest rate determination.[8] The time preference for money is distinct from inflation. That is because even in the case of zero inflation, parties still prefer to have money at the outset, as it gives them more options. The second component refers to the rate of interest reflecting various risks borne by the lender. One such risk is the risk of default by the borrower. The extent to which these risks are reflected in an interest rate depends on the type of debt, the currency of the debt, and the length of the deprivation. The time value of money is unrelated to the risks borne by the lender because the

---

5. Wetter J. Gillis, *Interest as an Element of Damages in the Arbitral Process*, 5 IFLR, 23, https://www.trans-lex.org/129800/_/wetter-jgillis-interest-as-an-element-of-damages-in-the-arbitral-process-5-iflr-dec-1986-at-20-et-seq/ (accessed 5 March 2025).
6. John Y. Gotanda, *Supplemental Damages in Private International Law*, Kluwer Law International, 1, 1 (1998).
7. Christina L. Beharry, *Prejudgement Interest Rates in International Investment Arbitration*, 8, 56 JIDS, 61, (2017) https://doi.org/10.1093/jnlids/idw006 (accessed 1 October 2025); Senechal and Gotanda, *supra* n. 2, at 495.
8. *The American Independent Oil Company v. The Government of the State of Kuwait*, Ad Hoc Arbitration, I.L.M. 21, Final Award, para. 174, 24 March 1982.

lender would still need to be compensated for the delay in payment even where he bears no risks.[9]

From a legal standpoint, there are three principal justifications for requiring a respondent to pay interest to a claimant that has succeeded on its damages claims. The primary rationale is to fully compensate claimant by restoring it to the position it would have enjoyed if the wrongful act had not occurred.[10] Indeed, if there were no delay between the date of the injury and date of compensation, claimant would be made whole by the tribunal's award, and an award of interest would not be needed. However, the time between the date of harm and the enforcement of an award can be quite lengthy and lead to increased financial loss to the claimant, ultimately leading to a position of uncertainty.

The second justification for awarding interest is to prevent unjust enrichment of a respondent. Respondents that retain and use the money owed to claimants during the resolution of the dispute enjoy an unfair benefit.[11] According to this rationale, respondent should be at least liable for the reasonable cost of borrowing the amount in question over the relevant period. The third reason for awarding interest is rooted in procedural efficiency. It encourages the parties to avoid disputes and, when they do occur, to resolve them in a timely manner.[12]

The analysis of economic and legal justifications reveals that they align in recognizing that the essential harm being redressed is the claimant's involuntary deprivation of capital. This deprivation results in a dual injury: the loss of the funds themselves and, essentially, the lost opportunity to utilize those funds during the period of delay.

[B] Determining Interest in Arbitration: How Is Interest Calculated

When presented with a claim for interest, an arbitral tribunal must address a wide range of issues. First, it must ascertain whether it has authority to award interest – a determination grounded in the agreement of parties, the applicable law or equitable principles. Once jurisdiction is confirmed, it must determine how interest award should be calculated. This requires a careful examination of which interest rate should be applied, whether simple or compound interest should be awarded and the time period during which interest is accrued. The issues arising under each of these considerations often intersect with legal, factual and economic dimensions, requiring a balanced and well-reasoned approach.

9. Beharry, *supra* n. 7, at 62.
10. Senechal and Gotanda, *supra* n. 2, at 496.
11. *Ibid.*
12. *Ibid.*

[1] Applicable Law

The obvious starting point for a tribunal's authority to award interest is the parties' arbitration agreement, or any other agreement relevant to the tribunal's determination of the dispute, such as the parties' contract or, in investment arbitration, applicable treaty.[13] Subject to the mandatory provisions of applicable law and public policy considerations, an agreement on whether, at what rate, and on what sums interest accrues will generally be determinative for payments covered by the interest provision.

Tribunals typically upload such contractual terms unless they conflict with overriding legal principles or violate public policy. This practice promotes the goals of party autonomy, respect for the intent of the parties, predictability and certainty concerning the legal rights of the contracting parties. Therefore, interest may not initially appear to be a complex issue, particularly when the legal basis for awarding it is explicitly set out in the applicable agreement or the law of a particular jurisdiction, for example, Finnish, Norwegian, and Swedish law.[14] However, as shown in §11.03[A][2] below, in international arbitration express terms explicitly addressing the tribunal's authority to award interest are relatively rare in practice, especially, when multiple jurisdictions are involved and the decision on interest must be made under conditions of conflicting laws, or when the applicable law provides arbitral tribunals with discretion to grant interest in arbitration without requiring the application of a specific rate or period. In such cases, the only guidance left to arbitral tribunals often comes from market-based economic principles.

Notably, while provisions addressing interest issue are common in international frameworks, they are typically not detailed. For instance, the Energy Charter Treaty states that arbitral awards 'may include an award of interest'.[15] Similarly, the US Model BIT also explicitly empowers the tribunal to award 'monetary damages and any

13. Lara Hammoud and Matthew Secomb, *Interest in ICC Arbitral Awards: Introduction and Commentary*, 15(1) ICC International Court of Arbitration Bulletin, 53, 54 (2004); John Y. Gotanda, *Damages in Private International Law*, in 326 Collected Courses of The Hague Academy of International Law, 189, 246-247 (2007).
14. *See* for Finland: Anders Forss, Marko Hentunen and Jerker Pitkänen, *Guide to Arbitration Places: Finland (version: 12 February 2024)*, Delos Dispute Resolution, https://delosdr.org/wp-content/uploads/2021/06/Delos-GAP-2nd-edn-Finland.pdf (accessed 18 May 2025): 'When Finnish law applies, the parties may agree how interest shall accrue on debts. Lacking such agreement, interest will accrue in accordance with the Finnish Interest Act (633/1982)'; *see* for Norway: Christian F. Galtung, *International Arbitration Law and Rules in Norway (verified on 2 August 2023)*, CMS, https://cms.law/en/int/expert-guides/cms-expert-guide-to-international-arbitration/norway (accessed 18 May 2025): 'The Norwegian Arbitration Act does not govern claims for interest that the arbitral tribunal has in the event of late payment of its fees and/or expenses. However, the preparatory materials for the Norwegian Arbitration Act indicate that the general rules on claims on interest as laid down in Norwegian Act relating to Interest on Overdue Payments) will apply'; *see* for Sweden: Fredrik Norburg, Anina Liebkind, Pontus Scherp, Marcus Axelryd, *Commercial Arbitration: Sweden (verified on 8 April 2025)*, GAR, https://globalarbitrationreview.com/insight/know-how/commercial-arbitration/report/sweden (accessed 18 May 2025): 'Parties are entitled to claim interest on their principal claim and costs. The Swedish Interest Act is not mandatory, and the parties are free to agree on an interest rate. According to the main rule under the Interest Act the interest rate is equivalent to the reference rate as determined by the Central Bank of Sweden, plus eight percentage points.'
15. Energy Charter Treaty, Lisbon, 34 I.L.M. 381 (1995), Art. 28(6) (17 December 1994).

applicable interest'.[16] The procedural rules of arbitral institutions may also address interest awards, as will be examined in §11.03[B] of this article. Whether international rules can serve as a basis for awarding interest also depends on how they are classified, either as procedural or as part of the substantive law that governs the dispute.

When there are no contractual stipulations indicating agreement between the parties on the issue of interest, arbitral tribunals look for a legal basis for their decisions with regard to interest. In practice, arbitrators have several options when it comes to applying a law. They may use: (i) the law applicable to the contract, (ii) the conflict rules, or (iii) the law of the place of arbitration.[17] Which law is applicable will depend on whether claims for payment of interest fall under the law applicable to the merits of the dispute or the law applicable to procedure. This distinction arises because interest can be seen both as a substantive right (compensating for delayed payment) and a procedural mechanism (regulating enforcement and the accrual of post-award interest).[18]

Determining which legal framework applies can significantly impact the tribunal's approach to awarding interest. If classified as a substantive issue, the applicable law governing the contract or claim will shape the determination of interest, including the rate and method of calculation. However, if treated as a procedural matter, interest may be subject to the arbitration rules, national arbitration statutes, or tribunal discretion. This distinction can be particularly relevant in cases where tribunals are required to assess statutory interest rates, equitable considerations, or commercial norms when making their decision.

Even where parties have expressly agreed on a tribunal's power to award interest, the applicable law therefore still plays a decisive role in determining the parameters of any interest to be awarded. As such, when using the law applicable to the contract as the basis for their decisions, arbitral tribunals may be confronted with a legal prohibition on awarding interest.[19] While even in extreme situations of Sharia law, arbitral tribunals tend to find a way to apply economic reasoning allowing granting interest. A notable trend is that the arbitral tribunals tried to balance Sharia law with international arbitration principles, particularly in cases involving parties from different legal traditions, and avoiding a strict religious interpretation by emphasizing the principle of party autonomy – if the contract allows interest, they may enforce it unless explicitly prohibited by local law.[20] This practice highlights the adaptability of international arbitration in balancing diverse legal traditions while ensuring economically relevant remedies. The following sections will explore how tribunals apply this authority in practice, particularly the methods used in calculating interest rates.

16. U.S. Model Bilateral Investment Treaty, Art. 34(1)(a), 34(2)(b) (2012).
17. Hammoud and Secomb, *supra* n. 13, at 54.
18. *Ibid.*, at 60.
19. Mark Wakim, *Public Policy Concerns Regarding Enforcement of Foreign International Arbitral Awards in the Middle East*, 21 N.Y. Int'l L. Rev. 1, 8-9 (2008).
20. Hammoud and Secomb, *supra* n. 13, at 55.

[2] *Applicable Interest Rates*

As pointed out by *John Y.* Gotanda, international arbitral tribunals are often confronted with claims that involve large amounts ranging from the millions of dollars.[21] This is particularly evident in arbitral award of *Yukos Universal Limited (Isle of Man) v. The Russian Federation*, where the amount of interest awarded was in excess of several billion USD.[22]

Although interest is regularly awarded in international arbitration, tribunals have taken different approaches regarding the applicable interest rate, the calculation methods, accrual period over which the rate is applied and their treatment of pre-and post-award interest. Prior to examining common practices in granting interest in §11.03[A] below, it is necessary to analyse theoretical framework of these matters.

The choice of interest rates is one of the key components of the interest calculation that can significantly impact the size of an award. Despite their substantial financial impact, interest rates rarely receive focused attention from parties or tribunals when presenting arguments or issuing awards.

Determining the applicable interest rates requires tribunals to balance legal principles, the parties' contractual intentions and prevailing economic realities. When calculating interest, tribunals generally consider three key components: (1) the appropriate **rate of interest**, (2) the **calculation method** (simple versus compound), and (3) the **period** during which interest accrues (pre- or post-award). The choice of interest rates follows a hierarchy of sources, starting with a rate agreed upon by the parties in their contract. In the absence of such provisions, tribunals may turn to statutory default rates or exercise discretion guided by fairness, market benchmarks like LIBOR, SOFR or EURIBOR, or the principle of the time value of money.[23]

In order to determine the rate at which interest accrues, the laws of many jurisdictions provide for tribunals to look first to the parties' agreement and enforce any provisions on the payment of interest, unless they contravene public policy.[24] While contractual rates are theoretically paramount, as explained in §11.03[A][2] below, their inclusion as a provision in the parties' agreement is rare, so that this situation leads tribunals to rely on statutory or market rates and supplementing gaps with commercial standards or equitable principles.[25] The rate in such statutes can vary widely. Some countries periodically set the rate of interest, typically basing it on market conditions; by contrast, other countries have fixed statutory rates which remain unchanged for years. As a result, they do not accurately reflect compensation for the

21. John Y. Gotanda, *A Study of Interest*, Villanova University School of Law Public Law and Legal Theory Working Paper No. 2007-10, 1-37, 1 (2007).
22. *Yukos Universal Limited (Isle of Man) v. Russian Federation, supra* n. 3, para. 1823.
23. Gisele Stephens-Chu and Joshua Kelly, *Awards of Interest in International Arbitration: Achieving Coherence Through Purpose*, 7 Indian J. Arb. L. 9, 28-30 (2018); Senechal and Gotanda, *supra* n. 2, at 502.
24. John Y. Gotanda, *Awarding Interest in International Arbitration*, 90 AM. J. Int'l L. 40, 50-51 (1996) https://doi.org/10.2307/2203750 (accessed 1 October 2025); For example, in *ICC Case No. 10619*, the tribunal upheld an agreed interest rate on late payments as stipulated in the contract; Hammoud and Secomb, *supra* n. 13, at 59.
25. Gotanda, *supra* n. 13, at 256 (2007).

loss of the use of money. Complex conflict-of-law questions can arise as to which statutory rate, if any, should apply. Commentators tend to favour application of the law of either the agreement or the currency of the award. But it has been held that 'arbitrators have the broadest powers to determine interest on the basis of the most appropriate rate, without resorting to any rule of conflict'.[26]

Beyond statutory provisions, some tribunals have resolved claims for interest based on general principles of law, such as the UNIDROIT Principles, which provide a framework for assessing interest claims in a balanced manner. The UNIDROIT Principles provide for interest at 'the average bank short-term lending rate to prime borrowers prevailing for the currency of payment at the place of payment'.[27] The Principles of European Contract Law (PECL) contains a similar provision.[28] Many commercial tribunals have relied on these instruments to award interest at market borrowing rates, including to 'fill the gap' left by the UN Convention on Contracts for the International Sale of Goods (CISG) Article 78 (which does not specify the applicable interest rate).[29]

Others have taken a more discretionary approach, determining the rate and nature of interest based on considerations of fairness and reasonableness, ensuring that the awarded interest aligns with equitable financial compensation.[30] In investment disputes, it is common for tribunals to award interest at market saving or borrowing rates such as the US T-bill rate or LIBOR[31] rate. Some tribunals have also added a certain percentage to the LIBOR rate to arrive at the approximate rate that international investors would have had to pay if they had been obliged to borrow the money.[32]

The approach taken by investment tribunals is closer to economic reality. It more accurately compensates a party for the loss of the use of money through an award of interest at a market rate, such as the US T-bill or LIBOR rate, and on a compound basis. Nevertheless, this approach has a serious drawback – it ignores the reality that businesses typically invest in opportunities that have a significantly greater amount of risk than the US T-bill or LIBOR rates. Accordingly, a tribunal should account for the

26. Guilherme Recena Costa, *37. On Pre-Award Interest Rates*, 40 under 40 International Arbitration, 591-612, 597 (2021).
27. International Institute for the Unification of Private Law (UNIDROIT), Principles of International Commercial Contracts, Art. 7.4.9 (2004).
28. Commission on European Contract Law, Principles of European Contract Law, Art. 9:508 (2002).
29. Recena Costa, *supra* n. 26, 603.
30. Senechal and Gotanda, *supra* n. 2, at 507.
31. Despite LIBOR was long regarded as a dominant benchmark for interest calculations in international arbitration, critical flaws have been revealed that ultimately necessitated its phase-out. The first major red flag emerged with the 2012 LIBOR scandal, where investigations uncovered systemic manipulation by panel banks submitting false quotes to benefit derivatives traders (The Economist, *The LIBOR Scandal*, July 2012). This undermined the LIBOR's credibility as a neutral benchmark. Mikhail Kalinin and Michael Peer, *The Lacking Interest in Interest Rates: Will the Phase-Out of LIBOR and Negative Rates Go Unnoticed by Arbitration Practitioners?* 37 Arb. Int., 735-748, 737 (2021) https://doi.org/10.1093/arbint/aiab031 (accessed 1 October 2025).
32. Sergey Ripinsky and Kevin Williams, *Damages in International Investment Law*, British Institute of International and Comparative Law, 363-391, 369 (2008).

underlying risk profile of the assets in the dispute in order to achieve the goal of full compensation.

Some tribunals have typically approached the rate of interest with one eye on ensuring full compensation. Despite differences and discretion of the tribunals, it is clear that the purpose of the award of interest plays a decisive role in selecting the appropriate rate of interest. As Mark Beeley and Richard E. Walck noted, arbitral decisions on interest rates frequently lack detailed reasoning, even though interest can materially affect the final quantum. The absence of standardized methodology has led to a range of outcomes influenced by the facts of each case, including the currencies involved, prevailing market conditions, and the conduct of the parties.[33]

Even when faced with relatively similar fact sets, tribunals may come to divergent decisions on the rate of interest to be awarded, with some preferring a risk-free rate and others choosing rates that reflect a higher level of risk. While that may, in some instances, represent compromises made to achieve a unanimous award, it may also reflect a relative scarcity of guidance and/or specific data on which to justify the award.[34]

In the absence of contractual provisions, the use of inconsistent methodologies, from risk-free benchmarks to risk-adjusted rates, has led to unpredictability in arbitral awards. However, we believe that addressing interest claims in the parties' submissions and enlarging the economic analysis in the reasoning of the arbitral award would promote fairness and uniformity in the award of interest.

[3] Simple Versus Compound Interest

In arbitration, the choice between simple and compound interest carries significant implications for achieving fair and commercially realistic compensation. Simple interest – calculated only on the principal amount – provides a straightforward, linear accumulation of interest over time.[35] While its ease of calculation makes it administratively convenient, its failure to reflect the compounding nature of real-world finance often results in under compensation for the prevailing party. In other words, in the simple interest scenario, the interest that accrues each period is not added to the base that is used to calculate interest in future periods.

However, compound interest is interest that is applied periodically, depending on the compounding period, to both the principal sum awarded and accumulated interest.[36] Tribunals increasingly recognize that compound interest better fulfils arbitration's compensatory purpose, especially in cases involving complex financial transactions, cross-border disputes or high-value claims.[37] In the finance world, compound

33. Mark Beeley and Richard E. Walck, *Approaches to the Award of Interest by Arbitration Tribunals*, JDIA, 53, 62 (2014).
34. *Ibid.*, at 62.
35. Enrik Haxhirexha, *Awarding Interest in Investment Arbitration*, CTEI Working Papers-04, 1, 33 (2014).
36. Black's Law Dictionary, 2nd ed., https://thelawdictionary.org/compound-interest/ (accessed 25 March 2025).
37. John Y. Gotanda, *Compound Interest in International Disputes*, Oxford U. Comp. L. Forum 1, 14 (2009).

interest is the international standard applied in most time value applications.[38] The treatment of interest, whether simple or compound, differs significantly between commercial and investment arbitration due to differences in legal frameworks, underlying principles and enforcement considerations. Compound interest is regularly awarded in investment treaty arbitrations.[39] The award in case of *The Compañia Del Desarrollo De Santa Elena SA v. The Republic of Costa Rica* is often cited by tribunals to explain that the use of compounding is not punitive in nature, but rather reflects the economic reality of investment – that of an investment opportunity being denied to the claimant by the respondent.[40]

In commercial arbitration, express authorization for arbitral award of compound interest from either the parties or arbitral rules is rare. While some jurisdictions such as Switzerland and Germany continue to prohibit the awarding of compound interest,[41] the relevance of these restrictions in today's financial landscape is questioned. The UNIDROIT Principles still take 'no stand on the question of compound interest'[42] on the basis that in some national legal systems 'compound interest is limited by rules of public policy aimed at protecting the non-performing party'.[43]

Modern financing and investment instruments almost universally rely on compound interest, raising legitimate debate over whether exceptions should be made in arbitration, particularly under the principle of party autonomy.[44] In contrast, some jurisdictions have adopted more flexible approaches. For instance, section 49(3) of the English Arbitration Act explicitly empowers tribunal to award 'simple or compound interest from such dates, at such rates and with such rests as it considers meets the justice of the case'. Therefore, commercial arbitration remains cautious in application of compound interest due to jurisdictional fragmentation.

Indeed, the adoption of compound interest reflects the majority of commercial realities, in that a loss of value incurred by a company, active in normal trading operations, implies the loss of use of that value.[45] The distinction between simple and compound interest highlights a broader tension between legal traditions that prioritize favouring predictability (simple interest) and economic principles demanding accuracy (compound). While compound interest has become standard practice in investment arbitration, its adoption in commercial arbitration remains fragmented. The trend towards market-aligned awards suggests that compound interest will eventually prevail, but harmonizing this across jurisdictions requires clearer standards.

38. *Ibid.*, at 15.
39. Hilary Heilbron, *Assessing Damages in International Arbitration: Practical Considerations*, JDIA, Jurisnet, 26-27 (2014).
40. *Compañia del Desarrollo de Santa Elena S.A. v. Republic of Costa Rica*, ICSID Case No. ARB/96/1, 1-204, 202 (17 February 2000), https://www.italaw.com/sites/default/files/case-documents/italaw6340.pdf (accessed 25 March 2025).
41. Swiss Code of Obligations (CO), Art. 105(3); German Civil Code (BGB) §289.
42. UNIDROIT, *supra* n. 27, Art. 7.4.10.
43. *Sempra Metals Ltd. v. Inland Revenue Commissioners*, 1 AC 561 (HL), 37 (2008).
44. Gotanda, *supra* n. 24, at 61.
45. Thierry J. Senechal, *Present Day Valuation in International Arbitration: A Five Principle-Based Framework for Awarding Interest*, SSRN, 1, 10 (2008) http://dx.doi.org/10.2139/ssrn.1122584 (accessed 10 November 2025).

[4] Pre-award and Post-award Interest

Based on its timespan factor, interest can be distinguished as pre-award and post-award, which is a critical component of the quantum in international arbitration.

International tribunals typically establish the interest accrual period by fixing both the starting date and the ending date, with this timeframe being shaped by several key factors.[46] These factors include the law applicable to a cause of action or form of loss, the conduct of the parties, date when the party's loss has accrued and, for post-award interest, any undertaking that the respondent will pay within a short period after the award. The fundamental consideration in awarding interest is its intended purpose. When the objective is compensatory, selecting an incorrect starting date can result in either excessive or insufficient compensation. Consequently, the determination of the time period for interest plays a crucial role in ensuring that the award fulfils its intended function effectively.

The purpose of granting pre-award interest in arbitrations is primarily to compensate the prevailing party for the financial loss incurred from the date the claims originated until the date arbitral award is issued.[47] This form of interest addresses two fundamental concerns: (1) providing complete financial redress for the period during which the claimant was deprived of funds, and (2) encouraging timely resolution of disputes by accounting for the opportunity costs incurred during the arbitral process. Pre-award interest remains an uncertain matter and tribunals often adopt different reasoning on pre-award interest rates.[48] Some tribunals prioritize strict adherence to the parties' agreement by applying explicit contractual interest clauses, while other tribunals refer to national statutory rates of the governing law.

The imposition of post-award interest plays an essential function in arbitration by discouraging losing parties from unjustly withholding payment or employing delay tactics after an adverse award. Unlike pre-award interest, which compensates for losses suffered during the dispute, post-award interest serves as a financial disincentive against non-compliance. In practice, post-award interest is frequently set at the same rate as pre-award interest. However, it may also be set at a higher rate to incentivize the respondent to promptly settle the awarded damages.[49]

It should be noted that some arbitral awards have not distinguished pre-award and post-award interest, with tribunals merging pre-award and post-award interest and ordering interest on damages to accrue until the date of payment.[50] While some scholars argued that whether approached as a matter of timing or as an issue

46. Stephens-Chu and Kelly, *supra* n. 23, at 26.
47. Matthew Secomb, *Interest in International Arbitration*, para. 2.143 (Oxford University Press 2019).
48. Mino Han and Ashutosh Ray, *Allocating Pre-Award Interest When a Procedural Delay is Byon Parties' Control* (1 September 2020) https://arbitrationblog.kluwerarbitration.com/2020/09/01/allocating-pre-award-interest-when-a-procedural-delay-is-beyond-parties-control/?utm_source=chatgpt.com (accessed 27 March 2025).
49. Gary B. Born, *International Commercial Arbitration* (3rd ed. Kluwer Law International, 2021) vol. II, Chapter 17.08[C].
50. *ICC case 5428*, Final Award, (1992) 3(1), ICC International Court of Arbitration Bulletin 16, 1988.

concerning the principal amount to which interest applies, these two forms of interest should be clearly separated.[51] This distinction helps to clarify their different purposes and minimizes the risk that either pre-award or post-award interest could be deemed unenforceable - potentially resulting in only part of the interest award being severed from the overall decision.

§11.03 DYNAMICS IN THE CRYSTALLIZATION OF INTEREST IN ARBITRATION

Granting interest remains one of the least standardized aspects of international arbitration, resulting in the diverse trends observed in practice, which reflect the vast impact of economic, cultural, and legislative developments at both international and domestic levels.

Numerous questions arise regarding what approach to granting interest should be considered standard in arbitration today, what changes can be expected and which practices should be regarded as pro-arbitration. A central issue is whether, from both legal and economic perspectives, interest claims carry the same weight as principal claims. This raises the question of whether interest claims should be regarded as merely derivative of principal claims or as equal to them. Consequently, it remains crucial to determine what level of reasoning in an arbitral award granting interest should be considered adequate and what criteria should be used to define the scope of it.

Another fundamental question is who the key trendsetters in this area are. Should this role be attributed to the parties, given their economic stake in arbitration? Or to arbitral tribunals as those who are responsible for substantive credibility and due process in arbitration? Perhaps arbitral institutions play the leading role, as neutral dispute resolution service providers aiming to ensure efficient proceedings. Or even, domestic courts given their direct impact on the final stage of arbitration - the recognition and enforcement of arbitral awards.

Beyond these key considerations, the analysis of trends related to interest in arbitration should, for the sake of completeness, take into account several alternative functions of interest, which are used by arbitral institutions to enhance the financial administration of proceedings. These functions, in turn, influence the overall economic outcome of arbitration, particularly in determining the amount in dispute, the costs of arbitration, and, in particular, accrual of interest on arbitration costs.

The following sections examine the trends in the treatment of interest in arbitration.

51. Thomas Walde, *Remedies and Compensation in International Investment Law*, 2(5) Transn'l Disp. Mgmt, 1, 24-25 (2005).

[A] Interest in Practice: Case-Based Observations

To reveal current stance on interest in arbitration, the analysis was conducted on a sample of twenty-one recently published ICC arbitral awards rendered between 2022 and 2024, in which monetary awards were granted (the Analysis).[52] While the sample provides illustrative insights, it is not intended to reflect a statistically comprehensive trend.

In the vast majority of cases, claims on interest have been subject to arbitration, with one exception; i.e., in Case No. 26123/JPA/AJP, interest was neither requested nor granted; therefore, the final award does not include an analysis of this issue.[53]

The Analysis has revealed several general trends and variations, which are outlined below.

[1] Reasoning for Granting Interest

A pattern observed in the selected awards is the frequent lack or even complete absence of reasoning in arbitral awards regarding the grounds for granting interest and the essential elements of its calculation. This pattern has persisted for over three

52. *(1) I.T. International Telecom Marine SRL v. Gignet, INC. and FB Sumarine Partners LLC,* ICC Case No. 27768/PDP, Final Award, 22 November 2024; *(2) Jack Rubenstein CT, LLC v. Naturalena Brands HK Limited a/k/a Naturalena Brands PTY Ltd and Naturalena Brands, Inc.,* ICC Case No. 27550/AB/XZG, 31 July 2024; *(3) Glass-Inspiration GmbH Design + Engineering v. M. G. McGrath, Inc. Glass & Glazing,* ICC Case No. 26994/FS/GL, Award, 29 May 2024; *(4) Sheldon Stein v. The Beneficient Company Group, L.P., Beneficient,* ICC Case No. 27439/PDP, Final Award, 23 April 2024; *(5) Uphealth Holdings, Inc. v. 1. Glocal Healthcare System Private Limited 2. Dr. Syed Sabahat Azim 3. Richa Sana Azim 4. Gautam Chowdhury 5. Meleveetil Damodaran 6. Kimberlite Social Infra Private Limited,* ICC Case No. 27329/PDP, Final Award, 15 March 2024; *(6) Focus Futura Holding Participações S.A. v. Risen Energy Co., Ltd.,* ICC Case No. 26404/PDP, Award, 05 September 2023; *(7) Zycus, Inc. v. Robertshaw Controls Company,* ICC Case No. 26220/PDP, Final Award, 01 September 2023; *(8) Mercedes M. Contreras Moncada v. Vision America International, LLC,* ICC Case No. 26123/JPA/AJP, Final Award, 30 August 2023; *(9) Puritan's Pride, Inc. v. Import IT, Ltd. D/B/A/ Ecmoho,* ICC Case No. 26981/PDP, Final Award, 30 June 2023; *(10) Janaúba i Geração Solar Energia S/A and others v. Trina Solar Energy Development Pte Ltd.,* ICC Case No. 26878/PDP, Final Award, 13 June 2023; *(11) Samsung Electronics Co., Ltd. v. Triller, Inc.,* ICC Case No. 27112/XZG, Final Award, 01 July 2023; *(12) Parque Solar Don Jose. S.A. de C.V., Villanueva Solar. S.A. De C.V. and Parque Solar Villanueva Tres, S.A. de C.V. v. Kino Contractor, S.A. de C.V., Enel Services Mexico, S.A. de C.V. (Formerly Kino Facilites Manager, S.A. de C.V.) and Enel S.P.A,* ICC Case No. 25587/JPA/AJP, Final Award, 28 July 2023; *(13) Polyplas Associates v. Mcneil & Nrm, Inc.,* ICC Case No. 27178/PAR, Final Award, 02 May 2023; *(14) Cardno Middle East Limited v. Central Bank of Iraq,* ICC Case No. 26290/AYZ/ELU, Final Award, 26 February 2023; *(15) Eureka Co. Ltd. v. JV LLC Oil Extraction,* ICC Case No. 26240/AZO/SP, Final Award, 18 October 2022; *(16) Office Create Corporation v. 1. Planet Entertainment, LLC and 2. Steve Grossman,* ICC Case No. 26300/PDP, Final Award, 3 October 2022; *(17) Claimant v. Respondent, ICC Case No. 26678/FS/GL,* Final Award, 30 September 2022; *(18) ACE Group International LLC and ACE Group Bowery LLC v. 225 Bowery LLC,* ICC Case No. 26805/PDP, Final Award, 21 September 2022; *(19) KR Analytical LLC v. Abacus Analytical Systems GmbH,* ICC Case No. 26406/HBH, Final Award, 27 May 2022; *(20) Romie Hospitality LLC v. Aamci & Associates LLC,* ICC Case No. 26476/PDP, Final Award, 02 May 2022; *(21) Protrade Systems, Inc. v. Nanovibronix, Inc.,* ICC Case No. 26098/PDP, Final Award, 15 March 2022 – (Jus Mundi Publications).
53. *Mercedes M. Contreras Moncada v. Vision America International, LLC, supra* n. 52.

decades indicating an apparent trend. In particular, a PwC study analysing nearly 100 tribunal awards over a twenty-five-year period (pre-2000s to 2015) found that only 40% of awards explicitly commented on what the payment of interest represents conceptually. In contrast, the remaining 60% of awards granted interest without explaining why it was awarded or what it was intended to compensate, making it difficult to determine the basis for the chosen interest rate.[54]

The lack of reasoning on the award of interest may be explained by the insufficient pleading of the parties on this issue, which has even been noted by some arbitral tribunals. For example, in the ICC Case No. 26220/PDP, despite the arbitral tribunal's proactive invitation for post-hearing submissions on pre- and post-award interest, including applicable rates, legal and factual details for computation, the tribunal noted that 'the legal arguments of the parties were thin and there was no precise calculation'.[55] Similarly, in the ICC Case No. 26476/PDP, the tribunal found that the statutory rate served as a useful guide, particularly given that 'the parties have not agreed to any other interest rate and have presented no evidence as to what interest rate would best reflect economic reality'.[56]

However, the Analysis has also demonstrated that the majority of awards include at least some consideration of the parties' positions, contractual provisions, determination of the applicable law governing interest, and references to the relevant statutory provisions. While it is also true that most arbitral tribunals avoided analysing interest calculations from an economic or financial perspective, considering themselves bound by contractual or statutory provisions and therefore adhering to them.

[2] Applicable Law

Arbitral tribunals generally recognize that if the parties agree in a contract on interest-related matters, including whether interest is simple or compound, the applicable rate, the accrual period and other relevant aspects, such provisions are binding and will not give rise to disputes in arbitration. Scholars have also observed that such explicit contractual provisions are either uncommon or, even when contracts specifically provide for the award of interest by setting rates and periods in advance, they often fail to adequately address the methodology that arbitral tribunals should adopt in applying interest.[57]

Therefore, one of the key issues that should be dealt with, when arbitral tribunals are deciding on granting interest, is what the legal basis for it shall be. Among the twenty analysed awards, nearly half involve cases where the applicable law coincided with the law of the place of arbitration, resulting in no extensive discussion on applicable law to interest. In other cases, the tribunals ruled that interest should be

54. PwC *Dispute Perspectives: Tribunals' Conflicts on Interest* (2016), 3, https://www.pwc.co.uk/tax/assets/tribunals-conflicts-on-interest-new.pdf (accessed 31 March 2025); Recena Costa, *supra* n. 26, 591-612; Beeley and Walck, *supra* n. 33, at 76.
55. *Zycus, Inc. v. Robertshaw Controls Company*, *supra* n. 52, paras 174, 346.
56. *Romie Hospitality LLC v. Aamci & Associates LLC*, *supra* n. 52, para. 153.
57. Beeley and Walck, *supra* n. 33, at 55.

governed by the law applicable to the merits of the dispute. In particular, the interest was considered according to the laws of Austria (ICC Case No. 26678/FS/GL),[58] Germany (ICC Case No. 26406/HBH),[59] New York (ICC Case No. 26098/PDP),[60] New Jersey (ICC Case No. 26220/PDP),[61] Iraq (ICC Case No. 26290/AYZ/ELU),[62] and Korea (ICC Case No. 26240/AZO/SP).[63] In contrast, in the ICC Case No. 27329/PDP, the arbitral tribunal determined that the law of the place of arbitration, i.e., the law of the State of Illinois, should apply to the interest claim, while Indian law governed the merits.[64] This decision highlights the different approaches to interest claims as substantive or procedural, which may be rooted in civil and common law, respectively.

[3] Applicable Rate

In the majority of cases where the contract provided for a specific rate, the arbitral tribunals applied it. However, it is rare for a contract to contain specific provisions on calculation of interest in event of a breach or dispute. Therefore, reference to statutory interest rates is not infrequent in commercial arbitration.[65] It is also notable that many statutory interest rates are fixed at levels far above market rates.[66]

In 80% of the examined cases, the parties and the arbitral tribunals referred to the statutory rates, indicating that, in the absence of a contractual interest rate, such a rate is to be applied. For example, in the ICC Case No. 26240/AZO/SP, the arbitral tribunal found that the interest rate requested by the claimant was the rate customary in the Euro area, i.e., the rate applied by the European Central Bank to its most recent refinancing operation plus 10%. However, as the disputed sale transaction had no connection to Europe and the parties had not agreed to apply the European Central Bank rate, the tribunal instead referred to the statutory provisions, in particular, to the law applicable to the merits of the dispute, i.e., Korean law.[67]

[4] Simple and Compound Interest

The Analysis showed that, in the vast majority of cases, parties requested simple interest at the statutory rate and, accordingly, arbitral tribunals granted it, being bound by the parties' requests or the applicable law, particularly where contractual or

58. *ICC Case No. 26678/FS/GL, supra* n. 52, para. 284.
59. *KR Analytical LLC v. Abacus Analytical Systems GmbH, supra* n. 52, para. 155.
60. *Protrade Systems, Inc. v. Nanovibronix, Inc.*, ICC Case No. 26098/PDP, *supra* n. 52, para. 184.
61. *Zycus, Inc. v. Robertshaw Controls Company, supra* n. 52, paras 348-350.
62. *Cardno Middle East Limited v. Central Bank of Iraq, supra* n. 52, paras 388, 444.
63. *Eureka Co. Ltd. v. JV LLC Oil Extraction, supra* n. 52, para. 210.
64. *Uphealth Holdings, Inc. v. 1. Glocal Healthcare System Private Limited et al., supra* n. 52, paras 399-402.
65. Recena Costa, *supra* n. 26, at 598.
66. Leonardo Giacchino, Thomas Sturma and Isabella Cotrupi, *What Premium To Use? The Setting Of Post-Judgment Interest Rates Using Commercial Rates In Investment Arbitration*, 5(1) JDIA 1, 11 (2018).
67. *Eureka Co. Ltd. v. JV LLC Oil Extraction, supra* n. 52, para. 210.

statutory guidance was clear. Consequently, simple interest was awarded in 90% of examined cases, with compound interest granted in only 10%.

This aligns with previous findings, as outlined in §11.03[A][4] above, that despite the prevalence of compounding in commercial transactions, simple interest remains the norm in most domestic statutes and tribunals are reluctant to award compound interest for no apparent reason.[68] At the same time, scholars tend to agree that compound interest should be the norm and is better suited to achieving the remedial goals of interest awards, regardless of whether interest awards are conceived in terms of compensation or restitution.[69]

However, for the sake of complete analysis, it should be noted that the PwC's research previously showed a different trend, with arbitral tribunals increasingly agreeing on the issue of compounding, whereas before 2005, the split between cases awarding simple and compound interest was 50:50; between 2010 and 2015, the split shifted to 13:87.[70]

Differences in observations could be explained by a lack of established practice resulting in different developments within a particular region or industry over a certain period of time. In this respect, two recent cases illustrate different approaches taken by the arbitral tribunals in exercising their discretion to deal with claims for compound interest. For example, in the ICC Case No. 27439/PDP, the arbitral tribunal noted that the claimant requested compound interest, which has historically been disfavoured in Delaware, but is not prohibited. The tribunal also noted that Delaware courts have in the past awarded compound interest on an equitable basis, when necessary to fairly compensate the prevailing party. Therefore, the tribunal found that 'compound interest is a more accurate mean of measuring the time value of money' and awarded post-judgment interest on the entire judgment amount from the date of the judgment at a rate of 5% above the Federal Reserve discount rate in effect on the date of the judgment, compounded quarterly in accordance with the statutory formula under Delaware law.[71]

In contrast, in the ICC Case No. 26878/PDP, the tribunal declined to grant compound interest at the statutory rate, stating that the parties to the dispute had not chosen to resolve the dispute in the local courts but in arbitration and therefore there was no reason why a statutory interest rate adopted to apply to actions in the local courts should apply to an international arbitration simply because it was seated in that state. Therefore, the tribunal considered it more appropriate to apply the interest rate in accordance with its interpretation of the contract and to confine itself to awarding

68. Recena Costa, *supra* n. 26, at 593.
69. *Ibid.*, at 610; Frederick Alexander Mann, *Compound Interest as an Item of Damage in International Law*, US Davis Law Review, 577, 578 (1988); Gotanda, *supra* n. 37; Beeley and Walck, *supra* n. 33, at 58.
70. PwC *Dispute Perspectives: Tribunals' Conflicts on Interest* (2016), 3, https://www.pwc.co.uk/tax/assets/tribunals-conflicts-on-interest-new.pdf (accessed 31 March 2025).
71. *Sheldon Stein v. The Beneficient Company Group, L.P., Beneficient, supra* n. 52, para. 9.15.

the interest intended to compensate a party for the time value of money, rather than to impose a penalty.[72]

[5] *Pre-award and Post-award Interest*

Arbitral tribunals usually consider pre- and post-award interest separately. The Analysis has revealed that both types of interest were granted in 74% of cases, post-award interest alone was granted in 16% and pre-award interest alone in 10%.

Exceptions include the ICC Case No. 26220/PDP, where the tribunal, in the absence of sufficient justification by the parties, used the law applicable to the merits, the law of New Jersey, which led to the recognition of the post-award interest, while no pre-award interest was granted, as the tribunal found that the claimant had insufficiently established entitlement to it.[73]

In contrast, in the ICC Case No. 27329/PDP, the arbitral tribunal dismissed the request for pre-award interest on future revenue, reasoning that it could result in double recovery to the claimant. Instead, the tribunal exercised its discretion to grant simple post-award interest, referring to it as a general practice in international arbitration.[74]

Another notable variation was the granting of post-award interest until either the amount awarded is paid in full or 'the entry of a judgment confirming the final award by a court of competent jurisdiction' as the arbitral tribunal decided in the ICC Cases No. 27550/AB/XZG and No. 27768/PDP.

[6] *Interest on Fees and Costs*

It should be noted that arbitral tribunals generally grant interest on the amounts of fees and costs, upon the respective request of a party. However, in the majority of cases, the parties did not request interest on these amounts, resulting in 60% of cases in which interest on fees and costs was not awarded.

For example, in the ICC Cases No. 27112/XZG[75] and No. 26098/PDP,[76] the arbitral tribunals found that since the claimant had not requested interest on fees and costs, no interest should be awarded.

In contrast, in some instances, the issue of awarding interest on fees and costs may be limited by statutory provisions, as in the ICC Case No. 26290/AYZ/ELU, the arbitral tribunal denied the claimant's request for interest on the arbitration and legal costs, finding that in this case interest should be awarded under Iraqi law, which provides that 'interest is equivalent to damages for delay in payment'. The tribunal

72. *Janaúba i Geração Solar Energia S/A and others v. Trina Solar Energy Development Pte Ltd.*, *supra* n. 52, para. 388.
73. *Zycus, Inc. v. Robertshaw Controls Company*, *supra* n. 52, paras 348-349.
74. *Uphealth Holdings, Inc. v. 1. Glocal Healthcare System Private Limited et al.*, *supra* n. 52, paras 399-402.
75. *Samsung Electronics Co., Ltd. v. Triller, Inc.*, *supra* n. 52, para. 172.
76. *Protrade Systems, Inc. v. Nanovibronix, Inc.*, ICC Case No. 26098/PDP, *supra* n. 52, para. 184.

noted that the claimant had not shown that Iraqi law would apply to the delay in payment (if any) of ICC arbitration costs and legal costs awarded by an arbitral tribunal, nor had it referred to any other provision of Iraqi law that would give the tribunal the power to award interest on costs.[77]

[7] Key Observations on Current Interest Practices

The Analysis highlights that disputes over interest in arbitration are multifaceted, involving a number of controversial positions on the questions of: (i) whether simple or compound interest should be applied, (ii) the interest rate, and (iii) accrual periods, based on the determination of the applicable law and interpretation of the contract. Although the observations from the analysed sample indicate a predominance of the statutory effect in calculation of interest, which is mostly simple, the economic reality suggests a shift towards the preference of compound interest. It is evident that unstable economies and economic market fluctuations no longer justify the use of statutory fixed interest, although it is predictable and traditionally used. The majority of the analysed arbitral awards reflect the understanding and willingness of arbitral tribunals to consider the application of compound interest upon agreement of the parties, which we believe is also an indication to parties to include such provisions in the contracts. It may therefore be expected that arbitral practice will continue to evolve in response to the challenges of economic and financial realities in recent years.

[B] The Role of Arbitral Institutions in Harmonizing Approaches to Awarding Interest in Arbitration

Variability in approaches to awarding interest in international arbitration raises the question of whether harmonization is feasible and what is the most appropriate place to ensure harmonization. Despite the widely recognized transnational nature of arbitration, seemingly straightforward issues remain subject to domestic legal regulations, creating contradictions when decisions must be taken and enforced on a broader international scale. For instance, it remains uncertain whether the determination of interest in arbitral awards shall be governed by the provisions of substantive law being inspired by civil law, or falls within the scope of procedural law, following the common law approach.[78]

The transnational nature of arbitration suggests that a reasonable international party would at the first place refer to the contract, as contractual provisions are unlikely to be disputed unless found to be contrary to public policy, particularly the international public policy of the country. Uncertainty arises, however, where the contract is silent on interest and, therefore, where interest has not been expressly waived, it may be considered appropriate to refer to the applicable law. This often involves the application of conflict of laws principles which, in an extreme hypothetical scenario,

77. *Cardno Middle East Limited v. Central Bank of Iraq, supra* n. 52, paras 388, 443-444.
78. Secomb, *supra* n. 47, paras 2.187-2.191, 3.27.

could lead to an overlap between civil law and common law approaches – each attributing different legal and economic characteristics to interest. Such a situation lacks transparency and predictability for international arbitration parties, demonstrating that the law governing the merits of a dispute or the law of the place of arbitration may not always be fully equipped to regulate interest.

As Mark Beeley and Richard E. Walck noted, 'presuming that there is no express provision in the clause itself, the next logical place to look for a power is in the arbitration rules selected (presuming of course that the proceedings are not entirely ad hoc)'.[79] Julian DM Lew and Matthew Secomb unilaterally agreed that 'a solution to the uncertainty associated with interest in international arbitration would be for each of the major arbitral institutions to include an article dealing with interest in their rules'.[80] This observation emphasizes the role of arbitral institutions as potential trendsetters in the development of guidelines for granting interest on sums awarded to parties in arbitration. Given the broad discretion that arbitrators frequently exercise in awarding interest, institutional rules may serve as a critical framework that balances predictability with the flexibility necessary to accommodate case-specific considerations.

Institutional arbitration rules can be broadly categorized into two groups based on their approach to awarding interest in arbitral awards.

The first group includes institutions whose rules are silent on the issue of awarding interest. These are: *(i)* institutions where the rules refer to interest only in terms of procedural or financial context, i.e., not related to granting interest on sums awarded in arbitration, such as the CCIR Rules,[81] FAI Rules,[82] ICC Rules,[83] ICAC Ukraine Rules,[84] ITOTAM Rules,[85] and Swiss Rules;[86] and *(ii)* institutions whose rules are entirely silent on the matter of interest, such as the DIS Rules,[87] GIAC Rules,[88] HKIAC Rules,[89] PCA Rules,[90] SCC Rules,[91] and VIAC Rules.[92] The absence of express provisions on awarding interest in these rules does not exclude the award of interest per se, but it gives greater weight to the applicable law and the contractual provisions agreed by the parties.

79. Beeley and Walck, *supra* n. 33, at 53.
80. Secomb, *supra* n. 47, para. 3.27; Julian DM Lew, *Interest on Money Awards in International Arbitration*, Making Commercial Law: Essays in Honour of Roy Goode, 543, 562 (Clarendon Press 1997).
81. Arbitration Rules of the Court of International Commercial Arbitration of the Chamber of Commerce and Industry of Romania 2025 (CCIR Rules).
82. Arbitration Institute of the Finland Chamber of Commerce 2024 (FAI Rules).
83. International Court of Arbitration of the International Chamber of Commerce Arbitration Rules 2021 (ICC Rules).
84. International Commercial Arbitration Court at the Ukrainian Chamber of Commerce and Industry 2025 (ICAC Ukraine Rules).
85. Istanbul Chamber of Commerce Arbitration and Mediation Center Arbitration Rules 2021 (ITOTAM Rules).
86. Swiss International Arbitration Rules 2021 (Swiss Rules).
87. German Arbitration Institute Rules 2018 (DIS Rules).
88. Georgian International Arbitration Centre Rules 2024 (GIAC Rules).
89. Hong Kong International Arbitration Centre Rules 2024 (HKIAC Rules).
90. Permanent Court of Arbitration Rules 2012 (PCA Rules).
91. Arbitration Institute of the Stockholm Chamber of Commerce Rules 2023 (SCC Rules).
92. Vienna International Arbitral Centre Rules 2021 (VIAC Rules).

The second group includes institutions whose rules explicitly address the issue of interest and grant arbitral tribunals express authority to award interest. Institutions in this group, including the AIAC Rules,[93] LCIA Rules,[94] SIAC Rules,[95] and WIPO Rules,[96] provide arbitrators with a range of discretionary powers, in particular:

- authority to order either simple or compound interest;
- power to award interest on any sum awarded against a party (as provided in the LCIA, WIPO, and AIAC Rules, whereas the SIAC Rules refer to 'any amount which is the subject of the arbitration');
- discretion to set the interest rate 'without being bound by legal rates of interest', as stated in the WIPO Rules. Similar provisions exist in the LCIA Rules, which additionally clarify that tribunals are not bound by the 'rates of interest practiced by any state court or other legal authority'. At the same time, the AIAC and SIAC Rules simply authorize arbitral tribunals to define the rate and determine such rest as they consider appropriate;
- authority to determine the period for which interest shall be paid, e.g., the WIPO and SIAC Rules grant tribunals discretion to set an appropriate period for interest payments. Similarly, the LCIA Rules provide this discretion but impose a restriction that the period must not extend beyond the date on which the award is complied with. The AIAC Rules adopt a comparable approach, specifying that interest shall accrue only until the date of payment of the whole or any part of the awarded sum.

To the second group, the ICDR Rules could also be included, as they explicitly grant arbitrators discretion to award either simple or compound interest. Furthermore, the ICDR Rules introduce additional considerations, requiring tribunals to take into account contractual provisions and applicable law. Moreover, unless the parties agree otherwise or the applicable law dictates, the ICDR Rules provide a default waiver of any right to punitive, exemplary, or similar damages.[97]

It could also be argued that institutional approaches to the question of the definition of the interest to be awarded by arbitral tribunals are influenced by an institution's adherence to a particular legal tradition. Institutions based in jurisdictions with a strong civil law tradition tend to remain silent on interest, as they consider it a substantive legal matter to be determined by the applicable law. Conversely, institutions with common law influences often empower tribunals with express authority to award interest.

This interplay between institutional rules and national legal traditions is evident in the similarities between some institutional and domestic arbitration rules. For example, the English Arbitration Act provides that, unless the parties agree otherwise,

93. Asian International Arbitration Centre Rules 2023 (AIAC Rules), Rule 6(i).
94. London Court of International Arbitration Rules 2020 (LCIA Rules), Art. 26(4).
95. Singapore International Arbitration Centre Rules 2025 (SIAC Rules), Art. 51(5).
96. World Intellectual Property Organisation Arbitration and Mediation Centre Rules 2021 (WIPO Rules), Art. 62.
97. International Centre for Dispute Resolution Arbitration Rules 2021 (ICDR Rules), Art. 31(4-5).

the arbitral tribunal has authority to award simple or compound interest (i) 'in respect of any period up to the date of the award' and (ii) 'from the date of the award (or any later date) until payment'.[98] Despite these influences, arbitral institutions are not bound to follow the approach of the jurisdiction in which they are incorporated. This certain degree of flexibility allows international arbitral institutions to act as key players in harmonizing the regulation of interest in arbitration, potentially bridging the gap between different legal traditions.

If arbitral institutions were to take a more proactive role in harmonizing approaches to the award of interest, one possible way forward would be to develop guidelines that enhance discretion of arbitral tribunals while ensuring greater transparency in interest-related decisions. A critical component of such harmonization would be to encourage arbitral tribunals to provide reasoned justifications for interest awards. This would include elaboration on the choice between simple and compound interest, the selection of interest rates, the relevant accrual periods and any other elements that affect the economic impact of awarding of interest.

Greater transparency in granting interest in arbitration would serve a number of purposes, including: (i) ensuring greater predictability of arbitral outcomes, thereby increasing confidence of the parties claiming interest, (ii) facilitating the cross-border enforceability of arbitral awards by evidencing that awarding interest is founded on reasoned decision-making rather than arbitral tribunals' discretion exercised in an unpredictable manner, and, finally, (iii) promoting greater consistency in arbitral practice by reducing the risk of conflicting approaches among different tribunals.

While complete harmonization of the regulation on granting interest across arbitral institutions may be seen as an ambitious goal, incremental steps towards a certain level of standardization could have a significant impact. For instance, this could include introduction of soft-law tools setting out best practices for awarding interest. In addition, empirical research on the awarding of interest in international arbitration could contribute to further development of institutional rules to ensure that they remain in line with evolving commercial realities.

[C] Alternative Institutional Perspective on Interest in Arbitration

As mentioned above, some institutional rules refer to interest only in a procedural or financial context. Therefore, to provide a comprehensive analysis of the role of interest in arbitration from an institutional perspective, the following aspects should be considered.

The alternative procedural roles of interest in institutional arbitration include: (i) consideration of interest for calculation of the amount in dispute and subsequently for calculation of arbitration costs, and (ii) accrual of interest directly on arbitration costs.

Regarding the first aspect, a widely accepted approach in institutional rules is that arbitration costs are generally calculated based on the amount in dispute. However, the weight given to interest claims may vary in correlation to the amount in dispute.

98. English Arbitration Act 1996, section 49(3) and (4).

For instance, the Swiss and FAI Rules explicitly provide that interest claims shall not be taken into account for determining the amount in dispute.[99] However, if the interest claims exceed the principal amount claimed, the interest claims alone shall be considered in calculating the amount in dispute for that claim. Conversely, the alternative approach exists whereby the amount in dispute is determined as the sum of claims for the principal amount and the accrued interest at the time of filing the claim. This approach is reflected in the ICAC Ukraine Rules.[100]

A different approach is seen in the ICC, ICDR, ITOTAM, and CCIR Rules, which, in the context of expedited proceedings only, explicitly exclude interest from quantification of the amount in dispute,[101] which may be explained by the fact that expedited arbitration assumes that the reasoning of awards should be as concise as possible, while ensuring clarity and comprehensibility. Therefore, awarding interest in the expedited proceedings is not expected to give rise to additional deliberations.

The possibility to exclude interest when determining the amount in dispute may also serve to balance the financial burden on parties while ensuring adequate remuneration for arbitrators. The reason for not taking the amount of interest into account when quantifying the amount in dispute often lies in the fact that arbitral tribunals primarily decide on the merits of the dispute, whereas decisions on interest are typically derivative. In practice, the decision to award interest tends to be made automatically in favour of the prevailing party, in line with the scope and amount of the interest claimed. However, a shift in arbitral practice could occur if interest claims were treated on an equal level with principal claims, with tribunals undertaking a substantial analysis of the quantification and methodology for determining interest. Such development could lead to a gradual trend towards including interest as a component of the total amount in dispute, which would subsequently increase the cost of arbitration.

Notably, the ICC, ITOTAM and CCIR Rules maintain a certain degree of flexibility by not explicitly addressing this issue in the rules for regular (not expedited) arbitrations. This allows to determine the amount in dispute upon case-by-case analysis. This approach recognizes that interest claims may vary in importance and require different levels of consideration.

With regard to the second aspect, the question of interest on arbitration costs remains rather controversial. In practice, arbitration costs are normally deposited by a party with an arbitral institution at the beginning of the proceedings and allocated by an arbitral institution at the end of the proceedings to cover the arbitrators' fees, institutional services and costs of arbitration, with any remaining funds being reimbursed to the parties. A hypothetical scenario arises where, if these funds were not held by the arbitral institution but instead invested by a party or an arbitrator, they could generate a financial benefit. However, arbitral institutions must ensure smooth financial administration, including guaranteeing proper remuneration for arbitral tribunals

99. Swiss Rules, *supra* n. 86, Art. 2.2; FAI Rules, *supra* n. 82, Art. 2.2(b).
100. ICAC Ukraine Rules, *supra* n. 84, Art. 15(1).
101. ICC Note to Parties and Arbitral Tribunals on the Conduct of the Arbitration under the ICC Rules of Arbitration (2021), para. 131 (ICC Note); ICDR Rules, *supra* n. 97, Art. 1(4), ITOTAM Rules, *supra* n. 85, Annex IV(1), CCIR Rules Annex V Art. 1(2).

at the end of the proceedings. In addition, most arbitral institutions operate as non-profit organizations, which also affects their treatment of deposited arbitration costs.

While most institutions adopt the same approach to interest on deposits, two different frameworks can be observed in the institutional rules. The first one, employed by the ICC, Swiss and FAI Rules, explicitly states that amounts paid as deposits or advances on costs do not yield interest for the parties or arbitrators. The second, followed by the LCIA and SIAC Rules, adopts a slightly different standpoint. Thus, the LCIA Rules provide that the advance payment for costs shall be the property of the LCIA, to be disbursed or otherwise applied by the LCIA in accordance with the LCIA Rules and invested having regard to the interests of the LCIA.[102] Similarly, the SIAC Rules provide that all deposits towards the costs of the arbitration shall be made to and held by the SIAC and any interest which may accrue on such deposits shall be retained by the SIAC.[103]

However, it is important to note that the absence of an explicit reference does not mean that claims relating to interest on deposits or advances on costs are excluded. A party may still submit such claims to be compensated by the other party under the general provisions as indicated above in §11.03[A][6] above. This possibility is explicitly addressed in the LCIA Rules, which provide that the party effecting the further advance payment for costs may request the arbitral tribunal to make an order to recover that amount as a debt immediately due and payable to that party by the defaulting party, together with any interest.[104]

Concerning the economic interests of arbitrators, it should be assumed that these are safeguarded by the right to request advances on fees. For example, the ICC Rules provide that advances on fees may be granted upon arbitrator's request and the completion of certain milestones in the arbitration, such as holding a case management conference in expedited procedure cases, establishment of the terms of reference, issuance of a partial award or holding a major hearing.[105]

The above analysis shows that interest in arbitration serves several procedural and financial functions that should not be overlooked, given their economic and commercial implications. Institutional rules frame the procedural role of interest, which influences calculation of the amount in dispute and the costs of arbitration, while the common objective remains to ensure a balance between the financial impact on the parties, the appropriate remuneration of arbitrators and the overall efficiency of the arbitration.

[D] Recognition and Enforcement of Interest Awards

International law, including the New York Convention on the Recognition and Enforcement of Arbitral Awards, does not establish a special regulation for the

102. LCIA Rules, *supra* n. 94, Art. 24(2).
103. SIAC Rules, *supra* n. 95, section IX, Art. 56.6.
104. LCIA Rules, *supra* n. 94, Art. 24(7).
105. ICC Note, *supra* n. 101, paras 180, 186.

recognition and enforcement of arbitral awards, in part of granting interest.[106] Therefore, such awards should be enforceable according to the general rules.

Reflecting the global shift towards arbitration-friendly policies, the prevailing trend in most jurisdictions is strongly pro-arbitration and pro-enforcement. This approach also extends to the enforcement of awards granting interest, for instance, reflected in the development of the practices in the United Kingdom and Ukraine.

In the United Kingdom, a turning point was marked with the enactment of the Arbitration Act 1996. Prior to this, under the Late Payment of Commercial Debts (Interest) Act 1998,[107] arbitrators were only empowered to award simple interest up to the date of the award. They had no authority to grant post-award interest except at the same rate as a judgment debt.[108]

Following the introduction of the Arbitration Act 1996, parties were granted significantly greater discretion regarding the tribunal's powers to award interest. The Act allows parties to agree on the tribunal's authority in awarding interest. In the absence of such an agreement, the tribunal has default powers to award simple or compound interest for any period, at any rate and with such rests as it deems justified, thereby formally recognizing the legitimacy of both pre-award and post-award interest up until payment.[109]

In the United Kingdom, a further trend has also been observed in relation to the enforcement of interest awarded in arbitration, which has been linked to the impact of international sanctions. This was evident in the Court of Appeal's decision to uphold the High Court's judgment in the case *Ministry of Defence & Support for Armed Forces of the Islamic Republic of Iran v. International Military Services Ltd*. In this case, the EU sanctions legislation was interpreted to the effect that no interest should accrue on the amount of a debt during the period when sanctions prevented the payment of such debt upon an arbitral award.[110] This case demonstrates the impact of external regulatory frameworks on the accrual and enforcement of interest in arbitral awards.

In Ukraine, local courts have shown a gradual transformation in their approach to post-award interest between 2015 and 2019. Prior to 2019, Ukrainian courts typically refused to enforce post-award interest, reasoning that courts lacked authority to intervene in arbitration and arbitral awards on the merits.

For instance, in 2015, the High Specialized Court of Ukraine ruled that when granting enforcement of an award, modifying the amount of interest to be recovered in a manner different from that specified in the foreign court decision was erroneous.[111]

106. Convention on the Recognition and Enforcement of Foreign Arbitral Awards (10 June 1958), 330 U.N.T.S. 38.
107. Late Payment of Commercial Debts (Interest) Act 1998, section 1(1).
108. Judgments Act 1838, section 17.
109. English Arbitration Act 1996, section 49.
110. *Ministry of Defence & Support for Armed Forces of the Islamic Republic of Iran v. International Military Services Ltd,* England and Wales Court of Appeal (Civil Division) Case No. A4/2019/2690, Judgment, EWCA Civ 145 (2020).
111. *Bank of Cyprus Public Limited Company v. [Entity] on recognition and enforcement of the LCIA award,* Decision of the High Specialized Court of Ukraine, Case No. 6-47255св14, 30 September 2015, http://reyestr.court.gov.ua/Review/52807508 (accessed 31 March 2025, translated from Ukrainian to English by authors).

During the period of 2015-2017, the courts have reconsidered several times the decision on the recognition and enforcement of the GAFTA award in part of granting of the compound interest in the case *Nibulon SA v. PJSC Rise,* and following the ruling of the Supreme Court further restricted the enforcement of the award of interest, reasoning that delegating the right to calculate interest to the party or state enforcement officers conflicted with Ukraine's principles of justice. The courts held that such delegation constituted intervention in the contractual relations established by the arbitration clause and, therefore, violated public order of Ukraine.[112]

In contrast, there has been a significant shift following the implementation of the pro-arbitration reform that was initiated in 2017, which in part of interest accrual on arbitral awards entered into force in 2019.[113] However, already in 2018, the Supreme Court adopted a new approach that also affected the aforementioned case of *Nibulon SA v. PJSC Rise,* recognizing that there was a gap in the law in part of calculation of interest during the period between the arbitral award and its enforcement. The Court held that determining a procedure for calculating a post-award interest would preserve a reasonable balance between the creditor's private interest and the public interest in enforcing the award. The Court further reasoned that since the accrual of interest until the debtor fulfils its obligations is not explicitly prohibited by law, post-award interest should generally be recognized and enforced.[114]

Therefore, the specific economic nature of awards on interest, particularly the absence of a fixed amount due and the use of a formula for interest accrual, has sometimes been equated with a lack of certainty or even finality of the award. This has led national courts in some jurisdictions to deny enforcement. However, a noticeable recent trend is the replacement of such restrictive practices with pro-arbitration approaches, recognizing the possibility of delegating implementation of the interest formula set in arbitral awards to domestic courts.

§11.04 CONCLUSIONS

Examining the legal and computational foundations of interest in arbitration reveals that interest is far more than a technical addition to awards; it is a fundamental mechanism for providing financial justice and safeguarding the economic value of compensation over time. This article has highlighted the important role interest plays in arbitral awards, both as a reflection of economic value of time and as a mechanism

112. *Nibulon SA v. PJSC Rise*, Case No. 759/16206/14-ц, Decision of the High Specialized Court of Ukraine, 23 September 2015, http://reyestr.court.gov.ua/Review/52411892 (accessed 1 October 2025), Decision of the Supreme Court of Ukraine, 26 October 2016, https://www.reyestr.court.gov.ua/Review/63793441 (accessed 1 October 2025), Decision of the Kyiv Court of Appeal, 23 February 2017, https://reyestr.court.gov.ua/Review/65040970 (accessed 31 March 2025, translated from Ukrainian to English by authors).
113. Civil Procedure Code of Ukraine (as amended on 1 January 2019), Art. 479(4-5); Elena Koch, *Transnational Recognition and Enforcement of Arbitral Awards*, 400, 142 (Odesa Simeks Print 2021, translated from Ukrainian to English by authors).
114. *Nibulon SA v. PJSC Rise*, Case No. 759/16206/14-ц, Decision of the Supreme Court of Ukraine, 15 May 2018, http://reyestr.court.gov.ua/Review/74630452 (accessed 31 March 2025, translated from Ukrainian to English by authors).

towards timely compliance. While the legal authority to award interest originates in the first place from party agreements, tribunals often must bridge contractual gaps by drawing upon applicable laws, procedural rules, and general principles.

From selecting the appropriate rate and accrual period to deciding between simple and compound interest, tribunals are tasked with balancing legal traditions, economic realities, and specific circumstances of each case. Notably, even in jurisdictions with strict prohibitions (e.g., Sharia law systems), tribunals increasingly harmonize religious doctrines with commercial realities, prioritizing party expectations. This practice emphasizes the adaptability of international arbitration in balancing diverse legal traditions while ensuring economically reasonable remedies.

The current trends in shaping interest in arbitration are developing on the basis of the economic background, which assigns significant economic value to arbitral awards granting interest and at the same time, within the legal framework, which limits the claiming of interest, the consideration of interest claims and the enforcement of interest awards. A chain reaction has been observed, leading to uncertainty regarding interest claims.

First of all, interest claims, being different in their nature in terms of civil law and common law legal traditions, may be considered a part of substantive or procedural law, contributing to uncertainty in determining the applicable law. Notwithstanding this, interest claims have traditionally been regarded as derivative of principal claims, particularly given their legal composition. This is reflected in the statutory provisions of most jurisdictions, which by default provide for simple interest and fix interest rates without encouraging any analysis of contemporary economic realities and their impact on the parties. In addition, the immunity of arbitral awards and the likelihood of equating interest provisions with imperative norms forming part of a state's public policy may create some confusion, in particular among: (i) parties that may be uncertain as to whether they are entitled to claim interest that is economically justified and not merely provided for by the applicable domestic law, (ii) arbitral tribunals that may be unclear as to the scope of their discretionary powers, if any, and (iii) domestic courts that may struggle to balance pro-arbitration recognition and enforcement of arbitral awards with public policy considerations.

In an attempt to resolve this equation with multiple variables, parties and arbitrators appear to have developed a risk-free approach – limiting interest claims to what is unarguably grantable, namely, simple interest at the statutory rate. As a result, a prevailing lack of reasoning has emerged in both requests for interest and the corresponding arbitral awards. Arbitral tribunals, bound by a party's requests, often refrain from engaging in substantive analysis, while parties tend to perceive interest claims as merely an extension of the 'costs follow the event' principle, despite the fact that interest claims should not be equated with claims for reimbursement of costs.

Economic reality, however, argues in favour of treating interest claims separately and on an equal footing with principal claims. In light of unstable global economic market, long-term multi-billion disputes could give rise to relatively independent interest claims. Given these circumstances, there is a widely held belief that leading arbitral institutions are well-positioned to introduce soft-law instruments to clarify the extent of arbitral tribunals' discretion to grant interest in line with economic realities.

A first step in such regulation could involve encouraging parties to incorporate clear contractual provisions on interest accrual in the event of a dispute. The second step would be to guide arbitral tribunals to proactively require parties to justify their interest claims from both legal and economic perspectives. Finally, tribunals should be encouraged to render reasoned awards on interest, explicitly recognizing its economic significance. Even in the absence of sufficient justification by the parties, tribunals could clarify that interest may be granted upon an appropriate request, thereby enhancing the completeness of the award and providing an educative function. Notably, there are already indications of such practices being implemented. The analysis has shown that arbitral tribunals generally recognize the importance of interest awards and show an increasing willingness to address issues such as compound interest, periods and rates based on the contractual provisions and taking into account the conditions of the economic environment.

At the level of domestic courts, a pro-arbitration trend has been steadily developing, reducing the scope of unpredictable outcomes for transnational parties. It is therefore reasonable to expect that contemporary arbitration is now well-equipped to process interest claims in alignment with economic market conditions – provided that all relevant stakeholders cooperate in ensuring a coherent and forward-thinking approach.

CHAPTER 12

Paving the Golden Path: The Road Beyond the Monetary Gold Problem in Investor-State Disputes

Clara Grønborg Juul & Julie Alexandra Bech Nosch[*]

§12.01 INTRODUCTION

Investor-state disputes have always been fraught with legal complexity, but few doctrines pose as thorny a challenge as the 'Monetary Gold problem.' The problem arises when a court or an arbitral tribunal ('tribunal') is called upon to adjudicate a dispute that by its very subject matter requires passing judgment on the rights and obligations of a state not party to the dispute. In such instances, the tribunal risks either straying beyond the contours of its jurisdiction or unduly restricting a party's access to legal recourse. Far from a theoretical curiosity, the Monetary Gold problem has arisen in numerous disputes concerning subject matters ranging from alleged conspiracies on snow crab fishing in the Barents Sea[1] to the territorial status of Crimea.[2]

At the time of writing, a ceasefire between Ukraine and Russia is being negotiated, but the conflict between Russia and the West continues unabated in the global economic sphere, where private entities on both sides are targeted through extensive sanctions. When such measures are enforced against foreign investors, they potentially violate the rights and protections accorded to investors under international investment treaties. States on either side frame this conduct as lawful, using the principles and

---

* This article was written by Clara Grønborg Juul and Julie A.B. Nosch in their personal capacity. The opinions expressed in this chapter are the authors' own and do not reflect the view of Gorrissen Federspiel or the Danish Defence Command.

1. *Peteris Pildegovics and SIA North Star v. Kingdom of Norway*, ICSID Case No. ARB/20/11, Award of 22 December 2023.

2. *JSC DTEK Krymenergo v. Russian Federation*, PCA Case No. 2018-41, Award of 1 November 2023.

defences accepted under public international law. Nowhere is this more present than in the rhetoric employed by the Russian Federation in its targeted measures against foreign investors from 'unfriendly countries'.[3]

This sets the stage for the Monetary Gold problem: Should an aggrieved investor commence arbitration proceedings against Russia for breaches of the rights enshrined in an investment treaty, Russia, for its part, may argue that its actions amount to lawful countermeasures under customary international law, a justified response to what it deems illicit sanctions. The result is a jurisdictional Gordian knot. If a tribunal entertains Russia's countermeasures defence, it must assess the legality of Western sanctions, veering dangerously close to ruling on the rights and conduct of a state not party to the arbitration. Yet if tribunals refuse to engage, either the aggrieved investors or Russia may find their right to be heard and legal rights rendered meaningless as geopolitics fray. Either course of action not only poses numerous pitfalls for challenges against the award but also challenges the general framework of international investment law.

Accordingly, this article examines the growing relevance of the Monetary Gold problem in investor-state dispute settlement and how tribunals may address this procedural deadlock. First, the article sets the scene of the regulatory framework in which the Monetary Gold problem may unfold. Second, the origins and depth of the Monetary Gold problem are analysed. Third, a proposal on arbitral case strategies is presented, based on an analysis of how tribunals have sought to navigate this procedural minefield – some with questionable ingenuity, others with considerable difficulty.

The purpose of the article is not to prescribe a definitive legal approach on how a tribunal should address the Monetary Gold problem, as this will inherently depend on the specific case at hand, but rather to offer strategic solutions to a pending procedural deadlock. To contextualise the Monetary Gold problem and illustrate how these strategies may play out, the article considers a Russian countermeasure defence for potential infringements on the rights of investors from 'unfriendly states'. The focus on Russia in the context of violations of Bilateral Investment Treaties is also warranted by the numerous cases pending against Russia. However, it is noted that other states may also be acting in violation of other bilateral investment treaties amid the ongoing economic conflict, potentially giving rise to investor-state arbitrations.

§12.02 SETTING THE SCENE OF THE MONETARY GOLD PROBLEM

This section unfolds in three parts. First, a general introduction to the regulatory framework of international investment law. Second, an overview of the broader 'countersanctions' employed by Russia, which may trigger investor-state arbitrations.

---

3. The term 'unfriendly countries' is used by Russia on the official lists stipulating the foreign states who have imposed restrictions of varying characters on Russia, *see* Jess Daly, 'Russia Creates New "Unfriendly Countries" List, Targeting Morality' (UNITED24 Media, 2 October 2024) https://united24media.com/world/russia-creates-new-unfriendly-countries-list-targeting-morality-2749 (accessed 1 October 2025).

Third, a description of the interplay between investment treaties and countermeasures under customary international law.

[A] The Regulatory Framework

Modern international investment law has developed by way of international treaties.[4] Today, more than 2,200 known bilateral investment treaties (BITs) are in force between various states.[5] The applicable law governing BITs is international law.[6] Although BITs are subject to independent negotiations and thus vary in structure and substantive provisions, they are remarkably similar in their content and protections.[7] Furthermore, many of the substantive protections of a BIT can be perceived as a codification of customary international law, namely the regulation of expropriation.[8] Beyond this basic protection, there is also a strong tendency for states to provide for broader protections in their BIT to attract foreign investments, for instance, provisions mandating host states to afford fair and equitable treatment (FET) to investors,[9] honouring legitimate expectations that may have influenced investment decisions.[10] FET provisions are prevalent in nearly all BITs.[11] Similarly, most BITs confer the right to Most Favourable Nation (MFN) treatment, generally granting foreign investors the right to receive the same level of treatment as other foreign investors and/or import more favourable provisions from other BITs the host state has entered.[12]

Notably, Russia has entered more than eighty BITs, including with a number of 'unfriendly countries', such as Ukraine, Canada and the United Kingdom, and several EU Member States like Germany, France, Finland and Denmark.[13] In many cases, Russian BITs provide an option of arbitration under the auspice of the Stockholm

4. Jörg Kammerhofer, *International Investment Law and Legal Theory: Expropriation and the Fragmentation of Sources*, 11 (Cambridge University Press 2021).
5. UN Trade and Development (UNCTAD) *Investment Policy Hub* (13 May 2025) https://investmentpolicy.unctad.org/international-investment-agreements/countries/57/denmark (accessed 1 October 2025).
6. Josefa Sicard-Mirabal and Yves Derains, *Introduction to Investor-State Arbitration*, 42 (Kluwer Law International 2018).
7. Maximilian Clasmeier, *Arbitral Awards as Investments: Treaty Interpretation and the Dynamics of International Investment Law*, 26 (Kluwer Law International 2016).
8. Ole Espersen et al., *Folkeret*, 210 (Christian Ejlers' Forlag 2003); Noah Rubins and Azizjon Nazarov, *Investment Treaties and the Russian Federation: Baiting the Bear?* 9 Business Law International, 100, 101 (2008).
9. Clasmeier, *supra* n. 7, 29 f.
10. *Ibid.*, 30.
11. Rubins and Nazarov, *supra* n. 8, 101.
12. Notably, there are different types of MFN clauses spanning in scope, and whether or not they extend to procedural aspects depend on their subject matter, *see* Sicard-Mirabal and Derains, *supra* n. 6, 57.
13. Blomstein, *International Investment Law and Russian Countersanctions; Countering the Counterstrike?* (29 November 2024) https://www.blomstein.com/neues/international-investment-law-and-russian-countersanctions (accessed 1 October 2025).

Chamber of Commerce Arbitration Institute for the settlement of disputes under the BIT.[14]

Global geopolitics has caused increased attention to be paid to modern international investment law and investor-state arbitration. The Russian annexation of Crimea in 2014 prompted several high-profile investor-state arbitration cases under the Russia-Ukraine BIT, such as *JSC DTEK Krymenergo v. Russian Federation*[15] and the infamous *Yukos v. Russian Federation* case,[16] both of which decided against Russia.

With the imposition of international sanctions against Russia following the invasion of Ukraine and the implementation of Russia's investor-hostile measures, the cases are likely to mount further, as will be explored in the immediate section. Whether the liberal framework of international investment law can and should withstand these challenges will remain to be seen.

[B] The Russian Economic Measures

On 25 April 2023, President Vladimir Putin signed Decree No. 302 'On the temporary management of certain property.' The decree provides for the temporary transfer of external management of assets situated in Russia that are owned or controlled by entities from 'unfriendly' countries.[17] The list of 'unfriendly countries' captures forty-nine countries, including the Group of 7 (G7) and European Union (EU) Member States.[18] Under Decree No. 302, temporary management will be transferred to the Russian Federal Agency For State Property Management, Rosimushestvo, which will have the competence to exercise almost all rights as owner.[19] Decree No. 302 was followed by the transfer of shares of the German state-owned Uniper and the Finnish state-owned Fortum on 25 April 2023.[20] On 16 July 2023, President Putin signed Presidential Decree No. 520, also transferring Carlsberg's shares in its subsidiary, Baltika Brewing Company, and French yoghurt maker Danone's shares in its Russian subsidiary.[21] According to Dmitry Peskov, a spokesperson for the Kremlin, the decree was adopted as a direct response to aggressive actions of the 'unfriendly countries',

14. *See*, among others, the Ukrainian-Russian BIT, Finland-Russian BIT, South-African-Russian BIT, Mongolian-Russian BIT etc.
15. *DTEK Krymenergo*, *supra* n. 2.
16. *Yukos Universal Limited (Isle of Man) v. The Russian Federation*, PCA Case No. 2005-04/AA227.
17. Noerr, *Putin Allows Seizure of Russian Assets of Foreign Companies* (26 April 2023) https://www.noerr.com/en/insights/putin-allows-seizure-of-russian-assets-of-foreign-companies (accessed 1 October 2025).
18. Tass, *Russia Adds Bahamas, Guernsey, Isle of Man to List of Unfriendly Countries and Territories* (24 July 2022) https://web.archive.org/web/20220730110440/https://tass.com/russia/1484099 (accessed 1 October 2025).
19. Noerr, *supra* n. 17.
20. Rosemary Griffin et al., *Russia Takes Temporary Control of Uniper, Fortum Power Assets*, S&P Global (26 April 2023) https://www.spglobal.com/commodity-insights/en/news-research/latest-news/electric-power/042623-russia-takes-temporary-control-of-uniper-fortum-power-assets (accessed 1 October 2025).
21. Alrud, *Baltika Carlsberg and Danone Russian Businesses Are Put under State Interim Administration* (17 July 2023) https://www.alrud.com/publications/64b4ddb7c80e48d019005d06/ (accessed 1 October 2025).

drawing upon justifications under public international law. Specifically, Peskov stated that '[t]his initiative mirrors the attitude of Western governments towards foreign assets of Russian companies.'[22] In general, the Kremlin has framed Decree No. 302 as 'an urgent response to the United States and other countries and international organizations whose actions, unfriendly and contrary to international law, illegally deny the Russian Federation, Russian legal entities and individuals property rights and/or restrict their ownership titles'.[23]

This is just one example of the broad range of economic measures that Russia has adopted in response to international sanctions. The Russian measures also extend to restrictions on dividend payments,[24] windfall taxes,[25] non-enforcement of patent rights[26] and subjecting certain transfers of property to government approval.[27] Most, although not all, of these measures target investors from 'unfriendly countries'. For simplicity, these measures can be described as the Russian 'countersanctions'.

A thorough analysis of the compatibility of each measure vis-à-vis the protections ensured by the relevant BIT in question would be unfeasible in this chapter, given the slight variations in the Russian BITs, and the fact that the assessment of a tribunal will always be based on the specific factual circumstances of each case. It would also not be necessary in the analysis of how tribunals may handle the Monetary Gold problem. However, in setting the scene of the problematic position of a foreign investor operating in Russia, and the pending relevance of the Monetary Gold problem, it is emphasised that specifically the utilisation of Decree No. 302 on the Temporary Transfer of Management, as highlighted in the introduction, would in present author's view constitute a 'text-book' BIT violation of expropriation without compensation.[28] Likewise for the legislatively imposed disregard of intellectual property rights, where patent holders associated with 'unfriendly countries' are entitled to 0% of proceeds

22. Alexander Marrow, Gleb Stolyarov and Anne Kauranen, *Kremlin Warns of More Asset Seizures after Move Gainst Fortum and Uniper*, Reuters (26 April 2023) https://www.reuters.com/business/energy/fortum-says-investigating-news-russian-asset-seizure-2023-04-26/.
23. President of Russia, *Executive Order on Interim Management of Certain Properties*, Presidential Executive Office (25 April 2023) http://en.kremlin.ru/acts/news/70986 (accessed 1 October 2025).
24. Jennifer Younan et al., *Russian Countersanctions: New Measures Targeting Foreign Investors in Russia*, A&O Shearman (11 May 2023) https://www.aoshearman.com/en/insights/russian-countersanctions-new-measures-targeting-foreign-investors-in-russia (accessed 1 October 2025).
25. *Ibid.*
26. Denis Khabarov et al., *Russia Adopts Zero Compensation to Patent Owners from Unfriendly Countries*, Baker McKenzie Global Sanctions and Expert Controls Blog (10 March 2022) https://sanctionsnews.bakermckenzie.com/russia-adopts-zero-compensation-to-patent-owners-from-unfriendly-countries/ (accessed 1 October 2025).
27. Raja Bose et al., *Between a Rock and a Hard Place: Claims Against Russia in Investment Treaty Arbitration*, K&L Gates Hub (20 April 2022) https://www.klgates.com/Between-a-Rock-and-a-Hard-Place-Claims-Against-Russia-in-Investment-Treaty-Arbitration-Part-II-of-II-4-20-2022.
28. *See Starrett Housing Corporation, Starrett Systems, Inc. and others v. The Government of the Islamic Republic of Iran, Bank Markazi Iran and others*, IUSCT Case No. 24 (14 August 1987) and *Tippetts, Abbett, McCarthy, Stratton v. TAMS-AFFA Consulting Engineers of Iran*, IUSCT Case No. 7 (29 June 2984) where the Iran-US Claims Tribunal in both cases found that a temporary transfer of management of a certain duration constitutes expropriation under international law and accordingly warrants compensation.

from the use of their patents.[29] Other more broadly adopted measures such as the windfall tax may fall within the lawful regulatory prerogatives of the host state, and thus not constitute a violation of the relevant BIT.

[C] Countermeasures and Bilateral Investment Treaties

As the BIT is an international instrument which creates legal obligations between contracting states, a breach of the BIT constitutes an infringement of an international obligation and thus an internationally wrongful act subject to the rules of state responsibility.[30] The wrongful act of states is regulated by the International Law Commission's 2001 Articles on State Responsibility for Internationally Wrongful Acts (hereafter 'ARSIWA'), which are largely a codification of customary international law.[31] ARSIWA Chapter V regulates Circumstances Precluding Wrongfulness for internationally wrongful acts, and specifically Article 22 regulates the application of countermeasures. If a Circumstance Precluding Wrongfulness is successfully invoked, the state's act is still regarded as a breach of its primary obligation, but its wrongfulness is precluded.[32] While acknowledging that there has been some debate in legal scholarship and case law on whether this would also exculpate the acting state from its obligation to pay compensation for said wrongful act, the present authors side with former Special Rapporteur on State Responsibility James Crawford, who argues that a successful invocation of countermeasures does in fact exculpate from its compensation obligations.[33]

Certain criteria must be met for a state to successfully invoke a countermeasures defence. These are codified in detail in Articles 49-54 of ARSIWA. These have been summarised as four cumulative criteria under customary international law by the ICJ in *Gabcíkovo-Nagymaros Project*:[34]

(1) The measure must be taken in response to a previous internationally wrongful act of another state and be directed against that state.
(2) The state taking the countermeasure must have called upon the state committing the wrongful act to cease its wrongful conduct or to make reparation for it.

29. Bose et al., *supra* n. 27; Decree of the President of the Russian Federation No. 299 of 1 March 2022 titled *On Amendments to Clause 2 of the Methodology for Determining the Amount of Compensation Paid to a Patent Owner When Deciding to Use an Invention, Utility Model or Industrial Design without His Consent, and the Procedure for Its Payment.*
30. United Nations Articles on Responsibility of States for Internationally Wrongful Acts (ARSIWA) as adopted by the Commission at its fifty-third session, in 2001, Art. 2.
31. Espersen et al., *supra* n. 8, 214; Martins Paparinskis, *Circumstances Precluding Wrongfulness in International Investment Law,* 31 ICSID Review, 484, 487 (15 Feburary 2016) https://doi.org/10.1093/icsidreview/siw007 (accessed 1 October 2025).
32. ICL Commentary to ARSIWA, Chapter V, para. 1.
33. James Crawford, *State Responsibility: The General Part,* 279 (Cambridge University Press, July 2013).
34. *Gabcíkovo-Nagymaros Project (Hungary/Slovakia)*, International Court of Justice, Judgment of 25 September 1997.

(3) The effects of a countermeasure must be commensurate with the injury suffered.
(4) The purpose of the countermeasure must be to induce the wrongdoing state to comply with its obligations under international law, and the measure must be reversible.[35]

These criteria are referred to as the 'Gabcíkovo-Nagymaros Project Criteria' in the following sections.

The law on countermeasures also mandates that the measure does not infringe upon peremptory rules of international law, as stated in Article 50 of ARSIWA and corresponding case law.[36] However, as stated by the UN Committee on Economic, Social and Cultural Rights, it is unlikely that economic sanctions or similar measures infringe upon such norms, as long as they do not inflict 'suffering upon the most vulnerable groups within the targeted country'.[37]

Thus, if countermeasures are invoked by Russia in an investor-state arbitration case regarding a potential violation of the investor's right under the BIT, the tribunal will essentially have to evaluate the illegality of the investor's home state's actions in order to decide upon whether the host state's countermeasures are lawful, without the home state being party to the proceedings. This question targets the crux of a jurisdictional challenge that may be posed to the tribunal, namely the *Monetary Gold* problem.

§12.03 THE MONETARY GOLD PROBLEM

The Monetary Gold problem derives its name from the 1952 *Monetary Gold* case before the ICJ.[38] The circumstances of the case were as follows: gold belonging to Albania, but confiscated by Germany during the Second World War, was to be distributed between Italy, France, the United Kingdom, and the United States under the 1946 Agreement on Reparation. However, Italy claimed entitlement to the entirety of the gold for damages accorded under an allegedly unlawful Albanian law of 1945.[39] Albania was, however, not party to the case. The ICJ found that:

> [i]n the determination of these questions — questions which relate to the lawful or unlawful character of certain actions of Albania vis-à-vis Italy — only two States, Italy and Albania, are directly interested. To go into the merits of such questions

35. *Ibid.*, paras 83-87.
36. International Law Commission, Draft articles on Responsibility of States for Internationally Wrongful Acts with commentaries, 2001, pp. 131 ff., *see* the 'Naulilaa' arbitration in note 6, p. 132 of the Commentary, citing the Committee on Economic, Social and Cultural Rights discussing the effect of economic sanctions on civilians.
37. *Ibid.*
38. *Case of the Monetary Gold Removed from Rome in 1943, Italy v. France*, United Kingdom of Great Britain and Northern Ireland and the United States of America ('Monetary Gold'), International Court of Justice, Judgment of 15 June 1954.
39. *Ibid.*, p. 7.

> would be to decide a dispute between Italy and Albania. The Court cannot decide such a dispute without the consent of Albania.[40]

This conclusion is founded on the fundamental principle of international law that the jurisdiction of an international court requires the consent of the State.[41]

The *East Timor Case*[42] before the ICJ raised a similar dilemma of proceedings between Portugal and Australia, where the distinct subject matter was found to be the lawfulness of the state of Indonesia's actions.[43] Here, the ICJ made a clear distinction between the substantive law and the law of jurisdiction. The Court underscored that even when the breach of an *erga omnes*[44] obligation is at issue, which is an obligation owed to all states, the Court did not have jurisdiction to rule on the matter when the obligation in question was breached by a state not party to the proceedings.[45] Even though a breach of an *erga omnes* obligation by one state can in principle be invoked by any other state before the ICJ, the ICJ held it could not assess such a breach committed by a state not party to the case.[46]

The applicability of the Monetary Gold principle in investor-state arbitration was confirmed in *Larsen v. Hawaiian Kingdom.*[47] The tribunal found that even though arbitral awards, contrary to judgments by the ICJ, are not binding upon third states, the *Monetary Gold* principle still applies.[48] The tribunal underscored that the question of jurisdiction is not contingent upon the award having binding effects on the rights and obligations of a third-party state, but rather whether the 'legal interests' of a third party are the 'very subject matter' of the proceedings.[49] This finding was supported by the statements of the ICJ in the *Nauru v. Australia*[50] case, which furthermore inquired whether the 'determination of the responsibility' of the third State not party to the proceedings would be a 'prerequisite' for the determination of the case before it.[51] Moreover, based on the *Nauru* case, the ICJ in *East Timor* stated that 'it is not necessarily prevented from adjudicating when the judgment it is asked to give might

40. *Ibid.*, p. 17.
41. This has been confirmed on several occasions by the ICJ, and in arbitral decisions investor-state disputes, i.e., in *Corn Products v. Mexico* (ICSID Case No. ARB (AF)/04/1), where the arbitral tribunal found it did not have jurisdiction to assess the wrongdoing of the American investor's home state, as the United States was not party to the proceedings.
42. *Case Concerning East Timor, Portugal v. Australia,* International Court of Justice, Judgment of 30 June 1995.
43. *Ibid.*, para. 33.
44. 'Erga omnes' refers to legal obligations or rights that apply universally to all states and are owed to the international community as a whole.
45. *East Timor, supra* n. 42, para. 29.
46. *Ibid.*; In the specific case, Indonesia had not even ratified the statute of the ICJ. However, this does interestingly not play a factor in the reasoning of the ICJ in para. 29, which in general terms states 'Whatever the nature of the obligations invoked, the Court could not rule on the lawfulness of the conduct of a State when its judgment would imply an evaluation of the lawfulness of the conduct of another State which is not a party to the case.'
47. *Larsen v. Hawaiian Kingdom*, PCA Case No. 1999-01, Award of 1 February 2001, para. 11.17.
48. *Ibid.*, para. 11.19.
49. *Ibid.*, paras 11.21-11.22.
50. *Certain Phosphate Lands in Nauru, Nauru v. Australia, International Court of Justice,* Judgment of 26 June 1992.
51. *Ibid.*, para. 55.

affect the legal interests of a State which is not a party to the case' as long as the 'rights and obligations' of that State did not 'constitute the very subject-matter of such a judgment'. The ICJ afterwards concluded that it could not exercise jurisdiction over Portugal's claims in the case, as 'it would have to rule, as a prerequisite, on the lawfulness of Indonesia's conduct in the absence of that State's consent'.[52] Note that *Larsen* inquires whether the 'legal interests' of third states form the 'very subject-matter' of the case at hand, while the ICJ in *East Timor* bases its conclusion on Indonesia's 'rights and obligations' forming the 'subject-matter' of the case and a determination of the wrongfulness of its actions being a 'prerequisite' to adjudicate the case. It is, however, unclear from the case law whether this difference in terminology bears any substantive implications on the legal assessment of the Monetary Gold principle.

Notably, the *Larsen* tribunal also highlighted an important exception to the Monetary Gold principle, namely, 'if the legal finding against an absent third party could be taken as given (e.g., by reason of an authoritative decision of the Security Council on the point), the principle may well not apply'.[53] In *Larsen*, such a decision could not be taken as a given, and the tribunal opted to dismiss the case altogether. The ICJ in principle acknowledged the same exception in *East Timor*, although the Court did not find that the Security Council and General Assembly resolutions confidently settled the question of the third-party obligations in the specific case.[54]

If Russia invokes countermeasures as a circumstance precluding wrongfulness, a tribunal will be faced with the Monetary Gold problem, as the invocation of countermeasures requires an assessment of the illegality of the previous wrongful act by another state not party to the dispute. For example, Decree No. 520, which orders the transfer of shares from Carlsberg's subsidiary, is directed against, *inter alia*, Denmark and Sweden as 'unfriendly countries', who have allegedly adopted unlawful sanctions against Russia and Russian entities. The legality of Western sanctions would arguably concern the very subject matter of the case and a determination of the legality or illegality of these sanctions could be a prerequisite to adjudicate Russia's claims before the tribunal.

The issue of the tribunal evaluating Western sanctions against Russia could also effectively be an evaluation of the legality of EU sanctions, given that the majority of the so-called unfriendly countries have implemented sanctions under EU regulations, notably Council Regulation 269/2014. The Court of Justice of the European Union (CJEU) has in a recent line of decisions starting from *Achmea*[55] taken a stance on its jurisdiction vis-à-vis arbitral tribunals with regard to questions on the application and interpretation of EU law. Notably, in *Komstroy*,[56] the CJEU found that also where neither the host state nor investor is an EU Member State or national, the fact that the arbitration agreement would entail evaluation of the application and interpretation of

52. *East Timor*, *supra* n. 42, paras 34-35.
53. *Larsen*, *supra* n. 47, para. 11.24.
54. *East Timor*, *supra* n. 42, para. 32.
55. *Slovak Republic v. Achmea B.V*, CJEU Case No. C-284/16 (6 March 2018).
56. *République de Moldavie v. Komstroy* LLC, CJEU Case No. C-741/19 (2 September 2021).

EU law renders it subject to the CJEU's jurisdiction.[57] The CJEU underscored that this is particularly the case where the seat of arbitration is placed within the EU subject to national court's jurisdiction with regard to setting-aside procedures.[58] The same analysis may apply where the seat is not located within the EU, but national courts have jurisdiction to (limitedly, although principally) review the award under enforcement proceedings. Hence, if a tribunal embarks upon an evaluation of the legality of sanctions adopted through EU Regulation 269/2014, it may risk post-award interference by the CJEU. The jurisdictional implications of the CJEU's approach in a Russia-investor arbitration have yet to be settled and would in any event depend on the specific circumstances of the case at hand.

The current geopolitical landscape can give rise to the Monetary Gold issue in various ways, and not only through an invocation of countermeasures as a Circumstance Precluding Wrongfulness. This has been seen in recent arbitral awards and national judgments, such as *Pildegovics and North Star v. Norway*[59] and *Law Debenture Trust Corporation plc v. Ukraine*.[60] In *Pildegovics*, the investor claimed that Norway had conspired with or incited Russia to unlawfully restrict the investor's access to snow crab fishing in the Loop Hole area of the Barents Sea. Here, the tribunal stated that assessing the claim 'would require the Tribunal to determine that the Russian Federation had acted unlawfully, which the Tribunal cannot do'.[61] In *Law Debenture Trust Corporation plc*, Ukraine argued before the Supreme Court of the United Kingdom that it had concluded contracts with the Law Debenture Trust Corporation, which was closely related to the Russian Federation, following threats of use of force by Russia. Accordingly, Ukraine pleaded that the contracts were null and void, as these had been concluded under duress. The Supreme Court carefully studied the principle of 'non-justiciability' and 'the acts of state doctrine',[62] which reflect the Monetary Gold principle under English Law. In its assessment, the Supreme Court found that English courts were in general barred from adjudicating the lawfulness under international law of the acts of foreign states.[63] However, the invocation of duress by Ukraine before the English courts could be limited to an assessment of 'duress' and accordingly voidability as regulated in English contract law. Given that the contracts were governed by English law, the English courts could legitimately adjudicate the issue under English contract law.[64]

57. Note, the EU law in question regarded the Energy Charter Treaty (ECT), an inter-state treaty, which had been concluded by the EU Council, pursuant to TFEU Arts 217 and 218. The CJEU found that the conclusion of the treaty by the EU Council rendered the ECT an EU act, thus an integral part of EU law.
58. Erica Stein and Quentin Muron, *Komstroy, PL Holdings, Micula: Closing the Door to Intra-EU Investment Arbitration – Again?*, 1 b-Arbitra Belgian Review of Arbitration, 7, para. 29 (2022).
59. *Pildegovics, supra* n. 1.
60. *The Law Debenture Trust Corporation plc v. Ukraine (Represented by the Minister of Finance of Ukraine acting upon the instructions of the Cabinet of Ministers of Ukraine)*, United Kingdom Supreme Court Case No. UKSC/2018/0192, Judgment of 15 March 2023.
61. *Pildegovics, supra* n. 1, para. 297.
62. *The Law Debenture Trust Corporation plc, supra* n. 60, paras 187-188.
63. *Ibid.*, para. 188.
64. *Ibid.*, para. 189.

Pildegovics and *Law Debenture Trust Corporation plc* are two recent examples of the growing relevance of the Monetary Gold problem globally and the various manners in which it can arise before both tribunals and courts alike. Moreover, following the award in *Pildegovics,* the Claimant applied for an annulment in 2024, alleging, *inter alia,* that the tribunal 'caused a denial of justice to Claimants and manifestly failed to exercise its powers by failing or refusing to decide several fundamental issues in dispute on the basis of its application of the Monetary Gold principle'.[65] This application has caused an International Centre for Settlement of Investment Disputes (ICSID) ad hoc Committee to issue a stay of the enforcement of the award and the matter has not been resolved as of the time of writing.

The question thus becomes: how shall a tribunal treat (or circumvent) the Monetary Gold problem if it should arise in an investor-state dispute under a BIT, whilst not jeopardising the award? The following section will address this question based on the decisions of recent tribunals faced with the invocation of the Monetary Gold problem.

§12.04 THE GOLDEN PATH FORWARD

As evidenced in the above, the Monetary Gold problem will undoubtedly challenge the wits and wisdom of tribunals, as they seek to ensure the due process rights of all parties, including those not directly involved. In an era of mounting geopolitical tensions, this issue is only set to grow in prominence.

The aim of this section is to address how the Monetary Gold problem has been addressed in international case law, and how it may apply to an Investor-State Arbitration against the Russian Federation. Thus, this section seeks to offer guidance on how the rights of foreign investors, grappling with hostile state measures amid geopolitical upheaval, may have their rights to redress and compensation safeguarded despite the challenges posed by the Monetary Gold problem. An analysis of case law reveals that tribunals have adopted a range of strategies when grappling with the Monetary Gold problem, the most notable of which present authors have identified and dubbed as:

(1) The Individual Rights versus Derivative Rights Approach.
(2) The Procedural Approach.
(3) The 'Very Subject-Matter' Approach.
(4) The Reframing Approach.
(5) The Authoritative Decision Approach.

The first two methods target the *Gabcíkovo-Nagymaros Project* criteria for lawful countermeasures under customary international law as set out above. Specifically, the Individual versus Derivative Rights Approach concerns the first criteria that '*the*

65. *Peteris Pildegovics and SIA North Star v. Kingdom of Norway,* ICSID Case No. ARB/20/11, Claimant's Request for annulment of the Award of 22 February 2024, para. 44.

measure must be taken in response to a previous internationally wrongful act of another State and be directed against that State' (emphasis added). The Procedural Approach targets the remaining three criteria. Each of these two approaches is directed towards handling the Monetary Gold problem following an invocation of a countermeasure and has been used in public arbitral case law where this international law defence has been pleaded.

If either of these two approaches is inapplicable, insufficient, or should the Monetary Gold problem arise outside the context of a countermeasures defence, the three other approaches demonstrate ways in which tribunals have tackled the problem. These approaches are based on case law not concerning countermeasures, but which still offer valuable insights into the ingenuity of tribunals – insights that may well prove instructive in investor-state disputes against the Russian Federation, as will be examined and highlighted in the following sections.

[A] The Individual Rights Versus Derivative Rights Approach

As previously noted, countermeasures may only be lawfully employed against another state in response to its internationally wrongful act.[66] Insofar as the current Russian countersanctions seek to target investors from 'unfriendly countries' based in Russia, this raises the question of whether these investors may be perceived as an extension of their home state and accordingly a viable target of countermeasures. In order to evaluate this, the tribunal must essentially evaluate whether the rights of investors are individual rights bestowed upon them directly through the BIT or rights derived from their home state, as party to the BIT.[67]

If investor rights are considered a derivative of their home state, the right inherently belongs to the home state and the host state can thus target these rights lawfully as a countermeasure.[68] In such a case, the damage to investors must be seen as an incidental loss and a predictable consequence of countermeasures.[69] However, if investors' rights are seen as direct and individual rights derived from the BIT, countermeasures targeting foreign investor rights in response to the wrongdoing of their home state will arguably be unlawful.[70] The qualification of investor rights is highly disputed in both case law and in international arbitration scholarship.[71]

66. *Gabcíkovo-Nagymaros Project*, *supra* n. 34, para. 83; ARSIWA Art. 49.
67. Jure Zrilič, *Are We in for a New Wave of Investment Arbitrations?*, Verfassungsblog on matters constitutional (21 March 2022) https://verfassungsblog.de/are-we-in-for-a-new-wave-of-investment-arbitrations/ (accessed 1 October 2025).
68. Martins Paparinskis, *Investment Arbitration and the Law of Countermeasures*, 79 British Yearbook of International Law, 264, 318 (2008) https://doi.org/10.1093/bybil/79.1.264 (accessed 1 October 2025).
69. The ILC commentary to Art. 49 states that countermeasures might have consequences for private parties, i.e., in a situation where 'as a consequence of suspension of a trade agreement, trade with the responsible state is affected and one or more companies lose business or even go bankrupt', *see* ILC (2001) Commentary to ARSIWA Art. 49, para. 5.
70. Paparinskis, *supra* n. 68, 332.
71. *Ibid.*, 334 ff.; Roland Portmann, *Legal Personality in International Law*, 11 (Cambridge University Press 2010).

A tribunal was faced with the question in *Corn Products v. Mexico*.[72] Mexico contended that a new tax on beverages containing high fructose corn syrup, which allegedly discriminated against an American investor, was enacted as a lawful countermeasure in response to the United States' prior violation of the North American Free Trade Agreement (NAFTA). In short, Mexico argued that investor rights were derivative and that Mexico could lawfully target the United States in response to its initial breach of NAFTA. However, the tribunal found that NAFTA bestows individual rights onto investors, different from the rights of their home states. Furthermore, the tribunal concluded that: '[the investor] is a third party in any dispute between its own State and another NAFTA Party and a countermeasure taken by that other State against the State of nationality of the investor cannot deprive that investor of its rights.'[73]

A hypothetical investor in a BIT dispute with Russia would be wise to argue for the individual rights approach in an attempt to sidestep the Monetary Gold problem. Should a tribunal adopt this analysis, a potential countermeasure defence could be rejected without further consideration because the target is not within the scope of lawful countermeasures, and the Monetary Gold problem would thus be avoided in its entirety.

However, the question of whether investor rights are either derivative or individual is not sufficiently settled to justify a rule of thumb.[74] When faced with the question, other arbitral tribunals have reached the opposite conclusion to that of the tribunal in *Corn Products*.

ADM v. Mexico arose out of the same beverage tax introduced by Mexico as in *Corn Products*, and Mexico again claimed a countermeasures defence.[75] The tribunal found that the substantial rights of the NAFTA agreement only existed on the international level between the home state and the host state thus designated the individual investors as mere beneficiaries or objects of those state rights and obligations.[76] Hence, Mexico could in principle target investors and investor rights as a response to an internationally wrongful act by the US.[77] Importantly, the tribunal in *ADM* made a distinction between the substantive rights and the procedural rights in NAFTA, finding that NAFTA did bestow individual procedural rights directly upon investors in order to enter arbitration proceedings with the host state.[78] However, the substantive rights at stake in those proceedings were derived from the home state and could thus in principle be suspended by the host state through lawful countermeasures.[79]

---

72. *Corn Products International, Inc. v. United Mexican States*, ICSID Case No. ARB (AF)/04/1, Award of 18 August 2009.
73. *Ibid.*, para. 176; Borzu Sabahi, Noah Rubins, and Don Wallace, Jr., *Investor-State Arbitration*, 532 (2nd ed., Oxford University Press 2019).
74. Paparinskis, *supra* n. 68, 267; Astrid Kjeldgaard-Pedersen, *The Legal Personality of the Individual*, 205 (Oxford University Press 2018).
75. *Archer Daniels Midland and Tate & Lyle Ingredients Americas, Inc. v. United Mexican States* ('*ADM*'), ICSID Case No. ARB(AF)/04/5, Award of 21 November 2007.
76. *Ibid.*, para. 176.
77. *Ibid.*, para. 180.
78. *Ibid.*, paras 173-174.
79. *Ibid.*, paras 179-180.

If a tribunal finds that investor rights are derived from the home state, Russian countermeasures against investors could in principle be invoked as a circumstance precluding wrongfulness against the home state's potentially wrongful acts, as in *ADM*.[80]

The legal treatment of the Monetary Gold problem before a tribunal will fundamentally depend on the theory followed by the tribunal. *De lege ferenda*, one could argue that investment treaties should state the nature of the investor rights explicitly.[81] Given diverging case law regarding the question of individual or derivative rights, it is difficult to formulate a decisive and predictive answer on how a tribunal may react to such a question.

Tribunals adhering to the derivative rights theory or facing the Monetary Gold problem in a context not affected by the question of individual or derivative rights have had to seek other approaches to avoid a material assessment of third state international responsibility. Accordingly, these are assessed in the following sections.

[B] The Procedural Approach

In order for a state to successfully invoke a countermeasure defence, the Gabcíkovo-Nagymaros Project criteria must be met. Recalling these as summarised by the ICJ:

(1) The measure must be taken in response to a previous internationally wrongful act of another State and be directed against that State.
(2) The State taking the countermeasure must have called upon the State committing the wrongful act to cease its wrongful conduct or to make reparation for it.
(3) The effects of a countermeasure must be commensurate with the injury suffered.
(4) The purpose of the countermeasure must be to induce the wrongdoing State to comply with its obligations under international law, and the measure must be reversible.[82]

To avoid the Monetary Gold problem, the investor could argue that the countermeasures defence cannot be invoked because one or more of the other cumulative requirements for lawful countermeasures have not been fulfilled (namely, criteria 2-4 above). This approach was taken by the tribunal in *ADM*. Here, the tribunal began its assessment of the countermeasures claim by evaluating the remaining criteria for the invocation of countermeasures beyond the first regarding a 'response to a previous internationally wrongful act of another State'. The tribunal found that the Mexican measure had not been adopted with the objective to respond to an unlawful act by the US, nor to induce the US to comply with its international obligations and that the

80. Kjeldgaard-Pedersen, *supra* n. 74, 212.
81. Paparinskis, *supra* n. 68, 268.
82. *Gabcíkovo-Nagymaros Project*, *supra* n. 34, paras 83-87.

Mexican measure in general did not meet the proportionality requirement. Accordingly, the tribunal could *ipso facto* dismiss the defence of countermeasures as a Circumstance Precluding Wrongfulness without having to assess the alleged international wrongfulness of the acts by the United States.[83]

Within the context of an investor-state dispute against the Russian Federation concerning countersanctions, an investor before a tribunal could adopt the Procedural Approach and argue that Russia has not fulfilled all the *Gabcíkovo-Nagymaros Project* criteria. The hypothetical exchange of pleadings on the issue could proceed as follows.

The Russian Federation could likely argue it has fulfilled criteria of 'calling upon the other state to cease its wrongful act' through its public statements condemning the international sanctions against the Russian Federation. Furthermore, the general rhetoric of the Kremlin that its measures are 'mirroring' the hostile measures taken by 'unfriendly countries' also speaks to the requirement that the countermeasure 'commensurate with the injury suffered'. One could also argue that the Russian Federation has sought to publicly portray that the measures are reversible,[84] as underscored by Peskov in addressing that Decree No. 302 'does not deal with property issues and does not deprive the owners of their assets. Because external management is temporary and only means that the original owner no longer has the right to make management decisions'.[85]

However, the investor could argue that the cessation of the international sanctions is not the true motive of the Russian countermeasures. When introducing Decree No. 320 on the temporary transfer of management, Peskov stated that '[t]he main purpose of the decree is to form a compensation fund for the possible application of reciprocal measures in response to the illegal expropriation of Russian assets abroad.'[86] While this statement does imply some level of reciprocity and proportionality, whether the objective of the measure is to induce the unfriendly states to cease their unlawful conduct abroad is likely to be a point of contention.

This assessment of each criterion will essentially depend on the material presented to the tribunal and the arguments advanced by Russia and a hypothetical investor. Nonetheless, the Procedural Approach as evidenced in *ADM v. Mexico* does offer an avenue for the investor to escape a Monetary Gold problem, despite the invocation of a defence on countermeasures.

[C] The 'Very Subject-Matter' Approach

As supported by the findings of the ICJ in *East Timor,* the tribunal may decide upon claims and issues which might affect the legal interests of third states peripherally, as long as a prejudication of the right, obligations or conduct of a third state is not central to the decision. The Monetary Gold principle is thus only applicable if the issue actually

83. *ADM, supra* n. 76, paras 151 and 160.
84. Marrow, Stolyarov and Kauranen, *supra* n. 22.
85. *Ibid.*
86. *Ibid.*

goes to the *very subject matter* of the dispute and the adjudication of third-party rights or conduct is a *necessary prerequisite* to assess the claims in the dispute.

Tribunals have relied upon this distinction in rejecting objections based on the Monetary Gold principle in cases such as *Raiffeisen Bank v. Republic of Croatia,* and *Addiko Bank D.D. v. Republic of Croatia,*[87] although the subject matter arguably to some extent touched upon legal interests of third states. Thus, an approach to avoid facing the Monetary Gold problem and its potential consequences is that the investor seeks to argue that the potential legal interests of a third state are not central to the claims of the dispute.

In the aforementioned *Pildegovics,* the tribunal broke down its analysis of each claim and subcomponents of the claim to assess to what extent the Monetary Gold principle actually affected each individual part. Based on this, specific claims might be deemed inadmissible due to the Monetary Gold principle, while the tribunal may find that the rights and interests of the third-party state do not actually go to the very subject matter of other claims. In this way, as mentioned earlier, the tribunal in *Pildegovics* rejected the assessment of only certain claims before it due to the application of *Monetary Gold.* Having acknowledged the risk of the Monetary Gold problem before it, the tribunal emphasised that 'in examining different aspects of the claims before it, the Tribunal will be mindful of the limits of its jurisdiction and of what is admissible and that may require the Tribunal declining to rule on parts of those claims'.[88] The approach adopted by *Pildegovics* hardly serves as an ideal outcome for the investor, given that parts of the investor's claims were effectively deemed inadmissible due to the Monetary Gold problem. Nonetheless, the 'Vital Interest Approach' highlights how tribunals have reacted to the Monetary Gold problem, should the investor not tread carefully. As of the time of writing, annulment proceedings are ongoing, with the investor claiming that the tribunal too extensively applied the Monetary Gold principle.

A key takeaway from *Pildegovics* is, however, that the Very Subject-Matter Approach can be used as a preliminary step to carve out the specific claims before the tribunal, which might be affected by the Monetary Gold principle. In the case of a Russian countermeasures claim, this would facilitate that the tribunal focuses its Monetary Gold analysis on only this defence, and whether a determination of third state conduct is a *necessary prerequisite* to assess the validity of the countermeasures defence. Here, the investor could argue that the determination of the countermeasures defence does not de facto require a decision on third state conduct, through the application of one of the ensuing methods, the Reframing Approach or the Authoritative Decision Approach.

87. *Raiffeisen Bank International AG and Raiffeisenbank Austria d.d. v. Republic of Croatia,* ICSID Case No. ARB/17/34, Decision on Respondent's Jurisdictional Objection of 30 September 2020; *Addiko Bank AG and Addiko Bank d.d. v. Republic of Croatia,* ICSID Case No. ARB/17/37, Decision on Croatia's Jurisdictional Objection of 12 June 2020.

88. *Pildegovics, supra* n. 1, para. 300.

[D] The Reframing Approach

When the legal interests of a third state *do* appear to be central to a claim before a tribunal, the tribunal has been seen to reframe the legal issue before it in order to avoid the Monetary Gold problem. In both *DTEK Krymenergo*[89] and *Pildegovics*,[90] the tribunal structured the analysis of the matters before it in a manner which did not require an adjudication upon third-state legal interests.

The award in *DTEK Krymenergo* was rendered in 2023. The case concerned investments made by a Ukrainian investor in Crimea that were impaired by the Russian Federation after the invasion of Crimea in 2014. The Ukrainian investor sought redress against Russia under the provisions of the Russian-Ukrainian BIT. A BIT only offers rights and protection to investors from one state party to the BIT (the home state) with regard to investments made in the territory of the other state party (the host state) and *vice versa*. Accordingly, in order to determine whether the Ukrainian-Russian BIT would be applicable to a Ukrainian investor regarding an investment located in internationally recognised Ukrainian territory under Russian occupation, the tribunal had to decide whether Crimea for the purpose of the dispute at hand should be regarded as a territory of the Russian Federation.

The Russian Federation claimed that the tribunal's decision on jurisdiction would essentially entail an evaluation of the sovereignty of Crimea, and that any such determination would be outside the jurisdiction of the tribunal.[91] Russia raised the Monetary Gold problem, as it stated that a territorial dispute was ongoing between Ukraine and the Russian Federation regarding the status of Crimea.[92] Hence, the tribunal's assessment would infringe upon the legal interests of Ukraine, a state not party to the dispute.[93]

As determining the territorial status of Crimea was a necessary prerequisite for determining the tribunal's jurisdiction and hence the merits of the case, the tribunal arguably had to frame the legal question of the territorial status of Crimea in a way that did not require an adjudication of Ukraine's rights, obligations, or conduct, which would risk invoking the Monetary Gold problem. The tribunal approached the question by limiting its analysis to a strict 'black letter' interpretation of the term 'territory' in the BIT, and whether this signified territory over which a state party had absolute sovereign powers or all territory under the effective control of the state. Holding that the term signified all territory under the effective control of a state party and finding that Russia's effective control over Crimea since 2014 was an undisputed fact before it, the tribunal concluded that Crimea formed part of the Russian territory within the meaning of the Russian-Ukrainian BIT. Henceforth, the Ukrainian investor owning an investment located in Crimea enjoyed the protection of the BIT.[94]

89. *DTEK Krymenergo, supra* n. 2.
90. *Pildegovics, supra* n. 1.
91. *DTEK Krymenergo, supra* n. 2, para. 215.
92. *Ibid.*, paras 222 & 227.
93. *Ibid.*, para. 222.
94. *Ibid.*, paras 250-299.

Notably, the tribunal addressed Russia's invocation of the Monetary Gold problem as a preliminary matter. The tribunal applied a strict definition of the Monetary Gold principle, derived from the original reasoning in *Monetary Gold*, and stated that the Monetary Gold principle only applies when 'the vital issue to be settled concerns the international responsibility of a third State'.[95] The tribunal underscored that the dispute before it concerned the 'alleged impairment of assets owned by that Ukrainian corporation in the territory of the Russian Federation', which did not relate to the 'international responsibility' of Ukraine.[96] Accordingly, the tribunal rejected that the Monetary Gold problem affected its jurisdiction over the case as such. The tribunal then proceeded to assess jurisdictional objections, including the territorial status of Crimea. This question, the tribunal reframed as described above to circumvent an adjudication of any international responsibility, rights, or obligations of a state not party to the dispute.

DTEK Krymenergo is for many reasons a controversial decision, and it arguably appears absurd that an investor-state tribunal determines questions related to the territorial dispute over the status of Crimea. Particularly in a context where international courts or organisations such as the ICJ or the United Nations, which are generally endowed with the competence and jurisdiction to decide issues related to sovereign disputes, have not been able to do so under the principle of state sovereignty.

Arguably, the decision in *DTEK Krymenergo* also demonstrates the *raison d'être* of the Monetary Gold principle, namely that the principle of state sovereignty requires the consent of a state for a court or tribunal to adjudicate matters regarding that state's rights and obligations. As stated in *Larsen*, the Monetary Gold principle is derived from the principle of consent under international law and is not dependent on the decision having binding effect on third parties or setting a binding precedent. Even though a tribunal's finding on the territorial state of Crimea is as such not binding under international law, it may still have the unintended effect of extending Russia's obligations under the BIT. One might wonder how this geopolitical situation played into the reasoning of the tribunal in *DTEK Krymenergo* when finding that the BIT definition of territory only required effective control, not sovereignty, over the territory. Paradoxically, in *DTEK Krymenergo*, recognising territorial rights and obligations of Russia over the internationally recognised Ukrainian territory of Crimea for the purpose of the BIT worked in favour of Ukraine by conferring investor rights and protection to Ukrainian investors. The decision hence strengthened Ukrainian investors' legal position under international law *vis-à-vis* the Russian state.

The Reframing Approach can also be identified in *Pildegovics*, where a dispute arose under the Latvian-Norwegian BIT. In this case, the Latvian investor claimed that Norwegian restrictions on snow crab fishing infringed upon the investor's investments in this industry. Among other arguments advanced, the Latvian investor alleged that Norway's non-recognition of certain fishing licences constituted an infringement of its investment as a foreign investor under the Latvian-Norwegian BIT. The fishing licences

95. *Ibid.*, para. 223, citing *Monetary Gold, supra* n. 38, 33.
96. *DTEK Krymenergo, supra* n. 2, para. 224.

were issued by Latvia under EU law and used for snow crab fishing by four vessels, mainly operating in Russian waters. Norway argued that this pleading would require the tribunal to assess whether Latvia had issued certain fishing licences lawfully and in general the 'EU's rights and obligations under the Svalbard Treaty, the NEAFC Convention, and UNCLOS.'[97] Accordingly, Norway sought to oppose the jurisdiction of the tribunal due to the Monetary Gold problem.

The tribunal reframed the legal issue before it and structured its analysis by assessing whether the fishing licences and vessels in question constituted an investment in Norway under the scope of the Latvian-Norwegian BIT. It concluded that neither the vessels, whose main activities took place in the territory of Russia, nor the licences, which were issued by Latvia, constituted investments in Norway.[98] The licences did not confer any rights upon the Latvian investor in relation to Norway, but were an EU requirement to undertake fishing in the whole North East Atlantic area.[99] Based on these findings, the tribunal did not find it had jurisdiction over claims arising from these fishing licences and vessels under the Latvian-Norwegian BIT.[100] Accordingly, the tribunal could reject these claims without considering questions of the lawful conduct, rights, or obligations of either Latvia or the EU.

To broadly illustrate how this may play out in an arbitration between an aggrieved investor from an 'unfriendly' country and the Russian Federation pleading a countermeasure defence, let us assume the hypothetical investor is Danish and the measure faced is undoubtedly expropriation without compensation. Expropriation is regulated under Article 4 of the Danish-Russian BIT, which stipulates (emphasis added):

(1) Investments of investors of either Contracting Party shall not be nationalized, expropriated or subjected to measures having effect equivalent to nationalization or expropriation (hereinafter referred to as 'expropriation') in the territory of the other Contracting Party except for measures taken in the public interest on a basis of non-discrimination and *against prompt, adequate and effective compensation. Such compensation shall amount to the value of the investment expropriated immediately before the expropriation or impending expropriation became public knowledge. The compensation shall be paid without delay, be freely transferable and shall include interest at the normal commercial rate established on a market basis from the date of expropriation until the date of payment.*

(2) The investor affected shall, have the right, under the law of the Contracting Party making the expropriation, to prompt review, by a judicial or other independent authority of that Contracting Party, of his or its case and of the valuation of his or its investment in accordance with the principles set out in this chapter.

In order to offer the tribunal a mechanism to avoid considering whether the countermeasure is lawful as a circumstance precluding wrongfulness under ARSIWA and

97. *Pildegovics, supra* n. 1, para. 137.
98. *Ibid.*, paras 270-275.
99. *Ibid.*, para. 275.
100. *Ibid.*, para. 299.

customary international law, the investor could argue that the Danish-Russian BIT does not allow for any exceptions to or exculpations from the obligation to pay compensation for expropriation. Arguably, the clear and detailed regulation of the right to compensation in cases of expropriation under Article 4 persists regardless of the reason for the expropriation. Accordingly, one could argue that the invocation of countermeasures as circumstance precluding wrongfulness, which as previously noted generally exculpates the acting state from financial liability related to the countermeasure, does not affect the specific right of compensation under Article 4, which is not dependent on liability of the state, but functions as an isolated mechanism. This would reframe the question of the validity of Russia's countermeasures defence into a question of the right and obligations arising from Article 4 of the Danish-Russian BIT.

The purpose of this example is not to opine on the legally correct application of Article 4 of the Danish-Russian BIT, and the present authors do not necessarily agree with the suggested interpretation of the BIT *vis-à-vis* the operation of countermeasures under international law. Nonetheless, this hypothetical example may serve to illustrate that reframing the issue could potentially be a case strategy for the investor to avoid the Monetary Gold issue related to the countermeasure defence.

[E] The Authoritative Decision Approach

The simplest approach to circumvent the Monetary Gold problem is to take advantage of the 'authoritative decisions' exception to the Monetary Gold principle stated in *Larsen* and implied in *East Timor*. Under this approach, the tribunal could either, to the extent possible, base its findings concerning third states on international authoritative decisions so that the 'legal finding against an absent third party could be taken as given' or can be framed as a 'finding of fact, not entailing or requiring any legal assessment'. The tribunal in *DTEK Krymenergo* arguably also relied on a consensus version of the 'Authoritative Decision Approach' when finding that Crimea was under effective occupation by Russia since 2014, as both parties agreed on this. Hence, no legal assessment of the state of occupation under international law was necessary.

As of the time of writing, no authoritative decision on the lawfulness of the international sanctions against the Russian Federation has been made. The invasion of Ukraine has been condemned in interim decisions by the ICJ, European Court of Human Rights (ECHR) and resolutions by the UN General Assembly (UNGA), although without explicitly endorsing sanctions against Russia.[101]

101. *Allegations of Genocide under the Convention on the Prevention and Punishment of the Crime of Genocide, Ukraine v. Russian Federation*, International Court of Justice, Decision on Provisional Measures of 16 March 2022; *Ukraine v. Russia (X)*, Case No. 11055/22, The European Court of Human Rights, Decision on Interim Measures of 1 March 2022; United Nations General Assembly Resolution A/ES-11/L.1 of 1 March 2022.

Thus, the investor could wait for an authoritative decision prior to commencing arbitration. Here, the question would be which decisions can be upheld as internationally authoritative. In *Larsen* and *East Timor,* UN Security Council and UNGA Resolutions were implied to be adequately authoritative, even though the argument essentially failed.[102] In the present political climate, it is unlikely that any authoritative decision will be made on the issue. Awaiting an authoritative decision on the matter would certainly sidestep the Monetary Gold problem – but only by foregoing arbitration, and accordingly redress, altogether.

§12.05 CONCLUSION

The Monetary Gold problem places the tribunal with the challenge of hearing and assessing the validity of the claims and objections presented by the parties, and avoiding any adjudication of a third state's rights, obligations, or conduct. If the Monetary Gold principle is not observed, the tribunal will transgress its jurisdiction, whereas if claims or objections are dismissed to a too wide extent based on this principle, the parties might claim an infringement on their right to be heard and access to justice. If not handled with caution, the Monetary Gold problem will either lead to procedural deadlock or jeopardise the enforcement of the award.

Based on an analysis of how tribunals have approached the Monetary Gold problem, different methods can be identified through which the tribunals have acknowledged the problem and the limitations it entails, yet have succeeded in determining the legal issues before them. These methods can be categorised as: (1) Individual Rights versus Derivative Rights Approach, (2) The Procedural Approach, (3) The 'Very Subject-Matter' Approach, (4) The Reframing Approach, (5) The Authoritative Decision Approach.

An application of one or more of these approaches can assist investors from 'unfriendly states' affected by Russian countersanctions in structuring their arguments before a tribunal, so that the Monetary Gold problem is handled appropriately and to their benefit.

As discussed in the above analysis, the extent to which each of these methods is likely to be successful will inevitably depend on the specific case at hand and the composition of the tribunal. It is the present author's belief that the Individual Rights Approach, in the alternative the Procedural Approach, offers the most clear-cut defence that should be advanced by the investor. The remaining methods may serve as inspiration for case strategies, which can also be used in cases if the Monetary Gold problem arises in a different context than countermeasures.

As the case law presented in this chaptershows, the Monetary Gold problem can arise in various ways in an investor-state dispute besides the invocation of countermeasures against a third state, including as part of a claim of duress imposed by a third state, a claim of conspiracy with/incitement by a third state, or a claim about the status under the BIT of a territory at dispute with a third state.

102. *Larsen, supra* n. 47, para. 11.24; *East Timor, supra* n. 42, para. 20.

Most of BITs were signed amidst the economic momentum of the late twentieth century,[103] following the end of the Cold War and the shift towards liberal market economics. In order to attract foreign investment, states globally pledged treaty-based protections against expropriation, discrimination, and other Machiavellian manoeuvres to curb hesitations from private economic actors to engage in historically unpredictable regimes. To ensure that the rights and protections of investors would prevail even if the geopolitical tapestry unravelled, the investment treaties sought to enshrine the right of redress through investor-state arbitration.

In the modern geopolitical landscape, where foreign states revert to the use of sanctions, tariffs, and other economic measures of geopolitical pressure, investors are not shielded from the political realities. Rather, as the geopolitical tapestry unravels, the separating lines between investors and their home state seem to blur, as private entities are perceived as viable targets in the inter-state conflict. In this environment, investor-state disputes are foreseeable, and the possible relevance in such disputes of third states' rights, obligations, or conduct is likely. Thus, engaged actors should understand and be prepared for the risks of the Monetary Gold problem and how it may be approached. In this context, parties to a conflict can learn and benefit from the strategic use of the five approaches identified.

The current geopolitical turmoil demonstrates that the late twentieth century's ideals of global free trade, prosperity through foreign investments, and peaceful relations through economic interdependence can no longer be relied upon. This geopolitical reality affects the fundamental objectives of the international framework of BITs, namely, to separate investors from identification with their home state and offer them protection independent of the changing diplomatic relations with the host state. Thus, in the intricate dance of international relations, where legal frameworks tango with geopolitical realities, the pivotal question arises: do investors truly enjoy protection without prejudice to the acts of their home state, or is this merely a peacetime privilege of flourishing diplomacy? The re-emerging relevance of the Monetary Gold principle points to the latter.

103. Michael Waibel et al., *The Backlash Against Investment Arbitration*, 46 (Kluwer Law International, 2010).

CHAPTER 13

'Security for Costs Against Russian Claimants in View of the Risk of Unenforceability of Adverse Costs Awards'

Tetiana Osypenko

§13.01 INTRODUCTION

The parties opting for arbitration to resolve their disputes expect guaranteed access to justice and, ultimately, an enforceable award.

A security for costs order by an arbitral tribunal is a type of interim measure that lies at the intersection of the above two interests and gives rise to the following considerations:

- the respondent's interest in enforcing a costs award as a way to recover financial losses it has suffered to fend off wrongful claims;
- the claimant's access to justice in pursuing its genuine claim;
- the predictability and flexibility of international arbitration, which are common yet sometimes conflicting aspirations of arbitration users.

For the sake of clarity, security for costs refers to security for costs of legal representation the respondent incurred to defend his case, and the tribunal's order for security for costs can be made against the claimant/counterclaimant in the dispute.[1]

Security for costs is generally considered a common law mechanism for securing the future costs order in favour of respondents. In arbitrations seated in civil law

1. 'Chapter 17: Provisional Relief in International Arbitration (Updated December 2023)', in Gary B. Born, International Commercial Arbitration, 3rd ed., (© Kluwer Law International; Kluwer Law International 2021), §17.01, [G], [e].

countries, security for costs (also known as caution judicature solve) has generally been taken with considerable caution and granted only in exceptional circumstances.[2]

At the same time, due to a raft of ever-expanding sanctions policies across the world, enforcement of foreign arbitral awards, including cost awards, under the New York Convention 1958 has arguably become at least more complicated and at worst effectively impossible in certain factual scenarios.

Against this background, security for costs stands as one of the potential solutions to mitigate the increasing risk of unenforceability of adverse cost awards against Russian claimants in Russia, countries that sanctioned Russia, and even so-called neutral jurisdictions.

This chapter analyses the measure in the context of Russian claimants in the following steps. In §13.02, the chapter describes the legal standards for granting security for costs under section 38(3) of the English Arbitration Act 1996 and Article 38 of the SCC Arbitration Rules. Sections 13.03 and 13.04 analyse the risk of unenforceability of adverse cost awards against Russian claimants in Russia and countries that sanctioned Russia within the lens of the criterion of the location of assets as part of the assessment of security for costs applications. Section 13.05 is devoted to the High Court judgment in *PJSC Tatneft v. Bogolyubov* case, dealing with security for costs against Russian claimants in the context of sanctions. Finally, the chapter draws conclusions on the relevance of the criterion of the location of assets of Russian claimants for the purposes of security for costs applications and the viability of the measure to mitigate the risk of unenforceability of adverse cost awards against Russian claimants.

§13.02 LEGAL STANDARDS FOR GRANTING SECURITY FOR COSTS UNDER SECTION 38(3) OF THE ENGLISH ARBITRATION ACT 1996 AND ARTICLE 38 OF THE SCC ARBITRATION RULES

Given its roots in common law, the mechanism of security for costs is first examined through the lens of the English *lex arbitri,* which not only reflects the influence of common law but also stands out as one of the few arbitration statutes to include an express provision on the matter. In view of the widely discussed amendments to the English Arbitration Act 1996 that are to enter into force in the near future, it is worth noting that the amended English Arbitration Act 2025 leaves untouched the provision on security for costs in section 38(3).[3] Then, the analysis of the institutional approach follows, with the focus on the SCC Arbitration Rules 2023. The provision on security for costs in the SCC Arbitration Rules bears crucial weight in light of the absence of an express provision on the security for costs in the Swedish *lex arbitri*.

2. 'Chapter 17: Provisional Relief in International Arbitration (Updated December 2023)', in Gary B. Born, International Commercial Arbitration, 3rd ed., (© Kluwer Law International; Kluwer Law International 2021), §17.02 [G] [4] [e], p. 601; Berger, Bernard, 'Security for Costs: Trends and Developments in Swiss Arbitral Case Law.' ASA Bulletin 28 (2010), no. 1: 7-81, pp. 7-9 https://doi.org/10.54648/asab2010005 (accessed 1 October 2025).
3. *Arbitration Act 1995*, https://www.legislation.gov.uk/ukpga/2025/4/enacted (accessed 18 May 2025).

Before delving into the specifics of the standard for assessment of security for costs applications, it must be emphasised that the first and foremost condition for ordering security for costs is the possibility of cost-shifting from the winning party to the unsuccessful party under the applicable law or rules. In this regard, both the English Arbitration Act 1996 and the SCC Arbitration Rules bestow discretion upon the tribunal to apportion costs of arbitration between the parties as it deems reasonable, subject to the parties' agreement.[4] Below, we describe the general standards for assessing security for costs applications under section 38(3) of the English Arbitration Act 1996 and Article 38 of the SCC Arbitration Rules 2023.

[A] The English Arbitration Act 1996

The English Arbitration Act 1996 in section 38(3) expressly provides for the power of the arbitral tribunal to order a claimant to provide security for costs.

To enforce the measure, the tribunal can, as per Article 41(6) of the English Arbitration Act 1996, issue a peremptory order and, failing the party's compliance, make an award dismissing the claim.

Prior to the 1996 reform of the English Arbitration Act, the authority to order security for costs was reserved for the national courts. However, this was criticised as an encroachment on the parties' agreement to avoid the courts and have their disputes decided by an independent and impartial tribunal of their choice.[5]

It should be emphasised that the specific provision for the jurisdiction of the arbitral tribunal to order security for costs in section 38(3) enhances party autonomy and contributes to legal certainty as compared to the Swedish *lex arbitri*, where security for costs is not specified as a distinct form of interim relief.

With respect to the standard for assessing security for costs applications, the English Arbitration Act 1996 provides little guidance, except that Article 38(3) explicitly excludes the non-residence criterion from the grounds on which security for costs order may be made.

This power shall not be exercised on the ground that the claimant is:

(a) an individual ordinarily resident outside the United Kingdom; or
(b) a corporation or association incorporated or formed under the law of a country outside the United Kingdom, or whose central management and control is exercised outside the United Kingdom.

In the context of Russian claimants, it can be inferred that nationality as such cannot be the criterion for granting security for costs. By contrast, the English Civil Procedure Rules – which apply where English court is asked to grant security for costs

4. English Arbitration Act 1996, section 61; SCC Arbitration Rules 2023, Art. 49(6), Art. 50. *See also*: ICC Arbitration Rules 2021, Art. 38(4)-(5); LCIA Arbitration Rules 2020, Art. 28.2-28.3.
5. 'Part 4: Chapter II – The Arbitral Proceedings', in Emmanuel Gaillard and John Savage (eds), Fouchard Gaillard Goldman on International Commercial Arbitration (© Kluwer Law International; Kluwer Law International 1999), pp. 655-708, p. 687.

– explicitly include the fact of residence or incorporation as a separate ground on which security for costs may be granted.[6]

That said, in international arbitration, the tribunal enjoys broad discretion to decide on the appropriateness of the measure, subject to the general duty of the tribunal in section 33 of the English Arbitration Act 1996.[7] Essentially, the tribunal can take into account, amongst other factors, the location of assets of the claimant when ruling on a security for costs application.[8]

In English-seated arbitrations, the CIArb Guideline on Applications for Security for Costs (*CIArb Guideline*) has been relied on as a useful source of reference, 'setting out the current best practice in international commercial arbitration in relation to security for costs applications'.[9]

The CIArb Guideline emphasises that granting security for costs must always be weighed against the risk of stifling a genuine claim and that the measure is appropriate only in particular circumstances. Arbitral tribunals should always ensure that they have the power to order security for costs under the applicable rules and laws, and that the parties are given a fair opportunity to present their case.[10]

Pursuant to Article 1 of the CIArb Guideline, arbitral tribunals have to take into account the following three criteria:

- the prospects of success of the claim(s) and defence(s);
- the claimant's ability to satisfy an adverse cost award and the availability of the claimant's assets for enforcement of an adverse cost award; and
- whether it is fair in all of the circumstances to require one party to provide security for the other party's costs.[11]

The above requirements merit more detailed consideration.

First, the tribunal shall undertake a prima facie assessment of claims and defences, but must never go as far as to prejudge the outcome of the case. In most cases, this criterion is not determinative for the purposes of the security for costs application,[12] unlike in the early dismissal procedure,[13] where the merits of the claims and defences are the focus of the tribunal's analysis.

6. *Merkin and Flannery on the Arbitration Act 1996*, pp. 399-400.
7. Harris, *The Arbitration Act 1996, A Commentary*, 4th ed. (2007), p. 190.
8. *Ibid.*; Merkin and Flannery on the Arbitration Act 1996, pp. 403-404.
9. Camilleri, Simon P., 'Between rags and riches: rethinking security for costs in international commercial arbitration', Arbitration International 37 (December 2021), no. 4, pp. 851-862, p. 856 https://doi-org.ezp.sub.su.se/10.1093/arbint/aiab036 (accessed 1 October 2025); ICC Dispute Resolution Bulletin 2020 No. 2, ICC-PO-2020-225, para. 4.2.
10. *CIArb Guideline on Applications for Security for Costs 2015*, pp. 1-4, https://www.ciarb.org/media/epgj4eb2/5-security-for-costs-2015.pdf (accessed 1 October 2025).
11. *Ibid.*, p. 3.
12. *Ibid.*, pp. 5-6.
13. An early dismissal procedure allows the tribunal to dismiss the claim on a summary basis if the party has no real prospect of succeeding in the claim. Notably, the English Arbitration Act 2025 in section 39A expressly empowers the tribunal, on an application of a party to the proceedings, to make awards on a summary basis.

Second, the circumstances that affect the claimant's ability to satisfy an adverse cost award and the availability of assets for enforcement shall be at the core of the tribunal's consideration. The CIArb Guideline lists as a relevant factor the risk of a cost award being unenforceable in the place of the claimant's residence or in the jurisdiction in which the claimant's assets are located. This factor, however, has rarely been successfully invoked due to the generally unproblematic enforcement of foreign arbitral awards under the New York Convention 1958. Further relevant circumstances for the purposes of the tribunal's assessment include the insolvency of the claimant and the existence of persons who stand to benefit from the award on the merits but bear no liability for a possible adverse cost award (e.g., third-party funders).[14]

To underscore, the concept of 'accepted commercial risk' may prevent the tribunal from granting security for costs if the respondent knew of the claimant's financial situation, place of residence and/or location of assets at the time of entering into a contractual relationship, and may be deemed to have accepted the risk of dealing with such a counterparty, including the possibility of unenforceability of an adverse cost award against him.[15]

Lastly, upon finding, based on the above criteria, that grounds for ordering security for costs exist, the tribunal must consider whether it would be fair to do so, having regard to the wider picture of the dispute and the overarching consideration of not stifling a genuine claim. For instance, the procedural history of non-compliance with cost orders by claimant or respondent, whether the cause of the claimant's impecuniosity may be attributed to the respondent's actions, as well as the timing of the application for security for costs should be factored into the tribunal's analysis.[16]

By way of example, in an ICC case seated in the United Kingdom, the tribunal relied on the criteria outlined in the CIArb Guideline while recognising the relevance of the applicable standard adopted in English civil litigation.[17]

In particular, the respective Procedural order provides as follows:

> 4.2. First, the Tribunal should consider the probability that the claimant will be unable to pay the likely amount of an award of costs assuming that the respondent's defence is accepted and that the award of costs is made and if so, second, should consider whether it fair and just in all the circumstances of the case to make an order for security.
>
> 4.3. This Tribunal adopts the two-stage analysis suggested in the Chartered Institute of Arbitrators Guidelines.

In assessing the probability that the claimant would not satisfy a costs award, the tribunal stated that it should consider persuasive evidence relating to all pertinent circumstances, such as the party's ability to fund the commencement of arbitral proceedings, the possible involvement of an undisclosed third-party funder, the party's conduct during the proceedings, including whether advances on costs were paid in a

14. *Ibid.*, pp. 7-9.
15. *Ibid.*, pp. 7-8.
16. *Ibid.*, pp. 9-12.
17. ICC Dispute Resolution Bulletin 2020 No. 2, ICC-PO-2020-225, paras 4.2-4.3.

timely manner, or any counterclaims advanced by the party requesting security, particularly where such counterclaims were based on the same facts as the original claims.[18] The tribunal notably omitted analysis of the prospects of claims and defences. Applying the standard to the circumstances of the case, the tribunal ordered the claimant to provide security for costs based on a set of factors pointing to the significant likelihood of the claimant's inability to satisfy the potential adverse cost award, such as the difficulties the claimant experienced in securing funding for the arbitration and its reliance on third-party funding, the fact that its legal fees in the arbitration had exceeded its equity, as well as the claimant's financial structure.[19]

Based on the above, the following conclusions may be drawn.

First, the Arbitration Act 1996 does not elaborate on the particular standard (conditions) for ordering security for costs and, in principle, the assessment of security for costs applications turns very much on the facts of the particular case. Second, the criteria set in international practice, such as the CIArb Guideline and ICC practice, are highly relevant in international arbitrations under English *lex arbitri*. Third, the relevance of civil litigation case law in international arbitrations should be limited to providing guidance in the particular circumstances (e.g., where the factual context is complex and has not been fleshed out in the relevant arbitration case law, as is the case with Russian claimants), and never reach the point of being binding precedents for English-seated tribunals. Finally, the robust 'internal' enforcement mechanism of security for costs enhances the practical effect of the measure, but at the same time reflects the underlying risks of limiting access to justice and implies the exceptional character of the measure in international arbitration.

[B] SCC Arbitration Rules

Article 38(1) of the SCC Arbitration Rules expressly provides for the power of the tribunal to order, at the request of a party, security for costs against the claimant or counterclaimant.[20]

The explicit inclusion of a security for costs provision in the SCC Arbitration Rules 2017 (and more recent editions of the SCC Arbitration Rules) provides essential legal certainty regarding the tribunal's authority to grant such a measure in SCC arbitrations, particularly in light of the absence of a corresponding provision under Swedish *lex arbitri*.[21]

18. *Ibid.*, para. 4.2.
19. *Ibid.*, paras 5.1-5.8.
20. SCC Arbitration Rules 2023, Art. 38 (1).
21. Patricia Louise Shaughnessy, 'Chapter 7: Interim Measures', in Annette Magnusson, Jakob Ragnwaldh et al. (eds), International Arbitration in Sweden: A Practitioner's Guide, 2nd ed., (© Kluwer Law International; Kluwer Law International 2021), pp. 177-200, p. 195, para. 44; Johan Sidklev, 'Chapter 23: Security for Costs in the SCC Rules', in Sherlin Tung, Fabricio Fortese et al. (eds), Finances in International Arbitration: Liber Amicorum Patricia Shaughnessy (© Kluwer Law International; Kluwer Law International 2019) pp. 437-446, pp. 439-440; Kristoffer Löf, Aron Skogman et al., 'Chapter 9: The Proceedings', in Annette Magnusson et al. (eds),

The wording of the provision in the SCC Arbitration Rules is notably more detailed in comparison to the English Arbitration Act. Article 38 stipulates that security for costs may be granted only in exceptional circumstances and further enumerates the relevant considerations that tribunals must take into account when determining such applications:

- the prospects of success of the claims, counterclaims and defences;
- the claimant's or counterclaimant's ability to comply with an adverse cost award and the availability of assets for enforcement of an adverse cost award;
- whether it is appropriate in all the circumstances of the case to order one party to provide security; and
- any other relevant circumstances.

The above criteria, together with the overarching 'exceptional circumstances' threshold, are consistent with prevailing international best practices on security for costs in international arbitration reflected in the CIArb Guideline.

From a practical perspective, the SCC Practice Note on Security for Costs for the period from 2017 to 2022 (*SCC Practice Note*) indicates that thirty-one applications for security for costs had been submitted during this time, which is a significant increase compared to the few applications prior to the introduction of the provision. This trend confirms that an express provision on security for costs facilitates more frequent recourse to the measure, thereby contributing to the development of case law on the matter and promoting a more structured and effective approach to its application. Notably, out of the thirty-one applications submitted, tribunals had granted security for costs in only two instances, underscoring the high 'exceptional circumstances' threshold imposed by the SCC Arbitration Rules for granting such relief.[22]

In this regard, the SCC Practice Note offers valuable insight into the circumstances that may (or may not) qualify as 'exceptional' for the purpose of granting security for costs.

In the first case where security for costs was granted, the tribunal weighed and balanced the criteria set out in Article 38 and ultimately deemed the claimant's insolvency during the course of the proceedings to constitute an exceptional circumstance justifying ordering security for costs. A notable element of the factual scenario was that the deadline for registering claims in the claimant's insolvency proceedings had already lapsed, thereby precluding the respondent from potentially enforcing a cost award within those proceedings.

International Arbitration in Sweden: A Practitioner's Guide, 2nd ed. (© Kluwer Law International; Kluwer Law International 2021), pp. 217-326, p. 300; Bruno Gustafsson, 'Chapter 10: Art. 38 of the SCC Rules – An Analysis of Security for Costs in TPF Arbitration', in Axel Calissendorff and Patrik Schöldstrom (eds), Stockholm Arbitration Yearbook 2019, Stockholm Arbitration Yearbook Series, vol. 1 (© Kluwer Law International; Kluwer Law International 2019) pp. 137-154, pp. 139-140.

22. Jake Lowther, Gaurav Majumdar, *SCC Practice Note on Security for Costs 2017-2022*, SCC Arbitration Institute, p. 3.

In the second case, a dispute arose in relation to the termination of a third-party funding agreement between an individual (claimant) and a third-party funder (respondent). The tribunal assessed the facts in light of the established criteria, including those provided in the CIArb Guideline, and determined that the claimant's failure to provide sufficient evidence of available funds in this particular context constituted an exceptional circumstance warranting the order for security for costs.[23]

In the remaining cases where security for costs was denied, the tribunals identified the crucial factors that weighed – individually and/or cumulatively – against granting the measure, as summarised below:

- the absence of a fundamental change in circumstances between the conclusion of the arbitration agreement and the application for security for costs, as the respondent was deemed to have accepted the risk of engaging with a counterparty in a precarious financial position;
- too late timing of the application ('a final award could be expected shortly'), 'relatively small' amount of claim, and the fact that most of the respondent's costs had already been incurred;
- the difficulty in assessing the prospects of claims and defences at the early stage of the proceedings;
- the mere fact that the claimant was registered in a foreign jurisdiction, which was known to the respondent at the time of entering into the contractual relationship;
- procedural history of the arbitration, e.g, the claimant's timely payments related to the arbitration proceedings, especially as opposed to the respondent's failure to pay its share of the advance on costs;
- the absence of specific evidence demonstrating the claimant's inability to satisfy a potential cost award, beyond an undisputed fact of limited financial resources, as well as the security for costs applications delving too deep into the merits of the dispute.[24]

Accordingly, SCC tribunals have granted security for costs applications only in exceptional circumstances, with the applications and the tribunal's assessment centring on claimants' alleged impecuniosity. That said, the risk of unenforceability of an adverse costs award at the location of a claimant's assets directly impacts the availability of assets for enforcement in Russia or elsewhere, as per Article 38(2)(ii), and should remain a valid ground for ordering security for costs.

***

Based on the brief overview of the standards for granting security for costs under the English Arbitration Act 1996 and SCC Arbitration Rules, it can be generalised that the risk of non-enforcement has been mostly assessed from the perspective of the extent of the impecuniosity of the claimant. Unlike in civil litigation, arbitration case law demonstrates that the risk of unenforceability of an adverse cost award at the

23. *Ibid.*, pp. 6-8.
24. *Ibid.*, pp. 10-32.

location of the claimant's assets has been rarely, if ever, successfully invoked. This is largely due to the successful operation of the 1958 New York Convention establishing a comprehensive framework for the recognition and enforcement of foreign arbitral awards in more than 170 Contracting States.

The situation, however, appears to have changed, as will be demonstrated in the next part.

§13.03 LOCATION OF ASSETS IN RUSSIA: THE RISK OF UNENFORCEABILITY OF ADVERSE COST AWARDS

It should be emphasised that the mere fact of a claimant's incorporation in Russia does not, in itself, constitute a sufficient ground for ordering security for costs, absent specific circumstances indicating a genuine risk of non-enforcement. That said, the location of assets in Russia may arguably present a serious risk that an adverse cost award rendered against a Russian claimant – whether sanctioned or not – will be unenforceable within Russia.

This part will outline the legal basis for denying recognition and enforcement of cost awards in Russia and consider the recent anti-arbitration stance of Russian lawmakers and courts through the lens of a risk of unenforceability of an adverse cost award.[25]

[A] Legal Basis for Denying Recognition and Enforcement of Foreign Arbitral Awards in Russia

The Russian Federation is a Contracting State to the New York Convention 1958.[26]

Article V of the New York Convention 1958 sets out an exhaustive list of grounds to refuse recognition and enforcement of a foreign arbitral award, which national courts are expected to interpret narrowly in line with the general pro-enforcement bias of the Convention.[27] In the context of our analysis, the public policy ground for denying recognition and enforcement as laid down in Article V.2.(b) is particularly relevant.

While Article 36 of the Law of the Russian Federation on International Commercial Arbitration (12 August 1993, as amended) does not entirely mirror the wording of Article V of the New York Convention 1958, Article 36.1(2) provides that recognition and enforcement of a foreign arbitral award may be refused if the court – either upon the request of the opposing party or ex officio – determines that enforcement would be contrary to the public policy of the Russian Federation.

Additionally, by virtue of Article 244.1.(3) of the Arbitrazh Procedure Code of the Russian Federation (*Arbitrazh Procedure Code*), the courts are authorised – at the

25. As designated by the Government Directive No. 430-r of 5 March 2022.
26. Contracting States, https://www.newyorkconvention.org/contracting-states (accessed 31 March 2025).
27. New York Convention 1958, Art. V; 'Chapter 26: Recognition and Enforcement of International Arbitral Awards (Updated March 2024)', in Gary B. Born, International Commercial Arbitration, 3rd ed. (© Kluwer Law International; Kluwer Law International 2021), §26.03, [B], [1].

request of the opposing party or ex officio – to refuse recognition and enforcement of an arbitral award rendered in a dispute involving sanctioned parties that falls within the exclusive competence of state commercial courts, as per Article 248.1.

[B] Anti-arbitration Stance of Russian Lawmakers and Courts

The anti-arbitration notion of Russian public policy underlying the risk of unenforceability of adverse cost awards is evident from the relevant legislative amendments and judicial practice regarding the enforcement of foreign arbitration agreements and arbitral awards.

Article 248.1 (paragraph 4) of the Arbitrazh Procedure Code, as introduced in 2020, essentially grants arbitrazh courts (state commercial courts, not to be confused with arbitral tribunals) exclusive jurisdiction in disputes involving sanctioned parties where the participation of such parties in foreign-seated arbitrations would create for them obstacles to access to justice. Based on Article 248.2 the sanctioned party may also request that a Russian court issue an anti-suit (anti-arbitration) injunction prohibiting commencing or continuing arbitral proceedings in a foreign arbitral forum.[28]

In its landmark judgment in *Uraltransmash v. PESA* dated 9 December 2021, the Supreme Court of the Russian Federation held that the mere fact of a party being subject to sanctions presumptively creates obstacles to its access to justice in arbitral proceedings seated in sanctioning countries.[29]

Below, we outline the 'anti-arbitration' practice of Russian courts with respect to the recognition and enforcement of arbitration agreements and awards following the 2020 sanctions-related amendments and the notorious *Uraltransmash v. PESA* case.

In the context of enforcement of arbitration agreements, there has been a series of judgments by Russian courts, disregarding arbitration clauses providing for seats and institutions in 'unfriendly countries' (EU, UK and other countries that introduced sanctions against Russia) and, notably, Asia (Hong Kong, Singapore) on the basis that sanctioned parties are unable to get a fair trial at contractually agreed arbitral forums.[30]

In its judgment No. A56-129797/2022 (*Ruschemalliance v. Linde)*, the Arbitrazh Court of Saint Petersburg and Leningrad Region opined that arbitration proceedings at HKIAC (with the seat in Hong Kong and English law applicable to the substance) would not provide a Russian claimant with a fair trial since the performance of the contract by

28. Arbitrazh Procedure Code of Russian Federation, Art. 248_1,-248_2.
29. Judgment of the Supreme Court of Russian Federation dated 9 December 2021, https://kad.arbitr.ru/Document/Pdf/99ce7aa2-7f06-4615-baa5-94473b980771/1f0d228b-cefb-435f-a5f1-8950060144da/A60-36897-2020_20211209_Opredelenie.pdf?isAddStamp=True (accessed 30 March 2025).
30. *See*, among others, Judgment of the Moscow Arbitrazh Court of 24 August 2022 No. A40-98907/22-3-711; Judgment of the Moscow District Arbitrazh Court of 3 February 2023 No. A40-98865/2022; Judgment of the Arbitrazh Court of Saint Petersburg and Leningrad Region of 1 December 2023 No. A56-84760/2023; Judgment of the Arbitrazh Court of Saint Petersburg and Leningrad Region of 5 December 2023 No. A56-103943/2023; Judgment of the Moscow City Commercial Court of 29 November 2023 No. A40-197598/2023.

Linde had been rendered illegal under the EU sanctions. Additionally, the Court stated that the following circumstances confirmed that the Russian party would not get a fair trial in arbitration proceedings at HKIAC. First, the Court noted that Hong Kong's legal system was heavily influenced by English law, which was bound to affect the tribunal's reasoning. The Court also posited that the Russian party would inevitably encounter difficulties in engaging local counsel to represent it in the arbitration due to reputational damage caused by the sanctions against Russia. Finally, the Court mentioned that the Russian party would, in any event, face problems with bank transfers as HKIAC's bank (HSBC) is a British bank. Therefore, the Court upheld its exclusive jurisdiction over the dispute under Article 248.1 (paragraph 4)of the Arbitrazh Procedure Code.[31]

It may be inferred from the above practice that an adverse cost award issued in breach of Article 248.1 stands a serious risk of unenforceability in Russia.

In this regard, the question arises: why would a sanctioned Russian claimant commence arbitration proceedings in 'unfriendly forums' instead of directly availing itself of an option of judicial remedy in Russian courts under Article 248.1?

First, a sanctioned party may commence proceedings before the foreign-seated arbitral tribunal based on the valid arbitration agreement after investigating the availability (location) of its counterparty's assets against which a possible award could be enforced. Given that Russian judgments are not widely recognised and enforceable, a counterparty's lack of assets in Russia entails poor prospects for the sanctioned party to enforce its claims.

Second, a Russian party may go to arbitration in a contractually agreed arbitral forum and become subsequently subject to sanctions in the course of the arbitration proceedings.

It should be noted that Article 248.1 (paragraph 5). of the Arbitrazh Procedure Code explicitly provides that the recognition and enforcement of a foreign arbitral award may be allowed if the sanctioned party did not object to the jurisdiction of the foreign-seated arbitral tribunal in the arbitration proceedings. Accordingly, if the sanctioned party, acting in good faith, commences arbitration proceedings outside of Russia on the basis of the arbitration agreement, the risk of unenforceability may be deemed, to a certain extent, lower for the purposes of a security for costs application. This would not negate, however, the risk posed by the overall hostile stance of Russian courts towards awards 'tainted by "unfriendly elements"' (e.g., by virtue of the seat, the location of the institution administering the arbitration proceedings, the jurisdiction of the applicable law, etc.).

In the context of enforcement and recognition of arbitral awards, in a judgment rendered in November 2022, the Stavropol Arbitrazh Court refused to enforce an LCIA award, with reference to the Presidential decrees adopted as 'countermeasures' to the Western sanctions. The creditor sought to enforce the award which concerned the obligations of the guarantor, being a debtor in the recognition and enforcement

31. Ruling of the Arbitrazh Court of St. Petersburg and Leningrad Region of 8 June 2023 No. A56-129797/2022, pp. 6-9.

proceedings, under the guarantee securing the performance by the seller (a company incorporated in Cyprus designated as 'an unfriendly state'). The Russian court assumed that the debtor was affiliated with or controlled by the seller incorporated in an 'unfriendly state'. The court stated, among other reasons for refusing recognition and enforcement of the award, that the withdrawal of funds of entities controlled by 'unfriendly states' would run contrary to the public policy of the Russian Federation.[32]

In another judgment dated 24 July 2024, the Supreme Court of the Russian Federation addressed the recognition and enforcement of an arbitral award issued in a FOSFA arbitration governed by the English Arbitration Act 1996. Notably, the tribunal was composed of arbitrators of Ukrainian, British, and Danish nationality. The Supreme Court, in its reasoning, presumed a lack of impartiality solely on the basis of the arbitrators' nationalities.[33]

Based on the above, it can be reasonably inferred that any – even rather indirect – implications of the sanctions and countersanctions regimes on the particular cost award will fall under the Russian notion of safeguarding public policy for the purposes of denying the recognition and enforcement of adverse cost awards against Russian claimants, whether sanctioned or not.

It is, therefore, argued that the location of assets in Russia should weigh heavily in favour of ordering security for costs. However, whether tribunals will opine that the risk meets the applicable standard, especially an 'exceptional risk standard' under the SCC Arbitration Rules, will depend on the particular circumstances of the case.

§13.04 LOCATION OF ASSETS IN THE EU: A RISK OF NON-ENFORCEABILITY OF ADVERSE COST AWARDS DUE TO SANCTIONS PROHIBITIONS

The location of Russian claimants' assets in countries that have introduced sanctions against Russia may also point to a serious risk of an adverse cost award being unenforceable for the purposes of a security for costs application.

Although the analysis in this part is limited to the risk of unenforceability in the EU Member States, the conclusions drawn may also apply to other jurisdictions that have sanctioned Russia insofar as the prohibitions under other sanctions programmes largely mirror those introduced by the EU.

In the context of security for costs applications (and international arbitration proceedings in general), Regulation (EU) No. 269/2014 and Regulation (EU) No. 833/2014,[34] establishing sanctions prohibitions, bear crucial weight for enforcement.

As per Article 5aa(1) of Council Regulation (EU) No. 833/2014, it is prohibited to engage, directly or indirectly, in any transaction with sanctioned entities, which

32. Judgment of the Stavropol Arbitrazh Court of November 2022 No. A63-7553/2022, p. 5.
33. Judgment of the Supreme Court of 26 July 2024 A45-19015/2023.
34. Council Regulation (EU) No. 269/2014 of 17 March 2014 concerning restrictive measures in respect of actions undermining or threatening the territorial integrity, sovereignty and independence of Ukraine; Council Regulation (EU) No. 833/2014 of 31 July 2014 concerning restrictive measures in view of Russia's actions destabilising the situation in Ukraine.

includes transferring and receiving funds under the cost award against Russian claimants.

That said, Article 5aa(3)(g) of Council Regulation (EU) No. 833/2014 exempts from the scope of the general prohibition transactions necessary to ensure access to justice and the recognition and enforcement of an arbitral award, namely:

> transactions which are strictly necessary to ensure access to judicial, administrative or arbitral proceedings in a Member State, as well as for the recognition or enforcement of a judgment or an arbitration award rendered in a Member State and if such transactions are consistent with the objectives of this Regulation and Regulation (EU) No 269/2014.

It is apparent from the wording that the exemption functions only with respect to awards rendered in Member States; that is to say, *the enforcement of awards rendered outside of the EU still falls under the prohibition in Article 5aa(1).*[35]

Article 2.1 of Council Regulation (EU) No. 269/2014 provides for the freeze of assets of sanctioned entities, prohibiting making available funds or economic resources to or for the benefit of the persons listed.

Under Article 5.1(a) of Council Regulation (EU) No. 269/2014, the release of frozen funds may take place under the following conditions:

- the funds or economic resources are subject to an arbitral decision rendered *prior to* the date on which the natural or legal person, entity or body was included in a sanctions list;
- the funds or economic resources will be used exclusively to satisfy claims secured by an arbitral award or recognised as valid in an arbitral award, subject to applicable laws and regulations governing the rights of persons having such claims;
- the decision is not for the benefit of a natural or legal person, entity or body listed;
- recognition of the decision is not contrary to public policy in the Member State concerned.

Essentially, it means that there is no legal basis for the enforcement of a cost award against frozen assets of a sanctioned party if the award was rendered after the party was put on a sanctions list.[36]

Enforcement against frozen funds can be further complicated by the operation of the public policies of the EU Member States, implementing the EU sanctions and establishing procedures for the operation of relevant exemptions and release of frozen funds.

---

35. Kristin Campbell-Wilson and Nataliya Mikhailovna Petrik, 'Chapter 2: Paving the Way for Justice: Arbitration and EU Sanctions Against Russia', in Patrik Schöldström and Christer Danielsson (eds), Stockholm Arbitration Yearbook 2023, Stockholm Arbitration Yearbook Series, vol. 5 (© Kluwer Law International; Kluwer Law International 2023) pp. 11-30, p. 27.
36. *Ibid.*, pp. 11-30, p. 18-19.

In this regard, we refer to a recent ruling by a Paris court dated 25 February 2025 (24/80821), wherein the court denied a Dutch company the ability to seize assets that had been frozen due to international sanctions against Iraq based on a lack of prior authorisation of the French Treasury.

Although the ruling was made in the context of Iraqi sanctions, it serves to showcase the difficulties successful parties may face in enforcing cost awards against Russian persons and entities in the EU.

Accordingly, the existence of the above restrictions on dealing with sanctioned entities creates a serious risk of unenforceability of a cost award for the purposes of the security for costs application.

It should be mentioned, however, that in the event of the serious risk of unenforceability in the EU, the availability of assets of Russian claimants in jurisdictions that have not sanctioned Russia might, albeit not necessarily, prevent tribunals from ordering security for costs. In that case, a tribunal may take into account the nature of the assets available, along with the possibilities for the claimant to dispose of those assets to avoid honouring the adverse cost award and the likelihood that the claimant will undertake such a course of action.

§13.05 *PJSC TATNEFT V. BOGOLYUBOV*: SECURITY FOR COSTS AGAINST RUSSIAN CLAIMANTS IN THE NEW CONTEXT

Given the absence, to the author's knowledge, of publicly available arbitral case law specifically addressing security for costs against Russian claimants, the English judgment in *PJSC Tatneft v. Bogolyubov* [2019] EWHC 1400 (Comm) may provide valuable guidance for assessing the risk of unenforceability in Russia in the context of Russian claimants.

To establish the factual background, the claimant (Tatneft) was incorporated in the Republic of Tatarstan, a constituent member of the Russian Federation. The defendants/applicants for security for costs (Gennadiy Bogolyubov, Igor Kolomoisky, Pavel Ovcharenko, Alexander Yaroslavsky) were Ukrainian nationals. The subject matter of the dispute related, in broad terms, to the alleged non-payment by Ukrainian businessmen for the oil supplied by Tatneft.[37]

The court derived the legal basis to order security for costs from Rule 25.13 of the English Civil Procedure Rules, which reads as follows:

> 25.13 (1) The court may make an order for security for costs under rule 25.12 if:
>
> (a) It is satisfied, having regard to all the circumstances of the case, that it is just to make such an order; and
> (b) one or more of the conditions in paragraph (2) applies
>
> (2) The conditions are –
>
> (a) the claimant is –

37. PJSC *Tatneft v. Bogolyubov [2019]* EWHC 1400 (Comm), p. 3, paras 3-4.

(i) resident out of the jurisdiction; but
(ii) not resident in a Brussels Contracting State, a State bound by the Lugano Convention, a State bound by the 2005 Hague Convention or a Regulation State, as defined in section 1(3) of the Civil Jurisdiction and Judgments Act 1982.

Having found that the condition in paragraph (2) was met (Tatneft was a Russian company), the court reiterated that security for costs shall be ordered against a foreign claimant in a non-discriminatory manner and that to justify ordering security for costs, a real risk of non-enforcement or additional burdens in enforcement in a foreign jurisdiction must be demonstrated.[38]

The court had to consider two aspects: (1) the risk of non-enforcement in Russia and (2) the risk of non-enforcement in Switzerland and Cyprus, where Tatneft had assets.

As for the first aspect, the court ultimately determined that there was a real risk of non-enforcement in Russia based on the following circumstances:

(1) the falling rate of enforcement of Ukrainian and English judgments in Russia within the period from 2015 to 2018;
(2) no bilateral enforcement treaty between the United Kingdom and Russia;
(3) the risk that an English court judgment will not be enforced by the Russian court on the basis of reciprocity;
(4) the risk of non-enforceability of a costs-order not accompanied by the decision on the merits in case of discontinuance of proceedings by Tatneft;
(5) the possibility of non-enforcement by considerations of public policy (Article 244(1) of the Arbitrazh Procedure Code);
(6) sanctions adopted by Russia against defendants.[39]

The court's reasoning on points (5)-(6) merits more detailed consideration.

On point (5), the court considered that Russian courts were empowered to refuse enforcement of a costs order if it would contradict the public policy of the Russian Federation (Article 244(1) of the Arbitrazh Procedure Code). The court, referring to relevant case law and expert opinions, inferred that Russian courts interpreted the concept of public policy 'expansively'. Next, the court referred to a set of factual circumstances pointing to the risk of non-enforcement in Russia based on public policy considerations. First, the merits of the dispute were regarded as issues of public importance by the then-Prime Minister of Tatarstan who 'sought to take it up with the Prime Minister of Ukraine'. Furthermore, the relations between the parties to the dispute 'had become by reason of tensions between Ukraine and Russia over Crimea highly politicised'. Kolomoisky had been subject of a criminal investigation and asset freezing in Russia, as well as public criticism from the president of the Russian Federation, while Bogolyubov and Yaroslavsky had been subject to the Sanctions

38. *Ibid.*, pp. 4-7, paras 6-11.
39. *Ibid.*, pp. 9-13, paras 21-39.

Resolution, and their assets had been frozen within Russia. Ovcharenko was considered 'a close associate of Mr Bogolyubov and Mr Kolomoisky'. Accordingly, there was a real risk that the Russian court would not enforce a potential costs order against Tatneft based on the expansive interpretation of the 'public policy' ground.

On point (6), the court addressed the risk of the non-enforcement of a cost order posed by the inclusion of Bogolyubov and Yaroslavsky in a sanctions list. The defendants were subject to sanctions that included 'Blocking of moneys, securities and property in the territory of the Russian Federation, as well as a prohibition for transfers out of the territory of the Russian Federation.' Upon detailed examination of each of the sanctions prohibitions, the court considered that those presented a real risk of non-enforcement of a cost order in favour of the defendants in Russia.

The court ultimately reasoned that each of the points (3)-(6) demonstrated a real risk of non-enforcement, and accordingly, if taken together with points (1)-(2), there was a clearly established real risk of non-enforcement.[40]

Turning to the assessment of the risk of non-enforcement against the claimant's assets in Switzerland and Cyprus, the court considered the statements of Tatneft as to the availability of assets for enforcement within the zone indicated in Rule 25.13. (2) (ii):

> (1) Tatneft states that it is the 99% owner of Tatneft Oil AG (TOAG), which is a company incorporated in Switzerland. TOAG, it says, is principally an investment holding company, with a total shareholder equity as at [sic] 31 December 2018 of CHF 453,273,431. Tatneft's shares in TOAG are held in bearer form in Switzerland. Tatneft has stated that the bearer shares are held in a safe deposit box at the branch of USB in Zug, Switzerland, under an arrangement between USB and TOAG. TOAG's major assets are said to include its largest subsidiary, Vamolero Holdings Ltd (VHL). VHL is also a holding company, whose principal assets are securities in Tatneft. Tatneft's shares in TOAG are said to be unencumbered.
>
> (2) Tatneft has recently stated that it also holds 100% of the shares in a Cypriot company, Tatneft Finance (Cyprus) Limited (Tatneft Finance). Tatneft's evidence is that Tatneft Finance had, as at [sic] 31 December 2018, total current assets of about USD 9 million, and total non-current assets of about USD 170 million. Its principal assets are said to include its wholly owned subsidiary, Colima Associated SA (Colima), a BVI company, whose main assets are ordinary shares in Tatneft.[41]

The court sided with the defendants' objections that the above assets might not be available for enforcement due to a number of circumstances, including, among others, the possibility for Tatneft to dispose of those assets with relative ease, which, in the court's opinion, was a course of action likely to be taken by Tatneft in view of

40. *Ibid.*, p. 13, para. 38.
41. *Ibid.*, pp. 13-13, para. 41.

'the very hard-fought litigation between parties which are on opposite sides not just of this case, but of wider issues'.[42]

Finally, having established that there was a real risk that the cost order would not be enforced, the court considered whether it was fair to order security for costs, having regard to all the circumstances of the case. The court acknowledged the additional reputational and financial burden that providing security would place on Tatneft. However, the court reasoned, based on the available evidence, that Tatneft had financial capacity to provide security and that the defendants would suffer substantial prejudice if a cost order were not enforced. Therefore, the court concluded that, in these circumstances, it would be just to order security for costs. Accordingly, the court ordered that Tatneft provide security for costs.[43]

Based on the above, the following conclusions may be drawn, which are relevant in the context of applications for security for costs against Russian claimants in international arbitration.

First, in disputes affected by sanctions, it can be reasonably inferred that there is a real risk that recognition and enforcement of a cost order against Russian claimants will be denied in Russia based on the expansive interpretation of the notion of 'public policy' by Russian courts.

Second, the availability of assets of Russian claimants in jurisdictions other than Russia does not automatically preclude ordering security for costs. This is provided that it can be demonstrated that the claimant can easily dispose of the assets and that there is a real risk that enforcement will have to be undertaken in Russia.

Third, if the claimant is financially capable of providing security for costs, the risk of stifling a genuine claim is mostly negated.[44] In such a case, ordering security for costs can be considered a just and balanced measure.

§13.06 CONCLUSIONS

The current political context surrounding Russian claimants has created a host of additional difficulties and risks in international arbitration, of which the risk of foreign arbitral awards being unenforceable by reason of alleged public policy violations due to sanctions is certainly one of the most pressing. The unenforceability of international arbitral awards can seriously undermine the legitimacy of international arbitration by rendering the entire time-consuming and costly process virtually useless for international arbitration users.

It is argued that, in appropriate circumstances, security for costs can serve as an effective tool to mitigate the risk of unenforceability of adverse cost awards in Russia and in the jurisdictions that have imposed sanctions on Russia. Under both the English Arbitration Act 1996 and the SCC Arbitration Rules, tribunals enjoy broad discretion in deciding on security for costs, with due regard to the need to balance the risk of

42. *Ibid.*, p. 15, paras 47-48.
43. *Ibid.*, p. 17, paras 54-57.
44. *Ibid.*, pp. 7-8, para. 7. *See also*: *Bestfort Developments LLP v. Ras Al-Khaimah Investment Authority* [2016] EWCA Civ 1099, para. 47.

non-enforcement – arising from various factors – against the overarching principle of ensuring access to justice. While a claimant's nationality or place of residence cannot, in itself, justify an order for security for costs, the location of Russian claimants' assets may constitute a specific circumstance indicating a serious risk of non-enforcement of an adverse cost award.

Such a risk arises primarily from the anti-arbitration stance of Russian lawmakers and courts refusing recognition and enforcement of foreign arbitral awards affected by sanctions based on the expansive interpretation of public policy. Russian courts can infer obstacles to access to justice for sanctioned parties in foreign-seated arbitration proceedings from the following:

- seat of arbitration in a country that has sanctioned Russia;
- applicable law of the jurisdiction that has sanctioned Russia;
- arbitrators of the nationality of a country that has sanctioned Russia;
- one of the parties of the nationality of a country that has sanctioned Russia.

At the same time, the risk of unenforceability in the EU arises from restrictions on transactions involving Russian parties and the imposition of asset freezes. A comparable risk may exist in other jurisdictions that have implemented similar sanctions frameworks.

All that said, before applying for security for costs against Russian claimants, the following considerations should be borne in mind.

First, some tribunals may take the view that parties choosing to contract with Russian counterparties today have, in effect, accepted the risk that a potential adverse cost award may be unenforceable. While the concept of assumed commercial risk is not explicitly addressed in the relevant provisions of the English Arbitration Act 1996 (section 38) or the SCC Arbitration Rules (Article 38), it has been consistently applied by SCC tribunals and is well established in international arbitration practice.

However, where the risk of non-enforcement was not reasonably foreseeable at the time the arbitration agreement was concluded, such a risk may meet the 'exceptional circumstances' threshold under the SCC Arbitration Rules. Furthermore, in ad hoc arbitrations governed by English *lex arbitri*, tribunals may arguably apply a lower threshold and order security for costs even if the risk of unenforceability was foreseeable at the time of concluding a contract.

Second, apart from the location of assets of Russian claimants, tribunals will take into account other relevant circumstances, such as insolvency of the claimant, the prospects of success of claims and defences, the history of non-payment of advances on costs, the existence of third-party funding and the terms of a funding agreement, as well as any bad faith attempts to move assets. It is argued that the combination of the risk of unenforceability of an adverse cost award at the location of assets and one of the above factors will stand a better chance of meeting the applicable threshold for ordering security for costs.

Third, if the risk of non-enforcement comes not from the claimant's lack of funds but from the unenforceability of a potential cost award – such as when foreign arbitral awards from 'unfriendly states' are denied recognition and enforcement – the concern that security for costs might stifle a legitimate claim becomes less pressing. This strongly supports the case for ordering security for costs.

Finally, security for costs has to be used reasonably to avoid exposing the award to challenges based on due process violations, which could undermine the very purpose of the measure to enhance the legitimacy and efficiency of international arbitration.

CHAPTER 14

Collective Arbitration: The History of Collective Consumer Arbitration and Its Future in Sweden

Raoul J. Sievers & Alexander Foerster

§14.01 INTRODUCTION

The notion of collective consumer arbitrations is not a new idea. Yet, particularly in the EU, it has recently become the subject of articles, dissertations, monographs, and dossiers.[1] In late March 2025, a seventeen-member working group appointed by the French Ministry of Justice rendered a report on the reform of French arbitration law, including the introduction of collective arbitral proceedings.[2] "Why now?," one may ask. In many EU Member States, dysfunctional court procedures increasingly deter consumers from asserting their rights. Despite current attempts to introduce collective redress procedures, observers note a freefall of the number of consumer disputes brought before courts. In many Member States, the inefficiency of the courts is deeply rooted in the realities of underfunded judiciaries and structural deficiencies of the legislative process. Already in 2013, scholars understood the ADR Directive (2013/11/EU) as promoting consumer arbitration.[3] More recently, the Representative

1. Cf. *Florian*, Class Action und Class Arbitration Waiver, 2024; *González Arango/Cruz*, Spain Arb Rev, 2017, 19; *Hanotiau/Schwartz*, ICC Dossier XIV: Class and Group Actions in Arbitration, 2016; *Kamilovska/Dushkovska*, Frontiers in Law, 2023, 126; *Konukpay*, Public and Private International Law Bulletin, 2019, 1; *Neumeier*, Asian Int'l Arb J, 2018, 143; *Strong*, in: International Arbitration and EU Law, 2024, 76; *Valasek/Hernández*, International Arbitration Report, 2021, issue 16, 37; *Van Zelst/Ten Brink*, Tijdschrift voor Arbitrage, 2019, 9.
2. Rapport et propositions de réforme du droit français de l'arbitrage, March 2025, p. 63; cf. for a summary of the report *Moody*, Working Group Proposes French Arbitration Code, Global Arbitration Review, March 31, 2025.
3. *Piers*, in: Arbitration in Belgium, 2016, 79, 87; *Reich*, 4 Penn St JL & Int'l Aff, 2015, 292, 331.

Actions Directive (EU) 2020/1828 introduced a right to collective redress across the EU in terms which, as authors noted,[4] left national legislators considerable leeway in implementing such redress in the form of collective arbitral proceedings.

This article examines the notion of such collective arbitrations as a means to resolve consumer disputes in Sweden. In Sweden, the number of consumer lawsuits has historically been low owing to widespread popularity of ADR in resolving disputes. Do the existing procedures sufficiently address the need to assert consumer rights, in particular in times of increasing mass and dispersed damages (*§14.02*)? Which benefits do collective arbitral proceedings offer (*§14.03*)? What can we learn from the history of class arbitrations in the United States (*§14.04*)? Do we need a blueprint for collective consumer arbitration in Sweden (*§14.05*)?

§14.02 CURRENT STATE OF CONSUMER DISPUTES IN SWEDEN

We shall first turn to the current state of consumer disputes in Sweden and examine both the role of the courts [*A*] and of ADR [*B*] in their resolution, as well as mandatory arbitration in disputes regarding redemption of shares [*C*].

[A] The Low Number of Consumer Lawsuits Before Swedish Courts

In Sweden, the number of consumer lawsuits before state courts has historically been very low. In 2012, Swedish civil courts recorded only 0.7 incoming cases per year per 100 habitants.[5] In comparison, the EU median for incoming civil cases per 100 habitants the same year was at 2.7 cases—nearly four times as high.[6] In a 2022 report, the international human rights organization *Council of Europe* further noted that between 2012 and 2021, the number of first instance civil and commercial litigation cases dropped by another decimal to 0.6.[7] The EU Commission's 2024 EU Justice Scoreboard observed similar developments in most Member States. On average, in 2022, roughly 30% less claims were brought before first instance civil courts than in 2012.[8] Yet, the number of incoming civil cases remains remarkably low in Sweden.

4. *Blackaby/Partasides/Redfern*, Redfern and Hunter on International Arbitration, 7th ed., 2023, para. 2.267.
5. The 2024 EU Justice Scoreboard, p. 2, figure 3.
6. The 2024 EU Justice Scoreboard, p. 2, figure 3.
7. Similar numbers can be found in Council of Europe, Judiciary at a glance in Sweden (2022), p. 2.
8. In 2022, first instance civil courts in Member States recorded only 1.935 new cases p.a. per 100 habitants (The 2024 EU Justice Scoreboard, p. 2, figure 3).

Figure 14.1 Average Number of Claims Brought Before First Instance Civil Courts per 100 Habitants[9]

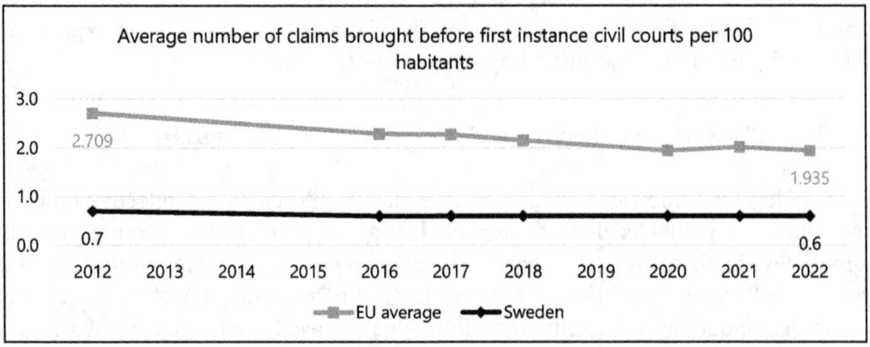

The low number of civil lawsuits may perhaps partly be explained by the rather consensus-minded, less litigious legal culture in the Nordics.[10] Another potentially contributing factor is that the distinct characteristics of Swedish civil procedure have contributed to the popularity of ADR and the avoidance of civil court proceedings. These relate to individual court procedures in consumer disputes [*1*] as well as to existing collective redress mechanisms [*2*].

[1] Deficits of Individual Court Procedures in Consumer Disputes

Comparative data from other EU Member States suggest a correlation between the levels of first instance civil court proceedings and the number of consumer lawsuits.[11] In this regard, the present findings of low civil court activities support the assumption that Swedish consumers seek to avoid court proceedings.[12]

This may very well be by choice. Yet, the EU Commission's 2023 Consumer Conditions Survey suggests a different view. While the trust of Swedish consumers in public authorities to protect their rights is remarkably high,[13] they are not nearly as confident with respect to the effectiveness of existing dispute resolution mechanisms. Only 26% of Swedish consumers agree that it is easy to resolve disputes with businesses through courts. This ranks the Swedes' satisfaction with their court system considerably below the 34%-average in all other Member States. In fact, when

9. Data is based on the 2024 and 2018 EU Justice Scoreboard, p. 2, figure 3.
10. Equally low numbers are recorded in fellow Nordic Member States Denmark (0.8) and Finland (0.2).
11. Cf. for Germany *Meller-Hannich/Höland/Nöhre*, Rückgang der Eingangszahlen bei den Zivilgerichten, Abschlussbericht, 2023, 207 et seqq. read in conjunction with the EU Justice Scoreboard's figures on the development of first instance civil court proceedings.
12. The assumption of low levels of consumer lawsuits in Sweden will subsequently be verified by reference to the EU Commission's Consumer Conditions Survey.
13. 80% of consumers trust public authorities to protect their rights as consumers, far above the EU average of 66% (EU Commission's Consumer Conditions Survey 2023, Sweden, p. 1).

experiencing problems with a business, 0% of consumers took the business to court.[14] Notably, while the survey also reflects a Swedish consensus-minded, non-adversarial mindset, unease in confrontational situations did not rank among the consumers' main reasons for avoiding dispute resolution.[15] Rather, Swedish consumers ranked significantly above the EU average in perceiving the claim as too small, in not expecting a satisfactory outcome,[16] and in finding the process too complex.[17]

[2] The State of Collective Redress Before Swedish Courts

A lack of legal mobilization for small claims may be addressed by collective proceedings, where individual legal costs are pooled, and a single consumer is represented by a group. Sweden is home to the oldest class action regime not only in the Nordics[18] but arguably in Europe.[19] On January 1, 2003, the Group Proceedings Act[20] (*GPA*) entered into force. Under the GPA, either an individual, a legal entity (section 4 GPA), a nonprofit organization (section 5 GPA), or a designated governmental authority (section 6 GPA) may initiate a group proceeding. The GPA stipulates certain preconditions for an action to qualify as a group proceeding. It is also an opt-in model, i.e., the consumer must proactively apply to join the action.[21] Notified consumers may join the group by notice to the court in writing as per section 14 GPA.[22] The general rules on litigation costs apply,[23] which include the Swedish adaptation of the English rule, i.e., "loser pays,"[24] Nevertheless, there are some particularities: as a standard rule, only a member of the Swedish Bar, an Advokat, may represent the claimant (an exception from the general principle that neither legal training, nor membership of the Swedish Bar is required to represent a party in Swedish courts). According to sections 38 et seqq. GPA, a success fee is allowed to a much wider extent than is otherwise the case in Swedish civil procedure. However, the respondent's adverse cost liability does not extend beyond legal fees at a "reasonable level" (*skäligt arvode*). This is deemed to be a compromise between incentivizing group proceedings and preventing abusive actions or strategic lawsuits against public participation (so-called SLAPP suits).[25]

14. EU Commission's Consumer Conditions Survey 2023, Sweden, p. 2.
15. EU Commission's Consumer Conditions Survey 2023, Sweden, p. 2.
16. There appears to be an overarching perception of Swedish civil procedure as a "defendant-friendly forum" (*Schoultz*, in: Outsourcing Legal Aid in the Nordic Welfare States, 2018, 43, 44).
17. EU Commission's Consumer Conditions Survey 2023, Sweden, p. 2.
18. British Institute of International and Comparative Law, Collective Redress: Sweden, p. 9; *Molavi*, 42 Nordic Journal of Human Rights, 2024, 32, 43.
19. *Gaudet*, Earth to Brussels, June 2, 2008, 29; *Lindblom*, ANNALS, AAPSS, 622, 231, 233. Though forms of collective redress mechanisms have existed in France since at least the 1970s (cf. European Commission—DG SANCO, Final Report on the evaluation of the effectiveness and efficiency of collective redress mechanisms, 2008, p. 111).
20. SFS 2002:599 Lagen om grupprättegång.
21. *Gaudet*, Earth to Brussels, June 2, 2008, 29.
22. Cf. for a detailed description of the procedure *Lindblom*, ANNALS, AAPSS 622, 231, 233 et seqq.
23. British Institute of International and Comparative Law, Collective Redress: Sweden, p. 7.
24. *Lindblom*, ANNALS, AAPSS, 622, 231, 236; cf. Chapter 18 of the Swedish Code of Civil Procedure.
25. British Institute of International and Comparative Law, Collective Redress: Sweden, p. 7.

While the GPA may have been the first, it is certainly not the most popular group action act in Europe today. Until 2021, only twenty-two group proceedings were initiated in Sweden under the Act,[26] far less than the anticipated twenty cases per year.[27] The procedural design of the Swedish group action did not succeed in establishing a worthwhile redress mechanism. In 2008, five years after the introduction of the GPA, a Swedish litigant received an average of merely EUR 37.62 per year in which they pursued a claim under a group proceeding.[28] Whereas the procedural design of the group action as an opt-in model may have contributed to the low case numbers,[29] its lack of popularity has mostly been connected to prohibitive financial risks, which follow from the general "loser pays" principle under Swedish procedural law.[30] In contrast to corresponding procedures in other jurisdictions, there are no designated public or private funds offering plaintiffs to seek recourse for legal expenses in actions under the GPA[31] (though plaintiffs have come up with models which significantly reduce financial risks).[32] An evaluation of the GPA five years after its introduction further noted that the assessment of the preconditions for group proceedings under section 8 GPA "tends to be complicated and drawn-out."[33] In addition to these regulatory shortcomings, the lack of popularity of collective procedures before Swedish courts has been attributed to structural deficits of courts in administering GPA proceedings, in particular, a general sense of inefficiency and a lack of expertise.[34] While it is too early to call the effects of Sweden's recent transmission of the Representative Actions Directive,[35] the unpopularity of the GPA and the aforementioned perception of structural inefficiencies of court-administered group proceedings cast doubt on its prospects of success.

[B] The Role of Consensual ADR in Consumer Disputes in Sweden

In fact, concerns over the inefficiency of existing dispute resolution mechanisms are the second most prominent reason for Swedish consumers not to assert their rights.[36] Insofar as Swedish consumers suppose that court proceedings are not designed in a

26. *Molavi*, 42 Nordic Journal of Human Rights, 2024, 32, 43 et seq. referring to *Wallerman Ghavanini*, 12 European Labour Law Journal, 2021, 498; cf. also British Institute of International and Comparative Law, Collective Redress: Sweden, p. 9 estimating the total number of proceedings below 25.
27. *Molavi*, 42 Nordic Journal of Human Rights, 2024, 32, 43.
28. European Commission—DG SANCO, Final Report on the evaluation of the effectiveness and efficiency of collective redress mechanisms, 2008, p. 116.
29. Cf. below under §14.03[A][1].
30. *Molavi*, 42 Nordic Journal of Human Rights, 2024, 32, 45.
31. *Lindblom*, ANNALS, AAPSS, 622, 231, 237. In recent years, the growing popularity and availability of litigation funders seems to make amends.
32. For instance, by way of a subscription model in the *Skandia case*, where a nonprofit organization used subscription fees (SEK 150 per consumer) to pay court fees and thereby shielded the individual consumers from recourse by the courts (*Lindblom*, SvJT 2005, 129, 155).
33. Evaluation of the Group Proceedings Act 2008, p. 3.
34. *Lindblom*, ANNALS, AAPSS, 622, 231, 238.
35. Lag (2023:730) om grupptalan till skydd för konsumenters kollektiva intressen.
36. EU Commission's Consumer Conditions Survey 2023, Sweden, p. 2.

way to efficiently resolve consumer disputes, the remarkable efficiency of ADR in Sweden will certainly have contributed to such perception.

In Sweden, disputes between a consumer and a business are commonly resolved before the Swedish National Board for Consumer Disputes (*Allmänna reklamationsnämnden*) (*ARN*), a state agency.[37] The ARN adjudicates disputes between a consumer and a business on a complaint filed by a consumer. The process is conducted exclusively in writing (section 19 ARN Act)[38] and primarily aims to find agreement between the parties (section 22 ARN Act). If such agreement cannot be found, the board will render an assessment of the matter in dispute in the form of a recommendation within ninety days (section 23 ARN Act). Under section 9 ARN Act, the ARN may administer collective proceedings upon filing by a group of consumers[39] or by the *Konsumentombudsman* (*KO*).[40] The KO is the Director General of the Swedish Consumer Agency (*Konsumentverket*), where consumers may file complaints against businesses. Such complaints do not automatically entail any procedure against the business but are merely reviewed by the agency's legal department, which then decides how to proceed. For complaints to result in a case, they must relate to a problem of great importance to many consumers and of strong consumer interest.[41] Notably, the proceeding under section 9 ARN Act is an opt-out mechanism, i.e., recommendations issued in such collective proceeding extend to all members of the group without the need for any sort of application or registration of the individual consumer.[42]

In 2024, the ARN registered 25,685 complaints.[43] As noted above, Swedish consumers virtually never initiate court proceedings. These 25,685 cases can, thus, be seen as the backbone of Swedish consumer rights enforcement. Yet, in the EU Commission's Consumer Conditions Survey 2023, only 46% of Swedish consumers agreed that it is easy to settle disputes with businesses in out-of-court proceedings, which is no more than 1% above the EU average.[44] In fact, only 7% of Swedish consumers reported having brought the matter to an out-of-court dispute resolution body (such as the ARN) when faced with a conflict with a business.[45] Furthermore,

37. Cf. for a historic and all the more instructive overview *Lundvik*, The National Board for Consumer Complaints, A Swedish Innovation for the Man in the Streets, 1984, 6.
38. Förordning (2015:739) med instruktion för Allmänna reklamationsnämnden.
39. Cf. *Bagner/Ribbeklint/Ewerlöf*, in: Class Arbitration in the European Union, 2013, 173, 175.
40. Proceedings under section 9 ARN Act are initiated by the KO in 91% of the cases (Information by the ARN upon request dated January 15, 2025).
41. For group proceedings initiated by the KO, cf. Umeå District Court, Case No. T 5416-04.
42. British Institute of International and Comparative Law, Collective Redress: Sweden, p. 12.
43. ARN Statistik, Antal inkomna ärenden åren 2022-2024.
44. EU Commission's Consumer Conditions Survey 2023, Sweden, p. 1.
45. EU Commission's Consumer Conditions Survey 2023, Sweden, p. 2. These 7% represent the share of consumers who experienced an issue, took action and filed a complaint with the ARN. The overall rate of consumers who experienced an issue and filed with the ARN should be even lower considering the share of consumers who experienced an issue but remained inactive which is not reflected herein.

since 1991, collective proceedings before the ARN have only been initiated in twenty-two cases.[46] Proceedings under section 9 ARN Act are thus even less frequent than group proceedings under the GPA.

[C] Mandatory Arbitration in Disputes Regarding Redemption of Shares

More than fifty years ago, the Swedish legislator introduced mandatory arbitration proceedings as a means of settling certain disputes under company law. Although the Swedish Companies Act[47] (*Companies Act*) includes certain provisions to protect minority shareholders, there are situations in which unprotected minorities have to withdraw their investments. Disputes about the buy-out and valuation of shares require special expertise and need to be resolved within a reasonable period of time. Thus, as many years of experience have shown, arbitral tribunals are better suited than state courts to achieve that goal.[48]

According to Chapter 22 of the Companies Act, a shareholder who holds more than 90% of the shares in a company shall be entitled to buy out the remaining shares of the other shareholders of the company. However, any person whose shares may be bought out is entitled to sell their shares to the majority shareholder. According to section 5 of the same chapter, disputes concerning the right or obligation to redeem shares or the determination of the buy-out price must be resolved through arbitration. The Companies Act explicitly refers to the Swedish Arbitration Act[49] (*Arbitration Act*) to govern the arbitration.

Arbitration can be initiated by either the majority shareholder or the minority shareholder. The majority shareholder must submit a written request to the company's board, specifying their chosen arbitrator. Similarly, the minority shareholder can initiate arbitration by delivering a notice under section 19 of the Act to the majority shareholder.

As a general rule, the majority shareholder is always responsible for the costs of arbitration, including the fees for arbitrators. However, under special circumstances, the arbitrators may require other shareholders to bear part of the costs. Arbitrators may issue separate awards on prejudicial questions, such as whether the majority shareholder has the right to redeem shares. This allows for a focused resolution of specific issues before addressing the redemption price.

Nevertheless, since the legislature cannot cut off the individual's path to state jurisdiction, arbitral awards rendered under the Companies Act may be challenged and reviewed not only on formal grounds but also on the merits.[50] The challenge is to be

46. Information by the ARN upon request dated January 15, 2025.
47. Aktiebolagslag, 2005:551.
48. Expert Report "Aktiebolagets kapital" leading to a recent reform of the Companies Act, SOU 1997:22, p. 264.
49. Lag (1999:116) om skiljeförfarande.
50. Section 22:24 Companies Act, Prop. 2004/05: 85, p. 474 and *Andersson/Johansson/Skog*, Aktiebolagslagen en kommentar, JUNO version 19, 22:24 comment 1.

brought before the Stockholm District Court (*Stockholms tingsrätt*). However, the majority of awards are accepted and successful challenges are very rare.

§14.03 THE NOTION OF COLLECTIVE CONSUMER ARBITRATION FOR MASS AND DISPERSED DAMAGES

While a considerable share of consumer disputes is resolved by ADR, in particular by the recommendation-based procedure of the ARN, there remains a vacuum of claims which Swedish consumers currently do not assert. These cases concern instances where consensual dispute resolution methods are exhausted or plainly insufficient and the consumers are left with court procedures which they consider futile, inefficient, and too complex.[51] These are the instances where conventional European redress mechanisms reach their limits. Which benefits can collective arbitral proceedings offer in comparison to both court [*A*] and consensual ADR procedures [*B*]?

[A] Addressing Deficiencies of National Court Procedures

In order to provide a desirable alternative to existing national court procedures, collective consumer arbitrations would have to address some of the deficits which have rendered existing court procedures unpopular among Swedish consumers. The broader discussion about the defining characteristics of commercial arbitration and its benefits as opposed to court procedures exceeds the scope of the present examination. However, there are two specific points presently to be made with respect to the structural benefits of a collective arbitral procedure, as opposed to existing collective redress mechanisms before Swedish courts, or most European courts for that matter.

The first point considers the aforementioned regulatory shortcomings. Regulatory shortcomings, individually, do not and cannot amount to a structural deficit of court proceedings. They can be resolved through regulation. Yet, regulatory shortcomings evolve into a structural deficit, where legal policy realities perpetuate them and inhibit their remediation through regulation in the foreseeable future. Therefore, the first point truly addresses current legal policy realities and whether they perpetuate the regulatory shortcomings of national court procedures [*1*]. The second point considers Swedish consumers' two most common reasons for inaction after a breach. The first reason is that their individual claims are too small. This is addressed by pooling the consumer's individual claim with a number of similar claims in a form of collective redress, as done in collective proceedings under the GPA. The second reason is that these collective proceedings are too inefficient. This may be addressed by the introduction of arbitral collective proceedings, which would allow consumers to benefit from the efficiency of arbitral institutions in administering disputes [*2*].

51. EU Commission's Consumer Conditions Survey 2023, Sweden, p. 2.

[1] *Legal Policy Realities*

Across the EU, the implementation of collective redress mechanisms has traditionally inspired significant influence of corporate lobby groups on the legislative process. As one example out of many, in Germany, attempts to introduce collective redress mechanisms have dependably entailed reports of associations exerting influence on pivotal procedural design features in ways rendering the process inefficient and undesirable. In the past, these reports have successfully triggered concerns over "American standards"[52] or a "professional plaintiff industry,"[53] which even transpired in the government's coalition agreement.[54] For the recent implementation of the Representative Actions Directive, a conglomerate of fourteen lobby organizations released a "Statement of the German Economy" opposing lenient provisions on standing and litigation funding to ensure that "collective actions cannot become an investment object."[55] The resulting legislation maintained existing limitations to standing and barred any possibility of profitable third-party funding, leaving consumer associations dependent on financing through public authorities.[56] As a consequence, the introduced collective action for redress was stripped of initially promising incentives and is widely anticipated to fall short of expectations.[57]

Similarly, in Sweden, discussions over the introduction of the GPA were met with well-funded reports claiming that courts would be "drowned in frivolous actions."[58] In response to these reports, proceedings under the GPA were, *inter alia*, designed as opt-in mechanisms.[59] While there are points to be made in its favor, the detrimental impact of an opt-in system on legal mobilization can hardly be overstated. Empirical research indicates that consumers have an inertia bias favoring inaction.[60] As a consequence, consumers opt into an opt-in mechanism just as rarely as they opt out of an opt-out mechanism.[61] For the present purposes, the procedural design feature of an opt-in mechanism shall merely serve to demonstrate the interplay between contrary interests in the parliamentary process and the influence of adverse legal policy realities on the design of an efficient collective procedure. It serves as an example to show that the interests involved in a parliamentary process are not necessarily for the benefit of the design of an efficient collective redress mechanism. At least with regard to

52. BDI (*Federation of German Industries*), Einführung amerikanischer Rechtsverhältnisse in der EU vermeiden ("Preventing the introduction of American legal standards in the EU"), August 15, 2017.
53. VCI (German Chemical Industry), Klageindustrie vermeiden ("Preventing a plaintiff industry"), May 17, 2018.
54. Coalition agreement between CDU, CSU, and SPD for the 19th legislative period, paras. 5937 et seqq.
55. Stellungnahme der deutschen Wirtschaft, May 5, 2023, p. 4.
56. *Röthemeyer*, VDuG, 1st ed., 2024, Part I, para. 101.
57. *Schneider/Conrady/Kapoor*, BB 2023, 2179, 2181; cf. for an overview over the history of lobby influence on collective redress legislations *Röthemeyer*, VDuG, 1st ed., 2024, Part I, para. 62.
58. *Lindblom*, ANNALS, AAPSS, 622, 231, 234 regarding the objections against the GPA in Sweden *af Sandeberg*, SvJT 2002, 782, 792.
59. *Molavi*, 42 Nordic Journal of Human Rights, 2024, 32, 45.
60. *Eisenberg/Miller*, 57 Vanderbilt Law Review, 2005, 1529.
61. *Molavi*, 42 Nordic Journal of Human Rights, 2024, 32, 44 et seq.

collective proceedings, reconciling these contrary interests has reliably defeated the purpose of advancing the true objectives of the legislative undertaking, i.e., to promote legal mobilization and procedural efficiency.[62]

In contrast, arbitral institutions have an inherent interest in efficient design and administration of the procedure. In fact, for each institution, its ability to promote procedural efficiency is its *raison d'être*. Consequently, international arbitral institutions are in a horizontal competition for the most efficient procedure. The same competition is fought out in a much more restrained manner on a state level, where legislators are frequently bound to cater to groups which pursue interests adverse to those of efficient redress. Meanwhile, like any regulatory competition, the one between institutions for procedural efficiency harbors the risk of market failure, i.e., a race to the bottom. From the perspective of a consumer, the danger of such a race to the bottom is embodied in the risk of a procedure that is efficient at all costs, including the neglect of procedural consumer protection. Yet, this risk is averted by the fact that any arbitration agreement referring consumer disputes to arbitration must be conscionable. Otherwise, it will be declared void. The voidness of the arbitration clause thus hangs over any institutional design of a collective consumer arbitration like a sword of Damocles. If the arbitration clause refers to an institutional procedure that infringes upon consumer rights, it will be deemed unconscionable. In *Mostaza Claro* and *Asturcom*, the ECJ further confirmed that the conscionability of an arbitration clause in a consumer contract is part of a European *ordre public* (as established in *Eco Swiss*)[63] and must therefore be assessed ex officio by courts, both in connection with set-aside proceedings[64] and in exequatur proceedings.[65] As a result, all institutions will be particularly mindful of designing a process that will not be considered unconscionable for the consumer. This effectively averts the risk of a race to the bottom and of efficiency at the expense of the consumer.

Thereby, the notion of collective consumer arbitrations may introduce a race between the arbitral institutions for the most efficient procedure as an alternative to currently observed adverse legal policy realities in the legislative process. Meanwhile, the institutional design of such a procedure can be expected to safeguard the consumer's procedural rights.

[2] Institutional Efficiency in Administering Collective Proceedings

In Sweden, the perception of inefficient administration of group proceedings under the GPA[66] eventually gave rise to the curious events of the *Skandia case*.

62. Cf. in detail on the politics of class action reform processes *Molavi*, Collective Access to Justice: Assessing the Potential of Class Actions in England and Wales, 2021.
63. *Eco Swiss v. Benetton*, ECJ decision of June 1, 1999, C-126/97, paras. 37 et seqq.
64. *Mostaza Claro v. Centro Móvil*, ECJ decision of October 26, 2006, C-168/05, paras. 34 et seqq.
65. *Asturcom v. Rodríguez Nogueira*, ECJ decision of October 6, 2009, C-40/08, paras. 52 et seqq.
66. Cf. above at §14.02[A][2].

In 2003, a nonprofit organization had initiated a group proceeding before the Stockholm District Court against *Skandia AB*. The action concerned claims for damages brought by policyholders under insurances concluded with *Skandia Liv* following losses incurred as a consequence of the sale of an asset management subsidiary by the parent company, *Skandia AB*.[67] At the same time, the KO set *Skandia Liv* a time limit of one month to pursue its own claims against *Skandia AB*, after which the KO, in turn, would initiate group proceedings against *Skandia AB*. Consequently, the management of *Skandia Liv* initiated arbitral proceedings against *Skandia AB* to determine *Skandia AB*'s liability to *Skandia Liv* for the incurred losses. *Skandia Liv's* CEO, Urban Bäckström, justified the initiation of the arbitration, stating that the alternative option of initiating court proceeding against *Skandia AB* before the district court would take "more than six years."[68] As a consequence, the group proceeding before the Stockholm District Court was withdrawn in May 2004[69] and the tribunal subsequently ordered *Skandia AB* to compensate *Skandia Liv* in approximately SEK 1.4 billion, which indirectly compensated the policyholders.[70] As a result, the arbitral award rendered the group proceedings superfluous. While *Lindblom*, who has published an article analyzing the case, is likely correct in noting that without the initiation of group proceedings (or the KO's threat thereof), *Skandia Liv* would not have pursued arbitral proceedings against *Skandia AB*,[71] one cannot help but wonder why the policyholders, or the KO for that matter, should not be afforded the opportunity to initiate such efficient arbitral proceedings against *Skandia AB* on their own terms.

In fact, the (brief) history of class arbitrations in the United States[72] has shown just how efficient collective arbitral proceedings can be. When the AAA reported on the current state of class arbitrations as *amicus curiae* in *Stolt-Nielsen* in 2009, it had registered 283 proceedings under its Supplementary Rules for Class Arbitrations only six years after their introduction.[73] Remarkably, the average disposition time for a class arbitration was only 630 days (median: 583 days)[74] compared to 1,196 days for a class action before a civil court (median: 1,068 days).[75] Thus, class arbitrations under the AAA were nearly twice as efficient as class actions in court.[76] This was also pointed out by Justice Breyer in his dissenting opinion in *AT&T Mobility L.L.C. v. Concepcion*, comparing statistics of Californian courts on class actions[77] to class arbitrations two years later:

67. *Strong*, in: International Arbitration and EU Law, 2021, 191 et seq.
68. *Lindblom*, NFT 2/2005, 123, 125.
69. *Lindblom*, SvJT 2005, 129, 156.
70. *Feldt*, Grupptalan, 2010, p. 44.
71. *Lindblom*, NFT 2/2005, 123, 126.
72. Cf. below at §14.04.
73. Brief for AAA as Amicus Curiae in Stolt-Nielsen, O. T. 2009, No. 08-1198, pp. 22, 23.
74. Brief for AAA as Amicus Curiae in Stolt-Nielsen, O. T. 2009, No. 08-1198, p. 24.
75. *Fitzpatrick*, 7 Journal of Empirical Legal Studies, 2010, 811, 820.
76. In contrast to the AAA, JAMS never published statistics on administered class arbitrations (*Strong*, 17 Harvard Negotiation Law Review, 2012, 201, fn. 27).
77. Administrative Office of the Courts, Class Certification in California, Second Interim Report from the Study of California Class Action Litigation, 2010, p. 18.

> Data from California courts confirm that class arbitrations can take considerably less time than in-court proceedings in which class certification is sought.[78]

While the duration of a class arbitration thereby exceeded the time of an average B2B arbitration, it was considerably more efficient than equivalent court proceedings.[79]

[B] Limits of Consensual ADR in Mass and Dispersed Damages

Taking consumer disputes to ADR rather than to the courts is a long-lived tradition in Swedish legal culture. In Sweden, considerable numbers of consumer disputes are resolved by the ARN.[80] Meanwhile, in times of globalized, interconnected trade, economic power has shifted from being distributed among a multitude of local players to being concentrated in the hands of internationally operating groups. This exposes an ever-growing number of consumers to the consequences of infringements by a comparably small number of companies. Mass and dispersed damages are the signs of a globalized economy. This raises the question whether ADR institutions, which are designed to resolve disputes between two parties, are fit to sufficiently cater to the collective needs of tens of thousands of consumers affected by the same breach of an internationally operating retailer or service provider. While the ARN does also administer collective proceedings under section 9 ARN Act, these proceedings are rare and the ARN may also reject cases that are perceived as too complex.[81]

Furthermore, in 2024, businesses complied with the recommendations of the ARN in (only) 76% of the cases.[82] The compliance rate further decreases in group proceedings under section 9 ARN Act. In the eleven cases in which the ARN sided with the KO, the businesses only followed the recommendations in seven instances (64%).[83] Taking into account the fact that Swedish consumers virtually never initiate court proceedings (irrespective of the outcome of previous ADR attempts), this leaves a significant vacuum in all remaining cases in which the consumers expressed their intention to assert their claim by filing with the ARN, but reverts to inaction upon the business' refusal to comply with the ARN's recommendations. A particularly high number of consumers is affected where such refusal follows recommendations at the end of collective proceedings under section 9 ARN Act. Similarly, the categorical rejection of asserted claims affects many consumers where they relate to mass or dispersed damages. In these instances, an arbitral collective redress mechanism would

---

78. *AT&T Mobility L.L.C. v. Concepcion*, 563 U.S. 333 (2011).
79. The same conclusion was reached by the AAA, Brief for AAA as Amicus Curiae in Stolt-Nielsen, O. T. 2009, No. 08–1198, p. 24.
80. Cf. above at §14.02[B].
81. Among other reasons, the ARN rejects claims that are too complex and time-consuming (British Institute of International and Comparative Law, Collective Redress: Sweden, p. 13). This happened in 16% of cases which were not previously withdrawn by the KO (Information by the ARN upon request dated January 15, 2025).
82. ARN Statistik 2024, I vilken utsträckning följer företagen våra rekommendationer?
83. Information by the ARN upon request dated January 15, 2025.

allow a consumer association, such as the KO, to collect these claims, secure funding,[84] and initiate efficient arbitral proceedings.[85]

§14.04 THE QUESTIONABLE HISTORY OF CLASS ARBITRATIONS IN THE UNITED STATES

As mentioned at the outset, collective consumer arbitration is not novel. Corresponding systems exist and have existed, most prominently in the form of class arbitrations in the United States. Perhaps unsurprisingly, the history of class arbitrations is not a story of consumer protection. It is a story of overworked state courts, of a Supreme Court Chief Justice in the 1970s with a penchant for ADR, of a judgment misunderstood for years, of inspiring arbitral procedural design, and of unmatched neglect of procedural consumer protection. To understand whether such neglect of consumer protection is an inherent flaw of consumer arbitration or the consequence of the specific purpose of its introduction in the United States, we must examine the history of American (collective) consumer arbitration.

The Supreme Court's path towards class arbitrations can be divided into two stages. From 1974 onwards, the Supreme Court increasingly turned away from its mistrust of arbitration and recognized its equivalence to state civil proceedings. In doing so, the Supreme Court laid the foundation for the emergence of consumer arbitration in the United States [*A*]. This was followed by the recognition of the competence of tribunals to decide on the admissibility of class arbitrations, which entailed their rise in the early 2000s [*B*]. Finally, it is worth examining the background to the subsequent decline of class arbitrations in the United States [*C*].

[A] The Rise of Consumer Arbitration in the United States

In *Wilko*, the Supreme Court demonstrated the profound mistrust of the U.S. judiciary towards arbitration that was prevalent in the 1950s. The Supreme Court adopted a general stance of suspicion towards arbitral tribunals, perceiving a potential for arbitrators to disregard the law with no effective means of ensuring compliance.[86] It was not until 1974, in *Scherk*, that the Supreme Court acknowledged the rationale of the Federal Arbitration Act[87] (*FAA*) as "reversing centuries of judicial hostility to arbitration agreements."[88] In the cases of *Moses Cone* and *Southland v. Keating*, the

84. In this regard, previous recommendations by the ARN favoring the consumers may provide a substantial argument to persuade third-party funders of the prospects of the claims.
85. For purposes of promoting legal mobilization the participation in previous ADR attempts may even be interpreted as an opt-in declaration by the consumer.
86. *Wilko v. Swan*, 346 U.S. 427, 436 (1953); cf. *Higginbotham*, 58 Duke Law Journal, 2008, 103, 109; *Orgel*, Class Arbitration, 2013, 102 et seq.; *Resnik*, 80 Notre Dame Law Review, 2005, 593, 620 (fn. 103).
87. United States Arbitration Act (Pub. L. 68–401, 43 Stat. 883, enacted February 12, 1925, codified at 9 U.S.C. Ch. 1).
88. *Scherk v. Alberto-Culver Co.*, 417 U.S. 506, 510 (1974).

Supreme Court expressed a more favorable view of arbitration generally.[89] In 1985, in *Mitsubishi Motors*, the Supreme Court continued in the same vein and stated that "we are well past the time when judicial suspicion of the desirability of arbitration and of the competence of arbitral tribunals inhibited the development of arbitration as an alternative means of dispute resolution."[90] In *McMahon*, the Supreme Court extended its arbitration-friendly approach to consumer disputes[91] before it finally overturned *Wilko* in its decision in *Rodriguez.*[92] The implications of these last two rulings for the significance of arbitration in employment[93] and consumer disputes[94] cannot be overstated.

In order to understand the rise of consumer arbitration in the United States from the beginning of the 1970s onwards, it is essential to examine the background to the Supreme Court's jurisprudence. And it is essential to know about *Warren E. Burger*, who was Chief Justice of the Supreme Court from 1969 to 1986. In the 1970s, Chief Justice Burger observed the population's growing dissatisfaction with the justice system due, in particular, to the increasing length and cost of proceedings.[95] In April 1976, he convened the *National Conference on the Causes of Popular Dissatisfaction with the Administration of Justice* in St Paul, Mississippi. The focus of the so-called *Roscoe Pound Conference*[96] was a debate on reducing the length and cost of proceedings and on ADR methods.[97] Chief Justice Burger urged the exploration and use of ADR to

---

89. *Moses H. Cone Memorial Hosp. v. Mercury Constr. Corp*, 460 U.S. 1, 24 (1983); *Southland Corp. v. Keating*, 465 U.S. 1, 2, 16 (1984) which was emphasized by the Supreme Court in the very similar case of *Perry v. Thomas*, 482 U.S. 483 (1987).
90. *Mitsubishi Motors Corp. v. Soler Chrysler-Plymouth, Inc.*, 473 U.S. 614, 626 et seq. (1985).
91. *Shearson/American Express, Inc. v. McMahon*, 482 U.S. 220, 226 (1987). This is consistent with the discussion of Sherman Act claims in *Mitsubishi Motors.* A week later, the decision in *Perry v. Thomas* (482 U.S. 483 (1987)) was also handed down, which, however, concerns the primacy of the FAA over incompatible national law and is thus dogmatically to be classified as a confirmation and continuation of *Southland v. Keating* (cf. also *Branson*, 12 Arbitration International, 1996, 161, 164).
92. The Court of Appeal had evidently been troubled by the inconsistency of the coexisting decisions in *Wilko* and *McMahon* and had consequently taken the initiative to declare the decision in *Wilko* obsolete. While the Supreme Court found little favor in the Court of Appeal's arrogation, it was now compelled to address the compatibility of the two decisions. The Supreme Court observed that *Wilko* was based on the "outmoded presumption of disfavoring arbitration proceedings" and, referring to *Justice Frankfurter's* dissenting opinion in *Wilko*, ultimately overturned the judgment (*Rodriguez de Quijas v. Shearson/American Express, Inc.*, 490 U.S. 477, 481 (1989)).
93. Cf. *Campbell v. General Dynamics Government Systems Corp*, 321 F. Supp.2d 142 (2004); *Circuit City Stores, Inc. v. Adams*, 279 F.3d 889 (2002).
94. *See*, for example, for claims under the Age Discrimination in Employment Act in *Gilmer v. Interstate/Johnson Lane Corp.*, 500 U.S. 20 (1991), for consumer sales contracts in *Hill v. Gateway 2000, Inc*, 105 F.3d 1147 (1997) and *Cavalier Mfg. v. Clarke*, 862 So.2d 634 (2003), for consumer loan agreements in *Wash. Mut. Fin. Group v. Bailey*, 364 F.3d 260 (2004) and *McKenzie Check Advance of Ms. v. Hardy*, 866 So.2d 446 (2004), and for contracts for work and services in *Allied-Bruce Terminix Cos. v. Dobson*, 513 U.S. 265 (1995) and *Carbajal v. H R Block Tax Services, Inc.*, 372 F.3d 903 (2004).
95. *Marchisio*, The Notion of Award in International Commercial Arbitration, 44.
96. The name goes back to the former dean of Harvard Law School *Nathan Roscoe Pound* (*Cameron*, The Global Pound Conference Series, Opening Address June 29, 2017).
97. *Wallace*, 80 Michigan Law Review, 1982, 592.

relieve the judiciary and mitigate the increasing length and cost of court proceedings.[98] Today, the *Roscoe Pound Conference* is considered by many to be the birth of ADR in the United States.[99]

Notably, all landmark decisions following the quarrel in *Wilko*, up to and including the recognition of the equivalence of arbitral and court proceedings in *Mitsubishi Motors*, were rendered during Chief Justice Burger's tenure. It is hard to imagine that the Supreme Court's newfound confidence in arbitration in the 1970s and 1980s was driven solely by a belief in the integrity of arbitration and not at least as much by an effort to relieve the judiciary and regain popular favor.[100]

[B] The Big Misunderstanding: *Bazzle* and Class Arbitrations

The Supreme Court's generous approach to arbitration clauses in consumer contracts did not go unnoticed in the legal departments of U.S. companies. In 1999, over 80% of all insurers and almost 70% of all financial service providers used arbitration agreements in their consumer contracts.[101] Why? Because an arbitration agreement and the imminent waiver of state court jurisdiction also meant the exclusion of recourse to class actions. In fact, the exclusion of class actions was far more important to companies than the advantages of a more efficient and cost-effective procedure.[102] The arbitration agreement was considered a "class action shield."[103] This raised the question of whether an arbitral class action, a class arbitration, is admissible, especially where the arbitration clause is silent on the issue.

This question led to the Supreme Court's decision in *Bazzle*, where the Supreme Court considered two consolidated class arbitration cases, *Lackey v. Green Tree Financial Corp.* and *Bazzle v. Green Tree Financial Corp.*[104] In both cases, Green Tree's arbitration clause was silent on the possibility of a class arbitration. In the first of the two cases, Lackey, the arbitrator declared the admissibility of the class arbitration. In the second case, Bazzle, the Dorchester County Court followed suit. In both proceedings, Green Tree unsuccessfully filed a motion to vacate.

The Supreme Court was thus faced with the question of whether the silence of the arbitration agreement regarding a possible class arbitration could be interpreted to

98. *Leathes*, Negotiation: Things Corporate Counsel Need to Know but Were Not Taught, 2017, 138.
99. Cf. *Holá*, Mediation in the Reflection of Law and Society, 2021, 96; *Marchisio*, The Notion of Award in International Commercial Arbitration, 44. This overlooks the significance of the decision in *Scherk* for arbitration, which laid the foundation for the Supreme Court's subsequent departure from *Wilko*.
100. Cf. also *Carbonneau*, Revue de l'Arbitrage 1988, 3, 30.
101. *Demaine/Hensler*, 67 Law and Contemporary Problems, 2004, 55, 63 et seq.
102. Meanwhile the efficiency of arbitral proceedings was the purported reason for the inclusion of arbitral agreements in consumer contracts, cf. *Sternlight*, 42 William and Mary Law Review, 2000, 1, 8 with further references.
103. *Dunham*, 16 Franchise Law Journal, 1997, 141; cf. *Drahozal/Wittrock*, 3 Entrepreneurial Business Law Journal, 2009, 275, 282 et seq.
104. *Green Tree Financial Corp. v. Bazzle*, 539 U.S. 444 (2003). Cf. for the procedural history up to the Supreme Court of South Carolina in *Bazzle v. Green Tree Financial Corp.*, 351 S.C. 244 (S.C. 2002).

infer its admissibility. Remarkably, however, the Supreme Court decided not to address this question. Instead, in a 5-4 decision,[105] the court concluded that the question of the admissibility of a class arbitration related to questions of procedural arbitrability and was therefore subject to the tribunal's discretion.[106] The Supreme Court ruled that this discretion had been violated in both proceedings, as the court had either itself taken the decision (Bazzle) or unduly influenced the arbitrator (Lackey).[107]

Thus, the plurality opinion[108] itself did not comment on the compatibility of class arbitrations with the FAA,[109] let alone in the case of a silent arbitration clause.[110] Meanwhile, the Supreme Court had not declared class arbitration incompatible with the FAA either, thereby casting significant doubt on the prevailing view among the lower courts denying their admissibility.[111] As a result, state courts subsequently transferred their authority to consolidate class arbitration proceedings and to assess their admissibility to the tribunals.[112] *Bazzle* also prompted the introduction of rules of procedure for class arbitrations by the AAA and JAMS.[113] On October 8, 2003, just over three months later, the AAA's *Supplementary Rules for Class Arbitrations* came into force. The *JAMS Class Action Procedures* followed in February 2005. Both institutional rules were based on the federal regulations on class actions in Rule 23 FRCP and reduced judicial involvement to a supervisory body in the individual stages of the proceedings.[114] The remarkable efficiency of the AAA in administering class arbitrations was pointed out above.[115] It is fair to say that *Bazzle* marked the beginning of the (brief) history of class arbitrations in the United States.

The decision in *Bazzle* is best understood against the background of the introduction of consumer arbitrations in the 1970s and 1980s. In the last years of Chief Justice Burger's tenure, he had succeeded in drastically reducing the number of class actions in court: 500 class actions in 1987 compared to 2,500 class actions in 1978. As

105. *Inter alia*, dissented by Chief Justice Rehnquist, previously a resolute supporter of Chief Justice Burger's undertakings to promote arbitration (*see infra* n. 117).
106. *Green Tree Financial Corp. v. Bazzle*, 539 U.S. 444, 451 et seq. (2003).
107. *Green Tree Financial Corp. v. Bazzle*, 539 U.S. 444, 453 et seq. (2003).
108. Due to the concurring opinion of Justice Stevens there was no concurring vote by a majority of Justices.
109. In his concurring opinion, Justice Stevens disagreed finding nothing in the FAA to suggest an incompatibility between the FAA and class arbitrations, *Green Tree Financial Corp. v. Bazzle*, 539 U.S. 444, 454 et seq. (2003).
110. In contrast, the dissenting opinion held class arbitrations to be inconsistent with the FAA where the arbitration clause remains silent on the issue, *Green Tree Financial Corp. v. Bazzle*, 539 U.S. 444, 455 et seq. (2003).
111. Cf. *Johnson v. West Suburban Bank*, 225 F.3d 366, 370 ff. (3d Cir. 2000); *Sagal v. First USA Bank, N.A.*, 69 F. Supp. 2d 627, 631 ff. (D. Del. 1999) (D. Del. 1999); *Howard v. Klynveld Peat Marwick Goerderler*, 977 F. Supp. 654, 668 (S.D.N.Y. 1997); *McCarthy v. Providential Corp.*, 122 F.3d 1242, 1244 f. (9th Cir. 1997); *Doctor's Associates, Inc. v. Hollingsworth*, 949 F. Supp. 77, 80 f. (D. Conn. 1996).
112. *Orgel*, Class Arbitrations, 2013, 161 et seq.
113. *Bryant*, SchiedsVZ 2021, 58, 60; *Born*, International Commercial Arbitration, 3rd ed., 2021, §10.08[A][2]; *Kent/String*, ICCA Congress Series No. 18, 2014, 853, 857.
114. A detailed description of the procedure exceeds the scope of the present article. German speaking may find a thorough examination in *Orgel*, Class Arbitrations, 2013, 161 et seq.
115. Cf. above at §14.03[A][2].

a result, many predicted the end of class actions in court.[116] However, from 1987—the first full year in office of his successor Rehnquist as Chief Justice[117]—he number of class actions increased dramatically. It reached its temporary peak in 2001 with 3,092 proceedings.[118] The U.S. civil justice system was once again teetering on the brink of overload. It is not unreasonable to assume that the Supreme Court's silence on the admissibility of class arbitrations in *Bazzle* was, once again, at least partly driven by an effort to relieve the judiciary.

[C] Neglecting Consumer Protection: The Fall of Class Arbitrations in the United States

Nowadays, class arbitrations lead a shadowy existence. This invites us to take a look at the judgments that have significantly contributed to this. In many ways, the issues that eventually gave rise to these decisions were a logical sequence to the Supreme Court's judgment in *Bazzle*: The Supreme Court still had to rule on whether ordering class arbitration is consistent with the FAA where an arbitration clause is silent on the issue [*1*] and, where the arbitration clause is, in fact, not silent on the issue but expressly excludes class arbitrations, whether such an arbitration clause is conscionable [*2*].

[1] **Stolt-Nielsen***: Class Action Shield*

In *Stolt-Nielsen*, in line with the general understanding of the Supreme Court's case law and twenty-one published AAA awards that relied on *Bazzle*, the tribunal had affirmed the admissibility of a class arbitration in a partial award, even though the arbitration clause remained silent on the notion of class arbitrations. Stolt-Nielsen moved to set aside the partial award, arguing that it was in manifest disregard of commercial practices in maritime law, which opposed the admissibility of class arbitrations. While the district court sided with Stolt-Nielsen and set the award aside, the Court of Appeal upheld the partial award, stating that Stolt-Nielsen's pertinent arguments had been sufficiently considered by the tribunal.[119] This brought the case before the Supreme Court.

The Supreme Court first took the opportunity to clarify that it had not ruled on the compatibility of class arbitrations with the FAA in *Bazzle*.[120] The court then turned to the admissibility of class arbitration in cases of silent arbitration clauses. The Supreme Court emphasized the fundamental importance of consent under the FAA ("arbitration

116. *Drahozal/Wittrock*, 3 Entrepreneurial Business Law Journal, 2009, 275.
117. Rehnquist had been a proponent of extending arbitrability under Chief Justice Burger and had followed Burger in this regard in all major decisions – except for a dissenting opinion in *Southland Corp. v. Keating*, which nevertheless emphasized the importance of judicial endorsement of arbitration (*Southland Corp. v. Keating*, 465 U.S. 1, 22 et seq. (1984)).
118. U.S. District Courts—Class Action Civil Cases Commenced, by Basis of Jurisdiction and Nature of Suit, During the twelve-Month Period Ending September 30, 2001 (www.uscourts.gov/judbus2001/appendices/x05sep01.pdf (no longer available) (accessed January 13, 2025)).
119. *Stolt-Nielsen S.A. v. AnimalFeeds Int'l Corp.*, 548 F.3d 85, 89 et seq. (2008).
120. *Stolt-Nielsen S.A. v. AnimalFeeds Int'l Corp.*, 559 U.S. 662, 679 et seq. (2010).

is a matter of consent, not coercion")[121] and referred to the differences in nature between conventional arbitration and class arbitration ("class-action arbitration changes the nature of arbitration").[122] In light of these differences, in the absence of express consent regarding class arbitrations, the court held that one may not presume an agreement to arbitrate to encompass the notion of class arbitration.[123]

Stolt-Nielsen has been interpreted as conflicting with the Supreme Court's pro-arbitration stance.[124] However, the decision is no less pro-arbitration than, for instance, the judgment in *Pyett* a year earlier.[125] Rather, the court recognized the fact that parties commonly opt for an efficient and flexible procedure when incorporating an arbitration clause and recalled that, to a certain extent, these characteristics may be compromised by class arbitrations.[126] The decision is not a departure from the past decades of pro-arbitration jurisprudence. However, it is a first impetus to a return to the FAA's guiding principles.

The reasoning applied to initiate such return is nevertheless a glorification of the true reasons for the incorporation of arbitration clauses in general terms and conditions at the time. One shall bear in mind that it was not the efficiency and flexibility of arbitral proceedings that inspired the standard clauses of the 1990s, but the exclusion of litigation out of concern for class actions.[127] In this respect, the Supreme Court was certainly correct in finding that a silent clause may not be interpreted in a way such as to imply the admissibility of class arbitrations. At the same time, however, the Supreme Court thereby solidified the arbitration clause as an effective class action shield.

[2] **Concepcion:** ***Class Arbitration Waiver***

Even before *Stolt-Nielsen*, businesses tried to avoid the risk of class arbitrations, in particular by way of their express exclusion through so-called class arbitration waivers. The conscionability of an arbitration clause including a class arbitration waiver was controversial between the circuit courts.[128]

In *Concepcion*, the district court had rejected an application to order arbitration under an arbitration clause including a class arbitration waiver. According to the district court, the effects of the class arbitration waiver were incompatible with California law, rendering the arbitration clause unconscionable.[129] The Court of Appeal upheld the district court's decision[130] and the case reached the Supreme Court.

121. *Stolt-Nielsen S.A. v. AnimalFeeds Int'l Corp.*, 559 U.S. 662, 681 et seq. (2010).
122. *Stolt-Nielsen S.A. v. AnimalFeeds Int'l Corp.*, 559 U.S. 662, 685 (2010).
123. *Stolt-Nielsen S.A. v. AnimalFeeds Int'l Corp.*, 559 U.S. 662, 684 et seq. (2010).
124. Cf. *Strong*, 17 Harvard Negotiation Law Review, 2012, 201 et seq.
125. *14 Penn Plaza LLC v. Pyett*, 556 U.S. 247 (2009).
126. *Stolt-Nielsen S.A. v. AnimalFeeds Int'l Corp.*, 559 U.S. 662, 685 et seq. (2010).
127. Cf. above at §14.04[B].
128. *Orgel*, Class Arbitrations, 2013, 261 et seq. with numerous references to case law and literature (in particular in fn. 434, 435).
129. *Laster v. AT&T Mobility LLC*, 584 F.3d 849, 853 (2009).
130. *Laster v. AT&T Mobility LLC*, 584 F.3d 849, 857 et seq. (2009).

The Supreme Court pointed out the rationale of the FAA, namely the implementation of efficient dispute resolution procedures and the rigorous enforcement of arbitral agreements.[131] It considered both objectives of the FAA to be impaired by the decisions of the district court and the Court of Appeal. The Supreme Court held that class arbitrations increased the duration and costs of proceedings and thus rendered the individual dispute resolution process less efficient, flexible, and confidential conflicting with the drafters' perception of the FAA.[132] In addition, the Supreme Court argued that arbitration was hardly suitable for complex proceedings such as class arbitrations owing to limited judicial review in the confines of section 10 FAA.[133]

In doing so, the Supreme Court quite indiscriminately declared arbitration unsuitable for the settlement of complex proceedings. This statement is not only in open contradiction to modern civil procedural practice, in which arbitration plays a particularly important role in highly complex proceedings. It also reveals a profound mistrust of the quality of arbitral proceedings and awards, which is reminiscent of the long-overturned conclusions in *Wilko*.[134] The court's reasoning is characterized by a strictly originalist understanding, which is deliberately confined to exploring the intent of the FAA's drafters. A modern interpretation of the FAA's purpose would certainly account for the fact that class arbitrations promote the efficiency of dispute resolution in a relative understanding, taking into consideration the sum of all disputes arising from a breach. In his dissenting opinion, Justice Breyer took another approach in comparing class arbitrations to class actions and emphasizing the former's efficiency.[135] Ultimately, the Supreme Court's majority was likely driven by the concern that doubts about the conscionability of class arbitration waivers could be detrimental to the popularity of arbitration clauses in consumer contracts and, thus, again, push the judiciary to the brink of overload.

The Supreme Court has maintained its stance on class arbitration waivers ever since, relegating class arbitrations to the shadows.[136] Until today, an arbitration clause including a class arbitration waiver remains one of the most effective defenses to collective redress in the United States.[137]

§14.05 THE FUTURE OF (COLLECTIVE) CONSUMER ARBITRATION IN SWEDEN

What does the future hold for collective consumer arbitration in Sweden? As a preliminary matter, it must be pointed out that the following references to consumer arbitrations in the United States must not be taken as warranting any conclusions based on comparisons between the current state of consumer dispute resolution in Sweden

131. Cf. *Shearson/American Express, Inc. v. McMahon*, 482 U.S. 220, 226 (1987).
132. *AT&T Mobility LLC v. Concepcion*, 563 U.S. 333, 348 et seq. (2011).
133. *AT&T Mobility LLC v. Concepcion*, 563 U.S. 333, 350 et seq. (2011).
134. Cf. above at §14.02[A].
135. *AT&T Mobility LLC v. Concepcion*, 563 U.S. 333, 363 (2011).
136. Cf. *Lamps Plus, Inc. v. Varela*, 139 S. Ct. 1407 (2019).
137. *Morris*, Class Action Review, 2024, p. 31.

and studies on the effectiveness of consumer arbitration in the United States. It is important to note that the diametrical differences between the legal cultures in the United States and Sweden prohibit any such comparisons. Yet, the references shall serve to dispel flat assumptions on the notion of (collective) consumer arbitration and offer a more differentiated view.

[A] Procedural Efficiency in Individual Disputes

The introductory endeavor into the reasons for Swedish consumers' inaction when facing misconduct by a business first revealed a remarkably widespread presumption that dispute resolution processes would take too long. In this context, the Swedish civil procedure's emphasis on oral hearings, which tend to elongate proceedings, has long lost out to the exclusively written process of the ARN. Swedish consumers might be correct in assuming that these processes, at an average duration of eighty-five days,[138] are simply out of reach for Swedish courts to match. But what happens in the 24% of cases where a business does not comply with an adverse recommendation?[139] In these cases, the consumers have undoubtedly displayed an interest in asserting a claim but were denied by the business' refusal to follow the result of the ARN process. Would not it be conceivable that in these instances, the KO initiates individual consumer arbitration claiming relief in accordance with the recommendation of the ARN?

To assess the efficiency of such proceedings, we may turn to the United States and the statistics on the duration of individual consumer arbitrations in times when mandatory arbitration clauses could be found in most consumer contracts. Besides class arbitrations, the AAA provided an efficient process for individual consumer arbitrations. In 2007, under the *Supplementary Procedures for Resolution of Consumer-Related Disputes*, an average consumer dispute was resolved within four months in an exclusively written process (which constituted 41% of cases)[140] and within six months where the process included in-person hearings.[141] The AAA's four-month average for a finally adjudicated written procedure is not far off the three-month duration of the ARN's recommendation process.[142] Moreover, such consumer arbitrations could be accelerated even further by recourse to the written submissions exchanged during the previous ARN process.

[B] Collective Arbitral Proceedings

Meanwhile, in a globalized economy with increasing mass and dispersed damages, collective redress has started to gain traction. Across the EU, including Sweden, such

138. British Institute of International and Comparative Law, Collective Redress: Sweden, p. 12.
139. Cf. above at §14.03[B].
140. Analysis of the American Arbitration Association's Consumer Arbitration Caseload 2007.
141. *Drahozal/Zyontz*, An Empirical Study of AAA Consumer Arbitrations, 2009, 7. These figures are supported by the statistics of the National Arbitration Forum for 2003-2004, *Fellows*, The Metropolitan Corporate Counsel, 2006, 32.
142. Cf. above at §14.02[B].

collective redress remains unpopular among consumers who have settled for swift ADR procedures. What if both could be combined, such as where a business refuses to comply with the ARN's recommendations at the end of a collective proceeding under section 9 of the ARN Act, or where allegations of mass or dispersed damages meet a business' categorical rejection of the asserted claims? What if, in these instances, a collective redress mechanism would allow a consumer association, e.g., the KO, to initiate a collective arbitral proceeding in annex to the previous ADR process?

The efficiency of institutional collective consumer arbitrations as well as its structural foundation, and the regulatory competition of arbitral institutions, have been explained above.[143] One of the remaining concerns raised with regard to consumer arbitrations is the fairness of the procedure and particularly the notion that consumers more frequently experience adverse outcomes in arbitration compared to litigation. While the ECJ, through its jurisprudence on the European *ordre public* in *Mostaza Claro* and *Asturcom*, has provided a reliable basis to ensure a fair procedural framework,[144] the notion of potentially unfair outcomes invites us to assess the success rates of consumers in consumer arbitrations in the United States. Amidst the rise of consumer arbitrations, in 1997, the AAA announced the establishment of a National Consumer Disputes Advisory Committee to develop a set of standards promoting fairness in the resolution of consumer disputes (the so-called Consumer Due Process Protocol).[145] While there are evident empirical difficulties in comparing outcomes in subsequent arbitrations to those in litigation,[146] a number of studies suggest that success rates generated by consumers in consumer arbitration are comparable to those experienced in litigation,[147] with the most comprehensive study on AAA consumer arbitrations finding that tribunals held in favor of consumer claimants on at least one of their claims in 53.3% of the cases.[148] This figure is, for instance, higher than the pertinent success rate of Swedish consumers in individual (39%)[149] or group proceedings (50%)[150] before the ARN.

The notion of largely comparable success rates of consumer claims in arbitration and litigation may further be supported by the fact that consumer arbitrations were, in fact, not unpopular among consumers.[151] The vast majority of consumer arbitrations were initiated by consumers (85.9%).[152] Thereby, the share of consumer-initiated proceedings in AAA consumer arbitrations is, for instance, significantly higher than the

143. Cf. above at §14.03[A][2].
144. Cf. above at §14.03[A][1].
145. *Shoneck/Currie*, A Guide to Understanding the American Arbitration Association's Consumer Due Process Protocol and Consumer Arbitration Rules, 2024, 2.
146. Cf. *Drahozal/Zyontz*, An Empirical Study of AAA Consumer Arbitrations, 2009, 7 et seqq.
147. *Fellows*, The Metropolitan Corporate Counsel, 2006, 32; supported by a comprehensive analysis of a number of studies by *Rudolph Cole/Frank*, 15 Dispute Resolution Magazine, 2008, 30. Meanwhile, there are serious concerns over outcomes in mandatory employment arbitration, *Colvin*, 8 Journal of Empirical Legal Studies, 2011, 1.
148. *Drahozal/Zyontz*, An Empirical Study of AAA Consumer Arbitrations, 2009, 47.
149. ARN Statistik, I vilken utsträckning fick konsumenterna rätt åren 2022-2024?
150. Information by the ARN upon request dated January 15, 2025.
151. Cf. for a comparative assessment of consumer surveys on mandatory arbitration, *Rudolph Cole/Frank*, 15 Dispute Resolution Magazine, 2008, 30.
152. *Drahozal/Zyontz*, An Empirical Study of AAA Consumer Arbitrations, 2009, 23, figure 1.

share of consumer-initiated proceedings in consumer lawsuits (i.e., either C2B or B2C) before German courts, based on data from 2015 (33.7%).[153]

[C] Concluding Remarks

In Sweden, the number of consumer lawsuits before state courts has historically been very low. While the less litigious legal culture in the Nordics may have contributed to widespread ADR in consumer disputes, the consensual nature of these mechanisms seems to virtually limit the scope of consumer rights enforcement. Where a business does not comply with non-binding recommendations, individual recourse to courts is unpopular due to prohibitive financial risks. Group proceedings are associated with overly complex and inefficient procedures. Collective arbitral redress promises to not only pool financial risks but to provide for an efficient dispute resolution process. This holds particularly true in Sweden, where the popularity of the KO and the ARN offer a unique opportunity to collect and assert claims through established institutions.

Meanwhile, the idea of collective consumer arbitration is not new and has, in the past, resulted in significant neglect of procedural consumer protection. Yet, an examination of the history of consumer arbitrations reveals that the neglect of consumer protection in the United States was a consequence of the introduction of collective consumer arbitration rather than an inherent flaw. Class arbitrations in the United States were little more than a byproduct of the judiciary's undertakings to relieve the courts and were gratefully picked up by business' legal departments. In contrast, the introduction of consumer arbitration with the goal of promoting legal mobilization is not destined to follow suit. Instead, it can offer a fair and efficient means to resolve consumer disputes where consensual ADR mechanisms are exhausted.

153. Calculated weighted average based on figures for 2015 in *Meller-Hannich/Höland/Nöhre*, Rückgang der Eingangszahlen bei den Zivilgerichten, Abschlussbericht, 2023, 207, figure 63 and official court statistics.

CHAPTER 15

Arbitration Across the Middle East: Same Same but Not the Same

Alain Farhad[*]

Despite being played on a global turf, international arbitration remains a game of local rules and practices. International arbitrators are expected to grasp and embrace the peculiarities of the jurisdictions in which they choose to arbitrate. They would be remiss not to do so, as the enforcement or the annulment of their awards is ultimately in the hands of local courts applying their own laws and jurisprudence. This is true of the Middle East, as it is of other parts of the world.

The Yearbook's readers, who may be more accustomed to the practice of arbitration in Nordic jurisdictions, might be interested in observing that the conduct of arbitral proceedings in Middle Eastern jurisdictions has remarkable peculiarities. They may have, for instance, read that the Dubai Court of Cassation has in the past few years annulled an award because the tribunal signed it on its last page only,[1] or that the Doha Court annulled another one because it was not issued in the name of the Emir of Qatar.[2] They will have seen that some litigants treat their arbitrators (and perhaps the whole process) as adversaries and attempt to intimidate them by launching court actions against them.[3] They may find such peculiarities intimidating or incomprehensible. Some may even look at them, with a degree of circumspection, as local idiosyncrasies disconnected from best practices found elsewhere.

* International arbitrator, Farhad Arbitration. The author wishes to acknowledge the work of Ms. Nakisa Saffarifard and Mr. Mazyar Javid on an earlier draft of this article and thanks them for their assistance.

1. *See, e.g.*, Dubai Court of Cassation, Commercial Appeal No. 156/2009 (dated 27 October 2009) and in general on the subject, Alain Farhad, *Two Steps Forward, One Step Back: A Report on the Development of Arbitration in the United Arab Emirates*, 35(1) Journal of International Arbitration 131-142 (2018) https://doi.org/10.54648/joia2018006 (accessed 1 October 2025).
2. *See* Qatar Court of Cassation, petition No. 64 of 2012.
3. *See, e.g.*, Global Arbitration Review, Sued Tribunal Cleared in time for Christmas, 18 December 2015, reporting on Dubai Court of Cassation Case No. 284 of 2015, 17 December 2015.

Perhaps compounding the complexity in the eyes of some external observers is the reality that within the Middle East, despite many similarities between legal systems, each jurisdiction has its own peculiarities. The local peculiarities found in one jurisdiction may therefore not be shared by its neighbours and vice versa. Neither the Middle East nor even the GCC are uniform regional blocs for the purposes of international arbitration.

Such views, while not entirely unfair, are however too often based on a superficial perception of Middle Eastern jurisdictions drawn from arbitration news headlines. These headlines, perhaps unsurprisingly, report on the most remarkable developments in each of these jurisdictions. True to the saying that people only notice trains when they are late, the bulk of the jurisprudential production in these jurisdictions, which is arbitration-friendly and therefore not newsworthy, is not reported.

Seasoned arbitration lawyers must not only be aware of these peculiarities, beyond sometimes overly simplified or incomplete news reports. They are also expected to apply them correctly. This article highlights some of the most remarkable differences that practitioners not accustomed to the Middle East might face when venturing into arbitration in some of its most popular jurisdictions. Although not an exhaustive review of all such quirks, it offers to help them navigate around some of the common pitfalls found in the author's experience of arbitration in some of the key jurisdictions in the Middle East: the United Arab Emirates, Qatar and Saudi Arabia.

§15.01 UAE

International arbitration in the United Arab Emirates (UAE) has experienced significant growth in recent years, positioning the country as a leading hub for dispute resolution in the Middle East. The UAE now consistently ranks among the most popular arbitration seats.[4]

This expansion has been driven by the UAE's strategic location, thriving economic business model, pro-arbitration reforms, and the growth of a sophisticated arbitration ecosystem. The UAE is thus now home to internationally recognized arbitration institutions and arbitration practitioners.

Despite its developing status as a global hub, the practice of arbitration in the UAE has retained a number of remarkable features, which may appear unusual to newcomers.

[A] Check Who's Authorized? Attention to Party Representation in the UAE

One of the more scrutinized formalities in UAE-seated arbitration – often surprising to foreign counsel – is the strict requirement for clear and formal proof of authority for individuals signing arbitration agreements or acting on behalf of a party in the

4. *See, e.g.*, GAR 100 Data Report in 2025, showing Dubai as the world's 5th most popular arbitration seat.

proceedings. While international arbitration generally accepts a broad range of indicators of authority, the UAE courts have ordinarily taken a far more conservative approach. They regularly require that signatories of arbitration agreements, especially when executed on behalf of corporations or government entities, hold express written authority to bind the party to arbitration. Powers of attorney, commercial licenses, board resolutions, or notarized authorizations are often demanded, particularly where the validity or scope of an arbitration agreement is challenged.

This approach stems in part not only from the broader approach to formalism in legal representation but also from Article 4(1) of the UAE Arbitration Law, which emphasizes the need for a party's representative to have 'special authority' to agree to arbitration.[5] UAE courts have historically interpreted this requirement stringently, annulling awards or refusing to enforce them where such authority is absent, incomplete, or improperly documented – even in the face of conduct suggesting ratification.[6]

In recent years, the Dubai Courts have somewhat softened their approach and have in some cases allowed evidence of apparent authority.[7] They now more easily accept that a party's signature on an agreement is presumed to belong to its authorized representative unless evidence is submitted to the contrary, thus establishing a rebuttable presumption of apparent authority. The burden is now on the party alleging its representative's lack of authority to prove it, and incidentally explain why it let an individual deprived of the requisite authority to sign an arbitration agreement on its behalf.

Despite these developments, the question of the power of the signatory to an arbitration agreement is still the subject of sometimes opportunistic challenges to the jurisdiction of arbitral tribunal. It thus remains a contentious issue, with which arbitrators in the UAE often have to grapple.

A similarly heightened level of formalism applies to the question of the proof of authority of legal representatives making submissions on behalf of a party in arbitration proceedings. While in many jurisdictions the question of a legal representative's authority is rarely controversial, that is a closely scrutinized threshold question in UAE arbitrations.

An arbitral tribunal seated in the UAE would be well advised to promptly verify that all representatives appearing before it possess the requisite authority to do so. This authority is typically granted through a notarized power of attorney (PoA), which must expressly empower the attorney to act in 'arbitration proceedings'. The absence of such explicit reference to 'arbitration' may lead to challenges regarding the attorney's authority.

Consequently, tribunals often review authority documents carefully to ensure they establish a clear and valid chain of authority to the legal representative. In practice, some tribunals go further by attaching the relied-upon PoAs to their awards.

5. Federal Law No. 6 of 2018 on Arbitration, Art. 4(1).
6. *See, e.g.*, Dubai Court of Cassation, Case No. 91 of 1998; Dubai Court of Cassation Case No. 577 of 2003; or Dubai Court of Cassation Case No. 287 of 2009, 11 May 2009.
7. *See, e.g.*, Dubai Court of Cassation Case No. 547 of 2014, of 21 October 2015; Dubai Court of Cassation Case No. 293/2015, of 27 January 2016.

It is also common for the Terms of Reference in the arbitration to include a paragraph confirming that both parties are satisfied with the PoAs presented by their counterparts.

Notably, this heightened level of scrutiny does not apply in the DIFC or ADGM, where a more flexible and internationally aligned approach is followed. Nonetheless, perhaps due to a degree of procedural caution – or 'contagious procedural paranoia' – arbitrators and parties in DIFC or ADGM-seated arbitrations may still adopt similar levels of scrutiny, particularly when there is a possibility that the award will need to be enforced onshore in the UAE.

Ensuring that representatives possess and can produce formal written proof of authority is not merely best practice – it can be determinative of the award's enforceability.

[B] Sign Here, and Here, and Here ... Signing Awards in the UAE, One Page at a Time

One of the most cited idiosyncrasies of arbitration practice in the Middle East is the requirement in the UAE that arbitrators sign each page of their awards.

Under Article 41 of the UAE Arbitration Law, the arbitral award must be in writing, signed by the arbitrators, and contain certain essential elements, including the place of issuance and the date.[8] While the text of the UAE Arbitration Law does not explicitly prescribe that each page be signed, the local courts have consistently interpreted signature requirements strictly, setting aside or refusing to enforce awards that were not signed on every page. In Case No. 403/2020 (dated 15 April 2020), the Dubai Court of Cassation refused to enforce an award rendered in a foreign-seated arbitration, which contained the signature of the arbitrator on the last page only and not on the pages containing the reasoning of the award.

Undoubtedly, this requirement, which is arguably *contra legem*, stems from an extension to arbitration by the UAE Courts of their own practice of signing court decisions on every page. Although some commentators initially suggested that this requirement may have loosened with the enactment of the 2018 Arbitration Law, the Courts quickly proved them wrong. Thus, several post-2018 decisions confirmed the requirement of signature on every page.[9]

In another recent decision in Case No. 109/2022, the Dubai Court of Cassation likewise found that the arbitrator's signature on the last page, which contained the dispositive section only (and not any part of the arbitrator's reasoning), did not satisfy the requirements of Article 41(3) of the UAE Arbitration Law. This, in the Dubai Court of Cassation's view, rendered the award void and unenforceable as a matter of UAE public policy.

Despite the absence of any statutory basis for this requirement, signing every page of an award therefore remains a procedural expectation in UAE-seated arbitration

8. UAE Federal Law No. 6 of 2018 on Arbitration, Art. 41.
9. *See, e.g.*, Dubai Court of Cassation, Case No. 403/2020 (2020).

proceedings. Article 41(6) of the UAE Federal Arbitration Law may, in theory, offer some relief to seasoned arbitrators concerned about the physical toll of signing lengthy awards. It allows for awards to be signed electronically.[10] Accordingly, subject to the parties' agreement and absent any contrary requirement for wet-ink signatures, arbitrators serving in the UAE may affix their electronic signatures to each page of the award, satisfying the formal requirement without resorting to repetitive manual signing. In practice, however, parties wary of the UAE Court's scrutiny often request wet-ink signatures on every page of an award.

It is also important to note that this requirement does not apply in the autonomous jurisdictions of the ADGM and the DIFC. However, UAE parties to arbitration proceedings will often request that awards issued in those jurisdictions also be signed on every page, despite there being no basis for such requirement. They ordinarily do so on the expectation that the awards may need to be enforced onshore, thus extrapolating from the UAE Courts' judicial requirements applied onshore.

§15.02 QATAR

Qatar has likewise witnessed a significant surge in arbitration activity in recent years. In 2024, the Ministry of Justice's Arbitration Affairs Department reported a 21% increase in the number of arbitration rulings, totalling eighty-five compared to seventy in 2023.[11]

At its own pace, carried by its own economic growth, Qatar is also establishing itself as a regional powerhouse of international arbitration.

[A] The Last Click: Emailing Arbitral Awards to the State

In the evolving landscape of arbitration across the Middle East, one feature of Qatar's arbitration regime stands out. The most original – and undeniably memorable – feature of the Qatari Arbitration Law is the obligation under Article 31(11) for arbitrators to transmit the final award to the government by email.[12]

Article 31(11) thus provides: 'The Arbitral Tribunal shall send to the administrative department in the Ministry concerned with the Arbitration affairs an electronic copy of the arbitral award or the decision ending the dispute, as the case may be, within two weeks from its issuance.'[13]

Behind this unusual requirement lies a deliberate and highly specific regulatory intent: to maintain a centralized record of legally impactful decisions. However, this requirement will not cease to puzzle practitioners and global users of international arbitration, accustomed to the privacy of arbitration proceedings and expecting the confidentiality of their outcome.

---

10. Federal Law No. 6 of 2018 on Arbitration, Art. 41(6).
11. *See* Daily Qatar News, 19 January 2025, https://dailyqatarnews.com/arbitration-rulings-rise-21-in-2024 (accessed 11 May 2025).
12. Qatar Law No. 2 of 2017, Art. 31(11).
13. *Ibid.*

This feature is not a dispensable formality. While, to the author's knowledge, there has been no reported court decision on the application (or misapplication) of this provision, its wording makes clear that it is mandatory. In a system where form is tightly linked to function, arbitrators must ensure that every aspect of award issuance – including this digital dispatch – is completed precisely and punctually (i.e., within two weeks of its issuance).

This feature is not unique to Qatar. Thus, Article 44 of the Saudi arbitration law contains a similar requirement, with the added constraint that in Saudi Arabia, the required governmental dispatch is not done by email but by hand and must be delivered with an Arabic translation of the award.[14]

This insistence on state notification reflects a distinct arbitration philosophy: arbitration, while private, is not entirely divorced from the state's interest in maintaining an orderly legal environment.

[B] In the Name of the Emir of Qatar ... or Not

Among the many procedural debates in the practice of arbitration in the Middle East, few appear as anachronistic as the question whether an arbitral award rendered in Qatar must be issued 'in the name of His Highness the Emir'.

In the now-notorious Qatar Court of Cassation Case No. 64 of 2012,[15] the Court took a formalist stance and annulled an arbitral award because it lacked that phrasing. The judges ruled that failing to issue the award in the Emir's name violated public policy – reasoning that, much like court judgments, arbitral awards in Qatar require the symbolic weight of state authority to be legally effective.

Despite the stir that it caused (and the anxiety it continues to cause for arbitrators sitting in Doha), this approach was in fact short-lived. Thus, in a pivotal 2014 decision (Petition No. 164 of 2014),[16] the Qatar Court of Cassation clarified that this requirement does not apply to international arbitration. In doing so, the Court noted that the New York Convention, to which Qatar acceded in 2003, does not mandate such specific formal requirements for foreign arbitral awards.[17] Furthermore, in Court of Appeal Case No. 2186 of 2019, the Court explicitly abandoned this requirement in the context of setting aside proceedings, holding that Qatar's 2017 Arbitration Law (Law No. 2 of 2017) lays out an exhaustive list of grounds for setting aside awards – and that the absence of reference to the Emir was not one of them.

Despite this course correction, for the years that followed, arbitral tribunals and arbitration institutions continued to debate whether it would be more prudent to include a reference to the Emir, out of an abundance of caution. This illustrates the

14. Saudi Arabia Arbitration Law, Royal Decree No. M/34, Art. 44 (2012).
15. Qatar Court of Cassation, Case No. 64 of 2012 (2012).
16. Qatar Court of Cassation, Petition No. 164 of 2014 (24 June 2014).
17. *See* generally on this subject, Khushboo Shahdadpuri and Hani Al Naddaf, *What's in a Name? The Validity of Arbitration Awards in Qatar*, Kluwer Arbitration Blog, 13 December 2021, http://arbitrationblog.kluwerarbitration.com/2021/12/13/whats-in-a-name-the-validity-of-arbitration-awards-in-qatar/ (accessed 29 September 2025).

ripple effect and the long-lasting procedural paranoia, which peculiar court decisions can sometimes cause in the practice of international arbitration in Middle Eastern jurisdictions. In the author's experience, this chapter has now been closed, and it is now widely accepted that at this juncture, awards issued in Qatar need not invoke the Emir.

§15.03 SAUDI ARABIA

The development of arbitration in Saudi Arabia has, in recent years, been the subject of much attention, which mirrors the enthusiasm displayed towards its ambitious economic development plans centred around its 'Vision 2030' programme.

Perhaps more than elsewhere in the Middle East, the practice of international arbitration is rooted in local traditions. Saudi Arabia's legal system is founded on Islamic Sharia, primarily the Hanbali school of jurisprudence. The new Arbitration Law promulgated by Royal Decree No. M/34 of 2012 has modernized many aspects, incorporating significant portions of the UNCITRAL Model Law. However, despite these modernization efforts, the practice of arbitration in Saudi Arabia comes with its share of noteworthy quirks.

[A] Not Just Any Arbitrator

One of the more intriguing features of the Saudi arbitration landscape is the specific provisions relating to those permitted to serve as arbitrator. Thus, Article 14 of the 2012 Saudi Arbitration Law (Royal Decree No. M/34 dated 24/5/1433H, corresponding to 16 April 2012)[18] requires as follows: 'The arbitrator shall be a natural person of full legal capacity, of good conduct and reputation. He may not be a minor, legally incapacitated, or deprived of civil rights due to a criminal conviction or a crime involving moral turpitude or dishonesty, even if he has been rehabilitated. If the arbitration is governed by Islamic Sharia, the arbitrator must be knowledgeable in the provisions of Islamic jurisprudence.'

Article 14 of the 2012 Saudi Arbitration Law thus decrees that an arbitrator must be a person of unimpeachable conduct and reputation – a standard that should raise no surprise. Where the dispute is entangled with Sharia principles, the law further insists that the arbitrator possess a working knowledge of Islamic jurisprudence, a requirement that has been the subject of much doctrinal commentary.[19] This requirement creates significant practical difficulties for parties and arbitration institutions seeking to appoint arbitrators in cases governed by Saudi law and where the seat of the arbitration is in the Kingdom. That is because the level of knowledge of Sharia required under the

18. Saudi Arabia Arbitration Law, Royal Decree No. M/34, Art. 14 (2012).
19. *See, e.g.*, Faris Nesheiwat and Ali Al-Khasawneh, *The 2012 Saudi Arbitration Law: A Comparative Examination of the Law and Its Effect on Arbitration in Saudi Arabia*, 13 Santa Clara J. Int'l L. 443, 451–452 (2015).

law is not defined and anyone's assessment of their own or other people's knowledge is subjective.

As a result, although the law does not mandate that arbitrators be Muslim, in practice, local courts may be more comfortable enforcing awards rendered by arbitrators whose curriculum vitae demonstrates experience with Sharia rules. Parties are therefore well advised to ensure that their choice of arbitrator, especially when dealing with Saudi-seated arbitrations, includes individuals able to navigate questions of Sharia compliance.

[B] More Signing ...

While the UAE Courts require the arbitrators to sign every page of their awards, Saudi law imposes a different signature requirement on all involved in the arbitration.

One of the more distinctive features of Saudi Arabia's arbitration framework is found in Article 33.3 of the 2012 Saudi Arbitration Law, which mandates that 'minutes of arbitration hearings must be signed by all parties, their representatives, tribunal members, witnesses, and anyone else in attendance'.[20] While this may raise eyebrows among international arbitration practitioners accustomed to hearing transcripts emailed by a reporter, this requirement reflects a deep-seated cultural and legal emphasis on formality and accountability in the Saudi legal tradition.[21]

In most jurisdictions, hearing transcripts are independently issued by a transcription service, provided with no expectation that each attendee will physically sign off on their accuracy. Saudi Arabia's approach draws its roots from Sharia principles and domestic litigation norms, where signed documentation is a cornerstone of evidentiary reliability and legal certainty. Thus, in Islamic law, especially under the Hanbali school, which is dominant in Saudi Arabia, *tawthīq* refers to the proper documentation of contracts, transactions, and testimony. Quranic verses (notably, Surah Al-Baqarah, 2:282) emphasize the importance of writing down agreements and having them witnessed and verified: '*O you who believe! When you contract a debt for a fixed term, write it down... and let a scribe write it down in justice ...*' (Qur'an 2:282) This verse underpins the Sharia-based practice of ensuring written evidence as complete, witnessed, and signed or acknowledged by all relevant parties.

In essence, the act of signing is not a mere formality – it is a juridical acknowledgment of what was said, done, and agreed upon during the hearing. The oversight of this requirement can expose the arbitral award to annulment proceedings or enforcement challenges before Saudi courts. The burden is therefore on the tribunal to ensure procedural compliance despite the obvious logistical complications, which this requirement presents.

20. Saudi Arabia Arbitration Law, Royal Decree No. M/34, Art. 33.3 (2012).
21. *See, e.g.*, Faris Nesheiwat and Ali Al-Khasawneh, *The 2012 Saudi Arbitration Law: A Comparative Examination of the Law and Its Effect on Arbitration in Saudi Arabia*, 13 Santa Clara J. Int'l L. 443, 455 (2015).

§15.04 CONCLUSION

This non-exhaustive selection of some of the key distinctive issues facing arbitrators and arbitration lawyers in some of the most popular arbitration jurisdictions in the Middle East serves as a reminder that even in a globalized legal practice, local quirks matter.

Seasoned arbitrators serving in an unfamiliar jurisdiction should not just assume that they can play the game of international arbitration by the rules they find most convenient or are most accustomed to. Comprehensive due diligence on the local requirements – both statutory and judicial practice – is indispensable. But the challenge is far from insurmountable. Arbitrators can seek assistance from the parties' submissions. They may also draw from a co-arbitrator's or an arbitral institution's greater experience of the jurisdiction in which they are serving.

Many Middle Eastern nations have embarked on a path of liberalization and modernization of their arbitration laws. They have adopted or adapted the UNCITRAL Model Law with local variations. This trajectory suggests that the region will continue to refine its legal frameworks to attract international commerce and investment. This welcome development does not, however, mean an abandonment of deeply rooted legal traditions and cultures. Engaging in international arbitration in the Middle East requires an appreciation for the intersection between evolving modern legislation and deeply ingrained legal traditions. Undoubtedly, the future points to a continued reconciliation between these time-honoured traditions and the imperatives of globalized dispute resolution, which will make the Middle East an ever more prominent player on the international arbitration stage.

CHAPTER 16

No Longer Sacred: A Cross-Jurisdictional Survey of Emerging Exceptions to the *Kompetenz-Kompetenz* Doctrine

Artem N. Barsukov[*]

§16.01 INTRODUCTION

The *kompetenz-kompetenz* doctrine is the principle that an arbitral tribunal has the power to rule on its own jurisdiction. This means that the arbitrators have the power to decide whether a valid arbitration agreement exists and whether a given dispute falls within its scope, rather than referring these questions to judicial authorities at the seat of arbitration.

By giving the tribunal the first say on matters of jurisdiction, *kompetenz-kompetenz* safeguards the integrity of the arbitral process. At the same time, the tribunal's decision on its jurisdiction is not necessarily final—it remains subject to judicial review, ensuring that basic judicial safeguards over arbitrability are maintained. The *kompetenz-kompetenz* doctrine reinforces party autonomy by ensuring that the arbitral forum chosen by the parties is respected, unless and until a court conclusively determines otherwise.[1]

Over time, *kompetenz-kompetenz* has been enshrined in key international instruments and national laws. While it does not explicitly provide for the *kompetenz-kompetenz* principle, the 1958 New York Convention laid the groundwork for it by obliging courts to refer parties to arbitration when an arbitration agreement exists,

* Artem expresses profound gratitude to Stephanie Day of Bennett Jones LLP for her tireless assistance in the preparation of this paper. Artem also wishes to thank Rika Schulz for her insights into the treatment of the *kompetenz-kompetenz* doctrine in Germany.

1. Gary B. Born, *International Commercial Arbitration*, vol. I, Chapter 7 (3rd ed. Kluwer L. Int'l 2021) (updated November 2023).

thereby implying that arbitrators may proceed despite challenges to their jurisdiction.[2] The UNCITRAL Model Law later explicitly codified the principle in 1985.[3] Article 16 of the Model Law provides that an arbitral tribunal "may rule on its own jurisdiction," including on any objections to the arbitration agreement.[4] The Model Law language and the philosophy behind it have since been adopted in the arbitration statutes of many jurisdictions across the globe. Today, virtually all major arbitration jurisdictions recognize the *kompetenz-kompetenz* doctrine. In a way, the doctrine has become synonymous with respect for party autonomy and arbitration as a dispute resolution process.

Indeed, for a time, the *kompetenz-kompetenz* principle seemed virtually unassailable, as jurisdictions around the world competed to be viewed as arbitration-friendly. However, with more experience came inevitable recognition that the doctrine has both positive and negative dimensions. The positive dimension of the doctrine—that arbitrators have the *power* to rule on their own jurisdiction—is accepted almost universally. The main divergence lies in the negative dimension, referring to the degree to which courts are *precluded* from intervening in jurisdictional disputes until an arbitrator has made a jurisdictional decision. The positive dimension of the doctrine is absolute, while the negative dimension is subject to qualification.[5]

This negative dimension of the *kompetenz-kompetenz* doctrine has increasingly caused courts to grapple with issues such as the standard of review applicable to an arbitrator's ruling on jurisdiction, the timing of judicial intervention, and the handling of parallel court proceedings in the context of stay applications in favor of arbitration.[6] As a result of this complexity, strict fidelity to *kompetenz-kompetenz* across various jurisdictions has gradually diminished, with both legislatures and courts increasingly carving out exceptions to this once-unassailable principle.

The objective of this paper is to review the current treatment of the *kompetenz-kompetenz* doctrine across key arbitral jurisdictions, with a focus on identifying emerging exceptions to the doctrine and discerning commonalities or patterns across those exceptions. It is hoped that this paper will serve as a useful tool for arbitration practitioners in tailoring arbitration clauses to clients' objectives and the jurisdictions connected to the performance of the underlying agreement. It is also hoped that, by identifying emerging trends, this paper will predict where many of the jurisdictions that still maintain fidelity to the principle may go next.

We will begin our examination with the author's home jurisdiction, Canada, and then move eastward across the globe to look at emerging rules and practices in England and Wales, Germany, Sweden, and Singapore.

---

2. *Ibid.*
3. UNCITRAL, *Model Law on International Commercial Arbitration*, U.N. Doc. A/40/17, annex I (June 21, 1985) (amended 2006).
4. *Ibid.*, Art. 16(1).
5. George A. Bermann, Chapter 4: Anticipatory Deference: What Will Courts Decide and Not Decide Before Enforcing an Agreement to Arbitrate?, in *Deference in International Commercial Arbitration: The Shared System of Control in International Commercial Arbitration* 79 (Franco Ferrari & Friedrich Jakob Rosenfeld eds, Kluwer L. Int'l 2023) [Bermann].
6. *Ibid.*, at 72-75.

§16.02 CROSS-JURISDICTIONAL SURVEY OF EXCEPTIONS TO THE *KOMPETENZ-KOMPETENZ* PRINCIPLE

[A] Canada

Canada is a federal state, with each province having its own set of arbitration statutes. Canada was an early adopter of the UNCITRAL Model Law, which, at the time, led to exponential growth of the use of arbitration in Canada, described as the "big bang of arbitration in Canada."[7] Today, all provincial international commercial arbitration statutes adopt the positive dimension of the *kompetenz-kompetenz* doctrine that mimics Article 16 of the Model Law,[8] as well as the doctrine's negative dimension via provisions that require courts to stay proceedings commenced in the face of an arbitration agreement.[9]

Despite this Canada-wide legislative scheme and Canada's firm commitment to positioning itself as an arbitration-friendly jurisdiction, over the last two decades, the landscape in Canada has shifted away from strict adherence to the *kompetenz-kompetenz* doctrine, with courts across the country increasingly introducing principled, ad hoc exceptions to general deference to arbitral tribunals. Canada's evolution in this regard has been very much in line with other parts of the Western World. Indeed, in certain aspects, Canada appears to have led the way, with the Supreme Court of Canada articulating principled exceptions in areas of consumer protection, access to justice, and bankruptcy and insolvency, which later found adoption in other jurisdictions. Lower Canadian courts have also followed the trend set by the Supreme Court, increasingly intervening in issues of arbitral jurisdiction, including by carving out exceptions for certain statutory rights.

The first harbinger of change was the 2007 Supreme Court of Canada case of *Dell Computer Corp. v. Union des Consommateurs.*[10] In that case, the Supreme Court of Canada held that courts retain authority to decide challenges to arbitrators' jurisdiction in certain circumstances[11] and carved out principled exceptions to the *kompetenz-kompetenz* doctrine to delineate the boundaries of permissible judicial intervention. Specifically, the court held that courts may rule on an arbitral tribunal's jurisdiction where: (i) a jurisdictional challenge raises a pure question of law; or (ii) the challenge involves a question of mixed fact and law but only requires a superficial examination of the evidentiary record.[12]

7. Cecil O.D. Branson, The Enforcement of International Commercial Arbitration Agreements in Canada, 16:1 Arb. Int'l 19, 23 (2000).
8. Model Law, *supra* n. 3, Art. 16.
9. *Arbitration Act*, SBC 2020, c 2, section 7; *Arbitration Act*, RSA 2000, c A-43, section 7; *The Arbitration Act*, 1992, SS 1992, c A-24.1, section 8; *The Arbitration Act*, CCSM c A120, section 7; *Arbitration Act*, 1991, SO 1991, c 17, section 7; *Arbitration Act*, RSNB 2014, c 100, section 7; *Arbitration Act*, RSPEI 1988, c A-16, section 6; *Arbitration Act*, RSNS 1989 c 19, section 7; *Arbitration Act*, RSNB 2014, c 100, section 7; *Arbitration Act*, RSN 1990, c A-14, section 4; *Arbitration Act*, SNWT 2022, c 14, section 8; *Arbitration Act*, RSY 2002, c 8, section 9.
10. 2007 SCC 34 [*Dell*].
11. *Ibid.*, para. 13.
12. *Ibid.*, para. 85.

Following *Dell*, which was decided under Quebec's distinct civil law regime, there were doubts as to whether the exceptions articulated by the Supreme Court would apply across Canada. In 2011, the Supreme Court of Canada's decision in *Seidel v. Telus Communications Inc.*[13] did away with that uncertainty, confirming that the exceptions articulated in *Dell* applied across all Canadian provinces while reiterating the importance of respecting the arbitral process.

The Supreme Court's decision to carve out exceptions to the *kompetenz-kompetenz* doctrine did not escape criticism. For instance, Frédéric Bachand, an arbitration scholar and Superior Court of Quebec judge, questioned the Supreme Court's suggestion in *Dell* that judges are better-suited to determine pure questions of law and opined that, even on questions of pure law, judges would benefit from a tribunal's own ruling on jurisdictional issues.[14] However, contrary to fears at the time, *Dell* and *Seidel* did not open the floodgates to courts ousting the jurisdiction of arbitral tribunals to hear jurisdictional challenges. Rather, Canadian commentators observed that "properly briefed courts ubiquitously and routinely refer to those two cases as preliminary steps in their analysis of the merits of stay applications. In the majority of such cases, jurisdictional issues are in fact remitted to arbitral tribunals for initial determinations."[15] On balance, *Dell* and *Seidel* did not significantly undermine the *kompetenz-kompetenz* doctrine in Canada.

It is worth noting that *Seidel* not only affirmed *Dell's* application across Canada but also introduced a further exception to the *kompetenz-kompetenz* doctrine in the area of consumer protection. In *Seidel*, the Supreme Court of Canada applied the "pure question of law" exception from *Dell* to permit courts to rule on arbitral jurisdiction over claims arising under a provision of consumer protection legislation that expressly permitted claims to be brought in court. In this case, Ms. Seidel, a customer of Canadian telecommunications company Telus, launched a class action alleging unfair practices under the British Columbia *Business Practices and Consumer Protection Act* (BPCPA).[16] Telus sought to enforce an arbitration clause included in its services agreement with Ms. Seidel to stay the action. The Supreme Court of Canada held that while arbitration agreements are generally enforceable, they cannot preclude court access when statutory rights expressly provide for judicial recourse.[17] Seeking to maintain a principled stance, the court also ruled that other claims brought by Ms. Seidel that fell under different provisions of the BPCPA, which did *not* expressly confer a right to judicial action, or that fell under general common law, were to be stayed in

13. 2011 SCC 15 para. 23 [*Seidel*].
14. Frederic Bachand, Kompetenz-Kompetenz, Canadian Style, 25:3 Arb. Int'l 435-437 (2009) https://doi.org/10.1093/arbitration/25.3.431 (accessed October 1, 2025).
15. Joel Richler, Competence-Competence in Canada: A Barometer of Court Support for Commercial Arbitration, 1:1 Can. J. Com. Arb. 13 (2020), https://www.canlii.org/en/commentary/doc/2020CanLIIDocs4071#!fragment//BQCwhgziBcwMYgK4DsDWszIQewE4BUBTADwBdoByCgSgBpltTCIBFRQ3AT0otokLC4EbDtyp8BQkAGU8pAELcASgFEAMioBqAQQByAYRW1SYAEbRS2ONWpA (no longer available) (accessed October 1, 2025).
16. S.B.C. 1986, c. 3, c.15.
17. *Seidel*, *supra* n. 13, para. 7.

favor of arbitration pursuant to British Columbia's *Commercial Arbitration Act.*[18] As a result, the effect of *Seidel* was limited to consumer disputes governed by legislative provisions that expressly preserve consumers' access to courts. In the years since *Seidel,* some Canadian provinces have introduced legislation to ban mandatory arbitration clauses in the context of consumer contracts altogether.[19] Such legislative provisions act as statutory exceptions to *kompetenz-kompetenz.*

Almost a decade after *Seidel,* the Supreme Court of Canada's decision in *Uber Technologies Inc. v. Heller*[20] expanded the consumer protection exception to create what has been referred to as "an access to justice" exception. While rooted in and closely tied to the consumer protection context, the access to justice exception provides a broader principled basis pursuant to which courts can depart from the *kompetenz-kompetenz* doctrine.

In *Uber,* the Supreme Court of Canada addressed the enforceability of arbitration clauses within the context of what has come to be known as "the gig economy." In this case, David Heller, a driver for Uber Eats, initiated a class action alleging that Uber had violated Ontario's *Employment Standards Act*[21] by classifying drivers as independent contractors rather than employees. Uber sought to stay the proceedings, invoking an arbitration clause included in its standard-form agreement, which mandated disputes be resolved through mediation and arbitration in the Netherlands under the ICC Rules, with upfront costs of approximately USD 14,500.[22] The Supreme Court of Canada found the arbitration agreement to be inoperative on the basis that it imposed prohibitive costs on Mr. Heller in pursuing mandatory arbitration, effectively denying him access to a remedy.[23] Ultimately, the court articulated a new exception to the *kompetenz-kompetenz* doctrine, wherein it allowed courts to stay arbitration proceedings (thus effectively ruling on the tribunal's jurisdiction) where, as in this case, there is a real prospect that a challenge to the tribunal's jurisdiction may never be resolved by the arbitrator.[24]

The third notable exception to the *kompetenz-kompetenz* doctrine was articulated by the Supreme Court of Canada in the 2022 case of *Peace River Hydro Partners v. Petrowest Corp.*[25] In this case, the Supreme Court of Canada unanimously held that superior courts across Canada have statutory jurisdiction pursuant to the Federal *Bankruptcy and Insolvency Act*[26] to declare an otherwise valid arbitration agreement inoperative, and to dismiss an application for stay of court proceedings in favor of arbitration if enforcing the arbitration agreement would compromise the orderly and efficient resolution of insolvency proceedings. The court outlined a non-exhaustive list

18. *Commercial Arbitration Act,* R.S.B.C. 1996, c. 55, section 15 (as it stood in 2011).
19. Consumer Protection Act, 2002, S.O. 2002, c. 30, Sch. A, section 7(2); Consumer Protection Act, CQLR c. P-40.1, Art. 11.1; Bill 4, Business Practices and Consumer Protection Amendment Act, 2025 (B.C.).
20. 2020 SCC 16 [*Uber*].
21. Employment Standards Act, S.O. 2000, c 41.
22. *Uber, supra* n. 20, para. 10.
23. *Ibid.*, para. 11.
24. *Ibid.*, para. 44.
25. 2022 SCC 41 [*Petrowest*].
26. Bankruptcy and Insolvency Act, R.S.C. 1985 c. B-3.

of factors that may be relevant in determining whether an arbitration agreement is inoperative in the context of bankruptcy and insolvency, including: (i) the effect of arbitration on the integrity of the insolvency proceedings; (ii) the relative prejudice to the parties to the arbitration agreement and the debtor's stakeholders; (iii) the urgency of resolving the dispute; and (iv) the effect of a stay of proceedings arising from the bankruptcy or insolvency proceedings.[27] These factors all emphasize concern about the impact that a stay of proceedings in favor of arbitration might have on third parties. As discussed below, courts of the United Kingdom have recently decided to follow a similar path, upending over a decade of jurisprudence.

In sum, there are three principled exceptions to the *kompetenz-kompetenz* doctrine that apply across Canada: (i) the question of law exception, (ii) the access to justice exception ("no reasonable prospect"), and (iii) the bankruptcy and insolvency exception.

Lower Canadian courts have since followed the trend established by the Supreme Court of Canada in *Uber* and *Petrowest*. For example, in a 2024 decision in *Orica Canada Inc v. ARVOS GmbH*, the Court of King's Bench of the Province of Alberta extended the access to justice exception from *Uber* to situations where arbitration is likely time-barred by local legislation and suggested that there may be other, additional scenarios where an exception to the *kompetenz-kompetenz* principle may be justified.[28] While this decision is only binding within Alberta, it may have a persuasive effect in other Canadian jurisdictions, prompting yet further exceptions to the *kompetenz-kompetenz* doctrine across Canada.

Finally, in *ONE Lodging Holdings v. American Hotel Income Properties REIT (GP)*,[29] the Supreme Court of the Province of British Columbia held that the *kompetenz-kompetenz* doctrine does not apply where the jurisdictional challenge concerns the existence of an arbitration agreement, as opposed to its scope or validity. Relying on the Supreme Court of Canada decision in *Dell*, the court held that question of whether an arbitration agreement exists can be decided by a court if it is a pure question of law or a question of mixed law and fact where the facts need only superficial consideration.[30] The ruling has the potential to overextend the courts' role in deciding jurisdictional challenges to arbitration agreements.

The cases canvassed above may at a first blush suggest that there is a rapid and significant departure from strict fidelity to *kompetenz-kompetenz* across Canada. However, a survey of jurisprudence and legislation in other key jurisdiction shows that Canada's approach is not fundamentally at odds with trends seen elsewhere in the world. In any event, the basic approach in Canada remains one of fealty to the *kompetenz-kompetenz* doctrine, *subject to* a closed—albeit growing—list of principled exceptions. As we will shortly *see*, the starting point of fealty to *kompetenz-kompetenz* is not necessarily found in every jurisdiction.

---

27. *Petrowest*, *supra* n. 25, paras 155-156.
28. 2024 ABKB 97.
29. 2024 BCSC 2179.
30. *Ibid.*, para. 39.

[B] England and Wales

A prime example of the above is England and Wales, where local legislation adopts a much less deferential stance towards tribunals' ability to rule on their own jurisdiction, and local courts have articulated a growing list of exceptions to the *kompetenz-kompetenz* doctrine over the years.

As a starting point, England and Wales has not adopted the UNCITRAL Model Law, although its arbitration legislation was influenced by it. While the English *Arbitration Act 1996*[31] incorporates the *kompetenz-kompetenz* doctrine via section 30, it also contains a unique provision in section 32 that allows parties to apply to English courts to have the court determine a tribunal's substantive jurisdiction as a preliminary point.[32] Although the High Court held in 2021 that section 32 is only available in rare circumstances,[33] it remains a significant departure from the *kompetenz-kompetenz* doctrine and the practice followed in other jurisdictions such as Canada, Sweden, and Singapore, where the default position is deference to the tribunal's competence to rule on its own jurisdiction, subject to limited principled exceptions.

Despite calls for section 32 to be struck in order to protect and respect the *kompetenz-kompetenz* doctrine,[34] it was kept in place in the new *Arbitration Act 2025*, but with certain amendments.[35] Prior to the amendments, absent agreement of the parties, an application under section 32 required both the permission of the arbitral tribunal *and* the court being satisfied that: (i) the determination of the question is likely to produce substantial savings in costs, (ii) the application was made without delay, and (iii) there is good reason why the matter should be decided by the court.[36] Section 14 of the *Arbitration Act 2025* removed the element of court's satisfaction, leaving only the requirement for permission of the arbitral tribunal. Further, section 5 of the *Arbitration Act 2025* amended section 32 to clarify that it can only be invoked if the tribunal has not yet ruled on its jurisdiction.[37] These amendments were intended to confirm that section 32 is available only as an alternative to the tribunal ruling on its own jurisdiction.[38] Because section 32 requires the permission of the tribunal or the parties, the Law Commission saw no hindrance to arbitration and the *kompetenz-kompetenz* doctrine.[39] The new *Arbitration Act 2025* thus carefully balances allowing

31. *Arbitration Act* 1996, c. 23 (UK).
32. *Ibid.*, section 32.
33. *Armada Ship Management v. Schiste Oil*, [2021] EWHC 1094 (Comm) para. 31.
34. Sir Richard Aikens, The Arbitration Act 1996: No Kind of Fault or Flaw? Three Problems on Jurisdiction and the Applicable Law of the Arbitration (address at Brick Court Chambers Annual Commercial Conference, October 13, 2022); Law Commission of England and Wales, *Arbitration Final Report*, Law Com. No. 404, at 102 (2023).
35. *Arbitration Bill* [HL] 2024-2025, 58/3 Parl. (U.K.), available at House of Commons Library https://commonslibrary.parliament.uk/research-briefings/cbp-10134/ (accessed October 1, 2025).
36. *Arbitration Act* 1996, *supra* n. 31, section 32.
37. *Arbitration Bill* [HL] 2024-2025, *supra* n. 35, section 5.
38. Law Comm'n, *Arbitration Final Report, supra* n. 34, at 103.
39. *Ibid.*, at 96.

preliminary court applications on matters of arbitral jurisdiction with maintaining respect for the arbitral process and its basis in consent of the parties.

Beyond this general principle, English legislation and case law recognize many of the same exceptions to the *kompetenz-kompetenz* doctrine that were articulated in recent years in Canada.

First, England and Wales has had a long-standing exception to the *kompetenz-kompetenz* doctrine where the existence of an arbitration agreement is genuinely in dispute. This is somewhat similar to Canada's "question of law" exception. The exception has been part of English law since at least 1993, when the English Court of Appeal held in *Harbour v. Kansa* that "[t]here will obviously be cases in which a claim that no contract came into existence necessarily entails a denial that there was any agreement to arbitrate."[40] This principle was subsequently affirmed in a 2007 decision of the England and Wales High Court in *Nigel Peter Albon v. Naza Motor Trading (No. 3)*,[41] where the court was asked to consider whether an arbitration agreement was valid, given that Mr. Albon asserted that his signature on the underlying joint venture agreement had been forged. Naza, the Malaysian company, sought to stay the English court proceedings in favor of arbitration under Malaysian law, as stipulated in the purported joint venture agreement.[42] In this case, the High Court refused to grant the stay and instead ordered a trial on the issue of forgery, staying the arbitration.[43] However, in other cases, where there is a "good arguable case" that an arbitration agreement exists, English courts will typically respect *kompetenz-kompetenz*, refer the parties to arbitration, and let the arbitral tribunal decide on gateway issues such as jurisdiction.[44]

Next, with respect to consumer protection, the English *Arbitration Act* expressly provides that arbitration agreements in consumer contracts for claims under a certain value (currently GBP 5,000) are automatically unfair and unenforceable against a consumer.[45] This provision effectively acts as a statutory exception to the *kompetenz-kompetenz* doctrine. Notably, the exception was recently expanded by the English Court of Appeal in a 2022 decision in *Soleymani v. Nifty Gateway LLC*[46] to apply to claims well over the GBP 5,000 threshold. In that case, the claimant, Mr. Soleymani, participated in an online auction hosted by Nifty Gateway, a US-based NFT marketplace, bidding USD 650,000 for a non-fungible token (NFT) associated with digital artwork. A dispute arose, and Mr. Soleymani refused to pay. In response, Nifty Gateway initiated arbitration proceedings in New York in accordance with the platform's terms of use.[47] The English Court of Appeal refused to stay court proceedings in favor of arbitration. In doing so, the court reasoned that the consumer protection

40. [1993] 1 Lloyd's Rep 455 para. 53.
41. [2007] EWHC 665 (Ch) [*Albon*].
42. *Ibid.*, para. 5.
43. *Ibid.*, paras 17-23.
44. *Noble Denton Middle East v. Noble Denton International Ltd.*, [2010] EWHC 2574 (Comm), para. 16 [*Noble Denton*].
45. *Arbitration Act* 1996, *supra* n. 31, section 91.
46. [2022] EWHC 773 (Comm) [*Soleymani*].
47. *Ibid.*, paras 8-15.

context is a "powerful factor" weighing in favor of having courts decide the issue of jurisdiction rather than leaving it in the first instance to the arbitral tribunal.[48] This decision bolsters both the consumer protection and access to justice exceptions to the *kompetenz-kompetenz* doctrine, affirming that when these important issues are at stake, national courts may be more willing to intervene.

Outside the consumer context, case law in England has generally demonstrated a tilt toward an "access to justice" exception to the *kompetenz-kompetenz* doctrine. For instance, in the 2009 decision in *Kaye v. Nu Skin,*[49] the English Court of Appeal refused to enforce an arbitration clause within a distribution agreement using virtually the same reasoning as the Supreme Court of Canada in *Uber*. Kaye was a 23-year-old distributor who had entered into an agreement with Nu Skin to sell its skincare products, achieving executive status in three years. Nu Skin subsequently terminated the agreement, alleging that Kaye's father had an economic interest in the arrangement, which breached the terms of the agreement. Kaye then commenced legal proceedings alleging breach of contract. Nu Skin applied for a stay of proceedings, asserting that the distribution agreement contained a binding arbitration clause which required parties to arbitrate their disputes in Utah, United States. Kaye was based in England.[50]

Despite finding that the agreement between Kaye and Nu Skin was a commercial rather than consumer transaction, the English Court of Appeal refused to stay its proceedings and undertook to make an independent determination on jurisdiction. The court held that further evidence should be heard to determine: (i) whether the arbitration clause was onerous and unusual given the disparity in bargaining power between the parties, (ii) whether in practice it might mean that Kaye had no real prospect of pursuing her claim, and (iii) how common foreign arbitration clauses are in distributorship agreements.[51] The clause, embedded in a standard-form contract drafted by Nu Skin, appeared to deprive Kaye of access to justice due to the significant burden of pursuing arbitration in a distant jurisdiction. The court undertook to resolve the question of the clause's validity rather than referring the question to the arbitral tribunal. The decision in *Kaye* indicates potentially strong willingness on the part of English courts to consider an "access to justice" exception to the *kompetenz-kompetenz* principle.

Finally, UK courts have very recently created their own version of the bankruptcy and insolvency exception. Prior to 2024, the law in England required a petition in bankruptcy to be stayed in favor of arbitration whenever a debt subject to an arbitration clause was not admitted, making referral to arbitration in such cases virtually automatic. This approach effectively prioritized arbitration and enshrined the *kompetenz-kompetenz* doctrine in the context of insolvency proceedings.[52] The law in

48. *Ibid.*, para. 86 citing *Golden Ocean Group Ltd v. Humpuss Intermoda Transportasi Tbk Ltd* (The "Barito"), [2013] EWHC (Comm) 1240.
49. [2009] EWHC 3509 (Ch) [*Kaye*].
50. *Ibid.*, paras 5-9.
51. *Ibid.*, paras 37-39.
52. *Salford Estates (No 2) Ltd v. Altomart Ltd* (No 2), [2014] EWCA Civ 1575, para. 22.

England fundamentally changed with the 2024 UK Privy Council decision in *Sian Participation Corporation (In Liquidation) v. Halimeda International Ltd*,[53] in which the Privy Council overturned nearly a decade of precedent to carve out an exception to the *kompetenz-kompetenz* doctrine in the context of bankruptcy and insolvency proceedings.[54] In this case, Halimeda International Ltd. advanced a term loan of USD 140 million to Sian Participation Corporation pursuant to an agreement containing an arbitration clause. When Sian defaulted, Halimeda filed for winding-up proceedings. Sian opposed, citing the arbitration agreement. The Privy Council held that winding-up proceedings should be stayed in favor of arbitration only if the debt is genuinely disputed on substantial grounds.[55] The court held that the mere existence of a dispute as to a debt covered by an arbitration agreement does not automatically necessitate a stay of insolvency proceedings. In reaching this decision, the UK Privy Council adopted a more interventionist approach, similar to but narrower than the approach taken by the Supreme Court of Canada in *Petrowest*, which empowered courts to declare arbitration agreements to be inoperative if enforcement of an arbitration agreement would compromise the orderly and efficient resolution of insolvency proceedings.

In sum, recent years have seen the *kompetenz-kompetenz* doctrine in England and Wales pulled in different directions by legislation and case law. While the 2025 reforms to the English *Arbitration Act* have moved—or at least clarified—the default position to be at a more deferential stance, English courts have been carving out increasing exceptions to the *kompetenz-kompetenz* doctrine, similar to those that have emerged in other jurisdictions such as Canada. On balance, England and Wales occupies a moderate position across the deference-intervention spectrum, though its courts are signaling increased willingness to carve out exceptions in situations that warrant it.

[C] Germany

As the name suggests, Germany is the originator of the *kompetenz-kompetenz* doctrine. Historically, before it adopted the UNCITRAL Model Law in 1998, Germany granted arbitrators the ultimate authority to determine their own jurisdiction, with no prospect of review by the courts, if the parties so agreed.[56] In doing so, German courts prioritized party autonomy, affirming that if parties had agreed to include the *kompetenz-kompetenz* principle in their arbitration agreement, arbitrators could make final and binding determinations on the existence and scope of arbitration agreements. In such circumstances, court interference was restricted to adjudicating the validity of the arbitration agreement. If the arbitration agreement was found to be valid, courts could not intervene in the tribunal's ruling on its own jurisdiction.[57]

53. [2024] UKPC 16 [*Sian Participation*].
54. *Ibid.*, paras 99-100.
55. *Ibid.*, para. 99.
56. Born, *supra* n. 1.
57. Peter Huber and Ivo Bach, Chapter IV: Jurisdiction of Arbitral Tribunal § 1040, in *Arbitration in Germany: The Model Law in Practice* 215 (Patricia Nacimiento et al. eds, 2nd ed., Kluwer L. Int'l 2015).

More recently, however, Germany has moved to occupy a position similar to England and Wales, signaling a fundamental policy shift away from strict fidelity to the *kompetenz-kompetenz* doctrine. Similar to the English *Arbitration Act*, Germany's arbitration law, found in the Tenth Book of the German Code of Civil Procedure (*Zivilprozessordnung* or ZPO), provides for a discrete avenue for court intervention.[58] In particular, under section 1032(2) of ZPO, until the arbitral tribunal has been constituted, a party may apply to court to determine whether arbitral proceedings are "admissible."[59] German courts have interpreted admissibility broadly to mean whether the arbitration agreement is valid and operative and whether the matter in dispute properly falls within the scope of the arbitration agreement.[60] In this sense, section 1032(2) is comparable to but more permissive than section 32 of the English *Arbitration Act 2025*, as it can be used unilaterally by either party, without requiring either consent of the other party or permission of the arbitral tribunal. Further, pursuant to section 1025(2) of ZPO, a section 1032(2) application is available even if the seat of arbitration is abroad or is yet to be determined.[61]

It is important to highlight that the above provisions of ZPO were at one point considered, but expressly rejected, for inclusion in the UNCITRAL Model Law.[62] This confirms that, despite being its originator, Germany today takes a somewhat less deferential stance towards the *kompetenz-kompetenz* doctrine compared to the international baseline.

In addition to this less deferential starting point, German legislation and case law also recognize many of the same exceptions to the *kompetenz-kompetenz* doctrine that have developed in Canada and England and Wales.

First, with respect to consumer protection, section 1031(5) of ZPO provides that an arbitration agreement involving a consumer must be contained in a separately signed document, meaning that German courts will refuse to refer a dispute to arbitration if an arbitration agreement is buried in standard terms and conditions and is not entered into separately by the consumer.[63] This rule seeks to ensure that consumers knowingly consent to arbitration. The rule is mandatory and cannot be waived.[64] By virtue of this legislative rule, consumers in Germany do not have to contest arbitral jurisdiction on the basis that the arbitration agreement was not properly brought to their attention, as was the case in Canada in *Seidel*.

Outside the consumer context, a limited "access to justice" exception—akin to the exception articulated in the *Uber* case in Canada in 2020—was effectively introduced in Germany two decades prior, in the 2000 *Plumber*[65] case. *Plumber* involved an

58. Zivilprozessordnung [ZPO] [Code of Civil Procedure], 10th Book, §§ 1025-1066, BGBl I 2005, 3202 (Ger.), https://www.gesetze-im-internet.de/zpo/ (accessed October 1, 2025).
59. *Ibid.*, 1032(2).
60. Higher Regional Court of Cologne, decision of October 1, 2011 - 19 SchH 7/11.
61. ZPO, *supra* n. 58, section 1025(2).
62. Report of the Working Group on International Contract Practices on the Work of Its Seventeenth Session, UN Document A/CN.9/246, 6.3.1984, 14, para. 55.
63. ZPO, *supra* n. 58, section 1031(5).
64. Docket No. III ZR 16/11.
65. Bundesgerichtshof, September 14, 2000, NJW 2000, 3720.

arbitration agreement included in a contract between a plumbing company and a builder, pursuant to which the plumbing company was responsible for the installation of heating and sanitary systems in a building. The plumbing company had concerns about the builder's ability to pay for the services rendered and demanded that it provide security. The relationship broke down, and the builder commenced a court action against the plumbing company notwithstanding the arbitration agreement.

The builder took the position that the arbitration agreement was void due to his inability to fund arbitration costs. The lower court dismissed the claim and referred the parties to arbitration. However, on appeal, the Federal Court of Justice found that the arbitration agreement was "incapable of being performed" under section 1032(1) of ZPO due to the builder's inability to fund arbitration costs. The fundamental animating principle underlying this decision, like in *Uber*, was access to justice. If the impecunious party were held to the arbitration agreement, they would be deprived of any avenue for recourse. Refusing to enforce arbitration agreements where they effectively bar any access to justice reflects basic notions of fairness.[66]

The *Plumber* decision represents a significant exception to the principle of *kompetenz-kompetenz,* as it allows German courts to step in and set aside an arbitration agreement solely due to one party's inability to fund arbitration costs. At the time it was released, *Plumber* attracted considerable criticism, not only for its effect on the *kompetenz-kompetenz* doctrine but also for potentially incentivizing self-serving behavior and creating unpredictability in international arbitration by virtue of undermining party autonomy.[67] In spite of these strong criticisms, the exception still stands today, underscoring the German judiciary's commitment to preventing situations where a party's impecuniosity effectively forecloses access to justice.

By contrast, Germany has been hesitant to introduce broad exceptions to the *kompetenz-kompetenz* doctrine in the insolvency context. Unlike in Canada and England, arbitration agreements are not directly affected by insolvency proceedings in Germany. In Germany, if a debtor or a trustee acting on behalf of a debtor disputes a claim that is subject to an arbitration agreement, the proper avenue through which to resolve the dispute, including any questions of jurisdiction, remains the competent arbitral tribunal. German jurisprudence has not yet developed an exception akin to the Canadian one in *Petrowest,* which enables courts to find an arbitration agreement inoperative when it might affect the efficiency or integrity of insolvency proceedings,[68] or the UK exception in *Sian Participation,* which requires a debt to be genuinely disputed on substantial grounds before a court will refer the dispute to arbitration. Indeed, German commentators have criticized the Supreme Court of Canada's decision in *Petrowest* as being too broad and potentially putting the basic principle of bankruptcy and insolvency law—namely, that insolvency administrators step into the shoes

66. Gerhard Wagner, Impecunious Parties and Arbitration Agreements, in SchiedsVZ | *German Arbitration Journal,* vol. 1, issue 5, 207 (Jörg Risse, Guenter Pickrahn et al. eds, Kluwer Law Int'l & Verlag C.H. Beck oHG 2003).
67. *Ibid.*
68. Chapter 2: Insolvency and Arbitration in the National Context: Germany, in *Insolvency in Commercial Arbitration: A German and International Perspective* 72 (Fabian van de Ven, Kluwer Law Int'l 2023).

of the debtor—on a slippery slope.[69] However, the Higher Regional Court of Cologne has held that Germany's "access to justice" exception continues to apply in the context of bankruptcy and insolvency proceedings, meaning that the *kompetenz-kompetenz* doctrine does not apply if the administrator lacks funds to pay for arbitration.[70]

In sum, Germany today adopts a comparatively less deferential stance toward the *kompetenz-kompetenz* doctrine, largely because its statutory framework permits either party to unilaterally ask a German court to rule on arbitral jurisdiction before an arbitral tribunal is appointed. In addition, German legislation and case law establish significant exceptions to the *kompetenz-kompetenz* doctrine in the areas of consumer protection and access to justice, with the latter potentially available solely on the basis of inability to fund the costs of arbitration. However, there is no exception for bankruptcy and insolvency proceedings.

[D] Sweden

Sweden occupies a unique place in this survey, in that it recently underwent a watershed transformation in its approach to the *kompetenz-kompetenz* doctrine as a result of legislative reform. Prior to 2019, Article 2 of the Swedish *Arbitration Act* allowed parties to apply to a Swedish court for a ruling on arbitral jurisdiction at any time—either before or during arbitration, and either before or after the appointment of the arbitral tribunal.[71]

In 2019, Article 2 was amended to limit court intervention to cases where the tribunal has expressly ruled that it has jurisdiction, and to impose a strict thirty-day deadline from the notification of the tribunal's decision for a party to seek judicial review.[72] The amendments also preclude courts from intervening in questions of arbitral jurisdiction without the parties' consent, except in the context of consumer transactions.[73] The legislative reform of 2019 can be said to have led Sweden to enshrine the *kompetenz-kompetenz* principle in its purest form. That is, outside of parties' agreement to the contrary and consumer transactions, the arbitral tribunal *always* gets to rule on its jurisdiction first, with courts' role effectively limited to judicial review.

Given the recency of these amendments, most of Swedish case law in this area was decided under the old, non-deferential framework. Consistent with the old framework, Swedish courts historically distinguished themselves from courts in other jurisdictions by conducting a comprehensive review of arbitral jurisdiction at the threshold stage, not only in respect of the existence, validity, and scope of arbitration agreements but also on issues that courts in other jurisdictions would typically refer to arbitration unless the parties expressly agreed otherwise.[74]

---

69. *Ibid.*, at 94.
70. Docket No 18 W 32/13.
71. *Swedish Arbitration Act* (SFS 1999:116), section 2 (prior to amendments by SFS 2018:1954).
72. *Swedish Arbitration Act* (SFS 1999:116), section 2, as amended by SFS 2018:1954.
73. *Ibid.*, section 4a.
74. Bermann, *supra* n. 5, at 85.

Yet, despite this more robust judicial scrutiny, which appears to conflict with the *kompetenz-kompetenz* principle, Sweden has managed to maintain a strong reputation as an arbitration-friendly jurisdiction.[75] This was achieved through thoughtful restraint, in which Swedish courts consistently balanced their broad oversight powers with respect for party autonomy, ensuring that only well-founded challenges to arbitration agreements were entertained. The careful balancing practiced by Swedish courts has led to early emergence of principled exceptions to the *kompetenz-kompetenz* principle, dating as far back as the early 1980s, decades before similar exceptions emerged in other jurisdictions such as Canada.

To begin, it has been the law in Sweden since the 1980 Supreme Court decision in *Tureberg-Sollentuna Lastbilscentral v. Byggnadsfirman Rudolf Asplund Aktiebolag*[76] that Swedish courts have the power to rule on the existence and validity of an arbitration agreement. As discussed above, a similar exception was not established in England and Wales and Canada until 1993 and 2007, respectively. Although the Supreme Court's ruling in *Tureberg-Sollentuna Lastbilscentral* did not expressly discuss the doctrine of *kompetenz-kompetenz*, the very fact that the court examined whether courts had jurisdiction over a dispute arising from a subcontractor agreement that incorporated an arbitration clause was a clear signal that Swedish courts may rule on the existence and validity of an arbitration agreement in the first instance. However, this decision should be approached with caution, as it was made long before the legislative reforms of 2019.

The Swedish Supreme Court followed up on this decision the next year, in *Case No. Ö1106-79/NJA 1981, p. 711*, where it articulated a form of "consumer transactions" and "access to justice" exceptions to the *kompetenz-kompetenz* doctrine.[77] The case before the Supreme Court involved a home buyer who sought to avoid an arbitration clause in a contract for construction of a single-family home. The Supreme Court observed that arbitration clauses in consumer contracts are often unreasonable, primarily because the costs of arbitration can impose a heavy burden on the consumer, who is typically the economically weaker party, thereby precluding access to justice. While the Supreme Court recognized that arbitration is often suitable to resolve matters arising from construction contracts due to their technical complexity, the court distinguished this specific case as being a consumer contract, as opposed to a complex construction contract, and undertook its own extensive review on matters of arbitral jurisdiction. In doing so, the Supreme Court effectively introduced an exception to *kompetenz-kompetenz,* which simultaneously addresses both the consumer protection and access to justice concerns.

As is the case in Germany, England, and certain Canadian provinces, today, the validity of arbitration clauses in consumer contracts in Sweden is largely governed by statute. In Sweden's case, the legislation effectively ousts the *kompetenz-kompetenz* doctrine in consumer disputes. Specifically, section 6 of the *Arbitration Act* provides that an arbitration agreement made before a dispute arises cannot be enforced against

75. *Ibid.*, at 90.
76. NJA 1980, p. 46, Supreme Court, Decision of February 12, 1980.
77. NJA 1981, p. 711, Supreme Court, Decision of June 12, 1981.

a consumer if the dispute concerns goods, services, or products for private use.[78] This carefully crafted rule safeguards consumers' right to have their disputes heard in court while also giving them an option to make an informed decision to arbitrate after they know the exact nature of the dispute.

Finally, in the insolvency context, like Germany, Sweden does not have a carve-out from the *kompetenz-kompetenz* doctrine. In *Case No. Ö 3504-01/NJA 2003, p. 3*, the Swedish Supreme Court held that creditors are bound by arbitration agreements entered into prior to the debtor becoming bankrupt.[79] In that case, creditors attempted to intervene in an arbitration concerning a claim made in bankruptcy proceedings, arguing that the arbitration agreement should not bind the estate because it was signed prior to bankruptcy. The Supreme Court disagreed, finding the creditors to be bound by the debtor's arbitration agreement. The Supreme Court held that this finding was consistent with section 16 of Sweden's *Bankruptcy Act*, which provides that if a creditor's right depends on the outcome of a particular trial, the result of that trial will determine the creditor's rights.[80] In effect, the Swedish Supreme Court refused to carve out an exception to the *kompetenz-kompetenz* doctrine for bankruptcy and insolvency proceedings. Where the claim is subject to an arbitration agreement, the arbitration can effectively decide the amount or existence of a creditor's claim, which they can then assert in bankruptcy proceedings.

The Svea Court of Appeal followed this general rule in *Advadis S.A., in bankruptcy, and Brodowsky v. Royal Unibrev A/S*,[81] where, during annulment proceedings, the appellant company, Advadis, argued in part that the arbitration agreement at issue was invalid because Advadis was bankrupt at the time of proceedings, and Polish law, which was the governing law of the agreement, provided that any arbitration agreement concluded by a bankrupt party loses its legal effect as of the date bankruptcy is declared. The Svea Court of Appeal dismissed the claim, holding that because Stockholm was the seat of arbitration, Swedish law applied, and, under Swedish law, bankruptcy estates are bound by arbitration agreements concluded by debtors prior to their bankruptcy.[82]

In sum, through legislative reform, Sweden recently transitioned from being one of the less deferential jurisdictions to effectively enshrining the *kompetenz-kompetenz* doctrine in its domestic law. Nonetheless, Swedish legislation and case law still provide for exceptions to the *kompetenz-kompetenz* doctrine in cases involving consumer transactions and access to justice concerns, similar to the practice in Canada, England and Wales, and Germany. However, like Germany, Sweden does not recognize an exception to the *kompetenz-kompetenz* principle in the context of bankruptcy and insolvency proceedings. On balance, following legislative reforms, Sweden occupies a similar position to that of Canada.

78. *Swedish Arbitration Act*, *supra* note 72, section 6.
79. NJA 2003, p. 3, Supreme Court, Decision of January 2, 2003.
80. *Swedish Bankruptcy Act*, SFS 1987:672 (Sweden), section 16.
81. Svea Court of Appeal, T 8043-13, March 20, 2015.
82. *Ibid.*

[E] Singapore

Of all the jurisdictions surveyed in this chapter, Singapore arguably maintains the most fidelity to the *kompetenz-kompetenz* doctrine, both in its legislation and in its jurisprudence.

Singapore law incorporates the doctrine of *kompetenz-kompetenz* in both its domestic act, the *Arbitration Act* 2001, and the *International Arbitration Act* 1994 (IAA).[83] Singapore's domestic *Arbitration Act* explicitly empowers arbitral tribunals to decide on their jurisdictional competence.[84] Similarly, the IAA incorporates Article 16 of the UNCITRAL Model Law, which grants arbitral tribunals power to rule on their own jurisdiction, including any objections with respect to the existence or validity of the arbitration agreement. In contrast to England and Wales and Germany, Singapore's arbitration legislation does not provide for any avenues for early court intervention on issues of arbitral jurisdiction.

Further, while courts of other UNCITRAL Model Law jurisdictions have attenuated the *kompetenz-kompetenz* doctrine over time through exceptions, Singaporean courts have remained steadfast in their commitment to the doctrine, repeatedly refusing to carve out exceptions and even criticizing courts of other jurisdictions that have done so. As a result, Singaporean courts permit themselves to examine issues such as the existence, validity, and scope of an arbitration agreement only in the clearest of cases, where there is no prima facie evidence of the existence of an arbitration agreement. Singaporean courts have ruled this to be a decidedly low threshold, leaving any contested issues concerning the scope or validity of the agreement for arbitral tribunals to resolve. The Singapore Court of Appeal expressly stated that to do otherwise "could significantly hollow the *kompetenz-kompetenz* principle of its practical effect."[85]

A prime example of Singapore's commitment to the *kompetenz-kompetenz* doctrine can be found in the case of *The Titan Unity*,[86] where the Singapore High Court addressed the application of the *kompetenz-kompetenz* doctrine in the context of a stay of application under the IAA. The plaintiff, Portigon AG, a German bank, initiated court proceedings against the charterers of the Titan Unity vessel, Oceanic Shipping Pte Ltd. Portigon alleged an error in the delivery of cargo with a value of around USD 3.7 million, for which it claimed it was the lawful holder of bills of lading as security for the shipment. Oceanic sought a stay of proceedings in favor of arbitration pursuant to section 6 of the IAA, on the basis that the bills of lading incorporated an arbitration clause. At issue was whether an arbitration agreement existed. Portigon argued that the arbitration clause had not been incorporated into the contract between the parties, the arbitration agreement was not properly dated, and the contractual carriers under the bills of lading were third parties, not Oceanic. The Singapore High Court held that it needed only to find a prima facie existence of an arbitration agreement and confirmed

83. *International Arbitration Act* (Cap. 143A, 2002 Rev. Ed.) (Sing.).
84. *Arbitration Act* (Cap. 10), section 21(1) [*IAA*].
85. *Tomolugen Holdings v. Silica Inv'rs Ltd.* [2015] SGCA 57 at para. 67.
86. [2013] SGHCR 28.

that this threshold would be met in all but the clearest of cases. The judgment reaffirmed Singapore's strong commitment to the *kompetenz-kompetenz* doctrine. The low prima facie threshold adopted by the High Court stands in sharp contrast with the more onerous "arguable case" standard adopted by the British Columbia Supreme Court in *One Lodging* and the England and Wales High Court in *Noble Denton*.

Consistent with its noninterventionist stance, the Singapore High Court recently refused to carve out an exception to the *kompetenz-kompetenz* doctrine in the context of consumer protection, taking a decidedly different approach from the Supreme Court of Canada in *Uber*. That decision was reached in a 2023 case in *Beltran v. Terraform,*[87] which involved a class action against Terraform Labs Pte Ltd., a Singapore-based blockchain technology company. Terraform sought to stay court proceedings in favor of arbitration, citing arbitration agreements that were embedded in the Terms of Use posted on its website. At issue in dispute was whether Terraform had established a prima facie case for the existence of valid arbitration agreements. The plaintiffs argued that the arbitration agreements were buried within the terms and conditions that were only accessible via hyperlinks on Terraform's websites and that these hyperlinks were obscure and lacked prominence. On this basis, the plaintiffs contended that they had not been given reasonable notice of the arbitration agreement prior to entering into contracts with Terraform. The court examined whether the plaintiffs had actual or constructive notice of these arbitration clauses, considering the nature of the website's Terms of Use, which did not require users to explicitly assent to the Terms of Use before using Terraform's website.

The High Court found that Terraform had established a prima facie case that a valid arbitration agreement existed, on the basis that it was "at least arguable," on the basis of the evidence of a pop-up notice which informed users of the applicable Terms of Use, the plaintiffs had notice of the arbitration agreement.[88] To this end, the court stated that it was "[n]ot unreasonable that [the plaintiffs] would ... have also noticed the hyperlink to the Terra Terms of Use, which contained the Arbitration Clause,"[89] and upheld the lower court's decision to refer the jurisdictional issue to arbitration. This decision stands in stark contrast with public policy in other jurisdictions. As noted above, German law explicitly requires arbitration clauses in consumer contracts to be contained in a separately signed agreement so as to protect consumers. Similarly, Sweden prohibits pre dispute arbitration clauses in consumer agreements altogether.

The High Court in *Beltran* directly addressed the "access to justice" exception carved out by the Supreme Court of Canada's in *Uber*, finding that it was "out of step with the prevailing stance in Singapore to support and facilitate arbitration ... [s]ubject to legislative intervention, it is questionable whether the court can or should strike down arbitration agreements on the grounds relied on in *Uber*."[90] *Beltran* thus marks purposeful divergence from the consumer protection-oriented approach adopted in other jurisdictions, where there is growing judicial willingness to carve out exceptions

87. [2023] SGHC 340 [*Beltran*].
88. *Ibid.*, para. 161.
89. *Ibid.*, para. 144.
90. *Ibid.*, para. 180.

from the *kompetenz-kompetenz* doctrine to protect consumers from being forced into expensive arbitration proceedings in remote jurisdictions.

Singapore's fidelity to the *kompetenz-kompetenz* doctrine also holds true in the insolvency context. In 2020, in *AnAn Group Pte Ltd. v. VTB Bank (Public Joint Stock Co)*,[91] the Singapore Court of Appeal articulated a test, which has since become known as the *AnAn* test, and which requires courts to dismiss or stay winding-up petitions in favor of arbitration if: (i) there is prima facie evidence of a valid arbitration agreement, (ii) the dispute falls within the scope of the arbitration agreement, and (iii) the debtor is not abusing the court process.[92] The Court of Appeal's decision in *AnAn* followed the then-current state of English law, setting a decidedly low threshold that effectively provides for automatic referral to arbitration unless there is evidence of abuse of process, which in and of itself entails a high threshold.[93] The Court of Appeal's decision in *AnAn* was recently followed by the Singapore High Court in the 2023 case of *Founder Grp (Hong Kong) Limited (in liquidation) v. Singapore JHC Co.*[94]

Following the dramatic reversal of English law in this area in 2024 in *Sian Participation*, there was a brief period of uncertainty as to whether Singapore would follow suit. However, that same year, the Singapore High Court confirmed in *Re Sapura Fabrication Sdn Bhd*[95] that Singapore continues to be governed by the *AnAn* test.

In sum, of all the jurisdictions surveyed in this chapter, Singapore by far maintains the strongest fidelity to the *kompetenz-kompetenz* doctrine, both through its legislation and its jurisprudence. Singaporean courts have consistently taken a deliberately pro-arbitration stance, requiring only the faintest evidence of an arbitration agreement to refer jurisdictional issues to arbitral tribunals and expressly refusing to carve out exceptions to the *kompetenz-kompetenz* doctrine where courts of other jurisdictions have done so.

§16.03 CONCLUSIONS AND PRACTICAL TAKEAWAYS

As from the survey presented in this chaptershows, the once-revered doctrine of *kompetenz-kompetenz* has faced increasing challenges, with courts around the globe increasingly adopting more interventionist and nuanced approaches. While it remains revered in certain jurisdictions such as Singapore and, to a lesser extent, Sweden, the *kompetenz-kompetenz* doctrine has seen a number of exceptions emerge in various jurisdictions through both legislative and judicial means, reflecting a shift towards greater judicial scrutiny of the arbitral process. This evolving landscape reflects the tension between maintaining party autonomy and ensuring effective functioning of the justice system.

The survey presented in this chaptershows that there is no universal approach to the *kompetenz-kompetenz* doctrine. Rather, key arbitral jurisdictions around the world

91. [2020] SGCA 33 [*AnAn*].
92. *Ibid.*, para. 56.
93. *Ibid.*, para. 36.
94. *Ibid.* [2023] SGHC 159.
95. [2024] SGHC 241.

fall along a spectrum. On the less deferential end of the spectrum, we find Germany, which, in addition to having significant carve-outs for consumer transactions and access to justice, allows parties to unilaterally ask a German court to rule on arbitral jurisdiction before the arbitral tribunal is appointed. Germany is followed by England and Wales, which has similar carve-outs, in addition to a fresh carve-out for bankruptcy and insolvency, but only permits an application to a court if the parties agree or if the arbitral tribunal consents. Canada and Sweden both sit in the middle of the spectrum, in that they adopt the *kompetenz-kompetenz* doctrine as the default rule but subject it to a growing list of principled exceptions. Finally, Singapore sits at the most deferential end of the spectrum, with both its legislation and jurisprudence maintaining strict fidelity to the *kompetenz-kompetenz* doctrine, subject to extremely limited exceptions.

The results of this survey carry a number of practical implications when it comes to drafting arbitration agreements and structuring transactions.

Admittedly, in the context of a *stay application*, the language of an arbitration agreement holds little influence over where such a challenge to the tribunal's jurisdiction may arise. This is because parallel court proceedings that invite a stay application can be conceivably commenced in any location that has sufficient connection to the underlying transaction.

Outside of stay applications, however, judicial challenges to the jurisdiction of an arbitral tribunal will typically be brought at the seat of arbitration. As a result, arbitration practitioners can influence the likely degree of judicial intervention in questions of arbitral jurisdiction by strategically selecting the seat of arbitration. If the client's preference is to preserve party autonomy and insulate the tribunal's decision-making from court intervention as much as possible, then it would be advisable to select a seat in Singapore, Sweden, or Canada. Conversely, if the client wishes to retain flexibility to bring a court application for an early ruling on jurisdiction, a German seat would be more advantageous. Finally, England and Wales provides a balanced option, as the *Arbitration Act* 2025 allows for judicial intervention, but only with the permission of the arbitral tribunal.

However, the choice of seat of arbitration will hold little sway in the context of consumer transactions, since consumers will almost always initiate parallel court proceedings in their home jurisdiction. For example, in the *Uber* case, the consumer commenced parallel court proceedings in the Canadian Province of Ontario, even though the arbitration clause specified Amsterdam, the Netherlands, as the seat of arbitration.

For this reason, clients with global operations who wish to resolve their consumer disputes efficiently and privately through arbitration would be well-advised to have different versions of consumer agreements, with tailored arbitration clauses for each jurisdiction. For example, the Swedish version of the agreement may not contain an arbitration clause at all, since Swedish legislation prohibits pre-dispute arbitration agreements in consumer contracts altogether. The German version of the agreement, for its part, should set out the arbitration agreement in a separate document. Furthermore, for the German, UK and Canadian versions of the agreement, clients may need to think creatively and offer to cover the consumer's reasonable arbitration costs in order to get around access to justice exceptions in these jurisdictions. Finally, the Singaporean version of the contract could contain a normal arbitration clause, given the high degree of deference to the *kompetenz-kompetenz* doctrine in that jurisdiction.

The findings of this survey may also be useful in corporate structuring, particularly in selecting the place of incorporation. The place of incorporation will typically determine which courts will have jurisdiction over any ensuing bankruptcy and insolvency proceedings. If a client wishes to resolve their disputes with creditors in a private and efficient manner afforded by arbitration, even in the event of bankruptcy or insolvency, they would be well-advised to incorporate in a jurisdiction that does not recognize an exception to the *kompetenz-kompetenz* doctrine in the context of insolvency proceedings, such as Germany, Sweden, or Singapore. Conversely, if the client rather prefers a "one stop shop" for resolving all of their disputes with their creditors, and does not mind the public nature of insolvency proceedings, it would be well-advised to incorporate in Canada or the United Kingdom.

The author hopes that arbitration practitioners in Sweden and elsewhere will find this paper and this survey helpful in advising their clients on the wording of dispute resolution provisions and the structuring of their transactions. The author intends to revisit this paper every five years to review how the state of legislation and jurisprudence has evolved across these key arbitral jurisdictions and to supplement this survey with newly emerging arbitral jurisdictions.

CHAPTER 17
Changing the Seat of Arbitration

Roman Zykov

§17.01 INTRODUCTION

A contract is fundamentally a balance of interests between the parties involved, reflecting the principle of party autonomy. Each party brings its own interests to the table, and the contract serves as a tool to harmonize these interests in a way that is mutually acceptable at the time of concluding the contract.

One of the elements of a contract is the dispute resolution clause. It is generally accepted that the same principles of formation, validity, modification, performance, and termination that apply to contracts equally apply to forum selection clauses, including arbitration clauses.

Arbitration agreements often include the choice of the legal seat of arbitration (or the place of arbitration) which:

> has a legal impact on various matters, such as the requirements relating to the appointment and challenge of arbitrators, whether and on what grounds a party can seek judicial review or setting aside of an arbitral award, which court is competent with respect to the arbitral proceedings, as well as the conditions for recognition and enforcement of an arbitral award in other jurisdictions.[1]

In this context, the seat is often chosen based on the country's reputation for legal neutrality, its arbitration law and case law, and efficient judicial mechanisms. Hence, the seat of arbitration is more than just an abstract legal concept; the choice of the seat may affect the parties' ability to rely on the legal system in which the arbitration is seated.

1. The UNCITRAL Notes on Organizing Arbitral Proceedings (2016), para. 28.

The UNCITRAL Notes on Organizing Arbitral Proceedings (2016) explain that the selection of the seat of arbitration is influenced by both legal and non-legal factors, the relative importance of which varies from case to case, such as:

(a) the suitability of the arbitration law at the place of arbitration;
(b) the law, jurisprudence and practices at the place of arbitration regarding:
   (i) court intervention in the course of arbitral proceedings;
   (ii) the scope of judicial review or grounds for setting aside an award; and
   (iii) any qualification requirements with respect to arbitrators and counsel representation; and
(c) whether the state in which the arbitration takes place, and hence where the arbitral award will be made, is a party to the New York Convention and/or to any other multilateral or bilateral treaty concerning the enforcement of arbitral awards.[2]

However, stability and even trust in a chosen legal system are not perpetual and over time can be distorted by unforeseen circumstances, ranging from natural disasters and pandemics to political or economic changes. The events of recent years, such as the global COVID-19 pandemic, military conflicts around the world and political shifts in various regions, have illustrated how quickly the conditions under which a contract was originally agreed to may change. While this has always been true in respect of long-term contracts, in the present dynamic times, even short-term contracts may require modification. As such, parties to an international arbitration agreement may find themselves in a situation where the chosen legal seat no longer offers the stability, safety, or impartiality that they had initially relied upon. This raises a critical question: whether the chosen legal seat of arbitration can be changed due to extraordinary circumstances?

Modification of forum selection clauses, including arbitration agreements, due to changed circumstances finds doctrinal support under the principle of *rebus sic stantibus,* which stipulates that a contract may be fully or partly inapplicable because of a fundamental change of circumstances. Some of the leading arbitration commentators have addressed this issue in their writings, albeit rather concisely.

For instance, in Redfern and Hunter in the Law and Practice of International Commercial Arbitration, it is noted that in rare cases, the arbitration seat may need to be changed without unanimous agreement if political conflicts, sanctions, or inaccessibility make the original location impractical, depending on the arbitration clause and applicable institutional rules.[3]

2. *Ibid.*
3. A. Redfern and M. Hunter, Law and Practice of International Commercial Arbitration (Sweet & Maxwell, 2004), 276. "Very occasionally it may be desirable to change the seat of the arbitration even if one of the parties does not agree. The need for a change may occur if, for example, through some political cause, the country in which the arbitration is to take place becomes inaccessible. International sanctions may be imposed (as with Iraq or the former Yugoslavia in the 1990s) making access difficult, if not impossible; or the country itself may be involved in conflict, internally or externally. Whether or not the place of the arbitration may be changed without the

According to J.P. Hernandez, an arbitration agreement, like any contract, may be revised under strict and exceptional circumstances (*rebus sic stantibus*) to adapt to changed conditions, including altering the arbitral seat, ensuring the agreement remains effective.[4]

Gary D. Born in his International Commercial Arbitration acknowledged that under the *rebus sic stantibus* doctrine, an arbitration agreement may be invalidated or modified if unforeseen, radical changes—such as extreme bias or hostility in the chosen arbitral seat—fundamentally undermine the agreement's fairness and original intent. Such circumstances must be exceptional and unforeseeable to justify overriding the parties' initial choice.[5]

Although this idea has not yet been embraced by the arbitration rules of arbitral institutes, some institutional publications raise this important issue. For example, the Secretariat's Guide to ICC Arbitration states the following:

> In extreme cases where the place of arbitration initially agreed upon can no longer function as such, and assuming that at least one party refuses to agree on a different place, it is conceivable that a party could apply to the arbitral tribunal to change the place of arbitration.
>
> The Court arguably has greater discretion to change the place of arbitration if it was initially fixed by the Court. However, the Court does not normally reconsider any of its decisions unless substantial new elements emerge that it did not previously take into account (see paragraph 3-406). Accordingly, only radically changed circumstances will normally prompt the Court to give serious consideration to a party's request to change the place of arbitration. Factors that the Court may take into account-other than the circumstances at the place of arbitration-include the stage the arbitration has reached and, in particular, whether the Terms of Reference have been signed or any decisions or awards have been rendered.

Professor Pierre Lalive also advocated the idea of adopting the principle voiced by Professor Arthur von Mehren, allowing a change in the arbitral seat not only when proceedings become "impossible" or dangerous but also when they become "unduly difficult."[6]

---

agreement of the parties depends on the arbitration clause or submission agreement, coupled with any institutional rules which may have been incorporated."

4. J.P. Hernandez, Changed Circumstances Affecting the Arbitral Seat (The Treaty Examiner, Issue 2, May 2020), 49-55. "the arbitration agreement is still a contract. As with other classes of contracts, a change of circumstances can result in the need to 'revise' or 'adapt' the agreement and allow it to display its full effects (rebus sic stantibus). It is recognized that this principle is generally applicable to arbitration agreements and the selection of arbitral seat, although the circumstances in which it can apply are strict and exceptional."
5. G.D. Born, International Commercial Arbitration (Kluwer Law International, 2021), 2238. "Under widely-recognized principles of national and international law, contracts may become invalid in the case of unforeseen, drastically-changed circumstances (e.g., rebus sic stantibus) that destroy the basis for the parties' bargain. If political, legal, or similar circumstances in the parties' agreed arbitral seat change fundamentally after the arbitration agreement is concluded, in an unforeseen manner, so as to make the chosen seat demonstrably biased and hostile towards one party, or towards any international arbitration, then it may be appropriate for the parties' choice to be invalidated or revised."
6. P. Lalive, On the Transfer of Seat in International Arbitration. In Law and Justice in a Multistate World: Essays in Honor of Arthur T. von Mehren (Brill, 2002), 525-526. "To sum up, it is this writer's considered opinion that arbitral practice should now fully support and implement—also

Indeed, in 1989, Professor Arthur von Mehren argued this principle at the Santiago de Compostela Conference held by the Institut de Droit International. This principle was codified in the 1990 Resolution related to Arbitration Between States, State Enterprises, or State Entities, and Foreign Enterprises. Article 3(d) of this resolution specifically stated that:

> d) Should it become unduly difficult to carry on an arbitration at the agreed place, the tribunal is entitled, after consultation with the parties, to remove the arbitration to such place as it may decide.[7]

Despite acknowledgment of this principle in legal literature, there is nearly no theoretical foundation for how it should operate. There is also limited case law addressing the issue of modifying forum selection clauses and arbitration agreements. However, case law demonstrates that it is possible.

In this chapter, I will explore the legal and factual considerations involved mainly in changing a seat of arbitration against the will of one of the parties, emphasizing the role of the arbitral tribunal in navigating these complex issues.

In summary, when addressing this issue, a tribunal will likely need to consider the following questions:

- Whether it is legally possible to change the seat, and what the legal requirements are.
- Whether the tribunal has the authority to change the seat of arbitration.
- Whether changing the seat affects the validity and enforceability of an arbitration agreement and the resulting arbitral award.
- What the circumstances for changing the seat of arbitration are.
- What should be considered when choosing the new seat of arbitration.

§17.02 THE POSSIBILITY OF CHANGING THE SEAT OF THE ARBITRATION

An arbitrator's starting point for assessing whether it is possible to change the seat should be to determine the applicable law of the arbitration agreement, and whether that law permits the adjustment of contracts. We will exclude the first part of the question from our analysis and just note that there are various methods for identifying the law, such as the law of the seat of arbitration, the law applicable to the main

in 'ordinary' international arbitrations (between private parties)—the ideas advocated by Professor Arthur von Mehren in 1989-1990, before the 'Institut de Droit International' in the case of arbitrations between States and foreign enterprises, not only when proceedings at the seat originally agreed upon would become, because of new circumstances, 'impossible' or dangerous, but already, as rightly expressed in the Resolution of Santiago de Compostela in 1990, when it would become 'unduly difficult' to carry on the arbitration proceedings at the place indicated by the parties in the arbitration clause."

7. English compilation of Resolutions (Institute de Droit International), 298. https://www.idi-iil.org/app/uploads/2019/06/Annexe-1bis-Compilation-Resolutions-EN.pdf (accessed October 1, 2025).

contract and the most closely connected law. Instead, we will focus on the second part of the question, i.e., whether the law permits the modification of contracts, including arbitration agreements, and if so, by which criteria the contract should be modified.

[A] The 26/62 Dilemma

Conceptually, modification (adjustment or adaptation) of contract terms involves a tension between two key legal principles: *pacta sunt servanda* and *rebus sic stantibus*.

The principle of *pacta sunt servanda* holds that agreements must be honored, regardless of subsequent changes in circumstances. This principle ensures the stability of commercial relationships and upholds the sanctity of contracts. However, the principle of *clausula rebus sic stantibus* provides that a contract may be modified or terminated if there are significant and unforeseeable changes in circumstances that render the performance of the contract impossible, illegal, or radically different from what was originally agreed.

This serves as a legal embodiment of the yin-yang concept, as reflected in the Vienna Convention on the Law of Treaties (1969), where Article 26 establishes the principle of *pacta sunt servanda*, while Article 62 enshrines the principle of *clausula rebus sic stantibus. The numbering of these articles is particularly symbolic in demonstrating this legal antagonism.*

Therefore, the 26/62 dilemma lies in balancing these two principles: how to maintain the integrity and stability of contracts while also recognizing the need for flexibility in the face of drastic or unexpected changes.

In the context of arbitration, this means that a tribunal must balance the parties' expectation that the arbitration will proceed in a particular manner with the understanding that certain unforeseen events may necessitate a change in the seat to preserve the fairness of the process. *This is where legal idealism interacts with legal realism.*

[B] National Laws on Modification of Contracts

As noted above, there are various principles for identifying the law applicable to arbitration agreements. Given that most arbitration laws contain either few or no basic rules about the formation, validity, modification, performance, and termination of arbitration agreements, it is accepted that general contract law also applies to arbitration agreements. Although this is not spelt out by the law, doctrinal sources in different jurisdictions provide confirmation to this effect.

While some national laws are silent about the possibility of modifying contracts, others have specific statutory provisions which permit modifications when performance becomes more onerous. Below are some examples of national rules in civil law jurisdictions that permit contract modification due to changed circumstances.

In France, Article 1195 of the French Civil Code establishes the following concise rule:

> If a change in circumstances unforeseeable at the time the contract was concluded makes performance excessively onerous for a party who had not agreed to assume the risk, that party may ask its co-contractor to renegotiate the contract. It continues to perform its obligations during the renegotiation.
>
> If renegotiation is refused or fails, the parties may agree to terminate the contract, on the date and subject to the conditions they determine, or ask the court by mutual agreement to adapt the contract. If no agreement is reached within a reasonable period, the judge may, at the request of a party, revise the contract or terminate it, on the date and on the conditions that he or she determines.[8]

In Germany, § 313 BGB sets forth the following:

> (1) If circumstances that became the basis of a contract have undergone serious change since the contract was concluded and if the parties would not have concluded the contract or would have concluded it with different contents had they foreseen this change, then adaptation of the contract may be demanded to the extent that, taking account of all the circumstances of the specific case, in particular the contractual or statutory distribution of risk, one of the parties cannot reasonably be required to uphold the contract without alteration.
> (2) [...]
> (3) If adaptation of the contract is not possible or if one party cannot reasonably be required to accept it, then the disadvantaged party may rescind the contract. In the case of continuing obligations, the right to terminate takes the place of the right of rescission.[9]

In the Netherlands, Article 6.258 (Unforeseen circumstances) of the Dutch Burgerlijk Wetboek reads as follows:

> (1) Upon a right of action (legal claim) of one of the parties to an agreement, the court may change the legal effects of that agreement or it may dissolve this agreement in full or in part if there are unforeseen circumstances of such a nature that the opposite party, according to standards of reasonableness and fairness, may not expect an unchanged continuation of the agreement. The court may change or dissolve the agreement with retroactive effect.
> (2) The court shall not change or dissolve the agreement as far as the unforeseen circumstances, in view of the nature of the agreement or of common opinion, should remain for account of the party who appeals to these circumstances.
> (3) [...][10]

Similar provisions are contained in Articles 478-480 of the Brazilian Civil Code, Article 1467 of the Italian Civil Code, Article 373 of the Swiss Code of Obligations (although only in relation to the contractual price) and others.

---

8. https://french-business-law.com/french-legislation-art/article-1195-of-the-french-civil-code/ (accessed October 1, 2025).
9. https://www.gesetze-im-internet.de/englisch_bgb/englisch_bgb.html (accessed October 1, 2025).
10. http://www.dutchcivillaw.com/legislation/dcctitle6655.htm (accessed October 1, 2025).

In Sweden, section 36 of the Contracts Act sets out:

> A contract term or condition may be modified or set aside if such term or condition is unconscionable having regard to the contents of the agreement, the circumstances prevailing at the time the agreement was entered into, subsequent circumstances, and circumstances in general. Where a term is of such significance for the agreement that it would be unreasonable to demand the continued enforceability of the remainder of the agreement with its terms unchanged, the agreement may be modified in other respects, or may be set aside in its entirety.
>
> Upon determination of the applicability of the provisions of the first paragraph, particular attention shall be paid to the need to protect those parties who, in their capacity as consumers or otherwise, hold an inferior bargaining position in the contractual relationship.

According to Dr. Finn Madsen, in Sweden:

> An arbitration agreement generally serves as the basis for a conventional arbitration. In the preparatory works, the arbitration agreement is described as a mixed agreement containing both procedural law and civil law features. [...] The civil law aspects lead, inter alia, to the agreement being governed by contract law rules regarding invalidity. Section 36 of the Contracts Act regarding the adjustment of unconscionable contract terms and the doctrine of frustration are applicable to the [arbitration] agreement.[11]

Notably, after Sweden introduced section 36 in 1976, similar provisions were included in the Contracts Acts in Denmark, Finland and Norway in the 1980s. Historically, these jurisdictions have had similar Contracts Acts for over a century.

In Sweden, there are several examples of national courts applying section 36 of the Contracts Act to arbitration agreements. In 1979, the Supreme Court set aside an arbitration clause in a commercial contract contained in the standard terms and conditions of the respondent, according to which all disputes had to be "settled according to Swedish law at the seller's choice by a Swedish general court or by arbitration according to law."[12] The Supreme Court set aside the arbitration clause on the grounds that there was a financial imbalance between the parties that would entail burdensome costs for the claimant if the dispute were decided in arbitration.

Furthermore, there have been other judgments in relation to consumer contracts in which Swedish courts have set aside arbitration clauses (before such clauses became prohibited in consumer contracts), taking into account the unequal procedural and economic capabilities of the parties.[13] Therefore, in the view of Swedish courts, the lack of due process or/and access to justice may warrant even the setting aside of arbitration clauses.

In the Russian Federation, Article 451 of the Civil Code (Modification and termination of a contract due to a fundamental change in circumstances) provides a more elaborate rule:

11. F. Madsen, Commercial Arbitration in Sweden (Oxford University Press, 2006), 45-46.
12. *NJA 1979* section 666. The quote is translated into English from Swedish by the author.
13. *See*, *NJA 1982* section 800. *NJA 1981* section 711.

(1) A fundamental change in the circumstances upon which the parties based their agreement at the time of contract formation shall serve as grounds for its modification or termination, unless otherwise provided by the contract or implied by its nature.
A change in circumstances is considered fundamental when it has altered to such an extent that, had the parties reasonably anticipated it, the contract would not have been concluded at all, or would have been concluded on significantly different terms.
(2) If the parties do not reach an agreement on aligning the contract with the substantially changed circumstances or on its termination, the contract may be terminated, or, on the grounds specified in paragraph 4 of this Article, modified by the court at the request of the interested party, provided the following conditions are jointly met [...][14]
(3) [...]
(4) Modification of a contract due to a fundamental change in circumstances may be allowed by court decision in exceptional cases, when termination of the contract would contradict public interests or result in damages for the parties that significantly exceed the costs necessary for the performance of the contract under the modified terms set by the court.

In sum, the concept of court-ordered contract modification due to a material adverse change of circumstances is accepted in some civil law countries.

In contrast, in common law jurisdictions, it is rare for a court to modify a contract at the request of just one party. However, certain circumstances or doctrines (such as frustration, equity and impracticality) in specific jurisdictions might allow for such contract modification.

In the United States, courts may modify contracts under equitable principles, such as **impracticability**, **frustration of purpose**, **duress**, or **unconscionability**. For example, if a contract becomes impossible to perform due to an unforeseen event, a court may intervene and adjust the terms or discharge the contract. Section 2-615 of the U.S. Uniform Commercial Code (UCC), although pertaining only to sales of goods ("Excuse by Failure of Presupposed Conditions"), reads:

> Delay in delivery or non-delivery in whole or in part by a seller [...] is not a breach of his duty under a contract for sale if performance as agreed has been made impracticable by the occurrence of a contingency the non-occurrence of which was a basic assumption on which the contract was made or by compliance in good faith with any applicable foreign or domestic governmental regulation or order whether or not it later proves to be invalid.

In the official comment No. 6 to Rule §2-615, the drafters stated that:

> In situations in which neither sense nor justice is served by either answer when the issue is posed in flat terms of "excuse" or "no excuse," adjustment under the various provisions of this Article is necessary, especially the sections on good faith, on insecurity and assurance and on the reading of all provisions in the light of their

14. The conditions are unforeseeability the time of contract conclusions, impossibility to avoid the circumstances, contract performance significantly distorts the parties' balance of interests, etc.

> purposes, and the general policy of this Act to use equitable principles in furtherance of commercial standards and good faith.[15]

Another possibility for changing the seat may be derived from the concept of forum non convenience. However, the party claiming the change of forum carries a heavy burden of showing that a trial in the agreed forum will be so manifestly and gravely inconvenient that the party would effectively be deprived of a meaningful day in court.

In *The Bremen v. Zapata Off-Shore Co.*, the U.S. court held that:

> "The forum-selection clause, which was a vital part of the towing contract, is binding on the parties unless respondent can meet the heavy burden of showing that its enforcement would be unreasonable, unfair, or unjust" and "unless the balance is strongly in favor of the defendant, the plaintiff's choice of forum should rarely be disturbed."[16]

Despite the differing approaches in civil and common law jurisdictions, it can be concluded that contract modification is possible under some laws in certain exceptional circumstances. Consequently, if we accept the argument that forum selection clauses are governed by the general rules of contract law, there is no reason why these rules would not apply to the modification of the seat of arbitration as well. Thus, the arbitral tribunal will have to make its own assessment in each case.

[C] *Lex Mercatoria* on Modification of Contracts

The concept of contract modification is also found in *lex mercatoria* rules, model documents and clauses, such as the UNIDROIT Principles of International Commercial Contracts (UNIDROIT Principles), the Principles of European Contract Law (PECL), the draft Common Frame of Reference (DCFR) and the ICC Hardship Clause 2020.

Article 6.2.3 of the UNIDROIT Principles of International Commercial Contracts provides that when unforeseen hardship arises in a contract, the party facing difficulties has the right to request renegotiations. They must do so promptly and provide clear justification for their request. Importantly, simply asking for renegotiation does not allow them to stop fulfilling their contractual obligations while discussions are ongoing. If the parties cannot reach an agreement after a reasonable period of negotiation, either side may take the matter to court. The court then has the authority to assess whether genuine hardship exists. If it determines that the circumstances warrant intervention, the court can either terminate the contract on fair and specific terms or adjust the contract's terms to rebalance the original agreement and restore fairness to both parties.

Article 6:111 of the Principles of European Contract Law and Book III Chapter I section 110 of the draft Common Frame of Reference (Variation or termination by court on a change of circumstances) adopt a similar approach whereby if circumstances change so dramatically that fulfilling the contract becomes extremely unfair or

---

15. https://code.dccouncil.gov/us/dc/council/code/sections/28:2-615 (accessed October 1, 2025).
16. *The Bremen v. Zapata Off-Shore Co.*, 407 U.S. 1 (1972).

burdensome, the parties must try to renegotiate the terms. This only applies if the change happened after the contract was signed, the parties could have reasonably predicted it when signing, and the contract does not already assign responsibility for such risks. If the parties cannot agree on new terms after good-faith negotiations, a court can step in. The court has two options: it can either end the contract with fair conditions or adjust the terms to balance the new situation fairly for both sides. The court can also order compensation if one party acted unreasonably by refusing to negotiate or breaking off talks in bad faith.

According to the ICC Hardship Clause 2020, contracts must be fulfilled even when circumstances make them more difficult or costly to perform than originally anticipated. However, if fulfilling the contract becomes extremely burdensome due to unexpected events beyond either party's control—events that could not reasonably have been foreseen or prevented—then both sides must negotiate in good faith to find fair solutions. When such negotiations fail to produce an agreement, either party can ask a judge or arbitrator to either modify the contract to restore balance or terminate it completely, depending on what is most appropriate under the changed circumstances.

The drafters of the ICC Hardship Clause 2020 recognized that "the solutions adopted by national laws may be substantially different from country to country. When the national laws request the parties to renegotiate the contract, and the renegotiation fails, the consequences of such failure may vary: under some laws the disadvantaged party will only be entitled to terminate the contract, while under others the disadvantaged party will have the right to request adaptation of the contract to the changed circumstances by the judge or arbitrator."[17]

Based on the above, it can be concluded that contract modification, and consequently the change of seat, is also supported by various codified *lex mercatoria.*

[D] Criteria for Changing the Seat

It has been demonstrated above that national laws and *lex mercatoria* employ a similar framework concerning contract modification. The criteria commonly include unconscionability and unforeseeability, both of which must be fulfilled in order to modify the contract. In particular:

(i) There must be circumstances that impose excessive burdens on one party and distort the contractual *status quo* (unconscionability).[18]

(ii) The circumstances must have been unforeseen at the time of concluding the contract (unforeseeability).[19]

17. https://iccwbo.org/wp-content/uploads/sites/3/2020/03/icc-forcemajeure-hardship-clauses-march2020.pdf (accessed October 1, 2025).
18. *See, The Rice Corporation v. Grain Board of Iraq and Iraqi Ministry of Trade* E.D. Cal. Order dated October 26, 2009, in *Fireman's Fund Insurance v. M.V. DSR Atlantic* 131 F.3d 1336 (9th Cir. 1997) "A contractual forum selection clause is prima facie valid and should be enforced unless enforcement is shown by the resisting party to be unreasonable under the circumstances."
19. *See, The Rice Corporation v. Grain Board of Iraq and Iraqi Ministry of Trade* E.D. Cal. Order (October 26, 2009): "Whatever 'inconvenience' [Plaintiff] would suffer by being forced to litigate

In addition to the above, depending on the applicable law, there may be other criteria, such as:

(i) The aggrieved party did not agree to assume the risk in the contract.[20]
(ii) The change of circumstances was outside the disadvantaged party's control.
(iii) The circumstances that permanently change the contractual balance cannot be overcome without adjusting the contract.[21]

Consequently, if an arbitrator (or judge) determines that the law permits contract modification, by applying these criteria (the scope of which depends on the applicable law) to the facts of the case, the arbitrator should be able to decide whether contract modification is warranted or not.

Finally, it is common among the various national laws, case law[22] and *lex mercatoria* that the burden of proof lies with the party seeking contract modification. Furthermore, some of the rules explicitly require a party seeking to modify the contract to request such an adjustment. In other words, the judge or arbitrator is not empowered to do it ex officio.

[E] Retroactive Effect of the New *Lex Arbitri*

One of the practical considerations regarding changing the seat due to changed circumstances is whether the new *lex arbitri* applies retroactively. For example, Article 6.258 of the Dutch Burgerlijk Wetboek states that "[t]he court may change or dissolve

in [Iraq] as it agreed to do was clearly foreseeable at the time of contracting ... Absent [showing that Plaintiff will for all practical purposes be deprived ofits day in court], there is no basis for concluding that it would be unfair, unjust, or unreasonable to hold [Plaintiff] to [its] bargain"; and "where it can be said with reasonable assurance that, at the time they entered the contract, the parties to a freely negotiated private international commercial agreement contemplated the claimed inconvenience, it is difficult to see why any such claim of inconvenience should be heard to render the forum clause unenforceable"; and "There is strong evidence that the forum clause was a vital part of the agreement, and it would be unrealistic to think that the parties did not conduct their negotiations, including fixing the monetary terms, with the consequences of the forum clause figuring prominently in their calculations."

20. Article 1195 of the French Civil Code, § 313(1) BGB, Art. 451.2(4) Russian Civil Code. *See*, also, *The Bremen v. Zapata Off-Shore Co.*, 407 U.S. 1 (1972) "where it can be said with reasonable assurance that, at the time they entered the contract, the parties to a freely negotiated private international commercial agreement contemplated the claimed inconvenience, it is difficult to see why any such claim of inconvenience should be heard to render the forum clause unenforceable." and "There is strong evidence that the forum clause was a vital part of the agreement, and it would be unrealistic to think that the parties did not conduct their negotiations, including fixing the monetary terms, with the consequences of the forum clause figuring prominently in their calculations."
21. Article 451.2(2) of the Russian Civil Code.
22. *See*, *The Bremen v. Zapata Off-Shore Co.*, 407 U.S. 1 (1972), in *The Rice Corporation v. Grain Board of Iraq and Iraqi Ministry of Trade* E.D. Cal. Order (October 26, 2009), the courts in dictum noted that since forum selection clauses are prima facie valid, the party opposing enforcement of a forum clause bears the burden of making a strong showing that [the clause] should be set aside.

the agreement with retroactive effect." Although this rule may not be explicitly stated in the laws of other jurisdictions, its existence and applicability may be inferred.

In a NAFTA case, *Pope & Talbot v. Canada*, the contract was silent on the seat. The tribunal had initially determined the original seat of arbitration to be Montreal, Canada, thereby acknowledging its authority to determine the seat of arbitration. The claimant requested that the tribunal relocate the seat of arbitration from Canada, citing concerns that the Canadian government's stance in state courts during annulment proceedings in other NAFTA awards effectively signaled a shift in Canada's policy toward NAFTA arbitration. The tribunal denied the motion based on, among other factors, that changing the seat would give rise to uncertainty as to whether "Canada's courts retain jurisdiction to review decisions and orders rendered prior to the change. That issue would surely guarantee very extensive litigation in both the United States and Canada."[23]

Therefore, as the new *lex arbitri* may differ from the previous one, the tribunal should consider how these two laws interact and whether changing the seat, and hence the *lex arbitri*, might prejudice either party and the arbitral award.

§17.03 THE AUTHORITY OF THE ARBITRAL TRIBUNAL TO CHANGE THE SEAT OF THE ARBITRATION

Another relevant element is the arbitral tribunal's mandate (authority) to modify the contract in the absence of the parties' consent. This involves a complex interplay of factors, including the terms of the arbitration agreement, the applicable law governing the tribunal's authority, and the arbitration rules. Consequently, the tribunal would face yet another dilemma, i.e., how to reconcile the principle of party autonomy and the tribunal's power to conduct the proceedings in such manner as it considers appropriate, while ensuring the equal treatment of the parties and their right to be heard.

The tribunal should analyze the arbitration agreement, applicable *lex arbitri* and arbitration rules.

[A] The Arbitration Agreement

As discussed earlier, an arbitration agreement is a contract in itself, which sometimes includes a clause specifying the seat of arbitration. When considering whether to change the seat of arbitration, the tribunal must look at the terms of the arbitration agreement.

Some arbitration clauses may contain provisions that grant the tribunal flexibility to change the seat of arbitration if exceptional circumstances arise. These provisions have seen increased use in recent times. For instance, in so-called waterfall arbitration

23. *Pope & Talbot v. Government of Canada*. Ruling concerning the investor's motion to change the place of arbitration, dated March 14, 2002. NAFTA case.

clauses, parties may provide for the possibility of changing the seat of arbitration, among other provisions.

In other cases, the contract may be more rigid, stipulating that the arbitration agreement cannot be altered by arbitrators. Should this be the case, the tribunal would be required to ensure that the contractual prohibition does not conflict with the provisions of the applicable contract law. As demonstrated in the preceding section, some national laws are framed in mandatory terms that exclude party autonomy on this issue.

Admittedly, the majority of arbitration agreements are silent on this issue, arguably granting the tribunal a discretion in deciding the matter. In such circumstances, the tribunal's ability to modify the seat may also depend on whether the parties' consent can be inferred from the circumstances surrounding the formation of the arbitration agreement. For example, if the agreement is silent on the issue of changing the seat, the tribunal may need to determine whether the parties would have reasonably agreed to such a change had they anticipated the extraordinary events that are now preventing the arbitration from proceeding at the originally designated location.

[B] The *Lex Arbitri*

The *lex arbitri* is another key factor in determining whether a tribunal has the authority to change the seat of arbitration. The *lex arbitri* governs procedural issues, such as the validity of the arbitration agreement, the appointment of arbitrators and the conduct of the proceedings.

While it may be prudent to check in each specific case, to my knowledge, no international arbitration law or framework currently explicitly grants the authority or prohibits a tribunal from changing the seat without the consent of the parties. In such cases, the tribunal must determine whether the applicable rules of contract law permit it to do so. In any event, the tribunal should maintain an open-minded approach towards changing the seat, as part of its fundamental obligations to uphold the equality of the parties, ensure the efficiency and integrity of the proceedings, and safeguard the enforceability of the resulting award.

[C] Arbitration Rules

Arbitration rules may provide additional guidance on whether the tribunal (or an arbitration institute) has the power to change the seat of the arbitration. As a preliminary remark, in our view, the arbitral tribunal is better positioned than the arbitration institute to assess the parties' arguments for or against changing the seat. However, this authority could also be granted to the arbitration institute.

Arbitration rules generally offer flexibility in arbitration proceedings and are designed to ensure that the process remains fair and efficient even in the face of extraordinary events. However, to our knowledge, presently, no institutional arbitration rules explicitly grant a tribunal (or the institute) the authority to change the seat without the consent of the parties. Professor Lalive mentioned in his article that, when the ICC Rules of Arbitration were revised in 1998, a proposal to include a provision explicitly granting the court the authority to alter the agreed seat was not accepted.[24] In my view, it is important that this issue is discussed and, hopefully, such a proposal will be considered in future revisions of the rules.

Redfern and Hunter in their famous treatise expressed the view that if the ICC Court has chosen the place of arbitration under its rules, "there does not appear to be any compelling reasons why it [ICC Court] should not designate a new seat if, in the opinion of the arbitral tribunal, it has become impossible to continue with the arbitration in that place."[25] Indeed, some arbitration rules authorize the institute to designate the seat of arbitration in the absence of the parties' agreement. Why stop halfway and not allow the arbitration institute to also modify the original seat if necessary? Notably, there have been some cases in which the original seat was sought to be changed by the institute under institutional arbitration rules.

One such case was reported by S. Jarvin, in which the ICC Court changed the previously designated seat of arbitration from Bangkok, Thailand, to Kuala Lumpur, Malaysia. The reason for changing the seat was the discovery that there were no laws governing arbitration in Thailand and that it was not yet bound by the New York Convention, which consequently undermined the enforceability of any award issued in Bangkok.[26]

However, in two other unpublished ICC Arbitration Cases No. 10373 and No. 10623 reported in several articles, the ICC Court declined to approve the change of the seat of arbitration. A dispute arose between a U.S. company and a state-owned Serbian company with the arbitration seat in Belgrade. Fearing that the final award would be annulled by Yugoslav courts, allegedly due to political motives aimed at protecting the state-owned company, the U.S. party requested the tribunal, and subsequently the ICC Court, to change the seat of arbitration. The decision of the tribunal (and subsequently the ICC Court) to refuse to move the seat of arbitration from Belgrade has been discussed extensively by leading arbitration commentators, although it can be concluded that no doctrinal consensus has been reached on this issue.[27]

To our knowledge, there have been several other unreported cases in recent times where the parties sought to modify the previously agreed seat of arbitration due to changed circumstances, though with varying outcomes.

24. Lalive, *supra* n. 6, 525.
25. Redfern and Hunter, *supra* n. 3, 277.
26. S. Jarvin, Le lieu de l'arbitrage, 7 ICC Bulletin 2/1996, 58.
27. Lalive, *supra* n. 6, 525-526; Y. Derains and E. Schwartz, A Guide to the New ICC Rules of Arbitration (Kluwer Law International. 1998), 202; G. Born, International Commercial Arbitration in the United States, (Kluwer Law and Taxation Publishers, 1994), 77; W. Laurence Craig, William W. Park and Jan Paulsson, Annotated Guide to the 1998 ICC Arbitration Rules (OUP, 1998), 104; M. Sherer. The Place or "Seat" of Arbitration (Possibility, and/or Sometimes Necessity of its Transfer?): Some Remarks on the Award in ICC Arbitration n° 10623, ASA Bull, 1/2003, 112-119; Knoepfler, Note on the Partial Award in ICC Arbitration Case No. 10373, Revue de l'Arbitrage, 413-421; A. Crivellaro, Note on the ICC Arbitration No. 10623, Decision of December 7, 2001, ASA Bull. 1/2003, 59 and 82.

To address this ongoing issue in contemporary arbitration, the Russian Arbitration Association has put forward the Anti-Sanctions Arbitration Protocol (ASAP), which is an opt-in component of the UNCITRAL Arbitration Rules developed in response to challenges arising from unilateral sanctions. In particular, paragraph 12 of the ASAP permits the arbitral tribunal to modify the place of arbitration:

> Should the place of arbitration and/or applicable *lex arbitri* render the arbitration agreement null and void, inoperative or incapable of being performed or otherwise adversely affect a party's ability to present its case, or enforce any resulting award by reason of relevant unilateral restrictive measures, the tribunal, at the request of a party, after giving the parties a rea-sonable opportunity to state their views, may change the place of arbitration and /or applicable *lex arbitri.*[28]

However, it remains to be seen whether leading arbitration institutions will adapt their rules to permit changes in the seat of arbitration. In the competitive landscape among major arbitration institutions, this new feature could certainly provide a distinct institutional advantage.

[D] The Court Ordered Change of Seat

There have been several instances in which state courts have intervened and ordered a change of the seat of arbitration. These cases typically arise when the original location becomes impractical or when the legal or political environment in that jurisdiction is deemed unsuitable for the arbitration process.

For example, in *Northrop Grumman Ship Systems, Inc. v. The Ministry of Defense of the Republic of Venezuela*, the U.S. court ordered that the arbitration take place outside of Venezuela, despite the parties' contract (for refurbishment of warships for the Ministry of Defense of the Republic of Venezuela) initially designated Venezuela to be the seat of arbitration. The court ruled that arbitration in the country would be impracticable, given the likelihood that the politically hostile environment would prompt Venezuelan courts to unfairly favor the Ministry in any related disputes. Following this ruling, the arbitral tribunal moved the proceedings to Brazil, where it awarded Northrop Grumman Ship Systems (later Huntington Ingalls) over USD 128 million. The district court subsequently enforced the arbitral award, concluding that the tribunal had not manifestly disregarded the parties' agreement or the law. In order to arrive at its decisions, the U.S. court required Northrop to show that: (a) conditions in the country made arbitration in Venezuela impracticable, i.e., would be "so gravely difficult and inconvenient" that Northrop would be "for all practicable purposes deprived of its day in court"; and (b) that Northrop could not foresee those conditions when it entered into the contract.[29]

---

28. https://arbitration.ru/upload/medialibrary/40d/a2ljucf4f6i0kfuz043967118yvspufg/DRAFT-ASAP-Prtotocol-and-Clause-Dubai-14-November-2024.docx (accessed October 1, 2025).
29. *Northrop Grumman Ship Systems, Inc. v. The Ministry of Defense of the Republic of Venezuela*, No. 20-60347 (5th Cir. March 10, 2021).

There also exist opposite examples when in similar circumstances the courts have upheld arbitration clauses and denied a party's application to change the seat. In *The National Iranian Oil Company v. Ashland Oil, Inc.*, the U.S. court upheld the arbitration clause with a seat in Iran. The dispute arose out of several long-term contracts for the supply of crude oil. Following the takeover of the American Embassy in Tehran in 1979, the U.S. President banned the importation of all oil from Iran not already in transit. Several cargoes of crude oil (worth nearly USD 283,000,000) were en route from the National Iranian Oil Company (NIOC) to Ashland Oil at the time, which received and refined the oil. However, despite NIOC's demand, neither Ashland nor its subsidiaries rendered any payment for the oil. NIOC subsequently commenced arbitration in Iran, but Ashland refused to participate in the proceedings because of the safety risks to Americans. However, Ashland did not agree to participate in an arbitration in any other country either. Thus, NIOC brought a lawsuit against Ashland in a U.S. federal district court. NIOC sought to compel arbitration in Mississippi and asked the court to appoint an arbitrator. The court denied NIOC's motion, finding that it lacked the power to order arbitration in Mississippi and that the conditions for unforeseeability and impracticability were not met.[30] The court also found that NIOC's reason for changing the seat of arbitration was a longer limitation period in Mississippi than the one in Iran. The district court decision was also upheld after appeal. The Court of Appeals summarized its judgment in a verse:

> There was an oil company from Iran
> whose lawyers devised a neat plan:
> that Ashland's contract might refute,
> the Iranians to the land of cotton ran.
> But their clever arbitration plan was spoiled;
> by an Act of Congress, the district court said, it was foiled.
> to rewrite their first deal.
> But their theories are only half-boiled.
> To arbitrate in Ole Miss is their prayer.
> Inconvenience or waiver makes it fair.
> But the contract is clear;
> we can't order arbitration here.
> Unless agreed, it's Iran or nowhere.[31]

30. *National Iranian Oil Company v. Ashland Oil, Inc.*, 817 F.2d 326 (5th Cir. 1987). "42. ...That NIOC—an instrumentality of the Islamic Republic of Iran—could not reasonably have foreseen in April 1979 that an American entity might find it impracticable to participate then or in the near future in an arbitral proceeding in Tehran defies credulity," and "44. ... Yet, as part of the revolutionary Government, NIOC certainly bears responsibility for creating the chain of events making it impossible for an American entity reasonably to travel to and to engage in quasi-judicial proceedings in Iran. Thus, NIOC cannot assert the doctrine of impossibility."
31. *National Iranian Oil Company v. Ashland Oil, Inc.*, 817 F.2d 326 (5th Cir. 1987).

In certain jurisdictions, the law allows for changing the agreed seat against the will of one of the parties, designating state courts as the new forum. For instance, Article 3 of the Swiss Act on Private International Law (1987) and Article 248.1 of the Russian Arbitrazh (Commercial) Procedure Code provide mechanisms for such jurisdictional transfers. If a valid arbitration agreement exists, these rules can effectively nullify it. In these situations, the option of changing the agreed seat of arbitration appears to be a less intrusive measure, aimed at preserving the agreement to arbitrate. It is widely accepted that parties choose arbitration specifically to avoid litigation in national courts. In the context of the ongoing battle of jurisdictions, the arbitration community—comprising institutions and arbitrators—should proactively take the initiative to self-regulate the change of seat, rather than leaving the decision to state courts to assume exclusive jurisdiction.

§17.04 THE IMPACT ON ENFORCEABILITY OF THE ARBITRATION AGREEMENT AND THE AWARD

One of the greater concerns when changing the seat of arbitration is the impact this may have on the enforceability of both the arbitration agreement and any subsequent arbitral awards. In international arbitration, enforceability is a crucial issue, as the effectiveness of arbitration as a dispute resolution mechanism hinges on the ability to enforce the awards globally.

The 1958 New York Convention on the Recognition and Enforcement of Foreign Arbitral Awards plays a critical role in ensuring that arbitral awards are recognized and enforceable in countries that are signatories to the Convention. When addressing this issue, the arbitral tribunal may wish to consider how its decision on the change of the seat may be treated in light of the grounds set out in Article V of the Convention.

It is a common feature in many arbitration rules that require an arbitral tribunal to take all necessary steps to ensure the enforceability of the award under the law. However, that does not mean that the arbitral tribunal must guarantee global enforcement of its award, but rather make every effort to ensure that the award meets generally accepted standards of enforceability, particularly those outlined in the New York Convention.

[A] Nullity of the Agreement or Award

A change in the seat of arbitration could potentially affect the validity of the arbitration agreement or any award rendered by the tribunal. The enforceability of an arbitration agreement is closely tied to the laws of the jurisdiction where the seat is located, and if the seat is changed, it could raise questions about the legal framework governing arbitration. For example, if the arbitration agreement is governed by the laws of a specific jurisdiction and the seat is moved to a different country with different arbitration laws, the agreement may need to be reviewed to ensure that it remains valid under the new jurisdiction's laws.

In some instances, a change in the seat could invalidate the arbitration agreement or the arbitral award if the relocation is specifically prohibited under the original agreement. However, such concerns can be mitigated if the tribunal demonstrates that the purpose of the relocation is to ensure equality between the parties and preserve the integrity of the arbitration.

[B] Breach of Mandate or Procedural Deviation

Another potential consequence of changing the seat of arbitration is that it could be viewed as a breach of the tribunal's mandate or a deviation from the agreed-upon procedure. Arbitration is a consensual process, and the parties generally enter into the arbitration agreement with the expectation that the process will unfold in a particular way, including that the seat of arbitration will not be changed. A unilateral change in the seat without the parties' consent may be seen as undermining the legitimacy of the arbitration and potentially leading to challenges of the arbitral award on the grounds of procedural irregularity.

However, if the tribunal can find the change of seat justified under the criteria discussed above, it may be able to mitigate these concerns. In its reasoning, the tribunal would need to demonstrate that the change was necessary in order to ensure the fairness and integrity of the arbitration.

[C] Arbitrability

When determining the new seat of arbitration, both parties and the tribunal should consider whether the dispute is arbitrable under the new *lex arbitri*. Since the New York Convention leaves it to the Contracting States to define the limits of arbitrability, the scope may differ across jurisdictions.

[D] Public Policy Considerations

Much has been said about public policy, but the following quotes offer the most concise yet comprehensive descriptions of it:

> Public policy does not admit of definition and is not easily explained. It is a variable quantity; it must vary and does vary with the habits, capacities, and opportunities of the public.[32]
>
> It is impossible to say what the opinion of a man or a Judge might be as to what public policy is.[33]

---

32. Kekewich, J., *Davies v. Davies* (1887), L. R. 36 C. D. 364; *see* also *Egerton v. Earl Brownlow*, 4 H. L. C. 1.
33. Jessel, M.R., *Besant v. Wood* (1879), L. R. 12 C. D. 620.

> Public policy is a very unruly horse, and when once you get astride it you never know where it will carry you.[34]

In some jurisdictions, a restrictive interpretation of public policy may render a change of seat illegitimate. In such cases, a prudent tribunal would consider the potential implications, particularly in jurisdictions where enforcement is likely to occur.

§17.05 ASSESSING THE FACTUAL CIRCUMSTANCES

Once the tribunal determines that: (i) the change of seat is legally permissible, (ii) the tribunal has the powers to change the seat of arbitration and (iii) a prospective arbitral award would be enforceable, it must then carefully assess the factual circumstances surrounding the case. This involves considering both legal and practical obstacles that prevent the arbitration from proceeding at the original seat and the external events that may have created these obstacles.

[A] Access to Justice, Fairness, Independence and Impartiality

Drawing from the case law reviewed in this chapter, one of the key factors for changing the seat has been whether the current seat impedes the parties' access to justice. This includes issues such as whether the local courts are functioning effectively and impartially, whether the parties can obtain the necessary legal resources (such as local counsel), and whether the tribunal can carry out its functions effectively.

When selecting the applicable law, arbitration rules, and legal seat of arbitration, the parties place significant trust in a legal system, expecting it to remain impartial, stable, consistent, and supportive of arbitration throughout the duration of the contract and beyond. However, the situation may change after the contract is signed and a party may be denied equal treatment as a matter of law or/and as a matter of fact.

While some facts supporting the change of seat can be easily assessed and evaluated by the tribunal, others may not be as clear-cut.

For example, a party may lodge sufficient evidence proving that it is unable, wholly or in part, to retain local counsel. This may be especially true in jurisdictions with a limited legal market and the dominance of just a handful of law firms that refuse to assist a party. There are recent examples of local counsel denying instructions from certain parties of a certain nationality due to the effects of unilateral sanctions, or even due to the existing sentiments against that nation. For instance, there have been many such examples recorded against Russian nationals in European countries in the past years. Clearly, the lack of local counsel undermines a party's ability to access local legal resources, which it expected to have at the time of signing the contract (legal advice on *lex arbitri*, representation in local courts, etc.) and it hinders fair and equal treatment

34. Burrough, J., *Richardson v. Mellish* (1824), 2 Bing. 252; quoted by Lord Bramwell in Mogul Steamship Co.; McGregor, Gow and others, 66 L. T. Rep. 6.

of the parties. It appears that a party can relatively easily demonstrate this fact to the tribunal.

In contrast, proving the subjective bias of a judge, let alone that of the national judiciary as a whole, is no easy task. In several cases, parties have attempted, with varying degrees of success, to demonstrate a lack of impartiality by referencing, among other sources, international studies,[35] affidavits from lawyers and law professors,[36] and research into recent case law from the relevant jurisdiction.[37]

It cannot be entirely ruled out that a judiciary with a long history of impartiality may suddenly develop a bias against a group of people due to political, social or even media pressure. For example, increasingly adversarial tensions between two countries may give rise to hostile sentiments in either or both countries and prompt the imposition of broad unilateral restrictions on the nationals of the other country. In this scenario, it would be difficult to imagine that companies of either country, especially if state-owned, would be treated impartially by the other country's local courts. Although the judiciary should remain independent of the government in most jurisdictions, there may still be uncertainty whether this is in fact the case. At the end of the day, the standard of "justifiable doubts" that applies to the impartiality and independence of

35. *See, The Rice Corporation v. Grain Board of Iraq and Iraqi Ministry of Trade* E.D. Cal. Order (October 26, 2009): "Plaintiff alleges in its Complaint that the forum selection clause is unreasonable because witnesses will be unwilling to travel to Iraq, the Iraqi judiciary is flawed, and the 2005 Country Report on Human Rights Practices deems Iraq an unfit venue to litigate this matter, which would ultimately deny Plaintiff 'its meaningful day in court.'"
36. *See, CH Offshore v. PDV Marina* [2015] EWHC 595 (Comm) "84. Mr Bravo's report states that the Venezuelan courts 'almost never' issue decisions adverse to PDVSA and its subsidiaries. But he has not apparently been asked to consider Mrs Padilla's evidence, as Mr Bentata has. Whilst Mr Bentata seeks to criticise Ms Padilla's reliance on various authorities as evidence that Astivenca can have a fair trial in Venezuela (because they are all employment or personal injury cases), he is silent on the actual question of whether or not Astivenca can have a fair trial. The inference must be that he does not consider that Astivenca cannot have a fair trial in Venezuela."

    The Rice Corporation v. Grain Board of Iraq and Iraqi Ministry of Trade E.D. Cal. Order (October 26, 2009), at 3 "Plaintiff supports its position with Sabah Al-Mukhtar's ('Al-Mukhtar') declaration, who is an admitted Iraqi attorney and a partner at a law firm in Baghdad, Iraq, and Plaintiff's attorney Janet K. Haines's ('Haines') declaration and supplemental declaration. Defendants argue Al-Mukhtar lacks personal knowledge and expertise to declare about the current situation in Iraq since he has lived in London for the past 29 years. Defendants also object to Haines' declarations, and the exhibits attached thereto of news articles concerning the political atmosphere and security situation in Iraq."

    McDonnell Douglas Corp. v. Islamic Republic of Iran, 591 F. Supp. 293 (E.D. Mo. 1984), at 15: "Defendant has submitted the affidavit of Dr. Hamid Varasteh as documentary evidence in opposition to the affidavit of Mr. Johnson. Dr. Varasteh's affidavit essentially contradicts the general conclusions of the Johnson affidavit in every respect. Submitted in addition to the affidavit evidence are English translations of two judgments in Iranian courts in favor of American companies in default judgment hearings. The totality of this evidence purports to indicate that plaintiff can expect a fair trial in Iran."
37. *See, Northrop Grumman Ship Systems, Inc. v. The Ministry of Defense of the Republic of Venezuela*, No. 20-60347 (5th Cir. March 10, 2021): "Finally, Jose Eloy Anzola, a Venezuelan lawyer and law professor, likewise opined that, based on his survey of post-1999 decisions of the Political-Administrative Chamber, the court was likely to intervene in arbitral proceedings in this case in a way that would 'seriously disrupt' the arbitration. Huntington Ingalls further drew the district court's attention to a particular decision by the Political-Administrative Chamber that effectively froze over $350 million of another foreign defense contractor's assets in connection with an arbitration on a $2 million contract."

arbitrators should also apply to the judiciary. The dictum "Justice must not only be done, but also be seen to be done"[38] which emphasizes the importance of both the actual delivery of justice and the appearance of fairness in the process takes on particular significance in today's fragmented world.

In *The Owners of Cargo lately laden on board ship or vessel Eleftheria v. The Eleftheria*, the English court set out the following criteria for establishing whether a party would be prejudiced by having to sue in a foreign court ("The Eleftheria criteria"):

(i) The party should be deprived of security for its claim;
(ii) The party should be unable to enforce any judgment obtained;
(iii) [...]
(iv) For political, racial, religious or other reasons, it should be unlikely that the party would receive a fair trial.[39]

Since then, the Eleftheria criteria have been applied by other courts,[40] and they have emphasized that there must be a strong evidentiary basis to establish the lack of fair trial in a foreign court.[41]

In *Heirs to the Sultanate of Sulu v. Malaysia*, the sole arbitrator acting under the UNCITRAL Arbitration Rules, in a preliminary award, designated Madrid, Spain, as the seat of arbitration as the arbitration agreement remained silent, and the parties did not reach any agreement otherwise.[42] Madrid, Spain, was selected based on its neutrality as a venue, given that none of the parties was Spanish. After Spanish courts vacated the sole arbitrator's appointment, the claimant requested the seat to be changed to Paris, France. The respondent failed to provide any comment on the change of seat. The arbitrator decided to change the seat to Paris, France and noted the following: (a) the circumstances that gave rise to the need to change the place of arbitration from Madrid to Paris were reasonably unforeseeable at the time the arbitration agreement was signed and at the date of the preliminary award; (b) the circumstances created a disruptive situation in the arbitration, with no analogous precedent known to date in Spain; (c) the Spanish court decisions were a supervening event that threatened to render the arbitration agreement inoperative or incapable of being performed, leaving the parties' legitimate expectations in the arbitration thwarted; (d) the Spanish court

38. Lord Hewart in *Rex v. Sussex Justices*, [1924] 1 KB 256.
39. *Owners of Cargo lately laden on board ship or vessel Eleftheria v. The Eleftheria* (Owners) [1970] P 94, [1969] 2 All ER 641, [1969] 2 WLR 1073, [1969] 1 Lloyd's Rep 237, 113 Sol Jo 407.
40. *See, Zephyrus Capital Aviation Partners Limited and Others And Fidelis Underwriting Limited And Others* [2024] EWHC 734 (Comm); *Vinmar Overseas Pte Ltd (Singapore) And PTT International Trading Pte Ltd*, The Court Of Appeal Of The Republic Of Singapore [2018] SGCA 65.
41. The high standard of proof is also upheld in some judgments without reference to the Eleftheria criteria. *See*, *CH Offshore v. PDV Marina* [2015] EWHC 595 (Comm) "84. Without any obvious enthusiasm, Astivenca suggests that there would be judicial bias in favour of Petroleo such that Astivenca would not receive a fair trial in Venezuela. The evidence comes nowhere near making good such a proposition to the necessary high standard."
42. *Heirs to the Sultanate of Sulu v. Malaysia*. Final Award, February 22, 2022.

decisions risked denying the parties access to justice in Madrid, since they would not be have been able to exercise their right to arbitration under the arbitration agreement.

In practice, it is challenging to propose a one-size-fits-all criterion for determining the unsuitability of a foreign court. The arbitral tribunal must make a case-by-case assessment based on the relevant factual matrix, as the arbitrator did in *Heirs to the Sultanate of Sulu v. Malaysia*. As a result, in some instances, the tribunal may find it justified to change the seat of arbitration, while in others, it may reject the party's request to do so.

[B] Logistical and Financial Barriers

In addition to legal access to justice, the tribunal must also consider whether logistical or financial barriers prevent the arbitration from being conducted at the original seat. If, for example, travel restrictions or financial sanctions make it impossible for party participants or witnesses to attend the hearings in local courts, or a party is prevented from paying the court or legal fees for auxiliary proceedings in local courts, an arbitral tribunal may be poised to change the seat of arbitration at the request of a party.

[C] New Laws

New laws, regulations and case law can have a significant impact on a contract as they can alter the legal environment in which the contract operates, affecting its validity, performance, or enforcement. This could include, among other things, the introduction of unilateral sanctions, tariffs, changes in tax laws, environmental regulations, and new court procedural rules, all of which could either enhance or complicate the performance of the contract. In some cases, these changes may lead to an argument for contract modification.

For instance, the introduction of unilateral sanctions by a government can impact contractual rights. In 2014, the EU introduced Regulation 833/2014, Article 11 of which prohibits the satisfaction of any claims arising from sanctioned persons. Furthermore, Article 13 provides that the Regulation shall apply within the territory of the EU.[43] Consequently, it could be argued that, if an arbitration is seated in the EU, the tribunal (regardless of the arbitrators' nationalities) may be required to apply Article 11 as mandatory law, potentially leading to the denial of the claims. In such a case, relocating the seat of arbitration to a neutral jurisdiction would be a viable option to preserve the contractual balance originally envisaged by the parties.

In the already discussed NAFTA case *Pope & Talbot v. Canada*, a party requested the tribunal to relocate the seat of arbitration from Montreal, Canada.[44] That request was made in light of several challenge proceedings against NAFTA awards in Canadian

43. Council Regulation (EU) No. 833/2014, July 31, 2014. https://eur-lex.europa.eu/eli/reg/2014/833/oj/eng (accessed October 1, 2025).
44. *Pope & Talbot v. Government of Canada*. Ruling concerning the investor's motion to change the place of arbitration, dated March 14, 2002. NAFTA case.

courts, where the Canadian government, as a litigant, argued that NAFTA Tribunals were not worthy of a high level of judicial deference[45] and the challenge of excess of jurisdiction aims at reviewing fundamental findings of law and fact by [NAFTA] Tribunals.[46] Those arguments made the claimant believe that Canada had changed its policy on NAFTA arbitration. The tribunal denied the motion based, in part, on the fact that the proceedings were nearly completed and changing the seat would not have been efficient. At the same time, in dictum, the court explained that the claimant's argument based on the Canadian government questioning some NAFTA awards before Canadian courts was insufficient for demonstrating that the Canadian policy on NAFTA arbitration had changed. As put by the tribunal in the case:

> Thus, it is certainly wrong to suggest that Canada's suitability as a place of arbitration may only be assessed by determining whether its courts have kept in check, an executive [Canadian government] otherwise free to make any legal arguments it wishes. After all, Canada's arguments before its courts are aimed at winning the day, and a Chapter 11 tribunal has no way of knowing in advance whether or when that day will come. For these reasons, the Tribunal concludes that there is a point where the behaviour of the executive in these matters must be judged on its own merits.[47]

There are various other legislative changes that may adversely affect a party's position at the seat of arbitration, potentially giving rise to an argument for contract modification, such as:

- If a new law introduces specific criteria as to the form of an arbitration clause.
- If under a new statute or case law the pending dispute becomes non-arbitrable.
- If a new statute or case law introduces requirements to arbitrators preventing the already appointed tribunal from continuing its work.
- If a new statute introduces some requirements to the arbitral institutions to administer cases seated in that jurisdiction (e.g., state registration).
- If the state of the seat withdraws from an international treaty, resulting in a manifest impairment of a party's procedural rights or the enforceability of the award.

Somctimes, new mandatory rules themselves may alter the entire dispute resolution mechanism previously agreed by the parties. For example, Article II of the Algiers Declaration (Claims Settlement) (1981) established the exclusive jurisdiction of the Iran-United States Claims Tribunal over claims between nationals of both states and the states themselves, albeit with some exclusions.[48] Article II has been applied in numerous Iran-U.S. cases, where the tribunal, despite the parties' initial forum

45. *United Mexican States v. Metaclad Corp.* 2021 BCSC 664 (May 2, 2001).
46. *S.D. Myers Inc. v. Canada.* Federal Court of Canada 2004 FC 38.
47. *Pope & Talbot v. Government of Canada.* Ruling concerning the investor's motion to change the place of arbitration, dated March 14, 2002. NAFTA case.
48. Declaration of the Government of the Democratic and Popular Republic of Algeria Concerning the Settlement of Claims by the Government of the United States of America and the Government of the Islamic Republic of Iran. January 19, 1981.

selection clauses, assumed jurisdiction and consequently relocated the seat to the Hague, the Netherlands, under Article VI(1) of the Algiers Declaration.[49]

[D] Threats to the Integrity of the Arbitration

A threat to the integrity of the arbitration, such as interference by authorities and involvement of state enforcement agencies, may justify a change in the seat of arbitration. Such actions create an environment where the fairness and impartiality of the proceedings are compromised, making it impossible for the tribunal to conduct a neutral and just arbitration process. In these circumstances, the tribunal may deem it necessary to relocate the seat of arbitration to a jurisdiction where the proceedings can be held without such external pressures or risks, thus ensuring the protection of the parties' rights and the overall integrity of the arbitration process.

In *Europa Nova Ltd v. Czech Republic*, the arbitral tribunal ordered that the place of arbitration be moved from Paris, France, to Geneva, Switzerland, based on the claimant's plea that intervention of the European Commission as well as actions taken by it and the EU courts in other unrelated arbitrations would impact the proceedings.[50]

In more hostile circumstances, such as in *Himpurna California Energy Ltd. v. Republic of Indonesia*, the tribunal however declined to change the seat of arbitration from Jakarta, Indonesia, despite the Jakarta courts issuing an injunction to suspend the arbitration, threatening a fine of USD 1 million per day if it proceeded, and an attempted abduction of the Indonesian arbitrator.[51]

[E] Impact of External Events

Lasting external events, such as natural disasters, pandemics, civil unrest and military conflicts, can also make it impossible to carry out the arbitration at the original seat. In such cases, the tribunal must assess the severity of these events and determine whether they have rendered the seat unfeasible for arbitration. Factors such as security concerns, the availability of infrastructure, and the ability to conduct hearings remotely or in person will all be important considerations.

§17.06 SELECTING THE NEW SEAT OF ARBITRATION

Once the prerequisites for changing the seat are met, the tribunal must then address the final question: which new seat will best ensure the continued fairness and neutrality of

49. *Halliburton Company, Imco Services (U.K.) Ltd. v. Doreen/Imco, the Islamic Republic of Iran*. Interlocutory Award (Award No. ITL 2-51-FT), IUSCT Case No. 31.
50. *WA Investments-Europa Nova Limited v. The Government of The Czech Republic*, PCA Case No. 2014-19, May 15, 2019.
51. *See*, When Arbitrators Act Without a Mandate; The Problematic Precedent Created by the "Arbitrator's" Decision to Change the Seat in the Heirs of the *Sultan of Sulu v. Malaysia*, 9 at https://cdn.prod.website-files.com/643fb88479ebe14441a89015/649aa9491f1b7e207de41457_Fietta%20LLP%20-%20When%20arbitrators%20act%20without%20a%20mandate.pdf (accessed October 1, 2025).

the arbitration process? This question can be divided into two parts. First, should the arbitral tribunal select from the options proposed by the parties, or may it draw from a broader range of jurisdictions? Second, by what criteria should the new seat be selected? These questions will be answered in the following.

[A] Choosing a New Seat

The first question is closely linked to two elements, i.e., (a) a party's burden of proof, and (b) the tribunal's mandate to decide only the issues, motions and claims that have been raised by the parties.

It is common knowledge that a party claiming something bears the burden of proof. Therefore, a party proposing a new seat of arbitration must demonstrate that the new seat will not possess the alleged deficiencies associated with the old one and will ensure the equilibrium of the contract. Similarly, a party defending the old seat while presenting a counterproposal for a new seat as a fallback position must demonstrate that the proposed new seat is at least not worse than the original one.

The arbitral tribunal may arguably only choose from the options proposed by the parties. If the arbitral tribunal selects a new seat that was not proposed by either party, the arbitral award may be challenged or its enforcement refused on the grounds of *extra petita*.

Finally, if the arbitral tribunal determines that neither of the proposed options fulfills the purpose of changing the seat, it may reject them without prejudicing the tribunal's decision to change the seat in principle. In such a case, the parties would not be required to reargue the issue of whether the criteria for the change are met, but instead would focus on identifying alternative new options for the seat.

[B] Criteria for the New Seat of Arbitration

This final part of the tribunal's analysis falls into two elements: (a) the criteria by which a new seat of arbitration should be selected (objective criteria), and (b) what the parties' considerations in selecting the initial seat in the contract were (subjective criteria).

As discussed above, section 3 of the UNCITRAL Notes on Organizing Arbitral Proceedings helpfully mentions several objective criteria influencing the selection of the place of arbitration:

(a) The suitability of the arbitration law at the place of arbitration.
(b) The law, jurisprudence and practices at the place of arbitration regarding: (i) court intervention in the course of arbitral proceedings; (ii) the scope of judicial review or of grounds for setting aside an award; and (iii) any qualification requirements with respect to arbitrators and counsel representation. and
(c) Whether the State where the arbitration takes place and hence where the arbitral award will be made is a Party to the New York Convention and/or to any other multilateral or bilateral treaty on enforcement of arbitral awards.

The Notes also add that, if it is expected that hearings will be held at the place of arbitration, other factors may become relevant in selecting the place of arbitration, such as: (i) the convenience of the location for the parties and the arbitrators, including travel to the location, (ii) the availability and cost of support services, (iii) the location of the subject matter in dispute and proximity of evidence, and (iv) any qualification restrictions with respect to counsel representation.

Potentially, there can also be other considerations that may be material.

For example, in *Heirs to the Sultanate of Sulu v. Malaysia,* the sole arbitrator outlined several criteria that were applied in his decision to change the seat from Madrid to Paris. According to him, moving the arbitration from Madrid to Paris would ensure that the proceedings remain free from local court interference, preserving the parties' autonomy over procedural and substantive rules until enforcement becomes necessary. France, and Paris in particular, offers an ideal setting for international arbitration, with a legal framework designed to support it. The French arbitration law empowers courts to assist when justice is at risk (Article 1505.4) while safeguarding arbitrators' authority to conduct proceedings without undue judicial intervention (Article 1448.1). This ensures fairness and due process. Paris is a globally recognized, neutral arbitration hub, independent of either party's home country. Its long-standing commitment to international arbitration is reflected in France's adherence to key treaties, including the New York Convention and the Geneva Convention of 1961. This legal environment guarantees the arbitration's neutrality and enforceability worldwide.[52]

Another consideration is the parties' initial vision for the forum, including the seat. These subjective factors may, of course, stem from the parties' pre-contract negotiations or prior dealings and need to be shown by a party. For example, in *Bancroft Life & Casualty ICC, Ltd. v. FFD Resources II, LLC*, the parties agreed that disputes would be resolved in state courts at Bancroft's place of registration, which, at the time of the conclusion of the contract, was the British Virgin Islands. However, when the dispute arose, it changed to St. Lucia, West Indies.[53] Bancroft asserted that the new forum should be in St. Lucia. In turn, the defendants had to show that the real intention was to litigate in the BVI, despite the language of the forum selection clause.

[1] The New Arbitration Law

As each case may have a distinct set of criteria that are essential for the new *lex arbitri*, it is important that the arbitral tribunal take them into account when choosing the new seat. The tribunal should, among other things, consider the quality of the new *lex arbitri* and ensure that the legal framework offers at least similar functionality to the previous one. This task would be simpler if the seat is transferred from one UNCITRAL Model Law jurisdiction to another. However, it may become more challenging, though certainly not impossible, if one of the seats involves a jurisdiction with a non-UNCITRAL-based *lex arbitri*.

52. *Heirs to the Sultanate of Sulu v. Malaysia.* Final Award, February 22, 2022.
53. *Bancroft Life & Casualty ICC, Ltd. v. FFD Resources II, LLC,* 884 F. Supp. 2d 535 (S.D. Tex. 2012).

The tribunal must also consider whether the new jurisdiction allows the type of dispute to be arbitrated. Some jurisdictions may have restrictions on the arbitrability of certain disputes. The tribunal must ensure that the new seat does not create new legal barriers to arbitration.

[2] The New York Convention

The tribunal should consider whether the new seat is located in a jurisdiction that is a signatory to the New York Convention. While other multilateral and regional treaties also permit the recognition and enforcement of arbitral awards, the New York Convention's 172 Contracting States make it the undisputed leader and a crucial factor in selecting a new seat.

[3] An Arbitration-Friendly Jurisdiction

Arbitration-friendliness can encompass various parameters, including acceptance of *kompetenz-kompetenz*, absence of qualification requirements for arbitrators and counsel, the existence of sustainable and favorable case law related to arbitration, overall support for the arbitral process (appointment and challenge of arbitrators by court, court-ordered interim measures, etc), a low percentage of the setting aside of arbitral awards and others. These factors are equally important in selecting a new place of arbitration.

[4] Impartiality of Local Courts and Legal Community

The recent past has shown that not only are neutrality and independence of the judiciary important but also those of other members of the legal community. While certain jurisdictions may rank highly for neutrality and independence in international surveys and indexes, it cannot be ruled out that, in practice, they may exhibit sudden bias against specific groups. A party requesting a change in the seat of arbitration must demonstrate to the tribunal that the proposed new seat does not suffer from the same deficiencies as the original one.

§17.07 CONCLUSION

Changing the legal seat of arbitration is a complex and nuanced process that requires careful legal and factual consideration. Tribunals must balance the need to preserve the integrity of the arbitration process with the practical realities of external events that may disrupt the original conditions under which the contract was concluded. By navigating these complexities, tribunals can ensure that the arbitration remains fair, efficient, and capable of delivering enforceable awards, even in the face of extraordinary challenges.

STOCKHOLM ARBITRATION YEARBOOK

1. Axel Calissendorff & Patrik Schöldström (eds), *Stockholm Arbitration Yearbook 2019*, 2019 (ISBN 978-94-035-0692-0).
2. Axel Calissendorff & Patrik Schöldström (eds), *Stockholm Arbitration Yearbook 2020*, 2020 (ISBN 978-94-035-2410-8).
3. Axel Calissendorff & Patrik Schöldström (eds), *Stockholm Arbitration Yearbook 2021*, 2021 (ISBN 978-94-035-3524-1).
4. Axel Calissendorff & Patrik Schöldström (eds), *Stockholm Arbitration Yearbook 2022*, 2022 (ISBN 978-94-035-1876-3).
5. Christer Danielsson & Patrik Schöldström (eds), *Stockholm Arbitration Yearbook 2023*, 2023 (ISBN 978-94-035-0358-5).
6. Christer Danielsson & Patrik Schöldström (eds), *Stockholm Arbitration Yearbook 2024*, 2024 (ISBN 978-94-035-4428-1).
7. Patrik Schöldström & James Hope (eds), *Stockholm Arbitration Yearbook 2025*, 2025 (ISBN 978-94-035-4979-8).